Living & Working in
FRANCE

● A Survival Handbook ●

David Hampshire

Survival Books ● Bath ● England

First published 1993
Second Edition 1996
Third Edition 1999
Fourth Edition 2002
Fifth Edition 2003
Sixth Edition 2004
Seventh Edition 2006
Eighth Edition 2006
Ninth Edition 2008
Tenth Edition 2012

Survival Books Limited
Office 169, 3 Edgar Buildings, George Street, Bath,
BA1 2FJ, United Kingdom
☎ +44 (0)1935-700060
✉ info@survivalbooks.net
🖥 www.survivalbooks.net

British Library Cataloguing in Publication Data
A CIP record for this book is available
from the British Library.
ISBN: 978-1-907339-44-8

Printed and bound in Singapore by International Press Softcom Limited

Acknowledgements

The publisher would like to thank all those who contributed to the successful publication of the 10th edition of *Living and Working in France* and previous editions of this book. In particular, thanks are due to Martin Hills and Jim Mace for research and updating this edition; Peter Read for editing; Lilac Johnston for proofreading and additional research; Di Bruce-Kidman for desktop publishing, photo selection and cover design; and Jim Watson for the cartoons and maps. Also thanks are due to the many photographers (listed on page 413) – the unsung heroes – whose beautiful images add colour and bring France to life.

Finally, a special thank you to the advertisers, without whose support it would be difficult to produce books in colour without them being prohibitively expensive.

Important Note

France is a diverse country with many faces, a variety of ethnic groups, religions and customs, as well as continuously changing rules, regulations, exchange rates and prices. A change of government in France can have a far-reaching influence on many important aspects of life, particularly taxes and social security. We cannot recommend too strongly that you check with an official and reliable source (not always the same) before making any major decisions or taking an irreversible course of action. **However, don't believe everything you're told or read – even, dare we say it, herein!**

Useful addresses and references to other sources of information have been included in all chapters and in **Appendices A to C** to help you obtain further information and verify details with official sources. Important points have been emphasised, in bold print, some of which it would be expensive, or even dangerous, to disregard. **Ignore them at your peril or cost!**

NOTE

Unless specifically stated, a reference to a company, organisation or product doesn't constitute an endorsement or recommendation. None of the businesses, products or individuals listed in this book (apart from the advertisers) have paid to be mentioned.

What Readers and Reviewers Have Said About Survival Books:

"If I were to move to France, I would like David Hampshire to be with me, holding my hand every step of the way. This being impractical, I would have to settle for second best and take his books with me instead!"
Living France

"We would like to congratulate you on this work: it is really super! We hand it out to our expatriates and they read it with great interest and pleasure."
ICI (Switzerland) AG

"I found this a wonderful book crammed with facts and figures, with a straightforward approach to the problems and pitfalls you are likely to encounter. The whole laced with humour and a thorough understanding of what's involved. Gets my vote!"
Reader (Amazon)

"Get hold of David Hampshire's book for its sheer knowledge, straightforwardness and insights to the Spanish character and do yourself a favour!"
Living Spain

"Rarely has a 'survival guide' contained such useful advice – This book dispels doubts for first time travellers, yet is also useful for seasoned globetrotters – In a word, if you're planning to move to the US or go there for a long term stay, then buy this book both for general reading and as a ready reference."
American Citizens Abroad

Contents

10. PUBLIC TRANSPORT 157

11. MOTORING 175

12. HEALTH 211

Publisher's Notes

♦ Frequent references are made in this book to the European Union (EU), which comprises Austria, Belgium, Bulgaria, Cyprus, the Czech Republic, Denmark, Estonia, Finland, France, Germany, Greece, Hungary, Ireland, Italy, Latvia, Lithuania, Luxembourg, Malta, the Netherlands, Poland, Portugal, Romania, Slovakia, Slovenia, Spain, Sweden and the UK. The European Economic Area (EEA) comprises the EU countries plus the European Free Trade Association (EFTA) countries of Iceland, Liechtenstein and Norway, plus Switzerland (which is an EFTA member but not a member of the EEA).

♦ Times are shown using the 24-hour clock, e.g. 10am is shown as 10.00 and 10pm as 22.00, the usual way of expressing the time in France (see also **Time Difference** on page 368).

♦ Prices quoted should be taken only as estimates, although they were mostly correct when going to press and fortunately don't usually change greatly overnight. Although prices are sometimes quoted exclusive of value added tax (hors taxes/HT) in France, most prices are quoted inclusive of tax (toutes taxes comprises/TTC), which is the method used when quoting prices in this book. To convert from other currencies to euros or vice versa, see 🖳 www.xe.com.

♦ His/he/him also means her/she/her (please forgive us ladies). This is done to make life easier for both the reader and the author, and isn't intended to be sexist.

♦ The French translation of many key words and phrases is shown in brackets in italics.

♦ All spelling is - or should be - British and not American English.

♦ Warnings and important points are printed in bold type.

♦ The following symbols are used in this book: ☎ (telephone), 📄 (fax), ✉ (internet) and 🖳 (email).

♦ Lists of Useful Addresses, Further Reading and Useful Websites are contained in **Appendices A, B** and **C** respectively.

♦ For those unfamiliar with the metric system of Weights & Measures, conversion tables are included in **Appendix D**.

♦ Maps of France – departments, airports and ports, TGV rail lines and motorways – are shown in **Appendix E**. A physical map of France is shown on page 6.

Beaujolais

Introduction

Whether you're already living or working in France or just thinking about it – this is THE BOOK for you. Forget about all those glossy guidebooks, excellent though they are for tourists; this amazing book was written especially with you in mind and is worth its weight in truffles. Furthermore, this fully updated and re-designed tenth edition is printed in colour. *Living and Working in France* is intended to meet the needs of anyone wishing to know the essentials of French life – however long your planned stay in France, you'll find the information contained in this book invaluable.

General information isn't difficult to find in France (provided you speak French) and a multitude of books are published on every conceivable subject. However, reliable and up-to-date information in English specifically intended for foreigners living and working in France isn't so easy to find, least of all in one volume. This book was written to fill this void and provide the comprehensive practical information necessary for a relatively trouble-free life. You may have visited France as a tourist, but living and working there is a different matter altogether. Adjusting to a different environment and culture and making a home in any foreign country can be a traumatic and stressful experience – and France is no exception.

Living and Working in France is a comprehensive handbook on a wide range of everyday subjects and represents the most up-to-date source of general information available to foreigners in France. However, it isn't simply a monologue of dry facts and figures, but a practical and entertaining look at life.

Adapting to life in a new country is a continuous process, and, although this book will help reduce your beginner's phase and minimise the frustrations, it doesn't contain all the answers. (Most of us don't even know the right questions to ask!) What it will do, however, is help you make informed decisions and calculated judgements, instead of uneducated guesses. **Most importantly, it will save you time, trouble and money, and repay your investment many times over.**

Although you may find some of the information in this book a bit daunting, don't be discouraged. Most problems occur only once and fade into insignificance after a short time (as you face the next half a dozen!). The majority of foreigners in France would agree that, all things considered, they love living there. A period spent in France is a wonderful way to enrich your life and hopefully please your bank manager. We trust this book will help you avoid the pitfalls of life in France and smooth your way to a happy and rewarding future in your new home.

Bon courage !

Survival Books
October 2011

1.

FINDING A JOB

Finding work in France isn't always as difficult as the unemployment figures may suggest, particularly in Paris and other large cities, depending of course on your profession or trade, qualifications and French language ability. Nationals of European Union (EU) and European Economic Area (EEA) countries have the right to work in France or any other member state without a work permit, provided they have a valid passport or national identity card and comply with the member state's laws and regulations on employment. The exceptions are Bulgarian and Romanian citizens who require a residence permit (*carte/titre de séjour*) to work in France until 2014, although they have been EU members since 2007.

EU nationals are entitled to the same treatment as French citizens in matters of pay, working conditions, access to housing, vocational training, social security entitlements and trade union rights, and their families and immediate dependants are entitled to join them and enjoy the same rights.

Nevertheless, there are still barriers to full freedom of movement and the right to work within the EU: for example, many jobs require applicants to have specific skills or vocational qualifications, and qualifications obtained in some member states aren't recognised in others (see **Qualifications** on page 25), although cross-border restrictions are gradually being outlawed by the European Commission (EC). There are also restrictions on employment in the civil service.

With the growth of the internet and the spread of broadband, it's possible to carry out many types of business 'remotely' and even from the comfort of your own home, but unless you have a company registered abroad you must still join the French system. This means not only paying French taxes and social security contributions, but also having your business 'approved' by the relevant authorities.

> ## ▲ Caution
>
> If you want to conduct two lines of business considered as different occupations (and the French have strictly defined 'job descriptions'), you'll need to pay two lots of taxes and social security contributions!

If you don't qualify to live and work in France by birthright or as an EU national, you must obtain a long-stay visa, which is dependent upon obtaining employment. However, France has had a virtual freeze on the employment of non-EU nationals for many years, which has been strengthened recently due to the high unemployment rate. The employment of non-EU nationals must be approved by the Pôle Emploi (formerly the Agence Nationale Pour l'Emploi/ANPE), which can propose the employment of a French national instead, although this is rare.

For a permanent position, the prospective employer must have advertised the post with the Pôle Emploi for at least five weeks and must also obtain authorisation to employ a non-EU national from the French Ministry of

Labour (Ministère du Travail, des Relations Sociales et de la Solidarité, ⌨ www.travail-solidarite.gouv.fr) or the Direction Départementale du Travail, de l'Emploi et de la Formation Professionnelle (DDTEFP) where the business is registered. The authorisation, which is a prerequisite to obtaining a long-stay visa, is sent to the Office Français de l'Immigration et de l'Intégration, formerly the Office des Migrations Internationales (OFII, 44 rue Bargue, 75732 Paris Cedex 15, ⌨ www.ofii.fr) for transmission to the appropriate French consulate abroad. The consulate notifies the applicant, who can then proceed with the application.

When the proposed monthly salary is above that for senior managers (around €3,500 per month), the application is usually approved; it's difficult for non-EU nationals to obtain permission for a lower-paid job unless they have unusual qualifications. However, this doesn't prevent unscrupulous employers taking on non-EU nationals illegally as poorly paid unskilled workers, particularly in the building industry.

There's an 'accelerated' programme designed to recruit foreign workers in fields where there has been a shortage of available employees, e.g. certain high-tech computer-related fields. This doesn't mean that anyone who can create a website is guaranteed a long-stay visa (there's normally a minimum salary level of around €27,000 per year) but it does make it easier for non-EU specialists with the requisite qualifications to find employment.

ECONOMY

France is one of the world's wealthiest countries and its fifth-largest economy (2010), with one of the highest per capita gross domestic products (GDP) in the EU (US$33,300 in 2010). The economy grew by 0.9 percent in the first quarter of 2011. In common with Europe's other 'major economies', France is in debt to the tune of some two-thirds of national income (compared with 62.6 per cent for Germany, 60.8 per cent for the US and 47.2 per cent for the UK). Since the start of the new millennium, inflation has generally been low at around 2 per cent (it was 1.9 per cent in mid-2011). France failed to reduce its national debt to meet an EU ruling that all member states must have 'balanced books' by 2004 (the rules were 'bent' as a result!).

France is among the world's largest exporters of both goods and services and in 2010 was ranked fifth in the world for total exports. The country has experienced an economic transformation in the last few decades, during which its traditional industries have been thoroughly modernised and a wealth of new high-tech industries created, although increasing competition, particularly from Far Eastern countries (known collectively as le low-cost!), has meant that traditional industries such as steel, clothing and textile production have become less competitive. Nevertheless, the manufacture of ships, cars, aeroplanes and defence equipment remains significant.

Less labour and capital intensive industries such as electronics, pharmaceuticals and communications have flourished since the '80s, although the largest growth in recent years has been in service industries, e.g. banking, insurance and advertising, which now account for over 70 per cent of GDP, compared with around 25 per cent for industry and under 3 per cent for agriculture. (Despite the continuing decline in the number of farms, France is still Europe's largest agricultural producer with almost 25 per cent of total EU production.)

French industry has increasingly looked beyond its own borders in the last few decades, during which it has been one of the world's leading investors in foreign companies. Conversely, in 2009 France was the third most popular among Organisation for Economic Co-operation and Development (OECD) countries for foreign investment and there was a record 22 per cent increase in 2010. France's answer to California's Silicon Valley, Sophia Antipolis on the Côte d'Azur, is the largest technology park in Europe with some 1,400 companies employing around 30,000 people, and a second park is under development nearby.

WORKFORCE

French workers enjoy an affluent lifestyle in comparison with those in many other western countries, with high salaries (especially for

EURO TUNNEL le shuttle

SAVE UP TO
50%*

Become one of our frequent travellers today!

PRICES FROM

£39

per car, each way*

BUY NOW & SAVE
0870 240 2268
eurotunnel.com/lwf

Gedess: 591170

* Terms and conditions apply.

FOLKESTONE · CALAIS

executives and senior managers) and excellent employment conditions (see **Chapter 2**). Much of the French 'working class' (France is supposedly a classless society) consists of skilled (*qualifié*) workers and technicians. French engineers are part of the elite (as in Germany) and highly respected. France has a well educated and trained workforce, and a strong emphasis is placed on training by employers. Even employees doing what many would consider menial jobs, such as shop assistants and waiters, have trade training (although seldom in politeness!) and aren't looked down on (the really menial tasks are generally undertaken by immigrants).

Most French don't dream of becoming entrepreneurs or businessmen but of working in the public sector, which constitutes some 25 per cent of the country's workforce compared with around 15 per cent in most other EU countries, and where benefits are second-to-none, e.g. up to three months' annual holiday and retirement at 55 or even 50!

WORK ATTITUDES

French firms have traditionally been expected to care for their employees and most have a paternalistic attitude. Experience, maturity and loyalty are highly valued (although qualifications are even more valuable), and newcomers generally find it difficult to secure a senior position with a French company.

The traditional hierarchical structure of French businesses, with little contact between management and workers, both of whom are reluctant to take on responsibilities outside their immediate duties, has given way to a more 'modern' reward-for-achievement attitude and relations between management and staff have generally improved. However, the French 'old boy' network is still alive and well and may prevent foreigners achieving the promotion they deserve (see **Industrial Relations** on page 23). 'Job hopping' as a way of increasing your salary or promotion prospects is rare in France.

As in the US, French employers tend to expect high standards and are intolerant of

mistakes or inefficiency. However, it's difficult and expensive to fire employees. When it comes to hiring new employees (particularly managers and executives) and making important business decisions, the process is slower in France than in many other developed countries. Many foreigners, particularly Americans, find that they need to adjust to a slower pace of working life. Most French managers and executives rarely take work home and they never work at weekends, which are sacrosanct.

Don't be misled by the apparent lack of urgency and casual approach to business – the French can be just as hard-headed as any other race. Business relations tend to be formal: colleagues usually address each other as *vous* rather than *tu* and often use surnames instead of first names, and socialising with work colleagues is rare. Attire is generally formal although in some companies Fridays are 'casual dress' days.

WORKING WOMEN

The number of working women has increased dramatically in recent years, and some two-thirds of French women (the vast majority under 40), including 70 per cent of women with one child, now work – the highest percentage in Europe outside Scandinavia. However, around 30 per cent of women work part-time, compared with just 5 per cent of men. Three-quarters of women are employed in distribution and transport, nursing and health care, education, secretarial professions and service industries such as retailing.

Male chauvinism is alive and well in France and most French women are more concerned with equal rights in the workplace and benefits (such as paid maternity leave and state-run nurseries) than the opportunity to reach the top. The fact that 'the best man for the job is often a woman' is rarely acknowledged by French employers, who are often reluctant to hire women if they think they're planning a family, not least because they must provide generous paid maternity leave. Women must generally be twice as qualified as a man to compete on equal terms, although the 1983 law on professional equality (*loi Roudy sur l'égalité professionnelle*) made it easier for women to break into male-dominated trades and professions. However, women still find it difficult to attain management positions, particularly in technical and industrial fields, where there has long been a tradition of prejudice against them.

Women have had some success in reaching the top in the professions and in sectors such as finance, insurance, the media, personnel, advertising and retailing. Career women are generally more accepted and taken more seriously in Paris, which has a more progressive outlook than the provinces (particularly the south, where opinions and attitudes lag behind the north). Nevertheless, over a quarter of France's 2.5m businesses are run by women, by far the highest proportion in Europe. Since 1997, women have had the right to earn 90 per cent of a full-time salary if they work a four-day week, e.g. taking Wednesday off to look after their children.

A woman doing the same or broadly similar work to a man and employed by the same employer is legally entitled to the same salary and other terms of employment. However, despite the Equal Pay Act of 1972, women's salaries are an average of around 15 per cent lower than men's. Around 17 per cent of women earn the minimum wage (see page 22), which generally reflects the fact that most women work in lower paid industries and hold lower paid positions than men (including more part-time jobs), rather than discrimination. (Employers with over 50 employees must publish a breakdown of pay and conditions for their male and female employees.)

However, the situation has improved considerably in recent years, and women are much less exploited in France than in many other western European countries. Women continue to face the additional hazard of sexual harassment, as 'flirting' is an unwritten part of French life, although it's likely to be less widespread or aggressive following the worldwide publicity given to the Dominique Strauss-Kahn case in New York. If it's any consolation, refusing a sexual advance from your boss rarely results in your losing your job, as it's difficult to fire employees.

SALARY

The Federation of European Employers publish an annual Pay in Europe report which can be purchased via their website (🖥 www.fedee.com), although it's expensive. French executive salaries were lower than the international average in the '70s and early '80s, but rose much faster than the rate of inflation in the '80s and were augmented by lucrative bonuses and profit-sharing schemes. They've now caught up and even surpassed those in some other Western countries, although in recent years university graduates and school-leavers have been willing to accept almost any wage in order to get a foot on the career ladder. Annual salary increases have been minimal since the recession in 2008.

☑ **SURVIVAL TIP**

If you have friends or acquaintances working in France or who have worked there, ask them what an average or good salary is for your particular trade or profession. If locality is your prime consideration, you can consult the website (🖥 www.salairemoyen.com) to ascertain the average salary in a particular area.

It's often difficult to determine the salary you should command, as salaries aren't usually quoted in job advertisements, except in the public sector where employees are paid according to fixed grades and salaries are public knowledge. Salaries may vary considerably for the same job in different parts of France. Those working in Paris and its environs are generally the highest paid, primarily due to the high cost of living, particularly accommodation. When comparing salaries, you need to take into account compulsory deductions such as tax and social security (see **Chapters 13** and **14**), and also compare the cost of living.

For many employees, particularly executives and senior managers, their remuneration is much more than what they receive in their monthly pay packets. Many companies offer a range of benefits for executives and managers that may include a company car, private health insurance and health screening, expenses-paid holidays, private school fees, inexpensive or interest-free home and other loans, rent-free accommodation, free or subsidised public transport tickets, free or subsidised company restaurant, sports or country club membership, non-contributory company pension, stock options, bonuses and profit-sharing schemes, tickets for sports events and shows, and 'business' conferences in exotic locations (see also **Chapter 2**). Many employees in France also receive an extra month's salary at Christmas, known as a 13th month's salary, and some companies also pay a 14th month's salary before the summer holiday period.

Salaries in many industries are decided by collective bargaining between employers and unions, either regionally or nationally. When there's a collective agreement, employers must offer at least the minimum wage agreed, although this is exceeded by most major companies. Agreements specify minimum wage levels for each position within

main employment categories in a particular industry or company, and often require bonus payments related to the age or qualifications of employees or their length of time with the company (*prime d'ancienneté*). This means that wage levels are effectively fixed. Cost of living increases for salaries above the *SMIC* aren't regulated by the government, although the collective agreement may provide for annual increases based on cost of living figures.

The introduction of the 35-hour week (see **Working Hours** on page 47) included guarantees that salaries couldn't be reduced from the levels paid on a 39-hour week basis. Government incentives available to employers for hiring additional workers did little to mitigate the cost of reducing the working week, and it's likely most salaries will remain static and pay rises will be few and far between for the next few years.

MINIMUM WAGE

At the lower end of the wage scale, there has been a statutory minimum wage (*salaire minimum de croissance/SMIC*) since 1950. When the cost of living index rises by 2 per cent or more in a year, the minimum wage is increased. In practice, the minimum wage rises each year, usually in July and especially when elections are coming up!

There's a lower *SMIC* for juveniles, those on special job-creation schemes and disabled employees. Unskilled workers (particularly women) are usually employed at or near the minimum wage, semi-skilled workers are usually paid 10 to 20 per cent more, and skilled workers 30 to 40 per cent more (often shown in job advertisements as '*SMIC + 10, 20, 30,*

Average Saleries	
Job Type	**Average Annual Salary**
Software Engineer/Programmer/Developer	€36,000
Senior Lecturer/Associate Professor	€37,000
Systems Engineer	€42,000
IT Consultant	€47,000
Project Manager	€51,000
Management Consultant	€56,000

in the public sector, where employees have long been known for their propensity to stop work at the drop of a beret. Recent years have seen strikes among public transport employees and among self-employed groups such as farmers, fishermen, truck drivers, doctors and other medical professionals, and strikes become increasingly common in the run-up to elections and in response to announcements of plant closures or sales to foreign investors.

For a time, strikes in private companies were almost unheard-of in France, but they've recently started to become a popular means of protesting against increasing threats to job security. In both the public and private sectors, strikes are often seen as the only effective means of communicating with the government and elected officials, as it's the government rather than employers who are expected to resolve most work-related issues. Despite negligible union membership (less than 10 per cent and falling), most workers in France are automatically covered by industry-wide and legally recognised collective agreements (*conventions collectives*).

Nevertheless, there has been a huge reduction in strikes in the last decade or so, a less confrontational relationship between employers and employees being due both to high unemployment and new legislation, requiring both sides to discuss their differences and imposing a 'cooling-off' period before a strike can be called.

40%'). Note, however, that many employees, particularly seasonal workers in the farming and tourist industries, are traditionally paid below the minimum wage (although the French government is increasingly clamping down and forcing employers to comply with the law).

Another type of minimum wage is the *revenu de solidarité active (rSa)* introduced in June 2009, which replaced the *revenu minimum d'insertion (RMI)* created in 1989, and the subsequent *revenu minimum d'activité (RMA)*, as a wage for job seekers who were no longer entitled to or didn't qualify for unemployment benefit. The *rSa* is now drawn by a staggering 3m people between the ages of 25 and 60. Those aged under 25 with two years employment in the preceding three years can (since 2010) also claim it. Rates vary depending on circumstances but start at €466 per month (2011) for a single unemployed person.

The wage is also designed to encourage people to seek work and complements low incomes for those who can only find short-time work, e.g. a single person earning €500 per month could claim €215 per month *rSa* in 2011. Non-EU nationals resident in France for at least five years are eligible. The minimum wage was €9 per hour in mid-2011, equal to gross pay of €1,365 per month for 151.67 hours (the standard under the terms of the 35-hour working week).

INDUSTRIAL RELATIONS

The French are notorious for their strikes (*grèves*, euphemistically known as *mouvements sociaux*), which are a common feature of French 'working' life – particularly

UNEMPLOYMENT

In an attempt to reduce high unemployment, recent governments have lowered some taxes and introduced a host of job creation schemes offering temporary (i.e. five-year) jobs in the public sector to school-leavers or those just out of training, conveniently taking them off the unemployment lists until after the next round of elections! In 2002, the 35-hour work week, designed to share the available pool of workers and stimulate new employment, generated a mere 1.3 per cent increase in employment (far less than expected by the government). In an attempt to avert further lay-offs, the government then increased minimum redundancy payments and officially defined 'economic redundancies' (*licenciements économiques*), which can be made only after an employer has undertaken certain procedures. As a result of these measures, combined with a general improvement in the economy, unemployment figures have reduced in recent years. In mid-2011, some 9.6 per cent of the workforce (just over 2.5m people) were officially unemployed, which is the lowest for over ten years.

Nevertheless, unemployment is still a major problem for those aged under 25, among whom it's almost three times the national average. France spends more on job creation schemes than any other EU country, yet has the worst job creation record in the OECD, and the government's recent attempt to introduce a 'youth employment contract' was a disaster (see **Indefinite-term Contracts** on page 45).

Other groups badly affected by unemployment are older people, women and blue collar workers, the last currently suffering unemployment rates five times as high as executives and managers. Although unemployment has hit manufacturing industries the hardest, no sector has survived unscathed, including the flourishing service industries in the Paris region. Some of the worst hit industries have been construction, electronics, communications, the media and banking.

The situation has been worsened, at least in the public mind, by a string of large business failures or 'reorganisations' which have involved hundreds or thousands of redundancies and the closing of entire branches or divisions, e.g. Air Liberté, Danone and Moulinex. Many companies have a total ban on recruitment and expect executives to accept fixed-or short-term contracts, rather than life-long security. Over a quarter of France's working population has a short-term contract (*contrat à durée déterminée/ CDD*), commonly known as 'precarious' employment (*emploi précaire*).

Although only half as many people as in the UK and Germany become unemployed each year (a quarter as many as in the US), only around 3 per cent find a new job within the year, compared with the European average of around 9 per cent (35 per cent in the US). Long-term unemployment is a huge problem, where the average period of unemployment is a year (the longest in Europe) and over a million people have been unemployed for over two years. Anyone aged over 50 who loses his job is unlikely to work again with an unlimited-period-of-employment contract (*contrat à durée indéterminée/CDI*) unless they're highly qualified and in demand.

UK citizens receiving unemployment benefit can continue to do so while job hunting in France, provided they register with the Pôle Emploi (see page 28, and can obtain a Job Seeker's Allowance while in France: obtain leaflets *UBL22* and *E303* from a UK Job Centre at least three months before you go.

EMPLOYMENT PROSPECTS

Being attracted to France by its weather, cuisine, wine and lifestyle is understandable but doesn't rate highly as an employment qualification. You should have a positive reason for living and working in France. Simply being fed up with your job or the weather isn't the best motive for moving to France. It's extremely difficult to find work in rural areas and isn't easy in cities and large towns (even Paris), especially if your French isn't fluent.

You shouldn't plan on finding employment in France unless you have special qualifications or experience for which there's a strong demand. If you want a good job, you must usually be extremely well qualified and speak fluent French. If you intend to come to France

without a job, you should have a plan for finding employment on arrival and try to make some contacts before you arrive.

If you have a job offer, you should ensure that it's in writing (preferably in French) and check that it isn't likely to be revoked soon after you arrive. France has a reasonably self-sufficient labour market and doesn't require a large number of skilled or unskilled foreign workers. However, in recent years, French companies have been keen to expand into international markets, which has created opportunities for foreign workers, particularly bilingual and tri-lingual employees. In recent years there has been a marked increase in French investment abroad, and France is experiencing a 'brain drain' as executives and entrepreneurs (and football players!) leave the country, creating something of a vacuum – particularly in high-tech industries such as information technology. There are some 2,000 affiliates of US firms in France, employing over half a million people.

Areas where there's currently a shortage of staff include banking, insurance and renewable energy industries, estimated to need over 100,000 extra employees in the next decade. Generally, there's a shortfall of around 10,000 to 15,000 graduates each year, and in 2010 it was estimated that there was a shortage of thousands of managers. There's also a shortage of butchers, computer technicians, hairdressers, hotel staff, lorry drivers, sales people and stonemasons.

Casual work can be found in tourism (e.g. at Disneyland Paris and other major theme parks), campsites, holiday centres and children's summer camps (*colonie de vacances*) and, of course, hotels and restaurants.

Before moving to France to work, you should dispassionately examine your motives and credentials, and ask yourself the following questions

♦ What kind of work can I realistically expect to do?

♦ What are my qualifications and experience? Are they recognised in France?

♦ Am I too old? Although discrimination on the basis of age, physical appearance, name and sexual preference is illegal, age discrimination is rife, where only around 40 per cent of men aged 55 to 64 work – the lowest percentage in Europe.

♦ How good is my French? Unless your French is fluent, you won't be competing on equal terms with the French (you won't anyway, but that's a different matter!). Most French employers aren't interested in employing anyone without, at the very least, an adequate working knowledge of French.

♦ Are there any jobs in my profession or trade in the area where I wish to live?

♦ Could I work as self-employed or start my own business?

The answers to these questions can be disheartening, but it's better to ask them before moving to France rather than afterwards.

⚠ Caution

An increasing number of people in France turn to self-employment or starting a business to make a living (see page 38), although this path is strewn with pitfalls for the newcomer. Bear in mind that only some 6 per cent of France's workforce is self-employed!

QUALIFICATIONS

The most important qualification for working (and living) in France is the ability to speak French fluently (see **Language** below). Once you've overcome this hurdle, you should establish whether your trade or professional qualifications and experience are recognised in France. If you aren't experienced, French employers expect studies to be in a relevant discipline and to have included work experience (*un stage*).

Professional or trade qualifications are required to work in most fields in France, where qualifications are also often necessary to be self-employed or start a business. It isn't just a matter of hanging up a sign and waiting for the stampede of customers to your door. Many foreigners are required to undergo a 'business' course before they can start work in France (see **Self-employment & Starting a Business** on page 38).

Theoretically, qualifications recognised by professional and trade bodies in one EU country should be recognised in France. However, recognition varies from country to country and in some cases foreign qualifications aren't recognised by French employers or professional and trade associations. All academic qualifications should also be recognised, although they may be given less prominence than equivalent French qualifications, depending on the country and the educational establishment. A ruling by the European Court in 1992 declared that where EU examinations are of a similar standard with just certain areas of difference, individuals should be required to take exams only in those areas, and a further directive agreed in June 2006 'entitled' qualified workers such as architects, estate agents, hairdressers and plumbers to set up shop in France. Nevertheless, it can take months and even years to obtain permission to work or start a business in France.

For certain jobs, you must show your police record (*casier judiciaire*) to a prospective employer, which lists convictions for 'serious' crimes, e.g. not parking tickets. You're the only person entitled to obtain a copy of your police record, from Le Centre du Casier Judiciaire National, 107 rue Landreau, 44300 Nantes.

A list of professions and trades in France can be found on the website of the Office National d'Information sur l'Enseignement et les Professions (ONISEP, ⌨ www.onisep.fr).

All EU member states issue occupation information sheets containing a common job description with a table of qualifications. These cover a large number of trades and are intended to help someone with the relevant qualifications look for a job in another EU country. For information about equivalent qualifications you can contact the Centre d'Études et de Recherche sur les Qualifications (CEREQ, ☎ 04 91 13 28 28/01 44 08 69 10, ⌨ www.cereq.fr) or ENIC-NARIC, run by the European Network of Information Centres (⌨ www.enic-naric.net).

A useful booklet, *Europe Open for Professionals*, is available from the UK Department for Education and Skills (☎ 0870-000 2288). Further information can be obtained from the Bureau de l'Information sur les Systèmes Educatifs et de la Reconnaissance de Diplômes of the Ministère de la Jeunesse, de l'Education Nationale et de la Recherche (☎ 01 55 55 10 10, ⌨ www.education.gouv.fr) and from the Ministère de l'Enseignement Supérieure et de la Recherche (⌨ www.enseignementsup-recherche.gouv.fr).

If you're contemplating working as a civil servant (*fonctionnaire*) in France, you can obtain details of the requirements, which include competitive exams and French nationality, from ⌨ www.service-public.fr (information about the scope and purpose of the website is available in English).

MEDICAL EXAMINATION

Most French employers require prospective employees to have a pre-employment medical examination performed by the employer's doctor (*médecin du travail*), who's certified to evaluate your fitness for the job for which you're applying. An offer of employment is usually subject to a prospective employee being given a clean bill of health. However, this may be required only for employees over a certain age (e.g. 40) or for employees in certain jobs, e.g. where good health is of paramount importance for safety reasons. (Once employed, most employees are entitled to an annual check-up by the *médecin du travail*.)

LANGUAGE

☑ **SURVIVAL TIP**

The most common reason for negative experiences among foreigners in France, both visitors and residents alike, is that they cannot (or won't) speak French.

Although English is the *lingua franca* of international commerce and may help you to secure a job in France, the most important qualification for anyone seeking employment is the ability to speak fluent French. Although most French children learn English at school and the majority of educated French can speak some English, many of them are reluctant to do so, as they have an ingrained fear of making mistakes and 'losing face'. (Results of a recent survey showed that two-thirds of French people claimed to speak only French and a mere 22 per cent admitted to speaking English 'well'.) The French are also extremely proud of their language (to the point of hubris) and – not surprisingly – expect everyone living or working in France to speak it.

If necessary you should have French lessons before arriving in France. A sound knowledge of French won't just help you find a job or perform your job better but will also make everyday life much simpler and more enjoyable.

If you come to France without being able to speak French, you'll be excluded from everyday life and will feel uncomfortable until you can understand what's going on around you. You must usually speak French if you wish to have French friends.

However bad your grammar, limited your vocabulary or terrible your accent, an attempt to speak French will be much better appreciated than your fluent English. Don't, however, be surprised when the French wince at your torture of their beloved tongue, pretend not to understand you even though you've said something 'correctly', or correct minor grammatical or pronunciation errors! The French honestly believe they're doing you a favour by pointing out your mistakes while they're fresh in your mind. (This also explains much of their hesitance to use English in public, for fear of being corrected themselves.)

If you don't already speak good French, don't expect to learn it quickly, even if you already have a basic knowledge and take intensive lessons (see **Learning French** on page 154). It's common for foreigners not to be fluent after a year or more of intensive lessons in France.

If your expectations are unrealistic, you'll become frustrated, which can affect your confidence. It takes a long time to reach the level of fluency needed to be able to work in French. If you don't speak French fluently, you should begin French lessons on arrival and consider taking a menial or even an unpaid voluntary job, which is one of the quickest ways of improving your French.

Your ability in French and other languages must be listed on your curriculum vitae (CV/ résumé) and the level of proficiency stated as follows: some knowledge (*notions*); good (*bien*); very good (*très bien* or *parle, lis, écris*); fluent (*courant*); and mother tongue (*langue maternelle*). When stating your French language ability, it's important not to exaggerate. If you state that your French is very good or fluent, you'll be interviewed in French, which may also happen even if you have only a little knowledge.

When doing business in France or writing letters to French businesses, communications should always be in French. Most business letters must be written in a very precise style with proper opening and closing greetings. See also **Unsolicited Job Applications** on page 32.

France also has over 70 regional languages, the most widely spoken including Alsatian (spoken in Alsace), Basque (Pyrenees), Breton (Brittany), Catalan (Roussillon), Corsican (Corsica), Gascon (southwest) and Occitan (Languedoc). In some areas, schools teach in the regional language as well as in French. However fluent your French, you may still have problems understanding these, as well as some accents – particularly those of the south – and local dialects (*patois*).

JOB HUNTING

As many as 60 per cent of job vacancies in France are never advertised but are filled by 'word of mouth'. When looking for a job, it's therefore best not to put all your eggs in one basket – the more job applications you make, the better your chance of finding the right (or any) job. Contact as many prospective employers as possible, by writing, telephoning or calling on them in person.

Whatever job you're looking for, it's important to market yourself appropriately. For example, the recruitment of executives and senior managers is handled almost exclusively by recruitment consultants. At the other end of the scale, manual jobs requiring no previous experience may be advertised at Pôle Emploi offices (see below), in local newspapers and on notice boards, and the first suitable applicant may be offered the job on the spot. Job hunting resources are listed below.

EU citizens who are receiving unemployment benefit in their own country can continue to receive it while job hunting in any other EU country, including France.

Employment Agencies

Government Employment Service

The French national employment service, Pôle Emploi (🖳 www.pole-emploi.fr) operates some 600 offices throughout France, providing both local and national job listings, although jobs on offer are mainly non-professional skilled, semi-skilled and unskilled jobs, particularly in industry, retailing and catering, and around 75 per cent of them are temporary (*intérimaire*) or short-term (*CDD*), although higher-level jobs are offered by specialist offices (see below). Offices are listed under *Administrations du Travail et de l'Emploi* in the *Yellow Pages* or Pôle Emploi in the *White Pages*; a list can be obtained from the Issyles-Moulineaux office (see above). Local jobs are advertised in Pôle Emploi offices and national listings can be found via a free weekly Pôle Emploi bulletin.

Pôle Emploi offices provide free telephones for calling prospective employers (not your mum!). The Pôle Emploi website provides access to many of its services, including a searchable database of job vacancies. To apply for most of the jobs listed online, you must contact a Pôle Emploi office, but a few of the listings give you the name and address of the company so that you can apply directly. The website also contains general information about job hunting in France (in French).

> For those wishing to start a business, special classes are provided which include writing a business plan, obtaining finance, grants, paperwork and legal requirements. All services are provided free of charge, although they must be approved by your counsellor.

The Pôle Emploi provides a comprehensive career resource library, including company listings, trade publications and a wide range of reference books, plus an individual career counselling service and advice on job opportunities and prospects in certain fields. Counsellors can review and (perhaps) translate your *résumé*, provide information about the job market, and assist you in evaluating your options and drawing up a job hunting strategy. The Pôle Emploi provides useful information in their *Préparer sa Recherché d'Emploi* document on their website (see above) which can be downloaded and printed, and their offices also provide free publications to assist job seekers.

If you're registered as unemployed, a personal counsellor is assigned to your case. Other services available to residents include intensive career workshops, mock interviews (on videotape), psychological testing and French language tuition (*perfectionnement de la langue française*), although complete beginners don't qualify.

Pôle Emploi services are available to all EU nationals and foreign residents in France. However, offices have a reputation for being unhelpful to foreign job-seekers unless they've previously been employed in France or are unemployed and receiving unemployment benefit. Being a government department, the Pôle Emploi isn't service-oriented and the

The European Employment Service (EURES) network covers all EU countries plus Iceland and Norway. Members regularly exchange information about job vacancies and you can have your personal details circulated to the employment service in selected countries, e.g. to the Pôle Emploi in France. Details are available in local employment service offices in each member country, where advice on how to apply for jobs is provided. In the UK, you can contact your local Employment Service, which publishes

quality of service varies with the region, the office and the person handling your case. If you would like the Pôle Emploi to (try to) find you a job before leaving your home country, you should complete an application at your local job centre, which will forward it to the Pôle Emploi.

Some Pôle Emploi offices specialise in certain fields and industries. For example, in Paris there are offices dealing exclusively with hotel and restaurant services, tourism, journalism, public works, civil aviation, the entertainment industry and jobs for the disabled. Around 20 Pôle Emploi offices are called *Points Cadres* and handle executive jobs. The Pôle Emploi also operates *Jeunes Diplômés*, a service for young graduates (🖳 www.jd.apec. fr); the Association Pour l'Emploi des Cadres (APEC, 🖳 www.cadres.apec.fr) for managers and engineers; and the Association Pour l'Emploi des Cadres, Ingénieurs, Techniciens de l'Agriculture (APECITA, 🖳 www.apecita.com) for professionals in the agriculture industry.

British Jobcentres can provide free leaflets entitled *Working in France* and *Working Abroad*.

La Cité des Métiers

La Cité des Métiers is a careers resource centre at the Cité de Sciences et de l'Industrie (known as 'La Villette'), where you'll find information on over 2,500 jobs, magazines and periodicals, mini-computers and staff to help with job applications. Its website (🖳 www. cite-sciences.fr – follow the links to Cité des Métiers) provides information about the various services and resources available, opening hours and job fairs and other exhibitions sponsored by La Villette.

information about working in France (ask for the Jobcentre Plus service). EURES also has a website (🖳 http://europa.eu.int/jobs/eures) where you can find contact information for job counsellors in the UK and other EU countries specialising in public sector jobs in France.

Recruitment Consultants

International recruitment consultants or executive search companies (*cabinet de recrutement*) or 'head hunters' (*chasseur de têtes*) acting for French companies and recruitment consultants in France (which are mainly to be found in cities and large towns) are suitable for executive and management positions, although many French agencies find positions only for French and EU nationals or foreigners with a residence permit. However, recruitment consultants were hard hit by the recession in recent years, particularly those dealing with executives and senior managers, and many French companies now do their own recruiting or promote in-house.

Consultants place advertisements in daily and weekly newspapers and trade magazines but don't usually mention the client's name, not least to prevent applicants from approaching a company directly. Unless you're a particularly outstanding candidate with half a dozen degrees, are multilingual and have valuable experience, sending an unsolicited CV to a consultant is usually a waste of time.

British people seeking work in France can obtain an *Overseas Placement List*, listing agencies that specialise in finding overseas positions, from the Recruitment and Employment Confederation in London

(☎ 020-7009 2100, 🖳 www.rec.uk.com – click on 'Jobseekers' and then on 'Consultancy Finder').

Many foreign (i.e. non-French) recruitment consultancies post job vacancies on the main internet job sites with links to their own recruitment websites. See **Internet** below for the addresses of the most popular online job hunting sites.

Temporary Agencies

Most employment agencies (*agence de travail temporaire/agence d'intérim*) are allowed to offer only temporary positions, although you can often secure a temporary job which leads to a permanent position. Due to the long annual holidays in France and generous maternity leave, companies often require temporary staff (France has the world's second-largest market for temps). Adecco, Manpower (between them the largest employers in the country with over 400,000 employees), Adia, SOS Intérim and Vediorbis are common in cities and large towns, and generally hire office staff and unskilled or semi-skilled labour. Look in the *Yellow Pages* under *Intérim, emploi (agences)*.

In addition to general temporary agencies dealing with a range of industries and professions, there are agencies specialising in particular fields such as accounting, banking, computers, construction, engineering and technical, hotel and catering, industrial, insurance, nursing and nannying, sales, secretarial and clerical. Most secretarial jobs are for bilingual or tri-lingual people with word processing experience (an agency will usually test your written language and word-processing skills).

To be employed by a temporary agency, you must be eligible to work in France and have a social security number.

You usually need to register with an agency, which entails completing a form and providing a CV and references (you can register with any number of agencies). Most temporary agencies have

websites, and it's often possible to review their vacancies and/or register online. When registering with a temporary agency, ensure that you know exactly how much, when and how you'll be paid. Your salary should include a payment in lieu of holidays and be net of social security contributions.

Newspapers & Other Publications

Most Parisian and regional newspapers have job sections (*offres d'emploi*) on certain days and most newspapers also post job advertisements on their websites. The most popular Parisian newspapers for job advertisements are *Le Monde*, *Le Figaro*, *France-Soir*, *Libération*, *Le Parisien* and *Les Echos* (the daily financial and stock exchange journal). The best newspapers depend on the sort of job you're seeking. If you're looking for a management or professional position, you should obtain copies of *Le Monde*, *Le Figaro*, *Libération* and *Les Echos*. *Le Figaro* provides a separate publication, *Carrières et Emplois*, on Wednesdays, which accumulates employment adverts from a variety of sources, and a job supplement, *Figaro Entreprises*, on Mondays. Those seeking employment as technicians, artisans, secretaries, sales clerks, factory workers and manual labourers should try *France-Soir* and *Le Parisien*. *Libération* has adverts for all job categories.

In addition to the above, there are many important regional newspapers in France, e.g. *Sud-Ouest* and *Ouest-France*. There are also a number of newspapers and magazines devoted to careers and jobs, such as *Carrières et Emplois* (which publishes

regional issues), *Carrières Publiques et Privées*, *Emploi*, *Entreprise et Carrières*, *Job Pratique*, *Le Mardi du Travail* and *Rebondir*. Specialist publications include *Courrier Cadres* for management level jobs (published by Pôle Emploi – see page 28), the *Journal de l'Hôtellerie* (🖥 www.lhotellerie.fr) for hotel and catering jobs, *L'Usine Nouvelle* for factory jobs and *L'Etudiant* for student summer jobs.

☑ SURVIVAL TIP

For links to the websites of the major French newspapers, see 🖥 www.onlinenewspapers.com/france.htm.

Most professions and trade associations publish journals containing job offers (see *Benn's Media Directory Europe*). Jobs are also advertised in various English-language publications, including the *International Herald Tribune*, *Wall Street Journal Europe*, and *France-USA Contacts* (fortnightly) – see **Appendix B**. You can also place an advertisement in employment wanted (*demandes d'emplois*) columns in most publications. It's best to place an advert in the middle of the week and to avoid the summer and other holiday periods.

Americans should obtain a copy of the *Directory of American Firms Operating in Foreign Countries*, and Britons should look for *Finding Work in France* (Careers Europe), available from Jobcentres.

Internet

The internet has hundreds of sites for jobseekers, including business, recruitment company and newspaper sites. Most of the main international job-finding sites have sections devoted to vacancies in France. Some of the best known are listed below (unless otherwise stated, sites cover all types of jobs in all parts of France).

◆ Pôle Emploi and newspaper sites (see above).

◆ Bale.fr (🖥 www.bale.fr) for IT and communications jobs.

◆ Cadremploi (🖥 www.cadremploi.com) for management jobs.

◆ Career Builder (🖥 www.careerbuilder.com).

◆ Career Guide (🖥 www.career-guide.com).

◆ Emailjob.com (🖥 www.emailjob.monster.fr).

◆ Emploi.com (🖥 www.emploi.com).

◆ Emploi Regions (🖥 www.emploiregions.com) for jobs in a particular region.

◆ Employment Guide (🖥 www.employmentguide.org.uk).

◆ Jobware International (🖥 www.jobware.com).

◆ Keljob (🖥 www.keljob.com).

◆ Monster (🖥 www.monster.fr).

◆ Offre-emploi.com (🖥 www.offre-emploi.com).

◆ Overseas Jobs (🖥 www.overseasjobs.com).

◆ Regions Job (🖥 www.regionsjob.com) for jobs in a particular region.

◆ StepStone (🖥 www.stepstone.com and follow the links for France).

◆ Talents.fr (🖥 www.talents.fr) for media and culture jobs.

Most of the above websites include articles about job hunting in France and information about work permits and qualifications. Don't forget to check the websites of large companies and international organisations.

International Organisations

International organisations with offices in France usually post job vacancies on their websites before taking out expensive advertisements or placing vacancies with recruitment consultants, and many now also accept applications online. The largest organisations in France include the OECD, the United Nations Education, Science and Cultural Organisation (UNESCO), the World Bank, the IMF and the International Labour Office – all located in Paris. The ability to speak French may not be of paramount importance to work for an international organisation and, in the case of the OECD and UNESCO, you may not even need a work permit if you're a citizen of a member country.

If you're an EU national, there are a variety of jobs connected with EU bodies, including the Council of Europe, the European Court of Human Rights and the European Parliament (all located in Strasbourg). If you're seeking employment with a foreign (e.g. British) company in France or a French company that does business with your home country, you should contact the relevant Chamber of Commerce, e.g. the Franco-British Chamber of Commerce (☎ 01 53 30 81 30, 🖥 www.francobritishchambers.com), which publishes a monthly review where you can advertise your skills.

Unsolicited Job Applications

Making unsolicited job applications (*candidature spontanée*) to targeted companies is naturally a hit and miss affair. It can, however, be more successful than responding to advertisements, as you aren't usually competing with other applicants. Some companies recruit a large percentage of employees through unsolicited *résumés*. When writing from abroad, enclosing an international reply coupon may help to elicit a response.

You can apply directly to multinational companies with offices or subsidiaries in France, and to French companies. Useful addresses can usually be obtained from local Chambers of Commerce as well as from the websites of multinational companies. Lists of foreign companies in France can be obtained from relevant consulates and embassies, e.g. there are around 2,000 British companies in France. Details of French companies can be obtained from the Chambre de Commerce et d'Industrie de Paris (☎ 08 20 01 21 12, 🖥 www.ccip.fr), which will provide lists of companies in particular fields or industries. French companies are listed by products, services and *départements* in *Kompass France*, available at libraries in France and main libraries and French Chambers of Commerce abroad, as well as via the internet (🖥 www.kompass.fr).

When writing for jobs, address your letter (*lettre de motivation*) to the personnel director or manager (*Chef du Personnel Directeur de Ressources Humaines*) or the relevant head of department (*Chef de Service*) and include your CV (*CV* or *résumé*) and copies of references and qualifications. Try to find out the person's name by phoning the company. If possible, offer to attend an interview and say when you'll be available. Letters should be tailored to individual employers and professionally translated, even if you think your French is perfect.

Details of translators can be obtained from organisations such as the Institute of Translation and Interpreting in the UK (☎ 01908-325250, 🖥 www.iti.org.uk). Note that some 90 per cent of French companies require hand-written letters from job applicants and submit them to graphologists (employers also use astrology, numerology and even more abstruse methods of selecting staff!). You should write on plain paper (but making sure you write straight) and make no mistakes (if you do, start again rather than make corrections). Model letters (*lettre type*) can be obtained from Pôle Emploi offices and on its website. There are many books available offering model business (and personal) letters, including the *Handbook of Commercial French* (Routledge) and *How to Address Overseas Business Letters* (Foulsham).

Your CV should be no more than two pages long and needn't include a complete career history; better to highlight relevant experience. It shouldn't contain foreign (i.e. non-French) abbreviations. Attach a passport-size photograph of yourself looking businesslike (not a grinning holiday snap!). Include character references, translated from English if necessary. Always follow up an application with a phone call a week or so after sending it.

Keep copies of all applications; this allows UK citizens to have their Job Seeker's Allowance extended for three months.

Networking

Networking (*faire du network*) is simply making business and professional contacts. It's particularly useful in France, where the majority of job vacancies are never advertised. The national employment agency, Pôle Emploi, recognises this and runs courses in networking. The keys to success are to look smart, smile, tell (almost) everyone you meet that you're looking for work, make a note of names and telephone numbers and follow them up, ask people for references – in short, not to be backward in coming forward.

It's difficult for most foreigners to make contacts among the French and many turn to the expatriate community, particularly in Paris. If you're already in France, contact or join expatriate social clubs, churches, societies and professional organisations.

A useful resource for English-speakers seeking contacts in Paris is *Paris Anglophone* (Frank Books), containing over 2,000 listings. Much of this information is available online at the Paris Anglo website (💻 www.paris-anglo.com), and there are a number of online forums dedicated to living in France which offer you a chance to network with those who already live there. Links to online forums and chat rooms about France can be found on the Paris Anglo site or at Expatica (💻 www.expatica.com), which has an active French section. Finally, don't forget to ask friends and acquaintances working in France if they know of an employer seeking someone with your experience and qualifications.

Temporary & Casual Work

Temporary and casual work (*travail temporaire/intérimaire* and *emploi de proximité*) is usually for a fixed period, ranging from a few hours to a few months (or work may be intermittent). Casual workers are often employed on a daily, first-come-first-served basis. Anyone looking for casual unskilled work in France must usually compete with North Africans, who are usually prepared to work for less money than anyone else, although nobody should be paid less than the minimum wage.

Many employers illegally pay temporary staff in cash without making deductions for social security. However, legally, pay must be aligned with that of permanent workers, and

most temporary workers found by agencies must have renewable contracts for 18 months or, in exceptional circumstances, 24 months. Temporary and casual work usually includes the following:

◆ office work, which is well paid if you're qualified and the easiest work to find due to the large number of temporary secretarial and office staff agencies;

◆ work in the building trade, which can be found by applying at building sites and through industrial recruitment agencies (such as Manpower);

◆ jobs in shops and stores, which are often available over Christmas and during sales periods;

◆ gardening jobs in private gardens (possibly working for a landscape gardener), public parks and garden centres, particularly in spring and summer;

◆ peddling ice cream, cold drinks and fast food in summer, e.g. on beaches;

◆ market research, which entails asking people personal questions, either in the street or house to house (an ideal job for nosy parkers with fluent French);

◆ modelling at art colleges (both sexes are usually required and you don't need to have a 'perfect' body);

◆ work as a security guard (long hours for low pay);

♦ nursing and auxiliary nursing in hospitals, clinics and nursing homes (temps are often employed through agencies to replace permanent staff at short notice);

♦ newspaper, magazine and leaflet distribution;

♦ courier work (own transport required – motorcycle, car or van);

♦ working as a deck-hand on a yacht, particularly on the French Riviera;

♦ driving jobs, including coach and truck drivers, and ferrying cars for manufacturers and car hire companies;

♦ office cleaning;

♦ baby-sitting.

A good source of information about temporary and casual work in France, particularly for students, is the Centre d'Information et de Documentation Jeunesse (CIDJ, 🖳 www.cidj.com). The website includes a listing of all the regional offices of the CIDJ in France. The Union Nationale Des Etudiants De France (UNEF, 🖳 www.unef.fr) publishes Le Guide Des Étudiants Salariés, a guide for students seeking part-time jobs in order to finance their studies, available by post (around €2) or downloadable from the website. American students can apply to the Council on International Educational Exchange (CIEE, ☎ 1-207 553 7600, 🖳 www.ciee.org).

Temporary jobs are available from agencies and are advertised in Pôle Emploi offices (see page 28) and on notice boards in expatriate clubs, churches and organisations, as well as in expatriate newsletters and newspapers. See also **Seasonal Jobs** below.

SEASONAL JOBS

Seasonal jobs are available throughout the year, the vast majority in the tourist industry. Many seasonal jobs last for the duration of the summer or winter tourist seasons, May to September and December to April respectively, although some are simply casual or temporary jobs for a number of weeks.

Seasonal jobs include most trades in hotels and restaurants, couriers and representatives, a variety of jobs in ski resorts, sports instructors, jobs in bars and clubs, fruit and grape picking and other agricultural jobs, and various jobs in the construction industry. Seasonal employees in the tourist industry have traditionally been paid below the minimum wage, although the authorities have clamped down on employers in recent years.

If you aren't an EU national, it's essential to check whether you'll be eligible to work in France, before your arrival.

⚠ Caution

French fluency is required for all but the most menial and worst paid jobs, and is equally or more important than experience and qualifications (although fluent French alone won't guarantee you a well paid job).

You may, if you aren't an EU national, also be required to obtain a visa. Check with a French embassy or consulate in your home country well in advance of your visit. Foreign students in France can obtain a temporary work permit (autorisation provisoire de travail) for part-time work during their summer holiday period and school terms (see **Chapter 9**).

Note that seasonal workers have few rights and little legal job protection in France, unless they're hired under standard employment contracts (usually CDDs), and they can generally be fired without compensation at any time.

Lists of summer jobs can be found via the internet, e.g. 🖳 www.pole-emploi.fr, www.cidj. com and www.jobs-ete-europe.com. There are many books for those seeking holiday jobs, including Summer Jobs Worldwide and Work Your Way Around the World (Vacation Work). If you speak French, you may be interested in 1,000 Pistes de Jobs (available from L'Etudiant, 🖳 http://librairie.letudiant.fr). See also **Employment Agencies** on page 28 and **Temporary & Casual Work** on page 33.

Hotels & Catering

Hotels and restaurants are the largest employers of seasonal workers, and jobs are available year round, from hotel managers to kitchen hands. Experience, qualifications and fluent French are required for all the best and highest paid positions, although a variety of jobs are available for the untrained, inexperienced and those who don't speak fluent French. If accommodation with cooking facilities or full board isn't provided with a job, it can be expensive and difficult to find. Ensure that your salary is sufficient at least to pay for accommodation, food and other living expenses (see **Cost of Living** on page 253).

The weekly trade magazine *L'Hôtellerie* (🖥 www.lhotellerie.fr) is a good source of hotel and catering vacancies, as is *L'Echo Touristique* (🖥 www.echotouristique.com). Both publications include job advertisements on their websites.

Holiday Villages

Some companies, such as Club Méditerranée (Club Med), operate both summer and winter holiday 'villages' throughout France for periods of around five months. Applicants should be aged between 20 and 30, fluent in French and at least one other language, and be 'personable'. Club Med recruitment offices are located in Lyon. English-speakers can apply online through Club Med's English-language recruitment website (🖥 www.clubmedjobs.com).

Summer Jobs

One of the most popular summer jobs in France – particularly among young people – is grape picking (*vendange*). Goodness knows why, as it's boring, hard work and badly paid. Over 100,000 foreigners are employed on French farms each summer, most of whom are 'professionals' from Morocco, Portugal and Spain who return to the same region each year.

Occupational hazards include sunburn, mosquito and other insect bites, cuts from secateurs, rashes on your arms and legs from chemical sprays, and incessant back pain from bending all day long. Accommodation and cooking facilities can be primitive, and the cost of food and accommodation is usually deducted from your wages.

The grape harvest begins in the south around mid-September and moves up towards Alsace by the middle of October. It's possible to move from area to area, particularly as growers recommend workers to each other. The best (often only) way to find work in a vineyard is to turn up and ask for a job (it's almost impossible to arrange work from outside France). Grape pickers can now obtain a *contrat vendange* valid for one month and renewable for a further month, which exempts them from paying social security charges. Note that grape-picking machines are reducing the number of people required each year.

Useful websites for finding grape-picking jobs include 🖥 www.grapepicking.co.uk, www. vinomedia.fr, www.viti-vini.com and the French government employment site, 🖥 *www.pole-emploi.fr*.

Other fruit-picking jobs include strawberries (May to mid-June), peaches (June to September), cherries (mid-May to early June), pears (mid-July to mid-November) and apples (mid-August to mid-October). The harvest begins early in the south, therefore it's possible to start in May and work through until October (or even mid-November if you pick frozen grapes on Mont Ventoux), following the sun as it ripens the fruit.

Note that fruit picking is sometimes paid at below the national minimum wage (see page 22), so you shouldn't expect to get rich. It isn't essential to speak French, but it certainly helps. Camping equipment comes in handy if you're fruit picking (other than grapes), as farmers often don't provide accommodation. Information about farm work can be obtained from the Service des Echanges et des Stages

Agricoles dans le Monde (SESAME, 🖥 www. agriplanete.com).

Holiday Camps

There are many children's and youth holiday 'camps' (*colonie de vacances*) in France, where French (and many foreign) parents sensibly off-load their offspring during the long summer break from June to September. These offer many job opportunities. Information about children's holiday centres is available from local Directions Départementales de la Jeunesse et des Sports, the addresses of which can be obtained from French embassies or from the *Yellow Pages*. You may also be able to obtain a job at a theme park, such as Disneyland Paris (see page 294). One of the largest British recruiters of summer seasonal workers is PGL Young Adventure (☎ 0844-371 0101, 🖥 www.pgl.co.uk), which operates around ten activity centres in France and recruits some 1,000 staff for work from May to September. PGL offers a variety of jobs, including couriers, group and entertainment organisers, chalet staff, sports instructors (particularly water-sports), teachers, caterers and cooks, and various support staff.

> ☑ **SURVIVAL TIP**
>
> Applications for summer jobs should be made by March for the following summer season; you can download information about employment with PGL from their website (🖥 www.pgl.co.uk) as well as submit an application online.

WINTER JOBS

Ski resorts require an army of temporary workers to cater for the annual invasion of winter sports enthusiasts. Such jobs can be a lot of fun. You will get fit, improve your French and make friends, and may even be able to save some money. Note, however, that although a winter job may be a working holiday to you (with lots of skiing and little work), to your employer it means exactly the opposite! Besides jobs in the hotel and catering trades already mentioned above,

a variety of winter jobs are available, including couriers, resort representatives, chalet staff, ski technicians, and (for the suitably qualified) ski instructors and guides.

As a general rule, the better paid the job, the longer the working hours and the less time off there is for skiing and other pleasurable activities. Employment in a winter resort usually entitles employees to a discounted lift pass (but no time to use it!).

Language Teachers

Language teaching (particularly English) is a good source of permanent, temporary or part-time work (many language schools need extra teachers in summer). This may entail teaching a foreign language at a language school or privately, or even teaching French to expatriates if your French is up to the task. Language schools don't always require a teaching qualification. A university degree and a respectable appearance may suffice, although you should take as many educational certificates with you as possible.

For English teaching, the three most widely recognised qualifications are the Certificate in English Language Teaching to Adults (CELTA), the Trinity Teaching English as a Second Language (TESOL) Certificates and the School for

International Training (SIT) TESOL Certificate; note, however, that an approved course costs around €1,400. Information about courses in the UK can be found in the *Times Educational Supplement* and in France from the University of London Institute in Paris (formerly the British Institute in Paris, ☎ 01 44 11 73 73, 💻 www.ulip.lon.ac.uk). Further information about teaching English in France is available from TESOL France (💻 www.tesol-france. org). The larger language schools, such as Berlitz, usually pay the lowest wages but are the most flexible regarding qualifications.

You could also try placing advertisements in French newspapers and magazines offering private lessons. You can also apply directly to state schools for a position as a language *assistant(e)*. The recent introduction of informal English classes into the early elementary school curriculum has created a shortage of teachers for this programme, and many schools are looking for part-time native English-speakers to teach games and songs to young children.

⚠️ **Caution**

Full-time teachers in French state secondary schools and universities must be French citizens and possess French teaching qualifications.

Part-time language assistants are usually paid only a nominal salary – much less than that offered to a qualified French native teacher. Further information about teaching in France can be obtained from the Ministry of Education (💻 www.education.gouv.fr).

AU PAIRS

The au pair system provides an excellent opportunity to travel, improve your French, and generally broaden your education by living and working in France. Single males and females aged between 18 and 27 from most countries are eligible for a position as an au pair. (Although 'au pair' is French, the French commonly refer to a *fille au-pair*; and the official French term is a *stagiaire aide-familiale*.)

Au pairs must usually have had a high school education or the equivalent and have a good knowledge of French, and they must attend French classes organised for foreign students.

If you're an EU national, you need only a valid passport and aren't required to arrange a position before arriving in France, although it's usually wise. Applicants from non-EU countries need a long-stay visa and require an 'engagement agreement' (*déclaration d'engagement*) with a French family and a certificate of registration for French classes at a language school. These must be presented to your local French embassy or consulate with your passport when applying for a visa.

Au pairs are usually contracted to work for a minimum of six and a maximum of 18 months. Most families require an au pair for at least the whole school year, from September to June. The best time to look for an au pair position is therefore before the beginning of the school year. You should apply as early as possible and not later than a month prior to your preferred start date or at least two months if you need a visa. There are also summer au pair programmes of one to three months between 15th June and 15th September. Enrolment must usually be made before 31st March. Au pairs employed for the summer only aren't required to attend French lessons.

Au pairs are usually placed in French-speaking families with children, although non French-speaking families and families without children can also engage an au pair. Working hours are officially limited to 30 per week, five hours per day (morning or afternoon), six days per week, plus a maximum of three evenings' baby-sitting. You should be given time off to attend French classes and religious services. Au pairs sometimes holiday with the family, or they may be free to take Christmas or Easter holidays at home. Choose a wealthy family and you may be taken on exotic foreign holidays (although they may be less likely to treat you as a family member)!

For your labours you're fed and lodged and paid 'pocket money' of around €320 per month. You're required to pay your own fare from your country to Paris (and back). If you're employed

in the provinces, your family will pay the rail fare from Paris to their home and back to Paris at the end of your stay. In Paris, a family may provide a *carte orange*, a monthly public transport pass.

An au pair position can be arranged privately with a family or through an agency. There are au pair agencies in France and many other countries, which can be found via the internet, e.g. 🖳 www.europa-pages. com/au_pair. Positions can also be found via magazines (such as *The Lady* in the UK) and newspapers, although you're usually better off using an agency. The better agencies vet families, make periodic checks on your welfare, help you overcome problems (whether personal or with your family) and may organise cultural activities (particularly in Paris).

An agency will send you an application form (questionnaire) and usually ask you to provide character (moral) and childcare references, a medical certificate and school references. Some agencies allow you to meet families in France before making a final decision, which is highly desirable, as you can interrogate the family, inspect their home and your accommodation, and meet the children who will make your life heaven or hell! Agency registration fees vary, although there are maximum fees in some countries, e.g. around £50 in the UK. You should contact a number of agencies and compare registration fees and pocket money, both of which may vary considerably (although the terms of employment should be similar). Pocket money is usually higher in Paris than in the provinces.

Many au pairs grow to love their children and families and form lifelong friendships. On the other hand, abuses of the au pair system are common in all countries, and you may be treated as a servant rather than a member of the family and be expected to work long hours and spend most evenings baby-sitting. Many families engage an au pair simply because it costs far less than employing a nanny.

If you have any complaints about your duties, you should refer them to the agency that found you the position. You're usually required to give notice if you wish to go home before the end of your agreement, although this won't apply if the family has broken the contract.

It's possible for responsible English-and French-speaking young women to obtain employment as a nanny (*nurse*, *nanny* or *nounou*, sometimes called *garde d'enfants*). Duties are basically the same as for an au pair job (see above), although a position as a nanny is a proper job with full employee rights and a real salary!

SELF-EMPLOYMENT & STARTING A BUSINESS

Being self-employed in France, as in most other countries, is no simple matter and requires planning, preparation (most foreigners don't do sufficient homework before moving to France), determination and a good deal of luck. While hoping for the best, you should anticipate the worst and have a contingency plan and sufficient funds to last until you're established (this also applies to employees). If you're planning to start a business, you must also do battle with the notoriously obstructive French bureaucracy (*bonne chance!*).

If you're an EU-national, you can work as a self-employed individual (*travailleur independent*) or as a sole trader (*entreprise individuelle* or *auto-entrepreneur*). A non-EU national with a long-term residence permit (*carte de résident*) can be self-employed or a sole trader. However, it's difficult for non-EU nationals to obtain a residence permit to become self-employed.

There are three main categories of self-employed people in France: *profession libérale* (e.g. accountants, doctors, lawyers, writers), *commerçant* (traders and shopkeepers) and *artisan* (craftsmen and tradesmen).

> ### ⚠ Caution
>
> To be self-employed in certain trades and professions, you must have an official status (*statut* or *régime*) and it's illegal simply to hang up a sign and start business.

For foreigners, self-employment options include foreign language teaching, translating, tour guiding, and representing a foreign company.

To work as a self-employed person you must usually have:

♦ qualifications and diplomas that are recognised in France for professions and trades requiring certification;

♦ a residence permit or for EU nationals, proof of residence in France;

♦ a tax registration certificate (*avis d'imposition*);

♦ a business permit (*carte de commerçant*) – see below;

♦ contracts or letters of intent from prospective clients (for those in service industries only);

♦ to register with your local social security (URSSAF) office and obtain a social security number (see page 242);

♦ to register with the relevant organisations (*caisses*) for health insurance and pension contributions; until recently, these depended on your activity, but the system is now being consolidated and a single organisation, the *Régime Social des Indépendants* (*RSI*, 🖥 www.le-rsi.fr), now handles all self-employed workers;

♦ to register for value added tax (*TVA*) at the office nearest to your business location if your turnover is over a certain limit (see page 266);

♦ to register with the appropriate organisation for your profession or trade within two weeks of starting a business, e.g. the Chambre de Métiers, the Chambre d'Agriculture or the Chambre de Commerce. You can obtain the address of the relevant body from your local town hall; for information about French Chambers of Commerce, contact the Assemblée des Chambres Françaises de Commerce et d'Industrie/ACFCI (🖥 www.acfci.cci.fr – English option).

♦ Registration with the appropriate professional or trade organisation is no longer necessary if you opt for the auto-entrepreneur system for new small businesses, i.e. up to €81,500 turnover for traders and up to €32,600 turnover for service businesses. to register at your local tribunal de commerce (for a commercial business).

Before being permitted to register as self-employed, you may be required to attend a business course (*cours/stage de gestion*) run by the relevant local organisation for your trade or profession, covering all aspects of business administration. Courses last from four to six days and can cost up to around €200. (Subject to approval of your new-business project and available funds, Pôle Emploi will pay for the course if you're unemployed and receiving benefits.) At the end of the course you're issued with a certificate (whether you understood anything or not!), which is a prerequisite for starting certain kinds of business. Most courses are held only in French, and in certain cases you may also need to pass an exam (also in French) to obtain a trading licence. The various organisations issue a certificate that must be presented to your local Chamber of Commerce when registering your business.

As a self-employed person in France you aren't entitled to unemployment benefit should your business fail and there are no benefits for accidents at work (except for artisans), although you're insured against invalidity. There's no sick pay for those in *professions libérales*, although *artisans* and *commerçants* are covered provided they've been paying social security contributions for at least a year. As a self-employed person you risk bankruptcy if your business fails, but no longer necessarily ruin, as since 1st January 2011 creditors have had no claim on your private estate if you operate as a sole trader limited company (*entrepreneur individuel à responsibilité limitée*). This protection covers auto-entrepreneurs, commerçants (retailers), self-employed sales agents, artisans, farmers and professions libérales.

It's wise to join a professional association, as they provide valuable information and assistance and may also offer insurance discounts. Most professional associations are organised locally. Check with your departmental Chambre de Commerce or with the local town hall for information about groups active in your area and profession. For information about the appropriate guild (chambre de métiers) for your profession, contact the Assemblée Permanente des Chambres de Métiers et de l'Artisanat (💻 www. artisanat.fr).

An increasing number of people are starting businesses (démarrer une entreprise) in France, despite the fact that the bureaucracy associated with it is among the most pernicious in the world, particularly for non-French speakers. However, registration has now been simplified and for the least complicated type of business (auto-entrepreneur) it can, in theory, be completed in a matter of minutes online, although if you need a licence or a loan to start a business, don't plan on getting it in a few weeks or even months, as it can take up to a year! Nevertheless, France is traditionally a country of small companies and individual traders, where the economic philosophy encourages and even nurtures the creation of small businesses. Many of these, however, exist on a shoe string.

Non-EU nationals require a licence (carte commerçante étranger) to start a business in France, and no commitments should be made until permission has been granted.

The majority of businesses established by foreigners are linked to the leisure and catering industries, followed by property investment and development. Types of business include holiday accommodation, e.g. bed and breakfast (chambres d'hôtes) and gîtes (chalets, apartments and cottages to let), caravan and camping sites, building and allied trades, farming (e.g. dairy, vineyards, fruit, fish and fowl), catering (e.g. bars, cafés and restaurants), hotels, shops, franchises, estate agencies, translation services, language schools, landscape gardening, and holiday and sports centres (e.g. tennis, golf, squash, shooting and horse-riding schools). Nevertheless, you should try to find a niche and not simply set up the same kind of business as lots of other expatriates.

Comprehensive information about setting up and running a holiday accommodation business in France are provided in our sister publication, Running Gîtes and B&B in France (Survival Books).

Basilique du Sacré-Cœur, Paris

2.
EMPLOYMENT CONDITIONS

French employees, particularly state employees, enjoy excellent employment conditions, which are variously dependent on the French Labour Code (*Code du Travail*), **collective agreements** (*conventions collectives de travail*), **an individual employment contract** (*contrat de travail*), **and the employer's in-house rules and regulations** (*règlements intérieurs/règlements de travail*).

Employees have extensive rights under the French Labour Code, which details the minimum conditions of employment, including working hours, overtime payments, holidays, trial and notice periods, dismissal conditions, health and safety regulations, and trade union rights.

> The Labour Code is described in a number of books, including the *Code du Travail* (VO Editions). Information about employment conditions is available from the Legifrance website (⌨ www.legifrance.gouv.fr), some of which is in English, and also from the government website (⌨ www.service-public.fr).

Collective agreements (*conventions collectives*) are negotiated between industry associations (*syndicats*) and employers' associations in many industries. These specify the rights and obligations of both employees and employers in a particular industry or occupation and include around 75 per cent of the workforce. Agreements specify minimum wage levels for each employment category in a particular industry or company. If an employer doesn't abide by the laws or the regulations, employees can report him to the works council or labour management committee. Where there's no works council or committee, the case is heard before an industrial tribunal (*conseil de prud'hommes*) comprising employer and employee representatives (elected by the workforce). When an employee is wrongfully dismissed, he's awarded damages based on his length of service.

Employment regulations are supervised by local work inspectors (*inspecteur du travail*) and the Direction Départmentale du Travail et de l'Emploi. Employment laws cannot be altered or nullified by private agreements. In general, French law forbids discrimination by employers on the basis of sex, religion, race, age, sexual preference, physical appearance or name, and there are specific rules regarding equal job opportunities for both men and women (see **Working Women** on page 20). In 2002, a law was introduced forbidding 'moral harassment', although regrettably this hasn't prevented a number of suicides (most notably by France Télécom employees under pressure from their bosses).

Salaried foreigners are employed under the same working conditions as French citizens, although there are different rules for certain categories of employee, e.g. directors, managers and factory workers. As in many countries, seasonal and temporary workers aren't always protected by employment laws and may have fewer legal rights than other workers. However, part-time employees receive the same rights and benefits (on a pro rata basis) as full-time employees.

This chapter covers the content of an employment contract and general employment conditions, and highlights points to check when negotiating the terms for a job, some of which apply to all positions and some to executive and managerial positions only. In addition to these points, you should enquire about your prospective employer and in particular whether he has a good reputation and prospects. A high turnover of staff should be a warning to look elsewhere!

EMPLOYMENT CONTRACTS

Legally, an offer of employment in France (and, in practice, regular salary slips for an indefinite-term contract – see below) constitute an employment contract (*contrat de travail/d'emploi*), although it's safer to obtain a formal written contract (especially before handing in your notice to a previous employer!). Employees usually have a formal contract stating such details as their job title, position, salary, working hours, benefits, duties and responsibilities, and the place and duration of their employment. Contracts usually contain a paragraph stating the date from which they take effect and to whom they apply.

⚠ Caution

Unless your contract specifies that you'll work only in the place of work listed, your employer is entitled to ask you to work elsewhere from time to time.

All employment contracts are subject to French labour law, and references may be made to other regulations such as collective agreements. Anything in contracts contrary to statutory provisions and unfavourable to an employee may be deemed invalid.

There are usually no hidden surprises or traps for the unwary in a French employment contract. Nevertheless, as with any contract, you should know exactly what it contains before signing it. If your French isn't fluent, you should try to obtain a translation, although according to French law any exclusion clauses must be 'clear and comprehensible'. If you cannot obtain a written translation (which is likely), you should at least have it translated orally so that you don't receive any nasty surprises later.

There are two main kinds of employment contract in France: an indefinite-term contract and a term contract.

Temporary Contracts

A temporary contract (*contrat de travail temporaire* or *intérim*) has no minimum or maximum duration and can be issued only in the following circumstances:

◆ to someone replacing a staff member who's temporarily absent (except if striking) and whose function is essential to the running of the business;

◆ to someone filling a post on an interim basis until a permanent staff member takes over;

◆ to cover a temporary, unforeseen and otherwise unmanageable increase in the workload of existing staff;

◆ for a seasonal business that requires additional workers at specific times of year, e.g. in agriculture for harvesting or in catering for peak periods;

◆ for workers in specific sectors (e.g. the theatre), where the use of temporary contracts is habitual.

Any other type of short-term contract is regarded as a fixed term contract (see below). A worker engaged on a temporary contract is known as a *salarié intérimaire* or simply *intérimaire*.

Fixed-term Contracts

A fixed-term contract (*contrat à durée déterminée/CDD*) is, as the name suggests, a contract for a limited period. This is normally a maximum of 18 months, although it's limited

Indefinite-term Contracts

An indefinite-term contract (*contrat à durée indéterminée/CDI*) is the standard employment contract for 'permanent' employees. Surprisingly, it doesn't have to be in writing (unlike a fixed-term contract), although you should insist on this; in fact, a standard contract form (*modèle de contrat de travail à durée indéterminée*) can be obtained from URSSAF offices. A *CDI* often includes a trial period of one to three months (three months is usual), depending on collective agreements, before it becomes legal and binding on both parties.

SALARY & BENEFITS

Your salary (*salaire*) is stated in your employment contract; salary reviews, planned increases, cost of living rises, etc., may also be included. Salaries may be stated in gross (*brut*) or net (*net*) terms and are usually paid monthly, although they may be quoted in contracts as hourly, monthly or annually. If a bonus is paid, such as a 13th or 14th month's salary (see below), this is stated in your contract.

General points such as the payment of your salary into a bank or post office account and the date of salary payments are usually included in employment conditions. Salaries above €1,500 per month must be paid by cheque or direct transfer (not cash), although it isn't wise to receive your salary in cash as it makes you subject to close scrutiny by the tax authorities!

You receive a pay slip (*bulletin de paie*) itemising your salary and deductions and you must keep your pay slips indefinitely, as they can be required to show proof of earnings (essential when you apply for a French retirement pension) or payment of social security or other insurances, even after your death!

Salaries must be reviewed once a year (usually at the end of the year), although employers aren't required by law to increase salaries which are above the minimum wage (see page 22), even when the cost of living has increased. Salary increases usually take effect on 1st January. See also **Salary** on page 21.

to nine months if a position is due to be filled permanently and can be extended to two years if the position is due to be suppressed (there's no minimum term). It can be renewed twice for a term no longer than the original contract, provided it doesn't exceed two years in total. A *CDD* must be in writing.

A *CDD* can be issued when a permanent employee is on leave (including maternity or sick leave), if there's a temporary increase in business, or at any time in the construction industry or for youth employment schemes.

*CDD*s are strictly regulated, mainly because they're considered a contributing factor to the ever-increasing 'precariousness' of employment (*précarité d'emploi*). For example, the salary of an employee hired on a *CDD* mustn't be less than that paid to a similarly qualified person employed in a permanent job. The employee has the right to an end-of-contract bonus (*indemnité de fin de contrat*) equal to 10 per cent of his salary, in addition to other agreed bonuses, although this doesn't always apply to seasonal employees.

Contracts for seasonal and temporary workers fall under the same rules as for a *CDD*.

13th Month's Salary & Bonuses

Many employers in France pay their employees a bonus in December, known as the 13th month's salary (*13ème mois*). A 13th month's salary isn't mandatory unless it's part of a collective agreement or when it's granted regularly, in which case this should be stated in your employment contract. In your first and last years of employment, your 13th month's salary (if there is one) and other bonuses should be paid pro rata if you don't work a full calendar year.

Some companies also pay a 14th month's salary, usually in July before the summer holiday period. A few companies, e.g. banks and other financial institutions, may pay as many as 15 or 16 months' salary. Where applicable, extra months' salary are guaranteed bonuses and aren't pegged to the company's performance (as with profit-sharing). In some cases, they're paid monthly (pro rata) rather than in a lump sum at the end or in the middle of the year.

Senior and middle managers often receive extra bonuses, perhaps linked to profits, equal to around 10 to 20 per cent of their annual salary, although these are more restricted since the recession began in 2008.

Employees of many French companies are also entitled to participate in bonus schemes (some tied to productivity) and profit-sharing schemes (*participation des salariés aux résultats de l'entreprise/système d'intéressement aux bénéfices*), which must (since 1994) be provided by any company with over 50 employees.

A new bonus-linked-to-profits (*prime-dividendes*) law was imminent in July 2011, making profit-sharing more equitable, subject to the following conditions. Companies employing over 50 people whose annual dividends to shareholders exceed those of the previous two years are to pay employees a bonus – the amount to be agreed between management and the labour management committee (see below). The average amount per employee is estimated at €700 and around 25 per cent of France's employees in the private employment sector are expected to qualify. Up to €1,200 can be paid without being subject to the principle social security contributions, but bonuses are included in taxable income. The scheme is voluntary for companies with fewer than 50 employees.

Some employers also operate optional investment plans (*plan d'épargne d'entreprise*), where the company holds a portfolio of securities on behalf of its employees, and share option schemes (*options sur actions*). If you're employed on a fixed-term contract, you're paid an end-of-contract bonus (*indemnité de fin de contrat*) equal to 10 per cent of your salary, in addition to other bonuses.

Companies with 50 or more employees must have a labour management committee (*comité d'entreprise*) comprising elected employees. The company pays an amount equal to 1 per cent of its payroll into the committee's fund, to be used at the discretion of employees to provide benefits such as private day-care, holidays, theatre discounts, holiday gifts and a staff Christmas party. As with training, some companies allocate extra funds to their *comité d'entreprise* as a means of attracting employees.

Expenses

Expenses (*frais*) paid by your employer are usually listed in his general conditions. These may include travel costs from your home to your place of work, usually consisting of a second-class rail season ticket or the equivalent amount in cash (paid monthly with your salary).

In the Paris area, most employers pay 50 per cent of the cost of an employee's *Carte Orange*, a monthly public transport pass. Otherwise, travelling expenses to and from your place of work are tax deductible.

Companies without a restaurant or canteen may pay a lunch allowance or provide 'luncheon vouchers' (*chèques* or *tickets restaurant*) that can be purchased for half their face value and may be used in local restaurants and some food shops.

Allowable expenses for travel on company business or for training and education may be detailed in your employment conditions or listed in a separate document.

Relocation Expenses

The payment of relocation expenses (*frais de voyage*) depends on your agreement with your employer and should be included in your employment contract or conditions. Most employers pay travel and relocation costs to France up to a specified amount, although you may be required to sign a clause stipulating that if you leave the employer before a certain period (e.g. five years), you must repay a percentage of the costs.

If you're hired from outside France, your air ticket and other travel to France are usually booked and paid for by your employer or his overseas representative. In addition, you can usually claim any onward travel costs, e.g. the cost of transport to and from airports. If you travel by car, you can usually claim a mileage rate or the equivalent air fare.

If you're relocating, an employer may pay a fixed relocation allowance based on your salary, position and size of family, or he may pay the total cost of removal. The allowance should be sufficient to move the contents of an average house, and you must normally pay any excess costs yourself. If you don't want to bring your furniture to France or have only a few belongings to ship, it may be possible to purchase furniture locally up to the limit of your allowance. Check with your employer. When your employer is liable for the total cost, he may ask you to obtain two or three removal estimates.

Generally, you're required to organise and pay for removals in advance. Your employer will usually reimburse the equivalent amount in euros after you've paid the bill, although it may be possible to get him to pay the bill directly or give you an advance.

> If you change jobs within France, your new employer may pay your relocation expenses when it's necessary for you to move house. Don't forget to ask, as he may not offer to pay.

WORKING HOURS

Traditionally, the French have had a flexible attitude to working hours, and the idea of fixed office hours is particularly alien to executives and managers. For example, taking a long lunch break, perhaps for a game of tennis or some other kind of 'game', isn't frowned upon, provided you put in the required hours and don't neglect your work. It isn't unusual for a parent to leave work early to collect children from a nursery, and some employees work only a half-day on Wednesdays, when children don't attend school.

However, in 2000, France introduced a mandatory 35-hour working week for all large employers, and on 1st January 2002 this became effective for all employers. The objective of the 35-hour week scheme, referred to as the 'working hours reduction' programme (*réduction du temps de travail* or *RTT*), was to dramatically reduce unemployment by spreading the existing amount of work across more workers. Companies were encouraged to negotiate with their employees to find ways of distributing the reduced working hours – including a seven-hour day, a four-and-a-half day week or even varying weeks within the same month. Some industries were allowed to recognise seasonal workload variations by granting extra time off during the off-season to compensate employees for longer hours necessary during peak times of the year.

These plans were considered radical disruptions of hard-won job security rights and privileges, and there were numerous one-day strikes and several large public demonstrations in protest against them. In fact, predictions (mostly governmental) that the scheme would create a million new jobs proved wildly optimistic and many of the original provisions have been amended and restrictions relaxed, so that the 35-hour week has generally become the 39-hour week and working practices have largely reverted to tradition, although some have changed irrevocably.

For many years, it wasn't usual practice to have scheduled coffee or tea breaks in France, but with the advent of the 35-hour week and its new 'flexibility' in scheduling, employers can (and do) establish mandatory break periods (*heures de repos*) to adapt working schedules to the new *RTT* rules. However, (non-alcoholic) drinks can usually be taken at an employee's work station at any time.

Many workers traditionally have a two-hour lunch break, particularly in the provinces, although this is no longer standard practice in most companies. Lunch may be anything from a marathon to a quick bite at a café. Eating at your desk is generally frowned upon unless you have urgent work to complete. In Paris, lunch breaks commonly start at 13.00, while in the provinces it's usually 12.00 or 12.30.

⚠ Caution

It may come as a nasty surprise to some foreigners to discover that many French employers (including most large companies) require employees to clock in and out of work. If you're caught cheating the clock, you can be dismissed.

Since the introduction of the 35-hour week, time-keeping requirements have become much more complex and most employees must be tracked to ensure that weekly, monthly and annual hours and days worked don't exceed the limits prescribed by the new laws.

The working week for round-the-clock shift workers is limited to 25 hours, and shift working is usually paid at higher rates as specified in collective agreements.

The good news is that weekends are sacrosanct and almost no office employees work at weekends. Even most shops are closed on Sundays (and many also on Mondays).

Flexi-time

Many companies operate flexible working hours (*horaire mobile/horaire flexible*). A flexi-time system requires employees to be present between certain hours, known as the block time (*temps bloqué/heures de présence obligatoire*), e.g. from 08.30 to 11.30 and from 13.30 to 16.00. Employees may make up their required working hours by starting earlier than the required block time, reducing their lunch break or working later.

Many large business premises are open from around 06.30 until 19.00, and smaller companies may allow employees to work as late as they like, provided they don't exceed the maximum permitted daily working hours.

Flexi-time rules are often complicated and may be contained in a separate set of regulations.

Overtime

In principle, if you work over 35 hours per week, you must be paid overtime or be given time off in lieu. Employees can be asked to do overtime but cannot be compelled to do over 220 hours per year, although this can be altered by collective agreements and/or the government. The total hours worked per week mustn't exceed an average of 44 over 12 consecutive weeks or an absolute maximum of 48 hours per week.

The minimum legal pay for overtime is the normal rate plus 25 per cent for the first eight hours above the standard 35-hour week (i.e. up to 43) and plus 50 per cent for additional hours (i.e. above 43). Employees can be granted time off in lieu at overtime rates (i.e. 1.25 hours for each hour of overtime worked) instead of being paid. Employees cannot be obliged to work on Sundays unless collective agreements state otherwise. If an employee agrees to work on a Sunday, normal overtime rates apply.

Salaried employees, particularly directors (*dirigeants*) and managers/executives (*cadres*), aren't generally paid overtime, although this depends on their contracts. Most of managers are subject to both *RTT* and maximum work time regulations, even though their work time may not be tracked on an hourly basis but measured in days per year. Directors, managers and executives generally work long

Before starting a new job, check that any planned holidays will be honoured by your new employer. This is particularly important if they fall within your trial period (usually the first three months) or before 1st May of your first year in the job, when holidays may not be permitted.

Some collective agreements grant extra days off (usually from one to three) for long service, and many grant additional days off in lieu of overtime or

hours, even allowing for their occasionally long lunch breaks, but are accorded additional holiday time to meet *RTT* requirements. For example, in Paris executives often work from 08.30 or 09.00 to 19.00 or 20.00. Senior staff in the south generally work shorter hours than those in Paris and the north, particularly on hot summer days.

HOLIDAYS & LEAVE

Annual Holidays

French workers enjoy longer holidays than those in any other country: an average of 39 days per year compared with 24 in the UK, 17 in Australia and just 14 in the US. French 'working' life revolves around holidays (*les vacances*); the majority of discussion is about holidays that have just been had or are coming up.

Under labour law, an employee is entitled to 2.5 days' paid holiday (*congé*) for each full month he works. After working for a full year, you're therefore entitled to 30 days off, which equals five weeks (including Saturdays, which are 'traditionally' counted as work days).

Legally, you earn your holiday entitlement over the course of a year that runs from 1st May to 30th April. Therefore, if you start work in January, by 1st May you'll have earned ten days' holiday, which you can take during the subsequent year, i.e. starting 1st May. By the next 1st May, you should have accrued a full five weeks' holiday, which is available to you over the next 12 months.

to meet *RTT* regulations. Employers cannot include official French public holidays (see below) in the annual holiday entitlement.

Employees are legally entitled to take up to four weeks' paid holiday in a single block between 1st May and 31st October, unless business needs dictate otherwise (although other agreements are possible). Most employees take a three-or four-week summer holiday between July and August and one or two weeks in winter (often around the Christmas and New Year holiday period).

Traditionally, August was the sole month for summer holidays, many businesses closing for the whole month. However, the government has been trying to encourage companies to stagger their employees' holidays throughout the summer, and it's becoming more common for employees to take their main summer holiday in July or between the two summer public holidays, 14th July and 15th August. Almost half of companies, particularly small businesses and local shops, close for the entire month of July or August, which naturally has adverse effects on the economy.

When a company closes during summer, employees are obliged to take their holiday at that time. Many large manufacturers are forced to close because their component suppliers shut during this period and they don't carry large enough stocks to keep them going. Even in those companies that remain open throughout the summer, roughly half of employees are on holiday during July and August.

There are various schemes designed to assist large and low-income families to go away on holiday, including holiday vouchers (*bon-vacances*) and holiday savings (*chèque-vacances*), to which certain employers contribute. Further information is available from the Agence Nationale pour les Chèques-Vacances (ANCV, 🖳 www.ancv.com).

Public Holidays

The only public holiday (*jour férié*) that an employer in France is legally obliged to grant with pay is 1st May (irrespective of which day of the week it falls on). However, most collective agreements allow paid holidays on some or all of the ten public holidays show in the table below. (Note: The Pentecost/Whit Monday holiday was officially abolished in 2004, but is still widely observed.)

When a holiday falls on a Saturday or Sunday, another day (e.g. the previous Friday or following Monday) isn't usually granted as a holiday instead. However, when a public holiday falls on a Tuesday or Thursday, the day before or the day after (i.e. Monday or Friday respectively) may be declared a holiday, depending on the employer. This practice is called 'making a bridge' (*faire le pont*). If a holiday falls on a Wednesday, it's common for employees to take the two preceding or succeeding days off.

In May there are usually three or four public holidays and it's possible to have a two-week break while only using a few days of your annual holiday. (In some years, France virtually grinds to a halt due to the *ponts de mai*.)

All public offices, banks, post offices, etc., are closed on public holidays, when only essential work is carried out. Note that foreign embassies and consulates usually observe French public holidays plus their own country's national holidays.

Maternity & Paternity Leave

The family is of fundamental importance in France, and female employees are entitled to extensive employment benefits with regard to pregnancy (*grossesse*) and infant care. Social security benefits are also generous and are designed to encourage large families (see page 243).

Maternity leave (*congé maternité*) is guaranteed for all women irrespective of their length of employment. The permitted leave period is 16 weeks: six weeks prior to birth (*congé prénatal*) and ten weeks afterwards (*congé postnatal*); leave is extended for the third and subsequent children as well as for multiple births or caesareans or other complications. A doctor may authorise additional time off, either before or after a birth, in which case a company must continue to pay your salary.

Women aren't obliged to inform their employers that they're pregnant, although if they don't they won't be entitled to benefits. It's normally to your advantage to do so in any case, as most employers are flexible regarding time off work in connection with childbirth and child care. For example, you're usually allowed to arrive late (especially if your journey to work involves travelling on public transport)

Public Holidays	
Date	**Public Holiday**
1st January	New Year's Day (*Nouvel An/Jour de l'An*)
March or April	Easter Monday (*Lundi de Pâques*)
1st May	Labour Day (*Fête du Travail*)
8th May	VE Day (*Fête de la Libération/Victoire 1945/Anniversaire 1945*)
May	Ascension Day (*Ascension*) – the sixth Thursday after Easter
14th July	Bastille Day (*Fête Nationale*)
15th August	Assumption (*Fête de l'Assomption*)
1st November	All Saints' Day (*Toussaint*)
11th November	Armistice Day (*Fête de l'Armistice*)
25th December	Christmas Day (*Noël*)

Parents also have the right to an additional year of unpaid parental leave (*congé parental*), which applies equally to parents of adopted children.

Employees have the right to take paid time off work to care for a sick child. The regulations allow 12 days a year for each child, although a doctor's certificate (*fiche médicale pour enfant*) must be provided.

Provided you don't extend your leave beyond the permitted period, your employer must allow you to return to the same job at the same or a higher salary, taking into account general increases in wages and the cost of living. See also **Sickness & Maternity Benefits** on page 244 and **Childbirth** on page 225.

Compassionate & Special Leave

Most companies provide days off for moving house, your own or a family marriage, the birth of a child, the death of a close relative, and other such events. Grounds for compassionate leave (*congé pour convenance personnelle*) are usually defined in collective agreements and may include leave to care for a seriously ill or disabled child (*congé de présence parentale*).

The number of days' leave granted varies according to the event, e.g. four days off for your own wedding (but not if you get married during a holiday!) and one day off to attend a child's wedding or the funeral of a parent (including in-laws), brother or sister.

Employees who have worked for a company for at least three years, and have worked for a total period of at least six years are entitled to take from between six and 11 months off – naturally without pay!

Sick Leave

Employees in France don't receive a quota of sick days as in some countries (e.g. the US), and there's no limit to the amount of time you may take off work due to sickness or accidents. You're normally required to notify your employer immediately of sickness or an accident that prevents you from working. You must also obtain a doctor's certificate (*arrêt de travail*) on the first day of your sickness, otherwise it will count as a day's holiday.

and to have more work breaks. You may also be entitled to a new chair and be exonerated from certain tasks. Employers are obliged to allow you paid time off for routine antenatal examinations. If you're breastfeeding, they must also reduce your daily work time by one hour for your child's first year, but aren't obliged to pay you for this hour.

New fathers are entitled to paternity leave (*congé paternité*) in addition to the three days off usually granted on the birth of a child (*congé de naissance* – see **Compassionate & Special Leave** below), provided they've been making health insurance contributions for at least ten months. The permitted leave period is 11 days for a single birth and 18 days for a multiple birth, which must be taken in a continuous period during the four months following the birth. You must notify your employer at least a month in advance of the days you wish to take. Both employees and the self-employed can claim a daily allowance of around €70. Fathers are entitled to a further three months' unpaid paternity leave. For more information on paternity leave, employees should contact their local CPAM or the self-employed the *caisse* to which they belong.

If you're off sick, you may leave home only between 10.00 and 12.00 and between 16.00 and 18.00 (these restrictions are apparently to prevent you from 'moonlighting').

For information about sickness benefits see **Sickness & Maternity Benefits** on page 244.

INSURANCE

All employers in France are required to publish a document listing the dangers and risks to the health and safety of their employees, and provide a minimum level of health and safety insurance.

All French employees, foreign employees working for French companies and the self-employed must contribute to the French social security (*sécurité sociale*) system. Social security includes healthcare (plus sickness and maternity benefits), compensation for injuries at work, family allowances, unemployment insurance, old age benefits (i.e. pensions), and invalidity and death benefits.

Contributions are calculated as a percentage of your gross income and are deducted at source by your employer. Social security contributions are high and total an average of around 60 per cent of gross pay, although some 40 per cent is paid by employers. For details, see **Social Security** on page 237.

Health Insurance

Comprehensive health insurance is provided by the French social security system (see page 237), but many industries and professions have their own supplementary health insurance schemes (*mutuelle*) that pay the portion of medical bills that isn't covered by social security – usually 20 or 30 per cent (see page 247). Membership may be obligatory and contributions may be paid wholly by your employer or split between you and your employer. Some employers, particularly foreign companies, provide free comprehensive private health insurance for executives, senior managers and their families. For further information about health insurance see page 247.

In addition to undergoing a medical examination before taking up employment, you may need to be examined by the company's *médecin du travail* on an annual basis,

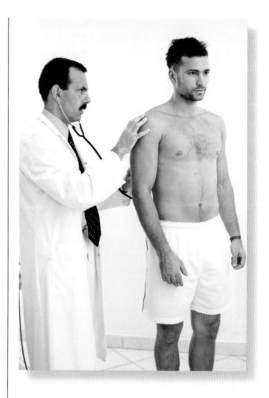

attesting to your continued fitness for your job, or at any time if there's a doubt about your physical condition. A medical examination may also be necessary as a condition of membership of a company health, pension or life insurance scheme.

Salary Insurance

Salary insurance (*assurance salaire*) pays employees' salaries during periods of sickness (*congé maladie*) or after accidents, and is provided under social security. After a certain number of consecutive sick days (the number varies with your employer), your salary is no longer paid by your employer but by social security, which is one reason contributions are so high. Some employers opt to pay their employees' full salaries for a limited period in cases of extended disability or illness, in which case state benefits are paid to the employer rather than to the employee.

Unemployment Insurance

Unemployment insurance (*allocation d'assurance chômage*) is compulsory for employees and is covered by social security contributions. In the last few years, the government has legalised a form of private unemployment insurance for some categories of self-employed people and owner-managers of small companies who aren't eligible for state unemployment insurance. Statutory unemployment benefit is available to those who are eligible.

RETIREMENT & PENSIONS

Your employment conditions may be valid only until the official French minimum retirement age (*retraite*), which is 60 for both men and women born before1st July 1951 in most trades and professions and civil servants (although some state employees can retire on a full pension at 55 or even 50).

Retirement ages were revised by the government in 2010 and those born after 1st July 1951 now have to work longer before retiring. If you were born in 1956 or after you'll have to work until the age of 62 before retiring. Those who have a certified partial and permanent disability may retire before these dates, plus those who started working at a young age and have the required number of paid-up social security quarterly payment periods, which varies and depends on exactly when they started working.

If you wish to continue working after you've reached retirement age, you may be required to negotiate a new employment contract, although you're usually permitted to do certain types of work after retirement (e.g. of an artistic or scientific nature), provided you were practising them alongside your main job before retiring.

In addition to contributing to social security, which provides a state pension (see page 246), most employees contribute to a supplementary company pension fund (*caisse complémentaire de retraite*). Almost every trade or occupation has its own scheme and in many companies it's obligatory for employees to contribute. The rates and details vary slightly, depending on whether you contribute to the fund for managers (*cadres*) or for non-managerial workers (*non-cadres*).

For further information see **Pensions** on page 246.

For further information see **Pensions** on page 246.

☑ **SURVIVAL TIP**

If your retirement pension is the product of employment years both abroad (e.g. in the UK) and France it may not be in your interest to take retirement at the minimum age in France. The formula used to calculate French state pensions takes into account average earnings over a minimum number of years, and if you work more years in France on a higher salary than previously to meet the minimum number of years required (they vary depending on your date of birth), your French pension should increase. Ask your local Pensions office (see page 246) for details.

EDUCATION & TRAINING

Employee training (*formation professionnelle*) is taken seriously, whether it's conducted in your workplace or elsewhere, and employers with ten or more employees must allocate a percentage of their gross payroll to employee education and training. Employers who are keen to attract the best employees, particularly those engaged in high-tech fields, usually allocate extra funds and provide superior training schemes (large companies often spend an amount equal to around 10 per cent of their payroll on training).

You're normally entitled to paid vocational training after two years with a company employing over ten people or three years with a company with fewer than ten staff and should apply at least two months in advance (four months if the training is to last over six months).

You're also entitled to unpaid time off for training (*congé individuel de formation*), although your employer may postpone this for up to nine months. Training may include management seminars, technical courses, language lessons or any other form of continuing education, provided it's relevant to the type of activity (*nomenclature des activités françaises/NAF*) carried out by your employer. If you need to learn or improve your French or another language in order to perform your job, the cost of language study is usually paid by your employer. However, not all employees benefit equally from training, which is decided by the employer.

It's in your interest to investigate courses of study, seminars and lectures that you feel will be of benefit to you (and consequently to your employer). Most employers give reasonable consideration to a request to attend a course during working hours, provided you don't make it a full-time occupation! (Time spent on training must be counted as working hours for the purposes of the 35-hour working week rules.)

Further information about training can be found via the internet portal set up by the Centres d'Animation et de Ressources de l'Information sur la Formation (💻 www. intercarif.org – click on 'Le réseau des CARIF-OREF' for a list of centres).

UNION MEMBERSHIP

There are numerous trade unions in France, many grouped into confederations, although French unions aren't as highly organised as those in many other developed countries, and their power and influence has been reduced considerably since the late '70s, when labour disputes and strikes (grèves) were common. Since then, union membership has declined dramatically, membership of the Confédération Générale du Travail (CGT) dropping from over 2.5m to around 1m today. Other major unions are the Confédération Française des Travailleurs Chrétiens, the Confédération Française de l'Encadrement/Confédération Générale des Cadres, the Confédération Française Démocratique du Travail and the Force Ouvrière.

Union membership includes only around a fifth of the total workforce and less than 9 per cent of the private sector workforce – the lowest proportion in the EU. Unions are strongest in traditional industries and services such as railways, automobile manufacturing and stevedoring, and have had little success in new high-tech industries. However, they're still capable of causing widespread disruption, as has been demonstrated in recent years.

All businesses with more than 11 employees must have a workers' (or works) council or a labour management committee comprising employee delegates (délégués du personnel) elected by and from the employees. The number of delegates increases in proportion to the number of employees, up to a maximum of 50. Delegates represent employees when they have questions or complaints for management concerning, for example, working conditions, job classification, wages, and the application of labour laws and regulations.

> Under French law, unions are allowed to organise on any company's premises and 'closed shops' are banned. With the exception of some public sector employees, e.g. the police, employees have the right to strike and cannot be dismissed for striking. Even where workers don't belong to a union, their rights are protected by labour laws.

In companies with over 50 employees, employee delegates must be elected to the board of directors and a labour management committee (comité d'entreprise) must be formed. Companies with separate locations (e.g. factories or offices) employing over 50 employees must have a local labour management committee (comité d'établissement), with representatives of this committee sitting on a central labour management committee (comité central d'entreprise).

In addition to matters relating to the terms and conditions of employment, any major changes to the operation, organisation and management of a company must be discussed with the committee before they can be implemented. However, a company isn't usually required to act on the opinion of the labour management committee.

OTHER CONDITIONS

Trial & Notice Periods

For most jobs in France there's a trial period (période d'essai) of one to three months, depending on the type of work and the employer (three months is usual). A trial period isn't required by law, although there's no law forbidding it. The length of a trial period is usually stated in collective agreements. During the trial period, either party may terminate the employment contract without notice or financial penalty, unless otherwise stated in a collective

A fixed-term contract (see **Employment Contracts** on page 44) can be terminated before the end of its period only in specific circumstances, i.e. when either the employer or employee has committed a serious offence (*faute grave*), due to an event beyond the control of both parties (*force majeure*), or with the agreement of both parties.

Under recent regulations designed to modernise labour law, an employee may terminate a fixed-term contract without penalty if he accepts a job with an indefinite contract.

If an employer commits a serious offence or illegally dismisses an employee before the end of his contract, the employee is entitled to be paid in full for the remaining period of the contract, plus 10 per cent of his salary and bonuses. If an employee commits a serious offence or unilaterally breaks the contract other than to accept a 'permanent' job, he may need to pay damages and loses his right to any bonuses. No compensation is payable if termination is due to *force majeure*.

Part-time Job Restrictions

Restrictions regarding part-time employment (*travail à mi-temps*) may be detailed in your employment conditions. Most companies don't allow full-time employees to work part-time (i.e. moonlight) for another employer, particularly one in the same line of business. You may, however, be permitted to take a part-time teaching job or something similar.

Changing Jobs & Confidentiality

Companies in a high-tech or highly confidential business may have restrictions on employees moving to a competitor (*clause de non-concurrence*), although strictly these aren't legal unless the employer offers employees a financial incentive not to change jobs. This is a complicated subject and disputes often need to be resolved by a court of law. French laws regarding industrial secrets and general employer confidentiality are strict. If you breach this confidentiality you may be dismissed and could be unable to find further employment in France.

agreement. If at the end of the trial period an employer hasn't decided whether he wishes to employ you permanently, he may have the right to repeat the trial period, but only once and only to the maximum period allowed by the collective agreement for the industry. After this period, if you haven't been officially dismissed, you're deemed to be hired 'permanently', irrespective of whether an employment contract exists.

Notice (*préavis*) periods are governed by the law and collective agreements, and usually vary with length of service. The minimum notice period is usually a month for clerical and manual workers, two months for foremen and supervisors, and three months for managerial and senior technical staff. The minimum notice period for employees with over two years' service is two months.

Although many employers prefer employees to leave immediately after giving notice, employees have the right to work their notice period and are usually allowed (if they ask) two hours a day off work to seek employment elsewhere. However, both parties can agree that the employee receives payment in lieu (*indemnité compensatrice de préavis*) of notice. Compensation must also be made for any outstanding paid annual holidays (*indemnité compensatrice de congés payés*) up to the end of the notice period, and all terminated employees receive a redundancy payment (*indemnité de licenciement*) of some sort (see **Dismissal & Redundancy** on page 56).

Acceptance of Gifts

Employees are normally forbidden to accept gifts (*accepter des dons*) of more than a specified value from customers or suppliers. Many suppliers give bottles of wine or small gifts at Christmas, which can usually be accepted without breaching this rule.

Dismissal & Redundancy

The rules governing dismissal (*licenciement*) and severance pay (*indemnité de licenciement*) depend on the size of a company, the employee's length of service, the reason for dismissal (e.g. misconduct or redundancy), and whether the employee has a protected status, such as that enjoyed by union and employee representatives, who can be dismissed only for 'gross misconduct'.

The two main reasons for dismissal are personal (*motif personnel*) and economic (*motif économique*), i.e. when a company is experiencing serious financial problems. An employee can be dismissed at any time during his trial period (usually the first one to three months) without notice or compensation. Thereafter, you can

be dismissed for personal reasons only in the case of a 'valid and serious offence' (*cause réelle et sérieuse*), e.g. stealing from an employer.

It's difficult for an employer to dismiss an employee unless he has demonstrated utter incompetence or is guilty of some form of gross misconduct. If an employee is accused of misconduct, a strict procedure must be followed before he can be disciplined or dismissed. He must be summoned by registered letter to attend a formal preliminary hearing with the employer, during which the alleged misconduct is discussed. He has the right to bring another person to the interview, either a colleague or an employee representative (whose name must appear on an official list). If dismissal could result, the employer must mention this as a possibility during the hearing. If the employer decides that the offence warrants dismissal, there's usually a cooling-off period before he can effect the dismissal. The grounds for dismissal must be stated in the dismissal letter, which must also be sent by registered post to the employee's home address.

A dismissed employee is entitled to severance pay if he has at least two years' service, and compensation in lieu of notice when a notice period cannot be observed. Payment must also be made in lieu of any outstanding paid holiday (*indemnité compensatrice de congés payés*) up to the end of the notice period, i.e. for earned holiday not yet used in the current year. Severance pay must equal at least 20 per cent of his average monthly salary for each year of service, i.e. 100 per cent if you've been employed for five years. Collective agreements may provide for increased severance pay. Severance pay may not be payable when an employee is dismissed for a serious breach of conduct – usually a criminal act.

If you're dismissed, you're also entitled to 'back to work assistance' and unemployment benefit (*allocation d'aide au retour à l'emploi/ARE*) from your local Pôle Emploi office and, in certain cases, to a relocation grant (*aide à la mobilité géographique*). The ARE unemployment benefit is up to 75 per cent of your previous salary for a period, which depends on your age and the length of time that you've contributed to unemployment insurance.

An employee dismissed for 'misconduct' can appeal against the decision to a union or labour court. If the employer didn't abide by the law or the regulations in a particular industry, the employee can have his case heard by his union or management committee. If there's no union or committee, the case is heard before an industrial tribunal (*conseil des prud'hommes*) comprising both employer and employee representatives (elected by the workforce). If the employee wins the case, he's entitled to severance pay and compensation (e.g. six months' salary or more) for breach of his labour contract, but he may not be reinstated. In order to avoid the expense and publicity of legal proceedings, most employers make an out-of-court settlement.

When an employee is dismissed for economic reasons, i.e. made redundant, the procedures are strictly regulated. As a result of several high-profile mass redundancies in recent years (notably Marks & Spencer, Danone and Moulinex) which prompted a number of demonstrations and strikes, legislation has been passed to tighten up the legal requirements in an attempt to discourage further plant closures and redundancies. (Unfortunately, these measures also tend to discourage businesses from taking on new employees.) Companies intending to fire at least ten workers within a 30-day period or at least 18 workers in a year, must consult the relevant administrative authorities as well as the works council or employee delegates before any steps are taken. This also applies in the case of any planned reorganisation or the sale or transfer of ownership of any portion of a company.

A company considering redundancies is obliged to table an 'employment protection plan' (*plan de sauvegarde de l'emploi*) disclosing its reorganisation and restructuring plans and their expected impact on employees.

Employers must propose specific action to try to prevent redundancies, including reducing working hours, retraining and redistributing workers within the company, and offering training programmes to allow workers to find new jobs outside the company. There must also be an explicit plan for calling back workers laid off if the economic situation improves or new jobs are created within the restructured organisation.

If you're thinking of employing a full-time, part-time or temporary employee, take care that you don't get embroiled in French employee legislation, particularly if you wish to terminate the employment.

 Caution

You should get an employee to sign a written statement of the terms of the termination of employment, or you could be sued for unfair dismissal.

At termination, it's customary to ask an employee to sign a receipt for amounts due (*reçu de solde de tous comptes*), although it has recently been ruled that this document doesn't limit the ex-employee's rights to claim further payments from his former employer.

A *cetrtificat de travail* should also be issued to an employee at the same time showing the period he was employed and his job title or function.

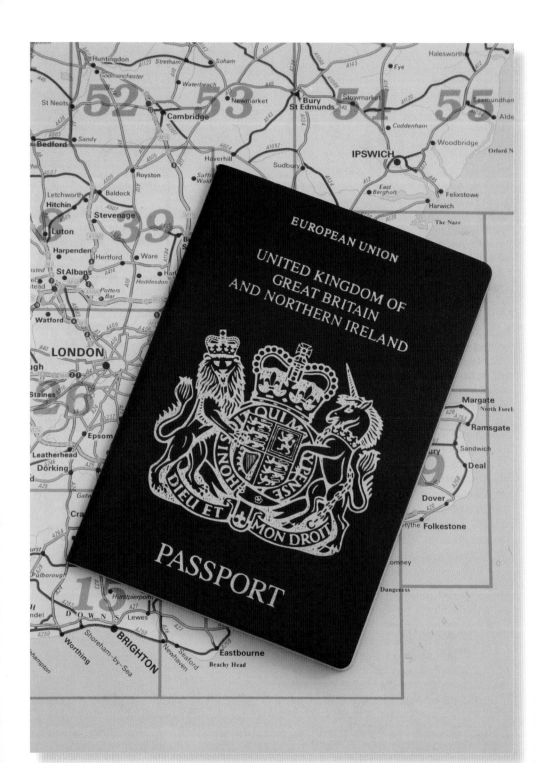

3.
PERMITS & VISAS

Before making any plans to visit France or live or work there, you must ensure that you have the necessary identity card or passport (with a visa if necessary) and, if you're planning to work there or stay long term, the appropriate documentation to obtain a residence and/or work permit, or for most EU nationalities, just proof of residence. There are different requirements for different nationalities and circumstances, as detailed below.

Immigration can be an inflammatory subject in France. The government has recently introduced new laws to curb non-EU immigration and is cracking down on illegal immigrants, who can be forcibly repatriated, although a controversial plan to send immigrant children 'home' was quickly abandoned. The new laws give the police wider powers to prevent illegal immigration and they can make random checks up to 40km (25mi) inside frontiers and at airports, docks, and road and rail terminals handling international traffic.

▲ Caution

Permit and visa infringements are taken seriously by the authorities, and there are penalties for breaches of regulations, including fines and even deportation for flagrant abuses.

Immigration is a complex and ever-changing subject and the information in this chapter is intended only as a general guide. You shouldn't base any major decisions or actions on the information contained herein without confirming it with an official and reliable source, such as a French consulate.

French bureaucracy (euphemistically called *l'administration*) is legendary, and you should be prepared for frustration caused by time-wasting and blatant obstruction on the part of officials. (This isn't necessarily xenophobia – they treat their fellow countrymen in the same way!) Often you may wonder whether the right hand knows what any other part of the body is up to (it usually doesn't) and you should expect to receive conflicting information from consulates, government departments, *préfectures* and town halls.

Red tape is a way of life in France, where every third person is a civil servant (*fonctionnaire*). In order to obtain a permit, you must complete numerous forms, answer dozens of irrelevant questions and provide mountains of documents with official translations to produce an impressive-looking *dossier*. When dealing with officialdom, you must persevere, as the first answer is always '*Non!*' Never take anything for granted where civil servants are concerned and make sure that you understand all communications. If in doubt, have someone translate them for you. You can sometimes speed up proceedings by employing a lawyer, although this is unusual in France and may be counterproductive.

While in France, you should carry your passport or residence permit (if you have one). You can be asked to produce your identification papers at any time by the police or other officials; if you don't have them, you can be taken to a police station and interrogated. You can carry copies, but you may be required to produce the originals within 24 hours. A residence permit or proof of residence serves as an identity card, which French nationals must carry by law.

VISITORS

Foreigners who aren't resident in France can visit the country for a maximum of 90 days at a time. EU citizens need only a national identity card to visit France; other foreigners require a passport. Visitors from EU countries plus Andorra, Australia, Canada, Croatia, Hong Kong and Macao, Iceland, Israel, Japan, Liechtenstein, Macedonia, Monaco, Montenegro, New Zealand, Norway, Serbia, Singapore, South Korea, Switzerland and the US don't require a visa, although certain conditions regarding the purpose of a visit apply to some of these countries. French immigration authorities may require non-EU visitors to produce a return ticket and proof of accommodation, health insurance and financial resources. All other nationalities need a visa to visit France (see below).

EU nationals who visit France to seek employment or start a business therefore have only 90 days in which to find a job or establish a business. However, Bulgarians and Roumanians still require a residence permit (*titre de séjour*) to work in France and if they don't have sufficient funds to support themselves their application for a residence permit will be refused. All other EU nationals plus nationals from Iceland, Liechtenstein, Norway and Switzerland no longer require a *titre de séjour*, but they should register with their local town hall within three months of arrival if they plan to live in France.

If you're a non-EU national, it isn't usually possible to enter France as a visitor and change your status to that of an employee, student or resident. You must return to your country of residence and apply for a long-stay visa (see below).

Non-EU citizens (except citizens of Andorra, Monaco and Switzerland and spouses of French residents – see below) who are staying with friends or family must obtain a 'certificate of accommodation' (*attestation d'accueil* – formerly *certificat d'hébergement* and sometimes referred to as *attestation d'hébergement*), valid for 90 days, before their departure and present it on arrival in France. Your hosts must apply for the *attestation* at their local town hall, police station or gendarmerie up to six months in advance of your arrival and mail it to you.

Note that you must spend at least 90 days outside France before you're eligible for another 90-day period in the country. If you're likely to want to return and require proof that you've spent the required period abroad, you should have your passport stamped at a police station, customs office or an office of the national police (*gendarmerie*) near your point of entry into France. You should ask to make a declaration of your entry (*déclaration d'entrée sur la territoire française*). Note also that visitors may not remain in France for over 180 days in a year.

VISAS

Visitors from EU countries plus Andorra, Australia, Canada, Croatia, Hong Kong and Macao, Iceland, Israel, Japan, Liechtenstein, Macedonia, Monaco, Montenegro, New Zealand, Norway, Serbia, Singapore, South Korea, Switzerland and the US don't require a visa to enter France, although certain conditions for some countries regarding the nature of the visit must be met. All other nationalities require a visa.

Some countries (e.g. Ireland and Italy) allow foreigners with close ancestors (e.g. a grandfather) who were born there to apply for a passport of that country, which can allow non-EU citizens to become 'members' of the EU.

⚠ **Caution**

If you require a visa to enter France and attempt to enter without one, you'll be refused entry.

If you're in doubt as to whether you require a visa, enquire at a French consulate before

making travel plans or go to the website of the Ministère des Affaires Etrangères (🖳 www. diplomatie.gouv.fr), where you can enter information about your situation to find the visa you require (on the English-language version of the site, click on 'Going to France'). Other useful sites include that of the Invest in France Agency (🖳 www.invest-in-france.org), which has general information on settling in France as well as details about visas; and 🖳 www.campusfrance. org, which contains information about studying in France, including the visa requirements for students; both are available in English.

A visa is stamped in your passport, which must be valid for at least 90 days after the date you intend to leave France. Visas may be valid for a single entry only or for multiple entries within a limited period. There are three main types of visa, as described below.

Short-stay Visas

A short-stay visa (*visa de court séjour*), also referred to as a 'Schengen Visa' (see below), is valid for 90 days and is usually valid for multiple entries as well as for free circulation within the countries that are signatories to the Schengen agreement (listed below).

A type of short-stay visa, often issued to businessmen, is a *visa de circulation*, which allows multiple stays of up to 90 days over a period of three years, with a maximum of 180 days in any calendar year.

An short-stay visa costs €60.

Schengen Visas

Germany is a signatory to the Schengen Agreement (named after a Luxembourg village on the Moselle River where the agreement was signed in 1995), which introduced an open-border policy between member countries. In autumn 2010, the 25 Schengen members were: Austria, Belgium, the Czech Republic, Denmark, Estonia, Finland, France, Germany, Greece, Hungary, Iceland, Italy, Latvia, Lithuania, Luxembourg, Malta, the Netherlands, Norway, Poland, Portugal, Slovakia, Slovenia, Spain, Sweden and Switzerland. Bulgaria and Romania are planning to implement the agreement later. The United Kingdom and Ireland aren't members, but are signatories to the Schengen police and judicial cooperation treaty.

So-called third-world citizens who aren't on the Schengen visa-free list can download a Schengen Visa application form the websites of French embassies, e.g. 🖳 www.ambafrance-uk. org/img/pdf_formulaire_sch_eng.pdf in the UK. Certain applicants for a Schengen visa must submit their visa application, together with all the necessary documents, in person at the French mission responsible for their place of residence.

A Schengen visa costs €60 and allows you to travel freely between all Schengen member countries. Under the Schengen agreement, immigration checks and passport controls take place when you first arrive in a member country from outside the Schengen area, after which you can travel freely between member countries for a maximum of up to 90 days in a six-month period.

Schengen visa holders aren't permitted to live permanently or work in Europe (short business trips aren't usually considered employment). Foreigners who plan to take up employment or a self-employed activity in France (or any Schengen country) may require a visa, even if their home country (nationality) is listed on the Schengen visa-free list.

Third-world nationals who are resident in France (or another Schengen country) can travel freely to all Schengen member countries without a visa, simply by showing their French residence permit and passport (or other valid travel document). New third-world nationals resident in France receive a Schengen ID card (existing third-world residents receive one when their paper residence permit expires).

Long-stay Visa

A non-EU national intending to remain in France for over 90 days, whether to work, study or merely holiday, must obtain a long-stay visa (*visa de long séjour*) before arriving and must apply for a residence permit within a week of their arrival. If you arrive without a long-stay visa, it's almost impossible to change your status after arrival and, if you wish to remain for longer than 90 days, you must return to your country of residence and apply for a long-stay visa. Non-EU parents with children aged under 18 must also obtain long-stay visas for their children.

A long-stay visa isn't necessary for EU nationals planning to stay longer than 90 days in France, although they should apply for a residence permit or register as a resident with their town hall within three months. Long-stay visas cost €99 for adults.

Au Pairs

To obtain a long-stay visa for an au pair position, you must usually have a contract (*déclaration d'engagement*) with a family and a certificate of registration for French language classes. The family or au pair agency must complete the application (*accord de placement au pair d'un stagiaire aide-familiale*), available from the office of the Direction Départementale du Travail et de la Main d'Oeuvre in the department where you'll be resident. Two copies of the application are returned to the family or agency, one of which is forwarded to you so that you can apply for a visa.

An au pair's residence permit (*permis de stagiaire aide-familiale*) is valid for six months and renewable for up to 18 months. For further information about working as an au pair in France, see **Au Pairs** on page 36.

Retirees

Non-EU retirees, except Iceland, Liechtenstein, Norwegian and Swiss nationals, require a long-stay visa to live in France for longer than 90 days, and should make a visa application to their local French consulate at least four months before their planned departure date. Non-EU retirees are issued with temporary residence permits, which must be renewed annually.

☑ SURVIVAL TIP

All non-employed residents must provide proof that they have an adequate income or financial resources (including health insurance for non-EU nationals) to live in France without working or becoming a burden on the state. A *titre de séjour* is preferable, for practical purposes, to a certificate of proof of residence, as it's more acceptable to officials.

Student Visas

There are three types of visa for non-EU nationals – '*non européens*' is the wording used by the French government on their website (🖥 www.service-public.fr) – planning to study in France, depending on the intended length of their stay:

◆ Schengen visa – A Schengen visa (see above) allows multiple entries but is valid for a maximum stay of three months only. Applications are made using a Schengen visa form (see **Applications** below) and the fee is the same. However, the requirements for a Schengen visa are the same as for a long-stay visa (see above).

◆ Temporary Long-stay Visa (*visa d'étudiant pour six mois avec plusieurs entrées*) – This allows multiple entries and is valid for three to six months. With this visa it's usually unnecessary to obtain a residence permit. The visa must, however, state that a residence permit is unnecessary, i.e. *le titulaire de ce visa est dispensé de solliciter une carte de séjour* or *le présent visa vaut autorisation de séjour*. Requirements are the same as for an ordinary long-stay visa (see above).

♦ One-year Visa – This visa is valid for between six months and a year but allows only a single entry. Applications are made using a temporary long-stay visa form (see above) and the fee is the same. On arrival in France, you must have a medical examination by a French doctor who's approved by the Office des Migrations Internationales (OMI) and apply for a residence permit (*carte de séjour d'étudiant*) – see **Residence Permits** on page 67.

Fiancé(e)s & Spouses

The status of the fiancé(e) or spouse of a French resident depends on the nationality of the resident, as detailed below.

Fiancé(e)s

Non-EU nationals coming to France to marry a French citizen may need to apply for a long-stay visa. France doesn't issue a 'fiancé visa'. If you plan to arrive in France less than three months before your marriage, it may be possible to enter the country on a short-stay visa and then regularise your situation immediately after your marriage, claiming full benefit of your status as the spouse of a French national. Make sure, however, that you declare your entry into France (by requesting a declaration of entry or having your passport stamped with the date you arrived).

Spouse

Non-EU nationals married to a French resident (whether of French or foreign nationality) for less than a year require a long-stay visa to enter France; they cannot obtain an extension (beyond 90 days) if they enter France as a visitor. It's usually fairly simple for someone married to a French national to obtain a long-stay visa, simply by presenting their marriage certificate and proof of the French partner's citizenship to the appropriate consulate.

Non-EU nationals who have been married to a French resident for more than a year may be permitted to enter France as visitors and then apply for a residence permit, although a long-stay visa is recommended (check with a French consulate abroad).

> The foreign spouse of a French citizen is automatically granted a permanent residence permit (*carte de résident* – see below) provided the couple have been married for at least a year. The non-EU spouse of an EU national resident in France is granted a temporary five-year residence permit (*carte de séjour*) permitting him or her to live and work in France.

The spouse and children under 18 of a non-EU national with a visa to work in France (*visa de séjour salarié*) may usually accompany him to France, although a visa is required for each family member. Applications for visas for family members must be made at the same time as the main applicant's visa application. Family members don't have the right to work in France unless they have their own *visa de séjour salarié*.

Applications

Applications for visas must be made to the nearest French embassy or consulate in your country of residence. Applicants for long-stay visas living in a country other than their country of nationality must apply in their country of nationality unless they've been resident abroad for at least a year.

You can usually apply for a visa in person or by post. If you apply in person, you should bear in mind that there are long queues at consulates in major cities (take a large book to read and get there early!). Check the opening hours and also the days they're open. Some consulates only deal with visa applications in the morning and/or close their visa section on one day a week. The documentation required for a visa application depends on the purpose of your visit to France. All applicants require the following:

♦ a passport valid for at least three months (90 days) beyond the last day of your intended stay in France;

♦ a ticket (or evidence of having booked a ticket) for your outward and return journey;

♦ the official visa application form(s), obtainable from a French consulate (in English in English-speaking countries) or via the internet (💻 www.service-public. fr – follow the links to '*Étrangers -Europe*' and then '*Étrangers en France*' and '*Entrée en France*'; the forms are listed on the right under '*Services en ligne et formulaires*' – the forms are only available in French via this website);

♦ a number of passport-size photographs on a white background (usually one for each application form, of which there may be up to eight!);

♦ a stamped, self-addressed envelope;

♦ the application fee, which is payable when the application is made. Fees for long-stay visas are €340 for visitors, €70 for employed people and €55 for students. No refund is made if the visa isn't granted.

Depending on the purpose of the visa, some or all of the following documents are also required:

♦ a 'validated' copy or official translation of your birth certificate or an extract from your civil status record dated within the last three

months, as well as those of your spouse and other members of your family;

♦ an affidavit stating that you've not been convicted of a criminal offence or declared bankrupt;

♦ evidence of accommodation: e.g. the title deeds to a property, a rental agreement or a 'certificate of accommodation' (*attestation d'accueil*) from a French family or friends with whom you'll be staying;

♦ evidence of financial independence, which may take the form of bank statements, letters from banks confirming arrangements for regular transfers of funds from abroad, or letters from family or friends guaranteeing regular support. Letters should be notarised (witnessed by a public notary). Students should have evidence of funds of at least €600 per month or €400 per month if their accommodation is free, in which case they should submit a letter from an organisation or institution guaranteeing accommodation or evidence of a scholarship or grant.

Evidence of financial independence isn't required by someone coming to France to take up paid employment, who must of course be able to supply an employment contract or equivalent (see below). Retirees must provide a copy of a pension book or other proof of regular income or confirmation from a French bank that their monthly income is adequate to enable them to live in France without becoming a burden on the state. The formula for calculating the income level required allows depends on the current cost of living.

♦ if you're a non-EU national taking up employment in France, a work contract (*certificat d'emploi*) approved by the French Ministry of Labour or the District Labour Department where the business is registered. This must be obtained by the prospective employer in France and sent to the Office Français de l'Immigration et de l'Intégration (OFII, 💻 www.offi.fr) for transmission to the appropriate French consulate abroad.

♦ an undertaking not to engage in any occupation without authorisation (on plain, unheaded paper and signed by you);

♦ a medical certificate issued by an OFII-approved doctor, which is necessary for most long-term visa applicants, including employees and their family members, students and au pairs. The examination must be carried out within three months of taking up residence in France. Applicants must pay a fixed fee.

♦ a health insurance certificate if you aren't eligible for health treatment under French social security (see page 237) and your stay is for less than six months. Note that some foreign insurance companies don't provide sufficient cover to satisfy French regulations, and you should check the minimum cover necessary with a French consulate in your country of residence and obtain a letter from your insurance company confirming that your policy is valid in France.

♦ If you plan to stay longer than six months and you're aged under 28, you must join the French social security system, which must be done when applying for your residence permit – see below. if you're a student, proof of admission from an approved educational establishment, stating that you'll be studying for at least 20 hours per week. This is usually a letter of admission (*attestation de pré-inscription*), when registering for the first time, or other evidence of registration (e.g. *certificat/ autorisation d'inscription*), depending on the level and type of studies.

♦ an agreement (*déclaration d'engagement*) with a French family and a certificate of registration for French language classes if you're an au pair (see page 36);

♦ a marriage certificate if you're a non-EU national married to a French resident (see page 354);

♦ written authorisation from a parent or guardian if you're aged under 18. (Additional documents are also required by non-EU students aged under 18.)

Documents should be translated into French, and translations must be made by a translator approved by your local French consulate, a list of whom (*liste de traducteurs*) is provided on request by consulates.

Students on a scholarship from the French government or a foreign government, or on an EU study programme or one arranged by a recognised international organisation require only a valid passport, completed visa application forms, photographs and a letter confirming the value of the grant and the duration of their intended stay. There's no fee for a visa for students on a scholarship.

 Caution

Visa applications usually take six to eight weeks to be approved, although they can take much longer and you should allow at least three months.

WORK PERMITS

The following information is of a general nature. For further details, contact your country's embassy in France or the commercial attaché at a French consulate. See also **Self-employment & Starting a Business** on page 38.

EU Nationals

EU nationals don't require a work permit; just proof of residence (a *titre de séjour* or a certificate from their town hall following registration there) which gives them the right to work in France. Restrictions to the right to work of nationals of the eight countries that joined the EU in May 2004 were lifted on 1st May 2006, but nationals of Bulgaria and Romania, which joined the EU in January 2007, still have restricted access to the French job market until 2014. For more information, check with your local French consulate or embassy.

Non-EU Nationals

A combined residence and work permit (*carte unique de séjour et de travail* or *carte de séjour salarié*) is issued to non-EU nationals coming to France to take up permanent employment. When you arrive, you have two months in which to apply for a temporary residence permit (*carte de séjour temporaire salarié* – see **Temporary Residence Permit** below) while your application for a *carte unique de séjour et de travail* or *carte de séjour salarié* is being processed (French bureaucracy at its inimitable best). To obtain this, you must present the following:

♦ a completed long-stay visa (*visa de long séjour*) application form (see above);

♦ an 'introductory' employment contract (a contract submitted by the employer stating that the position has been registered with the national employment agency and other relevant authorities);

♦ a medical certificate (from an examination carried out by an OFII-approved doctor).

Non-EU nationals wishing to start or manage a business or undertake any commercial activity in France must obtain a business permit (*carte de commerçant*). Business permits aren't required by holders of permanent residence permits (*carte de résident*), owners and investors in companies (not managers), and self-employed workers performing a service (rather than a commercial activity). An application for a business permit should be made abroad at a French consulate when applying for a visa. Your residence permit is stamped *non-salarié, profession libérale* and you aren't permitted to work as a salaried employee in France.

If you're already resident in France, you can apply for a business permit at your local town hall or *préfecture*. You must provide details relating to the incorporation of the prospective business, a detailed description of the proposed business activity, proof of financial resources, and an affidavit stating that you've not been convicted of a criminal offence or declared bankrupt.

It can take up to six months to obtain a business permit, although a temporary permit can be issued within a shorter period.

Students

After completing their first year of study, students can obtain a temporary work permit (*autorisation provisoire de travail*) for part-time (*mi-temps*) work, provided they have a residence permit (see below) and are attending an educational institution that provides students with French social security health cover or a scholarship (*bourse*).

They may work for a maximum total of 964 hours per year, which averages 18.5 hours per week for 52 weeks, or 60 per cent of full-time working (Algerians are limited to 50 per cent). On completion of their studies, students may remain on the same basis of part-time working, but if they take employment paying more than 1.5 times the current level of unemployment benefit (SMIC), they must register their change of status with the local *préfecture*, who will ensure that they're qualified to work in France in that capacity.

To apply for a work permit, you must submit your student card (*carte d'étudiant*) and residence permit, and a letter from the prospective employer (stating his name and address, the job title and description, salary, working hours, place of work and length of employment) to your local Direction Départementale du Travail et de l'Emploi. Secondary and technical school students under the age of 18 also need a letter of authorisation from their parents and a *certificat de scolarité*.

Written parental consent is required for anyone aged under 18 wishing to work in France.

RESIDENCE PERMITS

In general, all foreigners remaining in France for longer than 90 days in succession for any reason require a residence permit (*titre de séjour*) or (see **EU Nationals** above) a certificate showing that they have registered with their town hall. Where applicable, a residence permit holder's dependants are also granted a permit. Children can be listed on a parent's permit until the age of 18, although they require their own residence permit at the age of 16 if they're working.

Different types of residence permit are issued depending on your status, including permits for long-stay visitors (*visiteur*), salaried employees (*salarié*), transferees (*détaché*), family members (*membre de famille*), students (*étudiant*) and traders (*commerçant*). A combined residence and work permit (*carte unique de séjour et de travail* or *carte de séjour salarié*) is issued to non-EU nationals taking up permanent employment in France (see above).

There are two main categories of residence permit in France: a *carte de séjour* and a *carte de résident*. The *carte de séjour* is referred to below as a temporary residence permit and the *carte de résident* as a permanent residence permit.

Temporary Residence Permits

Until November 2003, a temporary residence permit (*carte de séjour*) was required by all foreigners aged 18 and above, both EU and non-EU nationals, who were to remain in France for over 90 days. A new law (called the *loi Sarkozy* after the then-future President) waived the requirement for EU citizens to obtain a *carte de séjour*, although the actual wording of the law is ambiguous. If you aren't sure whether your citizenship waives the requirement for a *carte de séjour*, you should contact the departmental *préfecture* in order to check whether one is required – particularly as you can be fined for failing to apply for one! The information below is provided on the assumption that a *carte de séjour* is required.

Whether or not you require a *carte de séjour* you must meet the criteria for residence, i.e. adequate financial means of support and, unless you qualify for state health benefits, private health insurance.

The period of validity of a temporary residence permit varies depending on your circumstances, as described below. Note, however, that a temporary residence permit automatically becomes invalid if you spend over six months outside France and it can be revoked at any time if you no longer meet the conditions for which it was issued (or if you obtained a permit fraudulently). The maximum permitted period of continuous residence in France for a holder of a temporary residence permit is three years.

EU Nationals

Unless advised otherwise (see above), EU nationals whether or not they're or will be working in France, no longer require residence permits (*carte de séjour de ressortissant d'un état membre de l'UE*) which were valid for ten years and renewable for further ten-year periods. Note that Bulgarians and Rumanians require a residence permit (until 2014) if they wish to work in France.

EU nationals who are unemployed and have no proof of income are issued with a one-year temporary residence permit, provided they have the means to support themselves during this period.

All EU nationals who live in France regularly in a law-abiding manner for a continuous five-year period (up to 6 months absence a year is permitted) are now automatically entitled to live permanently in France. A permanent residence permit (*CE séjour permanent*) is available, which is free and optional.

Non-EU Nationals

Non-EU employees must apply for a temporary residence permit (*carte de séjour temporaire salarié*) within two months of their arrival. This is valid for a maximum of a year and can be renewed two months before its expiry date, upon application and presentation of a new employment contract or verification of your continued employment. If you're taking up long-term employment, you must apply for a *carte unique de séjour et de travail* or a *carte de séjour salarié* (see above).

Employees transferred to a French company for a limited period (*statut détaché*) may not stay longer than 18 months initially, with a possible extension to 27 months. If you're taking up employment for less than a year, your permit is valid only for the period of employment. The permit has the annotation *salarié* or the name of the professional activity for which the contract was approved and lists the department(s) where the holder can be employed.

Non-EU spouses of EU nationals or French residents are granted a five-year residence permit (*carte de séjour*) permitting them to live and work in France. Dependants of non-EU nationals are entitled to a temporary residence permit marked '*vie privée et familiale*', prohibiting them from working in France.

Students

Students on a one-year visa (see above) should apply for a student's residence permit (*carte de séjour d'étudiant*), which is valid for a further year and can be renewed annually for the duration of the course. Students who have studied in France for the preceding two years and have a parent who has lived in France for at least four years don't require a permit.

Permanent Residence Permit

A permanent residence permit (*carte de résident*) is available for non-EU nationals and is usually issued to those who have lived in France for three consecutive years and speak fluent French (the exception is the foreign spouse of a French resident, who's automatically granted a permanent residence permit after one year of marriage). It's valid for ten years and renewable provided the holder can furnish proof that he's practising a profession in France or has sufficient financial resources to maintain himself and his dependants. A permanent residence permit authorises the holder to undertake any professional activity (subject to qualifications and registration) in any French department, even if employment was previously forbidden. See also **Citizenship** on page 343.

Applications

An application for a residence permit must be made to the *préfecture de police* in towns that have them, or to the local town hall (*mairie*) in small towns or the police (*gendarmerie/ commissariat de police*) in large towns and cities. If permits aren't issued locally, you'll be referred to the Direction de la Réglementation of your department's *préfecture* or the nearest *sous-préfecture*.

 Caution

Failure to apply for a residence permit within the specified period is a serious offence and can result in a fine.

In large towns and cities, many police stations have a foreigners' office (*bureau des étrangers*). In Paris, applications must be made to the appropriate police centre (*centre d'accueil des étrangers*) for the area (*arrondissement*) where you live. Centres are usually open from 08.45 to 16.30, Mondays to Fridays. Smaller towns may have a *bureau des étrangers* in the town hall, with limited opening hours, e.g. mornings only.

Students should apply to their local town hall or *préfecture* (there's a special counter at the *préfecture* in Paris). It's also worthwhile obtaining a student card (*carte d'étudiant*), which entitles you to certain privileges. Contact your school or university for details of how to apply.

If you arrive in France with a long-stay visa, you must apply for a residence permit within a week. EU nationals who visit France with the intention of finding employment or starting a business have 90 days in which to find a job and apply for a residence permit, if applicable, or register their address at the local town hall. Note that it isn't possible to do this while living in temporary accommodation such as a hotel or caravan site.

Documents

You'll be notified of the necessary documentation if you require a residence permit, which depends on your situation and nationality (and possibly on the issuing office!). The following documents are usually required by all applicants, including those from European countries (if applicable):

◆ a valid passport, with a long-stay visa if necessary, or a national identity card (EU countries only);

◆ a 'validated' copy or official translation of your birth certificate or an extract from your civil status record dated within the last three months (If you're accompanied by any dependants, they also require a passport, birth certificate and photographs. Note that British dependants must have their own passport irrespective of their age);

◆ a number (usually three) of black and white (white background) or, more usually, colour passport-size photographs;

◆ proof of residence, which may consist of a copy of a lease or purchase contract or a utility bill. If you're a 'lodger', the owner must provide an *attestation d'accueil* confirming that you're resident in his home (see above);

◆ two stamped, self-addressed envelopes;

◆ evidence of financial independence (see above);

◆ details of your French bank account;

◆ evidence of health insurance or a medical certificate from an OFII-approved doctor if you aren't covered by French social security. British retirees must produce a form E121GB available from the DSS Overseas Branch. If you're covered by French social security, you must produce your social security number.

In addition to the above, you'll be required to produce the following, as appropriate:

◆ a marriage or divorce certificate or other papers relating to your marital status (this isn't usually required by EU nationals, but British applicants require a copy of their marriage certificate because the maiden name of a married woman isn't included in a British passport). The spouse of a French citizen or of a foreigner resident in France must produce his or her marriage certificate and proof of nationality or legal residence of the spouse when applying for a residence permit.

◆ an employment contract or letter of employment if you're taking up employment in France (see page 44);

◆ a pre-registration or admission letter to an educational institution and/or a student's card if you're a student;

◆ an au pair contract (see page 36) and a certificate of registration for French language classes if you're an au pair; evidence of adequate financial resources (e.g. a copy of a pension book or other proof of regular income or confirmation from a French bank that your monthly income is no less than €500 per head) and private health insurance if you're a retiree or aren't working.

If you don't have the required documents, you'll be sent away to obtain them.

☑ SURVIVAL TIP

Certain documents must be translated by a notarised translator (listed under *Traducteurs – Traductions Officielles Certifiées* in the *Yellow Pages*), but you shouldn't have documents translated in advance, as the requirements often vary with the area or office and your nationality, and you may be wasting your time and money.

You'll be given a date (usually between 2 and 12 weeks after your application) when you can collect your permit (usually from the *préfecture de police*). In the meantime, or if it isn't possible to issue a residence permit immediately, you're given a temporary authorisation (*récipissé de demande de carte de séjour* or an *attestation d'application de résidence*) valid for up to three months and renewable. You should keep this as evidence that you've applied for your *residence* permit.

An initial *carte de séjour* valid for one year costs €340 for a 'visitor' (€55 for students), a renewal for one year or change (see below) €85 for a 'visitor' and €55 for students. Certain categories of people are exempt from these charges, including those on temporary work contracts and those who have stayed regularly in France for at least five years.

Most EU nationals no longer require a a *carte de séjour*.

Renewals & Changes

An application for renewal of a residence permit should be made one or two months before its expiry date. When you renew your residence permit, you must reconfirm your status and provide documentary evidence, as for the original application (see above). For renewal of a *carte unique de séjour et de travail* or a *carte de séjour salarié*,

you may be asked to provide proof that you've declared your income and paid your taxes for the previous year. If you're applying for a renewal of your residence permit and don't have all the necessary documents, you can apply for an extension (*prolongation*).

Other points to note are:

♦ If you're a student wishing to renew a residence permit, you require a certificate stating that you've attended classes during the past year and passed your exams (*certificat d'assiduité*).

♦ Retirees and other non-employed people can renew their permits for additional five-year periods provided they can prove that they still have adequate financial resources and private health insurance.

♦ There's a fee for the renewal of a residence permit (which varies depending on the type of permit), which is paid in the form of tax stamps (*timbres fiscaux*) purchased from a tobacconist (*tabac*).

♦ If a renewal application is refused, you must leave France when your permit expires.

If your circumstances change, you must inform the authorities so that your residence permit can be updated. If you move house, you must inform the town hall with jurisdiction over your new place of residence and produce proof of your new address. This is particularly important if you're in the process of renewing your residence permit, as the change of address must be recorded before a new permit can be issued.

If you're a non-EU national and want the status of your residence permit changed to allow you to work in France, you must undergo a process called *régularisation*. An application must be made to the *préfecture* with proof of residence, a written job offer, and a letter explaining why a French or EU national cannot do the job. The application is sent to the Direction Départementale du Travail for approval, which can take up to six months to obtain. Like renewals, there's a fee for having the status of a residence permit changed (see above).

4.
ARRIVAL

O
n arrival in France, your first task is to negotiate immigration and customs. In order to do so, you must have obtained in advance any necessary visas and permits (see Chapter 3). Once you've entered the country, you may need to register with your embassy or consulate and may want to find local sources of information, advice and help. This chapter contains information on all these topics, plus useful checklists of tasks that must be completed before your arrival in France or soon afterwards.

IMMIGRATION

France is a signatory to the Schengen agreement, whereby immigration checks and passport controls take place when you first arrive in a Schengen country, after which you can travel freely between them. This means that, when you arrive in France from another Schengen country, there are usually no immigration checks or passport controls. (Note that this doesn't apply if you're arriving from the UK or Ireland.)

Non-EU nationals arriving by air or sea from outside the EU must go through immigration (*police des frontières*) for non-EU citizens. If you require a visa to enter France and attempt to enter without one, you'll be refused entry. If you have a single-entry visa, it will be cancelled by the immigration official.

> ### ☑ SURVIVAL TIP
>
> If you think you'll need to prove your date of entry into France, you should obtain a declaration of entry (*déclaration d'entrée sur le territoire*), which may be wise in any case.

Immigration officials may ask non-EU visitors to produce a return ticket, proof of accommodation, health insurance and financial resources, e.g. cash, travellers' cheques and credit cards. If you're a non-EU national coming to France to work, study or live, you may be asked to produce documentary evidence. The onus is on visitors to show that they won't violate French law. Immigration officials can refuse you entry on the grounds of suspicion only. Young people may be more susceptible to interrogation, especially those with 'strange' attire, and should therefore carry an international credit card, a return or onward travel ticket, a student identity card, and a letter from an employer or college stating the purpose of their visit.

CUSTOMS

Those arriving from outside the EU (including EU citizens) are subject to customs checks and limitations on what may be imported duty-free. The shipment of personal (household) effects to France from another EU country isn't subject to customs formalities, although an inventory should be provided. There are no restrictions on the import or export of euros or foreign cash or securities, although if you enter or leave France with €10,000 or more in cash or negotiable instruments (see page 255), you must make a declaration to French customs.

If you require general information about customs regulations or have specific questions, contact the Centre de Renseignement aux Usagers des Douanes, 11 rue des Deux Communes, 93558 Montreuil Cedex (☎ 08 11 20 44 44 – on this number you can ask for the telephone number of your nearest centre, 💻 www.douane.gouv.fr) or your nearest customs office.

For information about the importation of pets, see page 357, and for vehicles see page 177.

Visitors

If you're visiting France (i.e. for less than 90 days), your belongings aren't subject to duty or VAT and may be imported without formality, provided their nature and quantity doesn't imply any commercial aim. This applies to the import of private cars, camping vehicles (including trailers and caravans), motorcycles, aircraft, boats (see below) and personal effects. All means of transport and personal effects imported duty-free mustn't be sold, loaned or given away in France, and must be re-exported before the end of the 90-day period.

If you enter France from another Schengen country (see above), you may drive slowly through the border without stopping. However, any goods and pets that you're carrying mustn't be the subject of any prohibition or restriction (see below). Customs officials may stop anyone for a spot check, e.g. for drugs or illegal immigrants. If you enter France from Spain – particularly if you're a single male – your vehicle is likely to be searched and 'inspected' by a sniffer dog. If a customs officer insists on inspecting everything in your car, there's nothing you can do to prevent him. If you arrive at a seaport by private boat, there are no particular customs formalities, although you must produce the boat's registration papers if asked.

If you arrive at a river port or land border with a boat, you may be asked to produce registration papers for the boat and its outboard motor(s). A foreign-registered boat may remain in France for a maximum of six months in a calendar year, after which it must be re-exported or permanently imported (and duty and tax paid).

Non-EU Nationals

If you're a non-EU national planning to take up permanent or temporary residence, you're permitted to import your furniture and personal effects free of duty. These include vehicles, mobile homes, pleasure boats and aircraft. However, to qualify for duty-free importation, belongings must have been owned and used for at least six months.

 Caution

Value added tax must be paid on items owned for less than six months that were purchased outside the EU. If goods were purchased within the EU, a VAT receipt must be produced.

To import personal effects, an application must be made to the Direction Régionale des Douanes in the area where you'll be resident. Customs clearance can be carried out by a customs office in an interior town in France, rather than at the border, but in this case you should obtain a certificate (*carte de libre circulation*) proving that you've declared your belongings on entry into France and are entitled to travel with them.

All items should be imported within a year of the date of your change of residence – in one or a number of consignments, although it's best to have one consignment only. After a year's residence in France you must pay French VAT (*TVA*) on further imports from outside the EU, except in certain circumstances, such as property resulting from an inheritance.

A complete inventory of items to be imported (even if they're imported in a number of consignments) must be provided for customs officials, together with proof of residence in your former country and proof of settlement in France. If there's more than one consignment, subsequent consignments should be cleared through the same customs office.

If you use a removal company to transport your belongings, they'll usually provide the necessary forms and take care of the paperwork. Many of the forms are now available online, either through the Customs website (💻 www.douane.gouv.fr – available in English) or by following the links on the Service Public site (💻 www.service-public.fr). If the removal company packs your belongings, ask for the containers to be marked 'Mover Packed', as this will speed the customs clearance process.

Always keep a copy of forms and communications with customs officials – both in France and in your previous country of residence. An official record of the export of valuables from any country will allow you to re-import them later.

Prohibited & Restricted Goods

Certain goods are subject to special regulations and in some cases their import (and export) is prohibited or restricted. This applies in particular to animal products, plants (see below), wild fauna and flora (and products derived from them), live animals, medicines and medical products (except for prescribed medicines), guns and ammunition, certain goods and technologies with a dual civil/military purpose, and works of art and collectors' items. If you're unsure whether any goods you're importing fall into the above categories, you should check with French customs.

To import certain types of plant, you must obtain a phytosanitary health certificate (*certificat sanitaire*). Details of the types of plant for which a certificate is required and how to obtain one can be obtained from a regional Service de la Protection des Végétaux or your country's customs department.

If you make it through customs unscathed with your car loaded to the gunwales with illicit goods, don't be too quick to break out the champagne in celebration: France has 'flying' customs officials (*douane volante*) with the power to stop and search vehicles at random anywhere within its borders (they often stop vehicles at motorway toll stations and major roundabouts on trunk roads).

REGISTRATION

All foreigners intending to remain in France for over 90 days must register with the local authorities, usually within a week of their arrival

and obtain a residence permit, although this is no longer mandatory for EU nationals who should, however, register with their local town hall within three months of arrival. Failure to apply for a residence permit, if required, within 90 days is a serious offence and may result in a fine. For further information see **Residence Permits** on page 67.

Nationals of some countries are required to register with their local embassy or consulate after taking up residence. Even if registration isn't mandatory, most embassies like to keep a record of their country's citizens resident in France (it helps them to justify their existence) and it can be to your benefit, e.g. in a personal, national or international crisis.

FINDING HELP

One of the main difficulties facing new arrivals in France is how and where to find help with day-to-day problems, particularly as many administrative matters are handled at a regional, departmental or even local level, rather than nationally.

The availability of local information varies according to your employer, the town or area where you live (e.g. residents of Paris are better served than those living in rural areas), your nationality, your French proficiency (there's an abundance of information available in French, but little in English and other foreign languages) and to some extent your sex (women are better served than men through numerous women's clubs). You should exploit the following sources of local information as well as social clubs (see page 300).

Company

Some companies, particularly international companies, employ staff to help new arrivals or contract this job out to a relocation consultant (see page 84). However, most French employers are totally unaware of (or uninterested in) the problems and difficulties faced by foreign employees and their families.

Colleagues & Friends

In France it isn't what you know but who you know that can make all the difference between success and failure. String-pulling (i.e. the use of contacts) is widespread, and when it comes to breaking through the numerous layers of bureaucracy, a telephone call on your behalf from a French neighbour or colleague can work wonders. Any contact can be of help, even professionals such as a bank manager or insurance agent (in many cases, such people will become friends). But take care! Although colleagues and friends can often offer advice and invariably mean well, you're likely to receive much irrelevant and even inaccurate information, and you should check everything you're told for yourself.

Local Community

Your town hall (*mairie*), which is often the local registry of births, deaths and marriages, passport office, land registry, council office, citizens' advice bureau and tourist office rolled into one, should be your first port of call for most kinds of local information, although even there you may be given inaccurate or irrelevant information. Your local community is usually an excellent source of reliable information, but you'll need to speak French to benefit from it.

Embassy or Consulate

Most embassies and consulates provide their nationals with local information including details of lawyers, interpreters, doctors, dentists, schools, and social and expatriate organisations, although some are more helpful than others (the British Embassy in Paris is supremely unapproachable).

The American Embassy has a particularly good website (🖳 http://france.usembassy.gov – click on 'U.S. Citizen Services'), which includes a good deal of information (in English) about living and working in France, including lists of English-speaking professionals, from doctors to private investigators. Much of the information comes from their popular *Blue Book: Guide for U.S. Citizens Residing in France*, which can be downloaded from the site or obtained from the US Embassy, 4, avenue Gabriel, 75382 Paris Cedex 08 (☎ 01 43 12 22 22).

Hand-holding Services

A number of English-speaking expatriates offer 'hand-holding' services to new arrivals. As with any service provider, some are worth their weight in gold while others are a complete waste of time and money, therefore it's essential to ask for and follow up references before paying a joining or annual membership fee (up to around €100 each). Services may range from help with house hunting and buying to finding tradesmen and completing tax returns.

Specific assistance is available to scientists and researchers and their families coming to work in Ile-de-France through services provided by the French Academy of Sciences. The Fondation Nationale Alfred Kastler (FnAK, 🖥 www.fnak.fr – available in 'English') and Science Accueil (🖥 www.saclay-scientipole. org/science-accueil/uk_index.htm – available in 'English') offer help finding accommodation and obtaining financial services, insurance and residence permits.

Expatriate Organisations

There's usually at least one English-language expatriate organisation in major French cities; in Paris, foreigners are well served by English-speaking clubs and organisations (see below) and there are several Anglophone organisations in the Bordeaux and Côte d'Azur regions. Contacts can be found through many expatriate magazines and newspapers (see page). An English-speaking counsellor in certain parts of France can be found via 🖥 www. counsellinginfrance.com.

In Paris, the American Church (☎ 01 40 62 05 00, 🖥 www.acparis.org), runs an annual newcomer's orientation series in October called 'Bloom Where You Are Planted'. The programme is designed to help foreigners adjust to life in France and consists of seminars on topics such as overcoming culture shock, survival skills, personal and professional opportunities, networking, enjoying France and its food, fashion, travel and wine.

The capital also houses the Association of American Wives of Europeans (☎ 01 40 70 11 80, 🖥 www.aaweparis.org), which is a member of the Federation of American Women's Clubs Overseas (FAWCO) and publishes the snappily titled *Vital Issues: How to Survive Officialdom while Living in France*; the Association France Grande-Bretagne (☎ 01 55 78 71 71, 🖥 www.afgb. free.fr – in French only), whose aim is to foster links between the two nations; The British & Commonwealth Women's Association (☎ 01 47 20 50 91, 🖥 www.bcwa.org); and WICE (☎ 01 45 66 75 50, 🖥 www.wice-paris.org), an anglophone expatriate organisation which operates a 'Living in France' programme for newcomers and doesn't like people to know what its acronym stands for!

Associations outside the capital include Anglophones Pau-Pyrénées (🖥 http://pau. anglophones.com, ✉ pau@anglophones. com), the Association France Grande-Bretagne Cannes (☎ 04 93 99 04 28) and the Mulhouse English Speaking Society (☎ 03 89 66 56 80). There are French 'versions' of the Round Table and 41 Club associations – La Table Ronde Française (🖥 www.tablerondefrancaise. com) and Le Club 41 Français (🖥 www. club41francais.asso.fr), which may have English-speaking members.

The British Community Committee (🖥 www. britishinfrance.com) publishes a free *Digest of British and Franco-British Clubs, Societies and Institutions*, available from British consulates in France (see **Appendix A**).

AVF

An organisation of particular interest to foreigners moving to France is the Union Nationale des Accueils des Villes Françaises (AVF). The AVF is a national organisation comprising around 350 local volunteer associations, which provide a welcome for individuals and families and help them settle into their new environment. Each association operates a centre where information and advice is available free of charge. The address of local associations can be found on the AVF website (🖥 www.avf.asso.fr), where some information is available in English, and there's a list of groups in each department as well as details such as whether information and services are available in English. Groups often contain at least one fluent English-speaker.

☑ SURVIVAL TIP

Foreigners planning to move to France can obtain information about particular areas from the Union Nationale des AVF, Relations Internationales (☎ 01 47 70 45 85, 🖥 www.avf. asso.fr).

CIRA

If you don't know which administrative department to contact for particular information (which is often the case in France), you can ask your local Centre Interministériel de Renseignements Administratifs (CIRA). As its name suggests, CIRA is a 'pan-governmental' organisation, which can answer questions on a range of subjects, including employment, finance, accommodation, health, consumer affairs, the environment and education. There are nine information centres (in Bordeaux, Lille, Limoges, Lyon, Marseille, Metz, Paris, Rennes and Toulouse) but only one central telephone number (☎ 3939).

The Disabled

Disabled people can obtain advice and help from the Association des Paralysés de France (🖥 www.apf.asso.fr), which isn't only for those who are paralysed, the Fédération des Associations pour Adultes et Jeunes Handicapés (APAJH, 🖥 www.apajh.org) and the Fédération Nationale des Accidentés de Travail et des Handicapés (🖥 www.fnath.org). See also **Disabled People** on page 354.

Disabled people looking for work or work-related information should contact the Association Gestion du Fonds d'Insertion Personnes Handicapées (AGEFIPH, 🖥 www. agefiph.fr, which provides contact details for the 18 regional associations).

If you're seriously and permanently disabled, you should apply to the Commission Technique d'Orientation et de Reclassement Professionel (COTOREP) for an invalidity card (*carte d'invalidité civile*), which entitles you to a number of benefits.

CHECKLISTS

Before Arrival

The following checklist contains a summary of the tasks that should be completed (if possible) before your arrival in France:

♦ Obtain a visa, if necessary, for you and your family members (see **Chapter 3**). Obviously this **must** be done before arrival.

♦ Visit France before your move to compare communities and schools, and to arrange schooling for your children (see **Chapter 9**).

♦ Find temporary or permanent accommodation.

♦ Arrange shipment of your personal effects (see page 85).

♦ Arrange health insurance for yourself and your family (see page 247). This is essential if you don't have a private insurance policy and won't be covered by French social security.

◆ Obtain an International Driver's Permit (IDP), if necessary.

◆ Open a bank account and transfer funds (you can open an account with many French banks abroad). It's wise to obtain some euros before arriving, as this will save you having to change money on arrival.

◆ If you don't already have one, obtain an international credit or charge card, which may be useful during your first few months, particularly until you've opened a bank account (or been paid). Note, however, that credit cards aren't universally accepted in France, particularly those without a microchip.

◆ If you don't already speak it fluently, learn as much French as possible (see **Language Courses** on page 155).

Don't forget to bring all your family's official documents, including birth certificates, driving licences, marriage certificate, divorce papers or death certificate (if a widow or widower), educational diplomas, professional certificates and job references, school records and student identity cards, employment references, copies of medical and dental records, bank account and credit card details, insurance policies and receipts for any valuables. You'll also need the documents necessary to obtain a residence permit (see page 67).

After Arrival

The following checklist contains a summary of tasks to be completed after arrival in France (if not done before):

◆ On arrival at a French airport or port, have your visa cancelled and your passport stamped, as applicable.

◆ If you aren't taking a car with you, you may wish to rent one for a week or two until buying one locally (see page 207). Note that it's practically impossible to get around in rural areas without a car.

◆ Apply for a residence permit (if applicable) at your local town hall or *préfecture* within a week of your arrival (see page 67).

◆ Register with your local embassy or consulate (see above).

◆ Check that your employer has applied for a social security card as soon as you start working (see page 242).

◆ Give the details of your bank account to your employer and anyone else who may be paying you.

◆ Arrange schooling for your children (see **Chapter 9**).

◆ Find a local doctor and dentist (see **Chapter 12**).

◆ Arrange necessary insurance (see **Chapter 13**) and **Car Insurance** (see page186).

☑ **SURVIVAL TIP**

Introduce yourself to your local mayor and invite your neighbours for an *apéritif* within a few weeks of your arrival. This is particularly important in villages and rural areas if you want to be accepted and become part of the community.

5.
ACCOMMODATION

I n most areas of France, accommodation (to buy or rent) isn't difficult to find, although there are a few exceptions. For example, in Paris, rental accommodation is in high demand and short supply, and rents can be astronomical. Property prices and rents vary considerably with the region and city. For example, around €120,000 will buy you a small detached modern house or a large property in need of renovation in Normandy or Brittany, Limousin or Poitou-Charentes but only a tiny studio apartment in Paris or a slightly larger one-bedroom apartment on the Côte d'Azur; a 50m² (500ft²) two-bedroom apartment in a reasonable area of Paris will cost you between €1,000 and €2,000 per month to rent but around 50 per cent less in a provincial city such as Bordeaux. In fact, property in Paris and on the French Riviera is among the most expensive in the world, although prices are reasonable in most other regions.

Accommodation accounts for around 20 to 25 per cent of the average family's budget and can be much higher in expensive areas. In cities and many towns, property isn't regarded as a good investment, and many people prefer to rent. (Tenants in France have security of tenure and rents are strictly controlled). Many Parisians rent their principal home but own up to three holiday homes, e.g. one in the country near Paris for weekends, one on the Mediterranean coast for summer holidays and another in the Alps for skiing. Around 25 per cent of executives (cadres) in the whole of France own a second home.

In cities and large towns, apartments are much more common than houses, particularly in Paris, where houses are rare and prohibitively expensive.

In rural areas there's a depopulation crisis due to the mass exodus of people from the land to the cities and factories in the last 30 years. Provincial France is losing its population to the cities at the rate of around 100,000 people a year. It's estimated that one in 12 properties is vacant and the number is even higher in some areas.

Some communities offer inexpensive or even free housing to families with school-age children in an attempt to preserve local schools and keep communities alive.

The French aren't particularly mobile and tend to move home much less frequently than people in some other countries, e.g. the UK and the US; homes are often kept in a family and passed down the generations.

For comprehensive information about all aspects of buying or renting property in France, see our sister publication, Buying a Home in France (Survival Books).

FRENCH HOMES

For many foreign buyers, France provides the opportunity to buy or rent a size or style of home that they could never afford in their home countries. In most areas, properties range from derelict farmhouses and barns to modern townhouses and apartments with all modern conveniences, from crumbling châteaux and manor houses requiring complete restoration to new luxury chalets and villas.

French homes are built to high structural standards and, whether you buy a new or an old home, it will usually be extremely sturdy. Older homes often have thick walls and contain numerous rooms. Most have a wealth of interesting period features, including vast fireplaces, wooden staircases, attics, cellars (caves), and a profusion of alcoves and annexes. Many houses have a basement (sous-sol or cave), used as a garage and cellar. In most old houses, open fireplaces remain a principal feature even when central heating is installed. In warmer regions, floors are often tiled and walls are painted rather than papered, while elsewhere floors are carpeted or bare wood, and walls are more likely to be papered. When wallpaper is used, it's often garish and may cover everything, including walls, doors and ceilings! Properties throughout France tend to be built in a distinct local (often unique) style using local materials. There are stringent regulations in most areas concerning the style and design of new homes and the restoration of old buildings.

In older rural properties, the kitchen (cuisine) is the most important room in the house. It's usually huge with a large wood-burning stove for cooking, hot water and heating, a huge solid wood dining table and possibly a bread oven. French country kitchens are worlds apart from modern fitted kitchens and are devoid of shiny formica and plastic laminates. They're often comparatively stark, with stone or tiled floors and a predominance of wood, tiles and marble. Kitchens in older apartments in Paris and other cities may be very basic, although modern fitted kitchens (with dishwashers, cookers and refrigerators) are usually found in new properties, and 'American kitchens' (i.e. open plan kitchens separated from the living or dining room by a bar or counter) are increasingly common. New homes usually also contain features such as deluxe bathroom suites, fitted cupboards, smoke and security alarms (see **Home Security** on page 94) and coordinated interior colour schemes. New homes are usually sold décorée, which means not only that they're decorated but also that they have a fitted kitchen.

Refrigerators (frigidaire or frigo) and cookers (cuisinière) are generally quite small.

Cookers in rural homes are usually run on bottled gas or a combination of bottled gas and electricity. Many homes have a gas water heater (chaudière) that heats the water for the bathroom and kitchen. Most houses don't have a separate utility room and the washing machine and drier are kept in the kitchen. A separate toilet (toilette or WC) is popular, and the bathroom (salle de bains) often has a toilet, a bidet, a bath (baignoire) and/or a shower (douche). Baths are more common than showers in older homes, although showers are found in most modern homes.

⚠ Caution

Note that many old, unmodernised homes don't have a bath, shower room or an inside toilet.

Many rural properties have shutters (volets), both for security and as a means of insulation. External shutters are often supplemented by internal shutters that are fixed directly to the window frames. In France, windows open inwards rather than outwards, as in most other countries. In the south and southwest, many rural homes have outdoor swimming pools, and homes throughout France have a paved patio or terrace, which is often covered. Old farmhouses invariably have a number of outbuildings such as barns, which can usually be converted into additional accommodation.

A huge variety of new properties is available in France, including city apartments and individually-designed, detached houses. Many new properties are part of purpose-built developments. Note, however, that many of these developments are planned as holiday homes and they may not be attractive as permanent homes (they're also generally expensive). If you're buying an apartment or house that's part of a development, check whether your neighbours will be mainly French or other foreigners. Some people don't wish to live in a commune of their fellow countrymen and this will also deter French buyers if you want to sell. Prices of new properties vary considerably depending on their location and quality (see **Property Prices** below).

"Mommy, Daddy, will I make new friends?"

The most important thing to me?
Is to make sure my child has the easiest time settling in to the new surroundings

"The friendliness of the Crown staff was terrific! I was treated as a person and not a job number. The Crown's kid's program was able to help my child quickly acclimate to the new environment. Thank you for making what could have been a very stressful situation completely a pleasure."
~Australia to Japan

Crown service offerings include:
* Home Search
* Visa & Immigration Services
* Family Assistance & School Search
* Household Goods Shipment & Warehousing
* Intercultural Training
* Spouse Career Support
* Pet Relocations

Tel. +33 13006 8000
paris@crownrelo.com
nice@crownrelo.com
lyon@crownrelo.com
crownrelo.com

Well Connected. Worldwide.™

CROWN ♛
RELOCATIONS

France's bold and innovative architecture, as portrayed in its many striking public buildings, doesn't often extend to private dwellings, many of which seem to have been designed by the same architect. However, although new properties are often lacking in character, they're usually spacious and well endowed with modern conveniences and services, which certainly cannot be taken for granted in older rural properties. Standard fixtures and fittings in modern houses are more comprehensive and of better quality than those found in old houses. The French generally prefer modern homes to older houses with 'charm and character' (which to the locals mean 'expensive to maintain and in danger of falling down'!), although new homes often have pseudo period features such as beams and open fireplaces.

Central heating, double glazing and good insulation are common in new houses, particularly in northern France, where they're essential. Central heating may be electric, gas or oil-fired. However, on the Côte d'Azur, where winter temperatures are higher, expensive insulation and heating may be

considered unnecessary (don't you believe it!). Air-conditioning has become more popular – encouraged by government tax incentives – but is by no means widespread, even in the south of France.

Note that most French families live in apartments or detached homes, and semi-detached and terraced properties built more than four or five decades ago are relatively rare. Some 45 per cent of the population lives in apartments (although less than 10 per cent in tower blocks), which are more common in France than in most other European countries. In cities and suburbs, most people have little choice, as houses are in short supply and prohibitively expensive. In the major cities there are many *bourgeois* apartments, built in the 19th or early 20th century, with large rooms, high ceilings and huge windows. Unless modernised, they have old fashioned bathrooms and kitchens and are expensive to decorate, furnish, heat and maintain. Many apartments don't have their own source of hot water and heating, which is shared with other apartments in the same building.

For details of typical homes in the most popular regions of France, see our sister publication, *The Best Places to Buy a Home in France* (Survival Books).

RELOCATION COMPANIES

If you're fortunate enough to have your move paid for by your employer, it's likely that he'll arrange for a relocation company (such as Crown Relocation, 🖳 www.crownrelo.com/crown/crwn_dir.nsf/relocountry/france – see inside front cover) to handle the details. There are fewer relocation consultants in France (most are based in Paris) than in many other European countries and they usually deal only with corporate clients. Fees depend on the services required, packages usually ranging from around €1,000 to €4,000.

The main service provided by relocation consultants is finding accommodation (for rent or purchase) and arranging viewing. Other services include conducting negotiations, drawing up contracts, arranging mortgages, organising surveys and insurance, and handling the move. Consultants may also provide reports on local amenities and services, such as schools, health services, public transport, and sports and social facilities. Some companies provide daily advice and assistance and help in dealing with officials.

Finding rental accommodation for single people or couples without children can usually be done in a week or two, while locating family homes may take up to four weeks, depending on the location and requirements. You should usually allow two to three months between your initial visit and moving into a purchased or rented property.

MOVING HOUSE

After you've found a home in France, it usually takes just a few weeks to have your belongings shipped from within continental Europe. From anywhere else the time varies considerably, e.g. four weeks from the east coast of America, six weeks from the west coast and the Far East, and around eight weeks from Australasia.

Customs clearance isn't necessary when shipping your household effects within the EU. However, when shipping your effects from a non-EU country to France, you should enquire about customs formalities in advance; if you fail to follow the correct procedure, you can encounter numerous problems and delays and may be charged duty or even fined. The relevant forms to be completed by non-EU citizens depend on whether your French home will be your main residence or a holiday home. Removal companies usually take care of the administration and ensure that the right documents are provided and correctly completed (see also **Customs** on page 73).

Members of FIDI and OMNI usually subscribe to an advance payment scheme that provides a guarantee. If a member company

fails to fulfil its commitments to a customer, the removal is completed at the agreed cost by another member company or your money is refunded. Some removal companies have subsidiaries or affiliates in France, which may be more convenient if you encounter problems or need to make an insurance claim.

American removal companies with offices in France include Biard International (🖥 www.biard.fr), Team Relocations (🖥 www.teamrelocations.com) and Grospiron International (🖥 www.grospiron.com).

Obtain at least three written quotations before choosing a company. Costs vary considerably, although you should expect to pay from €5,000 to €7,000 to move the contents of a three-to four-bedroom house. Note that prices may be higher in the summer and immediately after Christmas.

If you need to store your belongings between moving out of your old home and moving into your new one, most companies will do this for a minimal charge, e.g. €50 a month for up to 4.5m³ and around double in the Paris area, excluding insurance, although some companies provide free storage for a period. If you're flexible about the delivery date, most removal companies will quote a lower fee based on a 'part load', where the cost is shared with other deliveries. This can result in savings of 50 per cent or more compared with an 'individual' delivery, but make sure you don't leave essential items to be delivered as you may have to wait two or three weeks for them to arrive.

Make a list of everything to be moved and give a copy to the removal company. Don't include anything illegal (e.g. guns, bombs, drugs and pornography) with your belongings, as customs checks can be rigorous and penalties severe. Some companies won't take alcohol and some may be reluctant to take plants, although there are no restrictions on the import of most plants.

Give the shipping company detailed instructions how to find your French address from the nearest motorway (or main road) and a telephone number on which you can be contacted. Note also that if your new home has restricted access (or is surrounded by soft ground), you may incur additional costs (make sure you inform the shipping company in advance!).

Be sure to fully insure your belongings during removal with a well-established insurance company. Insurance premiums are usually 1 to 2 per cent of the declared value of your goods, depending on the type of cover chosen. It's prudent to make a photographic or film record of valuables for insurance purposes. Most insurance policies cover for 'all risks' on a replacement value basis. Note that china, glass and other breakables can usually be included in an all-risks policy only when they're packed by the removal company.

If you need to make a claim, be sure to read the small print, as some companies require you to make a claim within a few days, although seven is usual. Send a claim by registered post. Some insurance companies apply an 'excess' of around 1 per cent of the total shipment value when assessing claims. This means that if your shipment is valued at €30,000 and you make a claim for less than €300, you won't receive anything.

If you plan to transport your belongings to France personally, check the customs requirements of the countries you must pass through, in advance. If you're importing household goods from another European country, it's possible to hire a self-drive van in France. Hiring a van outside France isn't recommended, as you must usually return it to the country where it was hired. Generally, it isn't wise to do your own move unless it's a simple job. It's certainly no fun heaving beds and wardrobes up stairs and squeezing them into impossible spaces!

If you're taking pets with you, you may need to tranquillise them, as most pets are frightened (even more than people) by the chaos and stress of moving house. See also **Pets** on page 357.

Bear in mind when moving home that everything that can go wrong often does, so allow plenty of time and try not to arrange your move from your old home on the same day as the new owner/tenant is moving in. That's just asking for fate to intervene! See also the checklists in **Chapter 20**.

TEMPORARY ACCOMMODATION

On arrival, you may find it necessary to stay in temporary accommodation for a few weeks or months before moving into permanent accommodation or while waiting for your furniture to arrive. Some employers provide rooms, self-contained apartments or hostels for employees and their families, although this is rare and usually for short periods only.

Some hotels and bed and breakfast establishments cater for long-term guests and offer reduced weekly or monthly rates. In most areas, particularly in Paris and other main cities, serviced and holiday apartments are available. These are fully self-contained furnished apartments with their own bathrooms and kitchens, which are cheaper and more convenient than a hotel, particularly for families. Self-catering holiday accommodation is prohibitively expensive during the main holiday season (June to August) but may be affordable at other times.

One of the easiest ways to find temporary accommodation in Paris is through an agent such as Allô Logement Temporaire (🖳 www.allo-logement-temporaire.asso.fr – English version).

For information about French hotels, bed and breakfast and self-catering accommodation, and hostels, see **Chapter 15**.

BUY OR RENT?

If you're staying in France for only a few years, renting is usually the best option. It's also the answer for those who don't want the trouble, expense and restrictions associated with buying a property.

> ### ☑ SURVIVAL TIP
>
> Even if you're planning to buy, it's often prudent to rent for 6 to 12 months, in order to reduce your chance of making an expensive error. This allows you to become familiar with a region and its climate and gives you plenty of time to look around for a permanent home.

Renting is common in France, where some 45 per cent of the population live in rented accommodation. Tenants have security of tenure, and rental costs are strictly controlled under French law. It's possible to rent every kind of property, from a tiny studio apartment (bedsitter) to a huge rambling *château*.

If you decide not to rent but to buy, you should be clear about your long-term plans and goals. Buying a house or an apartment is usually a good long-term investment and preferable to renting over a period of five or more years, but you shouldn't expect to make a quick profit when buying property in France.

Rural property is considerably cheaper than in many other developed countries, and many foreign buyers find that they can buy a size or style of home that they couldn't afford in their home countries (e.g. prices are generally around half of those in the UK), although prices were increasing by an average of around 10 per cent for a number of years before the recent recession. In 2011, prices were slowly rising again in many areas, although increases were well below pre-recession rates.

For more information regarding buying or renting property in France, see our sister publications, *Buying a Home in France* and *The Best Places to Buy a Home in France* (Survival Books).

RENTAL ACCOMMODATION

If you want a long-term rental to move into as soon as you and your family arrive in France, avoiding temporary accommodation, you should start looking at least a month or two before your planned arrival date and will probably need someone on the spot to help. This may be your employer (if applicable), estate agent, or a property search agent or relocation company (see above). You can also use the internet and the local press and, if you're visiting the area, look at advertisements from owners wishing to rent privately on notice boards in supermarkets, bakers and newsagents. If you have friends living in your chosen area(s) who in turn have local friends and contacts, make use of their local knowledge, which can prove effective in finding something before it comes onto the market.

Try to avoid the *rentrée* months of September and October, when the French return from their summer holidays and (in university towns and cities) students may still be chasing accommodation. It's wise to make your search radius in the area you want as wide as possible – which will improve your chances of finding somewhere suitable – and not limit yourself to one town or city neighbourhood.

The Internet

There are numerous property websites offering rentals in France. Two of the most important – available in English – are 🖥 www.seloger.co.uk and www.french-property.com. The French National Federation of Estate Agents website (🖥 www.fnaim.fr – click on *louer*, then on *location* and complete the boxes) contains a wide choice of rentals, as does the property magazine *Logic-immo* (🖥 www.logic-immo.fr – click on *louer* and complete the boxes). Other property websites offering national coverage are 🖥 www.avendrealouer.fr and www.explorimmo.com. The property rental section of weekly free-sheets such as *Topannonces* (🖥 www.topannonces.fr) can also be accessed via the internet. Many property websites are updated daily and it's wise to consult them regularly.

Most websites offer free subscription to an email update which tells you about new property available in your chosen areas.

The Media

Good sources of rental accommodation include local newspapers, most of which have special property advertisement days, and free regional property magazines such as *Logic-immo*. Also useful are English-language newspapers published in France, such as *The Connexion* (🖥 www.connexionfrance.com), *The International Herald Tribune* (🖥 www.iht.com) and *The Riviera Times* (🖥 www.rivieratimes.com). You can also place a 'rental wanted' advertisement at no cost on notice boards in supermarkets, bakers and newsagents.

Most French newspapers have websites, many of which can be found via Online Newspapers (🖥 www.onlinenewspapers.com/france.htm).

Rental agents

There are numerous estate agency chains in France, including Foncia whose specialty is rentals (🖥 www.foncia.fr – full search and completion service). Agents deal with the majority of rentals, as most landlords don't have the time or desire to locate and liaise with tenants. You may never see the landlord (owner) as the agent looks after all administrative tasks. Agents are found in the *Yellow Pages* under *Agences immobilières* and *Locations d'appartements*. If you want a furnished rental (which is more difficult to find) look in the *Yellow Pages* under *Maisons, appartements, chambres meublés* (*location*).

Estate agents who handle sales and rentals shouldn't charge a registration fee, but property search agents may require an advance fee. The usual fee for renting unfurnished accommodation through a rental agent is one month's rent, payable when you sign the lease and pay the deposit to cover future possible damage and pay the first month's rent in advance. Thus your upfront outlay is three month's rent.

If you're investigating an area in person, look out for '*A LOUER*' estate agents' boards outside properties. Owners' home-made '*A LOUER*' boards tend to be for holiday or short-lets. *Notaires* can also act as rental agents.

Rental agents shouldn't be confused with 'property rental shops' (*marchands de listes de locations*) whose job is simply to supply and up-date addresses and details of properties for rent. Internet search engines have reduced the number of these list providers. If you do subscribe to a list service, you should only pay **at the end** of the up-dating period. A service lasting from one to three months costs between around €100 and €200.

Avoid 'agents' or owners who have only a mobile phone number (beginning 06) and check the fees you're expected to pay before signing the lease (see below).

Rents

Rents vary considerably depending on the size and quality of a property, its age and the facilities provided. In large cities, the district (*quartier*) – there are over 100 in Marseille, for example – and area (*arrondissement*) in which a property is located also have a considerable influence on rental costs. Prices, particularly for apartments, are calculated according to the number of rooms (*pièces*), excluding the obligatory kitchen, bathroom(s) and toilet(s) and any other 'utility' rooms, and the overall habitable floor area (in square metres) which includes any converted attic room provided the ceiling height is at least 1.8m. Room dimensions are rarely given in property descriptions, although the room's surface area may be mentioned.

A one-room apartment has a combined living and sleeping room, with possibly a separate kitchen, and is called a *studio*. A two-room (*deux-pièces*) apartment has either a bedroom or a room that converts immediately to a bedroom, and a living room. A three-room (*trois-pièces*) apartment has two bedrooms, a four-room (*quatre-pièces*) apartment may have three bedrooms or two bedrooms and separate dining and living rooms – an apartment with two bedrooms and a through lounge-dining room is a *faux quatre-pièces* – and so on. Apartment descriptions often begin with '*F*' or '*T*' followed by the number of rooms other than the 'utility' rooms. Thus '*faux F4*' is an abbreviation of '*faux quatre-pièces*'. The average size of a two-room apartment (*F2*) is around 50m² (538ft²).

Rental prices are also based on the prevailing market value of a property (*indice*), but the most significant factor is location: the region of France, the city and the neighbourhood. Rental prices are also dictated by supply and demand, and are higher in Aix-en-Provence, Cannes and Nice than in

Bordeaux, Lyon, Marseille, Strasbourg and Toulouse. Good quality three-room apartments in the more desirable neighbourhoods in the latter five cities were around €800 a month in mid-2011, while similar properties in equivalent neighbourhoods in Nice were around €1,000 a month.

Rental accommodation in Paris is always in short supply, and prices are among the highest in Europe, often double those in other French cities. In inner Paris, it isn't unusual to pay around €25 per m² and a tiny studio apartment of 20m² (215ft²) in a good area costs around €500 per month, a large two or three-bedroom apartment of 125m² (1,354ft²) in a top-drawer locality such as the 16th *arrondissement* can cost up to ten times as much, while the sky's the limit for a renovated apartment in a listed Haussmann building. A 60m² apartment with two bedrooms and a separate lounge advertised in mid-2011 in *De Particulier A Particulier* (the property magazine for private sales and rentals) in Montparnasse, near the Latin Quarter had a rental of €1,200 per month.

The lowest prices are in small towns and rural areas, although there's often a limited choice. Generally, the further a property is from a large city or town (or town centre), the sea, public transport or other facilities, the cheaper it is. Two-bedroom apartments or terraced village houses/cottages over five years old (*ancien*) in many departments cost under €500 a month, while three-bedroom (*quatre pièces*) detached houses with a garden in rural areas are around the same price as urban three-bedroom apartments.

Rental prices are often open to negotiation and you may be able to secure a 5 to 10 per cent reduction if there aren't any other interested parties.

▲ Caution

If you deal directly with a landlord, the lease should be vetted by a property professional with rental experience who's on your side. Some owners, for example, still ask for a 'key money/right to a lease' tax (*droit au bail taxe*), which no longer exists for rented accommodation.

Rental rates for short-term lets, e.g. less than a year, are much higher than for longer lets, particularly in popular holiday areas and notably for anything with a sea, lake or mountain view. If you rent on a weekly basis, you may experience up to five different seasonal weekly rates in a six-month period, from low to peak season, with the peak season rate up to three times as high as the low season. The rates depend on the standard, number of beds – including sofa beds – and the facilities provided. A *studio* sleeping four people costs around €600 a week on the Côte d'Azur in the peak season.

The rent for a *gîte* sleeping six is €250 to €350 per week in June and September, and €350 to €500 per week in July and August, higher if there's a swimming pool. However, when renting for several months outside the peak season, you can rent a two-bedroom property for around €500 in many regions.

CHARGES OR EXTRA COSTS

There may be extra costs (*charges*) in addition to the monthly rent, especially for those renting in apartment blocks; they're much less common if you rent a house or maisonnette. This is because while the landlord pays for major repairs and new equipment, the tenant pays for small repairs, rubbish collection and the general upkeep of the common areas in the building, grounds and outside areas, including lighting costs. Charges average around 10 per cent of the rent, but can be considerably more if you rent an apartment of *grand standing* in a residential block with large grounds or gardens, gatekeeper, concierge, electronic surveillance, gardener, swimming pool, tennis court and gym.

In a joint-ownership block of flats, the landlord or agent must tell the tenant exactly how the charges are split between the different apartments depending on their size. After consultation, a landlord can ask a tenant to contribute towards the cost of energy-saving improvements or installations in a property, which result in reduced heating bills, for at least two of the following:

♦ roof insulation;

♦ front, side and back wall insulation;

- double-glazing for windows in the above walls;
- replacement of the heating system or installation of a new boiler for bathroom hot water, or energy-saving adjustments to either;
- installation of heating equipment using renewable energy sources.

Landlords sometimes ask for interim or advance payment of projected extra costs, based on the previous year's costs or what appears likely to be spent in the coming year; any overpayments are adjusted, usually once a year. A detailed account should be sent to you one month before the annual adjustment date and you can review the bills (*pièces justificatives*). Alternatively, the landlord may stipulate monthly or quarterly payment of extra costs. If you rent long-term, but only occupy the property for part of the year, you still have to pay.

Check the accounts carefully, as landlords and managing agents (*syndics*) often make mistakes. Building repairs, facelifts (*ravalement*) and property tax (*taxe foncière*) aren't a tenant's responsibility, but residential or occupant's tax (*taxe d'habitation*) is if your rental period includes the 1st January.

Lift maintenance can form a major part of a building's running costs. The higher you are in a block the more (proportionately) you pay. Ground floor tenants shouldn't pay lift charges. In apartment blocks with a central heating unit, all accommodation must have its own meter unless this is technically impossible. Some older apartments, built before 1975, when this requirement came into force, fall into this category. All apartments heated by a central unit in the block must have heating appliances which can be regulated to different temperatures when required.

GARAGE OR PARKING SPACE

A garage isn't normally included with an apartment and must be purchased or rented separately. Modern apartment blocks generally have single lock-up garages (*box*), outside parking spaces – free, or rentable, if they're limited, for around half the price of garages – or locked underground parking with reserved parking spaces. Garages are snapped up

quickly and may not always be available. A simple *box* with just a light bulb and no tap costs from around €75 to €100 per month and garages of '*grand standing*' with a pit, taps and electrical points, double that. Centrally-located garages which aren't attached to apartment blocks and which are in towns with a parking shortage are in great demand and can cost even more. Apartment blocks in residential areas away from town centres usually have plenty of free parking spaces for residents and visitors.

Overnight street parking isn't recommended in town and city centres if you have a valuable car or if you want to protect your car's bodywork. If you can't find suitable parking, you could consider the special rates for residents (*tarif spécial résident*) offered by car parks such as those run by the VinciPark group (💻 www.vincipark.com).

☑ SURVIVAL TIP

Most property websites also carry advertisements for garage and parking space rentals, as does the website for *De Particulier A Particulier* magazine (💻 www.pap.fr).

BUYING A HOME

There are many ways of finding homes for sale in France, which include the following:

- **Newspapers & magazines:** including the English-language publications listed in **Appendix B**, weekly French property newspapers such as *De Particulier à Particulier*, *Le Journal des Particuliers*, *La Centrale des Particuliers* and *La Semaine Immobilière*, national newspapers in your home country and France (if you're looking for an expensive property), local magazines, papers and newssheets (which may have private property advertisements), property magazines published by the French estate agent chains (e.g. ORPI), and property advertisement magazines such as *Logic-immo*.

- **Property exhibitions:** which can be useful provided you plan your visit, including:

- checking that a show includes a reasonable number of exhibitors offering property in France;

- drafting a list of information to find and questions to ask;

- allowing plenty of time and visiting stands in order of priority;

- following up any useful leads and discarding irrelevant literature.

♦ **The internet:** there are many sites devoted to French property, including those run by French and foreign property agents (see **Appendix C**).

♦ **Discovery tours:** which are organised by a number of companies in various regions of France, allowing you to get a feel for an area and the type and prices of properties and maybe see a few properties that are available. For example, there's Moving to France (💻 www.moving-to-france. com), which organises property tours in Languedoc. However, these tours aren't cheap – around €1,100 per person in a double room for six days on a bed-and-breakfast basis, without the return travel costs – and you may prefer to arrange your own itinerary (see below).

A recent concept in house hunting is 'virtual discovery tours', whereby you can 'tour' properties on DVD or via the internet.

One company offering this facility is Real Property Tours (💻 www.realpropertytours. com). A lot of French estate agency websites offer this.

♦ **Visiting an area:** note that around half of French properties are sold privately and the only way to find out about them is to tour the area you're interested in, looking for FOR SALE (*A VENDRE* or sometimes simply *AV*) signs and asking locals or town hall officials if they know of properties for sale.

♦ **Developers:** some of whom sell direct, others via agents in France or abroad. Note, however, that developers needn't be licensed to sell property.

♦ **Property traders** (*marchands de biens*).

♦ **Estate agents** (see below).

Make sure you avoid national holidays (see page 50) when visiting France on a house hunting trip, and also the Monday before a holiday if it falls on a Tuesday and the Friday after if it falls on a Thursday.

When house hunting in France, it's advisable to take a calculator (to work out how few euros you'll get for your money), a mobile phone that works in France (and a charger and plug adapter), a camera and/or video camera, and instructions for remotely accessing your home answerphone, as well as a notepad, maps and contact numbers, and, if necessary, a dictionary or phrase book.

One of the best times to house hunt in France is September, when the country gets back into gear after the long summer holidays, when rested and refreshed estate agents have a backlog of property details on their desks, when flights and Channel crossings are cheaper and the roads less crowded than in summer, but when the weather is still pleasant for travelling around and viewing properties. The ideal house-hunting trip is between three and six days (but do your homework first).

Real Estate Agents

Only some 50 per cent of property sales in France are handled by real estate agents (*agent immobilier*). However, where foreign buyers are concerned, the vast majority of sales are made through agents or handled by *notaires* (see below). It's common for foreigners in many countries, particularly the UK, to use an agent in their own country who works with one or more French agents. A number of French agents also advertise abroad, particularly in the publications listed in **Appendix B**, and many have English-speaking staff (so don't be discouraged if you don't speak fluent French).

If you want to find an agent in a particular town or area, look under *Agences Immobilières* in the relevant French *Yellow Pages* (*pages jaunes*) available at main libraries in many countries. If using a local estate agent, it's best to go in person. French estate agents generally don't send you property details but expect you to be there, on the spot, and to visit houses immediately.

Qualifications

French estate agents are regulated by law and must be professionally qualified and licensed and hold indemnity insurance. To work in his own right in France, an agent must possess a *carte professionnelle*, which is granted only to those with certain professional qualifications or considerable experience. The *carte* must be renewed annually and its number and place of issue should be shown on the agent's letterhead.

Estate agents should also provide a financial guarantee for at least €75,000; without which they aren't entitled to handle clients' money. If an agent provides a guarantee for more than this amount, the name and address of the guarantor (i.e. bank) will also be shown on his letterhead. If an agent has a lower guarantee, you should pay your deposit to the notary or another legal professional involved in the sale.

Ensure that you're dealing with an agent who fulfils these requirements and, if in doubt, ask to see his qualifications and confirmation of the guarantees he offers.

Most French estate agents are members of a professional body, the main one being the Fédération Nationale de l'Immobilier (FNAIM, 🖳 www.fnaim.fr), the French association of estate agents. The Syndicat National des Professionnels Immobiliers (SNPI, 🖳 www.snpi.com) represents property agents and property managers, and the Union Nationale de la Propriété Immobilière

(🖳 www.unpi.org) is one of the national associations representing property owners' managing agents.

Foreign Agents

Very few foreign agents in France possess the coveted *carte professionnelle* (see above). Until recently, foreigners were permitted to act as self-employed 'sales representatives' (*agents commerciaux*) of French-registered agents, requiring no particular qualifications. This practice has now been outlawed, however, and you should avoid making any binding agreements with an *agent commercial* and certainly shouldn't pay any money to one or any unregistered 'property agent' or 'search agent'. In fact, you shouldn't even view properties with anyone who cannot produce a *carte professionnelle* (or who isn't employed by someone with one); if you have an accident while visiting a property, you won't be able to claim unless an agent is legal and registered.

> If you're dealing with an *agent commercial*, you should check that he's listed on the local *registre du commerce* (he should have a registration number and a *SIRET* number) and, preferably, that the agent he represents is a member of one of the recognised professional bodies (see above).

Members of the Federation of Overseas Property Developers, which is a member of the National Association of Estate Agents International Division (NAEA, UK ☎ 0192-649 6800, 🖳 www.naea.co.uk), are bound by a code of ethics requiring them to meet local licensing requirements and must therefore be French-registered if they have offices in France. The UK contact address is: National Federation of Property Professionals, Arbon House, 6 Tournament Court, Edgehill Drive, Warwick, Warwickshire CV34 6LG.

There may be advantages in using a foreign agent, particularly an English-speaking one who's experienced in selling to foreign buyers and is familiar with the problems they can encounter, but you should ensure that they're trading legally. Some UK-based agencies (e.g. My-French-House.com, ☎ 0845-123 5885 or 0113-216

4066, 🖥 www.my-french-house.com) offer a 'complete home-buying service', putting you in touch with property professionals such as French estate agents, *notaires*, lawyers and surveyors; you should carefully check any agreement or contract offered by such companies to ensure that your interests are protected.

If a foreign agent refers clients to a French agent or agents, he may share his commission with the French agent(s) or charge extra for his services – in some cases a great deal extra – and you should check what's included (and what isn't) in any prices quoted by foreign agents. See also **Fees** below.

Notaires

Around 15 per cent of property sales in France are negotiated by *notaires* (a peculiarly French official, whose functions aren't the same as a notary or notary public), who also have a monopoly on conveyancing for all property sales in France. *Notaires* have a strict code of practice and aren't, for example, permitted to display property details in their offices, which means that most have a working relationship with a number of estate agents.

When a *notaire* is the selling agent, his 'agency' commission isn't included in the asking price and is paid by the buyer, which

should be taken into account when calculating the overall cost of the property. However, the 'agency' fees charged by a *notaire* are usually lower than those levied by estate agents (see above), namely 5 per cent up to €45,735 and 2.5 per cent above this figure, but 5.88 per cent and 2.94 per cent respectively for new properties. *Notaire* fees are standard throughout France. Although there may appear to be a conflict of interest when a *notaire* is instructed by the seller but receives his fee from the buyer, in practice there are usually no problems. Value added tax/VAT (*TVA*) at 19.6 per cent must be added to all fees.

Fees

There are no government controls on agents' fees, although they're obliged to post a list of charges (*barème*) in their offices. Fees are usually levied on a sliding scale between 5 and 10 per cent: the cheaper the property, the higher the percentage, e.g. 10 per cent on properties priced at €20,000 reducing to 5 per cent on properties costing €150,000 or more. For expensive properties an agent's fee may be negotiable. An agent's fees may be paid by the vendor, the buyer or be shared, although it's normal for the vendor to pay, i.e. the fee is 'included' in the purchase price. A price quoted as *net vendeur* excludes the selling agent's fees; *commission comprise* (written as *C/C*) or *frais d'agence inclus* (*FAI*) indicates that the price includes the agent's commission. **Make sure when discussing the price that it's *C/C* or *FAI* and not *net vendeur*.**

Many foreign agents work with French agents and share the standard commission, so you usually pay no more by using a foreign agent. The agent's fee is usually payable on completion, but may be payable sooner.

If you're buying a garage separately through an agent, don't be surprised to find that the price includes a hefty agent's fee. Garage prices range from around €10,000 to over €50,000, depending on their location and services included.

When buying, check in advance whether you need to pay commission or any extras in addition to the sale price (apart from the usual fees and taxes associated with buying a property in France).

PROPERTY PRICES

Apart from the obvious points such as size, quality and land area, the most important factor influencing the price of a house is its location. A restored or modernised two-bedroom house may cost just €100,000 in a remote or unpopular area but sell for two or three times as much in a popular location. The closer you are to the coast (or Paris), the more expensive a property will be, with properties in certain areas of the Côte d'Azur the most expensive of all. A Charente farmhouse with a barn and land costs around the same as a tiny studio apartment in Paris or on the Côte d'Azur.

Note that when people talk about 'inexpensive' homes, they invariably mean something that needs restoring, which usually necessitates spending as much as the purchase price (or much more) to make it habitable. The French think that the British are particularly insane for buying up their tumbled down farmhouses and crumbling *châteaux*. Few Frenchmen (although it's becoming more common) share the British passion for spending their holidays and weekends up to their elbows in bricks and mortar! They do, however, have a grudging admiration for the British for their painstaking and sensitive restorations.

A slice of *la bonne vie* needn't cost the earth, with habitable cottages and terraced village homes available from around €100,000 and detached homes from as little as €125,000. In some rural areas it's still possible to buy an old property for as little as €25,000, although you usually need to carry out major restoration work, which can cost as much as building from scratch. Modern studio and one-bedroom apartments in small towns cost from around €40,000 and two-bedroom apartments from €50,000. A modern two-bedroom bungalow costs from around €75,000 and a rural two-bedroom renovated cottage from around €100,000. However, if you're seeking a home with several bedrooms, a large plot and a swimming pool, you'll need to spend at least €200,000 (depending on the area), and luxury apartments in Paris and villas in the south of France can cost many hundreds of thousands of euros.

In addition to the purchase price, you must allow for various costs associated with buying a house in France, which are higher than in most other countries and can amount to around 25 per cent of the purchase price for old properties and as much as 40 per cent of new properties (when most fees are included in the asking price). Note that prices may be quoted inclusive or exclusive of agency fees and the selling agent's fee. Make sure you know whether all agents' fees are included in the price quoted and who must pay them (usually the vendor). If you negotiate a reduction, check that the agent or vendor hasn't excluded some fees from the price (to be added later).

Property prices rose by an average of 4.2 per cent in the first quarter of 2011, but over the previous 12 months the average increase in house prices was less impressive, at 1.6 per cent. There is, however, a huge disparity between Paris and the provinces, with prices in Paris soaring and those in most regions fairly stagnant. It's becoming increasingly difficult to obtain an overall picture of the housing market in France, especially as in many rural areas there are few sales and it's also difficult to compare properties. In mid-2011, most notaires and agents reported slowing sales (particularly of new homes), and the consensus was that prices would stabilise or fall slightly for 2011 as a whole.

☑ SURVIVAL TIP

You can obtain up to date property prices from professional bodies such as the Fédération Nationale de l'Immobilier (FNAIM, 🖥 www.fnaim.fr), which publishes a quarterly report.

SECURITY

When moving into a new home, it's wise to replace the locks (or lock barrels) as soon as possible and fit high-security locks, as you have no idea how many keys are in circulation for the existing ones. Some apartments and houses may be fitted with door locks that are individually numbered; extra keys for these cannot be made at an ordinary *serrurerie*, and you must obtain details from the previous owner or the landlord to have additional keys cut or to change the lock barrels.

At the same time as changing locks, you may wish to have an alarm system fitted, which is the best way to deter intruders and may also reduce your home contents insurance (see page 249).

If you're likely to be leaving your home unoccupied for long periods, your insurance company may insist on extra security measures such as two, or even three, locks on external doors (one a mortise lock) and internally-lockable shutters (or grilles) on windows, which must be locked when the property is vacant. In high-risk areas, you may be required to fit extra locks and shutters, security blinds or gratings on windows.

However, no matter how secure your home, a thief can usually break in if he's determined enough, e.g. through the roof or by knocking a hole in a wall! In isolated areas, thieves can strip a house bare at their leisure and an alarm won't be much of a deterrent if there's nobody around to hear it.

If you have a holiday home, it isn't wise to leave anything of great value (monetary or sentimental) there. If you vacate a rented house or apartment for an extended period, it may be obligatory to notify your caretaker, landlord or insurance company, and leave a key with the caretaker or landlord in case of emergencies.

If you have a break-in, you should report it immediately to your local *gendarmerie*, where you must make a statement (*plainte*), of which you receive a copy. This is required by your insurance company if you make a claim. Note that a generous 'donation' to the local police at Christmas may encourage them to keep a watchful eye on your home when you're away.

Another important aspect of home security is ensuring that you have early warning of a fire, which is easily accomplished by installing smoke detectors. Following recent legislation, homes must have at least one smoke detector (*détecteur de fumée*) by March 2015. Battery-operated smoke detectors can be purchased from around €10. They should be tested weekly to ensure that the batteries aren't exhausted. You can also fit an electric-powered gas detector that activates an alarm when a gas leak is detected.

UTILITIES

As well as electricity and gas, French homes use oil (*fioul* or *fuel*) and wood (*bois*) for heating and hot water. Electricity and gas are supplied by the partially state-owned Electricité de France/Gaz de France (EDF/GDF, 💻 www. edf.fr and www.dolcevita.gazdefrance.fr), although commercial and household users now have a choice of private suppliers.

Your rental or real estate agent should be able to advise you on this. More information about utilities can be found in our sister publication, *Buying a Home in France* (Survival Books).

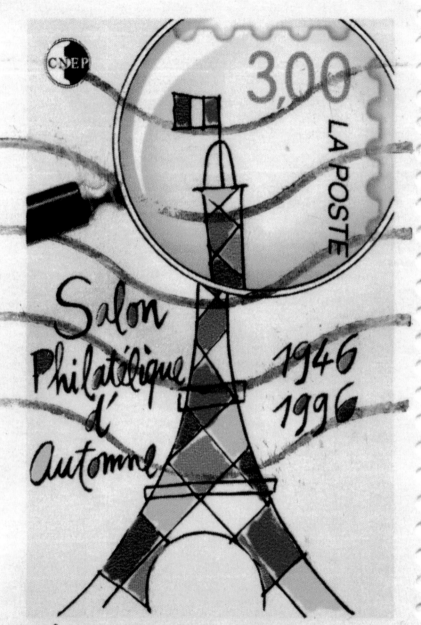

6.
POSTAL SERVICES

The French Post Office (*La Poste*) is a state-owned company, and post offices (*bureau de poste* or simply *poste*) in France are staffed by post office employees who are French civil servants (*fonctionnaires*); there are no post offices run by private businesses as in the UK, for example. However, privatisation of the postal service began in 2003; La Poste's monopoly of the handling of letters between 50g and 100g ended in 2006 – in theory; in September 2007 no alternative services were available! It was announced that the service would be completely liberalised by 2009 and later that La Poste would become a plc in March 2010 as a preliminary to privatisation, but in 2011 these plans were also abandoned due to the economic crisis! It remains, however, an objective of the present government to privatise La Poste although, as in the UK, there's considerable opposition both from employees and from the general public on social grounds.

There are around 17,000 post offices in France, 60 per cent of them in communes of fewer than 2,000 inhabitants but, as in other countries, those in the least populated areas are gradually being closed. The identifying colour used by La Poste is yellow, which is the colour of French post office signs, post vans and post boxes, which can be found in most villages, as well as towns and cities. The post office logo looks like a blue paper aeroplane on a yellow background.

> Signs for post offices in towns vary widely and include *PTT* (the old name for the post office), *PT, P et T, Bureau de Poste* or simply *Poste*. Post offices are listed in the *Yellow Pages* under *Poste: Services*.

In addition to the usual post-handling services, French post offices offer a range of other services. These include telephone calls, telegrams, domestic and international cash transfers, payment of telephone and utility bills, and distribution of mail-order catalogues. La Poste also offers email services (including free and permanent email addresses as well as e-commerce services for small businesses), banking services (including cheque and savings accounts, mortgage and retirement plans), currency exchange (*bureau de change*) and cash transfers. Post offices usually have photocopy and franking machines.

Main post offices usually have separate counters (*guichets*) for different services, e.g. cashing or depositing post office cheques (*CCP*), postal orders (*mandat*), *poste restante* and bulk stamps (*timbres en gros*), although some counters provide all services (*tous services/toutes opérations*). Before joining a queue, make sure it's the right one; if you join the wrong queue, you'll need to start again. If you need different services you must queue a number of times if there's no window for all services. Stamps are sold at most windows and most handle letters and packages (*envoi de lettres et paquets*), except perhaps very large parcels.

The Post Office produces numerous leaflets and brochures, and its website (📧 www.laposte. fr) contains information about all services, including a searchable database of post offices (the listings don't include opening hours or the times of the last collection each day), although La Poste recently abandoned its half-hearted attempt to translate its site into English.

French companies are usually slow to reply to letters. There's a tendency to ignore letters unless they're sent *avis de reception* (requiring a signature on delivery), which is recommended to avoid unnecessary delay; it's often necessary to follow up a letter with a telephone call.

BUSINESS HOURS

Business hours for main post offices in towns and cities in France are usually from 08.00 or 09.00 to 19.00, Mondays to Fridays, and from 08.00 or 09.00 to 12.00 on Saturdays. Main post offices in major towns don't close for lunch and may provide limited services outside normal business hours.

In small towns and villages, post offices close for lunch, e.g. from 12.00 to 13.30 or 14.30. Opening hours in rural areas vary considerably. Some village post offices are open for just three hours a day from 09.00 to 12.00, Mondays to Saturdays, while others are open from 08.00 to 12.00 and 13.30 or 14.30 to 16.30, Mondays to Fridays, and from 08.00 to 11.30 on Saturdays. In some villages opening hours are irregular, e.g. 07.00 to 10.30, 13.45 to 15.30 and 16.30 to 18.00, Mondays to Fridays, and 07.00 to 11.00 on Saturdays.

In Paris, a post office is open in each *arrondissement* from 08.00 to 11.00 (sometimes 13.00) on Saturdays. The central post office at 52 rue du Louvre, 1er is open 24 hours a day, every day (although after 19.00 only letters are dealt with), but it's best to avoid Saturday afternoons and Sundays unless it's urgent. The post office at 71 avenue des Champs-Elysées, 8e is open from 08.00 to 22.00, Mondays to Saturdays, and from 10.00 to 12.00 and 14.00 to 20.00 on Sundays. In other major cities and large towns, main post offices are also open for a few hours on Sundays.

LETTERS

The French letter post (*courrier*) delivery service used to have a reputation for being among the slowest in Europe and, although services have improved markedly in recent years, it's still far from reliable in many areas.

> Despite the fact that even second-class (*non-prioritaire*) letters, which aren't expected to be delivered rapidly, can sometimes arrive the next day, they can equally take eons, and although a 'priority' letter posted within France can generally be expected to arrive the next day (barring strikes or mishaps), four or five days isn't unusual!

Delivery times in Europe vary considerably depending on the countries concerned, e.g. two days for a letter from France to the Netherlands or Germany and around six days to Italy. Air mail (*par avion/poste aérienne*) from major French cities to the US takes five to ten days. Letters may arrive quicker when sent from main post offices. Strictly speaking, there's no longer a distinction between air mail and surface mail, as most international post is sent by air.

In addition to slow deliveries, post sometimes arrives in tatters. If you're sending anything remotely fragile, make sure that you pack it very carefully. Naturally, the post office takes no responsibility for late delivery or damaged post. Nevertheless, service is usually efficient – if not always friendly! Letter post rates apply only to letters and documents; other items may not be sent using this service, however small, but must be sent as 'parcels' (see page 102). Tariff (*tarif*) lists are available from all post offices.

Stamps

Stamps can be purchased at tobacconist shops (*bureau de tabac* – see page) as well as post offices. Coin-operated machines which used to be found outside main post offices have mostly been eliminated. Post offices also have machines that print postage labels for the amount required (*vignettes d'affranchisement* or *etiquettes*). Note, however, that these are printed individually and, if you have a large number of letters to post, you can wait a long time for all the labels to be printed. Self-adhesive (*auto-collant*) stamps for domestic letters up to 20g are sold in sheets of ten (*carnet*). It's also possible to buy and print stamps (even stamps using your own photographs!) via the internet, but first you need to create an account via 💻 www. laposte.fr. There's a handling fee of €5 for all orders (including other products) valued at less than around €40.

La Poste actively promotes the use of pre-stamped envelopes (*enveloppes prétimbrées*) – a service known as *le prêt-à-poster*. Not surprisingly, these are rather expensive when purchased individually, although savings can be made by buying in bulk. Stamped window envelopes (*avec fenêtre*) are also available, as are stamped envelopes with decorative designs (usually of local sights), stamped domestic postcards (*carte postale préaffranchise*) and international stamped envelopes (*enveloppe internationale*) for letters up to 20g. Blank pre-stamped envelopes are also sold by most hypermarkets and supermarkets. It's no longer necessary to affix an air mail (*par avion*) label or use air mail envelopes for international post, as all post is automatically sent by air to distant locations.

Official fiscal stamps (*timbre fiscal*), used to legalise documents, pay government taxes and motoring fines, etc., must be purchased from a tobacconist or a tax office and cannot be bought at a post office.

Addresses

The international identification letter for French addresses is 'F', which precedes the post (zip) code (*code postal*), although its use isn't obligatory. France uses five-digit post codes, where the first two digits indicate the *département* and the last three the town or commune or, in the case of Paris, Lyon and Marseille, a district (*arrondissement*); for example, 75005 indicates the fifth *arrondissement* of Paris. Paris addresses are often given with the *arrondissement* written, for example, 6ème/6e. To translate this into the post code, simply add 7500 to make 75006.

All post codes are listed by *commune* in alphabetical order in a yellow *Code Postal* booklet, available at any post office and via the post office website; they're also shown after each commune name in telephone books. Small villages (*lieu-dit*) often use the post code

of a nearby village or town, and the affiliated village/town name should be also included in the address.

Traditionally, the street address is written with a comma after the house number (i.e. 69, rue du Vin), but the post office advises that no punctuation should appear in the street and city lines of a 'properly' addressed letter, i.e. one that can be read by a machine! Similarly, the addressee's surname, the street name, the *lieu-dit* (if applicable) and the post town should all be written or typed in capital letters. A correct French address is shown below:

> **Monsieur ROUGENEZ**
> **Jean 69 RUE DES ESCARGAUX**
> **F-12345 GRENOUILLE VILLE**
> **France**

Many people include the department (or even region) name after the postcode, although this isn't necessary (and the post office discourages it).

CEDEX (*Courrier d'Entreprise à Distribution Exceptionnelle*) is a special delivery service for business post and where applicable is included in addresses after the town, sometimes followed by a number, e.g. 75006 PARIS CEDEX 09.

Post office (PO) boxes (*boîte postale/BP*) are shown in addresses as *BP 01*, for example and for some reason are usually given in addition to the street address.

It's customary for the sender (*expéditeur*) to write his own address on the back of an envelope.

Envelopes with printed boxes (*enveloppe précasée*) for addresses and postcodes are available from post offices and stationers. Note that French window envelopes have the window to the right of centre and not to the left (as, for example, in the UK).

Post & Letter Boxes

Post boxes (*boîte aux lettres*) are yellow and are usually on a pillar or set into (or attached to) a wall. There's always one outside post offices and railway stations and often one outside a tobacconist. It's best to post urgent letters at a main post office or railway station, as collections are more frequent and delivery is expedited.

In cities and at main post offices, there's often a choice of boxes: for example, one for local post (within the town, *commune* or *département*) and another for other destinations (*autres destinations* or *départements étrangers*). There may be other boxes for economy post (*tarif réduit*) or packets/periodicals (*paquets – journaux périodiques*). In Paris, there are often separate boxes for the city (i.e. postcodes beginning 75) and the suburbs (*banlieue*). There are also special post boxes labelled *pneumatique*, where post for addresses within the city and to

some suburbs is delivered within three hours (post is sent by compressed air under the streets of Paris).

French postmen/women (*facteur*) aren't obliged to deliver post to your front door unless it's on the street. If it isn't, you must install a letter box at the boundary of your property on the street. Home letter boxes must meet specific requirements as to size, accessibility, and how and where they're mounted. For example, the opening must be at least 23cm (9in) wide and 2.4cm (1in) high and the box must be at least 40cm (1ft 6in) but not more than 1.8m (6ft) above the ground. 'Approved' boxes can be purchased for around €10 in most DIY stores (in fact, smaller ones are usually more expensive). See the La Poste website for details or ask at your local post office if you plan to install your own letter box. (You may wish to give your postman a key to your letter box so that he can deliver items which won't fit through the slot, although postmen have a 'master' key, which opens standard boxes.)

If you live in an apartment block with a caretaker (*gardienne*), she may receive and distribute letters (and parcels) to tenants. Otherwise letters are put in your letter box in the foyer (make sure that it has a lock). Often letter boxes aren't large enough for magazines and packets, which are left in a common storage space. In some apartment blocks in main cities it isn't unusual for post to be stolen, therefore if possible you should install a letter box large enough to hold all your post or rent a post box at a main post office (see **Collections** below).

Deliveries

Except in main cities, there's usually only one post delivery a day, and in rural areas you may be able to have your outgoing post collected by your postman. If the postman calls with post requiring a signature or payment when nobody is at home, he'll leave a collection form (*avis de passage*).

Post is kept at the post office for 15 days, after which it's returned to the sender, therefore if you're going to be away from home for longer than 15 days you should ask the post office to hold your post (see **Collection** below).

If a letter cannot be delivered, e.g. because it's wrongly addressed or because the addressee has moved, it will be returned with a note stating, e.g. '*n'habite pas à l'adresse* indiquée – renvoyer à l'expéditeur. This is sometimes abbreviated to 'NPAI'.

If you want your post to be redirected, you must complete an ordre de réexpédition temporaire at least a week in advance. Identification is required for each member of the household. Post can be redirected indefinitely and the service costs around €22 for up to six months and around €3 per month thereafter. If you're moving house, you should complete a permanent change of address card (ordre de réexpédition définitif); this service also costs around €20 for six months and is renewable for a further six months.

You'll receive heaps of junk mail (courrier indésirable or publicité), e.g. unsolicited letters, retail brochures and free newspapers – estimated to amount to some 40kg per household, per annum. However, you should be sure to look between the pages of junk for 'real' post. It isn't unknown for foreigners to throw away important bills and correspondence during their first few weeks! The French tax authority is notorious for sending important forms and information in plastic wrappers that resemble those used for advertisements and junk magazines.

☑ SURVIVAL TIP

You may be able to reduce the amount of junk mail you receive by putting up a 'Pas de pub' sign or writing to the Syndicat des Entreprises de Vente par Correspondance, 60 rue de la Boétie, 75008 Paris.

Your postman may present you with a calendar each year around Christmas, designed to encourage you to tip him for thoughtfully delivering your post (albeit often late and mangled and supplemented by missives for various neighbours).

Collections

If you've received an avis de passage (see above), you must take it to your local post office, the address of which is written on the form. In large post offices there may be a window marked retrait des lettres et paquets. You usually need some form of identification

(pièce d'identité), e.g. your passport, carte de séjour or French driving licence, although this may not be requested.

A post office may refuse to give letters to a spouse if they're addressed to his or her partner, or to a house owner if they're addressed to his tenants or guests, although this often isn't a problem. You can give someone authorisation to collect a letter or parcel on your behalf by entering the details on the back of the collection form in the box marked 'vous ne pouvez pas vous déplacer', for which both your identification and that of the 'collector' is required. It's possible to set up a permanent authorisation (procuration) with the local post office granting permission for a spouse or other adult member of your household to collect registered or other post in your name using their own identity documents.

If you're going to be away from your home for up to a month, you can have your post retained by the local post office (garde du courrier – see below) for around €19 for up to two months. Alternatively, you can have mail redirected.

You can receive mail at any post office in France via the international poste restante service. If there's more than one post office in the town, include its name in the address to avoid confusion. Letters should be addressed as follows:

Marmaduke **BLENKINSOP**
POSTE RESTANTE
POSTE CENTRALE
Post code CITY NAME [e.g. 75001 PARIS]
FRANCE

Post sent to a poste restante address is returned to the sender if it's unclaimed after 30 days. Identification (e.g. a passport) is necessary for collection. There's a fee (equivalent to the standard letter rate) for each letter received.

If you have an American Express card or use American Express travellers' cheques, you can have post sent to an American Express office in France. Standard letters are held free of charge; registered letters and packages aren't accepted. Post, which should be marked 'Client Mail Service', is kept for 30 days before being returned to the sender. Post can be held for up to two months for €19 or forwarded to another office or address, for which there's a charge of €19 for less than two months, €23 for six months or €41 for a year.

Within France a 'change of address pack' is available from La Poste for €34 (6 months) or €52 (12 months) and €55 (6 months)/€100 (12 months) abroad. Other companies provide similar post-holding services for customers, e.g. Thomas Cook and Western Union.

You can rent a post office box (*boîte postale/BP*) at most post offices for an annual fee. All your post will be stored there and the postman will no longer deliver to your home, but you can arrange to be informed when registered or express post arrives.

PARCELS

The Post Office provides a range of parcel (*colis*) services, both domestic and international, under the Colissimo brand. Prices include both postage and various sizes of fold-flat cardboard boxes, each with a weight limit. Small packages to addresses in mainland France, weighing up to 3kg, cost €9.70. Medium-sized ones (up to 5kg) cost €11.40 and large ones (up to 7kg) €13.60. All should take no longer than 48 hours to deliver. Small sizes aren't available for international mail but medium sizes cost €27.20 to the rest of Europe and €36.50 to, e.g., the USA or Australasia: large ones cost €31.40 to Europe and €43 for further afield. International deliveries take four to eight days. The Colissimo range also includes special packages, e.g. for CDs or for one, two or three bottles. Minimal insurance is included on all these services but higher levels are available at extra costs.

⚠ Caution

A parcel is anything other than an envelope containing sheets of paper or card. If you wish to send someone a CD or a small gift, it must be sent as a parcel, which involves going to a post office. Parcels cannot simply be posted in a post box.

You can, of course, make up your own parcel, provided it conforms to size and weight limits to be found at 🖳 www.laposte.fr. If you're using express post, it's unnecessary to write on the envelope, as you must complete a form, containing your address and telephone number and those of the addressee, which is stamped and affixed to the parcel by post office staff. Parcels to addresses outside the EU must have an international green customs label (*déclaration de douane*) affixed to them.

For current tariffs ask at a post office or consult the La Poste website (🖳 www.laposte. fr). All services include minimal insurance against loss or damage in transit. Parcels posted in France must be securely packaged, and it's wise to buy padded envelopes (*à bulles*) or cardboard boxes sold at post offices. Padded envelopes come in four sizes and are obtainable from post offices. Boxes, padded bags and large envelopes are also sold in stationery shops.

When sending small parcels from a post office, use the window marked *Paquets* (if there is one). In larger branches, there's usually an automatic coin-operated weighing machine for packages.

Express

The fastest way to send letters or parcels abroad is via the *Chronopost International* service (called EMS in most other European countries), which serves around 220 countries. There are three services: 10, 13 and 18. Within France, the first of these services guarantees delivery by 10.00 the next day, the second by 13.00 and the last by 18.00. For international deliveries, there are varying tariffs for documents and goods and no fewer than nine zones, two of which cover countries both in and outside the EU (confused yet?). The minimum rate, for documents and goods weighing up to 500g is €33.10. Details can be found at 🖳 www.fr.chronopost.com.

An alternative service for international parcels is '*Postexport*', which is a postage-paid envelope designed for documents weighing between 20g and 2kg. This is much cheaper (and simpler to understand) than *Chronopost* or a courier service and takes on average only a day or two longer. Costs start at €2 for a 50g letter to Western Europe, delivered in three days. You can buy envelopes in advance and simply hand them in at any post office when you want to use them.

French railways (SNCF) also operate an express package and parcel service (*Service National des Messageries/SERNAM*, 🖥 www.sernam.fr) within France and to most European countries. The 'special express' service operates from door-to-door and the 'direct express' service from station-to-station. Charges vary depending on the speed of delivery, the distance, and whether the package is to be collected or delivered at either end.

DHL and UPS (🖥 www.dhl.com and www.ups.com) provide domestic freight services, which guarantee airport-to-airport delivery within four hours, plus optional delivery at the receiving end.

REGISTERED & RECORDED POST

Registered post is commonly used in France when sending official documents and communications, where proof of despatch and/or a receipt is required. You can send a registered letter (*lettre recommandée*) with (*avec*) or without (*sans*) proof of delivery (*avis de réception*). If you're sending items of value in an ordinary letter in France, you can insure it for an additional €7, which entitles you to claim for a loss of up to €800.

Under the declared value (*valeur déclaré*) system, you pay for insurance according to the weight of the package, starting at €14 for 250g and rising to €19.80 for 5kg. These fees provide cover of up to €600. For larger values, fees increase by €0.50 for each €100 of declared value for mail to a mainland France destination (mail to overseas French territories costs more). Parcels sent *recommandée* in Colissimo packages are covered against losses between €450 and €800. Compensation for domestic registered letters and parcels is known as *indemnité forfaitaire*.

For international post, registration costs €4.30

for compensation of €45 and €5.30 for compensation of €150. Under the *valeur declare internationale* scheme, it costs from €10 for a declared value of up to €500, rising to €29 for a value of €5,000. These fees are in addition to postage. The sender's address must be written on the back of registered letters. You receive a receipt for a registered letter or parcel. for both domestic and international mail.

A domestic recorded or 'tracked' service (*courier suivi*) enables you to check the progress of your post and find out when it arrives (via the internet).

It's possible to combine the recorded service with registered post (*le prêt-à-recommander suivi*) if you need a signed receipt and also want to be able to track your letter. Bar-coded envelopes for trackable registered letters are also available and it's even possible to send an electronic registered letter (see 🖥 www.laposte.fr for details).

Registered letters require a signature and proof of identity on delivery – normally of the person to whom they're addressed. If the addressee is absent when delivery is made, a notice is left and the letter must be collected from the local post office (see **Collections** above). When proof of delivery (*avis de réception*) is requested, a receipt is returned to the sender.

7.
COMMUNICATIONS

France has the third-largest telephone network in the world, and over 90 per cent of French households have a telephone. The French aren't, however, such habitual telephone users as some people, particularly North Americans, and they don't usually spend hours on the telephone; business people in particular would rather meet or exchange letters than conduct business over the telephone. France's telephone network is an odd mixture of the state-of-the-art and the antiquated.

Tariffs are reasonable by European standards (see below) and there's a range of service providers to choose from. France also has an efficient mobile telephone service, encompassing virtually the whole country.

Following the ending of the France Telecom (FT) monopoly in 2009, competition has substantially heated up, with Bouygues and Vodaphone the major entrants to the market. Although the landline network is still largely in the hands of FT, marketing through its Orange brand (🖥 www.orange.fr), it's possible to change the landline subscription to other suppliers, such as UK Telecom (🖥 www.uktelecom.uk,net), which offers billing in English (and sterling, if required), as well as cheaper rates for calls to the UK. The cost of the transfer is the same as for reconnecting to an existing FT line (see below).

Considerable savings can be made on domestic and international calls by shopping around for the lowest rates. Whoever is responsible for the landline, it's possible to have calls handled by pre-select (CPS) services, where use of a code diverts calls which are then charged independently of the landline subscription, often at lower tariffs. For those with second homes in France, a further option is international divert, where calls to a UK number can be switched automatically to a French one if you have a holiday home in France. The flat rate subscription covers any number of calls, while callers are charged at the UK rate for a local call.

EMERGENCY & SERVICE NUMBERS

The national emergency numbers (*services d'urgence et d'assistance*) in France are shown below.

Emergency Numbers

Number	Service
15	Ambulance (*Service d'Aide Médicale d'Urgence/SAMU*) or to contact a duty doctor out of hours
17	Police (*police-secours*)
18	Fire (*sapeurs-pompiers/feu centrale d'alarme*)
112	EU emergency number

If you aren't sure which emergency service you need (or cannot remember which number is for which service), it's best to call the EU emergency number (112), which will usually connect you to the emergency services switchboard for your department and dispatch the appropriate service (ambulance, police or fire) to assist you. In some areas, the 112 service may have personnel who speak English or other foreign languages, but you cannot rely on this, particularly outside the Paris area, Therefore, you must ensure that you and all family members know how to place an emergency call, give your name, street address or location, and request the appropriate service in reasonably clear French.

The Fire service number (18) is also useful as the *pompiers* handle the widest range of emergency situations in France, including road accidents and natural disasters, and will notify an ambulance or police if they believe the situation warrants it. Calls to emergency numbers are free from public and private telephones.

In addition to the national emergency numbers shown above, you should make a note of the number of your local ambulance service (*ambulance*), police station (*gendarmerie*) and fire service (*pompiers*), for which a space is usually provided in telephone books. Gas and electricity emergency numbers are listed in telephone directories under *EDF/GDF*.

Other numbers to note are the poison emergency service (*centre anti-poisons*), Samaritans (*SOS Amitié*) and various other help organisations listed at the front of telephone directories. There's

a 24-hour information/assistance telephone number (113) for problems associated with drugs, alcohol and smoking (*Drogue/Alcool/Tabac Info-Service*). There's also an internet helpline for women (*SOS Femmes*, 🖳 www.sosfemmes.com) and *Suicide Ecoute* for those contemplating suicide (☎ 01 45 39 40 00). Other emergency numbers deal with homelessness (115), child abuse (119) and missing children (116000).

In Paris, there's *SOS Médecins* (☎ 08 20 33 24 24 or 01 47 07 77 77) for an emergency doctor, and *SOS Dentaire* (☎ 01 43 37 51 00) for emergency dental treatment. Contact numbers for *SOS Médecins* in other parts of France can be found at 🖳 www.sosmedecins-france.fr.

In Paris and other main cities, there are emergency telephone boxes at major junctions, marked *Services Médicaux*, with direct lines to emergency services; and throughout France there are free SOS call boxes on motorways and some other major roads.

General information and help is available in English on ☎ 08 00 36 47 75 (or ☎ +33 1 55 78 60 56 from abroad) during normal office hours, Mondays to Saturdays. Other useful telephone service numbers (in French) include those listed opposite (calls are free unless otherwise stated).

INSTALLATION & REGISTRATION

If you're planning to move into a property without an existing telephone line (*ligne fixe*), you'll need to have one installed. In this case, you must normally visit your local FT office, which you'll find in the *Yellow Pages* under *Télécommunications: service*, although it may be possible to obtain a telephone number before moving to France. In either case, you must prove that you're the owner or tenant of the property in question, e.g. with an electricity bill, confirmation of purchase (*attestation d'acquisition*) or a lease (*bail*). You'll also require your passport or residence permit (*carte de séjour*). France Télécom publishes a *Set-Up Guide* in English.

If there's already a telephone line near the property, the charge is around €110. If you buy a property in a remote area without a telephone line, it may be expensive to have a telephone

Service Numbers

Number(s)	Service
1013	After-sales service and to report telephone breakdowns or line problems
1014	Private customer services
1016	Business customer services (or 08 25 33 11 22)
118xxx	Directory enquiries (see page 110)
118700	International directory enquiries
3000	For details of your current phone bill and 24-hour recorded information about FT's offers and call plans, which you can also book
3103	To pick up messages, if you subscribe to FT's *Top Message* service (see page 114)
3131	To find out the number of your last caller (see **Caller Identification** on page 115)
3201/3250	Weather forecast (€0.34 per minute)
3651	To prevent your number appearing on the telephone of the person you're calling (see **Caller Identification** on page 115)
3699	Speaking clock (*horloge parlante*)

installed, as you must pay for the line to your property. Contact FT for an estimate. A straightforward reconnection costs €55.

If you're restoring a derelict building or building a new house, you should have trenches dug for the telephone cable if you want a below-ground connection (you may be able to have an above-ground connection via a wire from the nearest pylon). This work can be carried out by FT, but their charges are high and it's possible to do it yourself, although you must observe certain standards. Details of the required depth of trenches and the type of conduit (*gaine*) to use, etc., can be obtained from FT.

When you visit the FT agency, you'll need to know what kind of telephone sockets are already installed in the property, how many telephones you want, where you want them installed and what kind of telephone you want (if you're buying one from FT). If you want a number of telephone points installed, you should arrange this in advance. You may also want to upgrade a line, e.g. to ADSL (see **Internet** on page 119).

You'll also be asked whether you want a listed or unlisted number (see **Directories** on page 109) and must inform FT where you want your bill sent and how you wish to pay it. If you plan to pay by direct debit, you must provide your account details (*relevé d'identité bancaire/ RIB*). You can also request an itemised bill at the same time.

You may be given a telephone number on the spot, although you should wait until you receive written confirmation before giving it to anyone.

It isn't possible simply to take over the telephone number of the previous occupant of a property. FT always changes the telephone number when the ownership or tenancy of a property changes.

You'll receive a letter stating that you have a mixed line (*ligne mixte*), which is simply a line allowing both incoming and outgoing calls. If you own a property and are letting it for holidays, you can arrange to have outgoing calls limited to the local area, or to regional or national calls only, but you cannot limit the service just to incoming calls.

To have a line installed takes from a few days in a city to weeks or possibly a month or more in remote rural areas, although 90 per cent of new customers have a line installed within two weeks. In certain areas there's a waiting list, and you can have a line installed quickly only if you need a telephone for your safety or security, e.g. if you're an invalid, in which case a medical certificate is required. Business lines may be installed quicker than domestic lines.

When moving into a home with a telephone line, you must have the account transferred to your name and a telephone number issued to you. This can usually be done within 48 hours. To do this, you can simply dial 1014 or go to the FT website (💻 www.orange.fr and click on 'fixe' and then 'ouvrir une ligne').

Some information is available on the English-language section of the FT website, but it's limited to business services and investment details. English-language assistance can be obtained by phone (☎ 08 00 36 47 75 or +33 1 55 78 60 56 from abroad) during normal office hours, Mondays to Saturdays. The charge for taking over an existing line is around €60.

If you're taking over a property from the previous occupants, you should arrange for the telephone account to be transferred to your name from the day you take possession.

☑ SURVIVAL TIP

Always check that the previous occupant has closed his account before you take over the line, or you may find his charges allocated to your new number.

Broadband

Broadband (le haut-débit) via ADSL (l'ADSL) is available in most urban areas, although it's patchy in rural areas and it remains questionable whether remote places will ever be connected as it's uneconomical. To find out whether broadband is available in your area, see the Orange website (💻 www.orange. fr), which contains detailed broadband cover maps for the whole of France. If broadband is available, installation costs the same as a standard line (see above). France Télécom

offers various combined phone and internet access packages for compulsive internet surfers (see **Internet** on page 119).

Yet another technological 'advance' is ADSL2, which offers even faster download and upload speeds (up to 20Mbits per second) but is currently available only within 1.5km of an 'exchange' and requires an upgrade to your ADSL box (supplied by most ISPs). To find out whether ADSis available to you, go to one of the following websites and enter your phone number or post code as required: 💻 www. degrouptest.com, www.dslvalley.com or www. zoneadsl.com.

An even faster connection (up to 100Mb/s), known as le très haut débit, is available to businesses in certain parts of the country and is expected to spread to the private sector in the coming years as part of France Télécom's 'Fiber to the Home' (FTTH) initiative.

If ADSL isn't available, it's possible to obtain a broadband connection via satellite or a mobile phone (e.g. with a 3G card and a laptop computer or PDA to connect to your phone).

For those whose French (let alone their 'techno-speak') isn't up to the complexities of all this, French telecommunications company Téléconnect offers an 'AngloPack' consisting of an English-language helpline (☎ 08 05 02 40 00) and English translations of all documentation and contracts. The service costs €29.90 per month, including two hours of 'free' calls; for details, see 💻 www. teleconnectfrance.com.

See also **Mobile Telephones** on page 116 and **Internet Telephony** on page 120.

Alternative Providers

There are now a great many alternative telephone service providers (i.e. alternatives to FT) in France, some of which advertise in the English language press (see **Appendix B**). To help find your way through the maze of alternative telephone providers you may want to consult a service such as BudgeTelecom (💻 www.budgetelecom.com) or Zone ADSL (💻 www.zoneadsl.com), where you can compare the available tariffs to see which is best for your calling pattern and review customer evaluations of the services available from each provider.

If you wish to use another provider (or several providers, for different types of call), you'll need to open a separate account with each. Note, however, that you must still have a line rental account with FT.

Telephones

You can buy a telephone (*téléphone*) from FT or any retailer. Cordless (*sans fil*) telephones are widely available. The standard French telephone connector is a large block with a single T-shaped blade-like plug. Adapter plugs allowing you to connect a standard RJ11 phone plug to a French phone point aren't easy to find in France, although they're available in some airport shops and larger computer stores, and it's preferable to buy them before you move to France, e.g. from Maplin (⌨ www.maplin.co.uk) or TeleAdapt (⌨ www.teleadapt.com). Note, however, that they cost around €40, so it would probably be cheaper to buy a new telephone! See also **Modems** on page 120.

DIRECTORIES

When you have a telephone installed, your name and number are usually automatically included in the next edition of your local telephone directory (*annuaire*), as well as the internet telephone directory. Like most telephone companies, FT sells its list of subscribers to businesses, but you can choose to have an unlisted number, which saves you from the dreaded telephone marketing, which is increasingly prevalent in France. There are three options (known as *Services vie privée*), all of which are free:

♦ **Orange list (*liste orange*)** – Your details aren't made available to businesses.

♦ **Chamois list (*liste chamois*)** – In addition to the above, your details aren't included in printed or electronic (e.g. online) directories.

♦ **Red list (*liste rouge*)** – In addition to the above, your number isn't listed in the directory or given out by directory enquiries.

The chamois and red options are particularly useful if you have a phone line reserved for a fax machine and don't want to be inundated with fax advertisements. Directories now include some mobile telephone numbers. You

can also ask for your email address, postal address and profession to be included.

Telephone directories are published by department (*département*). Not all directories are published at the same time (the issue date for new directories is shown at the front). Some departments have more than one volume (*tome*), e.g., the Paris *White Pages* (*Pages Blanches*) consist of five volumes and the *Yellow Pages (Pages Jaunes)* two.

Yellow Pages, which contain only business and official (e.g. government) telephone numbers, are included with the *White Pages* in one volume or published in a separate volume or volumes. When there's more than one volume, the index is included at the front of the first volume.

You can obtain a copy of *White or Yellow Pages* for other departments for a fee of around €7.50 per volume (☎ 08 00 30 23 02) or refer to them in libraries or at main post offices. There are also local *Yellow Pages (Les Pages Jaunes Locales)* in some areas (e.g. Paris), and 'business-to-business' directories (*Professionnels à Professionnels/PAP*) are published in national and regional editions as well as in a CD-ROM version. The *Yellow Pages* for the whole of France can also be accessed online at ⌨ www.pagesjaunes.fr.

Telephone directories (*both White* and *Yellow Pages*) contain a wealth of information, including emergency information and numbers, useful local numbers, FT numbers and services, tariffs, international country codes and costs, how to use the telephone (in English, French, German, Italian and Spanish), public telephone information, information about bills, directories and FT products, administration numbers, town plans and maps of the department(s) covered by the telephone book.

Subscribers are listed in the *White Pages* under their town or *commune* (or *arrondissement* in Paris, Lyon and Marseille, and not alphabetically for the whole of a department or city. It isn't enough to know that someone lives, for example, in the department of Dordogne, you must know the town.

You'll receive little or no help from directory enquiries (who aren't always helpful at the best of times) unless you know the town or village where the subscriber is located – in which case, you may as well look up the number yourself! The advantage of the listing system is that you can easily find the numbers of people in your town or village if you know their address but not their name. (A potential disadvantage is that other people can easily find your number!)

When your application for a telephone line has been accepted, you're given a voucher (*bon*) for a copy of your local telephone directory; the issuing office is usually housed in the same building as the FT agency.

Annual directories are supposed to be delivered to your door or building when they're available, but in some outlying areas delivery is haphazard at best. If you don't receive a directory, you can call ☎ 1014 and request one.

Directory Enquiries

For domestic directory enquiries, you can no longer simply dial 12, but must choose between umpteen services and endure a barrage of advertising (without being told how much you're being charged for the privilege!) before being given the number you want. All directory enquiries numbers begin 118, and costs start at around €0.34 per call. Some provide numbers outside France. Details of all directory enquiries services and their charges can be found on a dedicated website,

⌨ www.appel118.fr. For both domestic and international numbers, however, it's easier and cheaper to use an online telephone directory, e.g. ⌨ www.pagesjaunes.fr for France.

USING THE TELEPHONE

Using the telephone in France is simplicity itself. All French telephone numbers have ten digits, beginning with a two-digit regional code (01 for the Île-de-France, 02 for the northwest, 03 northeast, 04 southeast and 05 southwest), followed by another two-digit area code.

⚠ **Caution**

If you're calling within France, you must dial all ten digits, even if you're phoning your next-door neighbour.

Codes for the overseas departments (*DOM*), which have six-figure numbers, are as follows: French Guyana (05 94), Guadeloupe (05 90), Martinique (05 96), Mayotte (02 69), Réunion (02 62), Saint-Pierre-et-Miquelon (05 08). Monaco isn't part of France and has its own country code of 377.

Numbers beginning 06 are mobile numbers (see page 116), and those beginning with 08 are special (expensive) rate numbers (see page 114).

INTERNATIONAL CALLS

It's possible to make international direct dialling (IDD) calls to most countries from both private and public telephones. A full list of country codes, plus area codes for main cities and time differences, is shown in the information pages (*les info téléphoniques*) of your *Yellow Pages*. To make an IDD call you must first dial 00, then the country code, the area code (**without** the first zero) and the subscriber's number.

To obtain an operator from one of the four major US telephone companies dial 08 00 99 00 11 (AT&T), ☎ 08 00 99 00 19 (MCI), ☎ 08 00 99 00 87 (Sprint) or ☎ 08 00 99 00 13 (IDB WorldCom). (Note that these are French 08 00 numbers, not American 0800 numbers and that the latter aren't toll-free when

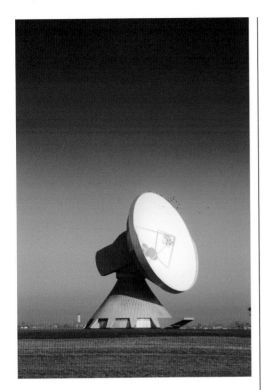

dialled from abroad.) These companies also offer long-distance calling cards that provide access to English-speaking operators, and AT&T offers a US Direct service, whereby you can call an operator in any state (except Alaska).

France Télécom publishes a useful free booklet, *Guide du Téléphone International*, containing information in both French and English.

Alternative Providers

If you're using a service provider other than France Télécom for your local or international calls you must normally dial a code to route your call to the appropriate telephone company. Each provider has its own code or procedure for accessing its network. It's possible to have subscriptions with several telephone providers, and each one will indicate to you what numbers you need to dial to route your calls correctly.

Alternatively, among the range of options available to FT landline subscribers is a facility whereby your phone line will route calls automatically to whichever of the alternative telephone providers you prefer, without your having to dial the extra numbers. If you have all your calls automatically routed via another provider, it's possible to revert to the FT system by dialling 8 before the number. This service, which is useful if there's a problem with your alternative provider, must be ordered in advance from FT and is free.

It's possible to use a callback service, such as those provided by Eurotelsat (💻 www.eurotelsat.com) and Kallback (💻 www.kallback.com). Calls are routed via the cheapest provider, and companies claim that you can save up to 70 per cent (compared with FT rates) on international calls. However, as the name suggests, you must dial an access number, hang up and wait for a call back (within seconds) before you can dial the number you want.

Recorded Messages

After dialling, you may hear the following recorded message: '*Le numéro que vous demandez n'est pas attribué; veuillez consulter le service des renseignements*' ('The number you've dialled is not recognised; please use Directory Enquiries').

If the number you're calling is engaged, you may hear an engaged tone (i.e. a series of short beeps) or you may hear a series of 'musical' tones followed by a recorded message: '*La ligne de votre correspondent est occupé; pour le rappeler automatiquement, appuyez sur la touche cinq*' ('The line you've dialled is engaged; for 'ring-back', press 5'). If you dial 5 before replacing the receiver, your telephone will automatically be called back by the number you're trying to reach as soon as it's free. There's no charge for this service. If the person you're calling is using *Signal d'Appel* (call waiting), you'll hear the following message: '*Veuillez patienter. Votre correspondant est en ligne. Nous lui indiquons votre appel par un signal sonore*' ('Please wait. The person you're calling is on the line and knows you're waiting'). If he doesn't clear the line within a few seconds, the message will give way to a normal engaged tone and you must redial.

Sometimes when lines are busy, you won't be put on hold but will be instructed to ring back later, e.g. *Toutes nos lignes sont indisponibles. Veuillez nous rappeler ultérieurement.*

Greetings

The usual French 'greeting' on the telephone is simply *Allô* inflected as a question (*'Allô?'*), but you'll sometimes hear the even blunter *'Oui?'* or the abrupt *'Je vous écoute'* ('I'm listening'). If you're calling via the operator, he may say, *'Ne quittez pas'* ('Hold the line'). 'I'm trying to connect you' is *'J'essaie de vous mettre en relation'*, and 'Go ahead' may be simply *'Parlez'* ('Speak').

Numbers

One of the most difficult things to do in any foreign language is to understand telephone numbers given to you orally. This is particularly difficult in French, as telephone numbers are dictated in the same way as they're written, i.e. normally two digits at a time. For example, 04 15 48 17 33 is *zéro quatre, quinze, quarante-huit, dix-sept, trente-trois*. It's therefore wise to practise your French numbers (particularly those from 70 to 100).

Note that the French don't say 'double' when two digits are the same: for example, 22 is *vingt-deux*.

Note also that some numbers aren't written in pairs, e.g. 0800 300 400; these are also spoken as written – in this case *zéro huit cents, trois cents, quat' cents*.

CHARGES

Deregulation of the telecommunications market has resulted in an intense price war, and considerable savings can be made on national as well as international calls by shopping around for the lowest rates. However, as there are now numerous alternative providers in France, it's impossible to list all their tariffs here, and only FT's are given in detail. (UK Telecom's are also listed, e.g. 🖳 *www.uktelecom.net).*

Comparisons between the rates offered by different service providers can be found via the internet (e.g. 🖳 www.comparatel.fr and www.budgetelecom.com). Line rental and call charges are explained below; for

information about installation and registration charges, see page 106.

Line Rental

The monthly line rental or service charge (*abonnement*) is €30 for a standard line or ADSL. If you use an alternative provider (other than FT), there may be a separate monthly fee in addition to your call charges, although most providers have dropped these.

Calls

Domestic Calls

France Télécom's tariffs depend on the destination and time of calls. Calls at peak times (*heures pleines*), which are Mondays to Fridays from 08.00 to 19.00 and Saturdays from 08.00 to 12.00, are charged at the 'normal' rate (*tarif normal*); calls at all other times (*heures creuses*), including all day on public holidays, are charged at a reduced rate (*tarif réduit*).

France Télécom no longer publicises its rates, however, but offers instead an array of 'all-inclusive' packages (*forfait*). Packages require a fixed monthly payment (e.g. between €1.50 and €10) in return for reduced rates or, in some cases, 'free' calls, which makes it all but impossible (deliberately!) to calculate what you're paying for each call or to compare rates with those of other providers.

A recent comparison between rates charged by the five major providers showed price variations of up to five centimes for a three-minute, off-peak local call, and a much wider range for a ten-minute, peak rate local call, with FT's charges – not surprisingly – generally the highest, although if you're a telephone addict you may find their 'unlimited use' (*illimité*) packages good value.

Alternative telephone service providers (see above) also offer a variety of call packages, consisting of a combination of varying initial charges and lengths followed by different per-minute charges and, in some cases, a single rate for all times of day and all destinations.

Calls from fixed telephones to mobile phones are more expensive with 'connection' charges and, often, higher per-minute rates compared with fixed-to-fixed or mobile-to-mobile rates.

The EU is currently seeking to introduce more comparability to all kinds of telephone services, so that all suppliers will have to conform to a standard way of explaining their charges so that like-for-like comparisons are possible.

International Calls

France Télécom tariffs for international calls are listed on its website and in mid-2011 were as shown in the table below.

Other telephone providers have different tariff structures for international calls. Most also offer a variety of discount plans, such as half-price on all calls to a designated ('favourite') country or to a number of overseas phone numbers (e.g. your mum's).

Special Rate Numbers

Special rate numbers, all of which begin 08, include those shown in the table on the next page (all charges apply from a fixed-line telephone; calls from a mobile cost more).

Other Charges

Charges for equipment rental, credit card calls and (if you use the same provider) internet connection will be included on your bill (see below), as will any charges for custom and optional services (below).

CUSTOM & OPTIONAL SERVICES

France Télécom provides a range of custom and optional telephone services, described as 'comfort services' (*service confort*). Almost all services can be ordered online from the FT website (💻 www.orange.fr), where you can also find a description of the services available – although their prices, which can change without notice, aren't always shown, but have to be established either by phone or a visit to a local FT branch.

FT branches are mostly confined nowadays to major towns and cities; those in other places are principally concerned with the sale of mobile phones and call packages and may be unable to help with other types

France Telecom Tariffs		
	Connexion charge	€ per minute
Mainland France:		
To fixed phones	0.11	0.014
To mobile phones	0.19	0.079
French Overseas Territories:		
To fixed lines	0.11	0.14
To mobile phones	0.19	0.25
Western Europe	0.069	0.11
Rest of Europe	0.28	0.502
North America	0.069	0.291
Australia & New Zealand	0,23	0.452

Special Rate Numbers	
Prefix	**Charge**
08 00/05 (*Numéro Vert*)	Free
08 01/10/11 (*Numéro Azur*)	Local call charge (€0.078 'connection' fee + €0.014 per minute off-peak and €0.028 peak)
08 20/21 (*Numéro Indigo*)	€0.11 connection fee + €0.12 per minute (€0.09 per minute for 08 20 20 and 08 20 25 numbers)
08 25/26/84/90	€0.11 connection fee + €0.15 per minute
08 91	€0.30 per minute
08 92	€0.45 per minute
08 93	€0.75 per minute
08 98	€1.20 per minute

of enquiry. *Services confort* can be ordered individually or as part of a package and include those below.

◆ **Call Barring (*Blocage d'Appels*)**: allows you to block all incoming calls

◆ **Call Transfer (*Transfert d'Appel*)**: allows you to divert calls to another number. Dial *21* followed by the number to which you wish your calls to be transferred, followed by the hash (#) key (*dièse*).

◆ **Call Waiting (*Signal d'Appel*)**: Tells you when another caller is trying to contact you when you're already on a call and allows you to speak to him without terminating your call. To activate, press the 'R' button followed by 2. If your phone doesn't have an 'R' button, just hang up briefly to change connections. Free service.

◆ **Call Waiting while Online ('*@llo*')**: If you have a shared line for telephone and internet access, this service allows you to 'see' an incoming call while you're online. The caller's number is displayed on your computer screen and you can take the call via the computer or the telephone or transfer it to an answering service.

◆ **Three-way Conversation (*Conversation à Trois*)**: allows you to hold a three-way conversation. Free service.

◆ **Reminder Call (*Mémo Appel*)**: allows you to programme your telephone to ring at a set time. To make a reminder call, dial *55* followed by the time you wish

to be called, using the 24-hour clock. For example, if you wish to be called at 15.30, you dial *55*1530 followed by hash (*dièse*) button.

◆ **Answering Service (*Top Message*)**: allows you to receive messages while you're on the telephone as well as when you're unable to answer the phone. If you've received a message, you'll hear an interrupted dial tone the next time you pick up the receiver – or possibly the time after that, or sometimes several days later! Free but, as indicated, unreliable.

◆ **Ring Back (*AutoRappel*)**: allows you to obtain an automatic call back by dialling 5 if the number you dial is engaged. Free service.

◆ **Caller Identification (*Présentation du Numéro/Nom*)**: This is available on telephones with a built-in display (or you can plug a display unit into your phone) and allows you to see either a caller's number or both his number and his name and business name. If you don't wish your details to appear on the telephones of anyone you're calling, you can dial ☎ 3651 before the number or opt for *secret permanent* (both free services). You can also find out the number of your last caller by dialling 3131 (free service).

◆ **New Number (*Annonce du Nouveau Numéro*)**: When moving out of a property, it's possible for callers to be advised of your new number for up to 12 months

♦ **Call Monitoring (*Allofact*)**: Monitor your calling habits over any period. Free but you must register by calling FT's order line (☎ 3000).

Some services require an annual subscription charge, others a fixed (per use) charge each time the service is used. As a result of increased competition, some services that were previously charged are now free. It pays to check with FT or read the advertising material that comes with your telephone bill to find out about the latest offers. For details of all custom and optional services, call ☎ 1014.

BILLS

France Télécom bills its customers every two months and allows you two weeks to pay your bill (*facture*). Bills include VAT (*TVA*) at 19.6 per cent, although an ex-VAT figure (*HT*) is shown as well as the total including VAT (*TTC*). Customers are encouraged to receive their bills online (via email), as with other utilities in France,

You can request an itemised bill (*facturation détaillée*) which lists all calls with the date and time, the number called, the duration and the charge; it's particularly useful if you let a home in France or lend it to friends. This service is free but must be requested a month in advance. You can monitor your calling habits over any period by using Allofact (see above) or via the FT website (🖳 www. agence.orange.fr).

Bills can be paid by post by sending a cheque to France Télécom, at a post office or at a local FT office. Simply detach the tear-off part of your bill and send or present it with payment. You can also pay your telephone bill by *titre interbancaire de paiement* (*TIP*) system, whereby your bank account details are pre-printed on the tear-off part of the bill, which you simply date, sign and return; or by direct debit (*prélèvement automatique*), which is recommended if you spend a lot of time away from home or are a non-resident, as it will ensure that you won't be disconnected for non-payment. If you're a non-resident, you can also have bills sent to an address outside France. If you pay your bills by direct debit, your invoice will specify the date of the debit

from your account, usually around 20 days after receipt of the invoice. Contact your local FT agent for information.

If you don't pay your bill by the date due, you'll receive a reminder (a letter or a telephone call) about a week after the due date. Late payment of a bill incurs a penalty of 10 per cent of the sum due. If payment still hasn't been made two weeks after the due date, FT may progressively reduce your telephone service (*service restreint*), depending on your payment record. If a reduced service is implemented, first international calls will be barred, followed by a restriction to local calls and finally to emergency calls only. You'll receive a letter before your service is disconnected and the bill must be paid immediately to prevent it being cut off. If you're cut off, you must pay the outstanding bill, a reconnection fee (as for a new connection, i.e. around €60) and you may also need to pay a deposit.

If you receive a bill with which you don't agree, you should pay your usual amount and contest the bill with your telephone company. They'll investigate it and won't disconnect you while it's in dispute, provided you pay something. Watch out for counterfeit bills produced by foreign companies; the give-away is the address to which to send the money, which is usually abroad.

MOBILE TELEPHONES

After a relatively slow start in introducing mobile telephones (*portable* or, increasingly, *mobile*), France is one of Europe's fastest-growing cellular markets. Mobile phones are now so widespread that some businesses (e.g. restaurants, cinemas, theatres, concert halls, etc.) ban them and some even use mobile phone jammers that can detect and disable every handset within 100m.

There are currently three mobile phone service providers: Bouygues, pronounced 'bweeg' (💻 www.bouyguestelecom.fr), France Télécom, operating under the Orange trademark (💻 www.orange.fr), and SFR (💻 www.sfr.fr). As in most other countries, the mobile phone market is a minefield: there are not only three networks to choose from but also a wide range of phones and a plethora of tariffs covering connection fees, monthly subscriptions, insurance and call charges. To further complicate matters, all three providers have business ties to one or more of the fixed telephone services (SFR with Cégétel, for example) and offer various deals combining mobile and fixed line services.

The major decision when buying a mobile phone is whether to take out a contract, whereby you pay a fixed monthly charge and obtain a certain amount of call time 'free', or to use a 'pay-as-you-go' scheme, where you pre-pay for your calls using a phone card. Note that, if you opt for pay-as-you-go, there's usually a time limit of one or two months on the use of each card; if

you don't make many calls, you may be wasting money on cards you don't use.

The most popular contracts usually give you a set number of hours of outgoing calls (e.g. two, three or five) for a flat monthly fee. Hours included in the fee may be limited to evenings and weekends or split between peak and off-peak calling times. Fees are usually reduced if you agree to a contract of 12 months or more, or order certain add-on features or services. You also accumulate 'points' which, in effect, give you a discount off a new phone. All mobile telephone bills must now include a complete list of calls made, including the duration and the time charged. New EU rules are designed eventually to make like-for-like comparisons of packages possible.

If you have a problem with a mobile phone service provider, you can call the Direction Générale de la Concurrence, de la Consommation et de la Répression des Fraudes (DGCCRF, ☎ 01 40 27 16 00 or 3939).

If you want to use a foreign mobile in France and avoid 'roaming' charges (though these are now limited throughout Europe – see **International Mobile Calls** below), it's usually possible to buy a SIM card, which will give you a French mobile number and allow you to make and receive calls in France. There are widely variable charges for connection to one of the French networks and you can choose between a monthly contract and a 'pay-as-you-go' card, which can be topped up (in values of €10, €20 and €35) as required. Note, however, that you must top it up at least once a year and frequently more often, or you'll lose your number and have to be reconnected. An alternative is to set up a SIM 'contract' in your home country, e.g. with 0044 (💻 www.0044.co.uk) in the UK.

There are now innumerable SIM card packages available in France, including those offered by supermarket chains such as Carrefour and Leclerc or electrical retailers such as Darty and Boulanger. Still more are available via the internet, whereby you buy a SIM card and top it up as required online, although again it's important to understand the contractual details of how often top-ups must be made. Often the time covered by a top-up will be lost if it isn't used quickly enough.

Text messaging (*envoyer des SMS/textos*) is as much an addiction in France as anywhere else, and the cost of texts sent and received within France is now limited by law.

All mobile phone numbers have the prefix 06, and calls to mobiles from a fixed phone in France are charged at higher rates than calls to another fixed line. Calls between mobile phones of the same company are generally discounted and most companies offer similar 'frequent caller' plans to those available for fixed phone services.

If you lose your phone, whether or not it's insured, you should phone your service provider immediately to report the loss and give the identification number of your phone (which, of course, you've written down somewhere you can find it quickly!). All new phones have an IMEI code, which appears beside the battery; if you can't find it, dial *#06# on your phone and it will be displayed. The contact numbers are: Bouygues ☎ 08 25 82 56 14 or +33 6 60 61 46 14 from abroad; Orange ☎ 08 00 10 07 40 or +33 6 07 62 64 64 from abroad; SFR ☎ 06 10 00 19 00 or +33 6 10 00 19 00 from abroad. You should also report the loss to the local police and, if the phone is insured, your insurer.

> ### ▲ Caution
>
> In recent years there has been widespread publicity regarding a possible health risk to users from the microwave radiation emitted by mobile phones. As yet it's unproven but the WHO took it seriously enough to issue a warning in 2011.

New mobile phones must now state the amount of energy absorbed by the user (known as the *débit d'absorption spécifique* or *DAS*). This is measured in watts per kilo (W/kg), and the maximum permitted *DAS* is 2W/kg for the head and body.

The French government has published a free leaflet, *Le Téléphone Mobile Santé et Sécurité*, containing guidelines for the 'safe' use of mobiles (including keeping them away from 'sensitive' body areas and not using them in poor reception areas, where they use maximum power), available from the Ministry of Health (🖥 www.sante.gouv.fr) and downloadable from their website. A mobile phone should be kept at least

15cm from a pacemaker, insulin pump or other electronic implant.

Further information about mobile phone use in France can be obtained from the Association Française des Opérateurs de Mobiles (AFOM, 🖥 www.afom.fr).

International Mobile Calls

New EU regulations, which came into force in July 2011, established the *Eurotarif*, setting ceilings for the costs of calls between one European country and another, popularly called 'roaming'. This was in response to revelations of outrageously high charges demanded by some operators and, according to the authorities, has had the effect of reducing charges by as much as 60 per cent. The maximum charge per minute is set at €0.35 for making a call and €0.11 for receiving one, plus VAT (at the local country's rate). Clients must be sent the costs of a call automatically.

In addition, in the case of very long calls, e.g. for prolonged access to the internet, downloading a film, etc., the *Eurotarif* sets a default limit of €50 (plus VAT), although customers can opt to change this should they wish. Details in English of all operators and their charges are shown by country at 🖥 http://ec.europa.en/information_society/activities/roaming/tariffs/in_ms/index/en.htm.

France Télécom tariffs for international calls are listed on its website and in mid-2011 were as shown in the table below.

Other telephone providers have different tariff structures for international calls. Most also offer a variety of discount plans, such as half-price on all calls to a designated ('favourite') country or to a number of overseas phone numbers (e.g. your mum's).

If you spend long periods abroad (e.g. at a second home), you may find it both cheaper and more convenient to run separate mobile phone arrangements in each country, provided you keep them up to date. Changing SIM cards is quick and easy to do.

PUBLIC TELEPHONES

Despite the increasing use of mobile telephones (see below), public telephone boxes (*cabine téléphonique*) can be found in all towns and villages, in post offices, bus and railway stations, airports, bars, cafés, restaurants and other businesses, and of course, in streets. Most telephone boxes are Perspex kiosks, and most public telephones (*téléphone publique*) accept telephone cards (*télécarte* – see below), *Cartes France Télécom* (see below) and bank debit cards, but many won't accept credit cards, particularly those without a microchip. Those accepting coins are now extremely rare, but may still be found at airports, main line railway stations and major bus stations (*gares routières*).

Public telephones are also available at some larger post offices, where you're allocated a booth and you pay for your calls at the counter afterwards. To make a call from a hotel room, you may be able to dial direct (after dialling 0 or 1, for example) or you may need to make calls via the hotel receptionist. Note, however, that hotels impose a surcharge (which can be 100 or 200 per cent!) on the cost of calls; cafés and restaurants also set their own charges. Most large hotels have public telephones in the foyer.

Public telephones are provided on high-speed trains (*TGV*) and allow both domestic and international calls. They can be operated with a *télécarte* or a *Carte France Télécom*. There are usually three telephones on each *TGV*, one in first class, one in second class and one in the bar. On some trains you'll see 'no telephone' signs, indicating that you aren't supposed to use your mobile phone.

Calls to emergency services can be made free from any telephone box, and all public telephones allow international direct dialling (IDD); international calls can also be made via the operator.

☑ SURVIVAL TIP

There are SOS (e.g. breakdown) telephones on motorways and at main junctions in Paris and other large cities (marked *Services Médicaux*), for use in the event of accidents or medical emergencies.

Telephone Cards

Télécarte

Telephone cards (*télécartes*) are available from post offices, railway stations, tobacconists, cafés, news kiosks, banks and various shops where the sign '*TELECARTE EN VENTE ICI*' is displayed.

Telephone cards are available in multiple values, e.g. €5 (for 50 units) and €15 (for 120 units). The values aren't necessarily directly comparable in either price or number of units from one supplier to another.

A new type of phone card is a scratch card, which gives you a code allowing you to make calls from a public or private telephone. France Télécom offers four such cards, called *Le Ticket de Téléphone*, allowing either national or international calls up to a fixed value. You scratch the back of the card to reveal the code, which must be dialled after the *Ticket* access code 3089 before you can dial the number you require.

Other telephone companies offer scratch cards (e.g. Kertel), which may provide better value than FT's cards. Many cards are on sale at supermarkets, newsagents, etc., as well as at La Poste, where they can also be 'recharged'.

Carte France Télécom

You can obtain a free telephone 'credit' card from FT, called a *Carte France Télécom (CFT)*, which can be used both in France and in over 40 other countries, calls being charged to your French telephone account. With a *CFT* you can make international calls to and from France but not from a foreign country to a country other than France.

Cards can be used with any public or private telephone; you simply dial an access code. You receive a detailed invoice for calls made with a *CFT* with your telephone bill every two months, or you can have your calls charged directly to a credit card.

Credit Cards

At major French airports, such as Charles de Gaulle (Paris), Lyon and Nice, as well as in most railway stations, there are public telephones that accept international credit cards, e.g. American Express, Diners Club, Eurocard, MasterCard and Visa. The cost of calls is automatically debited to your credit card account. Note that, although using credit cards is convenient, it can be very expensive. On some credit card phones there's a charge of 12 units (around €2) each time a card is used, although telephones have a button allowing you to make 'follow on' calls without paying this charge each time.

FAX

Now that most printers are equipped with scanners, the use of fax has declined considerably. For those who still want to use fax, modems, if not already installed in your computer, are cheap and easy to use. Although most of the outlets that once offered fax services, such as La Poste, no longer do so, individual shops, such as instant print shops, may still offer fax services. However, if you want to send a fax but not install a modem, there are a number of online facilities available, of which one,  www.fax-gratuit.net, as its name suggests, will send faxes free.

Beware of bogus fax bills (usually for hundreds of euros) purporting to be from FT. This is a Europe-wide scam and often includes 'the right to inclusion in an annual directory of fax owners'. The give-away is usually the address, which is often abroad!

INTERNET

There has recently been a proliferation of internet service providers (*fournisseur d'accès/FAI* or *serveur*), over 200 of which currently offer a variety of products at varying prices. Many offer packages that include telephone and TV services as well as internet access. France Télécom offers, under its Orange brand (formerly Wanadoo), a package that also includes email (see below) and on-line shopping. AOL Compuserve France (now linked with SFR) is the other major internet provider. Between them, Orange and AOL have some two-thirds of the market. Contact details for some of the major French internet service providers (ISPs) are shown below:

♦ **Alice France** (formerly Tiscali): www. aliceadsl.fr;

♦ **Budget Telecom:** www,budgettelecom. com;

♦ **Free:** www.free.fr;

♦ **Neuf Télécom (SFR):** www.adsl.sfr.fr;

♦ **Orange:** www.orange.fr;

♦ **Teleconnect:** www.teleconnect.fr;

♦ **UK Telecom:** www.uktelecom.uk.net.

For a comparison of ISP services and charges, consult one of the dedicated internet magazines (such as *Internet Pratique*) or visit the Budgetelecom website (www. budgetelecom.com), which provides information on current offers, customer evaluations and direct links to providers' websites.

There are many online shopping facilities, including railway and airline tickets, and you can even file tax forms and official documents online, as well as make tax payments. One advantage of French internet services is that junk mail is strictly controlled and therefore less of a nuisance than in many other countries. The leading French search engine (*moteur de recherche*) is called Voilà (www.voila.fr).

Internet 'cafés' (*webcafé*) are becoming increasingly popular in France, where over 1,000 communes have been awarded the appellation '*Villes Internet*' for providing public internet centres; the complete list of *villes internet* can be found at www.villes-internet.net.

Charges

France has a number of 'free' internet access services, where you pay only for your telephone connection time, not for access to the ISP. Alternatively, most service providers (including the free ones) offer various monthly plans which include all connection charges, usually at a rate that's lower than the standard telephone charges. As with telephone packages, there's a wide variety of charges for varying amounts of access (e.g. five or ten hours online), although most ISPs now offer packages including broadband internet connection and telephone (on a single line).

In Paris and other urban centres with cable television, it's possible to have a combined TV and broadband internet access package, while with the rapid spread of terrestrial digital TV (*television numérique terrestrial* or TNT), phone/internet/TV packages are increasingly offered. Recently a change in the law requires that VAT be paid on each element, rather than on the package as a whole, which has the effect of making these deals slightly more expensive.

Modems

Foreign modems usually work in France, although they may not receive faxes (Big Dish Satellite, 🖥 www.bigdishsat.com sells converters for this purpose).

Email

Email is variously called *email* (pronounced as in English and not to be confused with *émail*, meaning enamel), *mail*, *courier électronique*, *courriel* (short for *courier électronique*) and *mél* (the 'official' word and an abbreviation of *message électronique*). Useful email-related vocabulary includes @ (*arobase*), dot (*point*), hyphen (*tiret* or *trait d'union*) and slash (*slash*).

If you don't have access to the internet, La Poste offers the facility to send and receive emails via around 1,000 post offices as well as via its website (🖥 www.laposte.fr or www.laposte.net), where information about the service can be found. Messages can even be picked up via telephone (☎ 08 92 68 13 50). If you don't have a La Poste or Hotmail account, you can pick up your emails from another computer by going to 🖥 www.mailstart.com and entering your email address and password, although you're unable to download attachments. This service is free once a week; if you need to use it more often you can pay a small subscription (around €20 a year) for your own 'WebBox'. AOL users cannot use this service but they have an equivalent, called AOL Anytime, Anywhere.

If you want a French domain name or URL (i.e. one ending .fr), you must have a company registered in France and your site must be in French (other languages are optional). Domaine names can be registered via specialised agencies (e.g. 🖥 www.netim.com), whether for those with a .fr suffix or a less specific one such as .com or .org. The facility costs €11.90 plus VAT per annum.

> For a list of accredited domain name registrars (in France and other countries), go to 🖥 www.icann.org/registrars/accredited-list.html.

Internet Telephony

If you have a broadband internet connection, you can make long-distance and international phone 'calls' free (or almost free) to anyone with a broadband connection. 'Voice over internet protocol' (VOIP) is revolutionising the telecommunications market, although not, as once forecast, yet showing signs of making today's telephone technology (both land lines and mobile networks) obsolete.

A leading company in this field is Skype (🖥 www.skype.com), which is now owned by Microsoft, with over 50m users worldwide. Microsoft also has a popular system, MSN Messenger (🖥 http://get.live.com/messenger), and there are numerous other companies in the market – a web search for 'internet phone' will throw up dozens. All you need is access to a local broadband provider and a headset (costing as little as €15) or a special phone, and you're in business. Calls to other computers anywhere in the world are free, while calls to landlines are charged at a few centimes per minute.

Château d'Azay-le-Rideau, Loire Valley

8.
TELEVISION & RADIO

F rench television (TV) and radio broadcasting is partly state owned and partly private; two TV and five radio stations are under government control. Cable TV is available in the main cities and towns, although it's less common than in many other western European countries. Satellite TV was largely ignored by the French and was watched mainly by expatriates until the advent of digital satellite with its enhanced features and relatively easy installation and use. The leading service provider is CanalSat (with 30 per cent of the market and over 3m subscribers), followed by France Télécom SA (with its many internal divisions now known under the Orange brand), Suez, Canal+ and TF1. All broadcasting is overseen by the Conseil Supérieur de l'Audiovisuel (CSA).

TV and radio programmes are listed in daily newspapers, some of which (e.g. the Saturday edition of Le Figaro and the Sunday edition of Le Monde) provide free weekly programme guides with reviews and comments, and there's also a plethora of weekly TV magazines, including pocket (A5) size publications, e.g. Télé Poche and Télé Z, plus larger magazines. Guides are normally published two weeks in advance.

The annual World Radio TV Handbook (WRTH Publications, 🖳 www.wrth.com) contains over 600 pages of information and the frequencies of radio and TV stations worldwide.

TELEVISION

French TV is generally no worse than that in most other European countries, i.e. largely a succession of news, sport, talk and game shows, plus dubbed American films and sitcoms. Police detective series seem to be universally popular and those originally from the UK, America, Italy, Germany and other countries are regularly to be seen in dubbed form on French TV channels (French TV rarely shows foreign material in its original language), although there are occasional interesting documentaries and French series and films.

Standard

The standard for TV reception in France isn't the same as in most other countries, and TVs and DVDs (see below) operating on the PAL system or the North American NTSC system won't function properly (or at all) in France. Most European countries use a version of PAL, while France has its own standard called SECAM. If you want to import a TV it must be multi-standard, otherwise you should buy one in France. Most new television sets available in France contain automatic circuitry that can switch between SECAM and PAL. If you have a PAL TV, it's possible to buy a SECAM-to-PAL transcoder that converts SECAM signals to PAL. Note, that a SECAM-standard TV isn't required to receive most satellite broadcasts, which are different from terrestrial broadcasts.

TVs come in a wide range of screen sizes (measured diagonally). Among the most common are 48cm (19in) costing about €150; 55cm (21in) costing about €200; and 82cm (32in) costing about €350. All these would have built-in terrestrial digital TV (TNT, see below) flat LED screens and are HD-ready. Home cinema set-ups with screens as large as 150cm (59in) cost anywhere from around €1,400 to €3,000 or more, depending on the features.

Video & DVD Players

Videotapes are virtually obsolete in France, as elsewhere, replaced by DVDs, to the point that its is now difficult to find video cassette recorders (VCR) and players, although some units combine videotape players and DVD player-recorders.

DVDs will play properly on any TV and usually have the added advantage of offering a choice of languages; but be warned that many cheap French DVDs have no language options at all. Increasingly Blu-Ray DVDs are available alongside their conventional rivals, which are designed to provide better definition but only via high definition (HD) TVs. Most new TVs are HD-ready, although few channels yet transmit in HD, the number is slowly increasing and will ultimately become the standard. Blu-Ray DVDs aren't interchangeable with other DVDs. Although Blu-Ray players are usually also play conventional DVDs the reverse isn't true. The requirement to buy both a new TV and a new DVD player has made the expansion of Blu-Ray fairly slow. Films recorded on Blu-Ray discs, apart from the very newest releases, typically cost €15-25, compared with €10-20 for conventional DVDs.

In addition to conventional and Blu-Ray players and recorders, you can now buy equivalents that record directly on to a computer-style hard disk. The advantage of these is that they have the capacity to store literally hundreds of films; the disadvantage is that you cannot transfer their content, e.g. to play on another TV – you have physically to reinstall the whole unit. Such recorders cost between about €300 and €500, depending on the brand and its features.

When buying any TV equipment it pays to shop around. Hypermarkets and specialist chains such as Darty and Boulanger often have attractive special offers, notably for items that have been on display or used for demonstrations.

Terrestrial

France has six terrestrial stations broadcasting throughout the country (although reception is poor in some areas): France 2 and France 3 (both state-owned and operated by France Télévision), TF1, Canal Plus, M6 and Arte/France 5 (see below).

As in the UK, there's a progressive move to switch entirely to digital (numérique) television, the process scheduled to be completed by 2012. The change, rolled out regionally, is to a system called TNT (television numérique terrestrial). Depending on your location in relation to the transmitter, signals may be received by indoor or outdoor aerials or by satellite dishes. Given the geography of France, some locations are served only by satellite and householders there can claim government subsidies towards the cost of a dish and its installation.

However the signal is received, digital TV requires a decoder. For existing TVs, this means buying a set-top box, but all new TVs in France have inbuilt TNT decoders.

There's advertising (publicité or pub) on all French channels, although the government favours funding state-owned channels through increased license fees and has already reduced the number hours in which these channels can screen commercials. Main evening news programmes start at around 20.00 and last half an hour. These are usually followed by weather forecasts (prévision météorologique or simply météo), which often include a traffic forecast for the coming weekend, especially when a school holiday is approaching. The news and weather are usually followed by a film, serial or feature documentary on most channels. Note, however, that French TV channels aren't permitted to show films on Friday or Saturday nights, as this is deemed unfair competition for cinemas!

Films and some programmes are coded 10, 12, 16 or 18 in order to indicate their suitability (or unsuitability) for children of visible ages; the code is permanently displayed on the screen (except the 10 code, which is visible for only five minutes).

TF1

TF1 (Télévision Française 1, 🖥 www.tf1.fr) boasts 40 per cent of the viewing audience or double that of its nearest rival, France 2. Its programming is conservative, although it's usually of good quality, with the notable exception of mindless game shows and soaps. Its news reporting is generally weak, although popular.

France 2

France 2 (🖥 www.france2.fr) is more liberal and progressive in its programming. Programmes include event coverage and interviews. News coverage is fairly nondescript and similar to TF1's. France 2 runs several of the better American dramas (ER, for example, called Urgences) and during the week shows major films.

France 3

France 3 (🖥 www.france3.fr) shares much of its programming with France 2, augmented by regional news, documentaries and environmental programmes. The quality of programmes has improved in the last few years and they're generally more intellectual than those on TF1 and France 2.

Canal Plus

Canal Plus (or Canal+, 🖥 www.canalplus.fr) is Europe's largest pay channel (chaîne à péage) with the lion's share of the market. Apart from a few free-to-air (en clair) programmes, indicated in newspapers and programme guides by a + or * sign, the signal is scrambled.

To receive scrambled programmes you must obtain a decoder (décodeur), on which there's a returnable deposit (depôt de garantie) and pay a subscription. Canal Plus also carries advertisements. (See **Digital TV** on page 127).

Canal Plus specialises in films and sports programmes, particularly live soccer matches. It shows its share of second-rate films, although the selection has expanded to include many television premieres of hit films, both French and American.

Arte/France 5

Arte (pronounced 'artay', 🖥 www.artetv.com) and France 5 (also known as La Cinq, 🖥 www.france5.fr) broadcast on the same terrestrial frequency but on separate satellite and cable channels. Arte (from 19.00 until around 00.30 on terrestrial TV) broadcasts programmes in the languages of all the participating countries (Belgium, Switzerland, Spain, Poland, Austria, Finland and the Netherlands), although reception in France is usually dubbed or subtitled in French.

Arte provides a welcome cultural alternative to commercial broadcasting and its output consists largely of documentaries and cultural transmissions, foreign films in VO (version originale) with French subtitles, English comedy and no game shows. It's considered by many to be excessively highbrow and attracts only around 2 per cent of viewers.

France 5 broadcasts standard and educational programmes from 06.00 to 19.00.

France 24

This is France's answer to the BBC World Service and is mainly a 24-hour programme of news and current affairs, with discussions and interviews. It's available in several languages, including English. It has a high standard of news coverage, although obviously it will take time to earn the virtually universal trust that the BBC enjoys. In an excess of nationalistic pride, President Sarkozy declared soon after being elected that France 24 should broadcast only in French; apparently wiser arguments prevailed and the channel remains France's main medium for explaining what goes on from a French point of view.

M6

M6 (🖳 www.m6.fr) broadcasts mostly general entertainment programmes. It screens many American programmes and other mainstream shows plus soft-porn movies. It often has surprisingly good programmes considering its low profile and budget. Note that M6 is difficult to receive in some remote areas.

Foreign Stations

If you live close to a French border, you may also be able to receive foreign stations. In the Nord-Pas-de-Calais region it's possible to receive British and Belgian stations; those in northern Lorraine can receive Luxembourg TV; in Alsace many people watch German and Swiss TV; those near the Spanish and Italian borders can usually receive programmes broadcast in those countries; and in certain parts of the Côte d'Azur you can receive Télé Monte Carlo (which is also now available on most French cable and satellite networks).

Cable

With the rapid spread of satellite TV (and, notably, TNT) competition has virtually ceased in this area in France: a succession of mergers and acquisitions ended with the near-monopoly of Numericable (🖳 www.numericable.fr), whose market share has been said to be over 90 per cent. Their fibre-optic cable networks cover over 160 towns in France, where they offer up to 150 TV channels of which 15 are HD &/or 3D. They offer subscription packages including both fixed-line and mobile telephones and internet access from around €25 per month.

France has several channels, e.g. Canal Plus and Pink TV (see **Satellite** below), which are available by cable as well as satellite, and several available only to cable TV subscribers. Programme listings for cable services are included in French TV guides.

In some apartment blocks with cable service, you may not be able to receive all the programmes available to independent householders.

Satellite

France is well served by satellite TV (télévision par satellite). The primary source of English-language programmes is Sky Television (see below), but even if you don't wish to subscribe to Sky, you'll have access to around 100 English-language channels, including all the BBC channels (see **BBC** below) and ITV channels 1 to 4 on free-to-view (FTV, also called free-to-air/fta). To receive these channels, you must currently subscribe to Sky (their minimum package includes all three channels) or buy an FTV card.

The English language media in France (see **Appendix B**) is full of ads for satellite TV installation and equipment purchase, include decoders for both Sky and FTV.

Sky Television

In order to receive Sky television you need a Sky digital receiver (digibox) and a dish. There are two ways to obtain the equipment and the necessary Sky 'smart' card. You can subscribe in the UK or Ireland (personally, if you have an address there, or via a friend) and then take the Sky receiver and card to France, although for the first year of your contract the digibox must usually be connected to a telephone line; if you export it during this period and connect it to a foreign telephone line, Sky may terminate your contract. To receive Sky TV in France, a may need a 1.2m satellite dish, depending on your location.

Alternatively, you can buy a digibox and obtain a Sky card in France, although Sky receivers and cards are much more expensive there, but competition has reduced costs

in recent years (shop around). A number of companies advertise in the expatriate press or you can find them on the internet, e.g. 🖥 www. skydigi.tv/index.php and www.skyinfrance.co.uk.

You must subscribe to Sky to receive most English-language channels. If you subscribe to the basic package you'll have access to around 100 channels, including all the BBC's channels and ITV channels 1-4. Further information about Sky installation (in the UK) and programme packages can be found on Sky's website (🖥 www.sky.com).

⚠ **Caution**

There are strict laws regarding the positioning of antennas in urban areas, although in rural areas rules are more relaxed.

Digital TV

In March 2005, France became the last major European country to launch a digital terrestrial TV (DTT) service (known as *télévision numérique terrestre/TNT* and branded as '*télévision numérique pour tous*').

The joint venture between France Télévision and a group of cable and satellite operators made 14 free-to-air channels available (in MPEG-2 format), some of which are now also available in HD. Availability of TNT has been rolling out regionally and is expected to be completed by 2012, by which time analogue services will cease. Subsequently, the range of TNT may be extended: it was originally planned to include pay-TV channels but that has yet to happen. Set-top boxes are available for around €110, although it's possible to receive some (French) digital channels via an ordinary TV aerial.

Canal Plus (🖥 www,canalplus.fr, see above) is a subscription-only satellite TV service, originally analogue but now almost totally digital. Its main channel, largely showing films (including occasionally some with original soundtracks – *version originale* or *VO* – and French subtitles) is available free on TNT. Subscribers can opt for one of three packages (at €30-45 per month), with four-10 channels included and other paid options, such as sports channels, new films, and internet access or cable (where available).

BBC

The BBC no longer encrypts (scrambles) its mainstream channels from the Astra satellite that it shares with Sky, which means that you don't need a Sky Digibox to receive the BBC channels, including BBC interactive services; any digital satellite receiver will work.

The BBC's commercial subsidiary, BBC World Television broadcasts two 24-hour channels: BBC World (24-hour news and information) and BBC Entertainment (re-runs of UK general entertainment series and dramas). BBC World is free-to view, while BBC Entertainment is available via subscription TV packages, which usually also include BBC World. For more information and a programme guide contact BBC World Television (☎ 020-8433 2221). A programme guide is also listed on the internet (🖥 www.bbc.co.uk/tv).

Programme Guides

Many satellite stations provide teletext information, which includes programme schedules. The main French-language channels are included in most television listings in newspapers and magazines, but these may cover only 'prime time', i.e. the evening. Satellite programme listings are included in a number of British publications such as *What Satellite and Digital TV* (🖥 http://wotsat.techradar.com/inside-wotsat), available on subscription and from some international news kiosks.

If you don't have time to sift through all the available satellite channel listings to find programmes you're interested in, the Euro TV website (🖥 www.eurotv.com) can do it for you.

TV Licence

A TV licence (*redevance sur les postes de télévision*) is required by TV owners, costing €123 a year in 2011. The licence fee covers any number of TVs (owned or rented), irrespective of where they're located in France, e.g. in holiday homes, motor vehicles or boats, although you must pay for a separate licence for TVs in rented accommodation, e.g. *gîtes*. Even if you only have a foreign TV which you use solely for watching videos, you must have a valid licence.

If you import a TV capable of receiving French programmes, you must report the fact within 30 days of import to your local Centre Régional de la Redevance Audiovisuelle (listed under *Les infos administratives/Impôts et taxes* in the *Yellow Pages* – or you can obtain the address from your local post office).

The licence fee is now levied in conjunction with the *taxe d'habitation* and is therefore payable in December each year, although it's possible to pay in monthly instalments. If you're aged over 65 (on 1st January of the relevant year), paid no income tax in the previous year and live alone (or with other people in the same situation), you're exempt (*exonéré*) from paying for a licence. To obtain exoneration or to declare that you have no TV, apply to your regional Centre de la Redevance.

If you buy a TV in France, the retailer must inform the relevant authority and the TV licence fee will be added to your next residential tax bill. You'll be fined if you're discovered to have a TV without a licence when an inspector calls. If you don't pay the annual fee on time, you must visit the local *commisariat* to explain why and pay a fine (*agrandissement*) of 30 per cent for late payment.

If you dispose of your TV and don't replace it, you must notify the authorities, or you remain liable to pay the licence fee. (You may be asked whether you sold your TV so that the new owner can be sent a bill!)

DVDs

Recent films on DVD are expensive (over €25 for conventional ones and over €40 for Blu-Ray) although prices tend to fall rapidly with age and there are many special offers by supermarkets and other retailers. Most DVDs can usually be watched in English, although cheap ones may have no language options, so check the box before buying or renting.

☑ SURVIVAL TIP

DVDs may be encoded with a region code, restricting the area of the world in which they can be played. The code for Western Europe is 2, while discs without any region coding are called all-region or region 0 discs. However, you can buy all-region DVD players and DVD players can be modified to be region-free, allowing the playback of all discs (see 🖥 www.regionfreedvd.net and www.moneysavingexpert.com/shopping/dvd-unlock).

Films on DVD can be rented for around €3.50 per day. There are also automated 'kiosks' from which DVDs can be rented at the touch of a few buttons for as little as €1.70 (for six hours). You must pay a small membership fee (e.g. €2) to qualify for the lowest rate. Most hypermarkets carry a large selection of DVDs.

RADIO

Radio was deregulated in France in the '80s, since when scores of local commercial radio stations have sprung up, representing diverse ethnic groups, lifestyles and communities. Some English-language broadcasters have established radio channels in areas of high anglophone penetration. Local stations often have small catchment areas and low transmitting power, although many have been grouped into national networks. The largest is operated by NRJ, a popular Paris music station.

A radio licence isn't required in France.

French Radio

French radio is dominated by the five stations run by state-owned Radio France, although there are numerous independent stations.

Radio France

All five stations are available throughout France, although the frequencies vary from region to region. Information on all Radio France channels, including programme schedules, is available at 🖥 www.radiofrance.fr.

♦ **France-Bleu:** Mixes light music and 'easy listening rock' with regional features and interviews.

♦ **France-Culture:** Talks, debates and interviews on the arts and literature, much of it highbrow (some would say pretentious).

♦ **France-Info:** An all-news channel, with detailed news broadcasts every half an hour, followed by interviews and discussions of major issues. News stories and some features are repeated several times throughout the day.

♦ **France-Inter:** The main channel, broadcasting news bulletins, current affairs, magazine programmes, discussions, light music and plays. During the summer it broadcasts news bulletins in English (at 09.00 and 16.00).

♦ **France-Musiques:** Broadcasts mostly classical music, but also some jazz and 'world' music as well as cultural discussion programmes.

English-language Radio

Apart from English-language songs, there's little radio in English, although in a few areas there are English-language stations run by expatriates, e.g. Riviera Radio on 106.5FM in the south of France, Sud Radio on 96.1FM in the southwest, Lot radio on 88–89FM and occasional programmes on Radio Périgueux 103 on 102.3FM and Radio Plaisance on 95.9FM.

France's answer to the BBC World Service, Radio France Internationale (RFI), broadcasts in some 19 languages, including English (for five and a half hours per day – see 💻 www.rfi.fr/langues/statiques/rfi_anglais.asp) on short wave 11615KHz and 15605KHz.

The motorway system has its own radio network, and the Autoroute Info stations play popular music and carry frequent traffic and accident reports, often in English, German and Spanish during the summer holiday period. The frequency is indicated on signs along the motorway; 107.7 is often used.

If you're interested in receiving radio stations from further afield, you should obtain a copy of the *World Radio TV Handbook* (WRTH Publications, 💻 www.wrth.com).

If you have an internet connection and the appropriate software (e.g. Real Player, a free download from 💻 http://france, www.real.com, or Windows Media Player, a standard feature of Windows), you can listen to hundreds of radio stations via your computer ('internet radio'). What's more, you have a choice of live or recorded programmes, including classics that are no longer

broadcast. The BBC (see below) is one of many organisations offering this service, some of which broadcast only via the internet; search the web for 'internet radio' to find the main stations.

BBC

The BBC World Service is no longer available by radio in France, but only via satellite, i.e. as part of Sky or FTV satellite TV services. Exceptionally, it may still be received on the London medium wave frequency (648MW) in the northernmost parts of France.

You can also receive BBC national radio stations (on long wave) in most northern and western areas of France (the Nord-Pas-de-Calais, Normandy, Brittany, Pays-de-la-Loire, Île-de-France and Centre regions) and parts of Champagne-Ardenne, northern Burgundy. All BBC radio stations, including the World Service, are available via the Astra satellites.

BBC radio stations can be received via your PC using a Radio Player (which can be downloaded free from 💻 www.bbc.co.uk/radio) and, if you're really desperate, you can listen to recordings of BBC radio programmes via your computer at 💻 www.bbc.co.uk/worldservice/schedules/frequencies/eurwfreq.shtml.

Cable, Digital & Satellite Radio

If you have satellite TV, you can also receive many radio stations. For example, BBC Radio 1, 2, 3, 4 and 5, BBC World Service, Sky Radio, Virgin 1215 and many foreign-language stations are broadcast via the Astra satellites.

Digital satellite TV subscribers also have a choice of many French and international radio stations. Details are usually available in the monthly satellite subscriber newsletter.

9.

EDUCATION

France spends more per capita on education than most other developed countries (e.g. 20 per cent more than the UK) and has traditionally been noted for its high academic standards, although in the latest (2003) PISA survey by the Organisation for Economic Co-operation and Development (OECD), which compared the educational attainment of 15-year-olds in over 40 countries, France ranked was barely above the OECD average and behind Finland, Korea, the Netherlands, Japan, Canada, Switzerland, Australia and New Zealand (but above Sweden, Austria, Germany, Ireland, Spain and the US; the UK wasn't included in the survey).

The state-funded school system is supplemented by a comprehensive network of private schools, including many distinguished international schools. Around 15 per cent of French children attend private schools, most of which are co-educational day schools (education is almost exclusively co-educational and there are few boarding schools), but a private education has little snob value – and is considerably cheaper than in the UK, for example. Higher education standards are only average, however, with the notable exception of the elite *grandes écoles*, which are rated among the world's best educational establishments.

The French are proud of their schools and resent government interference, although there are almost continual 'reforms' of the education system. They have a respect, even a love, of learning and reforms are argued at great length and with surprising passion. Critics of the French education system complain that its teaching methods are too traditional and unimaginative, with most learning by rote. Classrooms are arranged in traditional style, with desks in serried ranks, and children spend much of their time copying information. It's also accused of being inflexible and training only the mind, rather than encouraging self-expression and personal development.

French schools place great emphasis on the French language (particularly grammar), arithmetic and the sciences.

Schools usually impose more discipline than most foreign children are used to (teachers may use any disciplinary method other than corporal punishment), as well as more homework (*devoirs du soir*), which increases with the age of the child (there isn't any at elementary level) and can become onerous, particularly for children used to the British education system.

French teachers generally have high expectations of pupils and the system is hard on slow learners and the not so bright. However, most state schools have 'special' education sections (*sections d'education spéciale/SES*) for children with learning difficulties due to psychological, emotional or behavioural problems and for slow learners, although these are beginning to disappear as education budgets are cut.

France has a highly competitive and selective examination system that separates the brighter students from the less academically gifted at around the age of 14. From primary school level, children are subjected to constant testing (at least twice a week in each subject). However, despite the generally high standards, there have been reports of an increasing number of children entering secondary education unable to read or write adequately.

Education in France is compulsory between the ages of 6 and 16, and state schools are entirely free, from nursery school through to university (free state schools have existed in France for over a century), but you have the right to educate your children at home (see **Home Education** on page 135).

Some 80 per cent of children continue their schooling beyond the age of 16 and there are around 2m students in *lycées*, private institutions, *grandes écoles* and universities. Free education is also provided for the children of foreign residents, although non-resident, non-EU students require a student visa (see **Chapter 3**).

> It was Napoleon who decided that children should study the same subjects, at the same level, at the same time in a particular region. Some 200 years later the system is largely unchanged and the syllabus and textbooks are broadly the same in all schools of the same level throughout France.

The standard curriculum means that children moving between schools can continue their education with the minimum disruption. Regions (or, rather, *académies* – see below) do, however, have a certain amount of autonomy in setting school timetables, and school holidays vary from region to region (see page 138).

Although the state provides a large proportion of the funding for the French education system, in recent years some of the responsibility has been transferred to regions (for *lycées*) and departments (for *collèges*).

Average class sizes have fallen overall in the last few decades, although they're still thought by some to be too large and the number of teachers is gradually being reduced, and it isn't unusual to find classes of 50 or more pupils. The average number of children per class is currently around 25.5 (nursery school), 22 (primary school), 24 (*collège*) and 27.5 (*lycée*).

Parent-teacher associations are common (if you wish to join, elections are usually held in October), and parent-teacher meetings, where parents can discuss a child's progress with teachers, are held regularly (there's usually one soon after the start of the first term). If you have a problem, you should contact your local education mediator.

Truancy is a rare offence in France, where a child can be expelled for forging a parent's signature in order to skip classes; parents of children who regularly play truant can be fined up to €2,000. Note, however, that in some areas (e.g. some Parisian suburbs), state schools are plagued by violence, vandalism and drug abuse – to such an extent that the French Education Minister recently proposed a police presence in 'problem' schools. There has also been an increase in bullying and racketeering among pupils, and a dedicated helpline called *Jeunes Violence Ecoute*, operated by the Fédération des Écoles, des Parents et des Educateurs (see **Information** below), is available to pupils and others who fear contacting the authorities or parents directly (☎ 08 00 20 22 23). There's also another helpline, *SOS Violences Scolaires* (☎ 08 10 55 55 00).

In an attempt to improve school discipline, all pupils and their parents must now sign a 'school life contract' (*contrat de vie scolaire*), confirming their willingness to cooperate with teachers and their commitment to education.

In recent years, there has been disquiet, particularly among *lycée* students, over class overcrowding and a shortage of teachers. Another increasing problem in state schools, particularly *collèges*, is teacher absenteeism and strikes (notably over the government's reforms of the pension system, so that teachers and other public sector workers must work longer for reduced pensions); it has been suggested that these are accelerating the drift towards the private sector.

INSURANCE

It's advisable that schoolchildren in France are covered by liability insurance for damage and injury to themselves and third parties while at school or travelling to and from school; insurance isn't obligatory except for school trips such as skiing holidays, but it's highly recommended.

Cover may be provided by your existing insurance policies (e.g. household), but it's likely to be the bare minimum. Basic school insurance (*assurance scolaire de base*), covering a child for all school-related activity, costs as little as €10 per year, but for a few euros more (between around €12 and €25 per year), you can cover your child for all eventualities, whether school-related or not; this is known as a *contrat scolaire et extrascolaire*.

Policies are often provided by parents' associations as well as by traditional insurance companies. Costs vary depending on the type of cover, the level of compensation in the event of an accident or injury, and the size of the excess (deductible) on a claim, which with cheaper policies may be €20 or €30. You can obtain a reduction if you 'remove' risks already covered by other insurance policies.

Some schools provide an insurance proposal form at the beginning of each school year, but you aren't obliged to take out this particular policy. When comparing insurance policies, check the cover provided, e.g. is your child covered outside term time?

Whatever cover you choose, the insurer should provide an *attestation d'assurance scolaire*, which you present to the school authorities.

ADAPTING TO THE SYSTEM

Generally, the younger your child is when he enters the system, the easier he'll cope; conversely the older he is, the more problems he'll have adjusting. Foreign teenagers often have considerable problems learning French and adjusting to French school life. In some schools, foreign children who cannot understand the language may be neglected and just expected to 'get on with it'. In your early days, it's therefore important to check exactly what your children are doing at school and whether they're making progress (not just with the language, but also with their other lessons). However, the authorities are coming to appreciate that the national policy of

immigrant integration requires that foreigners learn French and greater efforts are now being made, i.e. extra classes are available and an increasing number of regions offer free French lessons for the parents of foreign schoolchildren.

As a parent, you should be prepared to support your children through this difficult period. If you aren't fluent in French, you'll already be aware how frustrating it is being unable to express yourself adequately, which can easily lead to feelings of inferiority and inadequacy. It's also important for parents to ensure that their children maintain their native language, as it can easily be neglected (surveys show that the children of English-speaking residents are losing their ability to read and write English). See also **Language** below.

For many children, the experience of schooling and living in a foreign land is a stimulating challenge, providing invaluable cultural and educational experiences. Your child will become bilingual and a 'world' citizen, less likely to be prejudiced against foreigners and foreign ideas. This is particularly true if he attends an international school with pupils from different countries, although many state schools also have pupils from a number of countries and backgrounds. However, before making major decisions about your child's future education, it's important to consider his ability, character and needs. It's possible for children aged over 15 to experience the French school system before moving to France by participating in an international exchange programme such as that run by AFS International Youth Development (☎ 0113-242 6136, 💻 www.afsuk.org).

Parents with young children who are planning to move to France may be interested in En Famille France, an exchange organisation founded in the late '70s by Frenchman Jacques Pinault. It specialises in six-month exchange visits for children aged 9 to 13 between European countries and France. Children stay with a French family and attend a French school. One of the most important aspects of the scheme, however, is that children must be enthusiastic about the exchange. It can take up to a year to match two families, therefore you should make enquiries as early as possible. For further information contact En Famille International (☎ 05 57 43 52 48, 💻 www.enfamille.com – in English).

LANGUAGE

For most children, particularly those aged under ten, studying in French isn't such a handicap as it may first appear. The majority of children adapt quickly and most become reasonably fluent within three to six months (if only it were so easy for adults!). However, not all children adapt equally well to a change of language and culture, particularly those aged over ten (at around ten children begin to learn languages more slowly), many of whom encounter difficulties during their first year. On the other hand, foreign children often acquire a sort of celebrity status, particularly in rural schools, which helps their integration.

Indeed, totally non-French speaking children may initially be put in the class below their age group or made to repeat a year until their language skills have reached an adequate level. This can make the first few months quite an ordeal for non French-speaking children. However, some state schools provide free intensive French lessons (*classes d'initiation/CLIN* or *Français Langue Etrangère/FLE*) for foreign children and some have international sections for foreign pupils. It may be worthwhile inquiring about the availability of extra French classes before choosing where to live. Note, however, that while attending a *CLIN*, children may fall behind in other subjects.

Those who have particular difficulties with the language can take advantage of an *orthophoniste*, a specialist who deals with all sorts of speech and pronunciation problems. Foreign children are tested (like French children) and put into a class suitable to their level of French, even if this means being taught with younger children or slow learners. However, a child of six or seven must be permitted to enter the first year of primary school (*cours préparatoire/CP*), even if he speaks no French. An older child can be refused entry to the *CP* or another class and can be obliged to attend a *CLIN* against his parents' wishes. Once your child has acquired a sufficient knowledge of spoken and written French, he's integrated into a regular class in a local school.

The only schools in France using English as the teaching language are a few foreign and international private schools (see page 148), although a number of multilingual French schools teach students in both English and French. If your children attend any other school, they must study all subjects in French (except a few schools where a local language, e.g. Breton, is also used). If your local state school doesn't provide extra French classes,

your only choice will be to pay for private lessons or send your child to another (possibly private) school, where extra tuition is provided.

Some parents send a child to an English-speaking school for a year and then move them to a bilingual or French school, while others find it better to throw their children in at the deep end. Your choice should depend on the character, ability and wishes of your child. Whatever you decide, it will help if your child has some intensive French lessons before arriving. It may also be possible to organise an educational or cultural exchange with a French school or family before moving, which is a considerable help in integrating a child into the language and culture (see above).

Many state schools teach regional languages, including Alsatian, Basque, Breton, Catalan, Corsican, Provençal and Occitan. Where applicable, these are usually optional and are taught for around three hours a week, generally outside normal school hours. One exception is Breton, which is used exclusively in the early classes in certain schools in Brittany; another is Provence, where a small number of primary schools teach French and Provençal bilingually. See also **Language** opposite and **Learning French** on page 154.

You should also bear in mind that young children attending a French school can quickly lose their command of their native language, which may need reinforcing at home (e.g. through reading and writing, games, films and computer-based activities), and, if possible, regular trips to your home country or membership of a foreign-language club or association. Bilingualism is a complex subject; a detailed analysis of the issues involved and ways of dealing with them is contained in *A Parents' and Teachers' Guide to Bilingualism* by Colin Baker (Multilingual Matters).

HOME EDUCATION

Some 10,000 children are estimated to be educated at home in France, including the children of many expatriates. Those taught at home must reach a level of education similar to that attained by schoolchildren, including a reasonable level of maths, history, geography, science, spoken and written French and a foreign language, as well as having lessons in art, culture and sport.

> ☑ **SURVIVAL TIP**
>
> Home educators must inform the local town hall and education authorities at least a week before the start of each academic year and are subject to inspections a minimum of once a year.

A number of publications provide further information about home education, including *Apprendre Autrement* (for a copy, send a SAE to Marcel Mahl, 20 avenue de la Gare, 31230 L'Isle-en-Dodon) and *Oneto-One: A Practical Guide to Learning at Home, Age 0–11* (order at ⌨ www.nezertbooks.net). Other relevant websites include ⌨ http://ecolesdifferentes. free.fr, www.education-otherwise.org, www. freedom-in-education.co.uk and www. lesenfantsdabord.org.

INFORMATION

Information about French schools, both state and private, can be obtained from French embassies and consulates abroad, and from foreign embassies, educational organisations and government departments in France. The Fédération des Écoles, des Parents et des Educateurs (☎ 01 47 53 62 70, ⌨ www. ecoledesparents.org) provides free advice for parents on all aspects of education and careers, as does the Office National d'Information sur les Enseignements et les Professions (ONISEP, ⌨ www.onisep.fr), which has regional offices and publishes regional guides to education and careers.

The Association of American Wives of Europeans (☎ 01 40 70 11 80, ⌨ www. aaweparis.org), which is a member of the Federation of American Women's Clubs Overseas (FAWCO), publishes the *AAWE Guide to Education*, which claims to be the definitive guide to educating English-speaking children in France, with information on over 120 English language and bilingual school programmes throughout the country.

Useful websites include the Ministry of Education's site (🖳 www.education.gouv.fr), Eurydice (🖳 www.eurydice.org), containing information in English about the French education system, and the Service Public site (🖳 www.service-public.fr), which has sections on education (*enseignement*) and training (*formation*). The French Ministry of Education provides a nationwide free information service through Centre d'Information et d'Orientation (CIO) offices. For the address of your local CIO office, contact your town hall (*mairie*), which can also provide local information.

STATE SCHOOLS

Although French state-funded schools are called 'public schools' (*école publique*), the term 'state' has been used in preference to public in this book in order to prevent confusion, as a 'public school' in the UK is a private, fee-paying school. The state school system in France differs considerably from the school systems in, for example, the UK or the US, particularly regarding secondary education.

The Ministry of National Education, Youth and Sport is responsible for most of France's state education system, which divides the country into 28 'academies' (*académies*), confusingly not corresponding to the 22 regions, each of which is a group of several *départements* headed by a superintendent (*recteur*) and attached to at least one university. The *académies* set the curriculum and examinations (all schools in the same *académie* have the same exam questions), but a high degree of consultation ensures that standards vary little from *académie* to *académie*.

Children usually go to local nursery and primary schools, but attending secondary school often entails travelling long distances. One of the consequences of the depopulation of rural areas in recent years has been the closure of many schools, resulting in children having to travel further to school, although in most areas there's an efficient school bus service.

A general criticism of French state schools often made by foreigners is the lack of extra-curricular activities such as sport, music, drama, and arts and crafts. According to a recent Ministry of Education report, 60 per cent of pupils have no access to gymnasia or sports grounds and 20 per cent no access to a swimming pool, and 25 per cent of schools have inadequate sports facilities. State schools have no school clubs or sports teams and, if a child wants to do team sports, he must join a local club, costing around €150 to €200 per year. This also means that parents need to ferry children back and forth for games and social events (Americans will be used to this!).

However, although not part of the curriculum, a variety of sports activities are organised through local sports associations (e.g. Écoles Municipales de Sport), which may also organise non-sporting activities such as dance and music. Fees are low (e.g. €75 to €150 per year) and activities usually take place directly after school. Some organisations sell secondhand sports equipment. French state schools make limited use of computers; homework is always handwritten (usually, and for some obscure reason, on squared paper).

On the plus side, children are taught calligraphy (French handwriting may be quite different from the style you're used to), grammar (every French child knows the difference between a direct object and an indirect object!), philosophy and ethics, environmental studies and civics. And, in place of extra-curricular activities are 'discovery classes' at primary school level (see page 142) and – a uniquely French idea – an annual 'taste week' in October, during which schoolchildren are initiated into the finer points of *le bon goût*!

Note that class numbering in French state schools differs considerably from the US and British systems. The French system is almost the exact reverse of the US system. Instead of rising from 1 to 12, the French start in the 11th form (grade) at the age of six and end in the first form, followed by the *classe terminale*, the last year of a secondary high school (*lycée*) at age 18 or 19. If pupils fall behind at secondary school, they're often required to repeat a year (*redoubler*), although this is seldom the case in nursery and primary schools thanks to the introduction of a more flexible system of cycles.

Having made the decision to send your child to a state school, you should stick to it for at least a year to give it a fair trial. It may take a child this long to fully adapt to a new language, a change of environment and a different curriculum. If you need to change your child's school, you must obtain a *certificat de radiation* from his current school.

Enrolment

Children must attend a state school within a certain distance of their home, so if you have a preference for a particular school it's important to buy or rent a home within that school's catchment area (which may change periodically in accordance with demographic changes). You may make a request *dérogation*) for your child to attend a different school from the one assigned by your town hall, but you must usually have good reasons for such a request, e.g. another of your children already attends your preferred school, the preferred school is close to your place of work, or it teaches a unique course that you wish your child to follow, such as certain foreign languages. The transfer must be approved by the *directeurs* of both schools. Note, however, that free transport (i.e. a school bus service) may not be available for schools other than those in your allotted area.

Information about schools in a particular area can be obtained from the schools information service (*service des écoles*) at your local town hall.

To enrol your child in a French school you must compile an 'enrolment file' (*dossier d'inscription*) at your town hall (for primary schools) or at the *rectorat* school service (for secondary schools) and must provide the following documents:

◆ Your child's birth certificate or passport, with an official French translation (if necessary). If your child was born in France, you must produce your family record book (*livret de famille*) or birth certificate (*extrait de l'acte de naissance*).

◆ Proof of immunisation. In France, vaccinations are recorded in a child's health book (*carnet de santé*), which is issued to parents when a child is born. When you arrive in France, you're issued with a *carnet de santé* by your *mairie* for all school-age children. For more information, see **Children's Health** on page 228.

◆ Proof of residence in the form of an electricity or telephone bill in your name. If you don't have any bills, a rent receipt, lease or proof of property ownership (*attestation d'acquisition*) is acceptable.

◆ If your child is coming from another French school, a *certificat de radiation* issued by his previous school.

◆ Evidence of insurance.

You'll then be given a registration form to take to the school.

School Hours

State schools have now abandoned the four-day week (*semaine de quatre jours*) with Wednesday remaining free (a tradition dating back to the separation of church and state some 100 years ago, when parents were expected to arrange religious instruction for their children on Wednesdays) and Saturday lessons. A standard five-day, Monday to Friday, week is now the norm , however, there's currently a debate about limiting the length of school days by reducing the traditional two-month summer holiday. Contact your local education department or town hall to find out the position regarding school hours in your area.

School hours also vary depending on the type of school. Nursery school hours are from 08.30 or 09.00 to 11.30 or 12.00 and from 13.30 or 14.00 to around 16.30. There's a 15-minute break in the mornings and afternoons. Primary school consists of 26 hours per week, usually from 08.30 to 11.30 and 13.30 to 16.30. Secondary schools have the longest hours. In a *collège*, students attend school for 27 or 28 hours per week and in a *lycée* for around 30 to 36 hours (depending on the type of *lycée*). The school hours for a *lycée* are usually from 08.00 to 12.00 and 14.00 to 17.00, although some start at 09.00 and finish at 18.00. At both *collège* and *lycée*, children aren't obliged to remain in school if they have no lessons.

Most schools have a (free) bus, which collects children from outlying regions and returns them home at the end of the day. Due to the roundabout journey, this often adds considerably to the school day, although children often enjoy the journey and it's a good way for them to make friends. Many parents prefer to take children to and from school or take them to school and allow them to get the bus home. State schools and communities usually provide an after-school nursery (*garderie*) for working mothers.

Holidays

French children have the longest school holidays (*vacances scolaires*) in the world, with 117 days (excluding weekends in term time and some public holidays). They generally attend school for 160 days a year only, from early September until late June, although they compensate with long school hours and abundant homework (from primary school onwards). Winter and spring school holidays vary from town to town according to a system of zones (see table) in order to allow ski resorts to cope with the flood of children during these periods. Term dates may be modified to take account of local circumstances. Schools are also closed on public holidays (see page 50) when they fall within term time.

The year is made up of five terms, each averaging around seven weeks. Current and future term and holiday dates can be found on the Ministry of Education's website (💻 www.education.gouv.fr – click on '*Le calendrier scolaire*'). School holiday dates are published by schools and local communities well in advance, thus allowing parents plenty of time to schedule family holidays.

Usually you aren't permitted to withdraw your children from classes during the school term except for visits to a doctor or dentist, when the teacher should be informed in advance. In primary school a note to the teacher is sufficient, while in secondary school an official absence form must be completed by the teacher concerned and submitted to the school office. For absences of over two days, a doctor's certificate is required. If your child requires emergency medical care while at school, you'll be asked to sign an authorisation, as you will for school trips.

School Holiday Zones

Zone	Regions
A	Auvergne, Brittany, Languedoc-Roussillon, Lorraine, Lower Normandy, Midi-Pyrenees, Pays de la Loire and Rhone-Alpes.
B	Alsace, Burgundy, Centre, Champagne-Ardenne, Franche-Comté, Limousin, Nord-Pas-de-Calais, Picardy, Poitou-Charentes, Provence Cote d'Azur and Upper Normandy.
C	Aquitaine and Paris Ile-de-France.

The government issues instructions regarding student employment during the last term of the academic year. The rules apply to tertiary level students and students in secondary and technical schools aged 16 or older, although those in secondary education aged 14 or 15 are eligible for a permit for part-time summer employment, provided it's only light work and for not more than half the summer holiday period.

Provisions

Education is free in France, but pens, stationery and sports clothes/equipment must be purchased by parents. Most other provisions are provided in primary schools (ages 6 to 11) and in *collèges* (ages 12 to 15), although parents may need to buy some books, but everything must be purchased by parents for children attending a *lycée*. A number of passport-size photographs are required by secondary school students.

The average parent can expect to pay around €400 per year per *lycée* student (more for technical subjects), although low-income families may qualify for a 'back to school allowance' (*allocation de rentrée scolaire*) of around €250 for each child aged between 6 and 15. All grants must be applied for by the end of March for the following school year. It's also possible to buy secondhand books at the start of the term, when schools hold secondhand book sales (*bourse aux livres*).

Primary school children require the following articles:

♦ a school bag or satchel;

♦ a pencil case, pencils and crayons, stationery, etc.;

♦ gym shoes, shorts and a towel for games and exercise periods;

♦ a sports bag for the above if the satchel is too small.

Schools may provide lockers but seldom enough for all pupils, and lockers are often broken into in some schools.

Be warned that children are expected to bring a lot of books home each evening for their homework; these can be heavy and it's widely believed that carrying them can damage children's spines. The ministry is said to be looking into easing the burden, at least for small children. One suggestion has been to make text-books available online.

You may be given a list of items required (*liste des fournitures de rentrée*), which can run to three A4 pages, at the end of the summer term or the beginning of the autumn term (the latter causing parents to flock to the supermarket on the first day of school to buy everything that's required). Note, however, that some items are 'optional'; if in doubt, wait until term begins to see whether these are really required! Don't forget name tapes (*noms tissés*

sur ruban) for coats and sports equipment; you can order them from a *mercerie* or simply write on tape in indelible ink, but it's better to sew them into clothing rather than use iron-on tapes that can fall (or be pulled) off.

At nursery school, children usually take snacks for breaks but either go home for lunch or eat at the school canteen (*cantine*), where gourmet-style meals are available for around €1.50, paid a month in advance. The cost of lunch at a nursery or primary school varies with the area, the parents' income and whether they live within the catchment area. Lunch at a secondary school costs around €100 per term.

Children who have school lunches are called *demi-pensionaires*, those who go home for lunch *externes*. Taking a packed lunch isn't usually considered an option and may even be forbidden. Children are normally expected to eat everything when they have school lunch, which may consist of five courses (including wine – for the teachers!) and can last up to two hours, and there may be no 'tuck shop' or even vending machines – indeed, there are moves to ban the cosy arrangement whereby some schools earned money from permitting vending machines that sold sweets, snacks and fizzy drinks of the kinds specifically excluded from the regular school-meal diet.

With the exception of a few 'exclusive' schools, school uniforms are non-existent, although there may be dress codes regarding what may and may not be worn. There has recently been some debate over the introduction of uniforms, as in any case children usually devise their own 'uniforms', which can cost far more than a conventional school uniform. In some areas the theft by 'gangs' of designer clothes (e.g. by 'mugging') is widespread and has resulted in children being discouraged from wearing expensive clothes to school. Pupils are no longer allowed to wear any 'signs of religious affiliation' such as crucifixes or headscarves.

Nursery & Primary School Cycles

Nursery and primary schooling are divided into educational cycles (*cycles pédagogiques*). There are three cycles, each of three years' duration, as follows:

1. *Cycle des Apprentissages Premiers*, comprising the three sections of nursery school from the age of three to six (*les petits, les moyens* and *les grands* – see **Nursery School** below).

2. *Cycle des Apprentissages Fondamentaux*, comprising the final year of nursery school and the first two years of primary school (*cours préparatoire/CP* and *cours élémentaire 1/CE1*).

3. *Cycle des Approfondissements*, including the primary school years *cours élémentaire 2/CE2, cours moyen 1/CM1* and *cours moyen 2/CM2*.

Although each cycle normally lasts three years, it can be completed in two or four, depending on a child's progress. The decision whether a child is ready to progress to the next cycle is made jointly by a teachers' council (*conseil des maîtres de cycles*), the school director, the pupil's teachers and a psycho-pedagogical group. It's no longer possible to fail a year and have to repeat it, as the new system allows pupils to progress at their own speed and doesn't require them to repeat the same work as in the previous year. Parents are able to appeal against a school's decision regarding progression to the next cycle. A school record book (*livret scolaire*) is maintained for each child during the three cycles.

Pre-school

Children aged between two months and three years (in certain circumstances, and on an occasional basis, four years) can be left at a crèche (*crèche*), usually on the condition that both parents work. There are four kinds of crèche: 'collective' crèches (*crèche collective*) run by the local community, which are the most popular choice and therefore oversubscribed (only around 9 per cent of parents find places); 'minicrèches' (*mini-crèche*), which are similar to collective crèches, only smaller; parental crèches (*crèche parentale*), organised by groups of parents and limited to 16 children; and family crèches (*crèche familiale*), where you leave your children at the home of a 'maternal assistant' (*assistante maternelle*).

> ☑ **SURVIVAL TIP**
>
> If you leave your child with an *assistante maternelle*, you should ensure that she's accredited (*agréée*) by the Protection Maternelle et Infantile (PMI).

Crèches are usually open between 07.00 and 19.00 on weekdays. The cost of a *crèche collective* varies depending on the number of children accommodated, the parents' salaries and the commune; an *assistante maternelle* costs a minimum of €22 per day, but you can claim a state subsidy of at least 80 per cent. Visit your local Service de la Petite Enfance or Caisse d'Allocations Familiales (CAF) for details and be prepared to complete the usual hefty *dossier* before you receive any refunds. To find out about parental crèches, contact the Association des Collectifs Enfants Parents Professionels (ACEPP, 🖳 www.acepp.asso.fr).

If you need to leave your children only occasionally (i.e. both parents don't work full-time), children between three months and six years old can be left for up to a day at a time at a *halte-garderie* or *jardin d'enfants* or a *multi-accueil* centre (limited to 20 children); prices vary but can be as low as €2 per hour.

If your children need looking after for a short time before or after school, they can be accommodated by an *accueil péri-scolaire* or a *centre de loisirs sans hébergement* (minimum age three years), sometimes attached to a nursery school (see below).

If you can afford it, you can employ a child-minder (*garde d'enfant à domicile*) or nanny (*nounou*), who must, however, be declared to the authorities as a salaried employee and be paid at least the minimum wage (see page 22). Note, however, that you can obtain a tax reduction against crèche or childminding expenses.

Nursery School

Nursery schooling between the ages of two and six years is optional. France has a long tradition of free, state-funded, nursery schools (*école maternelle*) and has one of the best programmes in the world. Some 80 per cent of women with one child and around 50 per cent of those with three children work, and most make use of some form of nursery school. Around 30 per cent of children attend nursery school at the age of two, and most by the time they're four – a level of attendance matched only by Belgium.

In many areas facilities are in short supply and, although a place is theoretically available in nursery school for every three-year-old whose parents request one, you may need to enrol your child virtually at conception! (Normal enrolment takes place during the April before the start of the school year.) The place must be in a nursery school or an infant class (*classe enfantine*) in a primary school as close as possible to the child's home. Priority is given to children living in underprivileged areas, children with two working parents, children from families with three or more young children, and children who live too far from school to go home for lunch.

Nursery school hours are generally from 08.30 or 09.00 to 11.30 or 12.00 and from 13.30 or 14.00 to 16.00 or 16.30. Young children usually sleep for two hours after lunch. Children can attend for half a day, which many foreign parents prefer, particularly at first, when a child doesn't speak French. There may be a morning session on Saturdays, depending on the *département*, although this is optional.

Children may have lunch at the school canteen by arrangement (see **Provisions** above). For parents who are unable to collect their children when school is over, there's usually a supervised nursery (*garderie*) until around 18.00 for a small fee.

Nursery school has traditionally been divided into three stages, according to age: *les petits* – from two to four years, *les moyens* – from four to five years, and *les grands* – from five to six years. However, this isn't the official terminology. The three years of primary school from age three to six are included in the first of the new *cycles pédagogiques* (see above) and the last year is incorporated in the second cycle.

Nursery school is designed to introduce children to the social environment of school and to develop the basic skills of coordination. It encourages the development of self-awareness and provides an introduction to group activities. Exercises include arts and crafts (e.g. drawing, painting and pottery), music, educational games and perceptual activities, e.g. listening skills. During the final years, the rudiments of reading, writing and arithmetic are taught in preparation for primary school.

Primary School

Primary school (*école primaire*) attendance is compulsory between the ages of 6 and 11 for 26 hours per week. Schools are established and maintained by local communities, although overall responsibility lies with the state. Since the '80s, the primary school population has been decreasing, causing a reduction in the number of classes. In many rural areas this has led to the closure of schools and children having to travel to schools in neighbouring towns, or schools having to share teachers and equipment such as computers. There are several schemes in operation around the country to find better ways of organising primary education, particularly staff, half of whom are aged over 50 and reluctant to change. One scheme makes part-time use of graduates to assist teachers in an attempt to inject new blood into the system.

Each primary school has a director (*directeur/directrice*), who presides over the school council (*conseil d'école*). The council makes decisions regarding school regulations, communication between teachers and parents, school meals, afterschool care (*garderie*), extra-curricular activities, security and hygiene. The school council usually meets twice a year and comprises a teachers' committee (*comité des maîtres*), a parents' committee (*comité des parents*) and representatives of the local education authority and municipality. The parents' committee is the equivalent of the parent-teacher association (PTA) in many other countries.

The five years of primary school are structured as shown in the table below.

The subjects taught at primary school are divided into three main groups: French, history, geography and civic studies; mathematics, science and technology; physical education and sport, arts and crafts, and music. Minimum and maximum numbers of tuition hours are set for each group of subjects, up to a total of 26 hours per week. Teachers are allowed some flexibility in determining the hours so that they can place more emphasis on certain subjects for particular pupils, based on their strengths and weaknesses.

The main objectives of primary school are the learning and consolidation of the basics: reading, writing and mathematics. There are no examinations at the end of primary school, although a child's primary record is forwarded to his secondary school. However, all children are expected to be able to read and write French by the end of their first term in primary school, and are tested to see whether they're up to standard.

Primary school children have a notebook (*cahier de texte*) that they bring home each

Primay School Structure		
Age	**Form/Grade**	**Course**
6 to 7	11e	*cours préparatoire/CP*
7 to 8	10e	*cours élémentaire 1/CE1*
8 to 9	9e	*cours élémentaire 2/CE2*
9 to 10	8e	*cours moyen 1/CM1*
10 to 11	7e	*cours moyen 2/CM2*

(*classe de découverte*), when pupils spend one to three weeks in a new environment. It may be held in the country (*classe verte/classe de nature*), mountains (*classe de neige*), by the sea (*classe de mer*) or even abroad. It isn't a holiday camp and pupils follow their normal lessons, augmented by field trips and other extra-curricular activities. Not surprisingly, the most popular discovery class is the skiing trip, which usually takes place in January or February. Financial assistance is available for parents who cannot afford to pay.

Secondary School

Secondary education is compulsory until the age of 16 and includes attendance at a *collège* until the age of 15. At age 15, continuing education is decided by examination: students with the greatest academic aptitude going to a *lycée* (high school) until they're 18 (*cycle long*) to study for the *baccalauréat* and others following shortened studies (*cycle court*) in a vocational course. These include the study for a *brevet d'enseignement professionnel* (*BEP*) or *certificat d'aptitude professionnelle* (*CAP*), which can lead to a *baccalauréat professionnel*, in a 'professional' *lycée*.

At the end of *collège*, a certificate of competence is issued for particular skills, provided a certain level of language ability has also been attained. Students can repeat a year until they pass the final examinations, and few leave without a certificate.

The secondary school(s) your child may attend is primarily determined by where you live. In some rural areas there's little or no choice, while in Paris and other cities there are usually a number of possibilities. As in all countries, the schools with the best reputations and exam results are the most popular and are therefore the most difficult to gain entry to. Parents should plan well ahead, particularly if they want a child to be accepted by a superior *collège* or *lycée*. Some *collèges* are attached to *lycées*, with *collège* students granted preferential entrance to the *lycée*.

Collège

At the age of 11 all children attend a *collège* (formerly known as a *collège d'enseignement secondaire/CES*), headed by a *principal*.

day. Parents sign the book to verify that a child has done his homework and teachers use it to convey messages to parents, e.g. special items a child requires for school the next day. Some *assistantes maternelles* use a similar system, which provides a comprehensive record of a child's school years.

An hour's foreign language tuition per week is included in primary school years *CM1* and *CM2*. Most pupils (over 80 per cent) choose to learn English, although the French government is trying to encourage them to learn other foreign languages, including regional and immigrant languages, e.g. Arabic (all part of the losing battle to counteract the growing influence of the English language in France!). From the 2005/06 school year, it was intended that all *CE1* pupils be taught at least two foreign languages, although finding enough teachers to teach them has caused something of a setback to this laudable aim. Foreign language tuition is necessarily basic, and English-speaking parents shouldn't expect it to improve their children's English; in fact, they would be better off starting to learn a third language, i.e. in addition to French and English.

Homework is required from the start of primary school, and the transition from *CE1* to *CE2* can be a difficult one, children suddenly being subjected to increased pressure and having to undergo regular tests in all subjects.

One of the unique aspects of French primary education is the 'discovery class'

Each *collège* has a school council (*conseil d'établissement*) composed of administrative staff and representatives of teachers, parents, students and the local authorities. Its task is to make recommendations regarding teaching and other matters of importance to the school community.

The school year is organised on a trimester basis (a period of three months equating to a term), students being evaluated by teachers (*conseil des professeurs*) at the end of each trimester. This evaluation is particularly important, as it determines the future studies open to a student and the type of *baccalauréat* he may take (see below). Parents' organisations (*associations des parents/ délégués des parents*) also play an important role in determining a student's future studies. It's common for school class councils (*conseil de classes*) to recommend that a student repeat a year of *collège*. If the parents don't agree, they can appeal against the decision, although if they lose the appeal they must abide by the appeal commission's decision.

A few *collèges* offer boarding (*internat*), although this isn't as common as it used to be; arrangements are similar to those for an *internat* at a *lycée* (see below).

The four years of *collège* education are numbered from the 6th to the 3rd and are divided into two, two-year cycles:

♦ **Cycle d'Observation:** The first two years of *collège* (sixth and fifth forms) are called the 'observation' cycle, where all students follow a common curriculum. General lessons total around 24 hours per week and include French, mathematics, a modern foreign language, history, geography, economics, civics, physics and chemistry, biology and geology, technology, art, physical education and sport.

An extra three hours (*heure de soutien*) of lessons are set each week in subjects selected by the *collège* (usually French, mathematics and a foreign language), depending on individual students' needs. At the end of the fifth form, students move to the orientation cycle (fourth form) or repeat the fifth form.

♦ **Cycle d'Orientation:** The last two years of *collège* (fourth and third forms) are called the 'orientation cycle' because students are allowed some choice of subjects and can thus begin to decide the future direction (*orientation*) of their studies.

Students follow a common curriculum of around 25 hours of lessons a week in the same subjects as in the sixth and fifth forms. In addition to the core subjects, there are compulsory lessons in a second foreign language chosen from a list of options (*option obligatoire*), and optional classes (*options facultatives*) in a regional language or a classical language, i.e. Greek or Latin.

Decisions regarding future studies are made at the end of the third form (at around the age of 14), when exams are taken to decide whether students will go on to a *lycée* and sit the *baccalauréat* (see below), attend a vocational *lycée* or take an apprenticeship.

Technology fourth and third forms offer a more practical educational approach for students suited to a less academic form of learning. Students who attain the age of 14 or 15 and haven't reached the necessary level to move on to the fourth form are taught in small pre-vocational classes (*Classes Préprofessionnelles de Niveau/CPPN*). Here they receive extra lessons, particularly in French and mathematics, in order to enable them to continue their studies. Others move into preparatory apprenticeship classes (*Classes Préparatoires à l'Apprentissage/CPA*) – see **Vocational Lycée** below.

At the end of their last year at *collège*, students sit a written examination (*brevet des collèges*) in French, mathematics and history/geography. The *brevet* is the entrance examination to a *lycée*, although failure doesn't exclude students from going on to higher education.

Lycée

A *lycée* (headed by a *proviseur*) is roughly equivalent to a sixth form college in the UK and similar in standard to a grammar or high school (but higher than a US high school or two-year college). It provides an excellent education that's the equal of or better than any school system in the world. It's the aim of all ambitious students to attend a *lycée*, and competition for places is fierce. There are far fewer *lycées* than *collèges* and consequently there's less choice.

At a *lycée*, students are treated more like university students and aren't required to remain in school if they don't have a lesson. However, the informal, often casual, air contrasts with the constant pressure of monthly tests (*interrogation*) and the writing of formal dissertations in most subjects. It goes without saying that, unless a student is prepared to work hard, it's a waste of time attending a *lycée*. There are two types of *lycée*, described below.

In rural areas, *lycées* take students from a wide area and, because of the travelling distances involved, many offer boarding (*internat*) for four nights per week (Mondays to Thursdays) and a few accept boarders (*internes*) on Sunday nights.

At boarding schools, sports and social activities, as well as supervised homework periods, are generally organised in the evenings. Most *internats* are single-sex, but it may be possible for children of the other sex to rent a room nearby and dine at the school as well as taking part in evening activities – in which case they're known as *internes externés*! Costs are reasonable: around €2,500 per year for an *interne* and somewhat less for an *interne externé*.

General & Technology Lycée

A general and technology *lycée* (*Lycée d'Enseignement Général et Technologique*) prepares students for the general or technology *baccalauréat* (see below) or the technical certificate (*brevet de technicien/BT*). There are also professional *lycées* (*Lycées Professionnels/LP*) and *Centres de Formation d'Apprentis* (*CFA*) offering courses leading to vocational certificates (see **Vocational Lycée** below).

The course is divided into second (*seconde*), first (*première*) and final (*terminale*) years. Second form or *classe de seconde de détermination* is so called because it prepares students to choose the type of *baccalauréat* they'll take. Few second-form students specialise and work for a specific *baccalauréat*; exceptions are music, dance and certain technical subjects. During their second form, students study French, mathematics, a modern foreign language, history, geography, physics, chemistry, biology and geology, and have physical education and sports lessons.

They also choose subjects from one of the following two groups:

♦ **Academic:** introduction to economics and social studies and one or two other subjects from the following list: a second modern language, a regional language, a classical language, management, computers, information technology, artistic subjects and specialised sporting activities;

♦ **Practical:** one or two specialised technology subjects, such as industrial technology, science and laboratory technology, medical and social science, or applied arts. The inclusion of at least one technology subject is compulsory for students planning to progress to the first form and sit the corresponding technology *baccalauréat* (see below).

It's possible to transfer from a practical to an academic course or vice versa by way of a transition class (*classe passerelle*).

After the second form, students move on to one of the courses leading to the *baccalauréat* examination (see below). General and technology *lycées* also offer post-*baccalauréat* classes to students who have obtained a technology *baccalauréat* or a *BT*. These students can study for a further two years for the *brevet de technicien supérieur* (*BTS*), encompassing some 90 areas of specialisation. Holders of a *BTS* are deemed capable of entering a trade or occupation and assuming a responsible technical or administrative position.

The *BTS* programme has developed rapidly since its introduction due to good employment prospects, and it's often chosen in preference to a university course. It may also offer the possibility of a sandwich course providing practical experience in commerce or industry, and *BTS* students can apply for one of over 1,400 grants of around €450 to obtain work experience in another EU country.

Vocational Lycée

Vocational *lycée* (*Lycée Professionnel/LP*) courses lead to vocational certificates. These include the *brevet d'études professionnelles* (*BEP*) and the *certificat d'aptitude professionnelle* (*CAP*). The *BEP* certificate covers the range of knowledge required in a particular trade or industrial, commercial, administrative or social sector, rather than a specific skill. The *CAP* is more specialised and is awarded for skill in a particular trade, e.g. carpentry, plumbing or dressmaking. In addition to school lessons, the *BEP* and *CAP* programmes include practical periods with companies providing students with an introduction to the workplace.

After passing the *CAP*, students may be permitted to enter the 'special second form' (*seconde spéciale* or *spécifique*), where they undertake three years of technological studies leading to the *BT*. Students with a *BEP* or *CAP* can also take a technology or vocational *baccalauréat*, known as a *baccalauréat professionnel*, after a further two years' study (see below).

Almost every occupation in France has some form of recognised apprenticeship or certificate, including filing clerks, shop assistants and waiters, without which it's difficult to get a job in a particular field.

Baccalauréat

The *baccalauréat* (commonly called the *bac*) is taken at a *lycée* at the age of 18 or 19 and is an automatic entrance qualification to a French university. Those who pass are known as *bacheliers*. There are over 30 *baccalauréats* to choose from, but three main groups, as follows:

◆ **General *baccalauréat*:** The general *bac* is an academic diploma and prepares students for higher education rather than for a trade or profession. It enables students to continue their studies at university, in preparatory classes for a *grande école* (see below), in a higher technicians' section (*STS*), in a university institute of technology or in specialised schools. There are three main types of general *bac*: literature and classics; science; and economic and social sciences.

◆ **Technology *baccalauréat*:** This is awarded for general knowledge and for training in modern technologies. It's the first stage of higher technical training, usually at a university institute of technology or *STS* (see below), and occasionally at a university or *grande école*. There are eight types of technology *bac*: industrial; science and technology; laboratory science; medical and social science; agriculture; environment; hotel and catering; and music and dance.

◆ **Vocational *baccalauréat*:** Also known as the *baccalauréat professionnel*, this is chosen by an increasing number of students and has enjoyed huge success since its

introduction. The majority of those who pass the exam go straight into employment, although it also entitles them to enter higher education. A major feature of the vocational *baccalauréat* course is that students spend a quarter of their time training in industry.

Within these basic types, there are four 'series' (*série*) of *bac*: A, B, C and D in ascending order of difficulty and importance. For example, those wishing to study medicine usually take *Bac D*, and *Bacs* C and D are the most common among those wishing to attend a *grande école* (see below). Among students planning to go to university, *Bacs* A and B are common.

In the second form, students can choose to follow the vocational system (*système d'orientation*) or selection system (*système de sélection*). Those who choose the vocational system must sit the *baccalauréat* in subjects such as law, science, medicine, dentistry, pharmacy, management and economic sciences, social sciences or fine arts. The selection system is for those who wish to attend superior institutions of higher education. These students must pass the *baccalauréat* and a competitive examination, or pass the *baccalauréat*, provide a school record and attend an interview with an examining board. The selection system applies to institutes of technology (*IUT*), institutes of political studies (*IEP*), and post-*baccalauréat* establishments preparing students for the *BTS* or for entry to a *grande école* preparatory school (see below).

The courses taken during a student's final two years at a *lycée* depend on the type of *baccalauréat* selected. There are seven principal subjects in the first form and eight in *terminale*. The *baccalauréat* is taken in two parts, the first of which consists of an examination in the French language and literature (*baccalauréat de français*) taken in the first form. This must be passed before any

other exams can be taken. The second part of the *bac* is taken in *terminale*. Students who fail the *bac* can retake it the following year.

The French *baccalauréat* examination is marked out of 20, as are all French exams. An average of ten is a pass, 12/13 is quite good (*mention assez bien*), 14/15 is good (*mention bien*) and 16 and over is very good/excellent (*mention très bien*). Marks of 16 or more are extremely rare, so in reality a mark of 12 to 14 can be considered as good or very good and anything above 14 as excellent. Note, however, that not all subjects are regarded as equal, and some are 'weighted' in accordance with the type of *bac* according to a complex system of 'coefficients' (*coefficient*), although French is usually given the highest priority.

European universities and most US colleges recognise the French *baccalauréat* as an entrance qualification, although foreign students must provide proof of their English language ability to study in the UK or the US. A US university may grant credits to a *bachelier* allowing him to graduate in three years instead of four.

The international baccalaureate option (*option internationale du baccalauréat/OIB*) and international baccalaureate (IB) examinations are offered by some international *lycées* in France (and *lycées* with international sections) – see below.

Grandes Écoles Preparatory School

Grandes écoles preparatory schools (*classes préparatoires aux grandes écoles/CPGE* or *prépa* for short) are the first step for anyone with ambitions to attend a *grande école*, France's elite higher education institutions. Admission to a *prépa* is based on a student's grades in his final (*terminale*) year at *lycée* and the subjects chosen. For example, to attend a science *CPGE,* a student must take a C or D science *baccalauréat*. Usually, students require an average of 14 (*mention bien*) to be accepted.

Applications must be made by 1st May, i.e. before actually sitting the *baccalauréat*, with provisional selection based on school reports for the final year of *lycée* and teachers' reports. Successful students spend two years (one in the case of veterinary students) in a *CPGE*, which is generally an integral part of a *lycée*, although it may be housed within a *grande école*. Entrance to a *prépa* constitutes a first selection procedure, before the competitive examination (*concours*) for the *grande école*, taken at the end of the two-year period. This exam has a failure rate of around 90 per cent!

Students who fail the entrance examination may be permitted to remain at a preparatory school for another year and retake the exam if their grades are high enough. If they fail again they must change track, which for most students means going to a university. However, even partial success in one of the *CPGE* examinations can bring exemption from all or part of the *diplôme d'études universitaires générales* (*DEUG*), the examination taken at the end of the second year of university (see page 150).

PRIVATE SCHOOLS

There's a wide range of private schools (*écoles privées*) in France, including parochial (mostly Catholic) schools, bilingual schools, international schools and a variety of foreign schools, including US and British schools (see below). Together they educate around 15 per cent of French children. Most private schools are co-educational, non-denominational day schools (Catholic private schools usually admit non-Catholics and aren't allowed to promote Catholicism). Most private schools operate a Monday to Friday timetable. There are few private boarding schools (*internat*) in France, although some schools provide weekly (Monday to Friday) boarding or accommodate children with 'host' families.

The cost of private schooling can be surprisingly low, particularly for those used to UK fees: annual fees of €2,250 are common. Not surprisingly, private education is becoming increasingly popular and many schools are oversubscribed. Enrolment is often carried out on a first-come-first-served basis, and prospective pupils (and their parents) may have to arrive very early on enrolment day to be sure of a place – for admission to some schools, overnight camping is recommended!

For a list of private schools in a particular town or region, visit 🖥 www.servicepublic.

fr and search for '*Ecoles privées*' or contact your local Centre d'Information et d'Orientation (ask at your *mairie* for details). The Office de Documentation et d'Information de l'Enseignement Privé (ODIEP, 🖥 www.odiep.com) provides information about private schools from nursery to university level. UNAPEL (🖥 www.apel.asso.fr) provides information about parochial schools, while the Centre National de Documentation sur l'Enseignement Privé (🖥 www.enseignement-prive.org) publishes a list of all French private schools, as does Editions Fabert (🖥 www.fabert.com).

Bilingual, International & Foreign Schools

Some schools are classified as bilingual (*avec section bilingue* or *classes bilingues*) or international (e.g. *lycée international* or *avec section internationale*). Certain bilingual schools, such as the Ecole Active Bilingue in Paris, have US, British and French sections. The Ecole Internationale de Paris teaches in both French and English. Note, however, that the curriculum in most bilingual schools is tailored to children whose mother tongue is French. Places in bilingual and international schools are in strong demand and there are usually stiff entrance requirements.

> The only school in France teaching the UK curriculum is the British School of Paris (☎ 01 34 80 45 90, 🖥 www.britishschool.fr).

There are international schools in Aix-en-Provence, Bordeaux, Cannes, Grenoble, Lille, Lyon, Nice and nearby Sophia Antipolis, Saint-Etienne, Strasbourg and Toulouse, as well as in Luynes in Alpes-Maritimes and in Monaco. The Lycée International at Saint-Germain-en-Laye (near Paris) has nine national sections (American, British, Danish, Dutch, German, Italian, Portuguese, Spanish and Swedish). Each section aims to teach children about the language, literature and history of the particular language/country selected. All other lessons are taught in French. Where applicable, students who don't speak French are usually given intensive French lessons for three to six months. Most American and British schools are in the Paris area and on the French Riviera. Most English-language private schools offer a comprehensive English-as-a-Second-Language (ESL) programme, and number students from many countries.

Most private schools teaching in French provide intensive French tuition for non-French-speakers. Schools specialising in teaching non-French students are listed in our sister-publication, *The Best Places to Buy a Home in France*.

There are also private colleges for students aged 16 or older who need additional help with their *baccalauréat* studies or who wish to study subjects unavailable at their local *lycée*.

Private schools have smaller classes and a more relaxed, less rigid regime and curriculum than state schools. They provide a more varied and international approach to sport, culture and art, and often a wider choice of academic subjects. Many also provide English-language summer school programmes, combining academic lessons with sports, arts and crafts, and other extra-curricular activities. Their aim is the development of the child as an individual and the encouragement of his unique talents, which is made possible by the small classes. The results are self-evident and many private secondary schools have a near 100 per cent university placement rate.

Curriculum

Private schools in France teach a variety of syllabi, including the British GCSE and A Level examinations, American High School Diploma and college entrance examinations (e.g. ACT, SAT, achievement tests and AP exams), and the *OIB* and *IB* (see below). However, many schools offer bilingual children the French *baccalauréat* only. A number of private schools in France follow unorthodox methods of teaching, such as Montessori nursery schools and Rudolf Steiner schools, plus schools for children with special language requirements.

Some private schools offer an international baccalaureate option (*option internationale du baccalauréat/OIB*) in addition to the French *baccalauréat* examination. The *OIB* is intended for bilingual French students or foreign students with fluent French who are planning to enter a French university.

The *OIB* is a French exam and shouldn't be confused with the international baccalaureate (IB), which is classed as a foreign diploma in France. The IB, which originated in Switzerland in 1968 and has its headquarters in Geneva, is an internationally recognised university entrance qualification. As an international examination, it's second to none. It's taught in over 500 schools in around 65 countries but in only nine French schools, only three of which provide bilingual education: the Ecoles Actives

Bilingues Jeannine Manuel in Paris and Lille and the International School of Sophia Antipolis (ISSA) near Nice. In fact, the ISSA is the only IB school where classes are taught in both French and English.

Fees & Enrolment

There are two main types of private school in France: those that have a contract with the French government (*sous contrat d'association*) and those that don't (*hors contrat* or *école libre*). A private school with a contract must follow the same educational programme as state schools, in return for which it receives government subsidies and is therefore less expensive than an *hors contrat* school. A private school without a contract is free to set its own curriculum, receives no state subsidies and is consequently more expensive.

Private school fees also vary considerably depending on the quality, reputation and location of a school. Not surprisingly, schools in the Paris area are the most expensive. Fees at a Catholic private school that's *sous contrat* may be as low as €300 per year, whereas fees at an independent (*hors contrat*) international senior day school can be as high as €12,000 to €15,000 per year. Fees aren't all-inclusive, and there are additional obligatory charges, such as registration fees, as well as optional fees. For example, lunches may be included in school fees or charged separately, e.g. €100 to €150 per month.

You should make applications to private schools as far in advance as possible – you're usually requested to send previous school reports, exam results and records. Before enrolling your child in a private school, ensure that you understand the withdrawal conditions in the school contract.

HIGHER EDUCATION

France has numerous higher education (*enseignement supérieur*) institutions, including over 75 traditional universities (13 in the Paris region) and around 250 *grandes écoles* and *écoles supérieures* (see below).

French Universities

Universities are the weakest part of the French education system and are obliged to accept anyone who passes the French *baccalauréat* examination – some 30 per cent of secondary students (around 1m) – resulting in overcrowding, under-funding and generally mediocre standards. Lecture halls are packed and students have no tutorial system and little supervision.

These problems are exacerbated by the length of time it takes to obtain a degree in France, where the average leaving age is 29. Most courses aren't tailored to specific careers and, not surprisingly, a huge number of students fail to obtain a degree. Despite the high dropout rate, most people are opposed to limiting admissions, which they feel would compromise the principle of equality. However, the upshot is that unemployment among graduates is high and most universities have little prestige.

Although still famous (particularly among foreigners), the Sorbonne is little more than a building housing part of the sprawling Université de Paris, and it has lost much of its eminence within France to the *grandes écoles* (in fact, it's so overcrowded that conditions are said to be 'of third world standard'!).

Qualifications

Anyone who passes the French *baccalauréat* examination (see page 146) is guaranteed entry to a university, but not necessarily to study the subject of his choice. Schools of medicine, dentistry and pharmacy are attached to certain universities, and entry is restricted to the top 25 per cent of students with a *Baccalauréat* C. Other restricted entry institutions include schools of economics and law. One of the most difficult to gain acceptance to is a veterinary school, a popular and lucrative profession in France (where there are over 10m dogs!): there are just four veterinary schools in France, all with a highly competitive entrance examination.

Foreign students number around 130,000 or 10 per cent of university intake. Most are from North Africa, although there's a large number from EU countries, South America and China. There are quotas for foreign students at certain universities and for particular courses. For example, foreign students are limited to 5 per cent of the number of French students in medical and dental studies at universities in and around Paris.

Foreign students are admitted to French universities on the basis of equivalent qualifications to the French *baccalauréat*. French universities accept British A Levels as an entrance qualification, but an American high school diploma isn't generally accepted, and American students must usually have spent a year at college or have a BA, BBA or BSc degree.

All foreign students require a thorough knowledge of French, which is usually examined if a *baccalauréat* certificate isn't furnished. French language preparatory courses are provided.

There's a university entrance examination for mature students without a *baccalauréat*, although mature students are rare in France, where the idea of going back to school after working isn't popular.

Curriculum & Exams

During their first two years at university (called Stage I), students study a core curriculum, and in their second year they take the *diplôme d'études universitaires générales* or *DEUG*. There are nine types of *DEUG*, students being able to specialise in economic and social administration, law, literature and language, the arts, economics and management, science and technical studies, physical and sports studies, human and social sciences, and theology. The *DEUG* has a high failure rate, almost half of undergraduates failing to complete their degrees, although a new tutoring system, whereby older students help younger ones, has reduced the number who fail. Those who fail may be given a third year to pass, but no longer.

Those who pass the *DEUG* can take a degree (*licence*) in arts and sciences (equivalent to a BA or BSc) after a further year, or a further two years in the case of economics and law. The *licence* is classified as the first year of Stage II studies. However, a two-year *DEUG* or three-year degree has little value in the French job market, where competition for top jobs is fierce.

A *maîtrise*, roughly equivalent to an MA, is awarded after completion of the second year of Stage II studies, one year after gaining a *licence*. In certain subjects, e.g. science and technology, business studies and computer science, a *licence* isn't awarded, and after obtaining a *DEUG*, students study for a further two years for a *maîtrise*. Students can study for a further three or four years after receiving their *maîtrise* for a doctorate (*doctorat*) or Stage III degree.

Another type of degree, called a *magistère*, is awarded in certain subjects for three years' study after obtaining a *DEUG* or *diplôme universitaire de technologie* (*DUT*), the latter awarded on completion of a two-year course of study at a university institute of technology (*Institut Universitaire de Technologie/IUT*). The *magistère* course combines the acquisition of basic knowledge, an introduction to research and its practical application within a professional framework.

Recent reforms aim to 'harmonise' French higher education with that of other European countries by introducing a system known as *licence, master* and *doctorat* (*LMD*), and awarding students 'credits' (*crédits*) for each course. A *DEUG*, for example, is worth 120 credits and a degree 300.

Like most French schools, universities offer few extra-curricular sports and social activities (the most popular extra-curricular activity is the pursuit of love!). There aren't even inexpensive university bars in France.

Enrolment

Overseas students must complete an initial registration form (*dossier de demande de première admission en premier cycle*) and lodge their application by 1st February for entry the following October (the academic year runs from October to June). Application forms are available from the cultural sections of French embassies. Applicants must present a residence permit valid for at least a year or that of their parents if the latter have a residence permit.

Application must be made to three universities, at least two of which must be outside Paris. There's no central clearing system and applicants must apply to each university separately. Most French students normally apply via their school, which submits their applications for them.

Fees & Grants

University students don't pay tuition fees, and costs for foreign students are minimal. Between €150 and €300, depending on the options chosen, is sufficient to cover registration fees, including obligatory fees for health insurance and social security. Students aged over 26 are required to take out health insurance in their country of origin or insurance under the French social security system on arrival in France.

However, studies by the national union of students (UNEF) reveal that one in three French universities illegally demand admission fees. The fees may be quite modest but, in the case of highly sought-after courses, fees of several thousand euros may be demanded. The 2011 study also showed that, despite promises from the education ministry, there had been no improvement since the previous year, while complaints about this malpractice had been reported regularly since 2004. One possible reason that nothing has been done is that the government, which is desperately seeking to cut public spending, would probably have to compensate universities for the loss of their illicit revenues.

Note that students require numerous passport-size photographs (usually on a white background) and photocopies and translations of relevant documents.

Government grants (*bourse*) are awarded to 20 per cent of students. The maximum grant is around €3,000 per year, although most are less than €1,000. Some 12,000 grants of around €400 per month are available to students wishing to study abroad. To apply for a grant, students must prepare a *dossier social étudiant* by the end of April and submit it to the Centre National des Oeuvres Universitaires et Scolaires (CNOUS – see **Information** below). Scholarships are also provided by international organisations and foreign governments.

Banks make long-term, low-interest loans for quite large amounts if they judge the applicant to be a high-calibre student, i.e. one who will earn enough to repay the loan! Parents are obliged by law to support their children at university until they're 20, after which age they're officially financially self-reliant. One in three students support themselves during their studies by working part-time during terms and over holiday periods (see **Temporary & Casual Work** on page 33).

Accommodation

Students are eligible for a room in a university hall of residence, although places are limited and accommodation is generally poor. Students should expect to pay around €150 per month for a room in a hall of residence and between €225 and €300 per month for a private room (or more in Paris). Foreign students need around €600 to €1,000 per month to live in Paris (less in the provinces). Many students attend the nearest university to their home and treat university as an extension of school, particularly in Paris and other large cities where accommodation is expensive.

CROUS (see below) subsidise some university accommodation and student restaurants, but not all, therefore you should contact CROUS before choosing a university.

American Universities & Colleges

There are a number of American colleges and universities in France, including the American University in Paris (AUP), where all classes are taught in English and the 1,000-strong student body comes from over 70 countries. The AUP offers both BA and BSc degrees, and students can study for a BA in seven fields, including international business, art, history and European culture. Fees for a full academic

sections of French embassies provide information about higher education. A complete list of state and private universities in France, entitled *Le Guide des Études Supérieures*, is published annually by *L'Étudiant* magazine. All state universities are also listed on the Education Ministry's website (see above), and the Ministry has recently set up a new site aimed at making it easier for students who have obtained their *bac* to find a suitable course in France or abroad, obtain a grant and even find accommodation (🖥 www.etudiant.gouv.fr).

FURTHER EDUCATION

Further education generally embraces everything except first degree courses taken at universities, *grandes écoles* and other institutions of higher education, although the distinction between further and higher education (see above) is often blurred.

Each year many thousands of students attend further education courses at universities alone, often of short duration and job-related, although courses may be full-or part-time and include summer terms. France has many private colleges and other university-level institutions, some affiliated to foreign (usually US) universities, which include business and commercial colleges, hotel and restaurant schools, language schools and finishing schools.

Many educational institutions offer American MBA degree courses, including the European University in Paris and Toulouse. Among the most popular MBA subjects are banking, business administration, communications, economics, European languages, information systems, management, marketing, public relations, and social and political studies. Tuition fees are high and study periods strictly organised. Although most courses are taught in English, some schools require students to be fluent in both English and French, e.g. the European Institute for Business Administration (INSEAD) at Fontainebleau, one of Europe's most prestigious business schools. Many US universities also run summer courses in France.

Many further education courses are of the 'open learning' variety, where students study mostly at home. These include literally hundreds of academic, professional and

year are around €12,000, excluding health insurance, accommodation and deposits.

A popular American college in Paris is the Parsons School of Design (a division of New York's New School for Social Research), where students take a four-year Bachelor of Fine Arts (BFA) degree. The Paris American Academy, which specialises in fine arts, fashion, languages and interior design, also has a good reputation. There are many other American colleges in Paris offering courses in a range of subjects and degrees (from a BA to an MBA).

Information

The Centres Régionaux des Oeuvres Universitaires et Scolaires (CROUS, ☎ 01 44 18 53 00) are responsible for foreign students in France and provide information about courses, grants and accommodation. In Paris, students can contact the Centre National des Oeuvres Universitaires et Scolaires (CNOUS, 🖥 www. cnous.fr); for the website of other regional centres, enter www.crous-[name of city].fr.

The French Ministry of Education's website (🖥 www.education.gouv.fr) provides information about the organisation of the French university system, and the cultural vocational correspondence courses offered by private colleges. Many universities offer correspondence courses to students who want to study for a degree but are unable to attend a university due to their circumstances, e.g. health, distance, job or family commitments. These courses are particularly targeted at mature students. Over 30,000 students take part in correspondence courses taught through universities with distance learning centres, and through the Centre National d'Enseignement à Distance (💻 www.cned.fr), which prepares students for competitive exams and provides specific training.

The latest development in French education is 'virtual universities', where students can study via the internet (although they must take their exams in the 'real world'!). Universities offering 'virtual' courses include Pierre Mendès-France (in Grenoble), Nancy II, Paris-Dauphine, Paris-Sud, Sophia-Antipolis (near Nice) and the Institut d'Administration des Entreprises de Paris. Another type of course offered by universities and schools allows those in employment to enrol in evening courses. The Conservatoire National des Arts et Métiers (CNAM) and its regional centres admit students without any formal qualifications to a wide range of courses, many leading to a degree.

General information about local further education and training is available from town halls and libraries, and the French Ministry of Education provides a free information service through departmental Centre d'Information et d'Orientation (CIO) offices. See also **Day & Evening Classes** on page 309.

LEARNING FRENCH

If you want to make the most of the French way of life and your time in France, it's essential to learn French as soon as possible. For people living in France permanently, learning French isn't an option, but a necessity. Although it isn't easy, even the most non-linguistic person can acquire a working knowledge of French. All that's required is perseverance and a little help, particularly if you have only English-speaking colleagues and friends.

Your business and professional success and social life in France will be directly related to the degree to which you master French.

> ### Information
>
> A comprehensive list of schools, institutions and organisations providing French language courses throughout France is contained in a booklet, *Cours de Français Langue Étrangère et Stages Pédagogie de Français Langue Étrangère en France*. It includes information about the type of course, organisation, dates and costs, and other practical information, and is available from French consulates and from the Association pour la Diffusion de la Pensée Française (ADPF, 💻 www.adpf.asso.fr).

Most people can teach themselves a good deal through the use of books, tapes, DVDs, computer programmes and online courses (see **Self-help** below). However, even the best students require some help.

French classes are offered by language schools (see below), French and foreign colleges and universities, private and international schools, foreign and international organisations (such as the British Institute in Paris), local associations and clubs, and private teachers. Most universities provide language courses, and many organisations offer holiday courses year-round, particularly for children and young adults (it's best to stay with a local French family). Tuition ranges from courses for complete beginners, through specialised business or cultural courses to university level courses leading to recognised diplomas.

If you already speak French but need conversational practice, you may prefer to enrol in an art or craft course at a local institute or club (see **Day & Evening Classes** on page 309). In some areas the Centre Culturel provides free French lessons to foreigners. If you're officially registered as unemployed and have a residence permit, you can obtain free lessons (*perfectionnement de la langue française*) from the Pôle Emploi, although complete beginners don't qualify (contact your local Pôle Emploi office for information).

In some regions of France, foreign parents of schoolchildren are entitled to free French lessons to help both their children's and their own integration into French society. For information about exchange programmes for children and free French lessons, see **Adapting to the System** on page 133.

Self-help

There are numerous self-study French courses available, including those offered by the BBC (💻 www.bbc.co.uk/education/languages/french), Eurotalk (💻 www.eurotalk.co.uk) and Linguaphone (💻 www.linguaphone.co.uk). Websites offering free tutorials include 💻 www.france-pub.com/french, www.frenchassistant.com and www.frenchtutorial.com. A quarterly publication, *Bien-dire*, is aimed at adult learners (💻 www.learningfrench.com), and the About French language website (💻 www.french.about.com) provides copious information about the language and tips to help you learn.

There are several things you can do to speed up your language learning, including watching television (particularly quiz shows where the words appear on the screen as they're spoken) and DVDs (where you can select French or English subtitles), reading (especially children's books and product catalogues, where the words are accompanied by pictures), joining a club or association, and (most enjoyable) by making French friends.

Finding a French 'pen friend' while abroad is a good way to improve your language skills, and there are a number of websites aimed at putting people in touch for this purpose, including 💻 www.friendsabroad.com and www.mylanguageexchange.com.

Language Schools

There are many language schools (*école de langues*) in cities and large towns. One of the most famous French language teaching organisations is the Alliance Française (AF, 💻 www.alliancefr.org), a state-approved, non-profit organisation with over 1,000 centres in 138 countries, including 32 centres in France, mainly in large towns and cities. The AF runs general, special and intensive courses, and can also arrange a homestay in France with a host family.

Another non-profit organisation is the Centre de Liaisons et d'Echanges Internationaux (💻 www.agendaculturel.fr) offering intensive French language courses for juniors (aged 13 to 18) and adults throughout France. Courses include accommodation in their own international centres, with a French family, or in a hotel, bed-and-breakfast or self-catering studio. Junior courses can be combined with tuition in a variety of sports and other activities, including horse riding, tennis, windsurfing, canoeing, diving and dancing. The

British organisation CESA Languages Abroad (UK, ☏ 01209-211800, 💻 www.cesalanguages.com) offers advice and arranges language courses.

> ### ⚠ Caution
>
> Don't expect to become fluent in a short time unless you have a particular flair for languages or already have a good command of French.

Most language schools run various classes, and which one you choose will depend on your language ability, how many hours you wish to study a week, how much money you want to spend and how quickly you wish to (or think you can) learn. Language classes generally fall into the following categories: extensive (four to ten hours per week); intensive (15 to 20 hours); total immersion (20 to 40 or more). Some offer telephone lessons, which are handy if you're busy or don't live near a language school. Unless you desperately need to learn French quickly, it's best to arrange your lessons over a long period. However, don't commit yourself to a long course of study, particularly an expensive one, before ensuring that it's the right course. The cost of a one-week total immersion course is usually between €2,500 and €3,000! Most schools offer free tests to help you find the appropriate level and a free introductory lesson.

Train à Grande Vitesse (high speed train)

10.
PUBLIC TRANSPORT

Public transport (*transport public*) **services in France vary considerably depending on where you live. They're generally excellent in cities, most of which have efficient local bus and rail services, many supplemented by underground railway and tram networks, and French railways provide an excellent and fast rail service, particularly between cities served by the** *TGV* **(see page 160). France is also served by excellent international and domestic airline services, and extensive international ferry services, particularly along its northern coast.**

On the negative side, bus and rail services are poor or non-existent in rural areas (although the provision of public transport has recently been improved by the amalgamation of neighbouring communes into *agglomérations*), and it's essential to have your own transport if you live in a rural area. Paris has one of the most efficient, best integrated and cheapest public transport systems of any major city in the world. In addition to its world-famous *métro*, it boasts a comprehensive bus service and extensive suburban transport systems, including 'underground' (*RER* – see page 169) and overground rail networks and tramways.

The Paris tramway, which closed in 1957, reopened in December 2006 with the impressive title of *le Tramway des Maréchaux*, and covers 8km (5mi) of the southern part of the city, with 19 stops (the original tram network had over 1,000km of track!), although extensions are already planned.

Other cities have similar systems, and several have recently reintroduced trams. Most cities are moving towards more 'ecological' public transport systems, with, for example, buses running on bio-fuel or batteries, and encouraging or even obliging people to use them by restricting the circulation of private vehicles.

Thanks to government subsidies, public transport is generally inexpensive, although this doesn't stop the French from complaining about the cost. Various commuter and visitor discount tickets are also available.

Students visiting or living in France should obtain an International Student Identity Card (ISIC) and other young people an International Youth Card (IYC), both of which offer a range of travel discounts. They're available from most student travel offices and organisations. The French Government Tourist Office publishes a booklet, *France Youth Travel*, for those aged under 26. A number of local and regional organisations in France offer a *carte jeune*, which entitles the holder to discounts on local transport (and in some cases, driving lessons) as well as entertainment. The cost of a *carte jeune* varies according to age and the number of discounts offered.

AIRLINE SERVICES

The state-owned national airline, Air France (💻 www.airfrance.fr), is France's major carrier, flying to over 30 French, 65 European and 120 other destinations in over 70 countries. Air France and its various subsidiaries (including it's recently acquired partner, the Dutch airline

KLM, known collectively as Groupe Air France) together have a fleet of over 200 aircraft and carry 16m passengers annually. It provides a high standard of service and, as you would expect, excellent in-flight cuisine. Smoking is banned on both domestic and international flights.

International Flights

All major international airlines provide scheduled services to Paris, and many also fly to other main French cities such as Bordeaux, Lyon, Marseille, Nice and Toulouse. Air France shares many international routes with just one foreign carrier and is thus able to charge high fares. The lack of competition means that Air France's international and domestic flights are among the world's most expensive. However, some competition is starting to appear, and fares on some European and transatlantic flights have been reduced as a result of pressure by travel agents such as Nouvelles Frontières and no-frills airlines such as BMIbaby, EasyJet, Flybe and Ryanair.

British visitors are especially well served by cheap flights, particularly from London's Gatwick, Luton and Stansted airports, to many regional French airports, although routes change with alarming frequency. Booking online is the norm, which permits airlines to change their prices constantly. The recent surges in oil prices has led to many airlines imposing a fuel surcharge, and budget airlines levy surcharges for baggage and paying with a credit card, among other things. New regulations are supposed soon to have put an end to such practices to permit greater transparency when it comes to comparing costs, but it remains a minefield.

The latest development in UK-France services has been the opening by CityJet (🖳 www.cityjet.com) introducing flights from London City Airport to French provincial airports. The location of the London end, in the Docklands area, means that smaller aircraft are used, which are quicker to load and unload and therefore require shorter check-in times. Without the sort of surcharges imposed by Ryanair and not requiring expensive high-speed rail links from the more distant London

airports, CityJet fares can work out comparable to those of 'cheap' carriers for people living in or near central London.

Domestic Flights

Sadly, most of France's regional airlines have been swallowed up by Air France, which now dominates the domestic flight market, although there are still a few regional services, e.g. the Compagnie Aérienne Corse Mediterranée and Corsair, which operate flights to Corsica. Air France operates domestic services between major cities such as Paris, Bordeaux, Lyon, Marseille, Mulhouse/Basel, Nice, Strasbourg and Toulouse, many of which connect with international arrivals in Paris.

Competition on major domestic routes from *TGV*s (see below), e.g. Paris-Lyon and Paris-Marseille (which carries twice as many passengers as the corresponding air route), has helped reduce air fares, and flying is sometimes cheaper than travelling by train and quicker on most routes – provided you discount the time spent travelling from town centres to airport, queuing to check-in and security checks, and the time spent going from airport to the town centre after your arrival.

Any destination in mainland France or Corsica can be reached from any other in less than 100 minutes by air, although stricter security now means that check-in times can be an hour or more before departure.

TRAINS

The French railway network extends to every corner of France and is the largest in western

Europe, with over 31,000km (19,400mi) of track, serving around 5,000 passenger stations and carrying over 800m passengers per year. The French railway system is operated by the state-owned Société Nationale des Chemins de Fer Français (SNCF) and is one of the most efficient in Europe.

French high-speed trains (see **TGV** below) compete successfully with road and air travel over long distances, both in cost and speed. However, despite huge government subsidies and recent price increases, SNCF still manages to run up an annual deficit.

Under new EU rules, from 2012 French railway tracks can be used by any railway company and this has led SNCF to restructure its organisation to meet the new competition. There was outrage in France when a German carrier sought and won the use of the Channel Tunnel, but there was some corresponding satisfaction when it turned out that prospective services into France from Italy could not travel at TGV speeds because of the incompatibility of French and Italian equipment. Nonetheless, competition *is* coming, although to what extent it will benefit passengers is unknown.

A side-effect of the SNCF reorganisation is a move to use the stations (still owned by the company) to better effect. Already there's a massive programme of redevelopment in which new designs employing the latest environmentally-friendly and carbon-saving techniques are used. There's a greater concentration on making life easier and more comfortable for passengers, as well as opening the concourse to shops and other amenities attractive to the local populace in addition to travellers. This is already having the beneficial effect of generating further development in the often run-down areas traditionally found around main line stations. New services are being trialled throughout the network as well as new uses for station space, such as concerts, exhibitions and even sporting events.

Main Lines

Many things in France emanate from or are routed via Paris and this is also true of the railway system. (The Île-de-France region provides the SNCF with around two-thirds of its passengers.) There aren't many cross-country train routes, and it's often necessary to travel via Paris to reach a destination.

There are direct trains from French cities to many major European cities, including Amsterdam, Barcelona, Basle, Berlin, Brussels, Cologne, Florence, Frankfurt, Geneva, Hamburg, London, Madrid, Milan, Munich, Rome, Rotterdam, Venice, Vienna and Zurich. Some international services operate only at night, and daytime journeys may also involve a change of train. (The destination of a train is displayed on the outside of carriages.)

Stations

Paris has seven railway termini, each serving a main line (*grande ligne*) or a number, as shown in the table below.

If you buy a ticket for a journey starting in Paris, the departure station is indicated on it. All the stations mentioned above are on the *métro* and some are also on the *RER* (see

Paris Train Stations	
Station	**Regions & Countries Served**
Gare d'Austerlitz	Central and south-west France (including Toulouse), except *TGV Atlantique* routes, Spain and Portugal
Gare de l'Est	East (Nancy, Strasbourg), Germany and Eastern Europe
Gare de Lyon	The south and south-east (Lyon, Marseille, Côte d'Azur), including *TGV Méditerranée*, *Rhône-Alpes* and *Sud-Est* routes, Switzerland, Italy, the Balkans and Greece
Gare Montparnasse	Brittany and *TGV Atlantique* routes, including Bordeaux
Gare du Nord	The north, via *TGV Nord Europe* (Lille and London), and *Thalys* (Belgium, Holland and Scandinavian countries) services
Gare Saint-Lazare	The north-west (Dieppe, Cherbourg-Octeville, Le Havre, etc.)

extend into Belgium (*TGV Nord Europe*, with a service called *Thalys* linking Paris with Brussels and Amsterdam) but only as far as BordeMans and Vendôme (*TGV Atlantique*) and Marseille to the southeast (*TGV Méditerranée*). Other destinations are reached via a combination of dedicated *TGV* lines and mixed traffic lines.

The *TGV* network totals 5,500km (3,400mi) of dedicated and mixed lines, and there are six main lines (see map in **Appendix F**). A line now bypassing Paris means that some services (e.g. Lyon-Nantes and Bordeaux-Lille) are now direct and don't involve changing trains in Paris. It's even possible to travel by '*TGV*' from Rouen to Aix-en-Provence, although Rouen isn't usually served by the *TGV*.

Recent additions to the *TGV* network include a twice-daily service from Paris to Saint-Malo (in Brittany), and a Paris-Metz service (via Reims, Strasbourg and Nancy). Planned extensions include a Montpellier-Perpignan-Barcelona link (scheduled for completion in 2012), a Paris-Bordeaux service (via Tours and Angoulême, due for completion in 2013), and routes between Marseille and Nice in the southeast, and between Rennes and Le Mans in the northwest, although plans and estimated completion dates seem to change every few months. The TGV also operates between Paris and Switzerland (Berne, Geneva, Lausanne and Neuchâtel; Paris to Geneva, for example, takes around 3.5 hours.

Trains are often long, with up to 20 carriages and four engines, so finding your seat can be a challenge (see **Finding Your Seat** below). Trains are air-conditioned and include first-and second-class carriages, a bar/relaxation area, a shop, and sometimes a nursery. Carriages and compartments are colour-coded: red for first class, blue-green for second class and yellow for the bar. In second-class carriages, seats are arranged in airline fashion and are comfortable with reasonable space, pull down trays and foot rests. First-class seats are naturally more comfortable and roomy – and not always a lot more expensive. Luggage space is provided above seats and at the end of carriages. All TGVs are non-smoking.

All seats must be reserved and no standing passengers are permitted. The basic fare on the TGV is the same as on ordinary trains, except that there's a booking fee that varies

page 169). It's best to allow around a hour to travel between Paris stations, except between Gare Saint-Lazare, Gare du Nord and Gare de l'Est, which are close together (the Gare Saint-Lazare and the Gare du Nord are now linked by a fast underground connection). The main stations in Paris also provide access to the city's comprehensive suburban rail service (*réseau banlieue*).

TGV

The SNCF operates high-speed trains (*train à grande vitesse*, abbreviated to *TGV*) on most of its main lines (see map in **Appendix F**). Launched in 1981, these are among the world's fastest trains and set a new rail speed record of 574.8kph (over 350mph) in 2007. Double-decker *TGV*s (*Duplex*), which were introduced in 1995, have around 45 per cent more capacity than standard trains (up to 550 passengers) and no reduction in speed. Despite its rapidity, the *TGV* is as smooth and quiet as a conventional train. The TGV takes just three hours at an average speed of 300kph, to travel from Paris to Marseille.

TGV services operate to over 50 French cities, carrying over 40,000 passengers a day. It has revolutionised domestic travel in France and air travel on *TGV* routes has fallen significantly, e.g. Paris-Lyon, on which route there are around 35 trains per day in each direction, with over 75 per cent seat occupancy, carrying over 20,000 passengers daily.

To operate at maximum operating speed a *TGV* must run on special lines, which presently depending on the day and time of travel, and the length of the journey, but averages around 10 per cent of the ticket price; the fee is 'included' in the price quoted. Bookings can now be made up to 90 days in advance. Depending on the route and the time of travel, you may need to book weeks, days or just minutes before your departure. A new system allows those who miss their TGV train to exchange their ticket for one for the next ordinary train.

There are 'mobile-phone-free' (quiet) carriages on certain routes, and even loud conversation is frowned upon in first-class carriages. A recent initiative is the 'Intéractif Détente Train à Grande Vitesse' (iDTGV), which consists of two 'zones': the 'iDzen', where electronics (including mobile phones) are banned and you're provided with magazines, ear plugs and an eye mask to help you doze off, and the 'iDzap', where the opposite applies and you can even hire DVD players and games consoles.

On iDTGVs, you're invited to register your interests so that you can be 'matched' with like-minded travellers and arrange shared onward transport with them.

More attractive perhaps are the fares, which start at just €19 for a single journey and can be booked in English via Rail Europe (UK ☎ 08448 484 064, 💻 www.raileurope.co.uk) or in French at 💻 www.idtgv.com.

Eurostar

The Channel Tunnel – the world's most expensive hole in the ground – joins France with the UK by rail, surfacing at Coquelles (near Calais) in Pas-de-Calais and Folkestone in Kent. Thanks to a new high-speed line from Folkestone to London, opened in 2003, and moving the London terminal from Waterloo to St Pancras in 2007, the London to Paris journey time has been reduced to 2hr 15m.

The improvement comes at a price: a 'flexible' return fare costs over €400, although a 'fixed' return trip including a weekend booked

at least three weeks in advance can be had for just €70 and return tickets for under €100 can be purchased from London to other French cities via Paris. Note, however, that second class is very cramped and uncomfortable (worse than budget airlines) and you may find it pays to travel first class. A direct London to Avignon route commenced in 2003, but to date it has been under-promoted and is also limited to Saturdays in summer (timings ensure that the facility cannot be used for a day trip). Smoking is prohibited on all Eurostar trains.

You can obtain train information in English or make a booking by calling a UK number (☎ 01233-617575) or via the Eurostar (Le Shuttle) website (🖥 www.eurostar.com), where cheap late bookings can be made online – but only on Tuesdays! Cars can be taken through the Channel Tunnel using the Eurotunnel (Le Shuttle) service.

Other Trains

Standard trains have either electric (*Corail*) or gas turbine (*Turbotrain*) locomotives, which, although not in the *TGV* league, are fast and comfortable. Some branch lines operate *express* and *rapide* diesel trains. The slowest trains are the suburban *omnibus* services (some with double-deck carriages), which stop at every station. An *express* or *train express régional* (*TER*) stops only at main stations and is second in speed to the *TGV*. A *rapide* is faster than an *omnibus* but slower than an *express*. The SNCF also operates an extensive Motorail service.

Some non-*TGV* international trains, including *Trans-Europ-Express* (*TEE*) and *Trans-Europ-Nuit* (*TEN*), are first class only. Booking is necessary and a supplement is payable in addition to a first-class fare. Booking is recommended on all long-distance trains, particularly during peak periods, e.g. school and public holidays.

Facilities

Trains

♦ **Luggage:** Most trains have sections at the ends of carriages for the storage of large items of luggage as well as overhead racks for smaller items. Beware of luggage thieves when travelling on trains and try to store your bags in an overhead rack where you can keep an eye on them.

♦ **Restaurants & bars:** All TGV and most other fast trains have a bar-buffet and/or a restaurant car (*wagon-restaurant*) with waiter service. All rail catering is expensive and, with the exception of restaurant cars, of poor quality by French standards (it's better to take your own 'picnic'). On TGV and *Corail* trains, first-class passengers can order a tray meal at their seat, which should be done when making your booking (and is recommended, as queues for the restaurant car can be interminable). Some *Corail* services provide a Grill-Express and/or self-service restaurant and inter-city trains have a mobile drinks and snacks service (*minibar*) at your seat.

♦ **Toilets:** There are toilets on inter-city trains. If you accidentally drop something down one, be careful how you try to retrieve it: a man who dropped his wallet down a TGV toilet got his hand trapped when he tried to recover it!

♦ **Telephones:** Public telephones are available on TGVs and permit both domestic and international calls with a *télécarte* (see page 118). There are three telephones on each TGV: one in first class, one in second class and one in the bar. The use of mobile phones isn't permitted on most trains and there are signs indicating this, although many people ignore them.

♦ **Smoking:** Smoking is forbidden on all trains.

Stations

◆ **Platforms:** Note that station platforms (*quais*) aren't always clearly numbered, therefore you need to ensure that you're waiting at the correct one. Lines (*voies*) often have different numbers from platforms, which can be confusing. TGV platforms have a yellow line marked on the surface, outside which passengers must stand for safety. At smaller stations you may need to cross the track to exit the station; if so, you must take care! If you're seeing someone off at a main station, you must sometimes purchase a platform ticket, although it's unlikely that anyone will check that you have one.

◆ **Restaurants & bars:** Most stations have a restaurant in or near them and the main stations in Paris have a choice of restaurants, brasseries and snack bars, most serving good food at a reasonable price. Some, such as the Gare de Lyon restaurant, are famous for their cuisine. Station restaurants in small towns are often well patronised by locals, which is a good sign; indeed some station restaurants have Michelin rosettes. Snacks and drinks at station cafés and bars can be expensive and poor quality.

> At main stations in Lyon, Marseille and Paris (Gare de Lyon), there are kiosks where you can hire portable DVD players and discs (a service known as '*Cinétrain*').

◆ **Shops:** In a drive to increase revenue, the SNCF plans to create shopping centres in its 50 or so main stations; a 3,000m² precinct in Paris' Gare du Nord station was the first to open.

◆ **Luggage:** Luggage offices (*consigne*) are provided at most stations, where you're charged around €5 per item (including bicycles and wheelchairs) for 24 hours. There are also luggage lockers (*consigne automatique*) of various sizes, for which you must have the exact change; items can be left for up to 72 hours. Note that luggage lockers may be unavailable if there's a 'security alert'. Luggage trolleys are available free at main stations, although you need a €1 coin or token, which is refunded when the trolley is returned to a storage location (as in supermarkets). However, some stations have temporarily suspended luggage storage facilities due to stricter security measures.

Porters are available at most main stations and charge around €1 per bag. Those who are unable to carry their bags may request assistance from the reception desk (*accueil*) at any main station. You'll be charged €5 for this service.

The SNCF doesn't accept responsibility for lost luggage or luggage stolen from lockers, unless you can prove that there was negligence on its part or that the locker was faulty; even then the compensation is likely to be derisory. However, you can register (*enregistrer*) your luggage (including skis) for a fee, in which case you're entitled to compensation depending on the weight of your luggage. You must inspect your luggage when you collect it and make a claim by registered post within three days. The *Service Bagages à Domicile* leaflet, available at station information desks, provides information and current charges (☎ 08 25 84 58 45).

◆ **Parking & car hire:** Car parks are often provided close to railway stations, where long-term parking costs around €10-20 for the first 24 hours, reducing thereafter. Monthly parking tickets cost from around €70-180. You can hire (rent) an Avis car from around 200 main railway stations and leave it at any other station that operates the service. Cars can be booked at the same time as your train ticket.

◆ **Bicycles:** Bicycles can be hired from many stations and transported on trains (see **Cycling** on page 312). The SNCF publishes a brochure, *Guide Train + Vélo*.

Main railway stations may provide toilets, washing facilities, including hair dryers and showers, and some provide nappy/diaper-changing rooms. There are photocopiers and instant passport photograph machines at most inter-city and international railway stations.

Tickets

Tickets (*billet*) can be purchased by telephone (☎ 08 92 35 35 35) and via the internet (🖥 www.voyages-sncf.com), in addition to station ticket offices (at major stations staff

may speak English or other languages, e.g. German, Italian or Spanish), via ticket machines (*billetterie automatique*) at stations, and from rail travel centres and appointed travel agents. A ticket must be purchased and validated before boarding a train.

Single tickets are *aller simple* and return tickets *aller-retour*. All tickets are valid for two months. There are two classes on most trains: first class (*première classe*) and second class (*deuxième classe*), with the exception of *TEE* and *TEN* international trains, which are first class only.

Tariffs

There are two tariffs (*tarif*), depending on the day and the departure time of a journey:

♦ **Off-peak** (*tarif bleu*): usually from 10.00 on Mondays to 15.00 on Fridays, 08.00 on Saturdays to 15.00 on Sundays and 20.00 on Sundays to 06.00 on Mondays;

♦ **Peak** (*tarif blanc*): the intervening periods and on a few special days and public holidays.

The relevant period is indicated on timetables. A daily travel calendar (*Calendrier Voyageurs*) is published by the SNCF and is available free at stations; it's updated every six months. Fares are determined by the tariff applicable at the start of a journey, e.g. a journey that starts in the off-peak period and runs into the peak period is charged at the reduced ('blue') tariff. If you're discovered travelling in a peak ('white') period with a ticket that only entitles you to travel off peak, you must pay the higher fare and a fine. Various discounts are available (see below). The above tariff periods don't apply to TGVs.

Discounts

Season and other discounted tickets are available for various types of traveller, including those listed below.

♦ **Senior citizens:** The over-60s can buy a *Carte Senior*, which costs €50 and provides a 50 per cent reduction in off-peak periods and a 25 per cent reduction in peak periods. There's also a 25 per cent reduction on international journeys, and the card can be used on the national railway networks of several European countries. The *Carte Senior* is valid on all trains except regional trains in Paris and can be purchased from SNCF offices abroad as well as in France. *Carte Senior* holders are also entitled to discounts on entertainment and museum fees and other travel discounts. Even without a card, those over 60 are entitled to a 25 per cent reduction on all journeys starting in an off-peak period (known as the *tarif découverte senior*).

♦ **Children:** Children under the age of four who don't require a separate seat travel free; those who do are charged a standard fare of €8.20 one way (known as the *Forfait Bambin*), and children aged from 4 to 11 travel for half-fare. Those aged from 12 to 25 can save 20 or 50 per cent with a card called *La Carte 12-25*. Children aged from 4 to 14 can travel in the care of a *Jeune Voyageur Service* (*JVS*) host on selected routes for an additional fee of €35. For further information see the booklet, *Votre Enfant Voyage en Train* or *Guide Service Jeune Voyageur*.

Children aged under 12 can buy a *Carte Enfant +* (€65), which is valid for a year and entitles the holder and up to three other people (one of whom must be an adult) to travel at a 50 per cent reduction during off-peak periods and at a 25 per cent discount during peak periods. It also permits a family dog or cat to travel free. A *Carte Enfant +* doesn't include travel on Parisian suburban railways.

◆ **Students & apprentices:** Students and apprentices aged up to 23 can purchase weekly or monthly discount cards for all trains except *TGVs* (for which a monthly pass is available). *La Carte 12–25* provides a 50 per cent reduction in off-peak periods and 25 per cent at peak times. It's valid for a year and costs €49. The *Tarif Découverte 12–25* card also entitles holders a 25 per cent reduction on journeys started in an off-peak period.

◆ **Families:** Parents with three or more children under 18 can purchase a 'large family' card (*Carte Famille Nombreuse*), which costs €18, is valid for three years and entitles holders to discounts on all rail fares. The *Carte Famille Nombreuse* is available only to French residents, as it's a social service subsidised by the French government. Cards, which take up to ten days to obtain, can be applied for at SNCF stations, town halls and family benefit offices, where you must present identification for both parents, birth certificates or copies of your *livret de famille* or equivalent for each child, and a photograph of each family member.

◆ **Couples:** Any two adults travelling together have two options for reduced-price rail travel. The first, *Découverte à Deux*, provides a 25 per cent reduction on all first-or second-class travel on journeys starting in an off-peak period. The second, *Découverte Séjour,* provides a 25 per cent reduction on return journeys of less than 200km (124mi) which include a Saturday night stay.

◆ **Groups:** Groups of ten or more people of any age travelling together are entitled to discounts of varying amounts. Information is provided at SNCF stations. When included in a group, children aged 4 to 11 pay half the reduced fare.

◆ **Commuters:** Commuters can obtain a season ticket (6 or 12 months) called *Modulopass*, allowing a 50 per cent

reduction. Weekly (*hebdomadaire*) and monthly (*mensuel*) commuter tickets are also available. The cost varies depending on whether you want a ticket between two named stations (*trajets domicile-travail*) or a 'go-anywhere' card (*carte de libre circulation*). You must provide a passport photograph and present your passport or *carte de séjour*. Those who live over 75km (47mi) from their place of work may be entitled to an *abonnement de travail*, valid for a week or a month at a time. You need confirmation from your employer that you travel more than this distance daily.

Disabled passengers are entitled to a range of reductions, depending on the extent of their disability. In certain cases, a person accompanying a disabled person is entitled to travel free. Information is provided in the SNCF booklet *Guide Pratique du Voyaguer à Mobilité Réduite*.

◆ **Holiday ticket:** A holiday ticket (*billet séjour*) provides for a 25 per cent reduction on journeys of over 1,000km (620mi). An annual holiday ticket (*billet de congé annuel*) allows a one-time 25 per cent reduction on a journey over 200km (124mi). Tickets are valid for two months. Journeys must start during an off-peak period and there must be a Sunday between the outward and return journeys.

◆ **Advance purchase tickets:** *Découverte J8* and *Découverte J30* tickets entitle you to reductions by paying for your ticket 8 or 30 days in advance. Tickets are available only for the train specified. The SNCF booklet, *Le Guide du Voyageur*, available from main stations, provides further information about discounts.

Pets

You must buy a half-fare second-class ticket for a pet if it weighs over 6kg (13lb); it's also valid in first class. If a pet weighing under 6kg is transported in a bag or basket no larger than 45cm x 30cm x 25cm, the single fare is around €6, irrespective of the distance. Dogs must be muzzled. Holders of a *Carte Enfant +* (see

Children under **Discounts** above) are entitled to take a dog or cat with them free of charge.

Booking

Seats can be reserved on most trains (a nominal booking fee is included in the ticket price) and must be reserved on TGVs. The fee for a TGV booking varies depending on the time and day of the week. However, you can travel on the TGV following or preceding the one that you booked without changing your ticket. When reserving a seat you can choose between first or second class, and a window (*fenêtre*) or corridor (*couloir*) seat. All *TGV* tickets include a seat number. Bookings can be made up to two months before departure. Seats can be reserved by telephone (☎ 08 92 35 35 35) and both reserved and paid for online (🖳 www. voyages-sncf.com).

Seats can also be reserved via automatic ticket machines (see below). Eurostar bookings can be made by phone in English (☎ 08 92 35 35 39). At main stations, bookings may need to be made at a particular window (marked '*Locations*') and there may be a separate window for information ('*Renseignements*'). Tickets for seats that aren't paid for in advance must be collected from an SNCF station within 48 hours.

Ticket machines: Tickets can be purchased from ticket machines (*billetterie automatique*) at SNCF stations (the French love ticket machines and using them is usually preferable to queuing at a window). There are dedicated machines for main-line tickets, including those for *TGVs* (*billetterie automatique grandes lignes*).

Machines have touch-sensitive screens and some can be set to operate in various languages by pressing the appropriate flag symbol, e.g. the Union Jack for English (Americans must defer to the British in this rare instance).

Payment can be made in cash, although this is now mainly reserved for local journey ticket machines (*billetterie automatique lignes régionales*), which sometimes accept only coins. Tickets costing up to €760 can be paid for with a credit or debit card, which you insert in the machine when requested. Some *grandes lignes* machines accept only cards.

Ticket validation: With the exception of tickets purchased outside France and passes already marked with a validity date, all tickets are valid for up to two months and therefore must be date stamped in a validating machine (*composteur*) before you board a train. This includes booked TGV tickets (called '*Resa*') and the return ticket of a day return.

Insert one end of your ticket in the machine face up and a code number is stamped on the reverse (if you don't hear a satisfying 'chonk' or the stamp is illegible, try again).

> Validating machines have a sign '*COMPOSTEZ VOTRE BILLET* and are mounted on pillars at the entrance to platforms (*accès aux quais*); the SNCF is in the process of replacing existing orange machines, which often don't work, with new blue ones in an effort to reduce ticket fraud.

If you break a journey and continue it the same day, your ticket remains valid. However, if you break a journey overnight (or longer), you must re-stamp your ticket before continuing your journey. If you validate your ticket and then miss your train, and there are no more trains that day or you decide not to travel, you must go to the ticket office and have your ticket 'un-validated'.

There are ticket inspectors (who usually operate in threes) on most French trains, and failure to validate your ticket will result in a surcharge (if you're lucky) or a fine (if you aren't). If you argue with a ticket inspector, he's entitled to increase the penalty and persistent offenders face fines and/or prison. It's illegal to board a train without a ticket, even if you're merely seeing someone off. There are (controversial) plans to replace ticket inspectors on certain trains with a computerised ticket checking system called *Equipment Agent Seul* (*EAS*).

Refunds: If you buy a ticket for a specific date and seat and then decide not to use it, you can obtain a 100 per cent refund from any SNCF ticket office before and up to an hour after the scheduled time of departure. Thereafter (up to 60 days) you can reclaim only 90 per cent charge of the ticket price. A 10 per cent refund charge is also levied for all unreserved tickets, which must be returned within the validity period printed on the ticket. No refund is possible for a ticket costing €4.50 or less.

Refunds for *Découverte J8* and *Découverte J30* tickets are possible only up to four days before travel.

Finding Your Seat

To find your carriage, check the number on your ticket against the notice board showing the layout of trains (*composition des trains*) or the number on the outside of carriages. TGV carriage numbers or letters (which aren't always in numerical or alphabetical order!) are displayed on carriages alongside doors. Seat numbers are marked on tickets (e.g. '*VOIT 18:32*' = carriage 18, seat number 32) and displayed on the top of seats.

Night Trains

A range of sleeping accommodation is provided on night trains, depending on your budget and the size of your party, as detailed below:

♦ **Reclining seat** – You can (try to) sleep on a reclining seat (*siège inclinable*); there's no charge, but seats must be reserved.

♦ **Couchettes** – Couchettes (*places couchées*) are provided in four-berth compartments in first class and in six-berth compartments in second class, for which there's a booking fee depending on the type of train. Although a sleeping-bag sheet, pillow and blankets are provided, passengers don't usually undress, as compartments aren't segregated according to sex. Washrooms and toilets are provided at the ends of carriages.

♦ **Sleepers** – Sleepers (*voiture-lits*) provide sleeping accommodation for one to three people with a proper bed and private washing facilities. Single and double sleepers are provided in first class, and double and triple sleepers in second class. Each sleeper carriage has an attendant, who serves snacks and drinks. Trains display the TEN (*Trans Euro Nuit*) emblem on carriages when they cross borders. Sleepers cost around €100.

You should beware of thieves and armed robbers on overnight trains, especially those running along the Mediterranean coast and across the Italian border.

After a spate of robberies a number of years ago security locks were fitted to sleeping compartments; however, you should still take care before opening the door, as crooks sometimes pose as attendants. There are dedicated compartments for women travelling alone. Bookings can be made at SNCF offices, travel agencies and motoring organisations abroad, and at railway stations, rail travel centres and SNCF-appointed travel agents in France.

Information & Timetables

All SNCF rail enquiries are centralised on a premium-rate (€0.34 per minute) telephone number (☎ 3635 – press 1 for details of delays or cancellations, 2 for recorded timetable information or 3 to speak to someone). The SNCF head office is at 10 place Budapest, 75009 Paris (☎ 01 53 25 60 00, 🖳 www.sncf.com) and it has offices in many countries, including the UK (French Travel, 178 Piccadilly, London W1V 0BA, ☎ 0870-241 4243 or 0870-584 8848 for European tickets, 🖳 www.raileurope.co.uk). Rail information is also provided on the SNCF website (🖳 www.voyages-sncf.com).

SNCF publishes a free quarterly magazine in some countries, e.g. *Top Rail* in the UK, plus a wealth of free brochures and booklets detailing its services, including *Le Guide du Voyageur*, available from French stations. It also organises hotel accommodation, bus and coach services, boat cruises and package

holidays. The SNCF has teamed up with Expedia, one of America's largest online travel agencies, to offer flights, car hire, package holidays and other services (🖳 www.voyages-sncf.com).

At major stations, arrivals (*arrivées*) and departures (*départs*) are shown on large electronic boards. When you buy a ticket with a reserved seat, e.g. for a TGV, the departure time is printed on your ticket. French timetables (*horaire*) are usually accurate, particularly timetables for TGVs and other fast trains. Rail timetables are published in national, regional and local versions, and also for individual routes or lines, but can be all but indecipherable. (Some routes have separate timetables for each direction!)

SNCF also publishes three regional timetables: for the *Nord Est*, *Atlantique* and *Sud Est et Corse*. There are separate timetables and guides (*Horaires et Guide Pratique*) for TGV routes, and a *Lignes Affaires* timetable is published containing times for a selection of the most popular trains linking major centres from Mondays to Fridays. In most regions, a *Guide Régional des Transports* is available from local railway and bus stations. Rail timetables are updated twice a year: around 1st June and 24th September (exact dates vary annually).

Many rail services operate only from Mondays to Saturdays (*semaine*) and not on Sundays and holidays (*dimanches et fêtes*), and some run at different times on different days of the week. Before planning a trip, check that your planned travel dates aren't 'special days' (*jour particulier*) such as a public holiday, when there are usually restricted services – unless you have no option.

If your train is late and you want to find out what has happened to it, you can call ☎ 08 91 70 50 00.

METRO

A number of French cities have metros (*métro*) – underground railways or subways – including Lille (which had the world's first driverless system), Lyon, Marseille, Paris, Toulouse and most recently Rennes, whose *Val* system claims to be the world's smallest underground network. (The French will boast

about anything!) In most cities, public transport tickets and passes permit travel on all modes of transport, including the underground, buses, trams and suburban trains. No smoking is permitted on underground trains or in stations.

Paris

The Paris *métro*, which dates from 1898, is one of the world's oldest and most famous 'underground' railways, although some of it runs, spectacularly, overground. In the centre of Paris, you're rarely more than five minutes' walk from a *métro* station.

Trains operate from 05.30 until around 01.00 and there's a frequent service during the day with trains running every 40 seconds at peak times and every 90 seconds at other times. The *métro* is operated by the Régie Autonome des Transports Parisiens (RATP), and a single all-purpose ticket is valid for all public transport in the capital (*métro*, *RER*, buses and suburban trains). A flat fare is charged for journeys irrespective of distance, although you aren't permitted to break your journey and cannot make a round trip.

Tickets are sold at *métro* stations, bus terminals, tobacconists, RATP offices and ticket machines. A ticket for a single journey costs around €1.70 and ten tickets (called a *carnet* although actually issued as ten separate tickets) cost around €12. Children under four travel free and those under ten for half fare.

Métro stations are easily recognisable by a huge 'M' sign.

Métro and neighbourhood maps (*plan de quartier*) are displayed outside and inside stations, and there are computerised maps (*système d'information de trajets urbains/SITU*) at many stations: simply enter the name of the street you want and you're given a print-out showing the quickest way to get there, including on foot.

Main lines are numbered from 1 to 13, and the two supplementary lines are numbered 3b and 7b. To make sure you take a train going in the right direction, note the name of the station at the end of the line (or lines) you intend to travel on and follow the signs indicating that direction, e.g. *Direction Porte d'Orléans*. If you need to change trains, look for *Correspondance* signs. Up to six lines may cross at an intersection. When changing lines, there's often a long walk, although some stations have moving walkways.

You should be wary of pickpockets when travelling on the *métro*, particularly when boarding trains, as they tend to 'strike' just as the doors are closing, leaving you bag-less or wallet-less on the train as it pulls away.

Certain seats are reserved for the disabled, elderly or pregnant, although the French aren't usually eager to give up their seat and you may need to ask.

RER

The *RER* (*Réseau Express Régional*) is an express underground rail system that's independent of the *métro* and links most suburbs with the centre of Paris. It's much faster than the *métro* as there are fewer stops. There are four *RER* sectors (A, B, C and D), each comprising up to eight lines (e.g. A1, B2). Sectors A and B are operated jointly by the SNCF and RATP, and sectors C and D exclusively by SNCF.

The *RER* generally operates from 05.30 until around 00.30, with trains running every 15 minutes. Line B3 goes to Roissy-Charles de Gaulle airport, line C2 to Orly airport and line C5 to Versailles. Line A runs to a station at Marne-la-Vallée-Chessy built to serve Disneyland Paris. The *RER* also links Charles de Gaulle airport with the Gare du Nord, and the Gare du Nord with the Gare de Lyon.

> ### ⚠ Caution
>
> *RER* tickets must be machine-stamped before journeys commence and also, unlike *métro* tickets, when exiting an *RER* station.

Within the central area (*Ville de Paris*), a *métro* ticket is valid on *RER* trains. Outside this area the *RER* has a different ticket system from the *métro*, prices increasing according to the distance travelled. *RER* tickets can be purchased only at *RER* station ticket offices. A ticket for the central zone costs around €1.70, as for the *métro*.

Disabled Travellers

Disabled people who aren't in wheelchairs can book a free travel companion (*voyage accompagné*) a day in advance for *métro* and *RER* (and many bus) journeys between 08.00 and 20.00, Mondays to Fridays. Contact RATP – see below. The *métro* isn't suitable for wheelchairs, but *RER* lines A and B allow wheelchair access. An *RER* access guide is published for wheelchair users and available from the RATP head office, 54 quai de la Rapée, 75012 Paris (☎ 01 58 78 20 20 or 08 92 68 77 14). Information for disabled travellers is also provided on the RATP website (🖳 www.ratp.fr), and general information for disabled people in Paris on the websites of Pauline Hephaistos Survey Projects (PHSP, 🖳 www.accessinparis.org), which publishes a useful book, *Access in Paris*, the Association des Paralysés de France (🖳 www.apf.asso.fr) and a group called Mobile en Ville (🖳 www.mobile-en-ville.asso.fr).

Discounts

The RATP provides a selection of discount and season tickets, as follows:

♦ **Carte Orange:** The *Carte Orange* allows unlimited travel within the Ile-de-France. The cost varies according to how many fare zones you wish to include. The SNCF publishes a *Plan des Zones Carte Orange*.

A monthly card (*Carte Orange Mensuelle*) is valid for a calendar month, irrespective of when you buy it. A weekly card (*Carte Orange Hebdomadaire*) is valid for the current week if you buy it before Thursday or for the following week if purchased after Thursday. To buy a weekly or monthly *Carte Orange*, you need an identity card with your photograph, full name, address and signature. You must complete a *coupon vert* for a weekly card or a *coupon orange* for a monthly card the first time you buy one. After obtaining your identity card, you can buy a *Carte Orange* from ticket machines.

Weekly and monthly cards can be used within the applicable zones on all of Paris' public transport networks. If you commute to work for a company with more than ten employees, you pay just 40 per cent of the price of your season ticket, 40 per cent being paid by your employer and the remaining 20 per cent by central and local governments.

♦ **Carte Imagine-R:** In the Ile-de-France region (including Paris), schoolchildren and apprentices under 26 can obtain a *Carte Imagine-R*, which functions like a *Carte Orange* (see above). It's sold at train and underground stations.

♦ **Carte Navigo Annuel:** An annual ticket costing around €1,100 for unlimited travel on lines 1-5. It's also possible to buy a ticket covering any combination of lines, from two to five. You can pay monthly by standing order (*prélèvement*) at no extra cost.

♦ **Visitors' Tickets:** Visitors to Paris can enjoy unlimited travel by public transport, including the *métro* and *RER*, the SNCF Paris network, the bus network (including *Montmartrobus*, *Noctambus* and *Orlybus* – see **Buses & Trams** below), and the Montmartre funicular, by buying a *Paris Visite* ticket for zones 1 to 3, zones 1 to 5 or all eight zones plus Orlybus, Orlyrail, Roissyrail and Marne-la-Vallée-Chessy (for Disneyland Paris). Tickets can be purchased for one, two, three or five days. A *Paris Visite* ticket also entitles holders to discounts on admission fees to various tourist attractions and a 50 per cent reduction on the cost of bicycle hire.

A one-day *Mobilis* ticket is also available, the price of which depends on the number of zones required. Note that the Orlybus, Orlyrail and Roissyrail services aren't included in the *Mobilis* ticket.

Visitors' tickets are available from main *métro* and *RER* stations, Paris tourist offices, main SNCF railway stations and Paris airports.

Information

Prices for all RATP rail (and bus) tickets are available from *métro* stations and RATP offices. For RATP information, telephone ☎ 08 92 68 77 14 (in English) between 06.00 and 21.00 or consult the RATP website (🖳 www.ratp.fr).

BUSES & TRAMS

There's a nationwide campaign in France for 'car-free' cities, and there are excellent bus services in Paris and other major cities; many also have tram or trolley bus systems, including Bordeaux, Caen, Lyon, Le Mans, Montpellier, Nancy, Nantes, Nice, Orléans, Rouen, Strasbourg, Toulon and Valenciennes.

The town of Châteauroux (in Indre) recently became the first in France to offer free bus travel in order to persuade citizens to abandon their cars, and in Lille commuters are offered half-price bus travel. Other towns and regions have their own schemes that

allow a flat rate for use of buses, trams, etc., irrespective of the distance travelled.

However, in rural areas, buses are few and far between, and the scant services that exist are usually designed to meet the needs of schoolchildren, workers and shoppers on market days. This means that buses usually run early and late in the day with little or nothing in between, and may cease altogether during school holidays. (Note that a city bus is generally called an *autobus* and a country bus a *car* or *autocar*.) Smoking isn't permitted on buses.

The best place to enquire about bus services is at a tourist office or railway station. In large towns and cities, buses run to and from bus stations (*gare d'autobus/routière*), which are usually located next to railway stations. In rural areas, bus services are often operated by SNCF and operate to and from a railway station. An SNCF bus, on which rail tickets and passes are valid, is shown as an *autocar* in rail timetables. SNCF also provides bus tours throughout France. Private bus services are often uncoordinated and operate from different locations, rather than a central bus station.

Some towns provide free or discount bus passes to senior citizens (aged over 60) on production of an identity card, passport, or *carte de séjour* and proof of local residence.

There are no national bus companies in France operating scheduled services, although many long-distance buses are operated by foreign companies such as Euroways/Eurolines, Riviera Express and Europabus. Eurolines (💻 www.eurolines.com) operates regular services from the UK to over 50 French cities, including Bordeaux, Cannes, Lyon, Montpellier, Nice, Orléans, Paris, Perpignan, Reims, Saint-Malo and Strasbourg. Discounts are available to students and young people on some routes.

⚠️ Caution

Bus and coach passengers are required by law to wear seatbelts if they're fitted. Failure to do so renders you liable to a €135 fine.

Paris

Paris has over 112km (70mi) of bus lanes, so buses move at a reasonable speed. Operating hours vary, although buses are in service on most routes from 07.00 or 07.30 to between 20.30 and 21.00. On main routes, evening buses (*autobus du soir*) run until at least midnight. From Mondays to Saturdays, there's a bus every 10 to 15 minutes during peak hours on most routes and a reduced service after 20.30. On Sundays and public holidays, services are severely restricted on most routes. Night buses ('*Noctambus*') provide an hourly service on ten routes (a night bus map is available from *métro* stations).

As with the *métro*, a ticket for a single journey costs around €1.70 and ten tickets, called a *carnet*, around €12. The *métro* and buses use the same ticket. A ticket is valid for two sections or fare stages, marked *fin de section* at stops. Two tickets are needed for trips encompassing three fare stages and up to four tickets for trips to the suburbs.

Paris bus stops are indicated by a post with red and yellow panels marked with the name of the stop (e.g. a street or corner), as shown on route plans. Each stop displays the numbers of the buses stopping there, a map showing all stops along the route(s), and the times of the first and last buses. Most stops display a full timetable. The route number and destination is displayed on the front of buses and the route on the sides. Route maps are also displayed inside buses, and stops may be announced as you approach them.

To stop a bus, you must signal to the driver by waving your arm. On boarding a bus you must stamp (*composter*) your ticket by inserting it in the stamping machine (*composteur*) next to the driver. A ticket inspector (*contrôleur*) may ask to see your ticket and, if it isn't stamped, you'll be fined. If you have a *Carte Orange* or other pass valid on Paris buses (see **Discounts** above), show it to the driver as you board.

When you want a bus to stop, you signal to the driver by pressing a button or pulling a cord. A 'stop requested' (*arrêt demandé*) sign will light up above the driver's cab. Buses usually have separate entrance (*montée*) and exit (*sortie*) doors.

TAXIS

Taxi ranks (*station de taxi*) are usually found outside railway stations, at airports, and at main junctions in towns and cities. At some taxi ranks, e.g. at Charles de Gaulle airport, a button is provided to call a taxi when none are waiting. You can hail a taxi in the street, but it must be at least 50m (160ft) from a taxi rank where people are waiting. You can also call a radio taxi by telephone (usually provided at taxi ranks), but you must pay for the taxi's journey to the pick-up point. Some radio taxi companies operate a system whereby customers pay an annual fee for priority service. You can also hire chauffeur-driven cars (*voiture de place*) in most towns and cities, either by the hour or for a fixed fee for a particular trip.

Taxi drivers must obey strict regulations and can refuse to pick you up if you're obviously drunk or 'if your clothes are dirty or you have BO'! They're entitled to pick up additional passengers along the route, but may not charge them extra (except a fourth passenger). Drivers aren't usually permitted to accept fares outside their normal operating area (shown on the light on top of the vehicle), e.g. Île-de-France for Paris taxis.

In many cities there are simply too many cabs and the situation is exacerbated by unlicensed operators. Beware of illegal and unmetered cabs operating in main cities. If you're obliged to take one of these, agree the fare in advance.

Smoking isn't permitted in taxis. Drivers may refuse to carry animals (except guide dogs, which must be allowed), although most have no objection to small dogs; there's a set charge as there is for extra luggage, etc. Taxis adapted for use by the disabled are available in major cities, but must be booked. Consult the *Yellow Pages*.

⚠ Caution

Outside major towns, taxis can be expensive (e.g. €30 for a 20-minute ride). Note also that taxis in rural areas often double as ambulances.

It's possible to book a taxi online, e.g. 🖥 www.taxisbleus.com in Paris. Most mobile telephone service providers also allow you to contact a local taxi company in Paris and other main cities by dialling a short code.

Paris

Parisian taxis are among the cheapest in Europe and are ordinary cars fitted with a meter and a light on top. Taxi ranks are indicated by blue and white 'taxi' signs. A taxi for hire is indicated by a white light on the roof; an orange light means a taxi is engaged. When no lights are on or the meter is concealed by a black cover, the driver is off duty.

There are three fare rates, with the prevailing rate indicated by a small light on a taxi's roof beneath the main light. Rate A (around €0.77 per km) operates from 07.00 to 19.00, Mondays to Fridays, as far as (and including) the *Boulevard Périphérique*. Rate B (around €1.09 per km) runs from 19.00 to 07.00 and is also the day rate for journeys to the Hauts-de-Seine, Seine-Saint-Denis and Val-de-Marne departments. Rate C (around €1.31 per km) is the rate for the departments listed above between 19.00 and 07.00, the outer suburbs (*tarif banlieue*) and airports beyond the *Périphérique*. Rates are periodically charged by the licensing authority and current ones can usually be obtained from taxi ranks.

Rates are also displayed on the meter inside the taxi, and extra charges are shown on a notice in the rear left window. Taxi drivers cannot claim a return fare, whatever the destination. Note that very few Paris taxi drivers accept credit cards or cheques.

A useful website for information about taxis in Paris is 🖥 http://infotaxiparis.com (in English and French), which shows taxi rank locations current fares, etc. For further information or to make a complaint, write to the Service des Taxis de la Préfecture de Police, 36 rue des Morillons, 75015 Paris (☎ 08 21 00 25 25). For complaints you need to obtain a receipt (*bulletin de voiture*) and indicate the taxi number and the date and time of the fare.

11.

MOTORING

France has an extensive motorway network of over 9,500km (6,000mi), supplemented by a network (around 30,000km/18,500mi) of trunk roads, which vary from almost motorway standard dual-carriageways to narrow two-lane roads passing through a succession of villages where the speed limit is 50kph (30mph). French motorways are among Europe's finest roads, but they're also among the world's most expensive, being mostly toll roads.

Whereas motorways are often virtually empty, trunk roads are often jammed in the tourist season by drivers who are reluctant to pay or who cannot afford the high motorway tolls. They're particularly over-used by heavy goods vehicles (some 70 per cent of goods transported through France travel by road), although increasingly there are weight limits for vehicles approaching towns and villages, designed to force HGVs on to the *autoroutes*. If you're travelling long distances, it may be cheaper to fly or take a *TGV* than to use the motorways; it will almost certainly be quicker and less stressful. In rural areas, a car is generally a necessity, and driving can be enjoyable in remote areas, particularly outside the tourist season, where it's possible to drive for miles without seeing another motorist (or a caravan).

If you live in a city, particularly Paris, a car is usually a liability. Traffic density and pollution in cities is increasing (it's estimated that around 16,000 people die prematurely each year due to ailments cause by traffic-induced air pollution). Paris is one of Europe's most traffic-polluted cities and often experiences poor air quality in summer, with consequent restrictions on vehicle movement (see *pastille verte* on page 182); a reduction in road speed limits (*un pic de pollution*) is automatically triggered when air pollution reaches a certain level.

Parking in cities (especially Paris) can be a nightmare (dealing with parking constitutes 60 per cent of the Paris Highway Department's workload). Some cities have drastically cut the number of vehicles entering the central area with dramatic results. For example, Bordeaux has seen a reduction of 80 per cent in road accidents since restricting traffic, instituting a system of trams, buses and taxi-buses, and also encouraging people to cycle and walk. Some towns provide free buses and others have annual 'no car' days, although usually on Sundays,

The Mayor of Paris has radical plans to exclude all except residents' and essential service vehicles from the centre of Paris by 2012; the first phase saw the speed limit reduced to 30kph and this is to be followed by the pedestrianisation of the area surrounding Les Halles (itself currently being extensively redeveloped). A ban on all pre-catalytic converter vehicles is to be trialled in a dozen or so large towns in 2012. France is also in the forefront of the development of electric vehicles, which are now commercially available (see **New Cars** on page 179).

Rush hours are from around 06.30 to 08.30 and 16.30 to 18.30, Mondays to Fridays, when town centres are best avoided. A recent phenomenon, known as *l'effet des 35 heures*, is an advanced rush hour on Friday afternoons caused by workers on a 35-hour week knocking off early for the weekend. Paris, where traffic moves at around the same speed as a hundred years ago, is to be avoided by motorists at all times (except perhaps between 02.00 and 04.00). Friday afternoons are particularly busy on holiday weekends and also immediately before and after the lunch period – usually from around 12.00 to 15.00.

Traffic jams (*bouchon/embouteillage*) are notorious at the start and end of holiday periods, particularly on roads out of Paris and other northern cities, as sun-seekers flock southwards. Some areas and roads (particularly the *Autoroute du Soleil* – which some have dubbed the '*autoroute de la mort*') are to be avoided in July and August, when 6m French and over 1m foreigners set off on their annual holidays (*grandes vacances*).

The most important days to stay at home are the first weekends in July and August. Both dates are traditionally times when Parisians escape the city (*la départ*), and both the latter and the last Sunday in August are when they return (*la rentrée*). 14th July and 15th August are also best avoided, as many French take their summer holidays between these dates, both of which are public holidays.

Anyone who has driven in France won't be surprised to learn that it has a high 'accident' rate, although the figures can be misleading: although France has the highest number of road deaths (defined as those dying within 30 days of an accident) in Europe, at 67 deaths per million of population in 2009, it's still no more than the average in Europe.

Things used to be much worse, e.g. in the early '70s, when an annual road death toll of around 18,000 wasn't uncommon. Drastic measures introduced from 2002 (points on driving licences, speed cameras, heavier penalties) saw the number of fatalities decline by around 10 per cent over the 2002-06 period. These improvements continued to the point that, in 2010, the annual number of road deaths was under 4,000 for the first time in 50 years. Unfortunately 2011 has seen an increase, partly attributed to bad weather, with monthly totals up 20 per cent more than once. Government reaction has been to increase the number of speed cameras and speed-indicator signs, as well as further stiffening penalties.

The French are reluctant to use taxis when they go out for a meal or to a party (or even to let a non-drinking spouse take the wheel!), therefore it isn't surprising that some 40 per cent of accidents involve 'drunken' drivers (see **Drinking & Driving** on page 203); the most dangerous times for driving in France are consequently at night and on Sunday afternoons.

As you may know, the French drive on the right-hand side of the road. It saves confusion if you do likewise! If you aren't used to driving on the right, take it easy until you're accustomed to it. Be particularly alert when leaving lay-bys, T-junctions, one-way streets, petrol stations and car parks, as it's easy to lapse into driving on the left. It's helpful to display a reminder (e.g. 'Think right!') on your car's dashboard.

Always check your rear view and wing mirrors carefully before overtaking, as French motorists seem to appear from nowhere and zoom past at a 'zillion' miles an hour, especially on country roads. If you drive a right-hand drive car, take extra care when overtaking. It's wise to have an 'overtaking mirror' fitted.

Be particularly wary of moped (*vélomoteur*) riders and cyclists. It isn't always easy to see them, particularly when they're hidden by the blind spots of a car or are riding at night without lights. Many young moped riders seem to have a death wish and hundreds lose their lives each year. They're constantly pulling out into traffic or turning without looking or signalling. **When overtaking mopeds and cyclists, always give them a wide berth.** If you knock them off their bikes, you may have a difficult time convincing the police that it wasn't your fault; far better to avoid them (and the police).

Information about driving in France (and other European countries) can be found on the Automobile Association's website (⌨ www. theaa.com), from which a *European Motoring Advice* guide can be downloaded.

IMPORTING A VEHICLE

A new or used vehicle (including boats and planes) on which VAT (*TVA*) has been paid in another EU country can be imported free of French VAT by a French resident. If you buy a new car abroad on which VAT hasn't been paid (VAT should already have been paid on a secondhand car), VAT is due immediately on its arrival in France.

VAT is calculated on the invoice price if a vehicle is less than six months old or has covered less than 6,000km (3,728mi); otherwise a reduction is made depending on its age, and VAT is payable on the balance. It's therefore advantageous to buy a tax-free car and use it abroad for six months before importing it. However, if you're resident in France and buy a tax-free car abroad, you have a limited time to import it, e.g. two months when buying a car in the UK. The VAT rate is 19.6 per cent for all cars and caravans, and for motorcycles above 240cc.

⚠ **Caution**

In addition to VAT, customs duty must be paid on cars imported from outside the EU; there's no duty on cars imported from another EU country, provided that you produce purchase and registration documents.

The rate of duty varies with the country of origin (some countries have reciprocal agreements with the EU resulting in lower duty rates) and, of course, the value of the vehicle in France, calculated using the *Argus* guide to secondhand car prices.

Tax and duty must be paid in cash or by banker's draft at the point of importation or at the local tax office (*Hôtel/Recette des Impôts*) where you live. If you have a choice, it's preferable to pay at your local tax office. After you've paid VAT or confirmed that VAT isn't payable, you receive a customs certificate (*Certificat de Douane* 846A) permitting you to register the vehicle in France. Note that you require form 846A even when there's no VAT to pay, e.g. when importing a vehicle from another EU country.

An imported vehicle must be registered in France within three months. However, before you can register it, you must contact your local Direction Régionale de l'Environnement et de l'Aménagement (**DREAL**) listed in the *Yellow Pages*, who will send you a checklist of the documentation required. This may include the following:

♦ the customs certificate (*Certificat de Douane 846A*) mentioned above;

♦ the foreign registration document (*titre de circulation étranger*);

♦ a manufacturer's certificate of construction (*certificat/attestation de conformité*);

♦ proof of origin of the vehicle (*justification de l'origine du véhicule*) or a certificate of sale (*certificat de vente*);

♦ evidence that VAT has been paid in the country of origin (*déclaration d'impôt*);

♦ a registration request form (*demande de certificat d'immatriculation*) and a *demande d'identification* (confirming the vehicle's details);

♦ a test certificate (*rapport de contrôle technique*) not more than six months old if the vehicle is over four years old.

If you're planning to import a 'vintage' car, contact the Fédération Française des Véhicules d'Epoque (FFVE, ⌨ www.ffve.org) for information.

The recommended procedure for obtaining these documents is as follows:

1. Visit the DREAL with all your vehicle documents, including the vehicle identification number (VIN) and proof of your identity and address (plus copies just in case) and tell them you want to register a car. They should enter the VIN into their computer. If the number is recognised, which it should be if your car isn't too old and was manufactured for the European market, they'll give you a *certificat/ attestation de conformité* and ask you to pay around €30; you may then proceed to Step 2.

   If the VIN isn't recognised, you must contact the vehicle manufacturer to obtain a certificate (if your car has a non-European specification or has been modified, buy another car!). This will cost you up to €150, depending on the manufacturer, and you'll still have to pay the DRIRE €30 for the French certificate.

2. Go to your local Hôtel des Impôts and ask for a *déclaration d'impôt*. Present your car registration document, the *attestation de conformité* from the DREAL and your proof of residence and you should be given the appropriate form free of charge (unless the vehicle is brand new).

3. If the vehicle is over four years old, take it to a test centre (see below). If it fails the test, it must be repaired as required and

documentation provided to prove that this has been done (*justification*).

4. Take all the documents you've now amassed to the local *préfecture* (not a *sous-préfecture*, where you won't be able to get everything done on the spot but must wait while the paperwork is sent to and from the *préfecture*) and ask for a registration application form (*demande de certificat d'immatriculation*) and a *demande d'identification* (confirming the vehicle's details). Complete the forms, hand in your documents and wait. Note that your home vehicle registration document will probably be withheld by the *préfecture* (and you may never see it again), so keep a copy to send to your home registration authority, telling them that the vehicle has been re-registered in France. If your *prefecture* is far away, much of this procedure can be done online at 🖥 www.carte-grise.org.

5. Take all your documents to an insurance company or broker and to a garage or other outlet to obtain a registration document and registration plates (see **Vehicle Registration** on below). It's possible to do all the above in a day, but you should expect it to take **much** longer. It's important to have the correct documentation at each stage, otherwise you'll be wasting your time. If you import a caravan or camper van, even one manufactured in France, the fixtures and fittings are likely to need modifying to conform with French regulations (unless it was equipped in France), so you're advised not to attempt it but to sell your van in your home country and buy a new one in France. Although the British Caravan Council created a 'European' norm (EN1645) with the intention of facilitating the import of caravans to other EU countries, no other EU country has yet adopted it!

BUYING A CAR

Unlike people in most developed countries, the French generally drive cars manufactured in their own country. This isn't simply chauvinism, as French cars are relatively cheap and usually very good and, when they need servicing or break down, you can have them repaired at almost any garage in France. Needless to say, however, Japanese cars have become popular in recent years (Toyota have built a manufacturing plant in Valenciennes), while Fiat and Audi/VW are the bestselling foreign makes, and the two main French manufacturers, Renault and Peugeot-Citroën, which once shared three-quarters of the domestic market have recently suffered declining sales.

The availability of local service facilities is, of course, linked to the number of cars sold in France. Peugeot-Citroën and Renault dealers can be found in all large towns and there are also many Audi-VW, Fiat, Ford, Mercedes and Opel (General Motors/Vauxhall) dealers. Dealers for other makes are fewer and further between. It's difficult to find garages that can repair cars that aren't widely distributed in Europe, and the nearest dealer may be a long way from your home or workplace

If you buy a rare car (or a car that's rare in France), it's wise to carry a selection of basic spare parts, as service stations in France may not stock them and you may need to wait several days for them to be sent from abroad. On the other hand, if you're buying a French-made car with the intention of using it abroad, check that you'll be able to find spare parts for it.

The cost of running a car (e.g. insurance, taxes, petrol, servicing and depreciation) in France is among the highest in the EU. Those contemplating buying a 'sports utility vehicle' (SUV), known in France as a 'quat-quat' (short for quatre-quatre, meaning four-by-four), should note that there's additional purchase tax on such vehicles. To encourage purchase of 'green' cars (those with low carbon monoxide emissions) the government introduce a scheme (bonus-malus) whereby rebates were granted for the least polluting models and extra charges imposed on the worst. This is due to be wound up by the end of 2011, although it's likely that the 'malus' aspect will be retained. See also **Registration Document** below.

New Cars

New car prices are higher in France than in most other European countries, although lower than those in the UK, and many French people buy their cars in Belgium or Portugal, where most new cars are up to 20 per cent cheaper than in France. You should make sure, however, that the local French dealer of a car purchased abroad will agree to service it under the terms of the warranty. Since 1st October 2002, dealers have been allowed to operate anywhere in the EU and price differences should largely disappear within a few years. Personally importing a car from the US is usually much cheaper than buying the same car in France or elsewhere in Europe, but you must ensure that it's manufactured to French specifications or it may not be approved by the DREAL.

Making comparisons between new car prices in those countries which have adopted the euro currency is easy, but attention should be paid to the different levels of standard equipment and warranty levels. Most dealers will offer one or two extras free of charge, providing up to a 10 per cent discount on the list price, and some offer 'cash back' deals; you should shop around for the best package. French manufacturers have 'open days' through their retail stockists at least once a year, where giveaways and other promotions encourage test drives and large short-term purchase price discounts are offered. These events are announced through local media and often by door-stuffed junk mail.

The French government has in the past provided subsidies for owners who scrap old bangers and buy new cars. Designed to help French car manufacturers, such schemes have inevitably favoured imported models as much or more and so probably won't be repeated. Some dealers offer a hire purchase option (vente à crédit).

All new cars sold in France must now be labelled with their 'energy efficiency' (i.e. the amount of carbon dioxide their engines emit for every kilometre travelled), with colour codes ranging from dark green for the most environmentally-friendly models (emissions of less than 100g/km) to red for the most polluting (over 250g/km); there's a surcharge on the cost of a registration document for high-emission cars (see **Registration Document** below).

The environmentally-conscious can do even better than buying a dark-green-label car by investing in a vehicle that runs on a mixture of propane and butane, known as liquid-petroleum gas (LPG – *gaz de pétrole liquéfié*, *GPL* or *Gépel* in French), or convert a conventional car to run on LPG, which produces less harmful emissions than petrol, including around 15 per cent less carbon dioxide as well as less carbon monoxide. There are around 200,000 LPG-powered cars on French roads, manufactured by Daihatsu, Ford, Rover, Opel and others. Although new LPG cars cost more than ordinary cars (and conversion of an ordinary car is rarely economically sensible), fuel costs are around half as much as petrol, so that major savings can be made. Engine wear and noise are also reduced. Note, however, that LPG-powered cars aren't permitted to use certain road tunnels and they have been involved in a number of spectacular explosions. The *Guide GPL* is available from petrol stations supplying LPG and from the Comité Français du Butane et du Propane (🖥 www.cfbp.fr). See also **Fuel** on page 205.

Electric cars are gradually coming on to the market and are tax-free, as well as attracting government subsidies.

There's the usual chicken-and-egg problem of balancing car purchases with refuelling outlets (as happened earlier with LPG). The government is keen to speed this process but it hasn't been helped by a recent study that shows that, taking into account the impact of manufacturing and distribution, electric cars aren't nearly as green as was thought, to the point of being only carbon-neutral. In Paris, a car version of the successful *vélib* bike-hire scheme is due to be introduced in late 2011 under the name *autolib*, using exclusively electric vehicles.

Another option is the hybrid car, which can switch between types of fuel according to running requirements. Combinations of petrol or diesel and electricity or LPG are coming on to the market, but it's too early to establish whether their claims will prove to be justified.

It's possible to buy a car in France for which you don't require a licence. However, that's about the only advantage of vehicles, known officially as *voiturettes* but colloquially as *sans permis*; the disadvantages are that they're tiny (strictly two-seaters with no boot), have an official top speed of around 60kph/40mph (although downhill with a following wind they can reach a hair-raising 80kph/50mph), aren't allowed on motorways or dual-carriageways, make a deafening noise (inside!) and cost an alarming €7,500 for even a basic model. There is, however, a lively secondhand market in *sans permis* vehicles, which are often changed every two years.

Used Cars

Used cars (*voiture d'occasion*) in France are expensive compared with new cars and generally more expensive than in the UK, for example. It's often best to buy a car that's around two years old, as depreciation in the first two years is considerable. If you plan to buy a used car in France, whether privately or from a garage, check the following:

◆ that it has passed the official technical inspection (see below), if applicable;

◆ that it hasn't been involved in a major accident. A declaration that it's accident-free (*sans accident/non-accidenté*) should be obtained in writing.

◆ that the chassis number tallies with the registration document (see below), which should be in the name of the vendor when being sold privately;

◆ that the service coupons have been completed and stamped, and that servicing has been carried out by an authorised dealer;

◆ that the price roughly corresponds to those in the weekly *Argus* guide (see below);

◆ that you receive a guarantee, signed by the vendor, that the car isn't under a hire purchase agreement (*certificat de non-gage*);

◆ that you also receive a *certificat de non-opposition* confirming that the vendor agrees to sell you the car, i.e. you aren't stealing it!

◆ whether a warranty or guarantee is available; if so, obtain the relevant documents.

A *certificat de non-opposition* is valid for two months and a *certificat de non-gage* for one

You should pay within around 10 per cent of the *Argus* value, depending on the condition and the certified kilometre reading. Second-hand prices vary with the region and are generally higher in remote areas than in Paris and other major cities.

Note that all cars containing parts made from asbestos (*amiante*) are illegal (i.e. no one is allowed to buy or sell them) owing to the health threat posed to mechanics. As most pre-1997 vehicles have brake and clutch pads and gaskets containing asbestos, you should ask the seller for confirmation that asbestos parts have been replaced. If in doubt, have the vehicle checked before buying it.

VEHICLE REGISTRATION

When you import a car into France or buy a new or secondhand car, it must be registered at the *préfecture* or *sous-préfecture* in the department where you're resident within 15 days (although the process is usually carried out by the dealer in the case of a new car purchase). In Paris, registration is done by the *préfecture de police* or the town hall (*mairie*) of your *arrondissement*. If you import a car, you must obtain customs clearance and have it inspected by the DREAL before it can be registered (see **Importing a Vehicle** above).

Registration Document

A vehicle registration document is known as a 'grey card' (*carte grise*). *Sans permis* vehicles (see above) have a *mini-carte grise*, but the registration procedure is otherwise the same as with ordinary cars. It must be applied for at your local *prefecture*,

though a system for obtaining a registration document by post or online is currently rolling out regionally.

Cartes grises incorporate a tear-off portion, which must be completed by the vendor. You must present this and the sales certificate (*certificat de vente*), *certificat de non-gage* and *certificat de non-opposition* that you received from the vendor (see **Used Cars** above), technical inspection certificate, if applicable (see below), and a photocopy of your *carte de séjour* or passport, and complete a registration request form (*demande de certificat*

month only and you must re-register the car within this period (see **Vehicle Registration** below). A *certificat de non-gage* can be obtained from your *préfecture* or via the internet (🖥 www.interieur.gouv.fr). Never buy a car without a registration document, as it could be stolen.

Car dealers give warranties of 3 to 12 months on used cars depending on the age of the car and the model. Used car dealers, rather than franchised dealers, have the same dreadful (and well deserved) reputation as in other countries and caution must be taken when buying from them. If you're buying a used car from a garage, try to negotiate a reduction, particularly when you're paying cash and aren't trading in another vehicle.

All national and local (including free) newspapers carry advertisements for used cars. Specialist journals for used-car buyers include the monthly *Auto Journal* (🖥 www.autojournal.fr). *La Centrale des Particuliers* (🖥 www.lacentrale.fr) and *L'Argus* magazine (🖥 www.argusauto.com), all of which are published weekly, the last of which includes a guide to secondhand car prices. *L'Argus* updates prices every six months and they're used throughout the industry, e.g. by dealers buying and selling cars and by insurance companies when calculating values for insurance premiums and claims.

d'immatriculation), available in some cases from your *mairie* or *hôtel de ville*.

If you move home in the same department you must inform your *préfecture* of your change of address. However, if you move to another department, you must re-register your car with the new *préfecture* within three months.

⚠ Caution

You're recommended to re-register your car as soon as possible, as cars registered in another department (other than the one where you live) are prime targets for thieves and vandals.

You must present the tear-off portion of your registration document, your *carte de séjour* (if applicable) and proof of residence; you may also be asked for a *certificat de résidence* obtainable from your local town hall. The fee for a revised registration document is around €50.

EU legislation has introduced a national 'personalised' numbering system to remove the necessity for re-registration each time the owner moved to another French department (i.e. a car would retain the same registration number for life, as in the UK), which finally took effect from 2009. The new design shows the F (for France) and EU insignia in a blue band on the left, a seven-digit alphanumeric code (of two letters, three numbers and two letters in XX-NNN-ZZ format) in the centre and a departmental logo or coat of arms and department number on the right. The French government, which is keen to eliminate *départements* from the administrative structure, wanted to drop the department identification, but U-turned in the face of widespread protest. You can now choose which department to show on your plate, irrespective of where you live – which will probably lead to very few 75 (Paris) plates. When you receive a registration document with a new registration number, e.g. after importing a car or moving to a new department, you must fit new registration plates within 48 hours.

Registration plates are made on the spot for around €25 a pair by supermarkets and ironmongers (*quincaillerie*), on production of your registration document.

If a woman marries and changes her name, it's unnecessary for her to change her registration document. If you lose your registration document or have it stolen, you must report it to the police, who will issue you with a certificate allowing you to obtain a replacement from the *préfecture*.

The fee for a registration document varies according to the size of a vehicle's engine, termed 'fiscal horsepower' (*chevaux fiscaux*), which isn't the same as the actual horsepower (*chevaux DIN*) produced by the engine. Fee scales vary with the region; for example, they're up to 50 per cent higher in Paris than elsewhere. The website 🖥 www.carte-grise.org contains a calculator which shows the fees in all regions and for all models.

TECHNICAL INSPECTION

All cars over four years old are required to have a technical inspection (*contrôle technique* or CT) every two years, carried out at an authorised test centre (garages don't carry out tests, as they do in the UK, for example). Tests cover over 50 points, including steering, suspension, fuel tank, bodywork, seats, seatbelts, mirrors, windscreen, windscreen wipers and horn, all of which must be functional and in good condition, and emission levels. The points covered by the CT are frequently updated and expanded. Around 20 per cent of vehicles tested are found to be in unsatisfactory condition. Tested items are listed on a report (*certificat d'inspection/ autobilan*).

Tests take around three-quarters of an hour and must usually be booked. There's no fixed charge for a test and each centre can set its own rate, but the average is around €70. If your car passes the test, you receive a badge (*macaron*), which you must affix to your windscreen next to your insurance tab (the test centre may do this for you). You usually have two months' grace at the end of each two-year period in which to submit your car for a test. After this period, you can be fined for not displaying a valid badge on an increasing scale according to how overdue you are. If you buy a car over four years old that was last tested over six months previously, you must have it re-tested.

If your car fails the test for minor reasons (e.g. non-working bulbs, worn tyres, etc.) it's noted on the report and you're given two months to correct the problems. You should keep receipts for the work with your car documents in case you're stopped by the police and asked for them. More serious problems may require a repeat test to ensure the work has been done or, in extreme cases, you may be required to have your vehicle towed to a garage.

Cars over 25 years old can be classified as 'collectors' vehicles' (véhicule de collection), which means that they're exempt from the technical inspection under certain conditions (e.g. they can only be used at weekends and on certain roads in certain parts of the country), although an initial test is required to obtain a registration document.

Note that, even if your car passes the technical inspection, you can be fined if it isn't roadworthy, e.g. for each tyre without 1.6mm of tread over its entire surface. All new tyres purchased in France have bumps in the

grooves to enable you to check tyre wear; once the tread is worn down to the top of the bumps, it's time to fit new tyres.

A green disc (pastille verte) is provided by car dealers for new cars and can be obtained for older cars (petrol-driven vehicles manufactured since 1993 and diesel-engine vehicles manufactured since 1997) from a préfecture. The disc must be displayed inside the windscreen, and cars displaying it are the only vehicles allowed to circulate in cities such as Paris on 'bad air quality days' (level 3), known as pics de pollution. Discs should be renewed every two years. There are proposals in Paris to introduce a pastille noire for environmentally-unfriendly vehicles, such as sports utility vehicles, where they'll be banned from certain areas and on bad-air days.

ROAD TAXES

French-registered private vehicles no longer require a road tax certificate (vignette automobile), except certain camper vans. If you use a vehicle over 3.5 tonnes for your business, it must be taxed, and if you run a business with over three vehicles, you must pay tax on the fourth, fifth, etc. If you have vehicles that need taxing, you must declare them to the tax authorities when you acquire them and before 10th December each year. Forms 2856 and 2857 must be completed; these, along with other relevant information, can be found on the Tax Office's website (🖥 www.impots.gouv.fr).

If your vehicle requires a vignette, keep the receipt with your other car papers, as this proves that you didn't acquire it illegally and also enables you to obtain a replacement if it's stolen. If you need to replace your vignette, visit any tax office (Centre des Impôts) and produce your receipt. If you lose the receipt, you can obtain another from the issuing office, which keeps a record of payments.

Since January 2006, a tax has been added to the cost of a registration document for cars that emit more than a certain amount of carbon dioxide (see **Registration Document** above). The use of most motorways (autoroute) and certain bridges and tunnels is 'taxed' in the form of tolls (see **French Roads** on page 196).

DRIVING LICENCE

The minimum age for driving a car in France is 18, although *sans permis* vehicles (see above under **New Cars**) can be driven at 14. (For age restrictions on riding mopeds and motorcycles, see page 200) Those between 16 and 18 may follow an accompanied or 'anticipated' learning programme (*apprentissage accompagné* or *apprentissage anticipé de la conduite/AAC*, commonly known as *conduite accompagnée*) consisting of at least 20 hours' instruction by a qualified driving instructor, culminating in a written test (*épreuve théorique générale/ETG* or *code*), followed by (provided the test has been passed) 3,000km (1,875mi) of accompanied driving, which is a requirement for all learners, irrespective of age. The practical test cannot be taken until the age of 18.

 Caution

If you wish to accompany a learner driver, you must obtain your insurance company's permission.

The cost of a course of 20 hours' instruction, including the theory (*code*) and practical tests, is around €675, although 16-25 year olds can now obtain an interest-free bank loan to cover the cost and impoverished ones can take a course for €1 per day. Almost 200,000 teenagers each year opt for the accompanied apprenticeship and 80 per cent of them pass compared with only 50 per cent of those who start learning as adults.

Irrespective of your age, you now have three years (previously two) to pass the practical test after passing the theory test and may take it up to five times during this period; if you fail it on the fifth attempt or don't pass within the three-year period, you must retake the theory test as well as the practical (or give up!). If you fail the practical test, you must wait at least two weeks (or a month if you fail at the second or subsequent attempt) before you can retake it. Courses are available to those who pass (*stage post-permis*), although uptake is understandably low.

The practical part of the driving test has recently been increased and roughly doubled in time and, in accordance with new EU directives, tests will in future include the use of a car's instruments and systems, including checking tyre pressures and oil and water levels.

New drivers can run up fewer points on their licences and must observe lower speed limits than experienced motorists in the three years after passing their test (see **Points** below and **Speed Limits** on page 194). Drivers over 75 must pass a medical examination every two years in order to retain their licence.

A standard car licence (called a *permis B*) also entitles you to ride a motorcycle up to 125cc, provided you've held the licence for at least two years (although you must retake the theory exam if you've held a licence for over five years without riding a motorcycle).

You must have a licence *E(B)*, for which additional training is required, to tow a caravan or trailer weighing over 750kg (1,650lb) if it's heavier than your car or if the combined weight of the car and caravan/trailer is over 3.5 tonnes.

If a caravan or trailer exceeds 500kg (1,100lb), it must be insured and have its own registration document (see above).

A French driving licence is pink and contains a photograph. It's issued for life, and recent proposals to make licences expire when the holder reaches the age of 70 were dismissed, as were suggestions that French licences should be superseded by European ones. However, if your foreign licence has limited validity (UK licences expire when you reach 70), you may be unable to renew it in the country of issue and must apply for a French licence.

You can drive in France for at least a year on most foreign driving licences or an International Driver's Permit (IDP). An IDP must be obtained from the country where your current licence was issued. (If you hold a French licence and want an IDP for driving in other countries, it can be obtained from your *préfecture* on production of your current licence and two passport-size photographs; it's free and valid for five years.)

The Second EU Driving Licence Directive provides, among other things, for the mutual recognition of driving licences issued by EU member states. When EU citizens move from one member country to another, it's no

longer necessary to obtain a local driving licence after one year. However, a resident who commits a motoring offence in France involving a loss of licence points (see below) is obliged to exchange his foreign licence for a French one so that the penalty may be applied (non-residents escape the penalty but must still pay fines). Note also that most French officials (including *gendarmes*) are unaware of the aforementioned Directive and none too impressed when it's quoted to them.

You can expect the procedure to take at least two months, therefore you should apply to your local *préfecture* or *sous-préfecture* well in advance, i.e. before your year is up or, if you're an EU citizen, before your home licence expires. You'll need a valid, translated driving licence, proof of residence, your *carte de séjour* (if applicable), two passport-size photographs, a self-addressed registered envelope and the fee (currently around €25) in the form of fiscal stamps (*timbre fiscal*), obtainable from a tobacconist, as well as a copy of the penalty notice (*PV*) if applicable.

Some non-EU countries and some US states (e.g. Florida, Illinois, Kansas, Kentucky, Michigan, New Hampshire, Pennsylvania and South Carolina) have reciprocal agreements with France to waive the practical driving test,

but applicants must take the written test. If you need to take a driving test, it's wise to take a course through a certified driving school, some of which have sections for English-speakers.

The French authorities will confiscate your foreign driving licence and return it to the country of issue or retain it and return it to you when you leave France permanently. However, you should take a copy of your foreign licence before surrendering it, as your French licence will show that you have been driving only since it was issued, which may make life difficult if you want to hire a car and could also affect your insurance no-claims bonus. Should you subsequently return from France to the UK, this copy will also help you reinstate your UK driving licence,

If you're a UK citizen and become resident in France, you should note that the DVLA won't renew a British driving licence with a foreign address, so that when it expires you must either give a fictitious UK address or exchange it for a French licence. In the former case, to prevent 'misunderstandings' with the police, you should obtain a form F.45 (*enregistrement d'un permis de conduire de l'Union Européenne*), which you should staple to your UK licence; it's free, but (like everything to do with motoring documentation) can take a long time to obtain. If your UK licence is due to expire, you should take the F.45, along with the documentation listed above, to your *préfecture* in order to be issued with a French licence (take a good book!).

If you lose your French driving licence or it's stolen, you must report it to the police and obtain an acknowledgement (*récépissé de déclaration de perte ou de vol de pièces d'identité*), which is valid until a replacement licence is issued. Note, however, that a replacement licence may cost twice as much as the original.

Points

Driving penalties in France are based on a points system. Drivers normally start with 12 licence points, and between one and six points are deducted for each offence, depending on its gravity (see **Fines & Penalties** on page 195). Note that this is the reverse of the UK system, whereby points are *added* to your licence. However, new drivers are allowed to accumulate only six points during the three years after passing their test (two years if they've followed an accompanied learning programme) and, if they lose any points during this period, they must wait three years from the date of the offence to obtain the remaining six points. If they accrue six points during the probationary period, their licence is suspended and they must wait six months before being able to retake their test.

When an offence is registered, you receive a letter of notification from the *préfecture* stating the number of points lost and the number remaining. Points are automatically reinstated after three years but, if you lose all 12 points within this period, you receive a demand to surrender your licence within a week to your local *préfecture* and you're usually banned from driving for a minimum of six months (six years or more if you're convicted of manslaughter). Depending on your record, you may need to pass a written test, a practical driving test and/or medical and 'psycho-technical' examinations to regain your licence.

You can reinstate four licence points at any time (but not more than once every two years) by undergoing a two-day 'awareness course' (*stage de sensibilisation*) run by Améliorer la Sécurité et le Comportement des Usagers de la Route (ASCUR).

All drivers who have had a licence for less than two years and who lose four or more points are obliged to take an awareness course, which costs around €230 (but any fine you've had to pay is refunded!). To find your nearest ASCUR centre, contact your *préfecture* or visit 🖥 www.securite-routiere.equipement.gouv.fr. Courses are also run by a private company called Actiroute (🖥 www.actiroute.com).

The points system is explained in a booklet, *Permis à Points*, available from police stations and via 🖥 www.actiroute.com. See also **Speed Limits** on page 194 and **Traffic Police** on page 195.

CAR INSURANCE

As in mos other countries, car insurance is essential in France and driving without it is a serious offence, for which you can be fined and imprisoned. If you arrive in France with a vehicle that isn't insured there, you can buy a temporary policy valid for 8, 15 or 30 days from the vehicle insurance department of the French customs office at your point of entry. However, motorists insured in an EU country, Liechtenstein, Norway or Switzerland are automatically covered for third party liability in France (see **Green Card** below). The following categories of car insurance are available in France:

◆ **Third-party** (*responsabilité civile, minimale, tiers illimitée* and *au tiers*): the minimum required by law in France, which includes unlimited medical costs and damage to third party property;

◆ **Third-party, fire & theft** (TPF&T; *tiers personnes/restreinte/intermédiaire/vol et incendie*): known in some countries as part comprehensive – includes cover against fire, natural hazards (e.g. falling rocks), theft and legal expenses (*défense-recours*). TPF&T includes damage to (or theft of) contents and car stereo.

◆ **Multi-risk collision** (*multirisque collision*): covers all risks listed under TPF&T (see above) plus damage caused to your own vehicle in the event of a collision with a person, vehicle, or animal belonging to an 'identifiable person';

◆ **Comprehensive** (*multirisque tous accidents/tous risques*): covers all the risks listed under TPF&T and multi-risk collision (see above) and includes damage to your vehicle, however caused, and whether a third party can be identified or not. Note, however, that illegally parked cars automatically lose their comprehensive cover. Comprehensive insurance is usually compulsory for lease and hire purchase contracts.

Glass breakage (*bris de glace*) is often included in TPF&T comprehensive insurance, but you should check, as there may be an additional premium.

Driver protection (*protection du conducteur/ assurance conducteur*) is usually optional. It enables the driver of a vehicle involved in an accident to claim for bodily injury to himself, including compensation for his incapacity to work or for his beneficiaries should he be killed. However, if you have an accident while breaking the law, e.g. drunken driving or illegal parking, your comprehensive insurance may be automatically downgraded to third party only – or nullified altogether. This means that you must pay for your own repairs and medical expenses, which can be very expensive.

Additional insurance can be purchased for valuable contents and accessories. High-value cars must usually have an approved alarm installed and/or the registration number engraved on all windows in order to be insured against theft.

▲ Caution

Trailer owners should note that these are normally insured only when attached to your car and damaged in an accident; to insure them for theft, whether attached to your car or not, you must register them in their own right as if they were a caravan or another vehicle.

You should also check whether your insurance policy covers items stolen from your car. When motoring in France (or anywhere else), don't assume that your valuables are safe in the boot of your car, particularly if the boot can be opened from the inside.

Green Card

Although all motorists insured in an EU country, Liechtenstein, Norway and Switzerland are automatically covered for third party liability in France, British motorists should note that British insurance companies usually insist on your applying for a certificate of motor insurance (commonly known as a 'green card') if you're driving to France (or any other European country).

Most British insurance companies issue a green card for a maximum of 90 days per year. Nevertheless, you should shop around, as some companies allow drivers a green card for up to six months a year (e.g. Liverpool Victoria, ☎ 0800-015 4752) or even for an unlimited time, e.g. Saga, ☎ 0800-015 4752 (for the over-50s only). Another way round the restriction is to return to the UK for at least 24 hours after 90 days and obtain another green card!

If you're British and have comprehensive insurance, a green card is essential as it extends your comprehensive insurance abroad. There's usually no charge for a green card for a short period abroad (e.g. up to 5 days) but thereafter there may be a charge, e.g. around £1 per day.

If you drive a British-registered car and spend a period longer than the validity of a green card on the continent, you may need to take out a special (i.e. expensive) European insurance policy or obtain insurance with a European company. If you wish to import a foreign-registered car into France permanently, your (foreign) insurance company may refuse to insure it or will do so only for a short period, although EU residents can theoretically insure their cars in any EU country, therefore you may have no option but to buy a new car in France.

All French insurance companies provide an automatic green card (*carte internationale d'assurance automobile/carte verte*), extending your normal insurance cover to most other European countries.

Contracts

You'll initially be given a provisional insurance contract (*police d'assurance provisoire*) by your insurer or broker and will receive a definitive contract (*police définitive*) a few weeks later. With the contract is a green tear-off tab (*vignette*), which you must display in the windscreen of your vehicle as confirmation of insurance (*attestation d'assurance*). A special holder is usually provided. Each tab is valid for a limited period (e.g. six months) and you'll be sent a replacement automatically (provided you've paid your premiums!). Non-display of the insurance tab, even if it has fallen off the windscreen and is in the car, can result in a fine.

It's possible to insure a vehicle for less than a year (e.g. three months) and you can also insure a vehicle for a single journey over 1,000km (620mi). See also **Insurance Contracts** on page 236.

Premiums

Insurance premiums are high in France – an indication of the high accident rate, the large number of stolen and vandalised cars, and the high taxes (around 35 per cent) levied on car insurance. Premiums vary considerably according to numerous factors, including the type of insurance (see above) and car, your age and accident record and where you live. For example, premiums are highest in Paris and other cities and lowest in rural areas; they're lower for cars over three years old; drivers with less than three years' experience usually pay a 'penalty' and drivers under 25 also pay higher premiums. However, the maximum penalty for young drivers is 100 per cent or double the normal premium.

Some premiums are based on the number of kilometres (*kilométrage*) driven each year, and a surcharge is usually made when a car isn't garaged overnight. Shop around and obtain a number of quotations but beware of companies making 'special offers' of low premiums, as your policy may be cancelled if you make a claim! As elsewhere, the internet has websites comparing the premiums of different insurers (plus other insurance such as heath and household).

If you're convicted of drunken or dangerous driving, your premium will be increased considerably, e.g. by up to 150 per cent. Value added tax (*TVA*) at 19.6 per cent is payable on insurance premiums.

☑ SURVIVAL TIP

You can reduce your premium by choosing to pay a higher excess (*franchise*), e.g. the first €300 to €750 of a claim instead of the usual €125 to €250.

No-claims Bonus

A foreign no-claims bonus is usually valid in France, but you must provide written evidence from your present insurance company, not just an insurance renewal notice. You may also need an official translation. Always insist on having your no-claims bonus recognised, even if you don't receive the same reduction as you received abroad (shop around!). If you haven't held car insurance for two years, you're usually no longer entitled to a no-claims bonus in France.

A French no-claims bonus isn't as generous as those in some other countries and is usually 5 per cent for each year's accident-free driving up to a maximum of 50 per cent after ten years. If you have an accident for which you're responsible, you're usually required to pay a penalty (*malus*) or your bonus (*bonus*) is reduced. Your premium will be increased by 25 per cent each time you're responsible for an accident or 12.5 per cent if you're partly to blame, up to a maximum premium three-and-a-half times the standard premium. If you're judged to be less than 30 per cent responsible, you won't usually lose your no-claims bonus. However, if you've had the maximum bonus for three years, one accident won't reduce it even if you were at fault. All penalties are cancelled if you have no accidents for two years.

There's no premium increase if your car is damaged while legally parked (although you must be able to prove it and identify the party responsible) or as a result of fire or theft, and you should still receive your bonus for the current year. The same usually also applies to glass breakage.

Claims

Claims are decided on the information provided in accident report forms (*constat amiable d'accident de voiture/constat européen d'accident*) completed by drivers, as well as in reports by insurance company experts and police reports (see **Accidents** on page 201). You must notify your insurance company of a claim resulting from an accident within a limited period, e.g. two to five days.

After a car is reported stolen, 30 days must elapse before an insurance company will consider a claim. It often takes a long time – even years! – to resolve claims in France.

INSURANCE CLAIM FORM

PERSONAL INFORMATION

Last Name of Claimant   First Name
Address   Zip Code
Date of Birth   Social Security #   Telephone #
Cell #   Fax #   E-Mail Address

ACCIDENT / INCIDENT INFORMATION

If your car is damaged in an accident, you may take it to any reputable repairer (*carrosserie*), where the damage must usually be inspected and the repair sanctioned by your insurance company's assessor (*expert*), although sometimes an independent assessment may be permitted. Assessors normally visit different repairers on different days of the week, so you should arrange to take your car on the relevant day. (Some assessors have a weekly 'clinic' at their office where you can have damage inspected.) You should tell your insurer at least a day in advance so that he can advise the assessor. You may then be able to leave the car with the repairer or you may have to return it another day for the repair to be carried out. For minor repairs, an inspection may be unnecessary.

Cancellation

French insurance companies are forbidden by law to cancel third party cover after a claim, except in the case of drunken driving or when a driver is subsequently disqualified from driving for more than a month. A company can, however, refuse to renew your policy at the end of the current contract period, although they must give you two months' notice. If you find it difficult to obtain cover, the Bureau Central de Tarification can demand that the company of your choice provide you with cover, the premium being fixed by the Bureau.

Like other French insurance policies, a car insurance policy is automatically renewed annually unless you cancel it (*résilier*) in writing, and you must do so at least two months before the end of your annual insurance period,

although the notice period is sometimes only a month and in a few cases three months, therefore you need to check.

You may cancel your insurance without notice if the premium is increased by more than the official index (*indice*), based on the Index of Construction Costs published by INSEE, if the terms are altered, or if your car has been declared a write-off or stolen. Policies can also be cancelled without notice for certain personal reasons, such as moving house, a change of job, divorce or retirement. Standard cancellation letters (*lettre type de résiliation*) are usually provided by insurance companies and brokers.

Breakdown Insurance

Breakdown insurance (*assurance dépannage*) is provided by car insurance companies and motoring organisations (see page 208). If you're motoring abroad or you live abroad and are motoring in France, it's important to have breakdown insurance (which may include limited holiday and travel insurance – see page 250), including repatriation for your family and your car in the event of an accident or breakdown.

Most foreign breakdown companies provide multi-lingual, 24-hour centres where assistance is available for motoring, medical, legal and travel problems. Some organisations also provide economical annual motoring policies for those who frequently travel abroad, e.g. owners of holiday homes in France. If your car is registered outside France, you may be unable to obtain breakdown insurance from a French insurance company.

French insurance companies offer an optional accident and breakdown service (*contrat d'assistance*) for policyholders for an additional premium, which is adopted by some 90 per cent of French motorists. The breakdown service usually covers the policyholder, his spouse, single dependent children, and parents and grandparents living under the same roof. The 24-hour telephone number of the breakdown service's head office is shown on the insurance tab affixed to your windscreen.

If you break down, you simply call the emergency number and give your location, and a recovery vehicle is sent to your aid. Note, however, that although accidents are covered anywhere in France, in the event of a breakdown you need to be at least a certain distance from your home, e.g. 25 or 50km (15 to 30mi), depending on your policy. The service provides for towing your vehicle to the nearest garage and contributes towards the expenses incurred as a result of a breakdown or accident, e.g. alternative transport and hotel bills.

If your car is unusable for more than 48 hours in France and over five days abroad, your insurance company will usually pay for alternative transport home, e.g. first-class rail travel or car hire in France or tourist-class air travel. The retrieval of your vehicle is also guaranteed from within France or abroad. Such policies may include cover for personal accident, injury and illness, even when you aren't using your car, although they aren't adequate as a substitute for holiday and travel insurance (see page 250).

RULES OF THE ROAD

The following guide to road rules may help you to adjust to driving in France. Don't, however, expect other motorists to adhere to them (most French drivers invent their own 'rules').

All motorists in France must be familiar with the highway code (*Code de la Route*), available from bookshops throughout France (around €15), when they take their test, but most promptly ignore it as soon as they've passed. In fact, there isn't a single official highway code, but numerous versions of it produced by different publishers, e.g. Ediser and Rousseau!

The Prévention Routière publishes a leaflet in English called *Keep Right*, which highlights the major rules and conventions, and a similar guide, entitled *Welcome on France's Roads*,

including a list of common fines, can be downloaded from the Sécurité Routière website (🖳 www.securiteroutiere. gouv.fr – click on '*Les dépliants thématiques*' under '*Ressources*'). These are both rather basic, however.

For more detailed guidance, you should obtain the *Guide Pratique et Juridique de l'Automobiliste* (Editions Grancher), which explains the rights and obligations of car owners. If your French motoring vocabulary is wanting, *Hadley's French Motoring Phrase Book & Dictionary* (Hadley Page Info) is a handy reference.

Equipment

All motorists must carry a full set of spare bulbs and fuses, a red breakdown triangle), a dayglo reflective jacket (which must be within reach within the passenger area – *not* in the boot!), a fire extinguisher and a first-aid kit. An 'F' nationality plate (*plaque de nationalité*) must be affixed to the rear of a French-registered car when motoring abroad. All new-format French registration plates incorporate the nationality letter. Similarly, drivers of foreign-registered cars in France must have the appropriate nationality plate affixed to the rear of their cars; you can be fined on the spot for not displaying one.

The wearing of seatbelts (*ceinture de sécurité*) is compulsory for both front-and rear-seat passengers. Even passengers can be fined for not wearing a seatbelt (see **Fines & Penalties** on page 195). If you have an accident and weren't wearing a seatbelt, your insurance company can refuse to pay a claim for personal injury.

Studded tyres may be used from 1st November to 31st March (although this can be extended in bad weather) on vehicles weighing under 3.5 tonnes. Vehicles fitted with studded tyres or snow chains are restricted to a maximum speed of 90kph (56mph) and a '90' disc must be affixed to the rear. You can be fined for not having chains in your car in winter in mountain areas, even when there's no snow!

Lights & Horns

It's illegal to drive on parking lights (*codes* or *veilleuses*) at any time, although many French drivers do so.

> An EU 'directive' is expected to require motorists to use dipped headlights (low beam) at all times but its implementation date has yet to be announced. This requirement, pioneered years ago by Sweden, has met with much resistance, particularly in southern Europe, where both drivers and legislators protest that they don't have the problem of the midnight sun; motorcyclists also argue that they already use headlights in daytime, a safety measure that will be invalidated if cars do the same.

It's also illegal to use full beam (*pleins phares*) when you're following a vehicle or when a vehicle is approaching from the opposite direction; failure to dip your lights can cost you a penalty point on your licence. You should also use dipped headlights (*codes*) in tunnels and when driving onto and off cross-Channel ferries.

You should flash your headlights only to warn other road users of your presence, although the French usually do so to mean "Get out of my way!" and occasionally to warn other motorists of police speed checks and road blocks, which is illegal and punishable by a fine. Hazard warning lights (*feux de détresse* or *warnings*) may be used to warn other drivers of an obstruction, e.g. an accident or a traffic jam and should be used when being towed. In the event of an accident or breakdown, hazard lights may be used in addition to the warning triangle, but not instead of it.

The use of horns (*klaxon*) in built-up areas is restricted to situations where it's necessary to avoid an accident; in any case, a horn should be used as a warning signal and not as an expression of frustration (Parisian drivers please note!).

Children

The driver is responsible for all passengers aged under 13, who should travel in the back of a car whenever possible. It's dangerous to fit a child seat (even a rear-facing seat) in the front of a car fitted with a passenger airbag; some airbags can be disabled for this purpose. Babies weighing under 9kg (20lb), i.e. aged under around nine months, must ride in a rear-facing baby seat. Infants weighing between 9 and 18kg (20 and 40lb), i.e. aged between around nine months and three or four years, must ride in a front-facing child seat, and children over 18kg and up to ten years of age must ride on a raised seat and wear a standard seatbelt.

Mobile (cellular) phones (*portable* or *mobile*) shouldn't be used while driving, even with a 'hands-free' system. As with the non-use of seatbelts, you can be fined on the spot.

Priority

The traditional French rule that you should give way to traffic coming from your right (*priorité à droite*) still applies in some cases, and it's important to know what these are. Failure to observe this rule is the cause of many accidents – even among French drivers – and punishable by fines and licence penalties. The rules are as follows:

♦ You must give way to the right:

– at junctions marked by a triangular sign with a red border showing a black X, including junctions normally traffic-light controlled when the lights are out of order or flashing amber (see below). Note that any junction can be denoted by this sign and not only a crossroads.
– at roundabouts (see below);
– in car parks; wherever you see the sign '*Vous n'avez pas la priorité*' ('You don't have priority').

♦ You don't need to give way to the right (but should still take care):

– at junctions marked by a triangular sign with a red border showing a black X and the words *Passage protégé* underneath;
– at junctions marked by a triangular sign with a red border showing a broad vertical arrow with a thinner horizontal line through it;
– where the main road is joined by a private road or exit or a dirt track.

◆ Diamond-shaped yellow signs with a white border, which are posted at regular intervals (e.g. every 5km) on some major roads, indicate that you have priority at all junctions. If this sign has a thick diagonal black line through it, however, it means that you no longer have automatic priority at junctions and must obey individual junction signs (see above).

If you're ever in doubt about who has the right of way, it's wise to give way (particularly to large trucks!), and you should give way to trams and to emergency (ambulance, fire, police) and public utility (electricity, gas, telephone, water) vehicles when their lights are flashing or sirens sounding (or they don't look as if they're going to stop!).

Roundabouts

Vehicles on a roundabout (*sens giratoire* or *rond-point*) usually have priority and not those entering it, who are faced with a 'Give Way' sign ('*Cédez le passage*' or '*Vous n'avez pas la priorité*'). If there are no such signs (as most notably on the *Etoile* in Paris), vehicles entering the roundabout have priority. British drivers should note that traffic flows anti-clockwise round roundabouts and not clockwise.

Traffic Lights

The sequence of French traffic lights (*feux*) is red, green, amber (yellow) and back to red. Amber means stop at the stop line; you may proceed only if the amber light appears after you've crossed the stop line or when stopping may cause an accident. Traffic lights are often suspended above the road, although most are on posts at the side, with smaller lights at eye level for motorists who are too close to see the main lights (an excellent idea).

In Paris and other cities there's a two-second delay after one set of lights changes to red before the other set changes to green, to allow time for those who don't care to stop at red lights or cannot tell the difference between red and green (a significant proportion of Parisian drivers). You can be fined heavily and penalised four licence points (see below) for driving through a red light.

An amber or green filter light, usually flashing and with a direction arrow, may be shown in addition to the main signal. This means that you may drive in the direction shown by the arrow, but must give priority to pedestrians and other traffic. Flashing amber lights are a warning to proceed with caution and are often used at junctions at night, in which case you should be very careful and observe the priority signs (see above). Occasionally you'll see a flashing red light, meaning stop or no entry, e.g. at a railway crossing.

Level Crossings

Most level crossings have automatic barriers; red lights start flashing and a bell rings a few seconds before the barriers come down, indicating that you must stop. At crossings without barriers, a similar light system may be in operation, and there may be the classic French sign, '*Un train peut en cacher un autre*' (One train may conceal another). However, there are many level crossings without more than a warning road-sign; some of these are on closed lines but others are on little used lines (e.g. where a line is largely unused although not permanently closed because it's seen

to have 'strategic' importance) where trains occasionally pass. It's always wise to treat all level crossings with extreme caution.

Road Markings

White lines mark the separation of traffic lanes. A solid single line means no overtaking in either direction. A solid line to the right of the centre line, i.e. on your side of the road, means that overtaking is prohibited in your direction.

You may overtake only when there's a single broken line in the middle of the road or double lines with a broken line on your side of the road. Note, however, that if the gaps between the lines are short and the lines long you may overtake only slow-moving vehicles.

No overtaking may also be shown by the international sign of two cars side by side (one red and one black). Processions, funeral corteges, horse riders and foot soldiers mustn't be overtaken at more than 30kph (18mph).

Don't drive in bus, taxi or cycle lanes (you can be fined for doing so) unless it's necessary to avoid a stationary vehicle or another obstruction. Bus lanes are identified by a continuous yellow line parallel to the kerb. Be sure to keep clear of tram lines and outside the restricted area, delineated by a line.

Stopping & Overtaking

If you want or need to stop on a main road, you must drive your car completely off the road, but beware of ditches and soft verges (*accotements non-stabilisés*).

The French are obsessive over-takers and will do so at the most dangerous moments, often cutting in sharply within inches of your front bumper. It's therefore wise to decelerate when being overtaken (it's illegal to accelerate).

☑ SURVIVAL TIP

You must indicate left before and while overtaking; on single-carriageway roads you must indicate right when moving back into your lane, but this isn't necessary on dual-carriageways or motorways.

Many French motorists seem to have an aversion to driving in the right-hand lane on a three-lane road, in effect reducing it to two lanes, although it's an offence not to move to the right-hand lane if it's safe to do so. It's illegal to overtake on an inside lane unless traffic is being channelled in a different direction, although this is a favourite manoeuvre among impatient French drivers (and motorcyclists).

Loads & Trailers

Cars (and particularly roof-racks) mustn't be overloaded, and the luggage weight shouldn't exceed that recommended in manufacturers' handbooks. Carrying bicycles on the back of a car is illegal if they obscure the rear lights or the number plate. The police make spot checks and fine offenders.

The maximum dimensions for caravans or trailers are 2.5m (8.2ft) wide and 11m (36ft) long, or a combined length of 18m (59ft) for car and caravan/trailer. No passengers may be carried in a moving caravan.

On narrow roads, drivers towing a caravan or trailer are (where possible) required to slow or pull in to the side of the road to allow faster vehicles to overtake (although they rarely do). The speed limits for a towing car depend on the weight of the trailer or caravan (see **Speed Limits** below).

A special licence is required for towing heavy trailers or caravans (see **Driving Licence** on page 184).

Goods Vehicles

Goods vehicles over 7.5 tonnes are banned from roads between 10.00 on Saturday and 22.00 on Sunday, and from 22.00 on the eve of a public holiday to 22.00 on the day of the holiday. In Paris, goods vehicles aren't permitted to travel out of the city between 16.00 and 19.00 on Fridays to allow car drivers to get a head start for *le week-end*.

ROAD SIGNS

Although France generally adheres to international-standard road signs, there are also many unique signs with instructions or information in French. Of particular importance (if you wish to avoid an accident) are the signs relating to 'priority to the right'. Autoroutes du Sud de la France publishes a booklet explaining motorway signs and symbols, which is available from motorway toll booths or from the ASF (🖥 www.asf.fr).

Speed Limits

The speed limits in force throughout France are shown in the table below.

Speed Limits	
Road	**Speed Limits**
Motorways	130/110kph (81/69mph)
Dual-carriageways	110/100kph (69/62mph)
Other roads	90/80kph (56/50mph)
Built-up areas/towns	50kph (31mph) or as signposted

◆ Speed limits are reduced in rain (*par temps de pluie*), when the second limit shown above applies. When visibility is less than 50m (162ft), e.g. in fog or heavy rain, speed limits are automatically reduced to 50kph on all roads.

◆ Speed limits in built-up areas (*agglomération*) such as small towns and villages often aren't posted. Unless a lower speed limit (such as 40 or 45kph) is posted, the limit is 50kph and starts with the town or village's name sign, which usually has black letters on a white background with a red border. The end of the speed limit is indicated by the town's sign with a diagonal red line through it. A village sign with white letters on a dark blue background doesn't indicate a speed restriction unless otherwise indicated.

◆ Speed limits also apply to cars towing a trailer or caravan, provided the trailer's weight doesn't exceed that of the car. If the trailer's weight exceeds that of the car by less than 30 per cent, you're limited to 65kph (39mph); if the trailer is over 30 per cent heavier than the car, you mustn't exceed 45kph (28mph). A plate showing the permitted maximum speed must be displayed at the rear of the trailer. Cars towing trailers with restricted speeds aren't permitted to use the left lane of a three-lane motorway.

◆ Vehicles fitted with studded tyres or snow chains are restricted to 90kph (56mph)

and a '90' plate must be displayed at the rear.

◆ For two years after passing your driving test in France, you're designated a 'young' driver (*jeune conducteur*), irrespective of your age, and must display a *disque réglementaire*, consisting of a red capital letter A on a white background, on the back of any car being driven. During this period you mustn't exceed 80kph (50mph) on roads where the limit is normally 90kph, 100kph (62mph) on roads with a 110kph limit, or 110kph (69mph) on motorways with a 130kph limit. Visitors who have held a licence for less than two years are also subject to these speed restrictions, but aren't required to display a disc.

◆ There's a minimum speed of 80kph (50mph) on motorways in the outside (overtaking) lane during daylight, in dry weather on level surfaces and in good visibility, i.e. perfect conditions.

◆ The word *rappel* (reminder) is often displayed beneath speed restriction signs to remind motorists that the limit is still in force (although it's sometimes seen where a new limit is introduced!).

◆ Sleeping policemen (*ralentisseur* or *dos d'âne*) are common on many major and minor roads and are often accompanied by a 30kph (18mph) sign; if you don't slow down, you risk damaging your vehicle!

Speed limits are enforced by motorcycle traffic police and the use of radar speed checks is also widespread (including on motorways). The number has increased rapidly in recent years and new rules coming into effect in 2012 mean that there will no longer be warning signs of their presence just before each installation; instead there will be a general warning covering an unspecified length of road and there will also be more signs indicating to motorists the speed at which they're going. (Until this law comes into effect, you can find camera locations via 🖥 www.controleradar.org). Police also use concealed cameras to snap speeding motorists. French drivers often flash their headlights to warn other motorists of speed checks, although this is illegal, as are radar-detection devices (see **Fines & Penalties** below).

If your car has a GPS system, you can be 'caught' speeding by a Big Brother-style satellite surveillance system called 'Lavia' (short for *Limitation s'adaptant à la vitesse autorisée*). Note also that motorway toll tickets are timed and you can be convicted of speeding if you complete a section of motorway in less than a certain time!

French drivers routinely speed everywhere, generally at least 20kph above the speed limit and often far more: a recent motoring magazine survey (in the Var) found that the average speed on motorways was 160kph (100mph), i.e. 30kph (18mph) over the limit; and on major roads107kph (67mph) or 17kph (11mph) too fast!

Drivers rarely slow down for villages and are often irritated by motorists who do so. Usually you're 'allowed' to be 10 per cent above the limit, so if you're clocked at 55kph in a 50kph zone, or 99kph in an 90kph zone, you won't normally be penalised – but don't bank on it! See **Fines & Penalties** below.

TRAFFIC POLICE

In France, the *gendarmerie nationale*, which is actually a branch of the army, is responsible for road patrols outside towns and cities, and *gendarmes* use both cars and motorcycles. In towns and cities, it's the *police nationale*.

The police can stop motorists and ask for identification and car papers at any time (and also check your tyres, lights, etc.). This is known as a *contrôle*, and you'll routinely be asked for your driving licence (French if held), vehicle registration document (*carte grise*) and insurance certificate. It's wise to make a copy of all these documents and keep the originals on your person (you should not leave them in the car). Police may accept copies, provided you present the originals at a *gendarmerie* within five days; if you don't have even copies of the required documents, you'll be fined (see **Fines & Penalties** below).

If a vehicle isn't registered in your name, you'll also need a letter of authorisation from the owner. If you're driving a hired foreign-registered vehicle, you should ask the hire company for a 'hired/leased vehicle certificate'.

You're entitled to ask the name and particulars of any policeman or *gendarme* who stops you, but it's probably better to do so after you've found out what you've been stopped for!

Fines & Penalties

Fines can be imposed for a range of traffic offences. For offences not involving third parties (e.g. exceeding the speed limit or failing to stop at a *Stop* sign), police can demand an on-the-spot fine. On-the-spot fines are commonly applied to non-resident foreigners, whose vehicles are usually impounded if they're unable to pay. (French police may take you to a bank to allow you to withdraw cash!) It's well known that French traffic police target foreigners, although it's naturally officially denied. (It certainly looks suspicious when police officers produce pre-written tickets in English!)

Residents who are unable to pay fines on the spot are given 30 days to pay and fines are automatically increased (significantly) if they aren't paid on time, the penalties starting 45 days after the fine was imposed. A reduction is granted to residents who pay a fine on the spot or within 15 days. You can opt for your case to go to court rather than pay a fixed penalty, in which case you must usually pay a deposit (*amende forfaitaire*). The papers are sent to a police court (*tribunal de police*), where the case is dealt with in your absence. The case can be dismissed (although extremely rare) or the fine confirmed or increased. You receive the verdict in the form of an *ordonnance pénale* and have 30 days to appeal against the judgement, should you wish to do so. If you receive a fine by post (e.g. having been caught speeding by a camera), you must pay it within seven days or the fine is increased.

From 2013 all drivers are subject to the fines imposed by the EU country they're in, so ending an anomaly that allowed many offenders to avoid fines altogether or pay them at the rates applying where the vehicle was registered, which may have been much lower. This rule has been introduced following a report showing that foreigners are (even) more likely to break the law than residents – typically foreigners in any EU country exceed speed limits three times more often.

FRENCH ROADS

France has a good road system that includes everything from motorways (*autoroute*) to forest dirt tracks (*route forestière*). French motorways are excellent and most other main roads are also very good, although roads are generally poorer in areas with low traffic density (i.e. most of rural France) and the economic downturn has led to less frequent and thorough maintenance. Roads are classified as follows and are identified by their prefix and colour-coded markers:

Motorways

France boasts one of Europe's best motorway (*autoroute*) networks, totalling over 9,500km (some 6,000mi). The network is being continually expanded (2005 saw the completion of a continuous motorway route from Calais to Spain via Bordeaux; more recently, that of the A89 from Bordeaux to Switzerland, barring a short section in Dordogne; the A26/A31/A6/A7/A8 continuous *autoroute* Calais-Dijon-Lyon border to Italy; and the motorway box around Paris), therefore you shouldn't use a motoring atlas that's more than a year old. Good guides to French motorways and their services are *Bonne Route!* by Anna Fitter (Anthony Nelson) and Michelin's *autoroute* guide,

Because of the toll system (see below), driving on motorways is considered a luxury by many French people and consequently they have the lowest traffic density of any European motorways and are France's safest roads (although that isn't saying a great deal). Your

Categories of Road		
Prefix	**Signs**	**Classification**
A (*autoroute*)	Blue	Motorways – usually toll roads (*autoroute à péage*); usually marked red/yellow on maps
E (*route européenne*)	Green	European motorways or motorway-standard trunk roads traversing a number of countries, e.g. the *Autoroute de l'Est* (A4) is also the E25
N (*route nationale*)	Red	National trunk roads (financed by the central or regional government); usually shown in red
D (*route départementale*)	Yellow	Departmental roads (funded by departments); marked in yellow or white on maps
C (*route communale*)	White	Minor roads (funded by communes); marked in white on most maps
R (*route rurale*)	White	Minor roads in rural areas; marked in white on most maps
RF (*route forestière*)	Green	Forest tracks; shown only on local maps

risk of dying on a motorway – with the notable exception of the *Périphérique* (see below) – is around four times lower than on any other road.

Some motorways have colourful names, such as *Autoroute du Soleil* (A6/A7), *Autoroute l'Océane* (A11) and *Autoroute des Deux Mers* (A61). Signs on motorways inform you about interesting local sights and features, and regional motorway maps are distributed free by operators. There's also an excellent system of electronic information boards on overhead gantries, where various messages, including safety warnings and the time are displayed.

Tolls

Most motorways are toll roads (*à péage*), which have long been among the most expensive in Europe (more so now that half the motorways in southern France have been part-privatised). Motorway travel costs (2011) an average of €1 for 10mi/16km (€0.0625 per kilometre) for a car, e.g. €79.80 (about £65) from Calais to Marseille. There are five toll categories on most motorways, e.g. motorhomes and cars towing trailers or caravans are charged more than cars alone. Fees aren't standardised throughout the country and vary with the age of the motorway and the services provided. A new system of tolls has been introduced in some areas with higher tolls during peak periods. There are no tolls on the sections of motorways around cities. An *Autoroute Tarifs* leaflet and other traffic information is available from the Association des Sociétés Françaises d'Autoroutes (☎ 08 92 68 10 77, 🖳 www.autoroutes.fr). Tolls are often increased annually, usually in April.

If you use motorways regularly, it's worth paying via the Liber-T system, whereby you have a remote control 'box' fitted (attached to your windscreen just behind the rear-view mirror) which records your motorway use. This enables you to drive through the *Télépéage* lane without even having to wind down your window, tolls being deducted automatically from your bank account. You pay an annual subscription depending on your usage plus a deposit of around €30, refundable when you return the control box (both added to your first bill). If you use the motorway on your way to and from work you can also benefit from a reduction of up to 35 per cent in toll charges. For frequent users, the €29 annual subscription offers discounts of 20 per cent on journeys under 30km, 15 per cent for journeys of 30-60km and 10 per cent on those of 60km or over.

Télépéage badges can be obtained from offices of your local motorway company (Société d'Autoroutes – listed under *Autoroutes* in the *Yellow Pages*), which are usually situated near toll stations. You need to provide your bank details, proof of address and, to qualify for the work-use discount, confirmation from your employer that you drive to and from work.

UK residents can register for the Liber-T system online (🖳 www.saneftolling.co.uk) for a fee of €39.14 (which includes a €20 refundable deposit for the transponder). You receive a monthly invoice for toll fees (plus a €5 service charge), which is paid by direct debit.

Tolls are also levied for the use of major tunnels, e.g. Mont Blanc (Chamonix to Entrèves, Italy, 11.6km/7.2mi), Fréjus (Modane to Bardonecchia, Italy, 12.8km/8mi) and Bielsa (Aragnouet to Bielsa, Spain, 3km/1.86mi), and bridges, e.g. the Normandie, Saint-Nazaire, Tancarville and new Millau Viaduct.

Rest Areas & Service Stations

Most motorways (and *routes nationales* – see below) have rest areas (*aire de repos* or simply aire) every 10 to 20km (6 to 12mi) with toilets, drinking water and picnic tables. Toilets and telephones are also provided at motorway toll booths.

Twenty-four hour service areas (aire de service) are provided every 30 to 50km (19 to 31mi), with petrol stations, vending machines, shops, a café or self-service restaurant, and possibly an à la carte restaurant. Service areas cater for babies, young children, the elderly and the disabled, and some have motels and provide tourist information services. Service stations may also have facilities for minor car repairs.

Petrol prices on motorways are the highest in France and it's much cheaper to fill up at supermarkets, although garages within 10km (6mi) of a motorway are allowed to advertise their prices on the motorway, which has helped to bring down motorway prices in some areas.

Breakdown Services

If you break down on a motorway, you must park your car on the hard shoulder (bande d'arrêt d'urgence) and place an emergency triangle 30m (100ft) behind it. Free emergency telephones (poste d'urgence) are mounted on orange posts every 2km (1.25mi) on motorways and you may walk along the hard shoulder to the nearest phone, indicated by arrows. Each telephone is numbered and directly connected to the motorway security centre (Centre de Sécurité). Say whether you've broken down (tombé en panne) or have had an accident (accidenté), and give the number of your telephone and the location of your car in relation to it, i.e. before (avant) or after (après) the emergency telephone. A breakdown truck (dépanneuse) or first-aid help (service de secours) will be sent, as required. A multi-language service is provided, in English, German, Italian and Spanish on some motorways, e.g. the A7 between Lyon and Marseille.

Minor repairs of up to around half an hour are usually done on the spot. For anything more serious you'll need to be towed to a garage.

There are fixed charges for emergency repairs and towing, e.g. Monday-Friday 08.00-18.00, €114.50 for requesting a breakdown service and around €100 for repairing a vehicle on the spot. For towing it to be repaired at a

motorway aire, the breakdown company's own garage or the driver's choice of destination up to 5km (3mi) beyond the next motorway exit, the same price (€114.50) for vehicles weighing les than 1.8 tonnes or €141.50 for those weighing between 1.8 and 3.5 tonnes. At all other times, on-the-spot repairs cost €169.50 for all vehicles, while the other services cost, respectively, €171.75 and €212.50. All prices include 30 minutes' repair work; if the repair takes longer or towing is over 5km from a motorway exit, there are extra charges.

If you're unable to continue your journey, breakdown companies must provide free transport to take you and your passengers off the motorway and provide assistance in finding accommodation and alternative transport. See also **Breakdown Insurance** on page 189.

Other Roads

Unlike French motorways, main trunk roads (the former route nationale) are jammed by drivers (including those of heavy goods vehicles) who are reluctant to pay or cannot afford the high motorway tolls. If you must get from A to B in the shortest possible time, there's no alternative to the motorway. However, if you aren't in too much of a hurry,

want to save money and wish to see something of France, you should avoid motorways. Trunk and other secondary roads are often straight and many are dual-carriageways, on which you can usually make good time at (legal) speeds of between 90 and 110kph (56 to 68mph). On the other hand, trunk roads pass through towns and villages, where the limit is reduced to 50kph (30mph), which can make for slow progress. However, each year sees the construction of new bypasses to help speed the flow, particularly on much-trafficked routes.

In general, signposting is good, even in the most remote rural areas. However, only large towns or cities are usually signposted as you approach a ring road system, therefore you should plan your journey accordingly and make a note of the major destinations along your route.

> **⚠ Caution**
>
> Signposts indicating straight ahead usually point at or across the intended road, i.e. to the left or right, rather than vertically as in most other countries.

In towns, only the town centre (*centre ville*) and 'all directions' (*toutes directions*) may be signposted. If you don't want the town centre, simply follow the *toutes directions* or 'other directions' (*autres directions*) signs until you see a sign for where you want to go.

On mountain roads, driving conditions can be treacherous or even prohibitive, and studded tyres or chains may be obligatory. Many mountain passes are closed in winter (check with a French motoring organisation).

Paris

Paris is a beautiful city but should be avoided at all cost when driving, especially if you need to park there, which is usually difficult. If you cannot avoid driving in Paris, at least give the *Place Charles de Gaulle/Étoile* (at the top of the *Champs-Elysées*) a wide berth. One of the worst free-for-alls in the whole of Europe, it's a vast roundabout where 12 roads converge, all with (theoretical) *priorité à droite*. Because of the impossibility of apportioning blame in this

circus, if you have an accident, responsibility is automatically shared equally between the drivers concerned, irrespective of who had right of way.

The *Place de la Concorde* is, if anything, even worse, and a road to avoid unless you have a death-wish is the *Boulevard périphérique* (usually referred to simply as the *Périphérique*), an eight-lane race track around the city centre on which there's an average of one fatal accident a day! (There's also an inner ring road, which is slower but safer.)

Information

In June each year, the French Ministry of Transport issues a 'wily bison' map (*Carte de Bison Futé*) showing areas likely to suffer congestion and providing information about alternative routes (*itinéraire bis*), indicated by yellow or green signs with the word *Bis*. The map is available free from petrol stations and tourist offices in France and from French Government Tourist Offices abroad, as well as via the internet (🖳 www.bison-fute.equipement. gouv.fr). There are around 90 information rest areas throughout France, indicated by a black '*i*' and an *Information Bison Futé* sign. Green-arrowed holiday routes (*flèches vertes*) avoiding large towns and cities are also recommended.

Colour-coded traffic days and traffic jams (*orange* for bad, *rouge* for very bad and *noir* for 'stay at home') are announced via radio and television.

Up-to-date information about roads can be obtained by phoning the information line of the Centres Régionaux d'Information et de Coordination Routières (☎ 08 06 02 20 22), by tuning in to *Autoroute Info* (on 107.7FM) or via the internet, e.g. www.info-autoroute.com. General information about motorways, tolls and driving in France can be obtained from French Government Tourist Offices abroad (see page 286). Disabled travellers can contact the Ministère de l'Equipement, des Transports et du Logement, Direction des Routes, Service du Contrôle des Autoroutes (☎ 01 40 81 21 22).

FRENCH DRIVERS

France has some of the most dangerous drivers (*chauffard*) in Europe, who seem to use their brakes only when their horns or headlights don't work. Drivers of foreign-registered vehicles should be aware that many French drivers become apoplectic when overtaken by them. Most French people's personalities (yes, women's also!) change the moment they get behind the wheel of a car, when even the gentlest person can become an impatient, intolerant and even aggressive maniac, with an unshakeable conviction in their immortality.

The French themselves, however, have a quite different opinion of their driving: according to a survey by the Association Française de Prévention des Comportements au Volant, no fewer than 98 per cent consider themselves to be 'courteous' and 'responsible' – a sad case of self-delusion.

The French revere racing drivers (Alain Prost et al) and the majority of drivers are assailed by an uncontrollable urge to drive everywhere at maximum speed (women – young and old – often drive faster than men). To a French person, the racing line on a bend (which usually means driving on the wrong side of the road!) is *de rigueur* and overtaking is an obligation; me first (*moi d'abord*) is the French driver's motto.

Even when not overtaking or cutting corners, the French have an unnerving tendency to wander across the centre line, threatening a head-on collision with anything coming in the opposite direction.

When following another vehicle (and even when they have no intention of overtaking it), French drivers sit a few metres (or even centimetres) from its rear bumper trying to push it along irrespective of traffic density, road and weather conditions or the prevailing speed limit. They're among Europe's worst tailgaters, despite a law forbidding driving within two seconds of the car in front (referred to as the *distance de sécurité* and sometimes shown on motorways by arrows marked on the road surface).

Beware of lorries and buses on narrow roads, as lorry drivers believe they have a divine right to three-quarters of the road and expect you to pull over. Don't, however, pull over too far, as many rural roads have soft verges and ditches.

What makes driving in France even more hazardous is that for many months of the year French roads are jammed with assorted foreigners, including many (such as the British) who don't even know which side of the road to drive on, and whose driving habits vary from exemplary to suicidal.

Most French drivers have little respect for traffic rules, particularly anything to do with parking (in Paris, a car is a device used to create parking spaces). French drivers wear their dents with pride and there are many (many) dented cars in France – particularly in Paris (a '75' registration number acts as a warning to other motorists to keep well clear).

However, don't be too discouraged by the road hogs and tailgaters. Driving in France can be a pleasant experience (Paris excepted), particularly when using secondary country roads that are almost traffic-free most of the time.

If you come from a country where traffic drives on the left, rest assured that most people quickly get used to driving on the 'wrong' side of the road. Just take it easy at first, particularly at junctions, and bear in mind that there are other foreigners around just as confused as you are!

MOTORCYCLES

The French are keen motorcyclists and there are more bikers per head of population in France than in any other European country, although there's only one French motorbike manufacturer: Voxan, whose factory is at Issoire in Puy-de-Dôme (💻 www.voxan. com). Perhaps for this reason, the French

aren't generally prejudiced against bikers, as motorists are in many other countries.

Nevertheless, motorcycling is a dangerous pursuit: over 20 per cent of road casualties are motorcyclists and, over the same distance, a motorcyclist is 14 times more likely to have an accident than a car driver (although one has to wonder whether this is due to the intrinsic dangers of motorcycle riding or to the way most motorcyclists flout the rules of the road...).

Some rules apply to all motorcycles (collectively known as *deux-roues*), while others apply to certain types of motorcycle only. Speed limits for all motorcycles are the same as for cars – although you wouldn't think so. Motorcycles above 50cc are permitted to use motorways (tolls are lower than for cars, although the cost of a long journey can still be prohibitive). Dipped headlamps must be used at all times by riders of motorcycles over 125cc (see also below).

☑ SURVIVAL TIP

Third-party insurance is necessary for bikes, as well as passenger insurance. All bikes must also be registered (see page 181), have registration plates and carry a nationality sticker (*plaque de nationalité*). Approved crash helmets must be worn by all motorcycle riders and passengers.

When parking a bike in a city, lock it securely and if possible chain it to an immovable object. Take extra care when parking in a public place overnight, particularly in Paris, where bike theft is rife.

Mopeds

From the age of 14, children can ride a moped (variously known as a *cyclomoteur*, *scooter*, *vélomoteur* or *Mobylette*, the last being a trade name), with an engine capacity below 50cc and capable of a maximum speed of 45kph (28mph) – despite the contortions of riders attempting to eke an extra kph or two from their machines.

Mopeds must be registered and riders without a full licence must take a test (*brevet de sécurité routière/BSR*) consisting of a theory paper (*attestation scolaire de sécurité routière/ ASSR1*), taken at school, and five hours of practical training, four and a half of which must be on public roads, with a driving school (at a cost of around €100). Third-party insurance is necessary, and a metal tab with the owner's name (*plaque de nom*) must be attached to the handlebars.

Mopeds aren't permitted on motorways, and riders must use cycle paths where provided. Two-stroke petrol (*mélange deuxtemps*) is available at most petrol stations.

Mopeds can be lethal in the wrong hands (most teenagers have as much road sense as hedgehogs and rabbits) and many are killed each year. If you have a child with a moped, it's important to impress upon him the need to take care (particularly in winter) and not take unnecessary risks, e.g. always observe traffic signs and signal before making manoeuvres.

Other Motorbikes

Sixteen-year-olds can ride a motorcycle of up to 125cc (officially known as a *moto légère*), for which they require an A1 licence. The requisite theory test, the *ASSR2*, can be taken at school. Eighteen-year-olds can begin 'progressive training' (*formation progressive*) for a full motorcycle (*motocyclette* or *moto*) licence (*A*), although they're limited to bikes below 34 horsepower until they reach the age of 21.

A car licence (*B*) entitles you to ride a motorcycle of up to 125cc, provided you've been driving for at least two years (although you must retake the theory exam if you've held a licence for over five years without riding a motorcycle). However, it's recommended that you take a course of riding lessons with a *moto école*, which costs around €300. If you aren't at school, you can take an *attestation de sécurité routière* (*ASR*), which takes the place of the *ASSR1* and 2, with an adult education provider such as GRETA.

ACCIDENTS

If you're unfortunate enough to be involved in a car accident (*accident d'auto*), you must do the following in addition to the standard procedures that apply in all countries:

1. Stop immediately. Switch on your hazard warning lights and place a warning triangle

at the edge of the road 30m (100ft) behind your car, ensuring that it can be seen from at least 100m (325ft).

2. If anyone is injured, immediately call the fire service (*sapeurs-pompiers*) by dialling 18. Emergency phones (on orange pillars with '*SOS*' written on them) are positioned at 2km (1.2mi) intervals on motorways and every 4km (2.5mi) on other roads. To use them press and release the button marked '*pour demander au secours*' ('to summon help') and speak into the metal grille. Give the number of the telephone and as many other details as possible. The mobile (cellular) phone emergency number is 112.

   If you take an injured person to hospital yourself and he dies in your car, you could be sued for a great deal of money! If there are no injuries and if damage to vehicles or property isn't serious, it's unnecessary to call the police, unless another driver has obviously been drinking or appears incapable of driving. You must never leave the scene of an accident, however minor, before completing this procedure, as it's a serious offence.

3. If either you or the other driver(s) involved decides to call the police, don't move your vehicle or allow other vehicles to be moved unless necessary to unblock the road.

4. In the case of an accident involving two or more vehicles, it's standard practice for drivers to complete an accident report form (*constat amiable*) provided by insurance companies (keep one in your car). As the name implies, this is an 'amicable statement', where drivers agree (more or less) on what happened. It isn't obligatory to complete a *constat*, although an insurance claim made out in any other form can take longer to process. If your French isn't good, you may complete a *constat* in another language. At the bottom of the form there are a number of statements describing the circumstances of the accident. You should tick the boxes that apply, add up the number of ticks and enter the number in the box at the bottom. This prevents the form from being altered later.

Drivers must sign each other's forms. Always check exactly what the other driver has written before signing. It's particularly important to check the information entered on forms by other drivers against official documents, e.g. driving licence, car registration document and insurance certificate. Don't sign a statement, particularly one written in French, unless you're certain you understand and agree with every word. In the event of a dispute, a local bailiff (*huissier de justice*) should be called to prepare an independent report (*constat d'huissier*). If the police attend the scene of an accident, they'll also make their own report.

France has a national fund, the Fonds de Garantie Automobile (FGA, 🖳 www.fga.fr – the 'English version' of the site offers only a translation of the compensation law) that pays compensation to those injured and vehicles damaged by hit-and-run drivers. However, you can claim for damage to your vehicle only if the person responsible can be identified and is uninsured or insolvent. To make a claim, those in the southeast of France should contact the Marseille office at 39 boulevard Vincent Delpuech, 13255 Marseille Cedex 06 (☎ 04 91 83 27 27); those in all other parts of France should contact the Paris office at 64 rue de France, 94682 Vincennes Cedex (☎ 01 43 98 77 00).

⚠ Caution

If you witness an accident or its aftermath, it's a criminal offence not to try to assist anyone who's injured or in danger, at least by calling for help, and you can be fined up to €75,000 and imprisoned for up to five years for failing to do so.

Accident prevention is promoted by Prévention Routière (🖳 www.preventionroutiere. asso.fr). Other useful sites are those of the Fondation Anne-Cellier Contre l'Insécurité Routière (🖳 www.fondation-annecellier.org) and the Ligue Contre la Violence Routière (🖳 www. violenceroutiere.org).

DRINKING & DRIVING

Alcohol is reckoned to be a major factor in some 40 per cent of France's road 'accidents', i.e. over 2,000 deaths per year. The permitted blood alcohol concentration is 50mg of alcohol per 100ml of blood, but the amount you can drink and remain below the limit depends on whether you regularly imbibe, and your sex and weight. An 'average' man can generally drink a maximum of two small glasses of wine, two small glasses of beer or two 4cl measures of spirits; for most women the limits are even lower. Note that your alcohol level rises considerably when you drink on an empty stomach (which is why the French eat lots of bread!). The safest thing to do is not to drink at all when driving.

Random breath tests (*Alcooltest*) are carried out by the police, and motorists who are involved in accidents or who infringe motoring regulations are routinely tested for alcohol and drugs. If you're found to have over 25mg of alcohol per 100ml of air in your lungs, you're obliged to take a blood test.

Penalties usually depend on the level of alcohol in your blood and whether you're involved in an accident.

If you have an accident while under the influence of alcohol, your car and health insurance could be nullified. This means that you must pay your own and any third party's car repairs, medical expenses and other damages. Your car insurance premium will also be increased by up to 150 per cent.

CAR THEFT

Car theft is rampant in France, which has one of the highest rates of vehicle theft – and car burning! – in Europe (the theft of contents or accessories from motor vehicles is even more commonplace). If you drive anything other than a worthless heap, you should have theft insurance that includes your personal effects (see **Car Insurance** on page 186). It's particularly important to protect your car if you own a model that's desirable to car thieves, e.g. most new sports and executive cars, which are often stolen to order by professional crooks. In Provence, and on the Côte d'Azur in particular, stolen cars often find their way to Africa and may already be on a ferry by the time owners report them stolen.

It's wise to have your car fitted with an alarm, an ignition disabling system or other anti-theft device, plus a visible deterrent, such as a steering or gear lock.

When leaving your car unattended, store any valuables (including clothes) in the boot or out of sight. **Never** leave the key in your car, even when you're paying for petrol, and never leave your original car documents in your car. If possible, avoid parking in long-term car parks. Foreign-registered cars, particularly camper vans and motorhomes, are popular targets, especially when parked in ports. When parking overnight or when it's dark, parking in a well-lit area may deter thieves. If your car is stolen or anything is stolen from it, report it immediately to the police in the area where it was stolen. You can report by telephone but must go to

Champs-Élysées, Paris

the station to complete a statement. Report a theft to your insurance company as soon as possible.

Highway Piracy

Highway piracy (*les pirates de la route*) is an increasing problem in some areas, where foreign drivers are often targets. Gangs deliberately bump or ram cars to make drivers stop, usually late at night when there's little traffic about. A driver may also pose as a plain clothes policeman and try to get you to stop by flashing a fake badge or setting up a bogus road block. In the worst cases, thieves take not just the car and its contents, but even the clothes the victims are wearing. Travelling late at night can be hazardous and should be avoided if possible. See also **Crime** on page 346.

PARKING

Parking in most towns and cities (Paris excepted) isn't such a problem or as expensive as in many other European countries. However, parking is usually restricted in cities and towns and prohibited altogether in certain areas. Parking regulations may vary with the area of a city, the time of day, the day of the week, and whether the date is odd or even (seriously!).

In many towns, parking is permitted on the side of a street with odd-numbered houses for the first half of the month and on the 'even'

side for the second half of the month. This is called *stationnement alterné semi-mensuel* and is shown by a sign. (Note that the French for 'parking' is *stationnement*; *parking* means 'car park'.)

Parking may also alternate weekly or daily; parking on alternate days is indicated by a sign stating '*Côté du Stationnement – Jours Pairs*' (even) or '*Jours Impairs*' (odd). In Paris, signs may indicate that parking is forbidden on one side of the street at certain times, e.g. for street cleaning.

On-street parking is forbidden in many streets in the centre of Paris and other cities. Parking is forbidden in Paris on main access routes, designated as red routes (*axe rouge*). '*Stationnement interdit*' means parking is forbidden and may be accompanied by the sign of a 'P' with a line through it.

No parking may also be indicated by a '*Stationnement gênant*' sign with a picture of a lorry towing away a vehicle (if you park in a taxi rank or in front of a private garage, you're likely to find your car towed away or your tyres slashed!) or by yellow kerb markings. It's forbidden to park in front of a fire hydrant. In Paris, it's illegal to leave a car in the same spot on a public road for more than 24 hours. Parking a caravan on roads is forbidden at any time in Paris and some other towns and cities, and overnight parking in a lay-by isn't permitted anywhere in France, although you can stop for a rest if you're falling asleep at the wheel. On roads outside town limits, you must pull off the road to stop.

Blue Zones

In many cities and towns there are 'blue zones' (*zone bleue*), indicated by blue street markings. Here you can park free for one hour between 09.00 and 12.00 and from 14.00 or 14.30 until 19.00 from Mondays to Saturdays, with no limit outside these hours or on Sundays and public holidays. Parking isn't restricted between 12.00 and 14.00, meaning you can park free from 11.00 until 14.00 or from 12.00 until 15.00.

To park in a blue zone you must display a parking disc (*disque de contrôle/stationnement*) in your windscreen, which are available free or for a small fee from garages, travel agencies, motoring organisations, tourist offices, police stations, tobacconist and some shops. If you overstay your free time, you can be fined.

Ticket Machines

In most French cities, parking meters have been replaced by ticket machines (*horodateurs*). If a parking sign has the word '*Horodateur*' beneath it or there's a '*Stationnement payant*' sign, perhaps with '*Payant*' also marked on the road, it means that you must obtain a ticket from a nearby machine.

Parking must usually be paid for between 09.00 and 19.00, although it's free from 12.00 to 14.00 (even traffic wardens stop for lunch). The cost averages around €1 per hour (more at railway stations) and typically increases per half-hour on a sliding scale often up to a maximum of two hours. Machines usually accept all coins from 5 cents to €2. In some towns the first 30 minutes is free. Buy a ticket for the period required and place it behind your windscreen where it can be seen by a warden.

Car Parks

There are car parks (*parking*) in cities and towns, where parking rates vary considerably. Car parks in central Paris are more expensive. Long-term parking, e.g. at railway stations, is available in most towns for around €10 for the first 24 hours with a reducing scale thereafter. Monthly tickets can be purchased at a discount if you park frequently.

On entering most car parks, you take a ticket from machine, usually by pressing a button. You must pay before collecting your car, either at a cash desk (*caisse*) or in a machine – you cannot pay at the exit. After paying, you usually have around 15 minutes to find the exit, where you insert your ticket in a machine before the barrier.

Discounts

In most cities, local residents pay reduced parking fees by obtaining a permit from the town hall. This must be affixed to the right-hand side of your windscreen. Subscription cards for ticket machines are also available for residents and commuters. Disabled motorists are provided with free or reserved parking in most towns, shopping centres and at airports, but they must display an official disabled motorist's badge (*macaron*) inside their windscreen. Apply with your *carte d'invalidité* to the

Commission d'Education Spécialisée (CDES) if you're aged under 20 or the Commission Technique d'Orientation et de Reclassement Professionnel (COTOREP) if you're over 20. Disabled drivers can also obtain a European parking card (*carte européenne de stationnement*) entitling them to disabled parking privileges throughout Europe.

Fines

Fines for illegal parking are based on the severity of the offence, and increase if they aren't paid within three months. If your car is given a ticket (*papillon*) and isn't moved within an hour, it will be given a second ticket and after two hours a wheel clamp may be fitted or it can be towed way.

Paris has six car pounds (*fourrière*), where in addition to a parking fine you must pay a fee to release your car from a pound (or to have a clamp removed), plus a daily storage charge. However, if you don't collect your car within a certain period (which varies between 10 and 45 days), it may be sold.

Paris

Parking in Paris for anyone other than a Parisian is usually a nightmare (Parisians are world champions at the art of creative parking). Car parks in Paris are expensive and are often full. When visiting Paris, it's advisable use public transport, which is cheap, efficient, less dangerous and less stressful (see **Chapter 10**).

FUEL

Leaded petrol is no longer available and unleaded petrol (*sans plomb*) is available in two grades: 95 octane and 98 octane. Diesel fuel is called *diesel* (pronounced 'dee-ezel') or *gazole* or *gasoil* (both pronounced 'gazwal') and is available at all service stations. An increasing number of petrol stations (notably on *autoroutes*) also supply fuel containing biofuel. To help prevent errors, petrol pumps and hoses are colour coded; green for unleaded and black for diesel.

Liquid petroleum gas (LPG) is also available and there are around 1,800 petrol stations offering LPG (*GPL* or *Gépel*), particularly on motorways (a free map is available from petrol stations).

The cost of fuel has risen dramatically in recent years, although prices vary considerably depending on the area, town and petrol station. The cheapest source is usually hyper/supermarkets, while rural petrol stations and those on *autoroutes* are the most expensive. The costs per litre in mid-2011 were around €1.13 (diesel), €1.20 (ordinary unleaded) and €1.25 (premium unleaded). In some places a premium grade of diesel is also available, usually costing around €0.20 more than regular. LPG, which is the only fuel that has fallen in price recently, costs around €0.70 per litre.

> The general word for fuel is *carburant* and petrol is *essence*; *fuel* (or *fioul*) is heating oil, and *pétrole* is paraffin or oil (the black stuff that comes out of the ground).

To help tourists and travellers on motorways find inexpensive petrol, petrol stations within 10km (6mi) of a motorway are allowed to advertise their prices on the motorway, and a leaflet called *La Carte de l'Essence Moins Chère*, showing supermarkets a short distance from main routes, is available from French Government Tourist Offices.

Self-service petrol stations (*libre service*) are common and include most motorway and supermarket stations. Manned petrol stations are more common in small towns and villages. To ask for a fill-up, say '*le plein s'il vous plaît*'. Service may include cleaning your windscreen and checking oil and tyre pressures; tips aren't expected, although they won't be refused! When paying at self-service petrol stations, simply tell the cashier your pump number. Debit cards and major credit cards are accepted by most petrol stations.

There are 24-hour petrol stations on motorways, and some other stations have automatic pumps that accept debit or credit cards, which can be used when the station is open (to save queuing) or closed. Insert your card (you may need to lift a flap – *Soulevez le volet*) and you'll receive the following instructions, sometimes on an LCD display, sometimes by recorded message. (Some automatic pumps have instructions in English as well as French.)

♦ *Sélectionnez votre carburant*: 'Choose your fuel.' Press the button corresponding to the type of fuel you require.

♦ *Validez ou choix autre carburant*: 'Confirm or choose other fuel.' Press the button marked '*Val*' or change your choice of fuel.

♦ *Composez votre code confidentiel et validez*: 'Enter your PIN and confirm.' Enter the four-digit PIN for your card and press '*Val*'.

♦ *Impression ticket?*: 'Do you want a receipt?' Press '*Oui*' or '*Non*'.

♦ *Servez-vous jusqu'à €...*: 'Serve yourself to a maximum value of €...' Remove the nozzle and fill up without exceeding the value indicated. Replace the nozzle and your card will be returned to you. If you've requested a receipt, it will be printed automatically; you don't need to reinsert your card.

You may see *Veuillez patienter* between instructions, which means 'Please wait'. You may also be asked *Avez-vous une carte client?*, which means 'Do you have a customer loyalty card?'.

Many petrol stations provide services such as a car wash, vacuum cleaners and air, and often have a shop selling confectionery, snacks and canned and bottled drinks (which are usually expensive), newspapers and magazines, motoring accessories and sundry other items. Most petrol stations have toilets, sometimes located outside the main building, when it may be necessary to ask an attendant for the key. Routine servicing and repairs are also carried out at some petrol stations.

GARAGES & SERVICING

Garages are required to display a list of their charges for routine repairs and servicing, and many also display their hourly rate for different types of work, e.g. mechanical, electrical or bodywork. The quality of work is usually of a high standard and charges compare favourably with those in other European countries (they're usually much lower than in the UK).

It's generally cheaper to have your car serviced at a village garage than at a main dealer, although the quality of work may vary considerably from garage to garage. Note that when a car is under warranty it must usually be serviced by an approved dealer in order not to invalidate the warranty, although since 2002 dealers no longer have exclusive rights to servicing and the supply of spare parts, which were previously marked up by up to 400 per cent. (On the other hand, new car dealers are no longer obliged to offer after-sales service.)

If you need urgent assistance, particularly with an exotic foreign car, you're more likely to receive sympathetic help from a small general garage than a large specialist dealer.

If you drive a rare car, it's wise to carry a selection of basic spare parts, as service stations in France may not stock them and you may need to wait several days for them to be sent from abroad.

Garages are generally open from 08.00 to 19.00 and close for lunch between 12.00 and 13.30. Many garages close for the whole month of August. Some garages provide 24-hour breakdown assistance (at a price – see **Motoring Organisations** below)

Most garages don't provide a free 'loan car' (*véhicule de remplacement*) while yours is being serviced or repaired, although the idea is beginning to catch on. Otherwise your insurance company may do so or you can usually hire a car from a garage at a reasonable rate. Some garages will collect your car from your home or office and deliver it after a service, or will drop you off at a railway or bus station or in a local town and pick you up when your car is ready for collection.

CAR HIRE

Car hire (rental) companies such as Avis, Eurodollar, Europcar, Hertz, National Citer and Thrifty have offices in most cities and large towns in France and at major airports. Look under *Location de voitures* in the *Yellow Pages*. If you're a visitor, it's wise to book a hire car before arriving, although this is no guarantee that you'll get the car you book and won't save you having

to queue to complete the paperwork when you collect it. Fly-drive deals are available through most airlines and travel agencies. French railways (SNCF) offer inclusive train and car-hire deals, and a *France Vacances Pass* which includes car hire.

You can hire an Avis car from some 200 SNCF stations and leave it at any station operating the *Train + auto* scheme (leaflets are available at SNCF stations and include a map of participating stations).

Car hire in France is expensive, particularly for short periods, although rates have fallen in recent years. Prices, which include VAT (*TVA*) at 19.6 per cent, start at around €100 for a one-day rental of a small car such as a Peugeot 106 or Renault Twingo, but can vary widely from one company to another, so it pays to shop around. Rates also vary depending on your age and the number of years you've been driving. You may see small hire-cars marked '*Louez-moi de €55 par jour*' ('Hire me from €55 per day'); In fact, this is not a brilliant price for a day out, but a rate that applies only to hire contracts of at least a year.

Rates usually include 100km 'free', above which you pay around €1 per km. Reduced rates are available at weekends, usually from 12.00 on Friday to 09.00 on Monday, and rates fall considerably over longer periods, e.g. from €260 per week. There may, however, be a large excess (*franchise*), e.g. €2,500, and you may be charged extra (as much as €20 per day!) for collision damage waiver (CDW), which reduces or cancels the excess. It's possible to take out an annual insurance policy

Strasbourg

against having to pay an excess on hire cars for as little as €65 a year, for example with via Insurance 4 Car Hire (UK ☎ 020-7012 6300, 🖳 www.insurance4carhire.com), although you're covered only for a single period of up to 31 days.

Local hire companies are usually cheaper than the nationals, although cars must be returned to the pick-up point. Older cars can be hired from many garages at low rates. If required, check in advance that you're permitted to take a car out of France (usually prohibited).

To hire a car you must be a minimum of 18 years old, although most companies have increased this to 21 or even 25, and most also have an upper age limit of 60 or 65. Drivers must have held a full licence for at least a year. International companies require payment by credit card, although local firms may allow you to pay a cash deposit of €150 to €300 (or the whole hire period may need to be paid in advance). You may also need to produce a residence permit and other identification.

Optional extras include a portable telephone, luggage rack, snow chains and child seats. Instead of a standard car, you can hire a four-wheel drive car, estate car, minibus, luxury car or convertible, possibly with a choice of manual or automatic gearbox. Minibuses accessible to wheelchairs can also be hired, e.g. from Hertz.

Vans and pick-ups are available by the hour, half-day or day.

Cars can be hired in France through major international companies by booking through their offices in other countries and paying by credit card. This is a legitimate practice and can save 50 per cent or more on local hire rates. The telephone numbers of US-based hire companies can be obtained from international directory enquiries, although you may not be able to access toll-free (800) numbers.

MOTORING ORGANISATIONS

There are a number of motoring organisations in France, although membership isn't as large as in many other European countries. Breakdown insurance is provided by French insurance companies and most motorists take advantage of their low rates. Motoring organisations offer membership for individuals, couples and families and many offer 'premium' levels of membership that include additional services.

Other services provided by motoring organisations include vehicle serviceability checks, health and legal assistance, insurance and financial services, tourist services (e.g. a camping carnet and petrol coupons) and expert advice. Motoring organisations, like insurance companies, don't usually operate their own

breakdown rescue vehicles but appoint approved garages to assist members.

The principal French motoring organisations are the Automobile Club de France (🖥 www. automobileclub.org) and the Touring Club Francilien (🖥 www.touringclub.org).

PEDESTRIAN ROAD RULES

As in other countries, being a pedestrian is almost as dangerous as being a motorist; over 10 per cent of those killed on French roads are pedestrians. Pedestrian crossings (*passage à piétons*) may be distinguished by black and white or red and white stripes on the road, but can be indicated merely by a different kind of paving and they aren't usually illuminated, e.g. by flashing or static lights. Many have humps to encourage motorists to slow down, although you shouldn't assume that they will. In towns, pedestrian crossings are incorporated with traffic lights.

At a crossing with lights, pedestrians must wait for a green light (or green man) before crossing the road, irrespective of whether there's any traffic. You can be fined for crossing the road at the wrong place or ignoring pedestrian lights and crossings.

Pedestrians in France are generally better disciplined than those in many other countries and they usually wait for the green light, although where there's no crossing they're prone to wander across (and along) the road without even looking. Pedestrians must use footpaths where provided or may use a bicycle path when there's no footpath. Where there's no footpath or bicycle path, you should walk on the left side of the road (facing the oncoming traffic).

An increasing number of towns and cities have central pedestrian areas (*secteur piétonnier* or *zone piétonne*) barred to traffic, while other roads are often barred to pedestrians (indicated by an '*Interdit aux Piétons*' sign). Some have zones where pedestrians are supposed to have equal priority with cars, but don't bank on it!

⚠ Caution

Under a recent law, motorists are required to stop for pedestrians who indicate their intention to cross, whether there's a pedestrian crossing or not; however, old habits die hard and many drivers haven't yet taken the requirement on board, therefore it pays to be cautious. If you're within 50m of a pedestrian crossing you must use it and can be fined for not doing so.

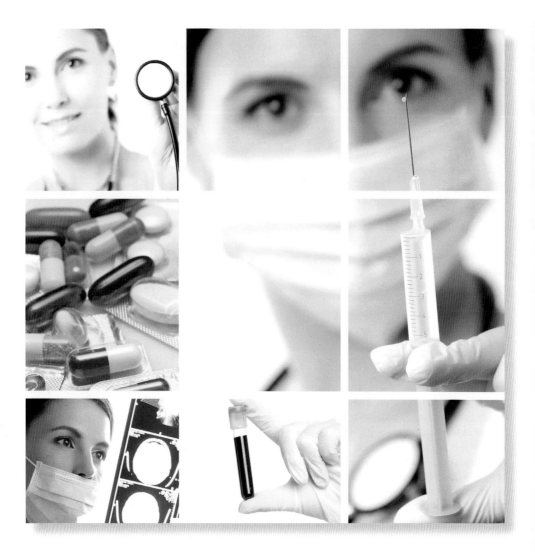

12.
HEALTH

The average life expectancy at birth in France has risen almost five years in the last two decades and is now the highest in the world after Japan: around 83 for women (compared with the EU average of 81.4) and 75.3 for men (the EU average). Almost half of male deaths between 15 and 45 are due to road 'accidents' and suicides (France has one of Europe's highest suicide rates for over 65s – over 3,000 per year). The infant mortality rate is around 3.29 deaths per 1,000 live births before the age of one year (around the European average), and a child born in France in 2007 had an even chance of living to be 100.

In fact, people are now living so long that a new 'category' of person has been created, le quatrième âge, which refers to those aged over 75 (those in le troisième âge are now positively wet behind the ears).

The quality of French healthcare and healthcare facilities is among the best in the world. The standard of hospital treatment is second to none, and there are virtually no waiting lists for operations or hospital beds. (Many British people obtain treatment in France at the expense of the British National Health Service to avoid the UK's long waiting lists!) Public and private medicine operate alongside one another and there's no difference in the quality of treatment provided by public hospitals and private establishments. However, local hospital services, particularly hospitals with casualty departments, are limited in rural areas. Nevertheless, private treatment costs around half as much as similar treatment in the UK, e.g. around GB£1,000 for a cataract operation, compared with GB£3,000 in the UK.

France has long been a nation of hypochondriacs (famously satirised by Molière in Le Malade Imaginaire), and the French visit their doctors more often than most other Europeans and buy large quantities of medicines, health foods and vitamin pills – in fact they're the European pill-taking champions.

Part of the reason for their addiction to medicine is that healthcare has always been free (the other reason is that the French are obsessive about their digestive systems).

The cost of healthcare to the state is escalating dramatically. France devotes a greater proportion of its GDP to healthcare than to defence or education, around half spent on hospitals, a quarter on doctors' salaries and a fifth on medicines. Yet the system is in dire financial straits (the annual overspend has reached several billion euros!). As a result, doctors are now subject to periodic checks on the necessity of their prescriptions and between 2003 and 2006 over 900 medicines were removed from the list of (4,500!) treatments reimbursed by the state.

A wide-ranging reform of the health service, aimed at 'treating you better while spending less', was approved by parliament in July 2004 and saw the introduction (in January 2005) of the 'regular doctor' system (see **Doctors** on page 217) and of a compulsory €1 levy on all consultations (see **National Health System** on page 214). Other 'reforms' being introduced progressively include the creation of a computerised health record for every resident. However, while most French people recognise the need for reform, they're reluctant to lose hospitals and the right to unlimited second opinions and an endless supply of free pills.

In general, French healthcare places the emphasis on preventive medicine rather than treating sickness. Alternative medicine (*médecine douce*) is popular, particularly acupuncture and homeopathy. These treatments are recognised by France's medical council (Ordre des Médecins) and homeopathic products are reimbursed by the national health service when prescribed by a doctor at a rate of 35 per cent off their (the health service's) *tarif de convention* (set price), which may be below the price you pay in a pharmacy.

France is the world leader in homeopathy; some 15 per cent of the population regularly consults homeopathic doctors and chemists (pharmacies) often have free leaflets explaining homeopathic treatments. Other types of treatment (e.g. osteopathy and chiropractic) are available but may not be reimbursed.

There are some 14,000 health associations for patients, families of patients and support groups in France – one for every conceivable ailment. A complete list, *L'Annuaire des Associations de Santé*, can be found at 🖳 www.annuaire-aas.com.

HEALTH RISKS

Despite the common stereotype of the French as wine-swilling gourmets stuffing themselves with rich food, many have become health freaks in recent years. Fitness and health centres flourish in most towns, and jogging (*footing*) has become fashionable. Smoking has declined considerably and is now a minority habit, although it's still more prevalent than in many other European countries and is estimated to kill 30,000 people each year (see page 231). Thankfully, however, smoking has been banned on all public transport, and in February 2008 all French bars, cafés and restaurants became smoke-free, greatly reducing the risk of suffering illness as a result of passive smoking.

Air pollution (caused by vehicles, not smokers!) is an increasing problem in Paris and other French cities (particularly Grenoble, Lyon, Marseille and Strasbourg), where it's blamed for a sharp rise in asthma cases. It's estimated that thousands of people die prematurely each

year as a result of air pollution. There's also a high and increasing rate of stress in cities.

The incidence of heart disease is among the lowest in the world, a fact that has recently been officially contributed in part to the largely Mediterranean diet. However, the French have a high incidence of cirrhosis of the liver and other problems associated with excessive alcohol consumption, and there has recently been an increase in the number of sufferers from Alzheimer's disease to over half a million (it affects around 10 per cent of those aged over 65 and 50 per cent of those over 85).

Among expatriates, sunstroke, change of diet, too much rich food and (surprise, surprise) too much alcohol are the most common causes of health problems. Nevertheless, when you've had too much of *la bonne vie*, you can take yourself off to a spa for a few weeks to rejuvenate your system (in preparation for another bout of over-indulgence).

France's spa towns, which are concentrated in the mountainous regions, include Dax, the country's first, and Salies-de-Béarn (in Aquitaine), Aix-les-Bains, Evian and Thonon-les-Bains (Rhône-Alpes), Alet-les-Bains, Amelie-les-Bains and Avène-les-Bains

(Languedoc-Roussillon), Chaudes-Aigues, Mont-Dore and Vichy (Auvergne), Dignes-les-Bains and Gréoux-les-Bains (Provence), Vittel (Alsace-Lorraine) and Lourdes (Midi-Pyrénées), where drinkers can expect miracles!

Among the most popular treatments offered at spas is thalassotherapy (*thalassothérapie – une thalasso* is the ultimate French 'short break'), a sea water 'cure' recommended for arthritis, circulation problems, depression and fatigue; it's even available on the national health service!

The claim that drinking red wine helps to reduce heart and other diseases – e.g. in *Your Good Health: The Medicinal Benefits of Wine Drinking* by Dr E. Maury (Souvenir Press) – has recently been challenged by other medical experts. However, it's generally agreed that drinking excessive amounts of red wine (or any alcohol) can destroy your brain and cause strokes and liver failure! As French producers sometimes warn buyers: *l'abus d'alcool est dangereux pour la santé, consommez avec modération* (alcohol abuse is dangerous for your health, consume in moderation).

Essential vaccinations, renewable every ten years, include tetanus, which is 65 per cent reimbursed or 100 per cent if given as part of a free health check-up (*bilan de santé*), available to those on *CMU*. Free flu jabs are available in October for over 65s and those with certain complaints.

You can safely drink tap water unless it's labelled as non-drinking (*eau nonpotable*), although the wine (especially Château Mouton Rothschild) is more enjoyable. Those who enjoy swimming in lakes and rivers, on the other hand, should be aware of the potentially fatal Weil's disease (*leptospirose*), transmitted through the urine of rats and other rodents, which is on the increase, particularly in Aquitaine.

EMERGENCIES

France's emergency medical services are among the best in the world but may operate in a slightly different way from those you're used to.

The action to take in a medical emergency depends on the degree of urgency. In a life-threatening emergency such as a heart attack, poisoning or serious accident, you should dial 15 for your nearest *Service d'Aide Médicale d'Urgence* (*SAMU*) unit. *SAMU* is an emergency service that works closely with local public hospital emergency and intensive care units, whose ambulances are manned by medical personnel and equipped with resuscitation equipment. *SAMU* has a central telephone number for each region and the duty doctor decides whether to send a *SAMU* mobile unit, refer the call to another ambulance service, instruct you to make your own way to hospital, or call a doctor for a home visit. In the most critical situations, *SAMU* can arrange transport to hospital by aeroplane, helicopter or, if appropriate, boat. If you call the fire brigade or police services, they'll request a *SAMU* unit if they consider it necessary.

You can also call the local fire brigade (*sapeurs-pompiers* or *pompiers*) in an emergency by dialling 18. The fire brigade and public ambulance services are combined, and the fire brigade is equipped to deal with accidents and emergency medical cases. It operates its own ambulances, which are equipped with resuscitation equipment, and the *pompiers* will arrive with a doctor.

If you need an ambulance but the emergency isn't life-threatening, call the local public assistance (*assistance publique*) or

Emergency Numbers		
Organisation	**Number**	**Emergency**
Ambulance (SAMU)	15	Serious medical emergencies
Police	17	Police emergencies
Fire Service	18	Fire, rescue and medical emergencies
General emergency	112	Pan-European emergency number

municipal ambulance (*ambulance municipale*) service. There are also private ambulances in most towns providing a 24-hour service, listed by town under *Ambulances* in the *Yellow Pages*. Ambulance staff are trained to provide first aid and oxygen. In small towns, the local taxi service also provides an 'ambulance' service.

You're billed for the services of *SAMU*, the fire service or the public ambulance service, although the cost is reimbursed by social security and your complementary insurance policy (see page 237), if you have one, in the same way as other medical costs (see **National Health System** below). In an emergency, any hospital must treat you, irrespective of your ability to pay.

There are 24-hour medical and dental services in major cities and large towns (numbers are listed in telephone directories). For example, in Paris, you can call SOS Dentaire (☎ 01 43 37 51 00) for dental emergencies. For other medical emergencies, you can contact SOS Médecins on ☎ 3624 from any part of France; details of the service can be found at 🖳 www.sosmedecins-france. fr. SOS doctors and dentists are equipped with radio cars and respond quickly to calls. In Paris and other main cities, there are emergency medical telephone boxes at major junctions marked 'Services Médicaux', with direct lines to emergency services. See also **Emergency**

& Service Numbers on page 105 and **Counselling** on page 231. If someone has swallowed poison, call your local 'anti-poison centre' (*centre anti-poison*), listed at the front of telephone directories.

If you're unsure who to call, telephone your local police, who will tell you who to contact or call the appropriate service for you. Whoever you call, give the age of the patient and if possible, specify the type of emergency. Keep a note of the telephone numbers of your doctor, local hospitals and clinics, ambulance service, poison control, dentist and other emergency services (e.g. fire, police) next to your telephone (and on your mobile phone).

If you're able, you can go to a hospital emergency or casualty department (*urgences*). Note that not all hospitals have paediatric units, particularly private hospitals and, if your child needs emergency treatment, you should take him to a hospital catering for paediatric emergencies. Check in advance which local hospitals are equipped to deal with emergencies and the quickest route from your home. This information may be of vital importance in the event of an emergency, when a delay could mean the difference between life and death.

NATIONAL HEALTH SYSTEM

France has an excellent, although expensive, national health system. If you qualify for healthcare under the national health system, you and your family are entitled to subsidised or (in certain cases) free medical and dental treatment. Benefits include general and specialist care, hospitalisation, laboratory services, medicines, dental care, maternity care, appliances and transportation. Those who don't automatically qualify can contribute voluntarily or take out private health insurance (see page 247).

Under the national health system, health treatment is assigned a basic monetary value (*tarif de convention*), of which social security pays a proportion, as shown in the table opposite.

NHS Benefits

Practitioner/Treatment	Reimbursement
Maternity-related care	100 per cent
Hospitalisation	80 per cent
Doctor, dentist and midwife services; consultations as an out-patient; basic dental care; miscellaneous items, e.g. laboratory work, apparatus, ambulance services	70 per cent
Spectacles	65 per cent
Services of medical auxiliaries, e.g. nurses and therapists	60 per cent
Medicines (see page 219 for details)	0 to 100 per cent

The above figures are intended only as a guide and should be confirmed with social security and practitioners, as they can vary depending on your circumstances and social security 'status'. For example, certain patients classified as needing serious long-term treatment, e.g. diabetic, cancer and cardiac patients, receive 100 per cent reimbursement for all treatment. The cost of buying or hiring medical equipment such as walking sticks, wheelchairs, and special pillows and mattresses is reimbursed up to specified limits.

The reimbursement you receive from social security applies to the *tarif de convention*, which isn't necessarily the same as the amount you pay. For example, if a blood test costs €75 and the *tarif de convention* is €60, you're reimbursed 70 per cent of €60 (€42), leaving you with a bill of €33. The balance of medical bills, called the *ticket modérateur*, can be reclaimed through a complementary health insurance scheme, to which many people subscribe (see **Private Health Insurance** on page 247).

Since 1st January 2005, €1 has been deducted from all reimbursements except those relating to treatment for children, women over six months pregnant and those on *CMU* (see page 239), in order to reduce the social security debt.

When choosing a medical practitioner, e.g. a doctor or dentist, it's important to verify whether he has an agreement (*convention*) with social security. If he has an agreement, he's known as *conventionné* and will charge the *tarif de convention*. If he has no agreement,

he's termed *non-conventionné* and the bill may be two to five times the *tarif de convention*; some *non-conventionné* practitioners are 'approved' (*agréé*) by social security, but only a small proportion of their fees are reimbursed. A few medical professionals are classified as *conventionné honoraires libres*; although they're *conventionné*, they're permitted to charge higher fees than the standard rates. These include practitioners who perform specialist treatment (*dépassement exceptionnel*) and those with a particular qualification or expertise (*dépassement permanent*). If you're in any doubt, you should ask what the fee is for a consultation or treatment and what percentage will be reimbursed by social security.

If you're a non-resident you may be asked to pay in cash, although cheques drawn on a French bank are acceptable. If you're unable to pay your portion of the bill (the *ticket modérateur*), you can apply to your social security payment centre (Caisse Primaire d'Assurance Maladie/CPAM) for a waiver (*prise en charge*). In the case of urgent or necessary treatment, approval is a formality.

If you're entitled to national health cover, you're issued with an electronic credit card-style card (*carte à puce*), called the *Carte Vitale*, which contains your social security number and covers all members of your family. (Children under 16 are included on only one parent's card.) A *Carte Vitale* has no expiry date but should be re-validated annually (and if your circumstances change in the meantime, such as moving house, an addition to your family or long-term treatment for a newly diagnosed illness) by machine in the town halls of most towns and cities or in a pharmacy.

At the beginning of 2007, the *Carte Vitale* began to be superseded by the *Carte Vitale 2*, which contains more information and a photograph of the holder (see **Registration** on page 75). The scheme is being rolled out regionally and will eventually cover all those eligible over the age of 16. It will simplify the transfer of information, while improving the security of patient data.

The idea behind the new system (like most health service innovations) is to save money by reducing a phenomenon known as *nomadisme*, whereby patients seek opinions on the same ailment from several doctors, which is estimated to cost €3bn per year. You can still consult specialists without a referral from your GP, but the reimbursement will be far lower and, in some cases, may be zero.

Reimbursement Procedure

When you visit a medical practitioner whose fees are wholly or partly refundable by social security, simply present your *Carte Vitale* and reimbursement will be automatically 'triggered', although you must still pay the doctor and wait for your bank account to be reimbursed (which should take place within five days).

> A charge of €1 added to all consultation fees as part of the government's effort to reduce the social security debt and this isn't reimbursed except in the case of treatment for children, women over six months pregnant and those on *CMU*.

If a medical practitioner isn't linked to the *Carte Vitale* system or isn't able to access a computer (there are still some who don't want the expense!), he'll complete a *feuille de soins*. The treatment provided and the cost of the consultation are listed on the form, which must be sent to your local CPAM for reimbursement. Don't forget to put your social security number (*numéro d'immatriculation*) and date of birth on the form (if it isn't already printed), and also to sign it before

sending it. If forms aren't correctly completed, they'll be returned and this will delay your reimbursement (which may take up to 13 days in any case).

If your doctor prescribes medicines, he'll give you a prescription (*ordonnance*) to take to a chemists. Many chemists (pharmacists) have systems enabling them to deduct the appropriate percentage of the bill reimbursed by social security, leaving you to pay only the unreimbursed portion. Some are also 'linked' to certain complementary insurance schemes, so that once you've registered with the chemist, you won't have to pay anything. Simply present your *ordonnance* and your *Carte Vitale* to the chemist. If your chemist isn't computerised (which is highly unlikely) or doesn't recognise your complementary insurer, you must pay 100 per cent for your medicines and make a claim for reimbursement. In this case, the chemist will give you a copy of the *feuille de soins*, with confirmation that the medicines have been issued, for you to send to your CPAM or insurer.

If you're requesting a reimbursement for services prescribed by a doctor, you must accompany the *feuille de soins* with a copy of the doctor's original prescription. You can save a number of *feuilles de soins* and send them together.

The refund is paid directly into the bank or post office account that you designated when you registered with social security. You receive a statement from the office, confirming the amount reimbursed. Normally, you automatically receive reimbursement of the 'complementary' sum (*ticket modérateur*) from your complementary insurance policy (sometimes before the social security refund). If you don't, you must send the social security statement to your complementary insurer. Always keep a copy of your *feuilles de soins* and check that reimbursements are received and correct, as it isn't uncommon for the system to break down.

To be reimbursed by social security for certain medical treatment, you must obtain prior approval from your CPAM. This may include physical examinations, non-routine dental care, contact lenses and non-standard lenses for glasses, certain laboratory and radiology tests, physiotherapy and speech therapy, and thermal and therapeutic treatments. Your medical practitioner will give you a proposal form (*demande d'entente préalable*) and, unless treatment is urgently required, you should apply at least 21 days before the proposed treatment and obtain a receipt for your application (if made in person) or send it by registered post. If you don't receive a reply from your CPAM within ten working days, it's deemed to have agreed to the request. See also **Social Security** on page 237.

DOCTORS

There are around three doctors (*médecins*) per 1,000 population in France (compared with 1.7 in the UK, 4.4 in Spain and 5.9 in Italy), around 45 per cent of them women, and there are excellent doctors throughout the country. However, finding a doctor who speaks good (or any) English can be a problem, particularly in rural areas. (Doctors' English tends to be limited to the names of medical conditions, most of which are the same in both languages!) The depopulation of many rural villages has created what have become known as 'medical deserts', where doctors are thin on the ground. A recent agreement with the medical unions hopes to address this by offering cash incentives to GPs who spend at least 30 days a year covering these areas. There are also plans to encourage the formation of health centres where a number of GPs operate and support staff providing various services, which would allow GPs more time to work in unpopulated areas.

Many embassies and consulates maintain a list of doctors and specialists in their area who speak English (and other foreign languages), and your employer, colleagues or neighbours may be able to recommend someone. Town halls and chemists also maintain a list of local practitioners. You can obtain a list of doctors registered with social security from your local social security office. General practitioners (GPs) or family doctors (*médecin généraliste*) are listed in the *Yellow Pages* under *Médecins: médicine générale* and specialists under *Médecins* followed by their speciality, e.g. *Médecins: gynécologie*

médicale. (There are as many specialists as general practitioners.) All French doctors and specialists are registered with the Ordre des Médecins.

Many French doctors are specialists in acupuncture and homeopathy, both of which are reimbursed by social security when performed or prescribed by a doctor or practitioner who's *conventionné* (see page 214). Osteopaths (*ostéopathe*), on the other hand, have only recently been 'recognised' by the French health service and only part of their fee is reimbursed. Until recently, you could choose to see any doctor or specialist at any time and weren't required to register with a particular doctor, which made it easy to obtain a second opinion, should you wish to do so. You're now required to appoint an 'acting doctor' (*médecin traitant*) and to obtain a referral from him before seeing another doctor or specialist, including a medical auxiliary such as a nurse, physiotherapist or chiropodist, but excluding a gynaecologist, ophthalmologist, paediatrician or a psychiatrist (for those aged under 26). Dentists are consulted directly.

It's normal practice to pay a doctor or other medical practitioner at the end of each visit, whether you're a private or social security patient (see **Reimbursement Procedure** on

page 216). A routine visit to a doctor costs €23 (€26 for treatment to a child), of which €1 isn't reimbursed by social security but is by some *mutuelles*; home visits cost more.

Many doctors are in single practices but an increasing number work in group practices, and there are also healthcare centres (*centre médical et social*), which may offer services that are usually unavailable at doctors' surgeries, e.g. health screening, vaccinations, dental care (*soins dentaires*) and nursing care (*soins infirmiers*).

Some centres specialise in a particular field of medicine, such as cancer or heart treatment. For example, as part of a Health Department initiative to fight breast cancer, women aged between 50 and 74 can obtain free screening (*dépistage*) at centres, a list of which are automatically sent (every two years) by the health service to women in this age group. Contact your doctor and ask him about this if you aren't about to receive the list. Although it isn't always necessary to make an appointment at a screening centre, it's preferable (unless you like waiting for hours). As when visiting a doctor, check whether the centre is *conventionné*.

In some areas, there are outpatient services (*centre de soins*) run by private organisations such as the Red Cross. You can obtain a list of local healthcare centres from your town hall.

Hours

Doctors' surgery hours may vary from day to day, e.g. morning surgery from 09.00 to 11.30 or 12.00, Tuesdays to Saturdays, and afternoons from 14.00 to 16.30, Mondays to Fridays. Certain periods may be set aside for appointments (*rendezvous*) and others for 'open consultation' (*consultation libre*), when no appointment is necessary; patients are seen in the order they arrive.

If your doctor is unavailable, his surgery will give you the name of a standby doctor (there may be a recorded message giving this information out of hours). If you need a doctor or medicines in a non-urgent situation and are unable to contact your doctor, your local police station (*commissariat de police*) will give you the telephone number of a duty doctor or the address of a pharmacy that's open. You can also call Pharmagarde (☎ 3237) to find the address of a pharmacy nearby that's open. If this isn't possible, dial

15 (there may also be a local 'emergency' number) and ask for the number of your nearest duty doctor. If you're unable to attend a surgery, your doctor may make a house call, although many won't.

Treatment

When you visit a doctor, you're invariably prescribed a number of medicines, which are liberally dispensed in France. (The standing of a doctor with his patients often depends on the number of medicines prescribed!) For some ailments you'll be prescribed a rectal suppository (*suppositoire*) which is the fastest way of getting drugs into the bloodstream (via the bowel or lower intestine), although this practice is dying out. Never take a suppository orally – they're usually difficult to confuse with oral pills, on account of their size and shape!

French doctors don't usually take your (or your child's) temperature, so if it's relevant you should do it yourself immediately before visiting a doctor. If medicine needs to be administered by a nurse, e.g. by injection, or other nursing services are necessary, your doctor or chemist will give you the name of a local nurse. Treatment can be administered at your home or at a nurse's office, and is paid for by social security.

Medical Examinations

Employees in France must (by law) have a medical examination when they're hired and annually thereafter. If you contribute to social security, you may be able to have this done by your family doctor, although your employer may require you to be examined by an appointed doctor. If you aren't covered by social security, you may have to be examined privately. In any case, you're issued with a medical certificate (*certificat de santé*).

A more thorough medical check (*bilan de santé*) is available free on demand every five years (a total of nine during a person's adult life) under social security. Technically it's mandatory for everyone to have a physical examination between the ages of 25 and 35 and between the ages of 45 and 55.

A couple must undergo a physical examination no more than two months prior to marriage, which includes a blood test and chest X-ray. You may also require a medical examination (and certificate) before being allowed to participate in certain sports, e.g. when joining a club.

In France, the results of medical tests (e.g. blood, urine, heart and smear) and X-rays are the property of the patient, who receives a copy, and doctors must provide medical records within a week of a request. You should keep these in a safe place, as you'll be asked to produce them if you require further treatment (in some cases even for treatment for a different condition). Furthermore, after an operation or other medical procedure you're entitled to access your *dossier* (ask your doctor). If you're denied access to your records, contact the Commission d'Accès au Documents Administratifs (CADA, 🖳 www. cada.fr). See also **Children's Health** on page 228.

MEDICINES

The French take a lot of medicines (*médicaments* – *drogues* are narcotics!) and are Europe's largest consumers of sleeping pills, tranquillisers and antidepressants such as Prozac and Valium. Medicines prescribed by doctors represent over 80 per cent of sales, and doctors habitually prescribe three or four different remedies for each ailment.

The French have traditionally been prescribed more antibiotics than other Europeans, a third of which are reckoned to be unnecessary or ineffective, and they have the highest incidence of anti-biotic-resistant bacteria in Europe, with the result that the government is now campaigning (among both doctors and patients) for a reduction in antibiotics prescription.

The cost of prescription medicines is controlled by the government, with some important exceptions such as Viagra or equivalents. Prices are reviewed twice a year, although there are no price controls on non-prescription medicines. Social security pays the whole cost of essential medication for certain illnesses or conditions, e.g. insulin and heart pills (labelled '100 per cent'), 65 per cent of medicines designated as important (with white labels), and 35 per cent for *médicaments de confort* (with blue labels) – see **Reimbursement Procedure** on page 216. A few medicines aren't reimbursed at all, including most contraceptive pills (see **Contraception & Abortion** on page 225).

Medicines are continually removed from the reimbursement or partly-reimbursed lists and over 200 were downgraded from 35 per cent reimbursement to 15 per cent in 2010. In addition, patients pay €0.50 for each medicine prescribed, although the health service limits annual payments per patient to €50, therefore if you're prescribed medicines 100 or more times in the same year, you'll pay a maximum of €50.

Note that medicines deemed to be 'ineffective' won't be reimbursed at all. (Of the 100 most prescribed medicines in France, almost a quarter are reckoned to fall into this category!) Information (in French only) about medicines commonly prescribed in France can be found on the website of the Association Française de Sécurité Sanitaire des Produits de Santé (AFSSAPS, 🖳 www.afssaps.fr). If you must pay for your own medicines, it can be expensive, e.g. €100 or more for a course of antibiotics.

The brand names for medicines often vary from country to country, so if you regularly take a particular medicine you should ask your doctor for the generic name. If you wish to

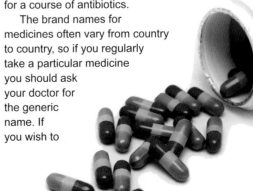

match a medicine prescribed abroad, you need a current prescription with the medicine's trade name, the manufacturer's name, the chemical composition and the dosage. Pharmacies may suggest an alternative if the medicine you want isn't available.

> As part of a government scheme to reduce health spending, chemists may propose a generic product instead of the brand on your prescription, as these are on average 30 per cent cheaper. Although you aren't obliged to accept the generic alternative, if you don't you may be required, depending on the French department where you live, to pay the *tarif de convention* and reclaim it from social security.

Note that under legislation which became effective in July 2003, social security reimbursement is based on the generic equivalent of branded medicines (if one exists). Generic products are usually identified by the prefix 'Gé'.

Most foreign medicines have an equivalent in France, although particular brands may be difficult or impossible to obtain. It's possible to have medicines sent from abroad and no import duty or value added tax (*TVA*) is payable. If you're visiting France for a short period, you should take sufficient medicines to cover the length of your stay.

Currently, a triangular 'traffic' sign with a red border and a black car symbol on a medicine packet indicates that it can cause drowsiness and that you shouldn't drive or operate machinery when taking it, but colour-coded packaging is being introduced to indicate the level of drowsiness caused by each medicine: yellow means 'drive with care', orange 'drive only with your doctor's permission' and red 'don't drive'.

Pregnant women should check with their doctor before taking any medication, including pain-killers.

Chemists

Prescription and non-prescription medicines are obtained from a chemist or pharmacy (*pharmacie*), denoted by a sign consisting of a green cross on a white background (which is usually illuminated and flashing when the shop is open). A chemist must own and run his own shop (chain chemists are illegal) and their numbers are strictly controlled, although there's at least one chemist in every town and many villages.

Most chemists are open from 09.00 to 19.00 or 19.30 from Mondays to Saturdays, although many close for lunch from 12.00 or 12.30 to 14.00 or even 15.00. Some are closed on Mondays and others may be closed on Saturday afternoons since the introduction of the 35-hour week. Outside normal opening hours, a notice giving the address of the nearest duty chemist (*pharmacie de garde*) is displayed in the chemist's window (the telephone numbers of local doctors on call may also be shown). This information is also published in local newspapers and listed in monthly bulletins issued by town halls.

In most cities, several chemists are open until late evening or early morning and in Paris a 24-hour service is provided by the Pharmacie Les Champs, 84 avenue des Champs-Elysées, 75008 Paris (☎ 01 45 62 02 41). There are also American and British chemists in the capital, stocking familiar American and British medicines.

Chemists are trained (and obliged) to give first aid and they can also perform tests such as blood pressure. They can supply a wider range of medicines over the counter without a prescription than is available in the UK and the US, although some medicines sold freely in other countries require a doctor's prescription in France. A chemist will recommend non-prescription medicines for minor ailments and may also recommend a local doctor, specialist, nurse or dentist. (Some chemists regard this type of recommendation as unethical and prefer to give you a list of practitioners).

French chemists are trained to distinguish between around 50 species of edible and poisonous fungi (*champignon*) and will tell you whether those you've picked are delicious or deadly. They're also trained to identify local snakes to enable them to prescribe the correct antidote for bites. Crutches (*béquilles* or, oddly, *cannes anglaises*), wheelchairs and other medical equipment can be hired from chemists, although they're often provided by hospitals, e.g. after operations, or may be provided on prescription by your GP.

Chemists shops aren't cluttered with the non-medical wares found in American and British chemists, although many sell cosmetics and toiletries (these are called *parapharmacies*, where you cannot buy certain medicines, such as painkillers) and most stock animal medicines and baby products, e.g. feeding bottles. Chemists are cheaper than a *parfumerie* for cosmetics but more expensive than a supermarket or hypermarket. Only a limited range of non-prescription medicines can be purchased in supermarkets and hypermarkets. A *droguerie*, which is a sort of hardware store selling toiletries, cleaning supplies, a wide range of general household goods, paint, garden supplies, tools and DIY supplies, shouldn't be confused with an American drug store.

Prescriptions

Prescriptions may be printed or handwritten; in the latter case, as in most countries, they're invariably illegible but a chemist will (usually!) be able to decipher them and will explain to you (and write on the medicine boxes) what you need to take when.

Whereas you must pay the full cost of non-prescription medicines, prescription medicines may be partly or wholly reimbursed by social security and/or your complementary insurance policy (see **Medicines** above). In fact, some non-prescription medicines can be obtained free (or at a reduced cost) on prescription.

You don't usually have to wait for prescription to be 'made up', as now (throughout the EU) original pack dispensing is standard practice. Pharmaceutical products are provided in pre-packaged form in the most commonly prescribed quantities. Doctors cannot prescribe for periods of longer than three months, therefore patients requiring regular repeat prescriptions usually visit their GPs once a quarter. Consequently, prescriptions for continuous-use conditions, e.g. high blood pressure or cholesterol, are usually packaged in one-month or three-month supplies.

Many French doctors prescribe homeopathic medicines, stocked by all chemists, many of which specialise in homeopathy.

HOSPITALS & CLINICS

France boasts a higher number of hospital beds in proportion to its population than most other European countries (8.7 per 1,000 compared with 7.6 in Spain and Italy and 6.9 in the UK), although the introduction of the 35-hour week and a recent shortage of doctors and nurses, particularly in the provinces, have led to the closure of many wards, and in the summer months, when staff are on holiday, some hospitals are forced to virtually close. There's also a shortage of certain specialists, e.g. anaesthetists, gynaecologists and ophthalmologists, partly due to a recent increase in malpractice lawsuits.

All cities and large towns have at least one hospital (*hôpital*) or clinic (*clinique*), indicated by a sign showing a red 'H' on a white background. Hospitals are listed in the *Yellow Pages* under *Hôpitaux*. There are many types of hospitals, both public and private (see below).

Like doctors and other medical practitioners, hospitals are either *conventionné* or *non-conventionné*. Every large town has at least one *hôpital conventionné*, which may be public or private, usually with a direct payment agreement with social security. Private

hospitals and clinics that are *non-conventionné* may also have an agreement (*agréé*) with social security, whereby around 30 per cent of the fees are usually paid by social security. For non-urgent hospital treatment, check in advance the reimbursement made by social security and, if applicable, the amount your complementary insurance policy or other private health insurance will pay.

If you're admitted to a hospital or other medical institution, you should be given a document outlining your rights (*charte des droits et libertés*).

Public Hospitals

There are generally three categories of public hospital: hospital centres or short-stay hospitals (*hôpital de court séjour*), medium-stay centres (*centre de moyen séjour*) and long-term treatment centres (*centre et unité de long séjour*). Hospital centres include general hospitals, *assistance publique* (*AP*) hospitals in Paris, specialist hospitals and regional centres (*centre hospitalier régional/CHR* or *centre hospitalier universitaire/CHU* when associated with a university). Public hospitals must accept all patients in an emergency irrespective of their ability to pay.

Medium-stay hospitals are usually for patients who have previously been treated in a short-stay hospital centre. They contain facilities for convalescence, occupational and physical therapy, and recuperative treatment for drug and alcohol abuse and mental illness. Long-term treatment centres are for those who are unable to care for themselves without assistance and include psychiatric hospitals and nursing homes for the aged (*maisons de retraite médicalisées*).

There are over 35 *CHU*s in France (12 in Paris), where medical students do their training. *CHU*s are rated among the best hospitals in France (indeed in the world), and professors and senior staff must undergo intensive training to secure their appointments.

Rural community hospitals are classified as hospital centres, although they're usually less well equipped than other short-stay hospitals and you should go to a large hospital if possible.

Not all hospitals have accident and emergency (*urgences*) departments, and you should check where your nearest A&E centre is to be found (see **Emergencies** on page 213).

Private Hospitals & Clinics

Most private hospitals (*hôpital privé*) and clinics (*clinique*) specialise in inpatient care in particular fields of medicine, such as obstetrics and surgery, rather than being full-service hospitals (the American Hospital in Paris is a rare exception). You should check in advance. The cost of treatment in a private hospital or clinic is generally much higher than in a public hospital, where a large proportion of costs are reimbursed by social security. However, some private hospitals participate in the French social security system and operate in the same way as public hospitals. These include the Paris hospitals listed below.

If your French is poor, you may prefer to be treated at a private hospital or clinic with English-speaking staff, as most public hospitals make little or no allowance for foreigners who don't speak French. There are a number of expatriate hospitals in the Paris area, including the American Hospital in Paris (☎ 01 46 41 25 25, 🖳 www.american-hospital.org) and the Hertford British Hospital, also known as the Hôpital Franco-Britannique (☎ 01 46 39 22 22, 🖳 www.british-hospital.org), which specialises in maternity care. Most staff at all levels in these hospitals speak English. Fees at the American hospital are much higher than at French hospitals, although they can

usually be reclaimed through the French social security system and most *mutuelles* and are accepted by most American medical insurance companies.

Long-term Care

The elderly are better catered for in France than in many other countries, although many old people are looked after at home by relatives (adult children are obliged by law to support ageing parents according to their means) and the cost of retirement homes and other accommodation can be prohibitive. Nevertheless, there are some 5,000 retirement homes in France, including public and private establishments, and they're becoming more common.

There are several types of retirement home (*maison de retraite*), which can be with or without medical support (*avec ou sans cure médicale*), They include a *foyer-logement* for those on low incomes; a *foyersoleil*, where accommodation for old and younger people is mixed; a *villageretraite*, where accommodation is in bungalows (*pavillon*), usually in a rural area (e.g. those operated by Seniorales®, 🖥 www.seniorales.com) with holiday-camp-style facilities and entertainment; and a *résidence avec services* or *résidence services*, consisting of apartments (normally two-room), some of which are offered unfurnished. Some communes run their own retirement homes (ask at your town hall), and some establishments offer temporary accommodation.

There are various state benefits for the elderly, and a new social security allowance, *allocation personnalisée à l'autonomie* (*APA*), was introduced in 2001 to help those requiring long-term care, who can also insure against becoming a burden on their children.

A traditional retirement home costs at least €2,000-3,000 per month and a long-stay hospital around €1,500 per month (more in Paris). *Village-retraite* accommodation costs between €1,000-2,000 per month (or from around €100,000 to buy) and apartments for one person €1,000-1,500 per month and €1,500-2,000 for a couple (depending on the size and location). On the other hand, for those who qualify, *foyer-logements,* cost much less.

Details of facilities for the elderly are contained in *Le Guide des Maisons de Retraite* (Pétrarque) and *Le Guide du Logement Senior* (Balland) and can be found on the site of the Association Française de Protection et d'Assistance aux Personnes Agées (🖥 www.afpap.org) and also on the website (🖥 www.plan-retraite.fr), which contains general information and a list of homes in Ile-de-France.

Accommodation

The basic hospital accommodation that is reimbursed at 80 per cent by social security is a two-or three-bed room (*régime commun*). A supplement must be paid for a private room (if available), although it may be paid in part or in full by your complementary or other private health insurance.

> You can usually rent a radio, TV or telephone for a small daily fee if they aren't included in the room fee. A bed is also usually provided for relatives if required. You must usually provide your own pyjamas, robes, towels and toiletries.

The best hospital accommodation is similar to five-star hotels, with food and wine (and prices!) to match. Catering in basic accommodation varies from good to adequate.

Children

Children aged 15 and under are usually treated in a paediatric unit well stocked with games, toys, books and other children. However, not all hospitals have paediatric units, particularly private hospitals. Children who require long-term hospitalisation may, depending on their health, be given school lessons in hospital.

Many hospitals permit a parent to stay with a child and some allow children, depending on their health, to attend during the day and return home at night. A free booklet, *L'Hôpital et l'Enfant* (in French), contains information and advice for parents with children in hospital.

Procedure

Except for emergency treatment (see page 213), you're admitted or referred to a hospital or clinic for treatment only after a recommendation (*attestation*) from a doctor or a specialist. Usually you're admitted to a hospital in your own *département*, unless specialist surgery or treatment is necessary which is unavailable there. If you wish to be treated in hospital by your own doctor, you must check that he's able to do so.

Except in the case of emergencies, you must provide the following documents on admission to a public hospital in order to receive reimbursement from social security:

♦ your social security registration card (*carte d'immatriculation*) or *Carte Vitale*;

♦ a doctor's certificate (*attestation*) stating the reason for hospitalisation;

♦ documents provided by your social security office (*caisse*) stating the conditions under which you're insured, e.g. if you're unemployed you need a document stating that you're entitled to unemployment benefits.

An employer must provide an *accident de travail* form when an employee is hospitalised as a result of an accident at work. If a woman is hospitalised to give birth or in connection with a pregnancy, she must have a *carnet de maternité* (see **Childbirth** below). If you aren't covered by social security, you must provide evidence of your health insurance (e.g. a European Health Insurance Card), salary or the ability to pay. If you're unable to pay, you may be refused treatment at a private hospital or clinic, except in an emergency.

Upon admission to a hospital you should receive an information booklet (*livret d'accueil*) containing meal schedules, information on visiting hours, a floor plan, doctors' names, hospital rules, and a description of the uniforms and name tags worn by hospital staff. If you don't receive it, ask for one.

Visiting hours are usually from 13.30 or 14.00 to 20.30 or 21.00 daily but tend to be flexible for immediate family members; visits can be made outside these hours in exceptional circumstances. In a private clinic there may be no restrictions on visiting hours.

Hospital stays are kept to a minimum and much treatment is performed on an outpatient basis (*hôpital de jour*) and your convalescence takes place at home (*hospitalisation à domicile/ HAD*), supervised by visiting doctors and nurses. The main exception to this rule is postnatal care (see **Childbirth** below). You can usually leave hospital at any time without a doctor's consent by signing a release form (*décharge de responsabilité*).

Costs

Hospital bills can be high, e.g. €200-300 per day for medicine, accommodation and meals plus several hundred euros for 'routine' surgery, or much more (running into thousands of euros) for a major operation. If you're paying the bill yourself for elective surgery, you should shop around, not just in France but in other countries, as the price can vary considerably. Note, however, that some operations are performed in France for half of the price in some other European countries.

If you're covered by French social security, 80 per cent of your hospital bill is usually paid by the state. (Some types of plastic surgery are also paid for, e.g. breast reduction in certain circumstances and some ear and nose operations.)

Patients covered by social security are charged a fixed daily fee (*forfait journalier/ indemnité journalière*) for meals of €18, unless hospitalisation was due to an accident at work or you're exempt on the grounds of low income, although some hospitals waive the charge on the day of admission. This fee is usually reimbursed by complementary health insurance.

If a medical bill is expected to be above a certain amount (which is increased annually in line with inflation), you can apply to social security for a *prise en charge*, which means that the full bill will be sent directly to social security. Otherwise, you must pay the bill when you leave hospital, unless you've made prior arrangements for it to be paid by your insurance company. You must pay for hospital outpatient treatment in the same way as a visit to a doctor or specialist (see **Reimbursement Procedure** on page 216).

Certain patients, classified as needing serious long-term treatment, receive 100 per

cent reimbursement, e.g. cardiac, diabetes and cancer patients. Pensioners receive free hospital treatment under social security, although up to 90 per cent of their pension may be deducted to compensate for the cost of treatment (while in hospital).

A stay at a spa is usually reimbursed at 70 per cent or higher when recommended by a doctor and approved by social security. Convalescence after a serious illness is often paid 100 per cent by social security.

CONTRACEPTION & ABORTION

Contraceptives are freely available in France and there are no age restrictions. A doctor's prescription is necessary for birth control pills (*pilule*) and certain contraceptive devices. Most birth control pills aren't reimbursed at all by social security, including all the latest pills; only some older pills are reimbursed. Condoms (*préservatif* – a preservative is a *conservateur* and Condom is a town in southern France) are widely available, e.g. in underground stations and high schools, and can be bought cheaply in chemists, supermarkets and other shops.

The 'morning-after pill' (*contraception d'urgence*) can be purchased without a prescription from chemists and is reimbursed (it's issued free to minors in an effort to reduce unwanted teenage pregnancies).

Abortion (*interruption volontaire de grossesse/IVG*) has been legal in France since 1974 and in 1982 became subject to reimbursement through social security, although it's a controversial subject. There has recently been a public outcry against the right of mothers to choose abortion if a problem is detected by an antenatal scan (some doctors refuse to perform scans as a protest against the 'legalisation of eugenics'), and the government may introduce legislation to restrict the entitlement to abortion.

Abortions must normally be performed in a hospital before the tenth week of pregnancy. There are no abortion clinics in France. Therapeutic abortions are allowed at any time during a pregnancy if the life of the mother is at risk or there's a high probability that a child will be born with a serious or incurable disorder. A doctor may refuse to perform an abortion, but in general abortion is available on demand for all except girls under the age of 18, who require the consent of a parent or guardian or a children's judge. A woman doesn't need the consent of the father to have an abortion, irrespective of her marital status.

Information

Further information about family planning can be obtained from the Mouvement Français pour le Planning Familial (🖳 www.planning-familial.org). There are also information centres (*établissement d'information*) and family planning centres (*centre de planification familiale*), staffed by specialised counsellors and medical professionals throughout France. These provide information and counselling (usually free) about contraception, abortion, and sexual and marital problems. Family planning centres also prescribe contraceptives, diagnose pregnancies, and provide gynaecological examinations and treatment.

CHILDBIRTH

Childbirth invariably takes place in a hospital, where a stay of at least five days and as many as 12 is normal, depending on factors such as the number of beds available and the mother's and baby's health. Most hospital maternity units are equipped with single and double rooms. You can choose to have a baby at home, but it's unlikely you'll receive support from doctors or other medical staff or from social security.

Procedure

As soon as your pregnancy is confirmed (by a blood test), your doctor will provide some general information about the progress of your pregnancy and a form to be completed and sent to the local Caisse d'Allocations Familiales (CAF), who will issue you with a reference number (and a card confirming it) relating to claims for family allowances. The CAF will also send you information about your entitlement to these and how to claim them.

You may be 'allocated' to a maternity hospital or clinic or, if you live equidistant from two or more, you may be given a choice, in which case you should visit the establishments (but ring first, as they aren't used to such visits) and talk to those who have given birth there before making your decision, as policies and procedures vary.

You must have blood and urine tests and should continue to see your doctor or a midwife at your chosen hospital each month. At the end of your 11th, 22nd and 33rd weeks of pregnancy, you're given an ultrasound scan (échographie) to check on the progress of the foetus.

☑ SURVIVAL TIP

If you don't wish to know the sex of your child, you should say so before each scan is made.

After the first scan, you'll be asked to take an additional blood test to check for the likelihood of Down's syndrome (syndrome de Down or Trisomie 21).

Expectant mothers are normally supervised by a midwife; it's possible to consult an obstetrician, but he'll usually become closely involved in a birth only if complications are expected or when it's classified as 'high-risk'. You can, of course, engage a private obstetrician to attend you before, during and after giving birth; this won't be paid for by social security but may be covered by private health insurance. In any case, you should register at the hospital, when a bed will be provisionally reserved for you at the appropriate time and, in theory, guaranteed for you whenever your baby decides to pop out.

Before booking a bed in a hospital or clinic, you should ask if it's conventionné (see page 214). Other things you may wish to investigate are whether your husband is allowed to attend the delivery, whether 'alternative' birthing positions (e.g. crouching or on your side) are permitted, which is less common in France than in many other developed countries, and what clothes and other articles you need to provide; at some hospitals, you need to provide only clothes.

If you wish to join antenatal classes at the hospital (or elsewhere), you may need to sign up for these well in advance, although usually around the sixth month is sufficient; if your French isn't good or you don't wish to join a class, it may be possible to arrange individual lessons.

One of the main topics of discussion at antenatal classes (and the subject of a special lesson) is the epidural (péridurale), which is usually the only form of pain relief offered during labour, and you should make it clear if you don't want an epidural (although you would be wise to keep your options open until labour begins!).

The French aren't great proponents of 'natural' birthing methods, and you're normally required to have a drip connected to your arm or hand, and heart-beat and breathing monitors strapped to your belly throughout labour. Almost nothing is left to 'chance', and if a baby is reluctant to make its appearance in the world, you'll be wheeled into the operating theatre for a caesarian section.

New mothers are strongly encouraged to breast feed (allaiter) rather than bottle feed (donner le biberon), although you're free to bottle feed if you prefer.

Births must be registered within three working days at the town hall of the district where they take place. In fact, this is done automatically if you don't do it yourself, but your signature won't appear on the birth certificate. Registration applies to everyone irrespective of their nationality and whether they're resident in France or just visiting. When registering a birth, you must produce a certificate signed by a doctor or midwife and the parents' passports or identity cards.

You should receive copies of the complete birth certificate (*acte de naissance – copie intégrale*) as well as 'summaries' (*extrait de l'acte de naissance*), which are required by various bodies, e.g. the tax office (see below). The hospital will issue you with a health record book (*carnet de santé*) for your child (see below). Children born to foreign nationals should be registered at the local consulate or embassy in order to obtain a national birth certificate and passport for a child, which may take several weeks and cost €100 or more.

Note than whenever someone born in France is required to produce his birth certificate, what is actually required is an extract (*extrait*) from the local record book, which contains details not only of his birth but also of his current status (*état civil*). Any such extract must be no more than three months old.

If you have private health insurance, don't forget to notify your health insurance company about the birth of a child. Also notify the tax office and make sure that your income tax payments are adjusted accordingly (see page 269).

You may give your child any name that isn't 'prejudicial' (whatever that means) and may be given either his father's surname or his mother's (maiden) name or both the parents' family names (hyphenated, in either order). Parents are asked to complete a *déclaration conjointe de choix de nom* at the time of registering a birth, but if you fail to complete a declaration the child is given the father's surname only.

Costs

Social security pays 100 per cent of most medical expenses relating to a pregnancy, including medical examinations and tests, antenatal care and the delivery. It even pays for a physical examination for the father – to check whether he's likely to survive the ordeal!

However, it's expensive to have a child in a hospital if you aren't covered by social security or don't have private medical insurance, in which case it may be cheaper to have your child abroad (or at home). For example, the cost of a midwife (see **Information & Support** below) is €17 for a consultation and €312.70 for a birth (rising to €344.50 for twins!). These are the *tarif de convention* costs since 2008, and there's a slight surcharge if births are on Sundays or public holidays!

To qualify for social security maternity benefit (*allocation pour jeune enfant*), mothers-to-be must undergo at least four antenatal examinations, during their third, sixth, eighth and ninth months of pregnancy. After your first examination you receive a certificate (*attestation de premier examen prénatal obligatoire*) that must be sent to your CAF to ensure that you receive your social security benefits.

Information & Support

Midwives (*sages-femmes*), who are qualified nurses with special training, handle most routine pregnancies and play an important part in childbirth. They're also responsible for educating and supporting pregnant women and their families. Midwives can advise women before they become pregnant, in addition to providing moral, physical and emotional support, both during pregnancy and after a birth.

All public hospitals and many private clinics offer childbirth classes, although these may take the form of discussions rather than instruction. French social security

also pays for physiotherapy (*kinésithérapie*) after childbirth.

Chemists can provide advice for pregnant women and new mothers concerning nutrition and supplements, and the care and feeding of babies. Your family doctor or obstetrician will advise you about postnatal examinations and check-ups.

In some areas there are mother and child protection centres (Centre de Protection Maternelle et Infantile/PMI) providing free services to pregnant women and children under the age of six, covered by social security. A list of local PMI centres is available from your town hall.

Many organisations provide counselling services for pregnant women, including SOS Bébé (🖳 www.sosbebe.org) and the English-speaking International Counselling Service (contact via the American Church – see below). A book of interest to mothers-to-be is *ABCs of Motherhood in Paris* published by Message, a Paris-based English-language mothers' support group; it's available from most Paris expatriate groups, including WICE (🖳 www. wice-paris.org) and the American Church (65 quai d'Orsay, 75007 Paris (☎ 01 40 62 05 00, 🖳 www.acparis.org), and via the Message Mother Support Group's website (🖳 www. messageparis.org).

CHILDREN'S HEALTH

France provides excellent healthcare for children, including a comprehensive programme of preventive treatment and a variety of dedicated medical facilities, and all children are required to have monthly check-ups during infancy and three checkups during their school years.

⚠ **Caution**

As in many other developed countries, there's a growing obesity problem in France, where over 15 per cent of children aged seven to nine are classified as obese and the obesity rate among teenagers has doubled in the last decade. Recent government measures (such as banning soft drink vending machines in schools) aim to tackle the problem, as well as that of teenage smoking.

Children can obtain a 'health kit' (*kit de santé*) from any of the 1,675 Centres d'Information et de Documentation Jeunesse (🖳 www.cidj.com). Booklets providing information for children about safe sex are available free from Crips d'Ilede-France (☎ 01 56 80 33 33). Information and help for parents of sick children are available from the Association Sparadrap (🖳 www.sparadrap. org – available in English), which publishes numerous books and leaflets.

Carnet de Santé

Children born in France are issued with a *carnet de santé* (health record book), in which is recorded every medical occurrence in their pre-adult lives, including vaccinations, childhood illnesses, general medical check-ups and surgery. It should always be taken with you on a medical visit with your child and must be produced when a child starts school. You can obtain a *carnet de santé* for children who weren't born in France from your local town hall on production of their passport, although some town halls may require 'persuasion'. If you're covered by social security, it's provided free; otherwise there's a small fee. Examinations, vaccinations (see below) and check-ups required during a child's first six years are listed in the *carnet de santé*. The *carnet de santé* may be superseded by the *Carte Vitale 2* in the near future.

Vaccinations

When you arrive in France, you should bring proof of your child's immunisations with you. Vaccinations against diphtheria (*diphtérie*), polio (*polio*) and tetanus (*tétanos*), collectively called *DPT*, and whooping cough (*coqueluche*) are given between the third and fifth months after birth (via three, monthly injections – usually in both thighs). *DPT* boosters are administered at 12 to 15 months and again at five to six years and are repeated thereafter at five-to six-year intervals.

All children must be vaccinated again tuberculosis (*tuberculose*) by means of a BCG (*BCG*) before the age of six years, but the vaccination isn't recommended before the age of two. There's controversy over its effectiveness, which can have adverse effects, such as causing an abscess or, in rare cases, paralysis, and some doctors won't administer it. However, without these compulsory vaccinations, your child may not be admitted to school.

Although it isn't compulsory, a multiple vaccination called ROR (or *rudirouvax*) against measles (*rougeole*), mumps (*oreillons*) and German measles (*rubéole*) is recommended between the age of 12 and 15 months. Vaccinations are provided free. Until the age of three, children are also supposed to have a daily dose of vitamin D and fluoride.

DENTISTS

There are excellent dentists (*dentiste*) throughout France, where there are around 330 dentists per 100,000 inhabitants – similar to Germany, Switzerland and the US, but fewer than Italy (550 per 100,000) and more than the UK (around 300).

Few French dentists speak fluent English ('Aaargh!' is the same in any language). Many embassies keep a list of dentists speaking their national language, and your employer, colleagues or neighbours may be able to recommend someone. Town halls maintain lists of local dentists, and local chemists may recommend one or narrow the choice for you. You can obtain a list of dentists registered with social security from your local social security office.

Dentists are listed in the *Yellow Pages* under *Dentistes*. Usually only names, addresses and telephone numbers are listed, and information such as specialities, surgery hours and whether they treat children (some don't) isn't provided.

Many 'ordinary' dentists are qualified to perform non-routine treatment, e.g. endodontics (*endodontie*) or periodontics (*paradontie*), carried out by specialists in many other countries, but some treatment is available only from a 'surgeon dentist' (*chirurgien dentiste*). Dentists also usually carry out routine teeth cleaning themselves, and hygienists are rare in France.

Hours

Dentists' surgery hours vary considerably but are typically 09.00 to 12.00 and 14.00 to 19.00. Some dentists have Saturday morning surgeries, e.g. 09.00 to 12.00. You must make

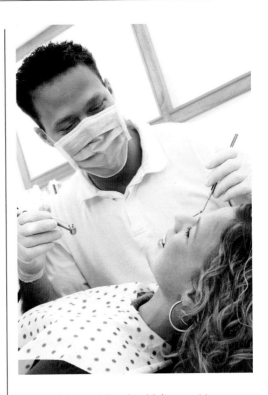

an appointment. You shouldn't expect to receive a reminder from a dentist that you're due for a regular check-up.

Many dentists provide an emergency service, and there are emergency services in most major cities. In Paris, there's a 24-hour home emergency dental service called *SOS Dentaire* (☎ 01 43 37 51 00).

Costs

Dental treatment can be expensive, e.g. €1,500 for a crown fitted by a 'specialist', although the normal charge is between €300 and €600. The *tarif de convention* (standard) costs are: check-up, fillings (*reconstitution coronaire*) start at €17 and tooth extraction €34, while plaque removal (*détartrage*) sets you back €29. There's no additional €1 charge as for doctor's consultations. As with doctors, however, you should check whether a dentist is *conventionné* if you want costs to be reimbursed.

Social security pays 70 per cent of the cost of dental care and prosthetic treatment, e.g. crowns and bridges. For orthodontic work, which is generally restricted to children under 12, you must obtain in advance a written description of the treatment required and an estimate of the cost for social security; you should be reimbursed 100 per cent of the cost.

However, these percentages apply to the theoretical cost of treatment as established by social security, which is often far lower than the actual cost. For example, the official cost of a crown is €107.50, therefore that the state will reimburse you only €75.25, whereas the cheapest metallic crown usually costs around €300, and a full ceramic crown can set you back up to €1,000 (dentists can charge what they like). You must pay the full cost of false teeth.

Sometimes it pays to have private treatment, as social security pays dentists only a small amount for some jobs (such as cleaning teeth) and they're therefore less likely to do a thorough job.

Always obtain a written estimate before committing yourself to a large bill. If you or your family require expensive cosmetic dental treatment, e.g. crowns, bridges, braces or false teeth, it may be cheaper to have treatment abroad. Alternatively, ask your dentist if he can reduce the cost by reducing the work involved.

Like doctors, dentists may give you a treatment form (*feuille de soins*), on which is listed the treatment provided and the cost. It's normal practice to pay a dentist after a course of treatment is completed, although if you're having expensive treatment such as a crown or bridge, your dentist may ask for a deposit .

OPTICIANS

There are no free eye tests for children or elderly people in France, where to obtain reimbursement (at 70 per cent) from social security it's necessary to have your eyes examined by an ophthalmologist (*ophtalmologue*), although you may have to wait weeks or even months for an appointment (the number of registered ophthalmologists is dwindling). An ophthalmologist is a specialist medical doctor trained in diagnosing and treating disorders of the eye, performing sight tests, and prescribing spectacles and contact lenses.

As with doctors, some ophthalmologists are *conventionné*, meaning that they charge the basic rate for a specialist of €28 for a consultation (or €44 if you haven't seen them in the preceding six months and aren't going to consult them again for at least six months),

whereas others (roughly half) aren't, which means that they charge more but you're reimbursed only at the basic rate. Treatment, including surgery, is reimbursed at only 65 per cent.

If glasses are necessary, the ophthalmologist writes a prescription, which you give to an optician, who's trained to test eyesight and to manufacture spectacles. To be reimbursed, you must choose an optician who's approved (*agréé*) by social security. Social security now pays 60 per cent (reduced in May 2011 from 65 per cent) of the cost of lenses and a 'basic' frame, if you require new glasses or if your spectacles are broken beyond repair. Note, however, that the approved cost of a basic frame (for adults) is €3 and of standard lenses €7.50, so your social security refund is hardly worth the paperwork! The balance may be picked up by a *mutuelle* if you have one. Larger refunds are available for contact lenses, bifocals or tinted lenses, but you may need prior approval from your *caisse*. If applicable, your optician will complete the necessary documents for social security.

Children aged under six are entitled to an unlimited number of pairs of glasses, reimbursed at 60 per cent (since May 2011) of €43 to €97 (frame plus lenses), depending on the correction required; children over six are reimbursed for only one pair per year.

Laser treatment for short-sightedness isn't reimbursed and costs around €1,000 per eye for the latest 'Lasik' treatment.

Some opticians test eyes as well as providing glasses, but these aren't reimbursed by social security, although some *mutuelles* cover the cost of optician-prescribed glasses. In Paris and other cities, there are large optical chains where spectacles can be made within an hour.

Prices for spectacles and contact lenses aren't controlled and are generally higher than in some other European countries (for example, soft contact lenses are cheaper in the UK and Germany), so it's wise to shop around and compare costs. Always obtain an estimate for lenses and ask about charges for eye tests, fittings, adjustments, lens-care kits and follow-up visits. Non-standard lenses can increase the cost of spectacles considerably. Ask the cost of replacement lenses; if they're expensive, it may be worthwhile taking out insurance. Many opticians and retailers offer insurance against accidental damage for a nominal fee. The French generally prefer spectacles to contact lenses, as the former are often a fashion accessory (or even a fashion 'statement'), but both are widely available.

It isn't necessary to register with an optician or optometrist (*opticien*). You simply make an appointment with the optician of your choice. Ask your colleagues, friends or neighbours if they can recommend someone. Opticians are listed in the *Yellow Pages* under *Opticiens* and ophthalmologists under *Médecins: ophtalmologie*.

It's wise to have your eyes tested before you arrive in France and to bring a spare pair of spectacles and/or contact lenses with you. You should also bring a copy of your prescription in case you need to obtain replacement spectacles or contact lenses urgently.

COUNSELLING

Counselling and help are available throughout France for various health and social problems, including drug and nicotine addiction, alcoholism, compulsive gambling, obesity, teenage pregnancy, rape, AIDS, attempted suicide and psychiatric disorders, as well as problems related to homosexuality, adolescence, marriage and relationships, child abuse and family violence.

There's a 24-hour information/assistance telephone number (☎ 113) for problems associated with drugs, alcohol and smoking (*Drogue/Alcool/Tabac Info-Service*). There are also self-help groups in all areas for problems such as alcoholism, gambling and weight control, e.g. Weight Watchers. There are psychologists (*psychologue*), psychiatrists (*psychiatre*) and psychoanalysts (*psychanalyste*) in public as well as private practice, and consultations with those in public practice may be reimbursed by social security.

The telephone numbers of various local counselling and help services (*Services d'Assistance*) are listed at the front of telephone books and include numbers for *SOS Amitié*, the French equivalent of the Samaritans, which provides a free counselling service in times of personal crisis. To find the number of your nearest *SOS Amitié* centre if you don't have a directory, call ☎ 01 40 09 15 22. SOS Help is an English-speaking Paris-based telephone crisis line in operation from 15.00 to 23.00 daily (☎ 01 46 21 46 46).

SMOKING

France has 12m smokers and, although numbers are falling, almost one in four children between 11 and 17 smokes, despite a law forbidding anyone under 16 from buying cigarettes. The incidence of smoking remains higher in France than in most other European countries, and it's estimated that over 30,000 deaths a year are directly attributable to smoking and that it adds some €8bn to the state healthcare bill.

The sale of cigarettes is strictly controlled by the state, which owns the French cigarette manufacturers and collects some €10bn in taxes annually from the sale of cigarettes and cigars; taxes have been dramatically increased to encourage people to stop smoking – and to compensate the treasury for any decline in the number of smokers (the average packet of 20 costs around €5) and loss of revenue from tobacco advertising, which is banned! (The result has been a significant increase in tobacco smuggling from neighbouring countries!)

> Cigarettes and other tobacco products can be purchased only at a licensed tobacconist (*bureau de tabac* or simply *tabac*).

Smoking was banned on all buses and trains in 2006 and is also forbidden in stations. No smoking is permitted on French domestic flights and all Air France flights. Smoking is also prohibited in all public buildings, clinics, hospitals, state and private schools, shops, offices and all business premises. However, owing to inevitable protests by proprietors and customers, it wasn't until February 2008 that French bars and restaurants finally lost the all-pervading smell of tobacco smoke beloved of devotees of the 'real' France.

Individuals who break the no-smoking laws can be fined, as can employers who fail to enforce the laws.

GIVING BLOOD & DONATING ORGANS

The collection of blood is organised on a rather ad hoc basis and if you wish to give blood you should look for signs advertising a local collection session or contact the Etablissement Français du Sang (EFS, 🖳 www.dondusang.net) to find out about sessions near you. You must be aged between 18 and 65 (60 for first-time donors) but you cannot give blood if you've had a blood transfusion at any time in your life, nor for four months after being tattooed or pierced.

If you spent over 12 months in the UK between 1980 and 1996, you may give blood only for non-therapeutic use, e.g. doctor training (owing to the perceived risk of passing on VCJD).

For information about donating organs, contact the Agence de la Biomédecine (🖳 www.agence-biomedecine.fr).

DEATH

Official Procedure

When someone dies in France, the attending doctor completes a death certificate (*constatation de décès*), but the medical cause of death is treated as confidential and doesn't appear on

death certificates. This can lead to problems if the body is to be sent abroad for burial, when a foreign coroner may require a post mortem examination.

If a death takes place at home in Paris, a coroner (*médecin de l'état civil/médecin légiste*) must be called, although elsewhere a family doctor can complete the death certificate. An inquest (*enquête judiciaire*) must be held when a death occurs in a public place or when it could have been caused by a criminal act. In the case of the death of a French resident, you should make several copies of a death certificate.

A death must be registered within 24 hours at the town hall in the district where it took place. Anyone can register a death, but you must present your own identification and that of the deceased. If the deceased was a foreigner, the town hall will require his passport or *carte de séjour*. The family record book (*livret de famille*) is required for a French citizen. Deaths of foreign nationals in France should also be registered at your local consulate or embassy.

Within a week of a death, you should inform banks, employer, retirement fund, insurers and *notaire*, as appropriate, as well as next of kin; within a month, a surviving spouse should apply for any pension refund (*réversion*); and within six months of a death you should provide a *déclaration des revenues* (on form 2042N) to the tax office showing all the income of the deceased's household between 1st January last and the date of death. See also **Wills** on page 280.

Euthanasia is illegal in France, where it's classed as murder, although the subject remains under discussion. A proposal to legalise euthanasia under certain circumstances was rejected in a vote by *sénateurs* (members of the Upper House) in January 2011.

Burial & Cremation

Cemeteries (*cimetière*) are secular and are usually owned by local authorities, who license a local undertaker (*pompes funèbres*) to perform burials. Before a burial can take place, the town hall must issue an 'act of death' (*acte de décès*) and a burial or cremation permit (*permis d'inhumer/de crémation*), as well as a permit to transport the body if it's to be buried outside the commune. You also need the mayor's permission to be buried in the commune where you have a second home. You should obtain at least six copies of the *acte de décès*. Bodies are normally buried or cremated within six days of death.

It's possible to reserve a burial plot (*concession*) for 15, 30 or 50 years or indefinitely. (You can even dig your own grave if you wish!) If a plot hasn't been reserved, the body will be buried in communal ground (*terrain communal*), where graves are maintained free of charge by the local authority for five years. After this period, the remains are disinterred and buried in a common grave. You're allowed to erect any monument but are responsible for the upkeep of a grave. There may be a diagram at the entrance to a cemetery indicating which plots are reserved and for how long.

It's common for a coffin to be left uncovered while friends and relatives pay their last respects, and you should inform the undertakers if you want the coffin closed.

Until recently there weren't many crematoria (*crématoire*) in France, although they can now be found in most large cities. You're entitled to scatter ashes anywhere except on a public right of way. Further information about funerals can be obtained from the Association Française d'Information Funéraire (💻 www.afif.asso.fr), which publishes its Charter of Ethics and Quality in English.

Costs

Dying in France is expensive and is best avoided if at all possible. However, since the state lost their monopoly on funerals at the end of the '90s the cost has been reduced, with the opening of 'supermarkets for the dead' such as the Roc-Eclerc chain (💻 www.roceclerc.com) – not without considerable opposition from other undertakers. Always obtain a quotation (*devis*) for a funeral in advance and make sure that you aren't paying for anything you don't want. Undertakers must, in any case, give you an example of a quotation detailing costs.

The cost of a basic funeral is set by the commune and the undertaker appointed by the commune is usually cheaper than an independent private company. The average funeral ('municipal' and private companies included) now costs around €4,000 for a burial and around €3,500 for a cremation. Prices for both burial and cremation start around €1,000 and can go up to around €8,000, with the cost of the coffin a major part of the price (undertakers can bury you only once and have to make the most of it!). The cost of cremation will, however, be a lot more if you want the ashes scattered from a helicopter on top of Mont Blanc!

Many people take out an insurance policy to pay for their funerals. Although banks will block the deceased's accounts (unless they're joint accounts), the next of kin may withdraw up to €5,300 to pay for a funeral, on production of the *acte de décès* and an undertaker's bill. The spouse or partner of a person who dies before retirement is also entitled to a death benefit (*capital décès*) to offset funeral costs, etc.

A 30-year burial plot can cost (without the cost of the tomb) between €150 and €500, depending on the area, and a perpetual plot between €1,500 and €4,000.

13.
INSURANCE

Most residents in France are covered by French social security (see page 237) and are entitled to higher benefits than residents of most other EU countries. Nevertheless, you would be unwise to rely solely on social security to meet your insurance needs. It's your responsibility to ensure that you and your family are legally insured, and French law is likely to differ from that in your home country or your previous country of residence, so don't assume that it's the same.

It's unnecessary to spend half your income insuring yourself against every eventuality, but it's important to insure against any event that could precipitate a major financial disaster, such as a serious illness or accident. There are a few occasions where insurance (*assurance*) for individuals is compulsory, including third party car insurance, third party liability insurance for tenants and homeowners, and mortgage life insurance if you have a mortgage. If you lease a car or buy one on credit, a lender will insist that you have comprehensive car insurance (see page 186).

Voluntary insurance includes car breakdown insurance (see page 186), third party liability insurance for schoolchildren, supplementary pensions, disability, health, household, dental, travel and life insurance (all covered in this chapter). If you fancy hunting in France, you can even take out insurance, costing from around €20, against being shot or having a leg chewed off by a *sanglier*!

If you're planning to take up residence in France, you should ensure that your family has full health insurance during the interval between leaving your last country of residence and obtaining health insurance in France.

In some countries (e.g. the UK), if you inform your insurance companies that you're moving abroad, your policies may be automatically be cancelled (and you may not be notified!). One way to cover yourself for this interim period is to take out a travel insurance policy (see page 250). However, it's better to extend your present health insurance policy than to take out a new policy. This is particularly important if you have an existing health problem that won't be covered by a new policy.

When buying insurance, obtain recommendations from friends, colleagues and neighbours. Compare the costs, terms and benefits provided by a number of companies before making a decision. Simply collecting a few brochures from insurance agents or making a few telephone calls could save you a lot of money. Premiums are often negotiable.

Further information can be found on the Service Public website (💻 www.service-public. fr) and from the Fédération Française des Sociétés d'Assurances (💻 www.ffsa.fr).

INSURANCE COMPANIES & AGENTS

Insurance is one of France's major business sectors, with over 500 French insurance companies and mutual benefit organisations to choose from, many providing a range of services while others specialise in certain fields only. The major insurance companies have offices or agents throughout France, including most large towns. Most insurance companies provide a free appraisal of your family's insurance needs.

Many of the largest companies, such as Groupement d'Assurances Nationales and Assurances Générales de France, which were previously government-owned, have now been largely privatised, although the government maintains considerable regulatory control over the insurance industry. The insurance sector is governed by regulations set out in the 'insurance code' (code des assurances) and insurance companies are supervised by the Direction Générale des Assurances.

☑ SURVIVAL TIP

If you find it difficult to obtain insurance cover, the Bureau Central de Tarification (🖥 www.bureaucentraldetarification.com.fr) can demand that the company of your choice provide you with cover, with the premium being fixed by the Bureau.

It's possible to take out certain types of insurance in another country, e.g. property insurance, although the policy must usually be written under French law. The advantages are that you have a policy you can fully understand (apart from all the legal jargon!) and can make claims in your own language. This is usually a good option for the owner of a holiday home in France. However, bear in mind that insuring with a foreign insurance company may be more expensive than insuring with a French company.

Since 1993, EU residents have been entitled to obtain insurance from any EU country and the Service Public website (🖥 www.service-public.fr) has links to the latest Ministry of Finance list of foreign and domestic companies licensed to sell insurance in France. In practice, however, it may be difficult or impossible to obtain insurance with a foreign company.

Insurance companies and mutuelles (see below) sell their policies in a number of ways. There are 'general agents' (agent général), which is a misleading term for agents who represent a single company and sell the policies of that company only, and brokers (courtier), who sell policies from a number of insurance companies and mutuelles. Most

mutuelles and some insurance companies also sell their policies direct to the public, transactions often taking place by telephone and post.

Note that it can be difficult to obtain impartial insurance advice, as brokers may be 'influenced' by the high fees offered for selling a particular policy. (Regrettably, you cannot sue an insurance agent for giving you bad advice or insure yourself against being uninsured!) Insurance agents, brokers and companies are listed in separate sections in the Yellow Pages under Assurances.

Mutual Benefit Organisations

A mutual benefit organisation (mutuelle) is an association made up of individuals who are grouped together, e.g. by profession or area, in order to insure themselves for a favourable premium. There are two kinds of mutuelle: one is a sort of provident society or sick fund, which is a non-profit organisation that ploughs its profits back into the fund, and the other an insurance company operating at a profit (hopefully). A provident mutuelle provides fixed tariffs irrespective of the number of claims and is greatly preferable to an insurance company.

Most trades and occupations have their own mutuelle, commonly providing supplementary health insurance and pensions. There are around 400 mutuelles in France and it pays to choose one that's widely recognised by medical practitioners. Further information about mutuelles can be obtained from the Fédération Nationale de la Mutualité Française (🖥 www. mutualite.fr).

Insurance Contracts

Read insurance contracts carefully before signing them. If you don't understand a policy, get someone to check it and explain the terms and the cover provided. Policies often contain 'traps' in the small print and, like insurance companies everywhere, some French insurance companies will do almost anything to avoid honouring claims. Therefore it pays to deal only with reputable companies (not that this provides a guarantee!).

Premiums

An insurance premium (cotisation) should be paid within ten days of the due date. If it isn't, you'll be sent a reminder; if it's still unpaid after 30 days your policy can be suspended. You will, however, still be liable to pay the premium. Bear in mind that insurance companies often take eons to bill new customers and in the meantime you should obtain documentary evidence that you're insured, e.g. from an agent.

You're usually issued with a provisional contract and, several weeks later, a definitive contract (the French love paperwork).

Claims

If you wish to make a claim, you must usually inform your insurance company in writing by registered letter within two to five days of the incident (e.g. for accidents) or 24 hours in the case of theft. (Household thefts must be officially reported within 48 hours.) Thefts should also be reported to the local police within 24 hours, as you must provide proof that you've filed a police report (*récépissé du dépôt de plainte*) when making a claim. In some cases, these are legal requirements.

An insurance company will normally send an adjuster to evaluate the extent of the damage, e.g. to your home or car. You should obtain legal advice for anything other than a minor claim. You can hire an insurance expert to negotiate with your insurance company on your behalf.

In certain cases, claims for damaged property (such as storm-damaged buildings or vehicles damaged by hailstones) aren't considered by insurance companies unless the government declares the situation a natural catastrophe or an 'act of God'. Claims concerning a government declared natural catastrophe/'act of God' situation can be made within ten days of the incident.

All insurance claim periods are calculated from the time you're aware of the incident (*sinistre*), which may of course be some time after it happened. So, if you're away from home when an incident occurs, your interests are protected.

Cancellation

Always check the notice period required to cancel (*résilier*) a policy. Insurance policies are normally automatically extended (*tacite reconduction*) for a further period (usually a year) if they aren't cancelled in writing by registered letter two or three months before their expiry date. If you don't cancel a policy,

you must pay the next year's premium, even if you no longer require the insurance. If you don't pay, you'll be sued for the whole premium plus the credit agency's fees and interest. Your name may also be added to a debtor's list, your bank account frozen and the bailiffs called, resulting in even more costs!

You may cancel an insurance policy before the term has expired without penalty if the premium is increased, the terms are altered (e.g. the risk is diminished), an insured object is lost or stolen or, in the case of home insurance, if you move. In certain circumstances you may cancel without penalty if your personal circumstances alter, e.g. you change jobs, are made redundant or retire, get married or divorced, or a member of your family dies. A cancellation for any of the above reasons must still be done in writing and sent by registered post.

SOCIAL SECURITY

France has a comprehensive social security (*sécurité sociale*) system covering healthcare, injuries at work, family allowances, unemployment insurance, and old age, invalidity and death benefits.

France spends more on 'welfare' than almost any other EU country: over 30 per cent of GDP. Total social security revenue is around €200bn per year and the social security budget is higher than the gross national product (GNP), i.e. social security costs more than the value of what the country produces! The government has proposed both reductions in benefits and increases in contributions to help lower the country's overall budget deficit (in 1978, the social services budget was 97 per cent funded by contributions, which by 2007 had fallen to 72 per cent, the remainder being covered by general taxation).

Not surprisingly, social security benefits are among the highest in the EU (the average household receives around a third of its income from social support payments such as family allowances and pensions), as are social security contributions. Total contributions per employee (to around 15 funds) average around 60 per cent of gross pay, some 60 per cent of which is paid by employers (an impediment to hiring staff). The self-employed must pay the full amount (an impediment to self-employment!), although the self-employed who operate a small business under the *auto-entrepreneur* system only pay their contributions as and when they have income. However, with the exception of sickness benefits, social security benefits aren't taxed; indeed they're deducted from your gross taxable income. Unsurprisingly, the public has been highly resistant to any change that would reduce benefits, while employers are pushing to have their contributions lowered.

Despite the high contributions, the French social security system is under severe financial strain due to an ageing population, which has contributed to a huge increase in spending on healthcare and pensions in recent years (France's health spending alone is around 10 per cent of its GNP – the highest in Europe).

Measures introduced in recent years include an enforced employee contribution towards 'the reimbursement of the social debt' (*contribution au remboursement de la dette sociale/CRDS* or *remboursement de la dette sociale/RDS*) – known unofficially as 'the social hole' (*le trou social* or more colloquially *le trou de la sécu*) – in addition to the existing employee levy (*CSG*) of 5.1 per cent (both contributions are levied against 95 per cent of total salary up to certain limits, which can be found at 🖳 www.legislation.cnav.fr). The combined *CRDS/CSG* now amounts to 8 per cent, which is only partly deductible from income taxes.

The Caisse Nationale d'Assurance Maladie (CNAM), which is part of the Ministry of Health and Social Security, is the public authority responsible for ensuring that social security policy is carried out on a national level, and for negotiating conventions and agreements with medical professions. Sixteen regional sickness insurance fund offices (Caisse Régionale d'Assurance Maladie/CRAM) deal with questions regarding accidents at work and retirement. They also coordinate the actions of local social security offices (Caisse Primaire d'Assurance Maladie/CPAM), of which there are around 130 throughout the country (at least one in each department), and which deal with everyday matters and reimbursements.

Information

Information about social security is available online, e.g. the Service Public site (🖳 www.service-public.fr) and the Assurance Maladie site (🖳 www.ameli.fr – it stands for *Assurance Maladie en ligne*), where some information is also available in English (click on 'Qui sommes nous?' on the home page).

For information in English (after the short introduction in French) about the French social security system, you can call the French Health Insurance Advice Line, set up by the CPAM of Manche but available to all residents (☎ 08 11 36 36 46). You can also visit 🖳 www.ameli.fr/assures-votre-caisse-manche.

There are a number of books (in French) about social security, including *Tous les Droits de l'Assuré Social* (VO Editions), and consumer magazines regularly publish supplements on various aspects of social security, particularly pensions and health insurance. If you have complementary health insurance through a *mutuelle* (see **Private Health Insurance** below) you'll receive a monthly or quarterly magazine containing the latest health care information.

annual income is below €9,029 (2011), you may be entitled to the most basic of state healthcare, known as *Couverture Maladie Universelle* (*CMU*) *de base*, provided you have lived in France continuously for three months. The *CMU* was introduced in January 2000 and is intended to ensure that all French residents have some social security cover. Information is available from your local CPAM office and on a dedicated government website (🖥 www.cmu.fr).

UK citizens wishing to claim family allowances in France must obtain a 'signing off paper' from the Child Benefit Office (PO Box 1, Newcastle-upon-Tyne, NE88 IAA, ☎ 0845-302 1444, 🖥 www.hmrc.gov.uk/childbenefit/contactus.htm) and may also need proof of income and health insurance. For further information, contact the Longbenton Contact Centre for Non-Residents Helpline, Department of Work and Pensions (formerly Department of Social Security), Benton Park View, Newcastle-upon-Tyne, NE98 1ZZ, UK, ☎ 0191-203 7010), which can send you a useful booklet (no. SA29) entitled *Your social security insurance, benefits and healthcare rights in the European Economic Area*, or visit the website of HM Revenue & Customs (🖥 www.hmrc.gov.uk) or the Department for Work and Pensions (🖥 www.dwp.gov.uk).

Eligibility & Exemptions

Your entitlement to health and other social security benefits depends on your nationality, your work status (e.g. whether you're employed, self-employed or retired) and your residence status.

Unless you're covered by a reciprocal social security agreement, you must normally contribute to French social security for a certain period before you're eligible for benefits. For example, you must contribute for three months before being entitled to family allowances, and you must contribute for at least a year before you can claim maternity benefits.

Different periods of salaried employment are required to qualify for 'cash' benefits (*prestations en espèces*), e.g. disability payments, and benefits 'in kind' (*prestations en nature*), e.g. free medicines. For example, for *prestations en espèces* you must have been in salaried employment for at least 120 hours in the last quarter, while for *prestations en nature* you must have been salaried for at least 200 hours. Full details can be obtained from your local social security office.

If you no longer meet the qualifying conditions, your benefits are extended for a maximum of a year from that date. (Benefits are extended indefinitely for the long-term unemployed, provided they're actively seeking employment.)

If you don't qualify for social security benefits, you don't have private health insurance and your

EU Nationals

If you're an EU resident visiting France, you can take advantage of reciprocal healthcare agreements. You should apply for a certificate of entitlement to treatment at your local social security office (or a post office in the UK). The paper form called an E111 has been superseded by a plastic card called a European Health Insurance Card (EHIC), and there have been a number of changes to procedures and conditions of use.

First, an EHIC must be applied for (by post, phone or internet) at least a month before travel and cannot simply be obtained the same day from a post office. An EHIC covers only one person and not a family, as did the E111. Its period of validity varies with the country of issue: in the UK, it's valid for three to five years (an E111 had to be renewed annually). However, you must continue to make social security contributions in the country where it was issued and, if you become a resident in another country (e.g. in France), it becomes invalid in that country.

Although an EHIC entitles you to much better cover than an E111 (which covered only emergency hospital treatment, whereas the EHIC covers 'any necessary medical treatment arising during a temporary stay in another EU member state'), it still doesn't entitle you to 100 per cent reimbursement of all medical expenses in France.

Rather, it gives you entitlement to the same cover as a French resident, i.e. normally around 70 per cent of routine healthcare and treatment costs. You can still receive a large bill from a French hospital, as the national health service assumes only a percentage of the cost! You're therefore recommended to enquire about the availability of 'top-up' insurance plans, covering the balance of costs.

If you incur medical costs in France, you must obtain a treatment confirmation (*feuille de soins*) and go to the local CPAM, the authority which deals with health insurance, to apply for reimbursement, which will be sent to you or credited to your UK bank account. Details of the procedure are included in the booklet that comes with the EHIC form. Note that it can take months for medical expenses to be reimbursed. Note that there have been reports of medical practitioners and hospitals in some countries, including France, refusing to accept the EHIC.

As soon as you have a permanent address in France, even if this is within the six month period the EHIC covers you for, you must obtain an E106 (for those below retirement age) or an E121 (for retirees), which is available in the UK from the International Pension Service (☎ 0191-218 7777). This form entitles you to cover while you transfer out of your home country's system (you must inform the relevant authority, e.g. the Department of Work and Pensions in the UK) and into the French system.

British visitors or Britons planning to live in France can obtain further information about reciprocal health treatment in France from the Department of Work and Pensions' Medical Benefits department (the same telephone number as above and below, of the International Pension Service) or, if they're of pensionable age, from the International Pension Service (☎ 0191-218 7777). Information about the EHIC in the UK can be obtained from the Post Office (☎ 0845-606 2030) and via the internet, e.g. 🖥 www.nhs.uk/nhsengland/healthcareabroad/ehic/pages/introduction.aspx.

Employees

France has social security agreements with over 40 countries (including all other EU countries and the US), whereby employees on a short-term assignment in France can continue to make contributions to social security in their home country and be eligible for social security benefits in France. An EHIC (see **EU Nationals** above) is required for the first year of employment and forms E102 and E106 for an extension.

The maximum period to which this arrangement applies is usually five years, although you may be required to contribute to French social security if you work in France for over two years. The exact terms of social security agreements vary from country to country and you should check before starting work in France. However, if you qualify to pay contributions abroad, it's usually worthwhile doing so, as contributions in most countries are much lower than those in France.

If you're from a country which doesn't have a social security agreement with France and are employed in France, your employer must declare you to the URSSAF (see page 243) and pay social security contributions on your behalf.

If you require just health insurance, it's much cheaper to take out private health insurance

(see page 247) than to pay high French social security payments. Private health policies also offer a greater choice of health facilities and may provide a wider range of benefits than social security.

Unemployed & Low Income

If you aren't employed, you may still be able to make contributions in your home country and claim benefits in France for a period. If you're unemployed and seeking work in France, you may be entitled to medical treatment for up to three months on presentation of form E119. Those on low incomes (e.g. under €7,771 for a single person and €11,657 for a couple in 2011) are exempt from social security contributions and also qualify for free complementary health insurance, the CMU complémentaire (see above under **Eligibility & Exemptions**). When you no longer meet the qualifying conditions, benefits are extended for a maximum of a year from the applicable date. In the case of long-term unemployed people actively seeking employment, benefits are extended indefinitely.

Non-salaried Americans aren't covered by French social security and must have private health insurance (see page 52). If you're receiving social security benefits in the US, you may be restricted regarding the number of hours you can work in France, e.g. 45 per month.

Students

If you're a student following a standard course at a French state-supported institution, you're usually covered by French social security. However, if you're attending a private institution, e.g. the American University of Paris, or are following a non-standard programme, e.g. French language and culture classes, you must have (and must produce evidence of) private health insurance (see below). Those coming to France under an exchange scheme must be covered for healthcare by the exchange authorities.

Retirees

Retirees receiving a state pension from another EU country are entitled to the same health benefits as French retirees. EU retirees over 60 going to live permanently in France aren't required to contribute to French social security, but must register with their local CPAM (and present forms E106 and E121). You're now required to have a form E121 for each member of your household. If you're receiving a state pension in another EU country, you may be subject to an annual check that you're still receiving it.

EU citizens who retired before qualifying for a state pension used to be able to receive French social security health cover for up to 30 months by obtaining a form E106 from their country's social security department. They had to have made full contributions in their home country during the previous two years and had to register at their local CPAM, present a copy of their carte de séjour/résident or temporary authorisation (récépissé de demande de carte de séjour), proof of their relationship with any dependants who didn't qualify in their own right (e.g. a marriage certificate), and their bank account details (relevé d'identité bancaire).

However, in 2007 the government changed the rules so that 'inactive' EU citizens taking early retirement in France could no longer pay for national health cover but had to take out private medical insurance, in most cases, until they had lived in France for a minimum of five years. This rule was challenged by the EU as discriminatory, since it applied only to non-French EU citizens. The government agreed to issue a new circular regularising the situation but when it did so in 2011 the rule remained unchanged. The EU may now launch the infringement proceedings it had earlier threatened but this process can take a long time, during which many people remain affected, particularly those with existing conditions that prevent them being accepted for full private medical insurance.

⚠ **Caution**

If you're planning to take early retirement in France, check whether you'll be covered under the national health system before making the move or that you can obtain (and afford) private health insurance. The change in the rules in 2007 (se above) forced a number of people who had already retired to France to move elsewhere following the withdrawal of their national health cover.

Registration

If you're working in France, your employer will usually complete the necessary formalities to ensure that you're covered by social security. If he doesn't, you must obtain confirmation that you're employed in France (*déclaration d'emploi*) and register at your local CPAM. Your town hall will give you the address or you can find it under *Sécurité Sociale* in your local *Yellow Pages*. In certain cases, you'll need to visit the *Relations Internationales* department of social security, e.g. if you're retired with a pension in another EU country.

You must provide your personal details, including your full name, address, country of origin, and date and place of birth. You'll also need to produce passports, *cartes de séjour* or proof of residence and certified birth certificates for your dependants, plus a marriage certificate (if applicable). You may need to provide copies with official translations, but check first, as translations may be unnecessary. You'll also need a rental contract or an electricity bill.

When you've registered, you'll receive a registration card (*Carte Vitale*), which looks like a credit card and contains a smart chip (*puce*). The card has your name and your social security number (*No. d'Immatriculation de l'Assuré*) printed on the front. Additional information is coded into the chip, which is needed to process any claim for reimbursement or services.

Contrary to some fears, there's no detailed information regarding your health or medical condition on the chip. However, at the beginning of 2007, the *Carte Vitale* began to be superseded by the *Carte Vitale 2*, which carries a photograph of the holder and the following additional information:

♦ the name of your regular doctor (*médecin traitant*);

♦ details of your complementary insurance, if any;

♦ details of a person to contact in an emergency;

♦ your permission to donate organs if applicable.

The *Carte Vitale 2* is linked to a computerised system known as a *dossier médical personnel*

(*DMP*), containing all your medical records and vital information such as your blood group and allergies. The cards are being issued initially to those making their first social security registration, and it will still take some years for all existing cards to be replaced. The existing *Carte Vitale* (the Mark 1 model) contains details of any on-going or chronic conditions you may have, for which healthcare may be provided free of charge.

Along with a *Carte Vitale*, you'll receive a certificate (*attestation*) containing a list of those entitled to benefits on your behalf (*bénéficiaires*), i.e. your dependants, and the address of the office where you must apply for reimbursement of your medical expenses. (This address is normally indicated in small type just above your name and address and is easy to miss.) Dependants include your spouse (if she isn't personally insured), dependent children under the age of 16 (or under the age of 20 if they're students or unable to work through illness or invalidity), and ascendants, descendants and relatives by marriage supported by you and living in the same household.

☑ SURVIVAL TIP

If you move home, acquire or need to change or transfer beneficiaries or find any errors in the information on your *attestation*, you must inform your CPAM. If a social security official makes a regular visit to your town hall, you may be able make changes to your records and ask questions during a scheduled visit.

Once you're registered with your local CPAM you can obtain information in French about the reimbursement of your medical expenses and the status of your 'medical account', your entitlements and the procedures to follow for reimbursement by telephone (☎ 3646). Calls are charged at local rates from land (home) lines. The service operates on weekdays between at least 08.30 and 16.00. Alternatively, or additionally, after the CPAM registration you can register online at the Maladie Assurance site (🖳 www.ameli.fr) to consult your medical account and reimbursements.

The date when your entitlement to social security benefits expires is shown on the certificate (*droits jusqu'au…*). Just before the end of the year when your benefits expire, you should receive a new certificate, along with instructions regarding how and where to update your card. There are machines in most public hospitals and in some town halls and an increasing number of chemists in which you can simply insert your *Carte Vitale* and update the chip. Alternatively, you can post the card to the office that sent it to you and ask for it to be updated. Make sure that you keep your certificate in a safe place, as you may be required to show it if you require services from a medical practitioner or chemist who isn't linked to the card system or whose computer is out of order.

Contributions

Social security contributions (*cotisations sociales* or *charges sociales*) are calculated as a percentage of your taxable income, although for certain contributions there's a maximum salary level. Contributions start as soon as you're employed or start work in France and not when you obtain your residence permit (*carte de séjour*) or proof of residence certificate.

Contributions are paid directly to the Union de Recouvrement des Cotisations de Sécurité Sociale et d'Allocations Familiales (URSSAF), which has 105 offices throughout France. URSSAF offices collect contributions for their area and send them to the central social security agency (Agence Centrale des Organismes de Sécurité Sociale/ACOSS) that distributes funds to the various benefit agencies, e.g. CNAF, CNAV and CRAM – the French love acronyms almost as much as paperwork.

It's possible to pay contributions monthly (actually, you pay ten monthly instalments from January to October based on an estimated total contribution; any necessary adjustment is made in November or December); you must apply before 1st December for monthly payments from the following 1st January.

The total social security contributions for employees (*salarié*) are an average of around 60 per cent of gross pay, some 60 per cent of which (i.e. around 35 per cent of gross pay) is paid by employers. The employees' portion comes to around 25 per cent of gross pay. All contributions are withheld from pay cheques, so no action is required (except to mourn the loss of so much hard-earned money!).

Salaried employees come under the general regime for salaried workers (*régime général des travailleurs salariés*). There are special regimes for agricultural workers (*régime agricole*), called MSA or GAMEX, and for miners, seamen, railway workers and various other state employees. All these are termed obligatory regimes (*régimes obligatoires*). It's also possible to make voluntary contributions (if you can't think of anything better to do with your money).

Benefits

Under French social security you're entitled to health, sickness and maternity, work injury and invalidity, family allowance, unemployment, and old age, widow(er)'s and death benefits, each of which is described below. With the exception of health benefits, these are known as 'cash' payments (*prestations en espèces*). Health benefits are known as payments 'in kind' (*prestations en nature*), e.g. free medicines.

Most social security benefits (*allocations*) are paid as a percentage of your salary rather than at a flat rate, subject to minimum and maximum payments. You must have been employed for a minimum period and/or earn a minimum salary to qualify for certain benefits, as detailed below.

Health Benefits

To qualify for health benefits you must have been employed for 600 hours in the last six months (or for six months at the minimum wage), 200 hours in the last quarter or 120 hours in the last month. There's no minimum qualifying period during the first three months after registration. For details of health benefits, see **Chapter 12**.

Sickness Benefit

To qualify for sickness benefit you must have been employed for 200 hours in the last three months (or six months if you're on the minimum wage). To qualify for extended cash sickness benefit you must have been insured for 12 months before your incapacity and for 800 hours of employment in the last 12 months. This includes 200 hours in the first 3 of the last 12 months or 2,080 hours at the minimum wage, including 1,040 hours during the first 6 of the last 12 months.

Employees who aren't automatically covered by sickness insurance can contribute voluntarily. As with unemployment benefit, sickness benefit is paid as a percentage of your previous salary (e.g. 50 per cent) rather than at a flat rate. A leaflet explaining sickness benefit is available from CPAM offices (listed at 🖳 www.ameli.fr). Information is also available on the Service Public website (🖳 www.service-public.fr).

Maternity Benefit

To qualify for maternity benefit you must have been insured for at least ten months before your pregnancy began and have been employed for 200 hours in the first three of the last 12 months or have made six months' contributions.

Payments are equal to your basic pay (up to a limit of around €2,700 per month), paid fortnightly throughout your maternity leave (for the duration of maternity leave). Benefits are payable for an extra two weeks before the birth if there are complications and for up to 12 weeks for multiple births. A monthly allowance or milk coupons are available for four months after the birth. Benefits are also paid for adoptions.

Employees who aren't automatically covered by maternity insurance can contribute voluntarily.

For details about the French social security system in English, go to 🖳 www.cleiss.fr and click on 'systèmes de sécurité sociale par pays' (right-hand side), then click on the Union Jack flag below 'France'.

Work Injury & Invalidity Benefits

Industrial accident insurance pays all medical and rehabilitation costs associated with work injuries (accident de travail) and provides a pension for you or your dependants in the case of injury or death. Insurance starts from your first day at work, with the variable contributions paid wholly by your employer.

A benefit of 60 per cent of earnings is paid (up to a maximum amount) during the first 28 days of disability and thereafter 80 per cent of earnings. Self-employed workers are excluded and are covered under the state sickness insurance programme. In the case of injury resulting in permanent total disability, a pension equal to 100 per cent of average earnings during the last 12 months is paid from the day following the accident.

In the case of partial disability, average earnings are multiplied by between 0.5 and 1.5 depending on the degree of disability. A lump sum payment is made if a disability is below 10 per cent. All necessary associated medical treatment, surgery, hospitalisation, medicines, appliances, rehabilitation and transportation are paid 100 per cent by social security. Those aged over 60 with at least 80 per cent invalidity are also entitled to an allocation compensatrice tierce personne (ACTP).

Family Allowances

France is a great place for large families (famille nombreuse), as there are high family allowances and other benefits (including lower taxes) to encourage couples to have more children.

To qualify for the basic family allowance (prestation or allocation familiale) you must have a carte de séjour or proof of residence and at least two children living at home with you, and your household income must be below a certain level (which depends on your circumstances).

You must have at least two children aged under 20 who are unemployed or earning no more than 55 per cent of the legal minimum wage (SMIC – see page 22). The monthly basic family allowances (2011) was €125.78 for two children, €286.94 for three children, €448.10 for four children and €161.17 for each subsequent child; these sums are increased by €35.38 for children aged between 11 and

16 and by €62.90 for children over 16. There's no allowance for the first child (to encourage you to have more!). A 'family supplement' (*complément familial*) of €163.71 is paid if you have children aged under six or have three or more children over the age of three and your household income is below a certain level. There are different schemes for agricultural, railway and public utility employees.

Other family allowances include:

♦ a birth or 'adoption allowance' (*prime à la naissance ou à l'adoption*), which pays €903.07 (2011) per child expected in the seventh month of pregnancy or twice as much (€1,806.14) for an adopted child;

♦ a 'starter allowance' (*allocation de base*) of €180.62 (2011) per month from birth until the child is three years old, plus additional amounts if one or both parents stops work or works part-time (these two allowances are part of the *prestation d'accueil du jeune enfant/PAJE*, which also includes an allowance for giving up work and for employing a child minder);

♦ a 'school start allowance' (*allocation de rentrée scolaire/ARS*);

♦ a 'single parent allowance' (*allocation de parent isolé/API*);

♦ a 'family support allowance' (*allocation de soutien familial*);

♦ a 'parental education allowance' (*allocation parentale d'éducation*);

♦ a 'special education allowance' (*allocation d'éducation spéciale*);

♦ a 'parental presence allowance' (*allocation de présence parentale*) for parents taking time off work to look after a sick or disabled child;

♦ an 'aid to resuming activity' (*aide à reprise d'activité des femmes/ARAF*) for women whose children are all at school;

♦ grants for employing a child-minder (*aide à la famille pour l'emploi d'une assistante maternelle agréée*);

♦ an allowance for moving house if you have (or are expecting) at least three children and need a larger home (*prime de déménagement*);

♦ various rent allowances for the low-paid, e.g. *aide personnalisée au logement* and *allocation de logement familiale*.

Most of these allowances, including the young child allowance, are means tested, although the child-minder allowance isn't and is equivalent to around 80 per cent of the cost (although the paperwork required to claim it is mountainous).

In addition to the above, there are various holiday benefits (*aide aux vacances*) for low-income families, including vouchers for holiday camps (*coupon vacances en camps et colonies*) and activity centres (*coupon centres de loisirs sans hébergement*), cultural and sporting activity vouchers (*chèque loisirs*), and family holiday vouchers (*coupon vacances familiales*).

If you're entitled to family allowances in another EU country, you must provide a certificate of termination of payments in that country.

Some family allowances are 'exportable' and paid to families with parents resident in France and children abroad, e.g. for education or health reasons. If one parent lives abroad with the children and is unemployed and the other lives and works in France, the parent in France is entitled to claim family allowances. If the parent abroad works and is paid family allowances by his country of residence, the difference is paid to the parent working in France (provided this is less than the French family allowance, which is likely).

For further information enquire at your local CAF in France or at a social security office abroad, or visit the CAF website (🖥 www.caf.fr).

PENSIONS

There's a crisis in state pension funding in France (and most of Europe), which has the largest proportion of inactive people over 55 in the EU, high unemployment, one of Europe's highest life expectancies, and around 40 per cent of 18 to 25-year-olds in full-time education. In 2010, the government extended the number of years some people are required to work in order to qualify for a full state pension on retirement.

The French pension system is largely unfunded, which means that the active population pays the pensions of those who are retired or otherwise inactive, known as a *régime de répartition*. As in many other countries, there are plans to transfer the burden from the public to the private sector, although this is creating controversy and social unrest.

The state pension schemes (the principal one for employees in business and industry and supplementary schemes for various government employees, small businessmen, shopkeepers and farmers) comprise both basic and supplementary pensions. Contributions are paid by both employers and employees and vary according to income. Certain non-employed people can contribute voluntarily to the state pension scheme.

Retiring in France

If you plan to retire while in France, you should check regularly that your pension contributions are up to date. A state pension is paid only when you cease fulltime employment and make an application to your regional sickness insurance fund office (Caisse Régionale d'Assurance Maladie/CRAM). The procedure is as follows:

♦ When you reach the age of 58, visit a retirement information centre (*point d'accueil*) to obtain information about retiring (contact a CRAM or visit the CNAV website 💻 www.retraite.cnav.fr to find your nearest centre).

♦ Four months before you reach the age of 60, you need to apply for a state pension (*demande de retraite personnelle* or *demande de retraite progressive* if you continue working part-time) as well as for any private pension to which you've been contributing. You can check on the progress of your application by calling Allô Retraite (☎ 3960).

The CNAV website also contains helpful information about retirement. If you're self-employed; refer to 💻 www.le-rsi.fr or www.cnavpl.fr, depending on whether you're classed as a *travailleur independant* or a *profession libérale*. In any correspondence with your local CRAM or CNAV office you need to give your full name, address, social security number and the number of your local social security office.

If you move to France after working in another EU country (or move to another EU country after working in France), your state pension contributions can be exported to France (or from France to another country). French state pensions are payable abroad, and most countries pay state pensions directly to their nationals resident in France. If you're salaried in France before your retirement there, following previous salaried employment in the UK, your local CRAM or CNAV office will handle your application for a UK state pension. They'll need your UK National Insurance number when you apply for your French state pension.

British pensioners should also note that, if
they were receiving a winter fuel allowance before
leaving the UK, they may be able to continue
to receive it in France; contact the International
Pensions Centre, Tyneview Park, Newcastle-upon-
Tyne NE98 1BA (☎ 019-1218 7777). Americans
who retire in France can receive their pensions (and
other benefits) via the Social Security department of
the French Embassy in Paris.

If you plan to retire to France, you should ensure
that your income is (and will remain) sufficient to live
on, bearing in mind devaluations if your pension or
income isn't paid in euros, rises in the cost of living
(see page 253), and unforeseen expenses such as
medical bills or anything else that may reduce your
income, e.g. stock market crashes.

Information about retirement homes in France
is contained in our sister publication, *Retiring in
France* (Survival Books).

PRIVATE HEALTH INSURANCE

If your stay in France is short, you may be
covered for emergency medical treatment
by a reciprocal agreement between your
home country and France (see **Eligibility &
Exemptions** on page 239), but this may not
cover you for routine treatment, for which you
may need to take out private health insurance.
This may take the form of a holiday and
travel policy (see below) or a comprehensive
international health policy (see below). It's
essential to make sure that you're fully covered
in France before you receive a large bill. If your
family isn't adequately insured, you could be
faced with some *very* high medical bills.

When changing employers or leaving
France, you should ensure that you have
continuous health insurance and, if you're
planning to change your health insurance

company, you should ensure that important
benefits aren't lost.

Once you become resident in France,
you must register with social security (see
Registration on page 242), which will cover you
for most of your medical expenses, although
you may wish to take out a complementary
health insurance (or 'top-up') policy (*assurance
complémentaire maladie*, commonly called
a *mutuelle*, although strictly a *mutuelle* is a
particular kind of benefit organisation), which pays
the portion of medical bills that isn't paid by social
security.

A complementary scheme may also provide
a supplementary pension, and the *Loi Madelin*
allows you to deduct your contributions from
taxable income provided you join the *mutuelle*,
which costs (depending on age) from around
€15.

Almost every trade or occupation has its
own complementary fund and in many cases it's
obligatory for employees to join. If you're self-
employed (*travailleur independent* or *profession
libérale*), you must take out a health insurance
policy (known in this case as an *assurance au
premier franc*) through your social security office
or through the relevant professional organisation.
Information about insurance for the self-employed
can be obtained from offices of the Caisse
d'Assurance Maladie des Professions Libérales.
If you aren't employed in France but have a
social security card (*Carte Vitale*), you can join
a complementary fund of your own choosing.
Premiums are normally quoted as a flat rate per
person covered, therefore unlike social security
health cover, insuring a large family will cost
considerably more than insurance for a single
person.

Many *mutuelles* base their reimbursements on
those of social security and reimburse a patient
only after social security has paid a proportion
of the fee. Therefore, in a case where social
security doesn't contribute, e.g. when a medical
practitioner isn't part of the national health system
(*non-conventionné, non-agréé*), a complementary
fund may also pay nothing. However, some
mutuelles pay the whole cost or part of the cost
of treatment or items that aren't covered or are
barely covered by social security, such as false
teeth and spectacles.

Some *mutuelles* reimburse the statutory
€1 charge on all consultations introduced in

October 2004 in the case of group policies (e.g. company schemes), but many don't on individual policies and you should check before taking out a policy.

Reimbursement applies only to the standard medical charges (*tarif de convention*). For example, if a blood test costs €50 and the *tarif de convention* is €40, your complementary fund will normally pay only the 30 per cent of the €40 that isn't refunded by social security. You must pay the €10 charged in excess of the *tarif de convention* yourself. However, for a higher premium you can insure yourself for actual charges (*frais réels*). Most policies offer different levels of cover.

It's sometimes necessary to have been a member of a complementary fund for a period before you're eligible to make a claim, e.g. three months for medical claims and six months for dental claims.

Different health practitioners 'recognise' different *mutuelles*. Reimbursement is triggered automatically in the case of those that are recognised, but an application must be made by those that aren't, which will involve you not only in a certain amount of paperwork but also in delays before receiving reimbursement.

Unfortunately, it's almost impossible to find out which *mutuelles* are most widely recognised. However, if you're likely to be using a particular practitioner (e.g. acupuncturist or physiotherapist) regularly, you should ask which *mutuelles* he recognises and consider joining one of those.

Details of *mutuelles* in your area can be found on the site of the Fédération Nationale de la Mutualité Française (💻 www.mutualite.fr – click on '*Trouver une mutuelle*') or simply look under *Mutuelles d'Assurances* in the *Yellow Pages*.

There are few foreign insurance companies which offer top-up policies for expatriates living in France. For UK nationals, Goodhealth Worldwide (now part of Aetna International), London office ☎ 0866-320 4023, 💻 www.aetnainternational. com) currently offers one, and a number of other international health policy providers (see below) are considering introducing such policies.

When choosing a complementary fund, ask friends, colleagues and neighbours for recommendations. Compare the costs, terms and benefits provided by a number of funds before making a decision.

It's wise to choose an insurer who's regulated, which means that after a certain period (e.g.

two years) they aren't permitted to alter your terms and conditions, increase the premiums if your health deteriorates with advancing years, or refuse to continue your insurance after an accident or illness.

International Health Insurance

Non-residents who spend time in different countries should take out an international health policy (sometimes referred to as private medical insurance or PMI), which should provide the following:

♦ immediate emergency healthcare;

♦ immediate access to a doctor;

♦ referral to a specialist if required;

♦ routine treatment, including dental treatment – if necessary in a hospital.

Dental Insurance

It's unusual to have full dental insurance (*assurance dentaire*) in France, as the cost is prohibitive. Basic dental insurance is provided under social security (see **Dentists** on page 229) and by *mutuelles* (see above). A *mutuelle* may offer additional cover for a higher premium. Most private health insurance companies offer dental cover (or extra dental cover) for

an additional premium, although there are many restrictions and cosmetic treatment is excluded. Where applicable, the amount payable by a health insurance policy for a particular treatment is fixed and depends on your level of dental insurance. It's often necessary to request 'pre-approval' for certain dental treatment and services, such as crowns, caps or bridge work. A list of specific refunds is available from insurance companies.

Other Health Insurance

In France, children are obliged to care for their parents if they're unable to care for themselves, but it's possible to take out insurance against becoming a burden on your children in old age or following an illness or accident (*assurance dépendance*). This can cost at least €300 to €500 per month, however, and may be much more, depending on your age and health. Policies can normally be taken out between the ages of 45 and 75, and contributions are tax-free.

Another kind of insurance recently introduced in France is the *garantie des accidents de la vie* (*GAV*), which pays out in the event of death or disability of a family member as a result of an accident, whether domestic or medical, an attack, or a natural or other disaster, e.g. a plane crash but not usually a road accident. *GAV* for an average family costs between €25 and €30 per month depending on the amounts paid, which vary with the severity of the accident (there may be a required minimum level of disability, e.g. 30 per cent).

HOUSEHOLD INSURANCE

Household insurance in France generally includes third party liability (*responsabilité civile*), building and contents insurance, all of which are usually contained in a multi-risk household insurance policy (*assurance multirisques habitation*).

Nine out of ten homeowners have a multi-risk policy, but not all policies cover the same risks: for example, while over 90 per cent of policies cover water damage, fewer than 90 per cent include third party liability, only around 75 per cent include theft, and just over half cover glass breakage.

All buildings under construction and major renovation or repair work on existing buildings must be covered by damage insurance (*assurance de dommages*) that guarantees the work for ten years after completion. It's the builder who's responsible for taking out this cover, but during the first ten years of the building's life it passes automatically to a new owner and will pay for damage caused by faults in the original construction.

For further information about household insurance, refer to our sister-publication *Buying a Home in France*.

THIRD PARTY LIABILITY INSURANCE

It's customary to have third party liability insurance (*assurance responsabilité civile*) in France for all members of your family. This covers you for damage done or caused by you, your children and even your pets, e.g. if your dog bites someone, although where damage is due to negligence, benefits may be reduced. Check whether insurance covers you against accidental damage to your home's fixtures and fittings.

> ### ☑ SURVIVAL TIP
> If you have children at school, they must also be covered by third party liability insurance (*assurance scolaire* – see Insurance on page 132).

Third-party liability insurance is usually combined with household insurance (see above), although it's usually adequate for modern domestic requirements. Third-party liability insurance (when not included in household insurance) is normally designed for businesses where cover may be necessary for the activities of a number of employees and, perhaps, the uses of power tools, vehicles, etc. Consequently the costs would probably be prohibitive for domestic purposes. Rates typically start in the hundreds of euros per year, rising to many thousands for large-scale needs; even then subscribers may need to pay an excess, e.g. the first €75 to €150 of a claim. If you're self-employed or run a business, you must also have third party liability insurance for 'managers' (*assurance responsabilité civile chef d'entreprise*), the cost of which depends on your line of work.

If you're letting a property, ensure that you're covered for third party liability in respect of your tenants, as most home insurance policies exclude such 'commercial' liability.

HOLIDAY & TRAVEL INSURANCE

ravel insurance (*assurance voyage*) is available from many sources, including travel agents, insurance agents, motoring organisations, charge and credit card companies, household, car or private medical insurers, and transport companies. Package holiday companies also offer insurance policies. However, most don't provide adequate cover, although you should take advantage of what they offer. For example, car insurance may include personal accident and health insurance (e.g. through Mondial Assistance) even if you don't use your car, but won't cover you for belongings or the cancellation of flights.

LIFE INSURANCE

Social security pays only some three months' salary or a maximum of around €8.838 (2011) to a widow or dependants, therefore a life insurance policy may be advantageous or even necessary. There are two kinds of 'life insurance' in France: life assurance (*assurance vie*) and death insurance (*assurance décès*). A life assurance policy is valid until you die and is essentially the same as a pension scheme, whereas a death insurance policy pays out only when you die. A life assurance policy benefits you, whereas a death insurance policy benefits your survivors.

A death insurance policy can also be useful as security for a bank loan and can be limited to cover the period of the loan; companies will usually place an age limit, eg. 80, beyond which cover is no longer provided. A life assurance policy can be a useful tax planning tool, reducing your tax rate on investment income. The term 'life insurance' is used for both types of insurance in this section, but you should ensure that you know which type of insurance you're buying.

Many companies provide free life insurance as an employment benefit, although it may be accident life insurance only, i.e. if you die as the result of an accident. If your employer doesn't provide life insurance (or if the cover provided is inadequate), you should consider taking out a private policy.

You can take out a private life insurance or endowment policy with numerous French or foreign insurance companies, although a life insurance policy that complies with and is intended to take advantage of French law is best taken out in France.

With all French life insurance policies you're entitled to a 30-day 'cooling off' period, during which you may cancel a policy without penalty.

New laws are removing many of the tax exemptions previously accorded to life assurance policies. In certain cases, however, premiums and dividends are tax-deductible and income from a life assurance policy is taxed at a low rate provided the policy is allowed to mature for at least four years and the fund is redeemed as a lump sum. Even if you make withdrawals during the investment period, only the growth element of the withdrawal is taxable. Because a life assurance policy reduces your income tax liability, it may also reduce your wealth tax liability (see page 277). If you take out a policy before moving to France, it will be exempt from French inheritance tax (unless you were aged over 70 when you took out the policy).

⚠ Caution

One possible catch with a life assurance policy is the *prélèvement libératoire*, a premium which exempts you from paying tax at the highest level and which may automatically be deducted unless you specify otherwise. Unless you're in the top tax bracket, you should benefit by not paying the optional *prélèvement libératoire*, but you must make it clear that you don't want to pay it. Seek the advice of an accountant before committing yourself to a contract.

You can choose the beneficiaries and the amount to be paid to them in the event of your death, which will obviously affect the amount you pay, as will your age and state of health, e.g. non-smokers are usually offered a 20 per cent reduction. You may pay as little as around €10 per month at the age of 30 for a benefit of €30,000, but premiums increase with age and there's a maximum age for taking out most policies, e.g. 45, 55 or 60.

Instead of taking a lump sum on retirement, you can opt for life annuities (*rente viagère*), whereby you're 'paid' a fixed amount each year for the rest of your life, but payments are subject to income tax (on a sliding scale according to your age. Note also that, when you die, payments stop and your spouse cannot continue to benefit from your pension, unless you make the annuity 'reversible' (*reversible*), in which case you receive a lower annuity but your spouse (if he survives you)

continues to receive either all or part of the annuity for the rest of his life.

You may have to pay a monthly minimum (e.g. €75) into a life assurance plan, although some plans allow you to make a minimum payment (e.g. €100) every three or six months.

Related beneficiaries (your spouse and children) aren't liable for French gift or inheritance tax, but unrelated beneficiaries are liable for inheritance tax at 60 per cent (see page 278), although they may be able to delay paying the tax until they're 70.

Finally, it's wise to leave copies of all life insurance policies with your will and with your lawyer. If you don't have a lawyer, keep copies in a safe place, but make sure your dependants know where they are! A life insurance policy must usually be sent to the insurance company upon the death of the insured, with a copy of the death certificate (see **Death** on page 232).

14.

FINANCE

France is one of the world's most sophisticated countries when it comes to financial
services and has the world's fifth-largest economy (2010), with GDP per head of
US$44,510 (around the same as the UK and slightly lower than the US). The annual
real GDP growth rate between 2003 and 2008 was, however, just 1.8 per cent, although
Inflation is historically low (around 2 per cent in mid-2011).

Financial services are provided by numerous
banks, the post office, investment brokers and
other financial institutions. Compared with
many other developed countries, particularly
the UK and the US, France isn't a credit
economy and the French prefer to pay in
cash or by cheque, debit card or charge
card rather than by credit card. In fact, many
French people don't understand the concept
of credit cards. Nevertheless, they're getting
increasingly into debt (*surendettement*) as they
spend beyond their means – so much so that
the government recently changed the law to
make personal bankruptcy possible.

If you plan to live permanently in France,
you must ensure that your income is and will
remain sufficient to live on, bearing in mind
exchange rate fluctuations (if your income
isn't paid in euros), rises in the cost of living,
and unforeseen expenses such as medical
bills or anything else that may reduce your
income (such as stock market crashes and
recessions!). Foreigners, particularly retirees,
often underestimate the cost of living in France
(see below) and some are forced to return to
their home countries after a few years. France
is one of the highest taxed countries in the
European Union (EU) when both income tax
and social security contributions are taken into
consideration.

When you arrive in France to take up
residence or employment, ensure that you
have sufficient cash, travellers' cheques, credit
cards, luncheon vouchers, coffee machine
tokens, gold, diamonds, etc. to last at least until
your first pay day, which may be some time
after your arrival. During this period you'll also
find an international credit card (or two) useful.

COST OF LIVING

No doubt you would like to estimate how
far your euros will stretch and how much
money (if any) you'll have left after paying
your bills. Anyone planning to live in France,
particularly retirees, should take care not to
underestimate the cost of living, which isn't as
low as is commonly supposed.

France is an expensive country by
American standards, and in recent years
many US visitors have found it difficult or
impossible to remain within their budgets.
(Americans will be particularly shocked by
the price of gasoline, electricity, clothing,
paper products and books, not to mention
social security contributions.) Even by British
standards, France is an expensive place to
live, with the notable exception of property
prices (Paris excepted). Manufactured goods
are (in general) more expensive than in the
UK, while services tend to be less expensive.
Social security costs are extremely high,
particularly for the self-employed, and the
combined burden of social security, income
tax and indirect taxes make French taxes
among the highest in the EU.

Your food bill will depend on whether you adapt to French eating habits or buy imported foods. Food in France costs around 25 per cent more than in the US but prices are similar overall to most other western European countries. From €400 to €600 should feed two adults for a month, excluding fillet steak, caviar and alcohol (other than a moderate amount of inexpensive beer or wine). Shopping abroad (e.g. via the internet) for selected 'luxury' items, such as electronic apparatus, computers and photographic equipment, can result in significant savings. English-language books can also be bought cheaply in the UK.

In the Mercer 2011 Cost of Living Survey (💻 www.mercer.com/costofliving) of 214 cities worldwide – one of the most respected annual surveys – Paris was ranked 27th, the only French city in the top 50. Luanda (Angola), Tokyo and Ndjamena (Chad) had the dubious honour of holding the top three places. The most expensive European cities were Moscow (4th), Geneva (5th), Zurich (7th), Oslo (15th), Berne (16th), Copenhagen (17th) and London (18th).

Other expensive European cities included Milan (25th), St Petersburg (29th), Rome (34th), Vienna (36th), Stockholm (39th), Helsinki (42nd), Prague (47) and Amsterdam (50th). Other selected rankings included Singapore (8th), Hong Kong (9th), Sydney (14th), Beijing (20th), Melbourne (21st), Tel Aviv (24th), Perth (30th), New York (32nd – the only US city in the top 50), Canberra (34th), Adelaide (46th), Toronto (59th), Vancouver (65th), Los Angeles (77th), Montreal (79th), Calgary (96th), Chicago (=108th), Washington (=108th), Ottawa (114th), Aberdeen (144th), Glasgow (148th), Birmingham, UK (150th) and Belfast (178th).

> The fundamental flaw with most cost of living surveys is that they convert local prices into $US, which means that ranking positions are as much (or more) the result of currency fluctuations than price inflation. Therefore in the last few years, the Eurozone, Australia, Switzerland, China and Japan, with their harder currencies, have become more expensive in dollar terms, while the UK and the US have become cheaper.

It's also possible to compare the cost of living between various cities, using websites such as the Economist Intelligence Unit (💻 http://eiu.enumerate.com/asp/wcol_wcolhome.asp), for which a fee is payable. There are numerous websites that will give you an idea of costs in France, such as 💻 www.numbeo.com/cost-of-living/country_result.jsp?country=france and www.expatforum.com/articles/cost-of-living/cost-of-living-in-france.html. However, you need to take cost of living data with a pinch of salt, as it may not be up to date, and price comparisons with other countries are often wildly inaccurate (and often include irrelevant items which distort the results).

It's difficult to estimate an average cost of living, as it depends very much on where you live and your lifestyle. There are also large differences in prices (and above all rents) between the major cities and rural areas. If you live in Paris, drive a Porsche and dine in expensive restaurants, your cost of living will be much higher than if you live in a rural area, drive a Renault Twingo and eat mostly at home. You can live relatively inexpensively by buying local produce whenever possible and avoiding expensive imported goods.

However, even in the most expensive cities, the cost of living needn't be astronomical. If you shop wisely, compare prices and services before buying, and don't live too extravagantly, you may be pleasantly surprised at how little you can live on.

FRENCH CURRENCY

In January 2002, the euro replaced the French franc, but although the franc has ceased to exist in France, it continues to be the official currency of Monaco, French overseas territories, such as Guadeloupe and Martinique, and many former French colonies, and is still 'used' in conversation by many French people. Older French people don't 'think' naturally in euros and commonly talk in francs (colloquially called *balles*). In fact, when referring to large sums (e.g. the cost of a property), some French people still refer to old francs (100 old francs were equal to one new franc), which became obsolete in 1958!

The euro (€) is divided into 100 cents (nostalgically called *centimes* by the French) and coins are minted in values of 1, 2, 5, 10, 20 and 50 cents, and €1 and €2. The 1, 2 and

5 cent coins are brass-coloured (and virtually worthless!), the 10, 20 and 50 cents copper-coloured. The €1 coin is silver-coloured in the centre with a brass-coloured rim, and the €2 coin has a brass-coloured centre and silver-coloured rim. (Euro coins contain so much nickel that they can cause skin irritation.) The reverse ('tail' showing the value) of euro coins is the same in all euro-zone countries, but the obverse ('head') is different in each country. French coins carry traditional designs (e.g. Marianne), the letters RF (*République Française*) and the date of minting. All euro coins can, of course, be used in all eurozone countries.

Euro banknotes (*billets*) are identical on both sides throughout the euro-zone and depict a map of Europe and stylised designs of buildings. Notes are printed in denominations of €5, €10, €20, €50, €100, €200 and €500, the last being available only on request (and approval!) from your bank. The size of notes increases with their value. Money is *argent* in French and *monnaie* means currency or change (*change* means exchange, as in *bureau de change*). To pay 'in cash' is either *en espèces* or *en liquide*, although the word *cash* is increasingly used.

The euro symbol may appear before the amount (as in this book), after it (commonly used by the French, who have been used to putting F after the amount) or even between the euros and cents, e.g. 16€50. Values below one euro are usually written using the euro symbol, e.g. €0,75, rather than with a US-style cent symbol, although small amounts (e.g. telephone call charges) are sometimes expressed as, for example, *3 ct €*. For information about writing figures in France, see **Writing Cheques** on page 263.

IMPORTING & EXPORTING MONEY

There's no limits on the import or export of funds and a French resident is permitted to open a bank account in any country and to export an unlimited amount of money from France. However, if you're a French resident,

you must inform the French tax authorities of any new foreign account in your annual tax return. Sums in excess of €10,000 (since 2007) deposited abroad, other than by regular bank transfers, must be reported to the Banque de France.

Similarly, if you enter or leave France with €10,000 or more in French or foreign banknotes or securities (e.g. travellers' cheques, letters of credit, bills of exchange, bearer bonds, giro cheques, stock or share certificates, bullion or gold or silver coins quoted on the official exchange), you must declare it to French customs. If you exceed the €10,000 limit and are discovered, you can be heavily fined.

When you arrive in France to take up residence or employment, you should ensure that you have sufficient cash (preferably deposited in a French bank account), travellers' cheques or deposit/credit card funds to last at least until your first pay day, which may be some time after your arrival. If you're planning to invest in property or a business that's financed with funds in a foreign currency (e.g. GB£ or US$), it's important to consider both present and possible future exchange rates (don't be too optimistic!). On the other hand, if you'll be earning your income in euros, this may affect your financial commitments abroad.

If you need to borrow money to buy property or for a business venture in France, you should carefully consider where and in what currency to raise finance. Note that it's difficult for foreigners to obtain business loans in France, particularly for new ventures, and you shouldn't rely on doing so.

It's possible to 'fix' the exchange rate to guard against unexpected fluctuations by buying a 'forward time option' from your bank or through a specialised currency exchange firm; the further in advance you buy, the more you pay. Note, however, that you may regret doing so if there's a big swing in your favour! When transferring or sending large amounts of money to (or from) France, you should be aware of the alternatives available, which include the following:

♦ **Bank draft (*chèque de banque*):** A bank draft should be sent by registered post. However, in the unlikely event that it's lost or stolen, it's impossible to stop payment and you must wait six months before a new draft can be issued. Bank drafts aren't treated as cash in France and must be cleared, like personal cheques. You should try to give a couple of days' notice if you require a bank draft.

♦ **Bank transfer (*virement*):** A 'normal' transfer should take three to seven days, but in reality it usually takes much longer and an international bank transfer between non-affiliated banks can sometimes take weeks! (It's quicker and cheaper to transfer funds between branches of the same bank than between non-affiliated banks.) In fact, the larger the amount the longer it often takes, which can be particularly awkward when you're transferring money to buy a property. When making a bank transfer, make sure that you have the full details of the recipient's bank account: if it's a foreign account, obtain the international bank account number (IBAN) and bank identifier code (BIC); if it's a French bank account, ensure that you give the name, account number, branch number (*code agence*) and the bank code (*clé*) or simply ask for a *relevé d'identité bancaire* or *RIB* (see page 261), which contains all this information. Otherwise, your money can be 'lost' while being transferred and it can take weeks to locate it.

♦ **SWIFT transfer:** One of the safest and fastest methods of transferring money is via the Society of Worldwide Interbank Financial Telecommunications (SWIFT) system. A SWIFT transfer should be completed in a few hours, funds being available within 24 hours, although even SWIFT transfers can take five working days.

> ### ☑ SURVIVAL TIP
>
> Since January 2008, the *Virement SEPA* system has been operating which simplifies euro payments, without using cash, to anyone located in Europe. The account receiving the payment should be credited within three working days. See 🖥 www.esepa.eu/e/view.xhtml for details.

The cost of transfers varies considerably – not only commission and exchange rates, but also transfer charges. If you plan to send a large amount of money to France or abroad for a business transaction such as buying property, you should ensure that you receive the commercial rate of exchange rather than the tourist rate, and shop around for the best rate. Always check charges and rates in advance and agree them with your bank (you may be able to negotiate a lower charge or a better exchange rate).

Smaller amounts of money can be sent by international money order from a post office or by telegraphic transfer, e.g. via Western Union (the fastest and safest method, but also the most expensive). Money can be sent via American Express offices by Amex card holders. It's also possible to send cheques drawn on personal accounts, although these take a long time to clear (usually a number of weeks) and fees are high. Post cheques can be cashed at any post office in France, and most credit and charge cards can be used to obtain cash advances. Don't rely entirely on a card to obtain cash, however, as they're sometimes 'swallowed' by cash machines and it can take a few weeks to retrieve them or obtain a replacement. Some machines refuse foreign cards for no apparent reason (if this happens, try another bank).

It isn't wise to close your bank accounts abroad, unless you're certain that you won't need them in the future. Even when you're resident in France, it's cheaper to keep money in local currency in an account in a country that you visit regularly, rather than to pay commission to convert euros. Many foreigners living in France maintain at least two accounts:

a foreign bank account for international transactions and a local account with a French bank for day-to-day business. If you open a euro account in another EU country, transfers to a French account are now subject to the same charges as domestic French transfers. If you're transferring from an account in France you should use the *virement européen* option (see box), although there's a limit of €50,000 per transfer. For transfers to the UK, euros and not GB£ must be transferred in order that the *virement européen* charges apply.

CHANGING MONEY

Most banks and main post offices in major cities have foreign exchange windows, and there are exchange bureaux (*bureaux de change*) in all major cities as well as at airports and major railway stations. Here you can buy or sell foreign currencies, buy and cash travellers' cheques, and obtain a cash advance on credit and charge cards. At airports and in tourist areas in major cities, there are automatic change machines accepting major currencies, including US$ and GB£.

Bureaux de change often have longer business hours than banks, particularly at weekends. Most offer competitive exchange rates and low or no commission (but check). They're easier to deal with than banks and, if you're changing a lot of money, you can usually negotiate a better rate, although generally banks offer better rates. Never use unofficial money changers, who are likely to short change you or give you a poor exchange rate. The euro exchange rate (*cours de change*) for most major international currencies is listed in banks and daily newspapers, and is also given online, e.g. 🖥 www.x-rates.com.

Prepaid Currency Cards

Prepaid currency cards are a new alternative to travellers' cheques and debit and credit cards, and can be used to withdraw cash from ATMs and to purchase goods in shops and restaurants, although few French businesses accept this form of payment. The cards, known by different names, are

offered by several finance companies including International Currency Exchange (which calls its card 'Cash2go'), Maestro ('I-Travel Prepaid'), Travelex ('Cash Passport') and Western Union ('Travel Cash Card'). Euros and US dollars are currently the only currencies available, and most companies allow 'loads' of between €150/US$200 and €7,500/US$10,000, the exchange rate being fixed when you 'load' the card. You're then given a PIN, which allows you to withdraw cash at ATMs.

Advantages of prepaid currency cards include greater security – if the card is lost or stolen there's no link between it and your bank account, unlike a debit card, for example, and the card has no name on it so there's no risk of identity fraud. Your cash withdrawals aren't subject to exchange rate fluctuations – which may be an advantage or a disadvantage, depending on whether the rate goes up or down. On the other hand, there are charges for most transactions, e.g. £2 for a cash withdrawal and £3 for a top-up. Read the small print carefully and make sure you understand all the associated charges before you take out a prepaid currency card. It's also worth comparing the charges with those incurred on a credit or debit card, which may well be lower.

If you lose your card or it's stolen, inform your card provider and they'll provide a replacement card, allowing you to re-access your funds. The use of CHIP and PIN on these cards also helps to keep them more secure if stolen or lost (although they aren't foolproof).

BANKS

There are two main types of bank in France: commercial and co-operative. The largest commercial banks have branches in most large towns and cities and include the Banque Nationale de Paris (BNP Paribas), Crédit Lyonnais and Société Générale. All three have now been privatised and, in order to compete with other larger European banks, have been seeking to merge. (Formal discussions between BNP and Société Générale were, however, blocked by the French government early in 2009, but in July that year approval was given for the merger of the Caisse d'Epargne – see **Savings Banks** below – and the Banque Populaire, as the former

was in difficulty.) Village branches are rare, although in many villages there are bank offices (*permanence*), which usually open one morning a week.

The largest co-operative banks are Crédit Agricole, Crédit Mutuel and BRED Banque Populaire. They began life as regional, community-based institutions working for the mutual benefit of their clients, but most are now represented nationally and offer a full range of banking services. Unlike commercial banks, each branch office of a co-operative bank is independent and issues its own shares. Anyone can become a member and invest in their shares, which is usually mandatory if you wish to take out a mortgage or loan, but isn't necessary to open a current account.

Crédit Agricole is the largest co-operative bank – in fact it's the largest retail bank in Europe, with around 10,000 branches and some 17m customers. (It's also the largest landholder in France.) Crédit Agricole is the only French bank to offer an English-language service (see **Foreign Banks** below). The top four French banks (Crédit Agricole, Crédit Lyonnais, Société Générale and BNP Paribas) are among the world's top ten banks. (In March 2003, Crédit Agricole bought Crédit Lyonnais, which, however, continues to trade as Crédit Lyonnais, albeit with fewer branches.) The Banque de France is the authority which sets interest rates and regulates other banks. All banks, including foreign banks, are listed in the *Yellow Pages* under *Banques*.

French banking has become highly automated in recent years, and all banks now offer an efficient and wide-ranging service, including online banking (for which there's sometimes a charge, e.g. €3 per month).

If you want to change banks, you should be aware of the restrictions and costs involved, e.g. you cannot transfer a mortgage or life insurance policy. In the former case, you can ask your new bank for a loan to pay off the mortgage with your old bank, although this is unlikely to be to your financial advantage. With some mortgages, you're liable for penalties if you redeem them before the agreed term. In the case of life insurance, you may be able to 'cash in' your policy, provided it has run for at least eight years (or you'll be liable for income tax on the amount you receive), but again there may be penalty charges. There are also charges for transferring other 'products', such as certain savings plans, although your bank manager may waive these. Send a recorded letter to your bank manager informing him of the accounts you wish to transfer and giving him the *RIB* (see page 261) from your new bank.

Post Office Banking

As in many other countries, the most popular banking facility in France is operated by the post office (*La Poste*), which also offers some of the 'cheapest' banking. In terms of the amount of money handled, *La Poste* is the country's third-largest 'bank' (after Crédit Agricole and Caisse d'Epargne). In rural areas, where the nearest bank is often many kilometres away, many people use the post office as their local bank. Another advantage of the post office is that many branches are open for longer hours than banks, although some aren't.

Post office accounts provide the same services as bank accounts, including international money transfers (by post and telegraph to many countries) and payment of bills. Post office account holders are issued with a (free) cash card for withdrawals from a cash machine located outside main post offices. Each transaction is confirmed with a receipt by post. The Post Office began offering mortgages in 2005.

Savings Banks

There are also savings banks, the largest of which is the Caisse d'Epargne (*caisse d'épargne* is also French for 'savings bank'), with over 400 branches. Savings banks are similar to British building societies and US savings and loan organisations, and offer savings schemes and loans for property and other purchases, although general banking services are limited compared with commercial and cooperative banks.

Foreign Banks

There are some 175 foreign-owned banks in France – more than in any other European country except the UK, although they have a relatively small market share. Most major foreign banks are present in Paris, but branches in the provinces are rare.

However, competition from foreign banks is set to increase, as EU regulations allow any bank trading legitimately in one EU country to trade in another. Among foreigners in France, the British are best served by their national banks, both in Paris and in the provinces, particularly on the Côte d'Azur. The most prominent British banks in France are HSBC with around 380 branches, followed by Barclays with around 100 branches, including at least one in all major cities.

> ☑ **SURVIVAL TIP**
>
> If you do a lot of travelling abroad or carry out international business transactions, you may find that the services provided by a foreign bank are more suited to your needs.

Foreign banks are also more likely to have staff who speak English and other foreign languages. However, many foreign banks (and some French banks) handle mainly corporate clients and don't provide banking services for individuals; even those that do may not operate in the same way as branches in their 'home' country or even have foreign-language-speaking staff. Barclays, however, has a national English-language service (☎ 08 10 06 06 60 or 01 55 78 70 30 or, from the UK, 0800-917 0157, 🖳 www.barclays.fr) and the Crédit Agricole also has an English-language service, known as 'Britline', based at its Caen branch (☎ 02 31 55 67 89, 🖳 www.britline.com).

Opening Hours

Normal bank opening hours are from 09.00 to 17.30 or 17.45, Mondays to Fridays, although banks may open any time between 08.30 and 09.30 and some close between 16.00 and 17.00. Larger branches may stay open until 18.30 or 19.00 on certain days or every day in cities. Banks at main railway stations in Paris are open from 09.00 until between 20.00 and 23.00, although they usually have long queues. In small towns, banks close for lunch from 12.00 or 12.30 until 13.30 or 14.00. Some banks open on Saturdays (e.g. 09.00 to 16.00) or just Saturday mornings since the official working week was reduced to 35 hours in 2000, although when a bank in a rural area opens on Saturdays it may close on Mondays.

Banks are closed on public holidays; when a public holiday falls on a Tuesday or Thursday, banks usually also close on the preceding Monday or the following Friday respectively.

At major airports such as Paris' Charles de Gaulle and Orly airports, *bureaux de change* are open from 07.00 to 23.00 daily. In Paris and other cities, private *bureaux de change* are usually open from 09.00 to 18.00, Mondays to Saturdays.

Using Banks

The following general points apply to French banking:

♦ For security purposes, most banks have two entrance doors, the second of which is opened only after the first has closed (intended to trap robbers as they attempt to flee with their booty). In some cases, you must press a bell and wait for a staff member to press a button to open the outer door.

♦ Banks usually have a more casual air than those in many other countries and most use open counters rather than protected teller windows, as most cash operations are now automated. They also don't have armed guards.

♦ When making payments into an account, a distinction is made between cash deposits (*versement en espèces*) and cheque deposits (*versement de chèques*), which must be listed on the paying-in form. Cheques must be signed on the back with the current account number written out. When paying in a foreign cheque, even one in euros, you usually – it depends on the bank – incur a charge (e.g. €15 up to a value of €300 or its equivalent or €25 for a larger amount), although charges are supposed to be the same as those for domestic transactions. When paying in a foreign cheque, even one in euros, you may incur a charge, e.g. 0.05 per cent for amounts up to €75,000 and €0.025 for higher amounts, with a minimum fee of €16.76 in both cases.

♦ When making a deposit 'manually', i.e. at a counter, you may not be given a receipt (*reçu* or *double*) and should request one if required.

♦ All regular bills, such as electricity, gas, telephone, mortgage and rent, can be paid by direct debit (*prélèvement automatique*) by your bank free of charge. A direct debit instruction form (*autorisation*) is provided.

This method of payment has the advantage that payments are automatically recorded on your monthly statement. Most banks offer a free online service, where you can consult your current and other accounts at any time. Bills can usually be paid online, although many banks charge for online services. If you need to pay an individual a regular sum, you can set up a standing order (*virement permanent*), which is also free. Note that if you don't pay a bill on time, interest (*majoration*) can be charged at 1.5 times the official rate.

◆ Many banks offer customers safe deposit boxes for an annual rent, e.g. from around €50 for the smallest box with contents insurance (included in the rental) up to a value of around €40,000. On-line secured digitized (*numérisé*) archiving of valuable documents is also offered for an annual fee by some banks.

◆ Buying stocks and shares is normally done through your bank, rather than a stockbroker (*agent de change/courtier*), although it's also possible to buy and sell directly, e.g. via the internet. Banks make a charge that's added to the broker's commission, plus VAT (*TVA*) at 19.6 per cent. New share issues can usually be purchased through advertisements in newspapers such as *Le Monde*. French banks also sell shares in their own unit trusts.

◆ If you have a problem with a bank, write to the mediator (*médiateur*), which all banks are obliged to have and whose name and address should be shown on your statements. Model letters (*lettre type*) in French, as well as the definitions of hundreds of banking and other financial terms, can be found on the website of the Fédération Bancaire Française (🖥 www.lesclesdelabanque.com – click on '*Particuliers*' and then on '*Lettres-Type*').

Opening an Account

You can open a bank account whether you're a resident or non-resident. It's better to open a bank account in person than by correspondence from abroad. Ask friends, neighbours and colleagues for their recommendations and go to the bank of your choice and introduce yourself. You must be aged at least 18 and provide proof of identity,

e.g. a passport (although you may need more than one form of identification), and your address in France if applicable, e.g. a utility bill.

You can open an account with a French bank while you're abroad, either by telephone or online. A number of French banks offer an English-language service, including the Crédit Agricole, whose service is called Britline (see 🖥 www.britline.com), and some British banks have branches in France, e.g. Barclays (see 🖥 www.barclays.fr).

☑ SURVIVAL TIP

If you open an account by correspondence, you must provide a reference from your current bank, including a certificate of signature or a signature witnessed by a solicitor. You also need a photocopy of the relevant pages of your passport and a euro draft to open the account.

Any account holder can create a joint account by giving his spouse (or anyone else) signatory authority. A joint account can be for two or more people. If applicable, you must state that cheques or withdrawal slips can be signed by any partner and don't require all signatures. However, in the event of the death of a partner, a joint account is blocked until the will has been proven.

Non-residents

If you're a non-resident (i.e. spend at least six months per year outside France), you're only entitled to open a non-resident account (*compte non-résident*). There's little difference between non-resident and resident accounts and you can deposit and withdraw funds in any currency without limit, although there may be limits on the amount you can transfer between accounts (an anti-money-laundering measure). Non-resident accounts have a ban on ordinary overdrafts (*découverts*), although loans for a car or house purchase are possible. French banks have increased the minimum deposit for non-resident accounts, which can be up to €3,000, although it isn't usually necessary to maintain this balance once an account is open.

Shop around for the best deal. It's possible for residents of the UK and Ireland to open a Crédit Agricole Britline account (www.britline.com) by post with CA Normandie, who only require a deposit of €225 or GB£150 to open a current account.

To open a non-resident account, you must usually produce two forms of identification, two 'proof of address' documents no more than three months old and a letter of recommendation from your existing bank. You can have documentation (e.g. cheque books, statements, etc.) sent to an address abroad.

If you're a non-resident with a second home in France it's possible to survive without a French account by using credit and debit cards, although this isn't wise and is an expensive option.

Residents

You're considered to be a resident of France if you have your main centre of interest there, i.e. you live or work there for at least half the year. To open a resident account you must usually have a residence permit (*carte de séjour*), proof of residence from your town hall or evidence that you have a job in France.

Current Accounts

The normal account for day-to-day transactions is a current or cheque account (*compte courant* or *compte de chèques*), which don't accrue interest. (It's illegal for banks in France to pay interest on current accounts.) Most people deposit their 'rainy day' money in a savings account. However, most banks will automatically transfer funds above a specified sum from a cheque account into an interest-bearing savings account.

Post office cheque accounts (*compte chèques postal*) are referred to by the initials *CCP*. Information about post office accounts is available online: there's a dedicated website (www.labanquepostale.fr) as well as the main Post Office website (www.laposte.fr).

When opening a cheque account, you should request a bank card, which can be used to pay bills throughout France (see **Cash & Debit Cards** below). Bank cards aren't cheque guarantee cards, which don't exist in France (see below). You'll receive a cheque book (*chéquier/carnet de chèques*) and your

bank card around two to three weeks after opening an account (although some banks don't issue a cheque book until an account has been operated for at least two months). You must usually collect your cheque book and bank card in person from your branch, although they can be sent to you abroad by registered post at your expense. New cheque books are issued automatically before your current one runs out, but you may have to ask for one.

Your bank will usually supply you with a number of slips showing your essential bank details (*relevé d'identité bancaire* or *RIB*, pronounced 'reeb'), which you can send to anyone who requires them. Many employers pay their employees' salaries into a bank or post office account by direct transfer (*virement*), therefore make sure that you give your employer your account details or you won't be paid!

You may withdraw any amount up to the balance (*solde*) of your account by cashing a cheque (*encaisser un chèque*) at the branch where you have your account or using your bank card. At any other branch of your bank, you can usually withdraw up to €500 per week but must provide identification and your cheque book. If the branch has a computer link to your branch, you may withdraw any amount up to the balance of your account.

Cheque clearing (*encaissement*) is quicker in France than in some other countries, and cheques from other branches of your bank may be cleared on the day of deposit, while cheques from other banks usually take around two days to clear (see **Statements** below).

⚠ Caution

Always make sure that cheques, including bank drafts (which aren't treated as cash in France), have been cleared before making a withdrawal against them.

Personal cheques are widely accepted throughout France and many people use them to buy everything from petrol to food, from restaurant meals to travel tickets. Many shops and businesses have cheque-writing machines

salaries over €1,500 must be paid by cheque or bank transfer.

It's illegal to post-date a cheque, as cheques are payable on the date presented irrespective of the date written on them and are valid for six months after this date. It's difficult to stop the payment of a cheque (*faire opposition à un chèque*) and it's usually possible only if your cheque book is lost or stolen, or the payee loses a cheque or has it stolen. It isn't normal to stop a cheque when, for example, goods or services aren't as specified.

If your cheque book is lost or stolen, you must notify your bank by telephone immediately or call the national helpline (☎ 08 92 68 32 08) and confirm the loss in writing. Any cheques written after you've informed your bank aren't your responsibility.

Writing Cheques

The design of a French cheque may be different from what you're used to. On the right-hand side is a box or line where the value of the cheque is written in numerals. The line *payez contre ce chèque* is where the value of the cheque is written in words. Write the name of the payee (or *moi-même* when writing a cheque for cash) next to the line marked *à* or *à l'ordre de*. The date line is in the lower right-hand corner above the signature position and is preceded by the town where the cheque was written (*lieu de creation* or simply *à*). French cheques also show your name and address.

When writing figures in France, or anywhere on the continent of Europe, the number seven should be crossed to avoid confusion with the number one, written with a tail and looking like a seven to many foreigners.

Beware also of French fours, as they can look like nines (which are written with a curly tail) or twos! You should use a comma to separate whole numbers and decimals (e.g. 123 euros and 45 cents is written €123,45), whereas a full-stop (period) or a space is used to separate millions and thousands, e.g. €1.234.567,89 or €1 234 567,89 is one million,

so that all you have to do is check the details and sign (there may be a sign such as *Les chèques sont rédigés automatiquement*). As there are no cheque guarantee cards, you're usually asked to produce identification, e.g. a passport or *carte de séjour*, when paying large amounts (e.g. over €100) by cheque.

Usually cheques are crossed (*chèques barrés*) and personal cheques aren't negotiable, i.e. they cannot be signed and endorsed for payment to a third party. They can be paid into an account in the name of the payee only (who must sign the back). This means that you cannot cash a cheque unless you have your own bank account. It's possible to obtain uncrossed or 'open' cheques (*chèques non-barrés*), although your bank is required to notify the tax authorities of all uncrossed cheques issued, as using uncrossed cheques is a good way of avoiding tax – a national sport in France. (For this reason, few people request uncrossed cheques!)

In theory, a trader can refuse to accept a cheque for goods or services or stipulate that cheques are only accepted for a minimum amount, unless their letter heading or cash till shows that they belong to a *Centre de gestion agréée* (see **Allowances** under **Income Tax** on page 270). The business's policy regarding cheques must be clearly displayed for customers. Traders can also refuse cash for anything above €3,000 (although most businesses are usually happy to accept any amount of cash at any time!). Non-residents in France are, in theory, allowed to pay a trader up to €15,000 in cash! In order to prevent tax evasion, French law also states that monthly

234 thousand, 567 euros and 89 cents – a nice healthy bank balance! If there's a difference between the amount written in figures and the amount written in words, the amount written in words is assumed to be correct.

The date is written in the standard European style; e.g. 10th January 2012 is written 10.1.12, not as in the US, 1.10.12. Most banks supply a specimen cheque showing how it should be written. If you make an error when writing a cheque, it isn't necessary to initial a correction.

Unless you have an overdraft facility, you should never write a 'rubber' cheque (*chèque sans provision* or '*chèque en bois*', literally a wooden cheque). Writing cheques for more than you have in your account is a criminal offence. If you accidentally overdraw (*mettre en découvert*) your account, your bank will send you a registered letter demanding that the necessary funds be paid into the account within 30 days. You also incur a fine (*frais*) of up to a maximum of €30 for a 'rubber' cheque made out for under €50 and a maximum fine of €50 for a cheque written for over €50, plus an unauthorised overdraft charge. (Persistent cheque bouncers can be fined from €400 to €35,000 and receive prison sentences of one to five years.)

In the meantime, you mustn't write any more cheques. If the funds aren't deposited within 30 days or if you overdraw your account twice within a 12-month period, your account will be closed! If this happens, you must return your cheque book to your bank (and also cheque books for other bank accounts in France); your name will be entered on a blacklist (*interdit bancaire*) maintained by the Banque de France, and you'll be unable to operate a cheque account at any bank in France for a year and your name will remain on the blacklist for five years.

If you're blacklisted, you may be unable to obtain a French mortgage or loan for years afterwards. Thousands of people are forbidden to operate bank accounts in France each year. If you can prove that overdrawing your account was due to the fault of another party, you can avoid being blacklisted. It's usually possible (and much safer) to ask for an overdraft facility, which costs around €4 per month.

Statements

Account statements (*relevé de compte*) are normally sent on a monthly basis, although you can usually choose to receive them weekly or quarterly. Your account details, such as your bank, branch and account number, are printed at the top of statements. It's also possible to obtain 'mini-statements' (showing your last few transactions) via cash machines (a facility known as *guichet automatique bancaire/ GAB*). You can check the balance of your post office account via telephone (*Audioposte*, which costs around €0.60 per call) 24 hours a day, including the last five transactions or all transactions during the last ten days. You're given a code to access your account. If you have a post office account, you can sign up for access via the internet (a service strangely called *Vidéoposte*), whereby you can check your balances and make most transactions, including buying and selling shares. Whereas some banks in France charge a monthly service fee for accessing your account online, *Vidéoposte* is free.

Two dates are usually shown on statements: the date a transaction was recorded by the bank (*date de traitement*) and the date the amount is credited or debited to your account (*date de valeur*). A cheque deposit, for example, may not be credited to the account until a few days afterwards, whereas a payment by card or cheque can be debited before the date it was handled! Bank statements may not show a cumulative balance, except at the end of the month,

making it difficult to check that you haven't overdrawn your account at any point.

Charges

There are no monthly charges on a cheque account, unless you want an overdraft facility, and no charges for transactions such as direct debits or (usually) standing orders, except when made overseas. However, banks normally charge around €35 per year for a bank card and may charge you if your account is left 'inactive' for a period. Some banks also charge for cash withdrawals (see **Cash & Debit Cards** below).

A leaflet (*Conditions et Tarifs des Principales Prestations Financières Applicables aux Particuliers*) is available from post offices listing the range of services and the costs associated with post office accounts, including savings account interest rates.

Cash & Debit Cards

Most banks offer customers a combined cash and debit card called a *carte bancaire* or *carte bleue* (both of which are abbreviated to *CB*), widely accepted throughout France. Confusingly, the term *carte bleue* is often also applied to credit and charge cards. Banks normally charge around €35 per year for a *CB* (€15 for a second card on a joint account). Although it's integrated with both the Visa and MasterCard/Eurocard networks, a *CB* isn't a credit card. However, for around an extra €10 you can have a *carte différée*, with which debits are made at the end of each month – with purchases made after the 19th or 20th of the month debited at the end of the following month – rather than immediately after each purchase (cash withdrawals are always debited immediately, even with a *carte différée*). The most common bank card is a Visa card (*carte bleue Visa*) card.

The key benefit of the *CB* is that it's accepted almost everywhere in France. It can therefore be used to pay for practically everything, including motorway tolls, parking, and train and bus tickets, and most shops accept payment by card for even small purchases, although a new system, called *Moneo* (see below) is designed to allow you to pay for items such as newspapers, bread and drinks with your *CB*. All bank cards have a microchip (*puce*), which was invented by a Frenchman, Roland Moreno, in 1974.

A standard *CB* allows you to withdraw up to around €900 per week from a cash machine (properly termed an automated teller machine or ATM – *distributeur automatique de billets/DAB*) operated by your own bank or similar amounts from another bank's machine (displaying a *CB* sign) in France or abroad, and to spend up to around €3,000 in France in a week or €4,500 abroad in a month without authorisation. The total amounts you can withdraw in a week if you make withdrawals in France and abroad in the same week are usually limited to the maximum weekly amount set by your bank in France. 'Gold' and other privilege cards allow you higher limits.

⚠ Caution

Some banks charge at least €1 each time you use one of their ATMs, and several charge for using other banks' ATMs (and there may be a 'handling' charge in small branches where clerks still pay out cash).

Note that an agreement between BNP Paribas, Barclays Bank (UK), Deutsche Bank (Germany), Scotiabank (Canada) and Westpac (Australia) allows card holders of any of these banks to use ATMs belonging to any of the others without charge. Take care when withdrawing cash from a machine at night, as some machines are popular venues for muggers.

You can also obtain account balances and mini-statements from a cash machine via your card. Some machines offer the option to display instructions in English and other languages. When using your *CB* in a cash machine or when making a purchase, simply enter your four-digit personal identification number/PIN (*code secret/confidentiel*) on the key pad provided. In an increasing number of shops, you must insert your card yourself into a slot in the key pad and wait for the message *'tapez votre code confidentiel'* before you enter your PIN; withdraw your card when you see *'retirez votre carte'*. There's no need to sign anything. (With most banks, it **isn't** possible to change your PIN, e.g. to a number you can easily remember!)

If you lose your *carte bleue*, report the loss to the central office (☎ 08 92 69 08 80) and inform your bank as soon as possible. Further information about French bank cards can be found on the website of the Groupement des Cartes Bancaires (🖳 www.cartes-bancaires. com – available in English).

Moneo

Moneo (sometimes written *Mon€o*) is a system, introduced in 2003, which works in a similar way as telephone cards. You 'charge' your bank card from your account (with between €20 and €100) using a special machine at your bank and use it like cash at retail outlets participating in the scheme (displaying a 'Mon€o' sign). These include bakers, bars, take-aways, newsagents and chemists. There has been some resistance from retailers, particularly bakers and tobacconists, to participation owing to commission charges of up to 3 per cent, but it's expected that an increasing number of outlets will accept payment by this method in the coming years.

As with a normal card payment, you must enter your PIN, but you don't receive a receipt; a display tells you how much has been debited from your card and the remaining credit balance. There are three types of *Moneo* card: green (an independent card, like a telephone card); blue (linked to your current account); and your ordinary *CB* with a *Moneo* chip – all

new *CB*s have the *Mon€o* logo and can be used in this way. You must pay between €7 and €10 a year, depending on the issuing bank, to use the system.

MORTGAGES

Mortgages or home loans (*hypothèque* or, more commonly, *prêt*) are available from all major French banks (for both residents and non-residents) and many foreign banks. The French post office also offers mortgages, but you must have been contributing to a plan or compte d'épargne logement (PEL/CEL) for at least 18 months to qualify. Most financial advisers recommend borrowing from a large reputable bank rather than a small one. Crédit Agricole is the largest French lender, with around 25 per cent of the French mortgage market. UCB is part of the French BNP Paribas group and specialises in arranging mortgages for foreign buyers.

In mid-2011, interest rates on fixed-interest euro mortgages ranged from 3.7 to 4.5 per cent and on variable-rate mortgages from around 3 to 4.5 per cent, depending on the borrower's credit rating and the term (insurance for both fixed and variable rate mortgages was an additional around 0.36 per cent).

Both French and foreign lenders have tightened their lending criteria in the last few years as a result of the repayment problems experienced by many recession-hit borrowers in the last few years. Some foreign lenders apply stricter rules than French lenders regarding income, employment and the type of property on which they'll lend, although some are willing to lend more than a French lender. It can be difficult for foreigners to obtain a mortgage in France, particularly if they have neither a regular income nor assets there. It's also possible to remortgage or take out a second mortgage on an existing property. In recent years, some French lenders have changed the terms of a mortgage offer at the last minute, forcing lenders to either pay a much higher rate or shop around desperately for a better deal.

It's possible to obtain a foreign currency mortgage, other than in euros, e.g. GB£, Swiss francs or US$. However, you should be wary of taking out a foreign currency mortgage, as interest rate gains can be wiped out overnight by currency swings and devaluations. It's generally recognised that you should take out a mortgage in the currency in which you're paid or in the currency of the country where a property is situated. In this case, if the foreign currency is devalued, you'll have the consolation of knowing that the value of your French property will have increased by the same percentage when converted into the foreign currency. When choosing between a euro loan and a foreign currency loan, be sure to take into account all costs, fees, interest rates and possible currency fluctuations.

If you need to obtain a mortgage to buy a home in France, you should shop around and compare interest rates, terms and fees (which can be very high) from a number of banks and financial institutions – not just in France but also in your home country. Bear in mind that mortgages in France are generally for a shorter period than in the UK and US, and therefore your repayments may be much higher.

More information about mortgages is provided in our sister-publication, *Buying a Home in France* (Survival Books).

VALUE ADDED TAX

Value added tax (VAT), called *taxe sur la valeur ajoutée* (*TVA*), accounts for around 45 per cent of government revenue (twice as much as income tax!). Most prices of goods and services are quoted inclusive of tax (*toutes taxes comprises/TTC*), although sometimes business supplies are quoted exclusive of tax (*hors taxes/HT*). The four rates of VAT are shown in the table below.

VAT is payable on goods purchased outside the EU but not on goods purchased in an EU country where VAT has already been paid, although you may be asked to show a VAT receipt to prove this. VAT on imported secondhand goods, on which VAT hasn't previously been paid, is subject to a complex calculation based on their secondhand value.

Business activity may or may not be subject to (*assujetti à*) VAT, and you should check with your local Centre des Impôts. Generally, a business providing a service (*prestation de service*) with an annual turnover of more than around €32,100 must register for VAT and charge VAT on sales and services. If VAT relates to sales (*vente*), these must exceed around €80,300 before registration is necessary. If you're self-employed (*travailleur indépendant*) or a sole trader (*entreprise individuelle*), you must register with the appropriate organisation (see **Self-employed** on page 38) and will automatically be given a VAT number.

With the exception of very small businesses, VAT returns must be made monthly and not quarterly as in some other EU countries. VAT refunds aren't paid automatically and must be applied for on certain dates. Make sure that you obtain and keep VAT receipts for all business-related expenditure. See also **Customs** on page 73.

INCOME TAX

Personal income tax (*impôt sur le revenu des personnes physiques/IRPP* – the information below applies only to personal income tax

Value Added Tax (*TVA*)	
Rate (%)	**Applicability**
0 (exempt)	Basic foodstuffs, children's clothes, medical and dental care, educational services, insurance, banking and financial services, and various transactions subject to other taxes
2.1 (super-reduced)	Medicines reimbursed by social security; newspapers and magazines
5.5 (reduced)	Certain foodstuffs (including most drinks and take-away food); agricultural products; non-reimbursed medicines; books; public transport; canteen food; cinema, theatre and concert tickets; travel agency fees
19.6 (standard)	All other services and goods

and not to company tax) in France is below average for EU countries, particularly for large families, and accounts for only 20 per cent of government revenue. The government has been reducing income tax levels for the past decade (corporation tax has also been reduced by 10 per cent to 33 per cent). However, when income tax is added to social security contributions (see page 243), regarded as a form of tax, and other indirect taxes, French taxes are among the highest in the industrialised world (at around 40 per cent in 2011).

Employees' income tax isn't deducted at source (i.e. 'pay-as-you-earn'), although the government has considered introducing such a system, and individuals are responsible for declaring and paying their own income tax. Tax is withheld at flat rates and at source only for non-residents who receive income from employment and professional activities in France, who must file a statement with the Centre des Impôts de Non-Résidents (TSA 10010, 10 rue du Centre, 93160 Noisy-le-Gtrand Cedex , ☎ 01 57 33 83 00) each year. Most taxpayers pay their tax a year in arrears in three instalments, although it can be paid in ten monthly instalments (see **Payment** on page 275).

⚠ Caution

The French tax authorities maintain computer records of tax declarations, employers and bank accounts to help them expose fraud, and can use social security numbers and access other government computer systems to identify residents and compare their declarations with their circumstances.

The French have a pathological hatred of paying taxes and tax evasion is a national sport (most people consider cheating the *fisc* a challenge rather than a crime). It's estimated that around a third of non-salaried taxpayers don't declare a substantial part of their income. Consequently, if your tax affairs are investigated, the authorities often take a hard line when they find you've been 'cheating',

even if you've made an 'innocent' mistake. If your perceived standard of living is higher than would be expected on your declared income, the tax authorities may suspect you of fraud (so contrive to appear poor !). In extreme circumstances, additional income tax or a higher rate of tax can be arbitrarily imposed by tax inspectors (*régime d'imposition forfaitaire*).

Indeed, individuals are encouraged – and even rewarded – to denounce tax dodgers! In any case, foreigners running a business in France are far more likely to be 'investigated' than natives: it's reckoned that foreign business accounts are checked every six years, whereas French farming families may avoid inspection for six generations!

As you would expect in a country with a 'billion' bureaucrats, the French tax system is inordinately complicated and most people don't understand it – not even the tax authorities, from whom it's difficult to obtain accurate (or even consistent) information, and errors in tax assessments are commonplace. Unless your tax affairs are simple, it's prudent to employ an accountant (*expert comptable*) to complete your tax return and ensure that you're correctly assessed. In fact, a good accountant will help you (legally) to save more in taxes than you'll pay him in fees. A list of registered tax consultants is available from the Conseil Supérieur de l'Ordre des Experts-Comptables (🖳 www.experts-comptables.fr) and details of Franco-British tax consultants are available from the French Chamber of Commerce in London (☎ 020-7092 6600).

Many books are available to help you understand and save taxes, and income tax guides are published each January, including the *Guide Pratique du Contribuable* (published by the Syndicat National Unifié des Impôts, 🖳 www.snui.fr), available in bookshops and newsagents' for around €7. The Service Public website (🖳 www.service-public.fr) also contains extensive tax information under '*Impôts*'.

It's possible to reduce your income tax bill by taking out a life assurance policy (see **Life Insurance** on page 250).

Liability

Your liability for French income tax depends on where you're domiciled, which is usually

the country you regard as your permanent home and where you live most of the year. A foreigner working in France for a French company who has taken up residence in France and has no income tax liability abroad is considered to have his tax domicile (*domicile fiscal*) in France. A person can be resident in more than one country at any given time, but can be domiciled only in one country. The domicile of a married woman isn't necessarily the same as her husband's but is determined using the same criteria as for anyone capable of having an independent domicile. Your country of domicile is particularly important regarding inheritance tax (see page 278).

Under the French tax code, domicile is decided under the 'tax home test' (*foyer fiscal*) or the 183-day rule. You're considered to be a French resident and liable to French tax if any of the following applies:

♦ your permanent home, i.e. family or principal residence, is in France;

♦ you spend over 183 days in France during any calendar year;

♦ you carry out paid professional activities or employment in France, except when secondary to business activities conducted in another country;

♦ your centre of economic interest, e.g. investments or business, is in France.

If you plan to live permanently in France, you should notify the tax authorities in your present country (you'll be asked to complete a form, e.g. a form P85 in the UK). You may be entitled to a tax refund if you depart during the tax year. The tax authorities may require evidence that you're leaving the country, e.g. evidence of a job in France or of having bought or rented a property there. If you move to France to take up a job or start a business, you must register with the local tax authorities (Centre des Impôts) soon after your arrival.

Double Taxation

French residents are taxed on their worldwide income, subject to certain treaty exceptions (non-residents are taxed only on income arising in France). Citizens of most countries are exempt from paying taxes in their home country when they spend a minimum period abroad, e.g. a year. According to the Convention for the Avoidance of Double Taxation and the Prevention of Fiscal Evasion, France has double-taxation treaties with over 70 countries, including all members of the EU, Australia, Canada, China, India, Israel, Japan, Malaysia, New Zealand, Pakistan, the Philippines, Singapore, Sri Lanka, Switzerland and the US.

Treaties are designed to ensure that income that has already been taxed in one treaty country isn't taxed again in another. The treaty establishes a tax credit or exemption on certain kinds of income, either in the country of residence or in the country where the income is earned. Where applicable, a double-taxation treaty prevails over domestic law. Many people living abroad switch their investments to offshore holdings to circumvent the often complicated double-taxation agreements. If you're in doubt about your tax liability in your home country, contact your nearest embassy or consulate in France.

The US is the only country that taxes its non-resident citizens on income earned abroad, although there are exclusions on foreign-earned income.

Leaving France

Before leaving France, foreigners must pay any tax due for the previous year and the year of departure by applying for a tax clearance (*quitus fiscal*). A tax return must be filed prior to departure, and should include your income and deductions from 1st January of the departure year up to the date of departure. The tax office will calculate the tax due and provide a written statement. A French removal company isn't supposed to export your household belongings without an official 'tax clearance statement' (*bordereau de situation*) confirming that all taxes have been paid.

Note that leaving (or moving to) France may offer an opportunity for 'favourable tax planning', i.e. tax avoidance rather than tax evasion. To take the maximum advantage of your situation, you should obtain professional advice from a tax adviser who's familiar with both the French tax system and that of your present or future country of residence.

Taxable Income & Exemptions

Income tax is calculated on both earned income (*impôt sur le revenu*) and unearned income (*impôt des revenus de capitaux*). Taxable income includes:

◆ base pay;

◆ overseas and cost of living allowances;

◆ contributions to profit sharing plans;

◆ bonuses (annual, performance, etc.);

◆ storage and relocation allowances;

◆ the cost of language lessons provided for a spouse;

◆ the value of a personal company car;

◆ payments in kind (such as free accommodation or meals);

◆ stock options;

◆ the value of home leave or holidays paid by your employer;

◆ children's education allowances;

◆ property and investment income (dividends and interest).

If you have an average income and receive interest on bank deposits only, tax on unearned income won't apply, as it's deducted from bank interest before you receive it.

Certain kinds of income are exempt from income tax, including payments from a complementary insurance policy or a

temporary accident and illness insurance policy, life annuities (*rentes viagères*) paid to invalids, military pensions, payments by social services, severance pay (up to certain limits), certain payments into a company holiday savings plan (*compte épargne-temps*), some contributions to a company holiday voucher scheme, allowances for obligatory training courses, gifts of home computers from an employer, and maintenance payments from a parent or guardian.

Allowances

Although the tax percentage rates in France are high, your taxable income is considerably reduced by allowances. These include the following:

◆ social security contributions, which aren't taxed and are deducted from the gross income of salaried employees;

◆ a 10 per cent allowance (*déduction forfaitaire*) for 'professional' or 'notional' expenses, to which all salaried taxpayers are entitled, unless such expenses are specified. (If your actual expenses exceed 10 per cent, you may itemise them and claim an additional allowance.) The standard minimum allowance is €421 and the maximum €14,157 (the maximum is around a quarter of this amount in the case of pension income – €3,660 in 2010).

The self-employed don't qualify for the 10 per cent allowance. If you're self-employed, however, you can obtain a reduction on your taxable income by joining your regional Association Agréée des Professions Libérales (commonly known as a *centre* de gestion), a government-sponsored body that regulates the income tax declarations of self-employed people. You must join within five months of your first accounting year (exercice comptable) and before the end of March in the year for which you want to claim a reduction. The joining fee is around €110. You must then pay an annual subscription of around €150 (payable at the end of the year). This means that, provided your taxable income is above around €9,000, joining is to your financial advantage (it's to your advantage anyway, as your accounts are less likely to be queried by the authorities!). If you aren't a member of a centre de gestion, your taxable profits are increased by 25 per cent before the progressive tax scale is applied.

Certain losses are also allowable against income tax (e.g. from letting furnished accommodation, and from agricultural and certain other investments), as are some expenses, e.g. support for a relative in need, taxes on historic or listed buildings, subscriptions to certain cultural organisations, improvements to a property you're letting or modifications to a property for an old or disabled person, the installation of a condensing gas boiler and capital invested in a business. The contribution sociale généralisée (CSG – see page 243) is also allowable under certain circumstances. The parents of a married dependent child may be able to claim an allowance against income tax. There are further allowances for those aged over 65 (on 31st December of the relevant tax year) who are still working and for those receiving an invalidity pension.

The figure you arrive at after deducting all allowances is your net taxable income (revenu net imposable).

Family Quotient

Families are taxed as a single entity, although you can elect for a dependent child's income to be taxed separately if this is advantageous (a dependant's income up to around €7,650 is exempt from income tax). The French income tax system favours the family, as the amount of income tax paid is directly related to the number of dependent children. Tax rates are based on a system of 'parts' (parts), reflecting the marital status of the taxpayer and the number of dependent children, as shown in the table below. The number of parts is known as the 'family quotient' (quotient familial/QF).

♦ A single, divorced or widowed person with no dependent children counts as 1 part.

♦ A single, divorced or widowed person with no dependent children, but one adult child, counts as 1.5 parts.

♦ A married couple with no dependent children counts as 2 parts. French law distinguishes between living with someone on an 'unofficial' basis (en union libre) and cohabiting with a spouse or 'official' partner (en concubinage). A partner can be made 'official' by entering into an agreement called a pacte civil de solidarité (PACS – see page 354). If you live en union libre, you're treated for tax purposes as two single people, whereas if you're 'pacsés' you're treated as a couple and are entitled to a number of tax

Family Quotient			
Dependent		No. of Parts Allocated	
Children	En Union Libre	Single/Divorced	Married/En Concubinage/Widowed
1	1.5	2	2.5
2	2	2.5	3
3	3	3.5	4
4	4	4.5	5

The above 'parts' increase proportionately for each additional child).

advantages; you must complete the relevant section of the tax return.

◆ Those with dependent children are allocated parts as shown in the table above. The first two children count half a part each, each subsequent child a full part.

Dependent children are usually classified as those aged under 18 and unmarried, or disabled children of any age. However, if children aged 18 to 25 are divorced or widowed and without children of their own, they can be claimed as dependants; a form requesting dependent status must be signed by the child and must be sent with the parents' tax return.

Calculation

The tax year runs for the calendar year, i.e. from 1st January to 31st December. The income tax rates for a single person (1 part) for 2010 income (2011 tax return) are shown in the table below:

Tax Rates (2010 income)

Taxable Income	Tax Rate	Cumulative Tax
Up to €5,963	0%	€0
€5,964 to €11,896	5.5%	€326.26
€11,897 to €26,420	14%	€2,359.48
€26,421 to €70,830	30%	€15,682.18
Over €70,830	41%	

Note that taxable income is income after the deduction of social security contributions and various allowances (see above). Your tax 'base' (*assiette fiscale*) is calculated by multiplying your taxable income within a particular bracket by the tax rate.

The tax rate for other taxpayers can be calculated (approximately) using the above table by multiplying the taxable income by the number of parts. For example, if you're a married couple with no children (2 parts), simply double the taxable income amounts shown, i.e. income up to €11,926 is exempt and income above that figure up to €23,792 is taxed at 5.5 per cent, etc. If you're a married couple with two children (3 parts), treble the taxable income shown. Note, however, that above certain thresholds, married couples pay less tax than widows or those living *en concubinage*, who pay less than single parents.

If your taxable income (2010) is below the thresholds (*seuil de nonimposition*) shown in the table below (for parts 1 to 5.5), you pay no income tax. If the tax due is less than €61 (known as the seuil de non-recouvrement or franchise), payment is waived (the generosity of the French government knows no bounds).

Taxable Income Thresholds

Parts	Taxable Income
1	€11,300
1.5	€14,281
2	€17,263
2.5	€20,244
3	€23,226
3.5	€26,207
4	€29,189
4.5	€32,170
5	€35,152
5.5	€38,133

The government web-site (⌨ www.impots.gouv. fr) contains a facility that allows you to estimate the tax payable on your previous year's income, simply by entering on-line income figures for your household, your marital status and number of dependent children. Tax varies with the status of children, and, above certain thresholds, married couples pay less tax than widows or those living *en concubinage* (*pacsés*), who pay less than single parents.

Reductions & Credits

Once you've calculated your tax 'base', you may be eligible for reductions (*réductions*) or credits (*crédits*) to this amount. (The difference between a reduction and a credit is that a credit can result in a negative amount of tax due – i.e. a refund – whereas a reduction cannot.) Tax reductions may apply to the following (there's no longer a reduction on life insurance premiums):

◆ children at school or university (around €61 per child at secondary school, €153 per child at a *lycée*, €183 per child in higher education in);

◆ 10 per cent of contributions to a *plan d'épargne retraite populaire* (savings account);

◆ contributions to a complementary health insurance scheme in accordance with the *Loi Madelin*;

◆ 50 per cent of the cost of home help up to €12,000 per year; the maximum allowance for the over 65s or a household with a

dependent child is €15,000 and increases to €20,000 if a member of the household has an officially recognised serious incapacity.

◆ costs of long-term care for elderly relatives (25 per cent up to a maximum ceiling of €10,000 per person);

◆ payments made to a former spouse;

◆ dividends from a French company;

◆ purchase of a new car running on GPL, a secondhand car converted to GPL or new cars running on another low-pollution fuel (such as electric vehicles): the credit in 2011 was between €400 and €5,000 per vehicle;

◆ purchase of forest or woodland;

◆ investment in an overseas company, a 'rural regeneration area' (*zone de revitalisation rurale*), a small or medium-size enterprise (PME) or an innovative job-creation project (*fonds communs de placement dans l'innovation*);

◆ management training expenses;

◆ union subscription fees;

◆ charitable donations.

Mortgages contracted after 1st January 2011 don't qualify for the limited-period tax relief on interest paid, which applies to earlier mortgages.

For 2011, if you have a child or children (who were aged under six on 1st January 2010) in registered day care and both parents work and earn less than a certain amount (or cannot work), you qualify for a tax credit (known as a *réduction d'impôt pour frais de garde*) of 50 per cent of your annual expenses up to €2,300 per child. If you employ a child-minder at home, you can claim an allowance for a home help (see above). You can also claim (2011) for a tax allowance of 30 per cent off the cost of home adaptations for elderly care or disabled persons, with a maximum of €5,000 for a single person and €10,000 for a couple.

Tax credits may also apply to the following: energy-saving home improvements; VAT on major items of domestic equipment purchased from and installed by a VAT-registered company; and those on low incomes (under certain circumstances) according to a scheme called *prime pour l'emploi*.

Self-employed

Those who qualify as self-employed in France include artisans or craftsmen (*professions artisanales*) such as builders, plumbers and electricians; those involved in trading activities such as shopkeepers, anyone buying and selling goods; and agents, brokers and property dealers. If you're a professional (*profession libérale*) such as an accountant, doctor or lawyer, or a freelance worker (*travailleur indepéndent*), such as an artist or writer, you may complete a *déclaration contrôlée* (form 2035) requiring you to keep accounts of income and expenses, including all related receipts and documents. If your earnings are below around €27,000, i.e. a *micro-entreprise* or *micro-BNC*, you must declare all earnings and qualify for a 50 per cent tax reduction.

Those in commercial enterprises, e.g. shopkeepers, should complete a normal tax return, unless their earnings are below around €76,500, in which case they may complete a *micro-BIC*. If your income is from letting a property privately, you can complete a *micro-foncier*, provided you've earned less than around €15,000; otherwise, you must complete form 2044.

The self-employed don't qualify for the 10 per cent allowance, although they can obtain a 25 per cent reduction by joining their local Association Agréée des Professions Libérales (see page 270). The self-employed can also claim against tax payments made to a *mutuelle*, provided the contract is drawn up according to the *loi Madelin*.

If you run a business from home, you must also pay *taxe professionelle*, although you can claim a reduction on your property tax.

UK Pensioners

If you're a UK national with a British state retirement or occupational pension and become a French resident, your pension will be taxed as income in France. However, you'll qualify for certain deductions, including the 10 per cent *déduction forfaitaire*. You'll also be exempt from social charges on your pension income provided you have a healthcare form E121 or E106. All UK pensions are paid in sterling and will need converting to euros for declaration to the French tax authorities.

You can usually have your pension paid directly into a French bank account, in which case you just need to keep a note of the euro amounts credited to your account for your tax return in France, but some occupational pensions cannot be paid into a foreign account. Government service pensions are taxed in the UK, irrespective of your place of residence or domicile, unless you transfer them out of the UK before you start receiving payments.

> ☑ **SURVIVAL TIP**
>
> The taxation of personal pensions is a complicated subject and you should obtain expert advice before retiring to France. Similarly, with regard to the taxation of 'tax-free' lump sums, which may be subject to French tax if received while resident in France.

If your UK pension is supposed to be taxed at source, you must advise the Inland Revenue that it will be taxed in France in order to avoid being taxed twice. You'll need to request form *FRA/Individuel* at your tax office in France, which will be stamped and sent to the Inland Revenue. British pensioners should also be aware of changes to the rules governing pensions introduced in April 2005, including a lifetime allowance.

Income Tax Return

You should be sent an annual tax return (*déclaration des revenus*) by the tax authorities in late February or early March of each year. From 2006 these have been pre-completed, therefore in theory all you have to do is check the figures (which won't include your UK pension received in euros) sign it and send it back, although the self-employed will inevitably have to enter new figures. If you aren't sent a form, you can obtain one from your town hall or tax office (look in the *Yellow Pages* under *Impôts, Trésor Public*). The standard return is the 2042 and there are supplementary forms for non-commercial profits (forms 2035,

2037), property income (2044), foreign-source income such as a pension or dividends (2047), capital gains on financial investments (2074), and other capital gains (2049).

There's no 'head of a household' in France (at least, not as far as the tax office is concerned), and either spouse or partner may complete and sign a tax return including all family members' income, although it's possible for children aged under 18 with their own income, e.g. income from an inheritance or their own earnings, to be independently assessed.

In the year of their marriage, a couple must provide three separate declarations: one for each partner for the period between 1st January and the date of the marriage, and a joint declaration for the period between the marriage and 31st December. An unmarried couple living together 'unofficially' (*en union libre*) is treated as two single people for tax purposes. If they enter into a *PACS* (see page 357), they're taxed as a couple from the year after making the agreement. (There was, however, a rush on unmarried couples contracting *PACS* in the second half of 2010, when the government generously allowed a joint declaration – for 2011 – as with marriages, between the date of the *PACS* and 31st December). A divorced couple continue to be taxed jointly at least until receipt of an *ordonnance de non-conciliation* (ONC).

French tax returns are complicated, despite attempts to simplify them in recent years. The language used is particularly difficult to understand for foreigners (and many French). Local tax offices (Centre des Impôts) will usually help you complete your tax return, either in person or via the telephone (☎ 08 10 46 76 87 – between 08.00 and 22.00, Mondays to Fridays, and from 09.00 to 19.00 on Saturdays) but, of course, mostly in French only.

Tax declarations can be made online, except for the first time you make a declaration; once you've been issued with a taxpayer number you can use the online facility, which is free and

allows you an extension of one to three weeks on the filing deadline (for some reason, the date varies depending on where you live).

You can make an appointment for a free consultation with your local tax inspector at your town hall. However, if your French isn't excellent you'll need to take someone with you who's fluent.

Alternatively you can employ a tax accountant (*expert comptable/conseiller fiscal*) to complete and submit the necessary forms (and take the blame for any errors!).

If you pay income tax abroad, you must return the form uncompleted with evidence that you're domiciled abroad. Around a month later you should receive a statement from the French tax authorities stating that you have no tax to pay (*Vous n'avez pas d'impôt à payer*). The French tax authorities may request copies of foreign tax returns. Americans who are going to be abroad on 15th April should ask for an *Extension Form*. US income tax returns cannot be filed with the IRS office in Paris but must be sent to the IRS in the US. IRS Publication 54, *Tax Guide for US Citizens and Resident Aliens Abroad*, can be downloaded from the IRS website (🖥 www.irs.gov/pub/irs-pdf/p54.pdf).

Although you're permitted to 'accidentally' under-declare by up to 5 per cent, you must pay the difference, and penalties for grossly understated or deliberately undeclared income and unjustified deductions range from 40 to 80 per cent, plus interest on the amount owed. Note also that you may make yourself liable for penalties if you display 'exterior signs of wealth' (*signes extérieurs de richesse*), so don't drive to the Centre des Impôts in your new BMW to deposit your tax return!

In 2011, tax returns needed to be filed by late May for employees or one month later for the self-employed. Late filing, even by one day, attracts a penalty of 10 per cent of the amount due. Changes in your tax liability may be made by the tax authorities up to three years after the end of the tax year to which the liability relates. Therefore you should retain all records relating to the income and expenses reported in your tax returns for at least three years, even if you've left France.

Payment

Sometime between August and December, you'll receive a tax bill (*avis d'imposition*). There are two methods of paying the bill: in three instalments (*tiers provisionnels*) or in ten equal monthly instalments (*mensualisation*).

Three Instalments

The more common method of payment is in three instalments. The first two payments, each comprising around a third (*tiers*) of the previous year's tax liability, are provisional (*acompte provisionnel*) and are payable by 15th February and 15th May each year. The third and final instalment, the balance of your tax bill (*solde*), is payable by 15th September. The tax authorities adjust your third payment to take into account your actual income for the previous year. Payment dates are officially 31st January, 30th April and 31st August, but the tax authorities allow you an extra two weeks (or 15 days) to pay bills. If you pay your tax bill late, you must pay a penalty equal to 10 per cent of your annual tax bill.

During your first year in France you won't have a previous year's tax liability (in France). Therefore the income tax computed with the information contained in the tax return filed at the end of May of the following year is payable in full by 15th September of the same year. In the following year, the normal procedure applies. The schedule below applies to a new arrival in France.

The 'end May' file date for tax returns is recent. In previous years it was the end of March. Check the *Date limite de Dépôt* (deadline date for filing your return) when you receive your *Déclaration* form.

Monthly Instalments

You can choose to pay your tax in monthly instalments (*mensualisation*) by direct debit, in which case you need to write to the collector of taxes in your tax region requesting this method of payment. If you make your request before 10th May, monthly payments will begin immediately (with an adjustment for any instalments already paid); if you apply after 10th May, they won't begin until the following January. Once started, monthly payments continue automatically each year unless you cancel them in writing.

Under this system, you pay one tenth of your previous year's tax bill on the 15th of each month from January to October. If your income is less in the current year than the previous year, the tax office will stop payments when it has received the full amount. On the other hand, if you earned more the previous year than the year before, the tax office will take a final balancing payment (*solde*), usually in December.

Monthly payments are a good budgeting aid, particularly if you're prone to rushing out and spending your salary as soon as you receive it. However, most people prefer to pay in three instalments, with the advantage that you can invest the amount set aside for tax until each payment is due.

Income Tax Payment		
Year	**Date**	**Action**
1 (arrival in France)		Tax payable in previous country of residence
2	End March	File tax return for first year's income
	15th September	Pay entire tax bill for first year
3, etc.	15th February	Pay first instalment of second year's tax
	End March	File tax return for second year's income
	15th May	Pay second instalment of second year's tax
	15th September	Pay final instalment of second year's income

PROPERTY TAXES

There are four types of local property tax (*impôt local*) in France: *taxe d'habitation* (referred to below as 'residential tax'), *taxe foncière* (or *taxes foncières*, referred to as 'property tax'), *taxe assimilée* ('sundry tax') and *contribution économique territoriale* ('new value added tax') which is now replacing *taxe professionelle* ('professional tax'). Taxes pay for local services, including rubbish collection, street lighting and cleaning, local schools and other community services, plus a contribution to departmental and regional expenses.

Residential and property taxes are payable, by both French and foreign residents, on principal residences (*maison principale*) and second homes (*résidence secondaire*) in France, although there's a reduction in residential tax for principal residences.

Forms for the assessment of both residential and property taxes are sent out by local councils and must be completed and returned to the regional tax office (Centre des Impôts) by a specified date, e.g. 15th November or 15th December for residential tax. They'll calculate the tax due and send you a bill.

In 2011, the government proposed a new (third) property tax on 'holiday' homes owned by non-residents, based on the rental value. However, this was challenged by the European Union and there was also considerable opposition from owners, not least from French nationals living abroad with homes in France. At the time of going to press it looked like the proposals would be dropped.

For further information on property taxes, see our sister-publication, *Buying a Home in France* (Survival Books).

WEALTH TAX

A wealth tax (*impôt sur la fortune/ISF*) is payable by each 'fiscal unit' (*foyer fiscal*), e.g. a couple or family, when its assets exceed €1.3m (2011), excluding your principal home in France if you're a resident. Tax rates apply on a sliding scale of as shown in the table below.

Wealth Tax Bands (2011)	
Wealth	**Tax Rate**
€1,300,000-€2,570,000	0.75%
€2,570,000-€4,040,000	1.00%
€4,040,000-€7,710,000	1.30%
€7,710,000-€16,790,000	1.65%
Above €16,790,000	1.8%

In 2012, the *ISF* will be simplified: a rate of 0.25 per cent will be levied on assets valued between €1.3m and €3m, and 0.5 per cent on assets valued above €3m, with a cumulative amount if both rates apply.

If you're domiciled in France (see **Liability** on page 268), the value of your estate is based on your worldwide assets. If you're resident in France but not domiciled there, the value of your estate is based on your assets in France only. Wealth tax is assessed on the net value of your assets on 1st January each year and is payable by the following 15th June by French residents, 15th July by other European residents and 15th August by all others. (The 30th September due date in 2011 was exceptional as the threshold was under government review when tax returns were being filed.) The amount payable is reduced by €150 for each dependant. The taxable estate doesn't include:

♦ 'professional assets' (*biens professionnels*), which may include shares in a company in which you're active, if they total at least 25 per cent of the equity;

♦ works of art and antiques;

♦ artistic and literary rights and commercial copyrights;

- the value of forest and woodland property;
- rural property let on a long-term basis;
- pensions and life annuities.

Newcomers to France benefit from a five-year exemption from wealth tax on any assets they retain outside France.

CAPITAL GAINS TAX

Capital gains tax (*impôt sur les plus-values*) is payable on the profit from sales of certain assets in France, including antiques, art and jewellery, securities and property, but a principal residence is exempt, provided you've occupied it for at least five years (or since construction if less than five years). Gains net of capital gains tax (CGT) are added to other income and are liable to income tax (see page 267).

Note that if you move to France permanently and retain a home abroad, you may be liable for CGT in that country. EU tax authorities co-operate in tracking down capital gains tax dodgers. For more detailed information on the subject on CGT, see out sister-publication, *Buying a Home in France* (Survival Books).

INHERITANCE & GIFT TAX

Dying in France doesn't free your assets from the clutches of the taxman, as the government imposes both inheritance and gift taxes.

Inheritance Tax

Inheritance tax – or estate tax or death duty – (*droits de succession*) is levied on the estate of a deceased person.

 Caution

Both residents and non-residents are subject to inheritance tax if they own property in France.

The country where you pay inheritance tax is decided by your domicile (see **Liability** on page 268). If you're living permanently in France at the time of your death, you'll be deemed to be domiciled there by the tax authorities, and if you're domiciled in France inheritance tax applies to your worldwide estate (excluding property), otherwise it applies only to assets in France. It's important to make your domicile clear so that there's no misunderstanding on your death.

When a person dies, an estate tax return (*déclaration de succession*) must be filed within six months of the date of death (within 12 months if the death occurred outside France). The return is generally prepared by a *notaire*. Inheritance tax is paid by individual beneficiaries, irrespective of where they're domiciled, and not by the estate. Tax may be paid in instalments over five or, in certain cases, ten years or may be deferred.

The rate of tax and allowances vary according to the relationship between the

Inheritance & Gift Tax Rates		
Value Above Allowance		**Tax Rate**
Spouse	**Children/Parents**	
Up to €8,072	Up to €8,072	5%
€8,072 to €15,932	€8,072 to €12,109	10%
€15,932 to €31,865	€12,109 to €15,932	15%
€31,865 to €552,324	€15,932 to €552,234	20%
€552,234 to €902,838	€552,234 to €902,838	30%
€902,838 to €1,805,677	€902,838 to €1,805,677	35%
Over €1,805,677	Over €1,807,677	40%

beneficiary and the deceased. French succession laws are quite restrictive compared with the law in many other countries. The surviving spouse (married or *Pacsé*) is, since 22nd August 2007, no longer subject to inheritance tax for legacies, while the children and parents of the deceased have an allowance of €159,325 each. After the allowance has been deducted, tax is applied on a sliding scale up to a maximum of 40 per cent (45 per cent is planned before the end of 2011) on assets over around €1,805,677, as shown in the table below (2011 rates).

There's an allowance of €15,932 for each brother and sister under certain circumstances, but the normal allowance is just €1,594, and the tax rate thereafter is 35 per cent up to €23,000 and 45 per cent above this amount. Mentally or physically disabled brothers and sisters aged over 50 who are unable to earn a living receive an allowance of around €46,000 in addition to the usual €15,932 or €1,594.

Any heir who doesn't benefit from any of the above allowances is entitled to €1,594 tax free. Between relatives up to the fourth degree, i.e. uncles/aunts, nephews/nieces, great uncles/aunts, great nephews/nieces and first cousins, there's a flat rate tax of around 55 per cent. For relatives beyond the fourth degree and for unrelated persons, the tax rate is around 60 per cent. (As you can see,

it's best to leave property in France to your spouse, children or parents, in order to take advantage of the higher tax allowances.)

Changes to inheritance tax rules that came into force in January 2007 include the option for a child to renounce his inheritance in favour of his children (so that they can inherit tax-free from their grandparents), permission to include your grandchildren in a legacy, and permission for childless couples to leave property up to a certain value tax-free to siblings and nephews/nieces.

Exemptions

Exemptions from inheritance tax include:

♦ payments from life insurance policies (many people take out a life insurance policy to reduce the impact of inheritance tax);

♦ certain buildings constructed between 1st June 1993 and 31st December 1996 and inherited for the first time (the first €46,000 of their value);

♦ historic or listed buildings;

♦ works of art donated to the state;

♦ certain woodlands and rural properties;

♦ legacies to charities and government bodies.

Certain expenses may also be deducted from inheritance tax, including the costs associated with a final illness, funeral expenses up to around €1,000, taxes (including income, wealth, property, residential and value added tax) from 1st January of the year of death until the date of death, notary's fees (for proving the will) and certain debts incurred by the deceased.

If you're resident in France and receive an inheritance from abroad, you're subject to French inheritance tax. However, if you've been resident for less than six years in France, you're exempt, or, if you paid the bill in another country, the amount is deducted from your French tax bill.

Gift Tax

France has a gift tax (*droits de donation*), which is calculated in the same way as inheritance tax (see above), according to the relationship between the donor and the recipient and the size of the gift. The thresholds for 2011 were:

Gift Tax Thresholds

Recipient	Gift Tax Exemption Threshold
Spouses/Partners	€80,724
Children	€159,325 (from each parent)
Grandchildren	€31,865 (from each grandparent)
Brother/Sisters	€15,932
Nieces/Nephews	€7,967

In addition to the above allowances, it's also possible to make a one-time cash gift of up to €31,865 to each child, grandchild/great grandchild or, in the absence of these descendants, to a niece or nephew, free of gift tax. This separate allowance is conditional on the donor being less than 80 years old (from 1st January 2010) and the beneficiary over 18 years old. The gift must also be declared to the tax authority.

☑ **SURVIVAL TIP**

Gift tax is payable on gifts in excess of the limits made between spouses, therefore assets should be equally shared before you become domiciled in France.

A registered disabled person, whatever their relationship to the deceased, receives an allowance of €159,325 due to their disability, to which they can add any other allowance that may ordinarily be entitled to through blood ties. For example, a disabled child is entitled to an allowance before gift tax of €159,325, plus a further €159,325 from each parent. Allowances are cumulative so that, for example, a child may receive gifts from both parents and grandparents, without one affecting the exemption limits of the other. If you're gifting real estate, then the situation can be made easier by gifting to your children a 'reversionary interest' in property, while you retain its 'life use'.

The allowances can be used every ten years, therefore a gift made every ten years is free of gift tax, provided it doesn't exceed the threshold limits. The limits on the amount that can be gifted free of tax depends on the relationship between the parties and, in some cases, the age of the donor. Any gifts made within six years of the death of the donor (*en avancement d'horie*) must be included in the inheritance tax return and are valued at the time of death rather than at the time of the donation. The payment of gift tax can be spread over a number of years, except in the case of the donation of a business.

WILLS

It's an unfortunate fact of life that you're unable to take your hard-earned assets with you when you take your final bow. All adults should make a will (*testament*) irrespective of how large or small their assets. The disposal of your estate depends on your country of domicile (see **Inheritance & Gift Tax** above). As a general rule, French law permits a foreigner who isn't domiciled in France to make a will in any language and under the law of any country, provided it's valid under the law of that country. If you're domiciled in France, you should make a French will.

Whatever type of will you wish to make, 'immovable' property (*immeubles*) in France, i.e. land and buildings, must be disposed of (on death) in accordance with French law.

All other property in France or elsewhere (defined as 'movables' – *meubles*) may be disposed of in accordance with the law of your country of domicile. Therefore, it's important to establish where you're domiciled under French law.

French law is restrictive regarding the distribution of property and the identity of heirs and gives priority to children, including illegitimate and adopted children, and the living parents of a deceased person. Under French law, you cannot disinherit your children, who have first claim on your estate, even before a surviving spouse, although you can delay their inheritance.

If you die leaving one child, he must inherit half of your French estate and two children must inherit at least two-thirds; if you have three or more children, they must inherit three-quarters of your estate. If a couple has no surviving children, the deceased's parents each inherit a quarter of the estate and the surviving spouse half (if only one parent is alive, the spouse inherits three-quarters). If there are neither children nor parents, the spouse inherits the whole estate apart from family possessions, half of which must go to any surviving brothers or sisters of the deceased.

The part of a property that must be inherited by certain heirs (*héritiers réservataires*) is called the legal reserve (*réserve légale*). Once the reserved portion of your estate has been determined, the remaining portion is freely disposable (*quotité disponible*). Only when there are no descendants or ascendants is the whole estate freely disposable.

If you take up residence in France and decide to have only a French will, check that it covers any assets you have in another country. It's possible to make two wills, one relating to French property and the other to foreign property. Opinion differs on whether you should have separate wills for French and foreign property, or a foreign will with a codicil (appendix) dealing with your French property (or vice versa). However, most experts believe it's better to have a French will for winding up your French estate and a will for any country where you own immovable property.

If you have French and foreign wills, make sure that they don't contradict one another, or worse still, cancel each other out, e.g. when a will contains a clause revoking all other wills.

Note the following information regarding wills in France:

♦ Marriage doesn't automatically revoke a will as it does in some other countries, e.g. the UK.

♦ Wills aren't made public and aren't available for inspection.

♦ Where applicable, the rules relating to witnesses are strict and, if they aren't followed precisely, a will may be rendered null and void.

♦ The role of the executor is different from that in many other countries; his duties are supervisory only and last for a year and a

Will and Testament

day. He's responsible for paying debts and death duties and distributing the balance in accordance with the will. The executor who's dealing with your affairs must file a *déclaration de succession* within a year of your death. At your death your property passes directly to your heirs, and it's their responsibility to pay any outstanding debts and their own inheritance tax.

♦ Winding up an estate takes much longer than in many other countries, and usually isn't given priority by *notaires*.

You should keep a copy of your will(s) in a safe place and another copy with your solicitor or the executor of your estate. Don't leave them in a bank safe deposit box, which in the event of your death is sealed for a period of time under French law. You should keep information regarding bank accounts, pensions and benefits, investments and insurance policies with your will(s), but don't forget to tell someone where they are! You should also make a separate note of your last wishes (e.g. regarding funeral arrangements) where your next-of-kin can find it immediately after your death, along with your social security number, birth, marriage, divorce and spouse's death certificates (as applicable), and the names and whereabouts of any children or other beneficiaries.

French inheritance law is complicated and it's important to obtain professional legal advice from someone familiar with the laws of all relevant countries when writing or altering your will(s).

Type of Will

There are three kinds of will in France: holographic (*olographe*), notarial or authentic (*authentique*) and secret (*mystique*), described below.

Holographic Will

A holographic (*olographe*) will is the most common form used in France. It must be written by hand by the person making the will (i.e. it cannot be typewritten or printed) and be signed and dated by him. No witnesses or other formalities are required. In fact it shouldn't be witnessed at all, as this may complicate matters. It can be written in English or another language, although it's preferable if it's written in French (you can ask a *notaire* to prepare a draft and copy it in your own handwriting).

A holographic will should be handed to a *notaire* for filing. He will also send a copy to the local district court, where the estate is administered. A holographic will can be registered in the central wills registry (*fichier de dernières volontés*). For anyone with a modest French estate, e.g. a small second home in France, a holographic will is sufficient. It costs around €50 if you prepare it yourself, including the registration fee.

Authentic or Notarial Will

An authentic (*authentique*) will is used by around 5 per cent of people and must be drawn up by a *notaire* in the form of a notarial document and can be handwritten or typed. It's dictated by the person making the will and must be witnessed by two *notaires* or a *notaire* and two other witnesses. Unlike a holographic will, an authentic will is automatically registered in the central wills registry. An authentic will costs on average around €150, including a percentage charge for the value of your estate.

Secret Will

A secret (*mystique*) will is rarely used and is a will written by or for the person making it and signed by him. It's sealed in an envelope in the presence of two witnesses. It's then given to a *notaire*, who records on the envelope that the envelope has been handed to him and that the testator has affirmed that the envelope contains his will. The *notaire* then files the will and notifies the district court where the estate is administered. A secret will costs the same as an authentic will (see above).

End of Life Will

A new type of will, made possible by a law passed in April 2005, is an 'end of life will' (*testament de fin de vie*), which contains instructions regarding medical treatment in the event of incapacitation, known as *directives anticipées*. The will, which is similar to a British 'living will', can either specify the type of treatment desired or appoint someone to decide on the appropriate treatment. An end of life will is valid for only three years and renewable for a further three years, yet must have been made at least three years before incapacitation.

Siddalls

Guiding you through the issues

Navigating through the French tax and inheritance rules can leave you not knowing which way to turn.

Tel: 0845 872 2268
Email: enquiries@siddalls.net

www.siddalls.net

inancial solutions for your life in France

15.
LEISURE

When it comes to leisure, few countries can match France for the variety and excellence of its attractions – from its outstanding natural beauty to the sophistication and grandeur of its cities. France is the world's most popular tourist destination, and tourism is the country's most important industry (the third-largest tourist industry in the world), earning the 'country' over €40bn annually and employing around a million people. Nearly 200m people visited France in 2010, over 15m of them going to Paris, where the Eiffel Tower is the most visited admission-charging monument in the world, attracting over 6m visitors annually). Visitor attractions are generally good value and many are free. Moreover, many places that aren't usually open to the public can be visited free on annual 'heritage days'(*journées de patrimoine*), usually the third weekend in September.**

France is one of the most beautiful countries in Europe and has the most varied landscape, offering something for everyone: magnificent beaches, spectacular countryside, mountains, rivers, lakes and seas. France also boasts vibrant nightlife, particularly in Paris, some of the world's finest wines, *haute cuisine*, an abundance of cultural activities, and rural tranquillity. The pursuit of *la bonne vie* is a serious business (most French rate the pursuit of pleasure and style way ahead of success and wealth) and even bons viveurs (*bons vivants* in French!) are spoilt for choice.

Paris is one of the world's great cities and is packed with national monuments. It's also one of the cleanest major capitals in the world (on the negative side, watch out for pickpockets, bag snatchers and canine waste). There's much to be enjoyed that's inexpensive or even free, not least its beauty and the extravagant street entertainment, both cultural and sartorial. Paris dominates the cultural scene in France, even more so than capital cities in most other European countries.

On the other hand, many provincial towns have a cultural centre (*maison de la culture*), where exhibitions, plays, music festivals, debates and art classes are held. There are many excellent provincial art galleries and museums, and art and music festivals are staged in all regions and major towns. Traditional folk festivals are held throughout the country, most notably in Brittany and the south; in fact, France boasts more festivals than any other European country.

Holders of a *carte famille nombreuse* can benefit from discounts at over 30 national museums and certain theme parks, including Parc Astérix and Futuroscope.

INFORMATION

Information regarding local events and entertainment is available from tourist offices (see below) and can also be found in local and foreign publications (see **Appendix B**). In most cities there are magazines and newspapers devoted to entertainment, and free weekly or monthly programmes are published by tourist organisations in major cities and tourist centres. Many city newspapers publish weekly magazines and supplements containing a detailed programme of local events and entertainment, particularly during the high season.

The Paris Tourist Office provides a 24-hour recorded information service for performances and shows in the capital (☏ 08 92 68 30 00 – press 2 for information in English) or you can visit its website (🖥 http://en.parisinfo.com – in English).

Tourist Offices

Most towns have a tourist office (*office de tourisme* or, in some smaller towns, a *syndicat d'initiative*, although the latter term is dying out). A directory listing 3,400 tourist offices is published by the Fédération Nationale des Offices de Tourisme et Syndicats d'Initiative (🖥 www.tourisme.fr – click on the US flag for information in English). Around 45 major cities and tourist areas have a *Loisirs Accueil France* office, open every day of the year, which makes hotel bookings for personal callers (for a small fee) anywhere in France, up to a week in advance. For information contact Loisirs Accueil France (🖥 www.loisirsaccueilfrance. com). A more recent development is a computerised tourist information service available in motorway rest areas (*aires d'autoroute*).

Each department and region of France has a tourist authority, and many of the regions have tourist offices in Paris. The main tourist office in Paris is the Office de Tourisme de Paris, 127 avenue des Champs Elysées, 75008 Paris (☏ 08 92 68 30 00, 🖥 http://en.parisinfo.com – both in English). There are also tourist offices at the Gare de Lyon and the Eiffel Tower which can be contacted via the above telephone number, plus tourist offices at international airports in Paris and other cities, where you can make hotel bookings. The Maison de la France (🖥 www.franceguide.com) provides tourist information about most regions and will send information. Information in English can also be found at 🖥 www.v1.paris.fr/en. Official interpreters are available on Paris streets during the main tourist season and wear armbands indicating the languages they speak.

Outside France, the French Tourist Office or Atout France (formerly Maison de la France) is a mine of information, promoting France as a tourist destination via 35 offices in 29 countries on all five continents.

☑ SURVIVAL TIP

If you write to a local tourist office for information, you should include an international reply coupon and shouldn't expect a reply in English, although most offices have staff that can understand letters written in English.

Opening Hours

Tourist offices in major cities are open daily, including Saturdays and Sundays. Telephone the tourist office or consult a guide book to check the exact opening hours. In major towns, reduced opening hours are in operation during winter, while in smaller towns and resorts, offices close for lunch (e.g. 12.00 to 14.00) and may be open only during the summer or winter, e.g. in ski resorts. The main tourist office in Paris (see above) is open from 09.00 to 20.00, the office at the Gare de Lyon from 08.00 to 20.00, Mondays to Saturdays, and the Eiffel Tower office from 11.00 to 18.00, May to September only.

Services

Most tourist offices will find you a hotel or hostel room locally for a fee, e.g. €2 to €6.50, depending on the standard. Many departments provide official booking services under the name *Loisirs-Accueil*, through which you can book a hotel, *gîte*, campsite or an activity or sports holiday. *Loisirs-Accueil* is operated by the Fédération Nationale des Offices de Tourisme et Syndicats d'Initiative (see **Information** above), which has its own website (🖥 www.loisirsaccueilfrance.com). Many tourist offices also change foreign currency, although they may not offer the best rates.

HOTELS

There are thousands of hotels in France (although *hôtels de ville*, *hôtels dieu* and *hôtels de police* **aren't** hotels!), with some 1,500 in Paris alone, catering for all tastes and pockets – from 'five-star palaces' (the French

classification system has just introduced a new 'palace' category) and *châteaux* to small family hotels, offering good food and accommodation, and good value. Children and animals are usually welcome.

Classification

Hotels are classified from one to five star de luxe by the French Ministry of Tourism, depending on their facilities and the type of hotel. This provides a guarantee of standards related to the price. Note, however, that stars are based on facilities, e.g. the ratio of bathrooms to guests, rather than quality, and you can often find excellent ungraded and one-star hotels. Two-star hotels are usually small family-run hotels, although nowadays many are linked to one another through independent hotel groups, such as Contact Hotels (🖳 www.contact-hotel.fr), with central booking arrangements.

Logis et Auberges de France

The backbone of the hotel network is the Logis et Auberges de France, the world's largest hotel consortium, whose trademark is a green and yellow sign of a fire burning in a hearth.

Logis members include over 3,500 privately run hotels/restaurants in the countryside (none in Paris). Members must conform to strict standards of comfort, service, hygiene, safety, quality of food and price. Most are one-or two-star hotels in popular locations, with prices ranging from around €50 to €100 per night for a double room. The Logis guide is available from French Tourist Offices. A number of Logis hotels can be booked through the '*Logis Stop*' service offered by Gîtes de France (see page 289). Contact the Fédération Nationale des Logis et Auberges de France (🖳 www.logis-de-france.fr – available in English) for information. A *Logis de France* handbook is available from bookshops and French Tourist Offices, as well as via the Logis website.

Chain Hotels

In addition to thousands of small family-run hotels, France has its share of soulless 'business' hotels, such as Ibis, Mercure, Novotel and Sofitel, although many have been refurbished and updated in recent years. International chains including Hilton, Holiday Inn and Intercontinental are represented in Paris and other major cities. One advantage of staying at chain hotels is that the standards and facilities are consistent and any hotel can book you a room at any other in the chain.

If you wish to indulge yourself, you need look no further than the Relais et Châteaux chain of over 250 independently owned elegant three-and four-star hotels (many occupying *châteaux* and other former stately homes) and exquisite restaurants (*relais*). They produce a guide detailing their establishments throughout the world, which is available from French Tourist Offices (see above) or the Centre d'Information, Relais & Châteaux (☎ 08 25 32 32 32 for bookings, 🖳 www.relaischateaux.com – available in English).

It's also possible to stay in many private *châteaux*, manors, abbeys and priories, 70 of which are listed in the *Château Accueil* directory available from French Tourist Offices or via the internet (☎ 01 47 20 18 27, 🖳 www.chateau-accueil.com – available in English). A *Bienvenue au Château* guide, covering northwestern France only, is available from the French Tourist Office. An excellent association of privately owned two-to four-star hotels where you're assured of peace and tranquillity is Les Relais du Silence (☎ 01 44 49 79 00, 🖳 www. silencehotel.com – available in English).

At the other end of the scale are a number of budget hotel chains such as Formule 1, which are common on the outskirts of towns and cities. From around €35 per night (breakfast costs around €6 per person) up to three people can share a room with a double and single bed and a TV. Shared toilets and showers are available in the corridors. You can arrive at any time of day or night.

☑ SURVIVAL TIP

If you arrive late, you can obtain the number of your room and the entry code by inserting the credit card used to book the room in the automatic reception machine (available in English). If the machine won't accept your card, press the *appel d'urgence* button near the entrance and a staff member will open the door for you.

For a list of Formule 1 hotels, write to Chain Hôtels Formule 1, Le Grand Champs, boulevard Rû de Nesles, 93160 Noisy-le-Grand Cedex (🖳 www.hotelformule1.com). Formule 1 is owned by Accor Hotels, who also own the Ibis and Etap chains and whose competitors include Mister Bed (🖳 www.misterbed.fr), Première Classe (🖳 www.premiereclasse.fr) and Villages Hotel (🖳 www.villages-hotel.com).

Hotel Guide Books

Most guide books list a selection of hotels and there are many hotel guides. The most comprehensive hotel (and restaurant) guide is the *Michelin Red Guide*, which includes both the humblest and poshest of establishments. Other good guides include *Les Routiers Guide to France* (Alan Sutton Publishing), which was originally designed for long-distance truck drivers but is now widely used by travellers in general who have discovered the value they offer; *The Good Hotel Guide* by Hilary Rubinstein (Papermac); and the *Guide to Hotels and Country Inns of Character and Charm in France* (Rivages). A complete list of hotels and guest houses, the *Annuaire des*

Hôtels et Pensions de Famille de Tourisme à Prix Homologués, is published annually by the French Tourist Office. An online guide to hotels can be found at 🖳 www.france-hotel-guide. com.

Facilities

You should ask to see a room before accepting it. Rooms with a private bath or shower may not always have a WC, although most now do, while rooms without a shower or bath usually have a washbasin.

Cheap hotels don't usually provide soap, or even towels. Beds often have long, hard, sausage-shaped bolsters (*traversin*) that serve as pillows (not the most comfortable). Usually the bottom sheet runs around them and substitutes for a pillow-case. In the wardrobe there may be pillows (*oreiller*), which, like bolsters, usually have no slips and are placed under the bottom sheet. Duvets are common. Staff in inexpensive hotels may not speak English.

Most hotels have central heating in winter and are uncomfortably warm. Air-conditioning is usually found only in luxury hotels and large modern hotels, particularly in the south. Some rooms have no curtains and are fitted with shutters or blinds, possibly located outside the window. Modern hotels may have electric roller shutters.

Most hotel rooms, except the very cheapest independent ones, are equipped with a TV, those in the north capable of receiving English-speaking BBC programmes. Satellite TV and free Wi-Fi internet access are common in hotels from two-star and up. All top-class hotel rooms have tea and coffee-making facilities, a radio and colour TV, bathroom or shower, a telephone, room service, and a mini-bar or refrigerator.

In general, French hotels don't cater well for business travellers. Few hotels have swimming pools, sports facilities or private parking. However, most hotels have photocopy, fax and email facilities; high class hotels may have a wireless connection system (*wi-fi* – pronounced 'wee-fee') in all rooms. Most hotels have a restaurant or at least a coffee shop and bar, and many of France's best restaurants are found in top-class hotels.

Hotel bulbs are usually dim and not ideal for reading in bed. Power points above wash basins are usually suitable only for electric razors. If you want to use a non-French hairdryer or travel iron, you must bring a French plug adapter.

BED & BREAKFAST

France has numerous bed and breakfast (*chambres d'hôtes*) establishments, particularly in villages and on farms; look for signs such as *ferme auberge*, *ferme de découverte/pédagogique/équestre* and *goûter à la ferme*.

Many *chambres d'hôtes* operate under the sponsorship of Gîtes de France (see **Self-catering** below) and are classified according to their comfort and environment with one to four ears of corn (*épi*). The cost is usually around €50 per night for a room (possibly with a private bath or shower) for two people including breakfast. Many *chambres d'hôtes* have accommodation for families and most serve meals (*table d'hôtes*). The standard of *chambres d'hôtes* is usually high and the home-cooked food delicious, owners being required to use fresh local produce.

When staying in bed and breakfast accommodation, it helps if you speak some French as your hosts may not speak any English (the Paris Tourist Board scrapped its *Hôtes Qualité Paris* scheme, designed to highlight B&B owners who had at least a smattering of English, almost as soon as it was introduced!).

Information

There are many guides to bed and breakfast, including the AA's *Guide to Bed & Breakfast in France*, Karen Brown's *French Country Bed & Breakfast* (Travel Press), Alistair Sawday's *Guide to French Bed & Breakfast* (Alistair Sawday Publishing), *Bed & Breakfast of Character and Charm in France* (Fodor's Rivages), *Charming Small Hotel Guides: France Bed & Breakfast* by Paul Wade & Kathy Arnold (Duncan Petersen Publishing), *French Country Welcome* (Gîtes de France) and *French Entrée Bed and Breakfast in France* by Patricia Fenn & Rosemary Gower-Jones (Quiller Press). All regional

tourist offices produce annual lists of *chambres d'hôtes*.

SELF-CATERING

France has an abundance of self-catering accommodation and you can choose from literally thousands of properties. The most luxurious dwellings have private swimming pools, tennis courts and acres of private parkland. Self-catering serviced apartments are provided in Paris and other major cities. Rates vary considerably and may be per person per night, or a fixed rate per night irrespective of the number of guests. Rates usually decrease for longer stays. See also **Temporary Accommodation** on page 86.

Unless somewhere has been highly recommended, it's best to book through a reputable organisation such as Gîtes de France.

Gîtes

The word *gîte* means simply 'home' or 'shelter' but is nowadays widely used to refer to any furnished self-catering holiday accommodation. A typical *gîte* is a small cottage or self-contained apartment with one or two bedrooms (sleeping four to eight and possibly including a sofa bed in the living-room), a large living-room/kitchen with an open fire or stove, and a toilet and shower room. There are usually shutters on the windows, stone or wooden floors with a few rugs and possibly bare stone

walls. There's usually a garden with garden furniture and possibly a swimming pool (which may be shared with another *gîte*).

Equipment

Properties are generally well equipped with cooking utensils, crockery and cutlery, although you're usually required to provide your own bed linen and towels (they can be rented for an extra charge but can be expensive). Equipment and facilities may include central heating, a washing machine, dishwasher and microwave, covered parking and a barbecue. Some owners provide bicycles and badminton and table tennis equipment. If you need a cot or a high chair, mention it when booking. Some basic food stuffs (e.g. sugar, salt and pepper) and essentials such as toilet paper and soap may be provided, but don't count on it.

Most *gîtes* in rural areas have a septic tank (*fosse septique*) and items such as sanitary towels, toilet paper (other than French toilet paper), disposable nappies, condoms, and anything made of plastic mustn't be flushed down the toilet.

Costs

The cost is usually calculated on a weekly basis (Saturday to Saturday) and depends on the standard, location, number of beds and facilities provided. The rent is higher for a *gîte* with a pool. The year is sometimes divided into low, mid-and high seasons, although many owners offer accommodation from June to September only. If you're making a late booking, try to negotiate a lower price, as it's often possible to obtain a large reduction if the owner is 'desperate' to fill a week or two.

Electricity, gas and water charges aren't always included, particularly outside the high season (June to August), and may be charged at high rates. There's usually a charge for cleaning, e.g. €35 to €65 per week, but this may be waived if you leave the place spotless. Heating (if necessary) is also usually extra and can be expensive. You may need to pay a small local tax (*taxe de séjour*).

Holiday Villages

Holiday villages and club resorts (such as Club Méditerranée) are increasingly popular among holidaymakers. They're usually self-contained with everything available on site, including shops, restaurants, swimming pools, and a wide range of sports and entertainment facilities. Most have children's clubs.

Inexpensive holiday village accommodation is available through Villages-Vacances-Familles (💻 www.vvf-vacances.fr), a non-profit organisation created in 1958 to provide holidays for low-income families. Villages-Vacances-Familles holiday villages provide child-minding and entertainment for children and are open to foreign visitors.

Holiday parks are similar to club resorts, except that sports and leisure facilities may be housed in a temperature-controlled plastic dome, such as Center Parcs' site at Les Bois-Francs near Verneuil-sur-Avre, around 120km (80mi) west of Paris (💻 www.centerparcs.com). Guests stay in villas set in attractive countryside or by the sea. Another chain of (around 450) holiday villages is Loisirs de France (💻 www.loisirsdefrance.com).

There are also many mobile home holiday centres in France, usually located on campsites

Booking & Deposits

It may be necessary to book six months in advance for popular areas in July or August, when there may be a minimum two-week rental period. Outside high season it's possible to find a *gîte* on the spot. When booking, you're usually required to pay a 'damage' deposit (*caution*), which cannot be more than 25 per cent of the rental charge and cannot be requested more than six months in advance. A deposit is termed either *arrhes* or *acompte*. When it's *arrhes*, you can back out of the agreement and forfeit your deposit; if the owner cancels he must pay you double the deposit. When a deposit is *acompte* it means that you have a binding contract: if you back out of the agreement, you must still pay the full rental fee, although you can claim damages if the landlord cancels your booking.

Information

Gîtes can be booked from abroad through French Tourist Offices, Gîtes de France or a travel agent. Many properties are let by holiday companies and associations, often as part of a holiday package. Properties are also let directly by owners through advertisements. Note that, if you rent directly from the owner, you may find it difficult to receive satisfaction or redress if you have a complaint.

The largest and most reputable self-catering organisation is Gîtes de France. Properties (called *gîtes ruraux*, as they're mostly in rural areas) are classified according to their comfort and environment, and are awarded one to four ears of corn (*épi*). For more information contact the Fédération Nationale des Gîtes Ruraux de France (🖳 www.gites-de-france.com – available in English), which publishes *Les Nouveaux Gîtes Ruraux*.

Clévacances is another major national organisation. Unlike Gîtes de France, Clévacances handles urban as well as rural properties. Properties are graded with one to five keys (*clés*), a similar system to GdF's *épis* or tourist board stars. Further information is available from the Fédération Nationale des Locations de France Clévacances (🖳 www.clevacances.com – available in English).

A handbook listing over 2,500 *gîtes* is published by the French Tourist Office in the UK, while tourist offices in most French *départements* publish a list of local *gîtes*. One of the most popular guides to self-catering accommodation in France is the *Guide des Locations Vacances Loisirs*, published quarterly. There are a number of books for self-caterers, including *Self-Catering France* by John P. Harris and William Hedley (Collins), *The Gîtes Guide* (FHG Publications) and *Guide Gîtes d'Etapes et Refuges France et Frontières* by Annick and Serge Mouraret (🖳 www.gites-refuges.com – available in 'English').

HOSTELS

There's a variety of inexpensive hostel accommodation in France, although fewer than in many other European countries.

Youth Hostels

Youth hostels (*auberge de jeunesse*) are open to members of national hostelling associations affiliated to Hostelling International (HI, 🖳 www.hihostels.com – available in English) and, despite their name, have no age restrictions. HI membership must be taken out in your home country and costs around €15 per year, or €10 if you're under 26. One-night membership of HI is available for around €3.

There are two French youth hostel associations: the Fédération Unie des Auberges de Jeunesse (FUAJ, 🖳 www.fuaj.fr – available in 'English'), operating over 200 youth hostels, and the Ligue Française pour les Auberges de Jeunesse (LFAJ, 🖳 www.auberges-de-jeunesse.com), both affiliated to HI.

French hostels are classified under three grades with accommodation usually in single-sex rooms with two to eight beds. The cost is generally from around €5 to around €15 per night (there are usually cheaper rates for groups), plus an additional hire charge for a sheet sleeping bag if you don't provide your own. Some hostels allow you to use your own sleeping bag. Breakfast costs from around €3.

The main advantage for budget travellers is that most hostels provide cooking facilities or inexpensive cafeterias. Hostels fill early in July and August, when you should book in advance, although some hostels don't accept bookings and restrict stays to four nights or less.

All hostels have a curfew at 22.00 or 23.00 (between 00.00 and 02.00 in Paris) and most are closed between 10.00 and 17.00, although some are flexible. There are restrictions on smoking and alcohol consumption and guests may be required to help with chores.

Other Hostels

In major cities there are *hôtels de jeunesse*, which are a cross between a hotel and a youth hostel, and *Foyers des Jeunes Travailleurs/ Travailleuses*, which are residential hostels for students and young workers. Ethic Etapes (formerly the Union des Centres de Rencontres Internationales de France, ⌨ www.ethic-etapes.fr) links *foyers* throughout France and publishes a list of members and services. Room rates are usually from around €12 to €20 per night for singles and €25 to €35 for doubles. *Foyers* usually have an inexpensive cafeteria or canteen. In many areas there are guesthouses providing dormitory accommodation from around €6 per night.

During July and August you can stay in student accommodation at most French universities. Rates are from around €8 per night and you can book through the Centre Régional des Oeuvres Universitaires et Scolaires (CROUS). Many monasteries and convents also accept paying guests and are listed in the *Guide des Monastères* available from bookshops.

In rural areas there are unmanned hostels or shelters providing dormitory accommodation called *gîtes d'étapes*. They're listed in footpath guides and marked on IGN walkers' maps, and are usually reserved for walkers, cyclists, horse riders and skiers. The rate per night is usually from €10 to €12. A list of *gîtes d'étapes* is included in *Accueil à la Campagne* available from the Fédération Nationale des Gîtes Ruraux de France. An even more basic form of shelter, common in remote hill and mountain areas, is a mountain hut called an *abri*.

Information about these can be obtained from local *Bureaux des Guides* or tourist offices.

A useful publication for young people seeking temporary accommodation is *Le Logement des Etudiants et des Jeunes* (Editions de Vecchi). The *Guide Gîtes d'Etapes et Refuges France et Frontières* by Annick and Serge Mouraret (⌨ www.gites-refuges.com) lists over 1,600 establishments providing inexpensive accommodation.

CAMPING & CARAVANNING

The French are Europe's keenest campers (although most remain within France) and have elevated *le camping* to a high level of sophistication and chic. There are over 11,500 campsites in France, including over 2,000 rural and farm sites, and France is Europe's largest camper van (*camping-car*) market, with around 18,000 vehicles sold annually.

You can also camp on a farm (*camping à la ferme*), although there are generally no facilities. A maximum of six camping spaces are permitted on farm land or in a park near a *château*. Off-site camping (*camping sauvage*) is restricted in many areas, particularly in the south of France, due to the danger of fires. For example, you need permission from the local Office des Eaux et Forêts to camp in state forests (*forêts domaniales*).

Classification

Campsites vary considerably from small municipal sites (*camping municipal*) with fairly basic facilities to luxury establishments with a wide range of facilities and amenities. Many sites are situated in popular hiking and climbing areas. Campsites are classified from one to four stars, as shown in the table below.

Many campsites have tents, caravans, mobile homes and bungalows for hire, and some provide (heated) winter accommodation.

Campsite Classification		
Star Rating	**Standard**	**Cost**
****	*très grand confort* (luxury)	€10 to 15
***	*grand confort* (high)	€8 to 10
**	*confort* (medium)	€5 to 10
*	*confort moyen* (basic)	€3 to 5

Some also provide fully-furnished luxury canvas 'houses' with all modern conveniences, including sprung mattresses, refrigerators, four-burner stoves and electric lighting. Some sites have facilities for the disabled, which is usually noted in guide books. French campsites are usually extremely clean.

Costs

Most sites have different rates for high season (*haute saison*) and low season (*basse saison*). The table above shows the approximate cost per person per night during high season, including a camping or caravan space, car parking and the use of facilities. Note that prices can vary considerably between campsites with the same star rating.

Some sites charge extra to use showers, sports facilities (e.g. tennis courts) and other amenities, such as ironing facilities or a freezer.

Booking

Booking is often possible at three-and four-star sites and is essential during the summer, particularly for sites on the coast and near lakes and waterways or if you require an electricity hook-up. Outside peak periods you can usually find a campsite without difficulty on the spot, but don't leave it too late in the day if you're in a popular area.

Information

The Fédération Française de Camping et de Caravanning (FFCC, 💻 www.ffcc.fr) publishes a *Guide Officiel* describing in detail the facilities at around 11,500 sites, including naturist and farm sites. It's available direct from the FFCC and from bookshops and camping, caravanning and motoring organisations. The FFCC also provides insurance for campers and caravanners and an international camping carnet. Many sites are members of other associations or groups, which include the following:

◆ Camping Qualité (💻 www.campingqualite. com – available in 'English'), with around 220 sites throughout France;

◆ Sites et Paysages de France (☎ 08 20 20 46 46, 💻 www.sites-et-paysages.com – available in 'English'; the home page begins: 'Meet your next fantastic holidays

in the heart of France's countries'!) with 52 members;

◆ Club Airotel (💻 www.airotels.com – available in 'English') with 58 campsites in France.

To find the most lavish campsites contact Castels et Camping Caravaning (💻 www.les-castels.com – available in 'English'), which has around 40 four-star sites in the grounds of beautiful châteaux or manors or in exceptional natural settings, and offers 'holidays for maximum sensations, passions and memories'.

Camping and caravanning guides are published for all areas and are available from local regional tourist offices. There are also many national camping guides, including *Camping à la Ferme* published by Gîtes de France (see above), Alan Rogers' *Good Camps Guide, France* (Deneway Guides) and the *Michelin Green Guide – Camping and Caravanning*, *Caravan and Camping in France* by Frederick Tingey (Mirador). The French Tourist Office (see page 286) publishes an excellent free booklet, *The Camping Traveller in France*. If you wish to rent a mobile home, caravan or tent on site, Alan Rogers' *Rented Accommodation on Quality Sites in France* (Deneway Guides) provides a comprehensive list.

If you're a newcomer to camping and caravanning, you may wish to join a camping or caravan club. Recognised clubs include the Camping & Caravanning Club in the UK (☎ 0845-130 7632, 💻 www. campingandcaravanningclub.co.uk) and the Camping Club de France (💻 www.

campingclub.asso.fr). Further information about camping and caravanning in France can be obtained from 🖥 www.campingfrance.com/fr (available in English) and numerous other websites.

NATURISM

France is the naturist capital of Europe, with many naturist beaches, villages and over 60 holiday centres, including a huge number of superbly equipped naturist camping centres. Topless bathing is accepted almost everywhere, even in Paris along the banks of the Seine, but nude bathing should be confined to naturist beaches and resorts.

The main naturist areas include Aquitaine, Brittany, Corsica, Languedoc, Provence and the Midi-Pyrénées. Cape d'Agde on the Languedoc coast is the largest naturist resort in the world, with a population of 40,000 from Easter to September. Naked day trippers are allowed in most resorts, although single male visitors aren't usually admitted (spoilsports!).

Information about naturist holidays can be obtained from the French Tourist Office, which publishes *France, a Land for all Naturisms*. If you aren't a member of a naturist association in another country, you must join the Fédération Française de Naturisme (🖥☐ www.ffn-naturisme.com) or pay a fee in proportion to the length of your stay. You must be aged 18 and require a colour (head and shoulders only!) photograph for your naturist 'passport' or carnet.

THEME PARKS

France has over 300 theme parks and similar attractions of varying size and scale, and these are increasing in popularity at the expense of traditional attractions such as *châteaux* (even in the Loire valley!). Details of all the major theme parks and attractions in France are provided by the annual *Guide Officiel des Parcs d'Attractions* (Guides Larivière). The following is a summary of the main parks.

Disneyland Paris

The most famous French theme park is Disneyland Paris, which is the fourth most-popular visitor attraction in the world. Its 23ha (56 acres) contain five themed 'lands', each with around 40 attractions, as well as shops and restaurants. There are six hotels and an 18-hole golf course on site. Disneyland is open year round, from 09.00 until 23.00 daily in spring and summer, and from 10.00 to 18.00 in autumn and winter, except for Saturdays and Sundays, when it closes at 23.00. It's best to avoid public holidays and weekends.

The entrance fee is a whopping €51 for adults and €45 for children aged 3 to 11; a combined pass for a day each at Disneyland and Walt Disney Studios (see below) costs around €108/€97. You can also buy combined passes for three, four or five days or, if you're addicted, an annual pass.

There's a surfeit of Disneyland Paris guides, including *Plan-Guide Disneyland Paris* and *Green Guide Disneyland Paris* (Michelin), *Disneyland Paris* (Fodor), *Disneyland Paris: The Guide* (Harmsworth) and *Disneyland Paris Berlitz* (Berlitz). Further information can be obtained direct from the Disneyland Paris website (🖥 www.disneylandparis.com – available in English).

> ### ☑ SURVIVAL TIP
>
> The best way to get to Disneyland from Paris is via the *RER* express suburban railway (see Chapter 10) on Line A terminating at Marne-la-Vallée/Chessy, a station specially built for Disneyland.

Near Disneyland is another Disney theme park, called Walt Disney Studios, where you can take a studio tour and pretend you're in Los Angeles.

Futuroscope

One of the most unusual French theme parks is Futuroscope (🖥 www.futuroscope.com – available in English) near Poitiers in Vienne, which is a cinematic extravanganza. Attractions include the Omnimax room, where a film is projected onto the inside of a domed ceiling; the Kinémax, housing a cinema with a screen that's higher than a seven-storey building; the Dynamic Motion Theatre, where the seats move in tune with the action; and the Magic

Carpet, with a 700m² (7,534ft²) screen in front and another beneath your feet.

Other Attractions

France's other major theme parks, aquariums and water parks include the following:

♦ **Aventure Parcs** – activity parks in Autrans (department 38), Biscarosse (40), Les Deux Alpes (38), Les Gets (74), Guyonvelle (52), Nançay (18), Quelneuc (56), Pays-des-Lacs (54), Serre-Chevalier (05), Trivisy (13) and Val Louron (65), where you can swing from the trees and bungee jump (🖥 www.aventure-parc.fr);

♦ **Bioscope** – a theme park in Ungersheim in Alsace devoted to 'man and the environment', open from June to November (🖥 www.lebioscope.com);

♦ **Cap Découverte** – an activity park in a converted coal mine at Blayeles-Mines in Tarn, where you can ski, toboggan, cycle, go-kart, skateboard and rollerblade all year round; open from February to December (🖥 www.capdecouverte.net – available in English);

♦ **Cité de la Mer** – includes Europe's deepest aquarium and the largest nuclear submarine ever opened to the public, in Cherbourg-Octeville; open from May to September (🖥 www.citedelamer.com – available in English);

♦ **France Miniature** – If you haven't much time and wish to see France in a day, all the major sites, in miniature, are at Elancourt, west of Paris; open from April to November (🖥 www.franceminiature.com – available in English).

♦ **Micropolis** – The theme of this park, in Saint Léons in Aveyron, is insects, including a giant beehive complete with swarming bees! Open from February to November (🖥 www.micropolis.biz).

♦ **Nausicaä** – one of the largest and most comprehensive aquariums in the world, near Boulogne; open all year round (🖥 www.nausicaa.fr – available in English);

♦ **Parc Astérix** – a traditional French theme park based on the popular comic strip, located near Paris' Charles de Gaulle airport; open from April to early October (🖥 www.parcasterix.fr – available in English);

♦ **Vulcania** – Experience volcanic eruptions and other seismic sensations near Clermont-Ferrand. Open daily all year round (🖥 www.vulcania.com – available in English).

♦ **Walibi** – watersport theme parks at Agen, Lyon, Metz and Roquefort (🖥 www.walibi.com – in English).

Funfairs and circuses are common in all areas, and sound and light (*son et lumière*) shows are held at historic sites during summer, including Les Invalides in Paris, the Palais des Papes in Avignon, and at many *châteaux* and stately homes, particularly in the Loire valley. The *son et lumière* at the ruined Château du Puy du Fou in Les Epesses between Nantes and La Roche in Vendée, from June to September (🖥 www.puydufou.com – available in English), is considered to be the most spectacular in Europe.

MUSEUMS & GALLERIES

France has around 7,000 museums and many important historical collections. There are

over 100 museums and some 500 historic monuments in and around Paris alone, ranging from one of the largest museums and galleries in the world, the Musée National du Louvre (🖳 www.louvre.fr) to some of the smallest and most specialised.

One of Paris's most popular art venues is the Centre National d'Art et de Culture Georges Pompidou (known as the Centre Pompidou), housing the Musée National d'Art Moderne, the Public Reference Library, with over a million French and foreign books, the Institute of Sound and Music and the Industrial Design Centre. Other important Paris museums and galleries include the Musée Rodin, Musée Picasso, Musée d'Orsay (superb!) and the Cité des Sciences et de l'Industrie.

Other members of the capital's museum and gallery collection include the Orangerie near the Place de la Concorde (housing Monet's grandest water-lily paintings), the Petit and Grand Palais just off the Champs-Elysées, the Cité de la Mode et du Design, the Musée du Quai Branly near the Eiffel Tower (dedicated to the art and culture of Africa, Asia, Oceania and the Americas), and the Musée de l'Erotisme in Pigalle – Paris's only museum open until 2 o'clock in the morning!

In addition to its national galleries, Paris boasts around 300 commercial galleries where admission is free. You can also visit a number of provincial museums, manor houses (*manoir*) and *châteaux,* gardens and businesses (particularly those connected with the food and drink industry), and even hydroelectric dams and nuclear power stations.

Opening Hours

National museums are usually open six days a week; the most common day for closing is Tuesday, but it's wise to check before you go. Most museums close on public holidays.

Most *châteaux* and other stately homes are open during the high season only, from May or June to September. Many are closed one day a week and most close from 12.00 until 14.00 for lunch.

Costs

Entrance fees are usually reasonable and on Wednesdays and Sundays entry is often half price or even free. Most museums offer free entry to those under 18 and a 50 per cent reduction for those aged 18 to 25 and 60 and over. Entrance to provincial museums is free for those aged under 7 and over 60 at all times.

A museums and monuments card (*Carte des Musées et Monuments*), providing entry to over 60 museums and monuments in the Paris area (for either one or three consecutive days), is obtainable from participating museums, the Paris tourist office, *métro* stations and French Tourist Offices abroad. The *Carte* allows you to bypass queues as well as saving you money.

Information

The French Tourist Office publishes a brochure in English, *Chateaux, Museums, Monuments*, listing 200 cultural attractions. A leaflet listing 128 gardens is available from French Tourist Offices, and keen gardeners may be interested in *Les Guides des Jardins de France* by Michael Racine (Guides Hachette).

Current museum and gallery exhibitions in Paris are listed in weekly entertainment magazines such as *Pariscope* and *l'Officiel des Spectacles*. Useful websites for museum information include 🖳 www.museums-of-paris.com and www.rmn.fr (site of the Réunion des Museés Nationaux, which operates 32 museums across France – available in English).

Centre Pompidou, Paris

CINEMA

French cinema has resisted the threat of television far better than the cinema in most other developed countries.

> The French are huge film fans, and Paris is the cinema capital of the world, with some 350 cinemas, most of which are packed every day (Parisians buy some 80 per cent of all cinema tickets sold in France).

Many cinemas in Paris show old films or reruns (*reprises*) of classics and many hold seasons and festivals featuring a particular actor, director or theme. Film lovers shouldn't miss the 'cinema days' (*journées du cinéma*) in summer, when films are shown non-stop for 24 hours at low prices.

Most old cinemas have been replaced by modern multiplexes, with ten or more screens and state-of-the-art technology. Cinemas listed as *grande salle* or *salle prestige* have a large screen (*grand écran*), comfortable seats, and high quality projection and sound standards. Some cinemas in Paris and larger towns are now equipped to show films in 3D. Smoking isn't permitted in cinemas, some of which are air-conditioned (a relief in summer). There are also private *ciné-clubs* in most cities.

France has a dynamic and prosperous film industry and some 200 French films are made each year. However, foreign (especially American and British) films are widely screened, sometimes before their general release in the UK or US! In Paris and other major cities, foreign films are shown in their original version (*version originale/ VO*) with French subtitles (*sous-titres français*). Dubbed films are labelled *VF* (*version française*). You may also come across *VA* (*version anglaise*), denoting an 'English'-language film made by a French-speaking director (beware!).

Films are classified and entrance may be prohibited to children under 18, 16 or 12 – listed as *interdit aux moins de 18/16/12 ans* – some form of identification (with a photo) may be required.

The time listed for each performance is usually ten minutes before the film starts. The last performance usually commences around 22.00 from Sundays to Thursdays and at 00.00 on Fridays and Saturdays. In Paris, performances are usually continuous from 14.00 until around midnight or 01.00.

Costs & Booking

Ticket prices range from €7 to €10 in Paris. Cinema chains such as Gaumont and UGC offer season tickets (*cartes privilèges*) for frequent customers; the Gaumont operates a 'membership' scheme. Cine-addicts can also obtain a *carte cinéma*, entitling them to discounts at most cinemas. Screenings on Mondays and/or Wednesdays are also often cheaper in many cinemas. Reduced price tickets are available for students, senior citizens, the unemployed, military personnel and families with three or more children. Children and students must produce a student card and senior citizens (those over 60) a passport, identity card or *Carte Senior* rail card.

You can buy tickets in advance, although this must often be done via a premium-rate automated telephone booking system, which will severely test your French comprehension.

Film Festivals

Europe's largest and most important film festival is the Cannes Film Festival, although access to films is limited to those in the film industry (or with the right contacts).

Major film festivals open to the public include the American Film Festival (Deauville in Calvados), the Comedy Film Festival (Chamrousse in Isère) and the Science-Fiction Film Festival (Avoriaz in Haute-Savoie).

Information

There are many French magazines devoted to films, including *Studio*, *Première* and *Positif*. English-language film magazines are also available from international news kiosks. An excellent website for film information is 🖥 www.cinefil.com, where you can find details (in French) of films showing in every department in France, including whether they're *VO* or *VF*.

THEATRE , BALLET & OPERA

High quality theatre, opera and ballet performances are staged in all major cities, many by resident companies.

Theatre

Parisian theatres include the famous Comédie Française (showing classics, i.e. plays by Molière, Racine, Corneille, Feydeau, etc.), founded by Louis XIV, and the Théâtre National Populaire (contemporary). Other than the classics, most French-language shows are translated hits from London and New York. There are also many café-theatres, where performances may not always be memorable but are usually enjoyable. Children's theatres in Paris and other cities perform straight plays, pageants and magic shows. There are also a number of English-language theatre venues in Paris, including the Théâtre Marie Stuart, ACT, Theatre Essaion, Voices and the Sweeney Irish Pub.

In the provinces, performances are often held in theatres that are part of a cultural centre (*maison de la culture* or *centre d'animation culturelle*), and the only national theatre outside the capital is the Théâtre National de Strasbourg. In addition to the large and luxurious state-funded theatres, there are many good medium-size and small theatres. Performances aren't always top quality, but there's plenty of variety. Performances usually start at 20.30 or 21.00 and theatres close one day a week. Smoking isn't permitted in theatres.

Ticket prices vary considerably depending on whether you go to a national or a private theatre. If you subscribe to 🖥 www.theatreonline.com you can obtain half-price tickets. Midweek matinee subscriptions are available at reduced rates. The Kiosque Théâtre (place de la Madeleine, 75008 Paris) sells half-price tickets on Tuesdays to Saturdays from 12.30 to 20.00 on the day of a performance, and many theatres offer student discounts. Just before a show starts, seats are often available at huge discounts. Students can obtain reduced price tickets from the Centre Régional des Oeuvres Universitaires et Scolaires/CROUS.

Obtaining theatre tickets in advance can be difficult, as many theatres allow booking only one or two weeks in advance and/or don't accept credit card bookings or use ticket agencies. However, bookings for certain shows can be made up to three weeks before a performance via the website, 🖥 www.theatreonline.com.

Drama festivals are popular and include the world-renowned Festival d'Avignon in July/August, encompassing drama, dance, film, concerts, exhibitions and many other events.

Ballet

The Paris Opéra Ballet has a history going back three centuries. Tickets are cheaper than their equivalents in London and New York but they're difficult to obtain, as most seats are sold by subscription months in advance. For information and booking details, see **Opera** below. Paris also boasts the Théâtre du Châtelet in the 1st *arrondissement*, where a variety of shows are staged, including ballet productions (🖥 www.chatelet-theatre.com). Modern and contemporary dance thrives in France and the Centre Pompidou stages some 'interesting' avant-garde programmes by French and international dance companies. Many small dance companies perform in small theatres and dance studios.

Opera

The Opéra de la Bastille (☎ 08 92 89 90 90) is France's major opera venue. Paris also boasts the celebrated Opéra Garnier in the 9th

arrondissement (details of both Paris operas can be found at 🖳 www.opera-de-paris.fr; tickets can be booked online or via ☎ 08 92 89 90 90) and the Théâtre du Châtelet in the 1st, where a variety of shows are staged, including opera productions (🖳 www.chatelet-theatre.com). France also has 12 regional opera companies, most notably those of Bordeaux, Lille, Lyon and Toulouse.

MUSIC

The French are great music lovers, although their tastes may differ from what you're used to in your home country.

> Some hypermarkets (e.g. Carrefour and Leclerc) have concert ticket booking or *spectacles* counters.

Classical Music

France has no world-renowned orchestras and few internationally famous performers, yet there's no shortage of classical music concerts, particularly in Paris, which boasts several major classical music concert halls, including the recently refurbished Salle Pleyel, the Théâtre des Champs-Elysées, the Théâtre du Châtelet (see above), the Salle Gaveau and the Maison de Radio France. These feature leading foreign orchestras and soloists as well as performances by the Orchestre de Paris, the Orchestre Philharmonique de Radio France and various other national and provincial orchestras (among the best are those of Bordeaux, Lille, Lyon and Toulouse).

The Parisian concert season runs from October to June. Students at the Conservatoire National perform regularly in the Paris *métro* and on the city's streets, as well as at the Cité de la Musique in northeast Paris, where there's a fascinating museum of musical instruments. Recitals of organ and sacred music are often held in churches and cathedrals, including Notre Dame de Paris, and many churches sponsor concerts with good soloists and excellent choirs. Paris also has a number of music halls where top international artists regularly perform. There's plenty of classical music outside the capital, although much of it's poorly advertised.

There are discounts at classical music concerts for senior citizens on production of identification or a *Carte Senior*. The main agency for tickets to almost any concert or cultural event in Paris is FNAC, 136 rue de Rennes, 6e (☎ 08 92 68 36 22, 🖳 www.fnac.com) and in the Forum des Halles, Level 3, 1–5 rue Pierre-Lescot, 1er (☎ 08 92 68 36 22). You can also buy tickets from the Virgin Megastore, 52 avenue des Champs Elysées, 8e (☎ 01 49 53 50 00).

Popular Music

French popular music is something of an acquired taste, being based on the traditional *chanson*, in which the words are far more important than the music. Even French rock music is rooted in this style and therefore, to American and British ears, a generation 'out of date'. This is reflected in the fact that the '60s rock star Johnny Hallyday, who's now nearing 70, and octogenarian crooner Charles Aznavour remain France's biggest box office draws. Foreign bands are much better known to French fans than any French group.

Most pop venues can be divided into those where you sit and listen, and dance clubs. The former (in Paris) include Bataclon, Bercy, Bobigno, Olympia, the Palais des Congrès and Zénith, although none of these is an 'automatic' stop on the world tour. Tickets for club performances cost around €15 and concerts €25 or more. Drinks are expensive in music clubs and may run to €15 for a beer.

Jazz

Paris is Europe's leading jazz venue and attracts the world's best musicians, while France as a whole hosts many excellent jazz festivals, including the Festival de Jazz in Paris in autumn, the Antibes-Juan-les-Pins Festival and the Nice Jazz Festival in July, one of the most prestigious jazz and blues festivals in Europe. France even has a nationally-funded National Jazz Orchestra.

Most jazz is performed in cellar clubs, where there's usually a cover charge and expensive drinks. Music starts at around 22.00 and lasts until around 04.00 at weekends and includes everything from trad to be-bop, free jazz to experimental.

Music Festivals

Open-air music festivals are common and popular in summer throughout the country, many of them staged in spectacular venues such as cathedrals and *châteaux*. Music festivals embrace all types of music, including classical, opera, chamber music, organ, early music, piano, popular, jazz and folk, many of which are listed in a booklet, *Festive France*, available from French Tourist Offices (see page 286).

Each year, over a weekend in May, in around 40 towns the bandstand (*kiosque à musique*) is given over to the performance of music of the Belle Epoque and 21st June is a national Fête de la Musique, when every French town becomes an open-air concert venue.

Information

French music magazines include the *Guide des Concerts* and *Les Activités Musicales*. Two publications provide a guide to what's on in Paris: *L'Officiel des Spectacles* and *Pariscope*, the latter with an English supplement.

SOCIAL CLUBS

There are many social clubs and organisations in France, including Ambassador Clubs, American Women's and Men's Clubs, Anglo-French Clubs, Kiwani Clubs, Lion and Lioness Clubs and Rotary Clubs, along with clubs for business people and others.

Paris is home to a number of clubs and societies founded and run by groups of expatriates, including national groups, e.g. American Citizens Abroad, the American Club of Paris and the Association of American Residents Overseas, the Association Franco-Écossaise, The Clan MacLeod Society of France, The Caledonian Society of France, The Paris Welsh Society and The Royal Society of Saint George).

University-based groups include the Alumnae Club of Paris, the Alumni of the University of Edinburgh in France, the Cambridge Society of Paris and the Oxford University Club, while professional associations include the Association of British Accountants in France, the Chartered Management Institute, the Institute of Directors, the Institution of Civil Engineers and the Institution of Electrical Engineers. There are also many women's clubs, including the American Women's Group of Paris, the British and Commonwealth Women's Association, the International Women's Club, WICE and MESSAGE – the Mother Support Group). Miscellaneous societies include the Association France Grande-Bretagne, the British Freemasons in France, French branches of British Guides in Foreign Countries and the Scouts, the English-speaking Union France, the Royal British Legion for ex-servicemen, the Salvation Army and the TOC H Association for elderly people.

During October, many organisations hold 'open houses' or other events to welcome new expatriates, including the popular 'Bloom Where You Are Planted' programme, organised by the American Church in Paris (see **Finding Help** on page 75).

Most private and international schools (see page 148) have an active parents' association and often need volunteers to help organise and run after-school activities for students.

There are also a number of English-speaking sports clubs in the Paris region, including the British Rugby Club of Paris in Saint-Cyr-l'Ecole (78), the Standard Athletic Club in Meudon-la-Forêt (92) and the Thoiry Cricket Club in Château-de-Thoiry (78), plus several arts groups, including The English Cathedral Choir of Paris, The International Players (an amateur drama group), the Paris Decorative and Fine Arts Society and The Royal Scottish Country Dance Society. There's also an English Language Library for the blind in the 17th *arrondissement*.

Outside the capital there are Anglophone clubs and societies in certain areas only, such as Dordogne, Bordeaux and the Côte d'Azur, although most are in Ile-de-France. A free *Digest of British and Franco-British Clubs, Societies and Institutions*, published by the British Community Committee, is available from the British Embassy in Paris (see **Appendix**

A). Details of English-language clubs are also included in our sister publication, *The Best Places to Buy a Home in France* (Survival Books) Other sources of information about English-speaking clubs are *The Connexion* and its various regional publications (see **Appendix B**), and the English-speaking church (see **Religion** on page 364).

For French speakers, the Accueil des Villes Françaises (AVF), a French organisation designed to welcome newcomers to an area, is an option (see page 75). And many local clubs organise activities such as chess, bridge, art, music, sports activities and theatre, cinema and local history outings. Ask your local town hall (*mairie*) for information.

NIGHTLIFE

French nightlife varies considerably with the town or region. In small towns, you may be fortunate to find a bar with music or a *discothèque*, while in Paris and other major cities you're spoilt for choice. Paris by night is usually as exciting and glamorous as its reputation, and it offers a wide choice of entertainment, including jazz and other music clubs, cabarets, discos, theme bars, nightclubs and music halls. The liveliest places are the music clubs, which are infinitely variable and ever-changing with a wide choice of music, including reggae, jazz, funk, rock and techno. High-tech discos are popular, where lasers and high decibels (not to mention drugs) combine to destroy your brain. Note that drunkenness and rowdy behaviour are considered bad taste and bouncers are often over-eager to flex their muscles. The most popular clubs change continually and are listed in newspapers and entertainment magazines.

The action starts around 23.00 or midnight and goes on until dawn (05.00 or 06.00). The admission fee to Parisian clubs is usually high, e.g. from €15 to €30, and generally includes a 'free' drink. Some clubs offer free entry but drinks are expensive.

A traditional and entertaining night out in Paris is to be had at one of the city's many cabaret venues, which include the Crazy Horse Saloon, the Folies Pigalle, the Lido and the Moulin Rouge. The entertainment doesn't

come cheap and runs to between €80 and €170 per head, depending on whether you just see the show or have champagne or dinner as well.

For those who prefer more sober entertainment, 'tea dancing' halls (*guinguette*) can be found throughout France. Old-style dance halls (*bal musette*), where dancing is to a live orchestra, are making a comeback in Paris and are popular with both young and old.

The French have even discovered the 'art' of making fools of themselves in public through karaoke (*karaoké*), which is becoming increasingly popular in Paris and other cities.

GAMBLING

French law forbids gambling for money... but exceptions are made for the stock market, national lottery, horse racing and casinos, all of which are state-controlled. Over 20m people regularly play LOTO, France's national lottery (*loterie nationale*). The LOTO and a plethora of scratch card systems are run by a company called La Française des Jeux (🖳 www.fdjeux.

com). Tickets and cards can be purchased at tobacconists.

Gambling on horse racing is also popular, with betting on the tote system controlled by the Pari Mutuel Urbain (PMU, 🖳 www.pmu.fr), which has branches at cafés throughout France. The most popular bet is the *tiercé*, which entails forecasting the first three horses to finish in the correct order; you can also choose four (*quarté*) or five (*quinté*) horses. Sunday is the most popular day for race meetings and the major races include the Prix de l'Arc de Triomphe, the Prix du Président de la République and the Prix d'Amérique.

There are over 170 French casinos, the largest being at Aix-les-Bains, Biarritz, Cannes, Deauville, Divonne and Evian. The most famous casino of all is that of Monaco (which is almost French). Gamblers must be aged over 18 and be smartly dressed. Blackjack and roulette are the most popular games. Details of all casinos can be found at 🖳 www.journaldescasinos.com, which is partly in English. However, French casinos have recently been losing out to online gambling – some 4m people are reckoned to use 'cybercasinos'.

BARS & CAFES

There's at least one bar or café in virtually every town and village in France, although the number has fallen from over 500,000 at the turn of the 20th century to around 60,000 today. In major towns and cities, watering holes include wine bars, café/bars, brasseries, bar-brasseries and tea-rooms (*salon de thé*). Although they don't have a reputation as hard drinkers, the French spend a lot of time in bars and cafés, perhaps nursing a single drink and playing games, such as *belote* (a mixture of bridge, rummy and solo, played with a standard card pack minus all cards below nine).

French café culture changed radically in February 2008, when all eating and drinking establishments became smoke-free.

Bars

A bar (*bar* or *bar-comptoir* – also known as a *zinc*, after the traditional zinc counters) sells alcoholic drinks and perhaps coffees and snacks, but doesn't usually serve meals. Bars have been rapidly disappearing throughout France, especially in Paris, and many more have been 'modernised' by the installation of TVs, video games, pinball machines (*flipper*) and piped music. There are also 'English' and 'Irish' pubs in Paris and other cities serving a range of British and other imported beers and 'authentic' (foreign) pub food. There are also wine bars in Paris and some other cities, where fine wines are served by the glass and snacks are available, although they're expensive and aren't common or popular.

A bar-brasserie or brasserie serves a wider selection of food than a café and is more like a restaurant.

Cafés & Salons de Thé

Cafés (or café-bars) and bistros serve alcoholic drinks, soft drinks, and hot drinks such as tea and coffee. They usually serve snacks (e.g. sandwiches) and ice-cream all day and may serve meals at lunchtime. If you just want a drink, don't sit at a table with a tablecloth, which indicates that it's reserved for customers wishing to eat. Most cafés have outside tables or terraces on the street, depending on the season and the weather.

Cafés are an institution and have been called the life support system of French culture. They aren't simply places to grab a cup of coffee or a bite to eat, but are meeting places, shelters, sun lounges, somewhere to make friends, meet lovers, talk, write, do business, study, read a newspaper or just watch the

world go by. Since February 2008, all cafés have been non-smoking.

As in other countries, there's a trend towards theme cafés, such as *cafés sports* (where you can watch top sports events on giant screens), and *cafés philos* (where you can indulge in a little philosophical debate over your absinthe).

A *salon de thé* is a tea-room serving tea and coffee, sandwiches, cakes and pastries, but no alcohol. Tea-rooms are fashionable in Paris (e.g. Angelina and Ladurée) and other major cities, but are more expensive than cafés or brasseries. Afternoon tea (*goûter* or *collation*) isn't usually served in France.

Opening Hours & Licensing

There are no licensing hours in France, where alcohol can be sold at any time of the day or night, although an official permit is required. Generally a bar or restaurant closes when the *patron(ne)* decides it will. Most bars and establishments selling alcohol open some time between 06.00 and 11.00 and close between 00.00 and 02.00. Many Parisian cafés open at 07.00 or 08.00 and close at around 14.00. Most brasseries and cafés open at around 11.00 and remain open until 23.00 or later. Cafés and bars near markets often keep the same hours as the market. Like restaurants, most bars and cafés close on one day a week (*jour de repos*), usually shown on the door.

The legal age for drinking in public establishments in France is 16, although children aged 14 to 16 may drink beer or wine when accompanied by an adult. Officially, unaccompanied children under 16 aren't allowed into establishments serving alcohol. However, there's virtually no enforcement.

Costs

The cost of drinks varies considerably with the establishment and its location. A bar or café must display its prices (*tarif de consommations*). At café terraces on major boulevards such as the Champs Elysées or the rue de Rivoli in Paris, you're charged two or three times as much as in a less fashionable street. You pay more for sitting at a table than standing at the bar and there's usually an even higher charge for a table outside or in the window. If you order a drink at the bar and sit down to drink it, you must pay more! Beware of high prices at railway stations and airports and in tourist areas.

RESTAURANTS

No other country is so devoted to its cuisine and the French are among the world's most avid eaters (the French rarely snack but eat civilised meals). They like nothing more than to talk about food and wine (sex and even politics lag way behind). Good French food is noted for its freshness, lack of artificial ingredients and preservatives (the French are fighting a rearguard action against the onslaught of GM food and crop spraying), and exquisite presentation. French cooking is an art form and master chefs are national heroes, although French food reflects not only the expertise of its chefs but also the attitude of the customers, who are among the most discerning, yet also among the most conservative, in the world.

Almost everyone can afford to eat out, and culinary treats await you around every corner. However, not all restaurants offer good value (*rapport qualité-prix*) and it's possible to eat badly in France. One simple rule is to frequent establishments packed with local residents.

☑ **SURVIVAL TIP**

If you want good French food without breaking the bank, look out for establishments awarded a single knife and fork and marked with a red 'R' (*repas*) in the *Michelin Red Guide*.

Top-class restaurants are classified by Michelin (which awards them one to three stars/*étoiles*) and Gault-Millau (up to four chef's hats/*toques*). Ratings are reviewed annually, and there are usually fewer than 20 restaurants in the whole of France with three Michelin stars. Paris is widely recognised as the gastronomic capital of the world and has more restaurants than any other city, although Lyon has more Michelin-starred chefs and the southwest claims to be France's gastronomic heartland. Every region of France has its specialities, which it proudly offers and jealously guards (see **French Cuisine** below).

Surprisingly, many restaurants (including expensive ones) are lacking in what might be assumed to be a quintessentially French quality: ambience. In particular, it isn't unusual for restaurants to be brightly lit, so it pays to check before booking a 'candle-lit dinner' for two.

The good news (for the majority of the population) is that from February 2008 all French restaurants became entirely non-smoking.

Given the quality and variety of French cooking (and the strength of French chauvinism), it's little surprise that most restaurants serve French food, and foreign restaurants are somewhat thin on the ground (except in Paris), although the choice is gradually widening. In Paris, the abundance of African, Middle Eastern, Vietnamese and West Indian restaurants reflects the colonial history of France, although foreign restaurants rarely make the top grade. In the provinces, Italian restaurants are the most common (many serving mainly pizzas), followed by Chinese and, increasingly, Greco-Turkish kebab restaurants. Indian restaurants are scarce. If you're used to spicy foreign food, however, you may find familiar dishes disappointingly bland in France.

Types of Restaurant

Eating houses encompass a wide range of establishments; some of the most common are described below.

Auberge

An *auberge* (or *hostellerie* or *relais*) was originally a coaching-inn or hostelry. Today it's generally an alternative name for a restaurant and may no longer provide accommodation. An *auberge de jeunesse* is a youth hostel.

Brasserie

A brasserie (or bar-brasserie) is a down-to-earth café-restaurant serving meals throughout the day (unlike a restaurant) and often remaining open until the early hours of the morning, particularly in Paris. See also **Bars & Cafés** on above.

Bistro

A bistro (*bistro* or *bistrot*) is generally a small, simple restaurant (or café-restaurant), although they can be trendy and expensive, particularly in Paris and other cities. The hallmark of a bistro is basic French cuisine at reasonable prices. They also provide a place to meet and talk and a stage for musicians. Unfortunately, like cafés, bistros have long been in decline and their numbers have fallen dramatically in the last few decades.

Buffet & Fast Food

A *buffet* is a self-service restaurant, usually found in railway stations and airports. A *libre-service* (or a *self*) establishment is a self-service cafeteria often found in department stores, hypermarkets and shopping centres, in motorway service stations and in city centres. There are many US-style fast food outlets in Paris and other French cities, including McDonald's (which has even invaded the Champs Elysées in Paris and the Promenade des Anglais in Nice and has around 1,000 outlets) and Quick (the Belgian competitor to McDonald's with around 325 outlets and entertaining 'Franglais' menus) as well as pizzerias and pancake stalls (*crêperies*).

Relais Routier

A *relais routier* is a transport café, although these are nothing like the 'greasy spoon' establishments found in other countries and are usually excellent, good value restaurants (mostly on trunk roads) patronised by all travellers, particularly truck drivers (a car park full of trucks outside any establishment is usually an excellent sign).

Restaurant

A restaurant is a serious eating place that serves meals at normal meal times and isn't somewhere for just a drink or snack, unless it's a café-restaurant. Note that you can expect to spend two to three hours or more over a meal in a top-class restaurant.

Rôtisserie

A rôtisserie specialises in grills, although it may serve a wide range of other dishes.

Food

Although the French eat much the same meals as those in most other countries, they may have a different emphasis.

> Breakfast isn't important to most French, which usually consists of just coffee (mainly), tea or hot chocolate. This may be accompanied by croissants or rolls (or a *baguette*), butter and jam (often dunked in coffee or chocolate!).

Lunch is sacred and the most important meal of the day. It's generally served from 12.00 until 14.00, when nearly everything closes in rural areas, although most people lunch around 12.30 in the provinces and at 13.00 in Paris. You'll find it difficult to get a hot meal almost anywhere in rural areas after 14.00 or 14.30.

Sunday lunch is the main gastronomic event of the week for French families and often lasts over three hours. Many restaurants put on an elaborate Sunday menu (at a higher price), although inexpensive set meals are usually also unavailable.

Dinner is usually served from 19.00 until 21.30 or 22.00, although in main cities many restaurants stay open until midnight. Usually dinner is a lighter meal than lunch. A meal eaten late in the evening, perhaps after a cinema or theatre visit, is called supper (*souper*) and may be eaten as late (or early) as 02.00.

French Cuisine

French cooking (*cuisine*, which also means 'kitchen') is divided into a range of categories or styles including the following:

- ◆ *Cuisine bourgeoise* (or *cuisine paysanne/traditionelle*) consists of plain fare such as meat or game stews and casseroles made with wine, mushrooms and onions, with a liberal dose of garlic and herbs. *Cuisine bourgeoise* is commonly found in *relais* (see above) and middle-class restaurants and, although sometimes lacking in imagination, is universally popular, particularly among those with hearty appetites.

- ◆ *Cuisine minceur* is gourmet food for slimmers (invented by Michel Guérard) and is the most delicious slimming food in the world. It's similar to *nouvelle cuisine* (see below) but with the emphasis on the avoidance of fat, sugar and carbohydrates.

- ◆ *Cuisine régionale* (or *cuisine des provinces/campagnarde*) is cooking that's particular to one of the 22 regions of France (see map in **Appendix F**), each of which has its own style of cooking and specialities, often influenced by that of a neighbouring country. *Cuisine régionale* was traditionally based on the availability of local produce, although many well known regional dishes are becoming increasingly difficult to find in restaurants, while others have become ubiquitous.

- ◆ *Haute cuisine*, the cream of French cooking and naturally the most expensive, although not as popular as it once was, comprises a vast repertoire of rich and elaborate sauces made with butter, cream and wine, and a variety of exotic ingredients such as truffles, lobster and wild boar.

- ◆ *Nouvelle cuisine* is a healthier version of *haute cuisine* with the emphasis on freshness and lightness, i.e. pretty food in small portions artfully arranged on large plates. The accent is on minimum cooking to retain natural flavours, with sauces designed to enhance rather than mask the taste of the main ingredients. Chefs are encouraged to experiment and create new dishes; indeed, if master chefs wish to retain their ratings in the gastronomic bibles, it's mandatory. *Nouvelle cuisine* has become less fashionable in recent years.

Vegetarian Food

The French have a generally unsympathetic (or uncomprehending) attitude towards vegetarians (*végétarien*), who are thin on the ground, although gradually increasing in number. You need to be courageous to be a vegetarian in France, where the number of carnivores (per capita) is exceeded in Europe only in Belgium.

You'll constantly be asked why you're a vegetarian and have to explain that chicken, pork (including bacon pieces or *lardons*), sausage and fish are in fact types of meat (see **Vegetarian & Vegan Food** on page 331).

There are only a few vegetarian restaurants in the major cities, although crêperies and pizzerias usually serve vegetarian dishes and you can request vegetarian food (e.g. an omelette) as an alternative to the listed dish in most restaurants, as there's unlikely to be a vegetarian option. A useful book for vegetarians wanting to eat out is *Vegetarian France* (Vegetarian Guides/Editions La Plage), which lists over 150 vegetarian establishments, including some hotels. Vegans (*végétalien*) will find it almost impossible to eat out.

Food to Avoid?

The French have a recipe (or half a dozen) for everything that walks, crawls, slithers, jumps, swims or flies – no living thing is safe from the French cooking pot! However, irrespective of how repulsive something may be in its natural state, the French usually contrive to make it taste (and possibly even look) delicious.

If you're at all squeamish or fussy about what you'll eat, it's wise to learn what to avoid, which may include frogs' legs (*cuisses de grenouilles*), snails (*escargots*), bird's wing (*aile*), little eels (*anguillette*), brain (*cervelle*), tripe (*tripes*), lung (*mou*), brawn or boar's head (*hure*), sweetbreads/pancreas (*ris* – rice is *riz*), calf's innards (*fraise de veau*), kidney (*rognon*), liver (*foie*), tongue (*langue*), pig's head/brawn (*fromage de porc/tête*), calf's head (*tête de veau*), testicles (*rognons blancs/animelles*), horsemeat (*cheval*: France is Europe's second-largest consumer of horse meat after Belgium), pig's trotters (*pieds de porc*), pig's ears (*oreilles de porc*), pig's tail (*queue de porc*), and a variety of songbirds, including blackbirds (*merles*), buntings (*ortolans*) and warblers (*beguinettes*). If you don't like garlic, avoid anything that's *à l'ail* (although it's good for you).

Menus & Prices

Menus with prices must be displayed outside restaurants, with the exception of small village restaurants, where you're offered whatever is being served on a particular day. All restaurants must offer a fixed-price menu (*menu à prix fixe, menu conseillé, menu formule* or simply *menu* – the word for 'menu' is *carte*) with from three to seven courses (commonly four), and many offer a choice of fixed-price menus.

A fixed-price menu may offer a choice between two or three dishes for each course, although in humble village restaurants there's usually no choice, but the price may include wine. The more expensive the menu, the wider the choice of dishes and the larger the number of courses (see below). You can also order separate dishes from the *carte* (the French don't use the term *à la carte*!), which may not be an option in basic restaurants, although it invariably works out much more expensive. Watch out also for the words *en supplément* (sometimes abbreviated to *en suppt*) after items on a menu, as you'll be charged extra!

A *menu dégustation* or *menu gastronomique* is often served in a top-class restaurant and can cost hundreds of euros. It consists of many small portions of the specialities of the house, designed to display the chef's expertise, each of which may be served with a complementary (but not complimentary!) wine.

The sign of good food, a frequently changed menu and an unpretentious establishment, is often a hand-written menu (possibly on a blackboard outside).

Most restaurants are more than happy to cater for children. Some have a children's menu (*menu d'enfants*) and many local restaurants provide a free (or low-priced) place setting (*couvert*) for a young child eating from his parents' order.

Fixed menu prices range from as little as €10 per head in a village café/restaurant up to €150 or more at a two-or three-star Michelin gastronomic shrine.

Although menu prices are low compared with those in many other countries, the cost of wine, coffee and other drinks may be high (wine is often three or four times supermarket prices and not always served at the appropriate temperature). Those on a tight budget and with limited time may prefer to eat in a self-service restaurant (*self*), where you can eat well for around €10. Holders of a *carte famille nombreuse* can benefit from discounts at a number of restaurant chains, including Buffalo Grill.

Menu prices are legally required to include tax and service, although some restaurants still add 15 per cent for service (see **Tipping** on page 368). Pressure from French restaurateurs caused former president Jacques Chirac to reduce the rate of VAT from 19.6 to 5.5 per cent (the rate applying to take-away food) and then spent years trying, eventually successfully, to have the change endorsed by the EU Commission.

When the idea received EU approval, concessions were required, such as that the reductions should either be passed on to customers &/or used to hire (and train) more staff. The effect was patchy, with some restaurants indicating particular items that had been reduced, rather than the contents of the menu overall, while others simply ignored the whole thing and kept the extra money. President Sarkozy has recently said that nonetheless, he had no intention of increasing VAT on restaurant food.

Courses

There are usually three or four courses (a starter, main course, cheese and/or dessert). The first course or starter (*entrée*, which doesn't mean 'main course', as in British English, while *hors d'oeuvre* is a dish of assorted cold food served as a starter) may vary from a hearty soup in a no-menu establishment to a range of exquisite, mouth-watering concoctions in a top-class restaurant.

The main course (*plat principal* or simply *plat*) is traditionally a meat course, although you can choose fish (vegetarian options are rare – see **Vegetarian Food** above), and is accompanied by vegetables (often *haricots verts*) and/or chips. In inexpensive restaurants it's common to use the same knives and forks throughout a meal (which may even be required!).

The cheese course is served after the main course and precedes the dessert. A good cheese board contains local cheeses made from cow's, goat's and possibly even sheep's milk. In cheaper restaurants, you may have no choice of cheeses. The dessert course comes after cheese, or after the main course if there's no cheese course.

Finally you'll be offered a small cup of strong black coffee, possibly accompanied by a bowl of *petits-fours*. Coffee isn't usually included in a fixed-price menu.

Wine

In France, wine is regarded as a necessary accompaniment to even the humblest of meals. The French value quality rather than quantity and will gladly stretch a good bottle between four people rather than guzzle a bottle of cheap wine each.

If wine is included in a fixed-price menu, it's shown on the menu (*vin compris*) and includes, within reason, as much (table) wine as you want. You must pay for drinks other than wine (except tap water). When drinks are included (*boisson comprise*), you can usually choose between wine, beer and mineral water, but must usually pay for anything more than a quarter of a litre of wine or a small bottle of beer or water per head.

In restaurants serving good food, the cheapest house wine (*vin de la maison/vin du patron*) is often good. In cheaper eating places, house wine may be undistinguished but can be ordered by the glass (*verre*) or carafe (*carafe*), which usually come in litre, half-litre (50cl) and quarter-litre (25cl) sizes. Wine may also be served in a jug or pitcher (*pichet*). If there's no house wine or wine by the carafe, wine will probably be expensive,

Children under 14 aren't permitted to drink alcohol in a restaurant (see **Opening Hours & Licensing** on page 308).

Other Drinks

It isn't mandatory to drink wine with a meal and you can drink tap water (*eau du robinet*) or mineral water (*eau minérale*), beer, cider (excellent with pancakes) or nothing at all. If you want free water, ask for a *carafe d'eau fraîche* or *eau du robinet*, which must be provided by law, or you may be served mineral water, which you'll have to pay for. Drinks such as beer and mineral water have the same mark-up as wine

Opening Times

Many restaurants close on one day a week, often on Sundays or Mondays. Always check in advance, as some restaurants close on unexpected days, e.g. Saturdays. Most restaurants also close for one or two months a year for a holiday (*fermeture annuelle*). Those in winter holiday resorts may close for part or the whole of the summer, while those in summer resorts generally close in winter. Many top-class Paris restaurants close for the whole of August.

Booking

Always book for popular restaurants, inexpensive restaurants offering exceptional value, and any restaurant in a holiday resort, especially for Sunday lunch. Top-class restaurants (particularly those that are Michelin or Gault-Millau rated) are often booked up months ahead. If you're eating at one of these gastronomic temples, you should reconfirm your booking a few days before.

Information

There are innumerable publications relating to French restaurants. Two invaluable books are the *Michelin Red Guide* and the *Gault-Millau Guide de la France*. The *Gault-Millau* (published only in French) is primarily a restaurant guide but includes a selection of hotels. It isn't as comprehensive as the *Michelin Red Guide* but makes up for it with its mouth-watering descriptions of the gastronomic delights on offer. The annual *Guide des Relais Routiers* is essential for those driving through France, and guides to local restaurants are published in all areas and available free from tourist offices.

A priceless little book packed with useful information and containing an excellent dictionary of menu terms is *The Pocket Guide to French Food and Wine* by Tessa Youell & George Kimball (Carbery), while *Bon Appétit* by Judith White (Peppercorn) is a handy, pocket-size menu dictionary.

LIBRARIES

France isn't well provided with libraries (*bibliothèque* – *librairie* is a bookshop). Most French people don't do a lot of reading and consequently libraries aren't popular.

Paris is better served than most cities and also boasts the Bibliothèque d'Information Publique in the Centre Georges Pompidou and the Bibliothèque Nationale, both of which are free (although the latter is open only to graduate students and bona fide researchers), as well as the new Bibliothèque de France, which isn't free. The Bibliothèque Nationale (⌨ www.bnf.fr) contains a copy of every book published in France. The Bibliothèque de France is the world's largest library and is open from 10.00 to 19.00 on Tuesdays to Saturdays and from 12.00 to 18.00 on Sundays; a day pass costs €3.

In addition to public libraries there are private libraries in Paris and other major cities. The American Library in Paris (☎ 01 53 59 12 60, ⌨ www.americanlibraryinparis.org) is open Tuesdays to Saturdays from 10.00 to 19.00 and houses the largest collection of English-language books in France. Other English-language libraries in Paris include the

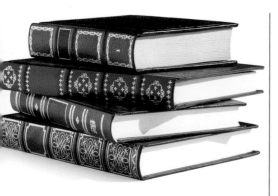

Benjamin Franklin Documentation Centre and the Canadian Embassy Special Library. The British Council in Paris (☎ 01 49 55 73 00) no longer has a lending library, but still operates a 'Knowledge and Learning Centre' (open Mondays to Fridays from 14.00 to 18.00).

Many other libraries are reference (*consultation sur place*) rather than lending libraries and don't allow members to borrow books. When you're allowed to borrow books, you need a library membership card (not always free).

As in other countries, traditional libraries are being replaced by *médiathèques*, where as the name suggests the coverage extends much beyond books as such. Some even include small art galleries, performance areas, etc.

DAY & EVENING CLASSES

Adult day and evening classes, on a plethora of subjects, are run by various organisations in all cities and large towns, and even in many small towns and villages. These include expatriate organisations such as the Women's Institute for Continuing Education (WICE, ☎ 01 45 66 75 50), some of which provide classes for children (e.g. English), particularly during school holidays. French universities run non-residential language and other courses during the summer holiday period.

Among the most popular classes with foreigners are those related to cooking (and eating) and wine. A full list of companies offering cookery courses and gastronomic breaks is included in the *Reference Guide to Travellers in France* available from the French Tourist Office. The most famous French cookery school is the École Cordon Bleu (🖥 www.cordonbleu.edu – in English).

Many famous French chefs have founded cookery schools, including Auguste Escoffier, Michel Guérard, Roger Vergé and Paul Bocuse, the 'English' version of whose website (🖥 www.bocuse.fr) includes the following description of the Restaurant Bocuse: 'Located at 4km in the north of Lyon on the edges of Saône not far from the bridge of Collonges, this house of family became the road of all the greedy ones.' Stick to cookery, Paul.

Adult further education programmes are published in many cities and regions, and include courses organised by local training and education centres. Local newspapers also contain details of evening and day courses. See also **Further Education** on page 153 and **Language Schools** on page 155.

Tour de France

16.
SPORTS

S ports facilities in France are generally good, although lacking in some rural areas. Recreational sports don't play an important part in most French lives, and school and university sports participation is low compared with many other countries. When they do participate in sports, the French generally prefer solo to team sports. Among the most popular participation sports are *boules*, cycling, fishing, hiking, horse riding, hunting, swimming, tennis and skiing. On the other hand, the French (especially men) are as keen sport spectators as the people of most other countries.

When the French decide to take a sport seriously, they do it with a vengeance, as is the case with skiing and tennis, where France has unrivalled facilities. The latest sport to get similar treatment is golf, which although still exclusive, is one of the fastest growing sports in France. Many less well known sports are popular in the summer in the French Alps and the Pyrenees, including rock climbing, white water rafting, glacier skiing, mountain biking, grass skiing and off-road driving.

The French Government Tourist Office (see **Chapter 15**) and other tourist offices are excellent sources of sports information. The FGTO publishes a free brochure, *France for Active Holidays*, describing many of France's sporting attractions. Many specialist publications promoting sporting events and listing local sports venues are available from regional and local tourist offices. Sports fans may be interested in the all-sports daily newspaper *L'Équipe*, which publishes fixtures, results and details of all sporting events in France, plus major events abroad.

Many other indigenous and foreign sports are played in France, where groups of expatriate fanatics play American football, baseball, boccia, cricket, croquet, pelote (pelota/jai-alai), polo and softball. For information about local expatriate sports facilities and clubs enquire at tourist offices, town halls, embassies and consulates (see **Appendix A**).

AERIAL SPORTS

France has a historical and abiding passion for aviation and the love affair extends to all aerial sports, including light-aircraft flying, gliding, hang-gliding, paragliding, parachuting, sky-diving and ballooning.

The Alps and Pyrenees are excellent venues for aerial sports, particularly hang-gliding (*delta plane*) and paragliding (*parapente*). The Pyrenees are reckoned to be the best mountains in Europe for paragliding. There are flying clubs at most airfields, where light aircraft, including microlights (*ULM*) and gliders can be hired. Parachuting and freefall parachuting (sky-diving) flights can also be made from many private airfields. The south of France is an excellent place to learn to fly, as it's rarely interrupted by bad weather. For further information contact the Aéro-club de France (💻 www.aeroclub.com) or the Fédération Française de Vol à Voile (💻 www.ffvv.org).

Ballooning is also popular, and there are balloon meetings throughout France, particularly in summer. It's an expensive sport, however, and participation is generally limited to the wealthy, although you can enjoy a flight (in someone else's balloon) for around €200.

BOULES

There are three principal games of *boules*: *boules lyonnaise*, *pétanque* and *le jeu provençal* (or *La Longue*), from which *pétanque* derived. It's generally recognised that *pétanque* is easier to play, as no special playing area is required and the rules are simpler.

For most people, *pétanque* is a pastime or social game rather than a serious sport. It's played throughout France, but particularly in the south, where most village squares have a pitch (*piste*) and many towns have a special arena called a *boulodrome*. It isn't unusual, however, to find people playing on almost any patch of ground – even in the middle of the road! The more uneven the surface the better, although grass is totally unsuitable. The other essential requirement is an unlimited supply of *pastis*.

The Fédération Française de Pétanque et de Jeu Provençal (FFPJP, 🖳 www.petanque.fr) has over 500,000 members.

CLIMBING & CAVING

France has the best rock-climbing and some of the best mountaineering 'facilities' in Europe. The French have always been avid climbers and France has some of the world's leading exponents. If you're an inexperienced climber, it's advisable to join a club and 'learn the ropes' before heading for the mountains. You'll need a guide when climbing in an unfamiliar area, particularly when climbing glaciers. Mountain guides are available in the main climbing areas, which include Briançon, La Chapelle, Embrun, La Grave and Pelvoux in the high Alps; Chamonix and St-Gervais in Savoie-Dauphiné; Gavarnie, Luchon and Saint-Lary in the mid-Pyrenees; and Bastia in Corsica. Guides are available at mountaineering schools and in many smaller resorts and should be members of the International Federation of Mountain Guides Associations (IFMGA, known in French as the UIAGM and in German as the IVBV, 🖳 www. ivbv.info), which has strict standards.

A number of climbers lose their lives each year in France, many of them inexperienced and reckless (or just plain stupid). Many more owe their survival to rescuers, who risk their own lives to save them. Mont Blanc, Western Europe's highest peak at 4,800m (15,780ft), has seen a record number of deaths in recent years and over 1,000 in the last 20 years. Needless to say, it's highly dangerous to venture into the mountains without proper preparation, excellent physical condition, adequate training, the appropriate equipment *and* an experienced guide.

Information about climbing clubs is available from the Club Alpin Français, officially called the Fédération Française des Clubs Alpins et de Montagne (FFCAM, 🖳 www.ffcam.fr).

CYCLING

France is one of Europe's foremost cycling countries, and cycling is both a serious sport and a relaxing pastime. Bicycles aren't expensive and can be purchased in supermarkets and hypermarkets. Mountain biking (*VTT*) is also a serious sport in France with sponsored events and even professional races. There are *VTT* trails in many areas, although bikes aren't permitted on hiking tracks.

Cyclists must use cycle lanes (*piste cyclable*) where provided and mustn't cycle in bus lanes or on footpaths. You should wear reflective clothing, protective head gear, a smog mask (in cities) and a crucifix in Paris! Cycles must be roadworthy and fitted with a horn or bell and front and rear lights. A cyclists' safety manual, *Premiers Trajets de l'Enfant à Vélo*, specifically aimed at children, is available from La Prévention Routière (🖳 www. preventionroutiere.asso.fr).

Transporting & Renting Bikes

The government is keen to encourage cycling and many trains are equipped with bicycle storage areas. You can travel with your bicycle (as 'hand' baggage) on any day of the week on over 2,000 short-distance trains, marked with a bicycle symbol in timetables (subject to space).

Bicycles can also be rented from over 200 SNCF stations in the principal tourist regions, particularly on the coasts. SNCF usually provides three types of bicycle. Payment can be made in cash, by cheque or by credit card at certain stations, when no deposit is necessary. Payment is made when you return the bike, which can be to the station you rented it from or any other station renting bikes. Bikes can be booked in advance.

> A list of stations where you can rent a bike is contained in a brochure, *Guide Train + Vélo*, available from SNCF stations.

Some *métro* and RER stations in Paris also rent bikes. Bicycles can also be rented from bicycle shops (*marchand de vélos*) in Paris and other cities and towns, but it's around double the rate charged by SNCF.

Tour de France & Other Events

The *Tour de France* is the ultimate challenge on wheels and is probably the toughest sporting event in the world. It's also France's and the world's largest annual sporting event and is watched by some 20m people along the route. The *Tour de France* is held in July and consists of three weeks of cycling on the toughest roads

in France and its neighbouring countries (even in the UK). The route and length of the race changes each year, towns paying handsomely to be a 'stage town', but it always finishes on the Champs-Elysées in Paris.

France has other important road races, including the Paris-Nice in March. Professional track racing is also popular and includes the *Six Jours Cycliste de Paris*.

Associations, Clubs & Information

Keen cyclists may wish to join the Fédération Française de CycloTourisme (FFCT), 12 rue Louis Bertrand, 94207 Ivry-sur-Seine Cedex (🖳 www.ffct.org) or the Fédération Française de Cyclisme (FFC, 🖳 www.ffc.fr). There are cycling clubs in all medium to large towns and tours are arranged in most cities and many tourist areas.

Among the best maps for cycling are the Michelin yellow maps (scale: 1cm = 2km). Many books are written for cyclists, including *Cycling France* by Jerry H. Simpson (Bicycle Books), *Cycle Touring in France* by Richard Neillands (Oxford Illustrated Press), *France by Bike* by Karen and Terry Whitehill (Cordee) and *Cycling in France* by Susi Madron (George Philip), who also operates the UK's largest French cycling holiday company, Cycling for Softies (☎ 0161-248 8282, 🖳 www.cycling-for-softies.co.uk).

FISHING

There's excellent fishing in rivers, lakes and ponds throughout France, many of which are stocked annually with trout, grayling and pike. Fishing is permitted on beaches and other public areas of seafront but not in ports, and there are restrictions on the type of equipment you may use and the kind of fish you may catch (e.g. you aren't allowed to catch young fish); the amount of shellfish (especially sea urchins and oysters) you may gather is also strictly limited. For details, contact the regional Direction des Affaires Maritimes (a list of addresses can be found at 🖳 www.mer.equipement.gouv.fr/ administration/02_serv_prox/01_dram_ddam/ directions_regionales.htm).

Almost all inland waters, from the tiniest stream to the largest rivers and lakes, are protected fishing areas. Fishing rights may be owned by a private landowner, a fishing club or the state. Wherever you fish, however, you must have a fishing permit and you must pay a fishing tax (*taxe piscicole*) by means of a *timbre fiscal* (obtainable from tobacconists). Permits are sold by fishing tackle shops, whose staff can advise you on the best local fishing spots, and in some cases by local cafés. Always carry your fishing permit with you, as wardens (who patrol most waters) may ask to see it.

> To obtain a permit to fish state-controlled waters, you must in effect join a recognised fishing association, which will issue your *carte de pêche* as part of an annual membership. For a list of associations, ask at a tackle shop or contact the Fédération Nationale de la Pêche en France (FNPF, 🖳 www.unpf.fr).

Signs such as *pêche réservée/gardée* are common and denote private fishing. Many of the best fishing waters are in private hands, although it may be possible to obtain permission to fish from the owners.

The fishing season varies with the area and type of fish, but is typically from around 1st March to 15th September for category 1 waters and from 15th January to 15th April for category 2. Fishing regulations vary from department to department. Boats can be hired on inland waters and from sea ports, where deep-sea fishing expeditions are organised. Sea fishing is better in the Atlantic than the Mediterranean.

Further information can be obtained from the Office National de l'Eau et des Milieux Aquatiques (ONEMA, formerly the Conseil Supérieur de la Pêche, 🖳 www.csp.ecologie. gouv.fr) or the Union Nationale pour la Pêche en France (see above). Various websites offer information about fishing in France, including 🖳 www.peche-direct.com and (for trout fishers) 🖳 www.pechetruite.com. A brochure, *Angling in France*, is available from the FGTO (see **Chapter 15**). Information about local fishing areas and fishing permits is available from local tourist offices and town halls. There are a number of books on fishing in France, including *Fly Fishing in France* and *Pêche Française* by Phil Pembroke.

FOOTBALL

Association football or soccer (*le foot* – pronounced to rhyme with the English word loot) is generally reckoned to be France's national sport, with over 7m players.

The French soccer league has four divisions, and teams also take part in a national cup competition (*coupe de France*). The first division has 18 teams and top clubs include Auxerre, Bordeaux, Lille, Lyon, Marseille, Paris Saint-Germain and St Etienne (and Monaco). Football takes a break from Christmas Eve until the end of January, in common with many other European countries. Amateur football is widely played and there are clubs and leagues in all departments.

Further information is available from the Fédération Française de Football (🖳 www.fff.fr) and, at local level, from town halls and *mairies*.

GOLF

Golf is one of the fastest growing sports in France. The largest number of golf clubs are found in Normandy, Brittany, the southwest, the Côte d'Azur and the Paris region. Many courses have magnificent settings (seaside, mountain and forest) and many are linked with property developments. Properties on or near golf clubs, which may include life membership, are becoming increasingly popular with foreigners seeking a permanent or second home.

There are courses to suit all standards, and green fees are low in comparison with many other European countries (particularly the UK), although they may vary with the season; fees at clubs are higher at weekends and on public holidays than during the week. In fact, most golfers prefer to pay and play than to pay an annual membership fee. Most courses require a minimum handicap.

Golf holidays are popular and are a major source of revenue for golf clubs. Most courses welcome visitors and some clubs have special rates for groups. A golf pass is available in some parts, allowing visitors to play at a number of courses in a particular area.

Most clubs have driving ranges (known as *practices*!), practice greens, bunker practice areas, a clubhouse (possibly a *château*),

swimming pools, saunas, Jacuzzis and steam baths, as well as the usual expensive bone-jarring, muscle-wrenching apparatus. Most clubs permit visitors, although there's usually a high hourly or daily fee. Some clubs are small and extremely crowded, particularly during lunch hours and early evenings. Some first-class hotels have fitness rooms. Gym, training and exercise classes are provided by sports centres and clubs throughout France and these often charge reasonable rates.

HIKING & RUNNING

France has some of the finest hiking (*tourisme pédestre*) areas in western Europe. Spring and autumn are the best seasons for hiking, when the weather is cooler and the routes less crowded, although the best time for mountain flowers is between May and August. There are pleasant walks in all regions but most serious walkers head for the Alps, Pyrenees, Vosges, Auvergne and Jura mountains.

France has six national parks, all with an inner zone where building, camping and hunting are prohibited, and 85 state-run natural reserves that were created to preserve the most-threatened areas of national heritage, which are ideal for hikers.

France has the finest network of walking trails in Europe, including some 30,000km (18,600mi) of footpaths known as the *Grande Randonnée* (*GR*) network. Started in 1947, the network has since been expanded into every corner of France under the guidance of the Fédération Française de la Randonnée Pédestre (FFRP, 🖳 www.ffrandonnee.fr). The FFRP issues permits and provides insurance, although these aren't compulsory. A *GR de pays* is a country walk and a *Promenade Randonnée* (*PR*) a one-day or weekend excursion from a *GR*.

In mountain areas there are refuge huts on the main *GR* routes, although these are usually open only in summer. They're basic but much better than being stranded in a storm. The cost is around €10 per night or less if you're a member of a climbing association or a club affiliated to the Club Alpin Français (🖳 www.ffcam.fr). More comfortable accommodation is provided by France's 130 *Rando Plume* establishments – B&Bs conveniently located

restaurant and bar. Many clubs are combined with country or sporting clubs boasting a luxury hotel, restaurant, swimming pool, gymnasium, tennis courts, billiards, croquet and *boules*. You can hire golf clubs and a trolley at all clubs and possibly also a buggy. In major cities, there are indoor driving ranges where membership can be obtained (on a monthly or annual basis).

France hosts a number of international golf tournaments as part of the European tour, including the French Open, the Mediterranean Open, the Cannes Open and the Lâncome Trophy.

For more information about golf, contact the Fédération Française de Golf (🖳 www.ffgolf. org). A full list of golf courses in France, together with photographs and an online booking service can be found at 🖳 www.golfinfrance.f9.co.uk; comprehensive information is also available from the website of *Golf Magazine* (🖳 www.francegolf. fr) and the European Tour (🖳 www.europeantour. com). Another useful website for French golfers is 🖳 www.golf.com.fr. The Institut Géographique National (IGN) publishes a general golf map of France (ref. 910).

GYMNASIUMS & HEALTH CLUBS

There are gymnasiums (*gymnase*) and health clubs (*club de forme*) in most towns. Most have

join in). Hunting rights are jealously guarded and hunters pay €1,500 per year or more for the privilege of hunting in some areas.

A licence isn't required for a shotgun and French hunters are notoriously bad marksmen; around 50 people are killed by hunters each year (often other hunters). Many are inexperienced and some are downright dangerous, especially if they've been at the bottle before taking to the land. Although they won't deliberately shoot you (unless you're a conservationist or *garde-chasses*), it's advisable to steer clear of the countryside during the hunting season.

The minimum age for hunting is 15 (although those under 18 must have parental consent) and a permit (*permis de chasser*) is necessary. Hunters must pass a practical as well as a theoretical exam set by each Fédération Départementale des Chasseurs (FDC, 🖥 www.fdc[number of department].com, e.g. 🖥 www.fdc24.com for Dordogne) to obtain a permit.

It's possible to apply to the Association pour la Protection des Animaux Sauvages (🖥 www.aspas-nature.org) for your land to be designated a 'refuge', although this won't do much for your local popularity! Note that hunting within 150m (500ft) of a house is forbidden, although some hunters ignore this rule. Where hunting is forbidden it's usually shown by a sign ('*chasse interdite/gardée*'). Certain areas are denoted as *réservé pour repeuplement*, which means that hunting access is prohibited in order to allow wildlife to reproduce; red public notices are attached to the perimeter.

For further general information about hunting in France, contact the Office Nationale de la Chasse (🖥 www.oncfs.gouv.fr). Local information, including the dates of the hunting season, can be obtained from your Direction Départementale de l'Agriculture et de la Forêt or Fédération Départementale des Chasseurs

for hikers. There are hiking clubs in most areas, all of which organise local walks, usually on Sundays. Local footpaths include forest paths (*routes forestières*) and 'little walks' (*petites randonnées*), usually between 2km and 11km.

The basic source of information for the *GR* network is the Institut Géographique National (IGN) map number 903 (*Sentiers de Grandes Randonnées*), showing all *GR* trails. The FFRP (see above) publish a series of topographic guides (*Topo-guides*), available in English and French, covering all of France's long-distance footpaths, and an annual *Rando Guide*. The Michelin 1,100 orange series maps (scale 1:50,000 or 1cm = 500m) are good for walking, although for the ultimate in detail you need the IGN *Rando* series of 2,000 maps. A route-planning CD ROM is available from retailers or the IGN website (🖥 www.ign.fr – available in English) for around €40.

Among the best English-language books for hikers in France are *Classic Walks in France* by Rob Hunter and David Wickers (Oxford Illustrated Press), *Walking in France* by Rob Hunter (Oxford Illustrated Press) and *Walking Through France* by Robin Neillands (Collins).

HUNTING

France has 1.6m registered hunters (*chasseurs*), more than all other European countries combined. Hunting is a key part of the masculine culture (only a few women or *mairie*. There are many magazines devoted to hunting in France.

▲ Caution

Before buying a property, you should be aware of any hunting rights on or adjacent to your land and check before planning any fencing or walling that this won't raise objections. Although hunters don't have the right to hunt on private land (*propriété privée*) without permission, when land has traditionally been used by hunters they won't bother to ask.

RACKET SPORTS

Tennis is by far the most popular racket sport in France; squash and badminton are also played, but facilities can be poor. There are two main kinds of racket club: sports centres open to all, and private clubs. Sports centres require no membership or membership fees and anyone can book a court. Clubs tend to have little or no social aspect and there may not even be club nights or tournaments. Most towns and villages have municipal courts that can be rented per hour. Some hotels have tennis and squash courts, and organise coaching holidays throughout the year.

Local information about racket sports facilities is available from *mairies*, travel agents and tourist offices.

Tennis

Tennis's popularity has grown tremendously in the last few decades and there are courts in most towns and villages, although in small villages there may be one court only and it may be in poor repair. One of the reasons for the popularity and high standard of tennis in France is that there are hundreds of covered and indoor courts, enabling tennis to be played year round.

Tennis was long regarded as an elite sport in France and remains that way in many private clubs, which are usually expensive and exclusive and rarely accept unaccompanied visitors. Membership runs to several hundred euros per year and most clubs have long waiting lists.

France has many tennis schools and resorts, and in Paris and other cities there are huge tennis complexes with as many as 24 courts, open from 07.00 to 22.00 daily. Many tennis clubs provide saunas, whirlpools, solariums and swimming pools, and most have a restaurant.

Further information about tennis can be obtained from the Fédération Française de Tennis (www.fft.fr).

Squash & Badminton

There are squash clubs in most large towns, although many have only one or two courts. There are also many combined tennis and squash clubs. The general standard of squash is low due to the lack of experienced coaches and top competition, although it's continually improving, encouraged by the recent success of France's top male players, Thierry Lincou and Grégory Gaultier. Rackets and balls for racket-ball (a 'simplified' version of squash played with a larger, bouncier ball and shorter rackets) can also be hired from most squash clubs.

Some tennis centres also provide badminton courts and there are around 600 badminton clubs, although facilities tend to be poor.

Further information can be obtained from the Fédération Française de Squash (🖥 www. ffsquash.com) and the Fédération Française de Badminton (🖥 www.ffba.org).

RUGBY

Most rugby in France follows the rugby union code (15 players a side), although rugby league (13 players a side) is also popular, particularly in Carcassonne and Perpignan.

The national rugby union team (*les tricolores*) competes in the annual Six Nations championship along with England, Ireland, Italy, Scotland and Wales, home games being staged at the Parc des Princes or the Stade de France in Paris.

French rugby owes its popularity (and existence) to clubs rather than schools or universities. It has its stronghold in the southwest of the country (the *Midi*), where every town has a team. Among the most famous clubs are Agen, Bayonne, Béziers, Brive, Narbonne and Toulouse. French clubs compete in an annual European Cup competition with British clubs. There's even a British Rugby Club in Saint-Cyr-l'Ecole in Yvelines near Paris.

Further information is available from the Fédération Française de Rugby website (🖳 www.ffr.fr), where you can find a list of clubs in your region.

SKIING

Both downhill skiing (*ski alpin*) and cross-country skiing (*ski de fond/ski nordique*) are very popular in France, although downhill skiing is greatly preferred.

France is Europe's number one destination for serious downhill skiers and some 15 per cent of the French population ski regularly. France boasts over 3,000km 2 (over 1,150mi²) of skiing areas spread over six mountain ranges, which between them have the largest number of resorts and the most extensive network of ski lifts in the world (over 4,000).

Most resorts have a range of ski lifts, including cable cars, gondolas, chairlifts and drag lifts. Drag lifts are usually 'Pomas' for single riders, rather than two-person T-bars, common in Austria. Lifts are marked on *piste* plans, as are all runs, which are graded green (for beginners), blue (easy), red (intermediate) and black (difficult).

Ski resorts provide a variety of accommodation, including hotels, self-catering apartments and chalets. Accommodation is more expensive during holiday periods (Christmas, New Year and Easter), when lift queues are interminable and runs overcrowded. During public and school holidays (see pages 50) the crowds of school children may drive you crazy, both on and off piste.

Cross-country skiing (*ski de fond/ski nordique*) doesn't have the glamorous and exciting image of downhill skiing, but it's nevertheless a popular sport in France. It appeals to both young and old, the fit and the unfit, as it can be enjoyed at any pace and over any distance and a variety of terrains.

Cross-country skiing has the advantages over downhill skiing of cheaper equipment, no expensive lift passes, no queues **and** fewer broken bones! Trails, usually consisting of two sets of specially prepared tracks (*pistes de ski de fond*), are well signposted. Some resorts have floodlit trails for night skiing.

If cross-country skiing is too much like hard work and downhill skiing old hat, you may wish to try something more exciting such as freestyle, off-piste, speed, heli-or 'extreme' skiing or snow-boarding (*surfing*). Snow-boarding is particularly popular and is taught in most resorts. The French invented 'extreme' skiing, which involves negotiating slopes steeper than 60 degrees.

Heli-skiing, where helicopters drop skiers off at the top of inaccessible mountains, is illegal in France. However, 'powder hounds' can ski into un-navigable areas and be picked up by helicopter (if they're lucky) or can be dropped by helicopter on mountains in Italy or Switzerland (where heli-skiing is legal) and ski back to France.

Other activities may include paragliding, parasailing, hang-gliding, snow-shoe walking, dog-sledding, tobogganing, snowmobiling and, for the seriously suicidal, snow-joering (being towed on skis by a horse!), bob-sleighing and ice-diving.

Most winter resorts have heated indoor swimming pools, gymnasiums, fitness centres, saunas and solariums, along with a variety of other indoor activities, including tennis, squash, ice-skating, curling, indoor golf and tenpin bowling. There's an excellent choice of restaurants and bars in most resorts, although they can be expensive. Other entertainment includes discos, cinemas, nightclubs and casinos.

Summer skiing is available in Alpe d'Huez, Les Deux Alpes, La Plagne, Tignes, Val d'Isère and Val Thorens and can be combined with other sports such as tennis, swimming, golf, horse riding, grass skiing, fishing, water-sports, hiking, climbing and a range of other activities.

If you're a newcomer to downhill skiing, it's worth enrolling in a ski school to learn the basics; it's much safer (particularly for other skiers) than simply launching yourself off the nearest mountain. France has 11,000 instructors and all French resorts have ski schools (École de Ski Français) where classes are organised at all levels, from beginner to competition. Ski school costs from around €170 to €200 per person for courses of three to five days (nine to 12 hours) for groups of two to eight people. Individual lessons are also available but are understandably more expensive. Not all instructors speak English; those who do are most likely to be found at the most popular resorts, e.g. Chamonix.

Always abide by the International Ski Federation's (FIS) Safe Skiing Code, which can be found on, for example, 🖥 www.boardsure. com/safety_information/isfssc.php. Further safety guidelines are contained in the booklet *Pour Que la Montagne Reste un Plaisir*, available from tourist offices and ski hire shops in resorts. General information about health and safety for skiers can be obtained from the Médecins de Montagne website (🖥 www. mdem.org).

For further information about skiing and other winter sports, contact the Club Alpin Français (🖥 www.ffcam.fr), the Fédération Française de Ski (🖥 www.ffs.fr) and the Association des Maires des Stations Française de Sports d'Hiver (also known simply as

SkiFrance, 🖥 www.skifrance.fr – available in 'English'). The latest weather and snow conditions are available via telephone (☎ 08 92 68 08 08), internet (e.g. the France Météo website, 🖥 www.meteofrance.com), teletext, in daily newspapers and direct from resorts. The FGTO (see **Chapter 15**) publishes a *Winter Holiday Guide*.

SWIMMING

Swimming (*natation*) is one of the country's favourite sports and pastimes. Beaches vary considerably in size, surface (sand, pebbles, etc.) and amenities. Most resorts provide beach clubs for the young (*club des jeunes*) and all but the smallest beaches have supervised play areas where you can leave young children for a fee. Otherwise, most beaches are free.

Most French beaches are noted for their cleanliness; in a few areas public beaches are dirty and overcrowded, although this is very much the exception. Officially, 96 per cent of French beaches are 'clean' and over a third have been awarded an EU 'blue flag' (*pavillon bleu*) for the quality of their water (97 out of 271 beaches), although many that fail the tests are dangerously polluted. The dirtiest beaches are on the northern coast between Calais and Cherbourg, the cleanest around Nice (although not all). The pollution count must be displayed at the local town hall: blue = good quality water, green = average, yellow = likely to be temporarily polluted, and red = badly polluted.

A list of blue flag beaches can be found on the Blue Flag website (🖥 www.blueflag.org – in English) and a list of 'black flag' beaches on that of the Surfrider Foundation Europe (🖥 www.surfrider-europe.org – the 'English' version of the site is 99 per cent in French!), which draws attention to what it considers to be unacceptably high levels of pollution.

Sea swimming is dangerous at times, particularly on the Atlantic coast, where some beaches have very strong currents. Most beaches are supervised by lifeguards who

operate a flag system to indicate when swimming is safe. You should observe flags and other beach warning signs. When a beach is closed or swimming is prohibited, it's shown by a sign (*'baignade interdite'*). There are stinging jellyfish in parts of the Mediterranean and along the Atlantic coast but no (harmful) sharks.

Swimming pools (*piscine municipale*) can be found in most French towns. Paris now boasts around 35 public pools, including a floating pool on the river Seine (opened in 2006 to complement the annual 'Paris-Plage' initiative, which transforms 3.5km of the Seine river bank into a sandy beach for five weeks of the summer).

Most swimming pools and clubs provide swimming lessons (all levels from beginner to fish) and run life-saving courses. Since 2003, all French children have been required to follow a 'learn to swim' programme and take swimming tests at regular intervals.

France also has a number of huge water-sports centres with indoor and outdoor pools, slides, flumes, wave machines, whirlpools and waterfalls, plus sun-beds, saunas, solariums, Jacuzzis and hot baths.

WATER SPORTS

Popular watersports include sailing, windsurfing, waterskiing, jet-skiing, rowing, canoeing, kayaking, surfing, barging, rafting and sub-aquatic sports. Wetsuits are recommended for windsurfing, waterskiing and sub-aquatic sports, even in summer. Rowing and canoeing are possible on most lakes and rivers, where canoes and kayaks can usually be hired (rented).

France has Europe's best surfing beaches, on the extreme southwest Atlantic coast, including Biarritz (the capital of European surfing), Capbreton, Hossegor and Lacanau.

Scuba diving and snorkelling are popular, particularly around the coasts of Brittany, the French Riviera and Corsica. There are clubs for most water-sports in all major resorts and towns throughout France, where instruction is usually available. France has over 8,500km (5,300mi) of inland waterways, controlled by Voies Navigables de France (VNF, 💻 www.vnf. fr), and it's possible to navigate from the north coast to the Mediterranean along rivers and canals. Canals aren't just for pleasure craft, and millions of tonnes of freight are transported on them annually. Except for parts of the Moselle river, all French waterways provide free access.

French residents must obtain a certificate of competence to pilot power boats of 9 to 50hp; separate certificates are required for inland waters (*permis fluvial*) and coastal waters, including rivers within five nautical miles of a harbour (*permis mer*). You must have an International Certificate of Competence (ICC), which is valid for five years, to hire a boat over 15m (50ft) long.

Be sure to observe all warning signs on lakes and rivers. Take particular care when canoeing, as even the most benign of rivers have 'white water' patches that are dangerous for the inexperienced. Some rivers have strong currents and require considerable skill and experience to navigate. It's sensible to wear a lifejacket, whether you're a strong swimmer or a non-swimmer. On some rivers there are quicksand-like banks of silt and shingle where people have been sucked under.

France has literally hundreds of harbours and sailing is a popular sport in France, which has some 750,000 yacht owners, and numerous sailing clubs and schools. Boats of all shapes and sizes can be hired in most resorts and ports, from motorboats to barges and houseboats (*pénichette*) accommodating 10 to 12 people. In contrast, many inland waters are devoid of sailing boats, and inland sailing clubs are few and far between. If you prefer to let someone else do the work, there are hotel barges, some with heated swimming pools, air-conditioning, and even suites with four-poster beds!

If you wish to berth a boat in France, you must find a caretaker (*gardien/ne*) to look after it. The cost of keeping a yacht on the Atlantic coast is much lower than on the Mediterranean, although even there it needn't be too expensive provided you steer clear of the most fashionable ports. Mooring fees vary considerably depending on the size of boat, the time of year and the location, e.g.

a 15m boat would cost €26.95 a day at La Rochelle in winter (double in the summer), while a superyacht could cost some 50 times that in Saint-Tropez; permanent moorings can cost €3,000 per metre per year or more.

Further information about inland waterways can be obtained from Voies Navigables de France (VNF, 🖳 www.vnf.fr). The FGTO (see **Chapter 15**) publishes a free booklet, *Boating on the Waterways*. A book which may be of interest to boat owners is *The French Alternative: The Pleasure and Cost-Effect of Keeping your Boat in France* by David Jefferson (Waterline).

17.
SHOPPING

France is one of Europe's great shopping countries, and shops are designed to seduce you with their artful displays of beautiful and exotic merchandise. Paris is a shoppers' paradise, where even the shop windows are a delight, although it isn't the place for budget shoppers. One of France's main attractions is its markets, which take place regularly in almost every town and many villages, where almost everything can be bought, in a uniquely French atmosphere.

Most towns have a supermarket or two and, on the outskirts of large towns, there are usually huge shopping centres with hypermarkets, do-it-yourself (DIY) stores and furniture warehouses. In many city centres there are pedestrian streets (*rue piétonne*), where you can walk and shop without fear of being mown down by cars and motorcycles – although you're still at the mercy of skateboarders and rollerbladers.

The French don't usually make good servants, and shop staff are often surly and unhelpful, particularly in department stores, where you can wait ages to be served while staff chat among themselves (in France the customer often comes last). On the other hand, one of the delights of French life is the art with which even the simplest purchase is wrapped – especially if you say it's a gift (*pour offrir*).

In Paris and other cities and tourist resorts, you must be wary of pickpockets and bag-snatchers. **Never** tempt fate with an exposed wallet or purse or by flashing your money around.

For those who aren't used to buying articles with metric measures and continental sizes, a list of comparative weights and measures is included in **Appendix E**.

PRICES

French retailers are among the world's most competitive and have smaller profit margins than those in many other countries. Price fixing isn't permitted, except on books, although the *Loi Lang* (named after Culture Minister Jack Lang) allows only up to a 5 per cent discount off manufacturers' 'recommended retail prices'. Prices of bread and pharmaceuticals are government controlled.

Some products are particularly expensive in France and are worth importing. These include electronic and audio equipment, cosmetics, furniture, books, paint and similar products, and almost anything that's manufactured outside the EU. Among the best buys in France are pottery, decorative glass, kitchenware, quality clothes (including children's), fashion accessories, toys, domestic electrical equipment, wines, spirits (but not imported ones), luxury foods and perfumes.

SALES & BARGAIN SHOPPING

There are relatively few bargain shops in France (certainly compared with the UK or US), although there's usually at least one cheap 'bazaar' in each town.

The French generally don't go in for secondhand goods, and charity shops are virtually non-existent, apart from the those of Emmaüs (🖥 www.emmaus-france.org), an international charitable organisation with around 120 shops in France, and a few *dépôts-vente*, where you can leave unwanted clothes (or other articles) and receive 50 per cent of the selling price when they're sold.

On the other hand 'boot sales' (known as *foire à tout* in the north and *vide grenier* in the south) are becoming increasingly common (see **Markets** on page 329). There are secondhand bookshops in most large towns and cities. See also **Clothing** on page 334 and **Furniture & Furnishings** on page 337.

It's possible to buy goods direct from factories, with discounts of between 30 and 70 per cent, although factory shops aren't nearly as common as in the US. Most of them are to be found in the north and east of France, although the factory-shopper's Mecca is Troyes in Aube, where there are around 230 'factory' outlets. Keen bargain hunters may want to track down *The Factory Shop Guide for Northern France* by Gillian Cutress & Rolf Stricker, which is now out of print, *Le Guide France-Europe des Magasins d'Usine* (Editions du Seuil) and *Paris Pas Cher* (Flammarion).

You should be wary of fake goods, as some 70 per cent of all fake products are copies of French brands, reckoned to cost the country 30,000 jobs and €6bn in lost sales annually. Perfumes are a favourite target, but counterfeit goods include leather products, CDs and DVDs, household goods and food. Even French truffles, which can cost as much as €650 per kilo, have been 'counterfeited' by the Chinese in recent years. If you're buying a designer item (i.e. a handbag) in a market and the price seems too good to be true – then it probably is!

SHOPPING HOURS

Shopping hours vary considerably according to the city or town and the type of shop. Food shops cannot legally open for more than 13 hours per day, and other shops are limited to 11 hours per day. Food shops outside Paris (such as bakeries) are open from as early as 06.30 or 07.00 until 12.00 or 12.30, and again from between 15.00 and 16.00 until 19.00 or 20.00. Non-food shops usually open from 09.00 or 10.00 to 12.00 and from 14.00 until 18.30 or 19.30. Small shops tend to tailor their opening hours to suit their customers rather than their staff.

Large shops and super/hypermarkets remain open at lunchtime, although smaller stores usually close, except perhaps on Fridays and Saturdays. Most hypermarkets are open from 09.00 until between 20.00 and 22.00, Mondays to Saturdays.

France is generally closed on Sunday, although some village shops, particularly *boulangeries*, *charcuteries* and *pâtisseries*, open on Sunday mornings. There's widespread opposition to Sunday trading from unions and small shopkeepers, although French shops are permitted to open on five Sundays a year and those in designated 'tourist' areas (e.g. coastal and ski resorts) can open on any Sunday. Many shops (and some other businesses) are closed on Monday mornings or all day Mondays, particularly those that open on Sundays.

In many cities and towns, shops have a late-opening day (*nocturne*) once a week, e.g. Wednesdays in Paris, until between 20.00 and 22.00. It's generally best to avoid shopping on Wednesdays if possible, as many children are off school and go or are taken shopping on that day. Paris and some cities have food shops that stay open until 22.00 or 00.00 and

a few that open 24 hours. Many small Parisian boutiques open at around 10.00 or 10.30 until 19.00 or 19.30. Some shops close for the whole of August or for another month in the year.

Shops and restaurants often indicate the days they're open or closed, e.g. every day (*tous les jours* or *TLJ*), every day except Monday (*sauf lundi*), and Saturdays, Sundays and holidays (*samedis, dimanches et fêtes* or *S, D & F*). Most shops close on public holidays (see page 50) and most (except some newsagents') shut on 1st January, 1st May, 14th July and 25th December.

SPECIALIST FOOD SHOPS

Buying food is a serious business in France, where the range and quality of fresh food is without parallel. The French have a passion for eating, and shopping for food is a labour of love and not to be rushed. When they have time, people usually shop in small specialist food shops and markets rather than in large, soulless supermarkets and hypermarkets. Despite intense competition from supermarkets and hypermarkets, traditional, small, family-run shops still thrive in villages and small towns and enjoy some 60 per cent of the general retail trade and around 50 per cent of the food trade. Although their numbers are decreasing – more as a result of the depopulation of rural areas than competition from supermarkets – they survive by offering personal service (advice, tastings, etc.) and high quality, as well as providing a meeting place for locals.

When living in France, one of the best ways to integrate with the local community is to support local businesses. The quality and range of food provided by small shops varies considerably, so shop around to find those that you like best and become a regular customer. In many rural villages, there are mobile shops (*marchands ambulants*) selling bread, meat, fish, dairy products, fruit and vegetables. They usually visit once or twice a week. Ask your neighbours what days they call and listen for their horns. Despite the availability of almost any fruit and vegetable at almost any time of year (from somewhere in the world), the French tend to eat only what's in season locally (i.e. in France) and generally avoid imported produce.

> Food is sold by the kilo or by the 'piece' (*pièce*). *Une livre* (not to be confused with *un livre*, meaning 'book') means 'pound' (either in weight or in money) and is equivalent to half a kilo or 500g.

Farmers and producers sell their produce direct to the public and you'll often see signs such as '*produits de la ferme – vente directe*' in country areas for fruit, vegetables, wine (and other drinks), cheese, pâté, honey, eggs and other foods. You can also pay in advance, usually annually, for a weekly or monthly supply of fresh fruit and vegetables direct from a local producer, whereby the grower makes up a basket of seasonal produce, which you must usually collect. There's also a growing trend to 'pick your own' fruit and vegetables. (If you're tempted to pick mushrooms in the forest, take them to a chemist and check that they're safe to eat.)

Boucherie

Most villages and all towns have a butcher's shop (*boucherie*) selling all kinds of meat, including pork, although generally speaking pork is the preserve of the *charcuterie* (see below). A *boucherie* doesn't sell horse meat (*cheval*), which is sold by a specialist horse butcher (*boucherie chevaline*), denoted by a sign with a horse's head (it's also sold in some supermarkets and hypermarkets) and is similarly priced to beef (many people believe it's the best of all meats, although its popularity has waned in recent years). A butcher may also sell poultry, although this is sold exclusively by specialist poultry shops (*volailler*) in some towns. Butchers will often cook meat purchased from them at little extra cost and many also sell spit-roasted chickens and other cooked meats.

The French are voracious carnivores and are second in Europe only to the Belgians in the quantity of meat they consume per capita. When the French kill an animal for food, nothing is wasted, not even the ears and tail, not to mention its innards and private parts (offal), which is highly prized. The French are puzzled by many foreigners' aversion to eating certain parts of an animal. However, since the 'mad cow disease' (*maladie de la vache folle*) epidemic, butchers must display details of the life and manner of slaughter of all bovines, including the country or area of origin, on a *ticket de pesée* attached to the joint or carcass. Unless your French is particularly good, you're better off buying your meat pre-packed from a supermarket. However, if your French is up to the task, your local butcher is a better choice and is usually an excellent source of cooking tips.

☑ **SURVIVAL TIP**

Butchers often open on Sundays but close all day on Mondays or just in the morning, whereas supermarkets (which have a meat counter) are open on Mondays.

Boulangerie

Thanks to a 19th-century law, all towns and villages above a certain size must have a baker (*boulangerie*) or an outlet selling bread (*dépôt de pain*), e.g. a café, newsagent's, supermarket or petrol station. The French love their daily bread (many old country homes have a bread oven) and won't keep bread for more than a few hours (let alone freeze it – heaven forbid!), although consumption has fallen from some 84kg per head per year in 1965 to around 40kg today (or from 230g to around 110g – half a baguette – per day).

When foreigners refer to French bread, they usually mean a *baguette*, although there are many other varieties of loaf. *Pain* (or *pain parisien/gros pain*) is the thickest and longest, while the narrowest and shortest is the *ficelle* (literally a 'piece of string'). Other common types of loaf are *flûte* and *bâtard*. Note also that otherwise identical loaves are often cooked in different ways, e.g. in a mould (*moulé*) or on a flat baking tray or tiles (*pavé*) and you should specify which you prefer.

French bakers are producing an increasingly wide variety of 'non-standard' breads, including wholemeal bread (*pain complet/intégral*), *pain de campagne* ('country' bread, made with a blend of white, wholemeal and rye flour), *pain de seigle* (rye and wheat bread) and *pain au son* (with added bran). Unlike a *baguette* or *pain*, these can be kept for a few days. Wholemeal or mixed-grain *baguettes* are sometimes available. *Pain de mie* is a tasteless sandwich loaf used for toast (or feeding ducks), although *pain de mie complet* is a slight improvement.

A *boulangerie* also sells *croissants*, chocolate *croissants* (*pains au chocolat*), *brioches* (a type of bun), special breads made with raisins and nuts (e.g. almonds, hazelnuts or walnuts) and a limited range of cakes and biscuits, although for fancy cakes you need to visit a *pâtisserie* (see below). Bakers sometimes also sell sandwiches and other snacks, such as quiches and mini-pizzas. Like bread, *croissants* vary considerably in quality and taste, and it's well worth shopping around for the best. It's best to avoid packaged *croissants*.

Bakeries usually close on one day a week, although in a town with more than one they won't all close on the same day. When the only baker in a village closes, bread (usually *baguettes* and *pains* only) is usually available from another outlet, such as the village café.

Charcuterie

A *charcuterie* (literally pork butcher's) is a delicatessen selling mostly cooked meats, plus pâtés, pies, quiches, omelettes, pizzas, salads and prepared dishes. Each region has its own pork specialities, as does each *charcutier*. A *charcuterie* may also have a *rôtisserie*, where meat and poultry is spit-roasted. A *charcutier* may also be a caterer (*traiteur*), who can create delicious dishes for two or a banquet for 100.

Confiserie

A *confiserie* is a high-class confectioner, not to be confused with a common sweet shop (which don't exist in France). Each town has a *confiserie*, where you can buy hand-made chocolates and confectionery made with every fattening (and expensive) ingredient under the sun. They may also make excellent home-made ice-cream. A *confiserie* isn't the place to buy children's mass-produced sweets, best bought in bulk at the supermarket, but confectionery to win somebody's heart. A *confiserie* may be part of a cake shop (*pâtisserie* – see below).

Crémerie

A *crémerie* ('dairy shop') sells butter, cream, cheese, eggs, yoghurt, ice-cream, and a variety of other foods, many with nothing to do with milk. Surprisingly, *crémeries* don't usually sell fresh milk. They're mainly found in rural areas where there are lots of cows, such as Normandy and the Jura.

Both salted (*demi-sel*) and unsalted (*doux*) butter (*beurre*) is available, made from both pasteurised and unpasteurised (*cru*) milk. (Low-fat, margarine-like spreads are available in supermarkets, although they aren't normally used as a substitute for butter.) A *crémerie* usually sells dozens of cheeses, many of which cannot be found elsewhere. If it doesn't, there's probably a cheese shop (*fromagerie*) nearby (see below).

Épicerie/Alimentation Générale

A grocers or general store (*épicerie/ alimentation générale – épicerie* is literally a 'spice shop') sells most everyday foods, including butter, cheese, coffee, fruit, vegetables, wine and beer, plus a range of preserved and packaged foods. Many general stores are now self-service (*libre-service*). Prices are usually considerably higher than in supermarkets; you pay for the convenience and personal service. In Paris and other cities, many grocers stay open late.

Fromagerie

France produces around 400 varieties of cheese, including many made with unpasteurised milk (*lait cru*). This practice is under threat from Brussels' eurocrats, although under the French *AC* system it's illegal to make cheeses from pasteurised milk! Many thousands of cases of food poisoning are attributed to cheese each year, although nobody knows for sure whether the cheese is infected before, during or after it's made.

Imported cheeses are rare, although the French make their own 'foreign' cheeses, particularly Emmenthal. Goat's milk cheese (*fromage de chèvre*) is popular and comes in numerous varieties (and prices). It's also possible to buy sheep's milk cheese (*fromage de brebis*).

When buying a soft cheese such as brie or camembert, you should state whether you want it ripe (*fait*) or unripe (*pas fait*). A sell-by-date of around three weeks ahead of the purchase date on pre-packaged camembert is a good indicator for *pas fait*.

Pâtisserie

A *pâtisserie* is a cake shop, selling wonderful (but expensive) home-made pastries, fruit tarts and chocolate éclairs, and perhaps home-made ice-cream. It's possible to buy just one or two slices (*une part*, not *tranche*) of a fruit tart or flan or a whole one. Every town and region tends to have its own specialities. Cakes are made to order for special occasions. All creations are beautifully wrapped, even when you buy just a single *tartelette*.

Poissonnerie

Fishmongers' (*poissonnerie*) are rare in inland France compared with other food shops, although fish stalls are common in markets. Fish isn't an inexpensive alternative to meat and is often expensive, although it's reasonably priced in fishing ports – even more so if you buy directly off the fishing boats – and mussels (*moules*) can be purchased for around €3-4 per kilo.

Most foreigners find it difficult to identify the myriad types of fish sold in France, which vary from region to region. The most common species include anchovy (*anchois*), bass (*basse*), bream (*acarne*), eel (*anguille*), haddock (*aiglefin* – haddock is smoked haddock), mackerel (*maquereau*), monkfish (*baudroie/lot*), mullet (*barbeau*), octopus (*pieuvre*), plaice (*carrelet*), salmon (*saumon*), sardine (*sardine*), sea bass (*bar/loup*), skate (*raie*), sole (*sole*), squid (*calamar*), trout (*truite*), tuna (*thon*), turbot (*turbot*), whitefish (*blanc*) and whiting (*merlan*). Fish are cleaned, scaled and 'topped and tailed' free on request.

Common shellfish (*coquillage*) include clams (*clovisse/flie/palourde/vernis* according to size), cockles (*bulot/coque*), crab (*crabe*), crayfish (*langoustine*), lobster (*langouste* or *homard*), mussels (*moules*), oysters (*huîtres* – see below), prawns (*crevette rose*), scallops (*coquille Saint-Jacques*) and shrimps (*crevette*). The 'queen' of mussels, *moules de bouchot* from Normandy's Mont St Michel bay, recently became the first seafood to be awarded an *AOC*.

France is by far Europe's largest producer of oysters, which aren't just for millionaires and cost as little as €5 per kilo in fishing ports, although they can cost twice as much in markets and supermarkets. Oysters are, however, usually sold by the dozen and not by weight, and the price varies with the category or size. They're 'properly' eaten raw (despite

periodical 'scares'), although they're equally tasty when cooked.

All fish must be labelled with its source (e.g. wild or farmed), the location of the catch (if wild), and its commercial and scientific names. There are three quality grades: *Label Rouge* (top quality, like meat), *Certification de Conformité Produit/CCP* (medium quality) and *Qualité Aquaculture de France* (basic quality).

Health Food Shops

There are few 'health food' shops in comparison with many other developed countries (e.g. the UK) – the French believe all food is healthy (except McDonalds) – and they sell meat products as well as vegetarian and vegan food (see **Vegetarian & Vegan Food** below). The best known chain is Naturalia France.

Foreign Food Shops

French supermarkets sell few foreign foods, with the exception of biscuits, coffee and tea, confectionery, preserves, Italian pasta, Chinese and Vietnamese foods, delicatessen foods (e.g. *charcuterie*) and perhaps a few cheeses, particularly Dutch (many French people are unaware that there are any British cheeses!). You may also find American hamburger buns, and British-style (sliced) bread, marmalades and sauces, e.g. HP and Worcester. There may be wider ranges, even including curry-making products, in supermarkets in areas where there are many foreign residents or tourists, sometimes in a 'tastes of the world' (*gouts du monde*) section.

Foreign food shops are common in Paris and some other cities (notably Toulouse). In Paris, Galeries Lafayette features a British Food Hall and the Grande Épicerie de Paris is an international grocery store selling foods from the UK, the US and other countries. Other American food shops in the capital include Thanksgiving (4th *arrondissement*) and The Real McCoy (7th). Marks & Spencer returned to the Champs Elysées in November 2011 with British food, and there are plans for a franchised network of Marks & Spencer Simply Food shops throughout France.

Foreign food can be ordered from abroad via the internet, although prices are inevitably high.

MARKETS

Markets are a common sight in towns and villages and are an essential part of French life, largely unaffected by competition from supermarkets and hypermarkets. They're colourful, entertaining and an experience not to be missed, even if you don't plan to buy anything.

There are generally three kinds of market in France: indoor markets, permanent street markets and travelling open-air street markets that move from neighbourhood to neighbourhood on different days of the week or month. Many small towns hold a market or fair once a month, usually on the same date each month.

The *raison d'être* of the French market is fresh food – meat, fruit, vegetables, fish, cheese, bread, etc. – most produced locally, although it's generally more expensive than in supermarkets. In many markets a wide range of live 'food' is available, including snails (the best quality snails for festive occasions can cost around €1 each), lobsters, crabs, ducks, chickens, guinea fowl, pigeons and rabbits. Most rural food markets have a selection of stalls run by organic farmers. A variety of other goods are commonly sold in markets, including flowers, plants, clothes and shoes, ironmongery, crockery and hardware.

Specialist markets (particularly in Paris) include antiques, books, clothes, stamps/postcards, flowers, birds and pets. Antique and flea markets (*marché aux puces*) are common throughout France, the largest regular market is held at Saint-Ouen in Paris, with 7km (4mi) of shops selling secondhand goods, antiques and curios (*brocante*). It's open every Saturday, Sunday and Monday from 07.30 until 19.00. Paris also has a number of smaller flea markets. However, don't expect to find many bargains in Paris, where anything worth buying is snapped up by dealers.

Elsewhere, Lille stages the *Grande Braderie de Lille* on the first weekend in September, which is the largest flea market in Europe with 100km of stalls! In the provinces there are also *foires à tout* or *vide-grenier* (a cross between a flea market and a car boot sale), where you can turn up some real bargains, particularly fine china, e.g. Limoges. For further money-saving tips, see **Sales & Bargain Shopping** above.

The most popular days for markets are Wednesdays and Saturdays, although they can be found somewhere every day of the week except Mondays. In the provinces, markets are often held in the mornings only, from around 06.00 until 12.00 or 13.00 (shrewd shoppers get there before 09.00). You need to get up with the birds to shop at some wholesale markets (e.g. in Paris), open from around 04.00 to 08.00.

Each district (*arrondissement*) in Paris has at least two or three weekly street markets, some of which close for lunch, e.g. from 13.00 to 16.00, and continue until 19.00 or 20.00. There are Sunday morning markets in many towns.

To find out when local markets are held, ask at your local tourist office or town hall. Market days may be listed on a sign when entering a town, which may also indicate any parking restrictions). A useful guide to French markets is Anne Gregg's *Tarragon & Truffles* (Bantam Books).

DEPARTMENT & CHAIN STORES

Among the most famous department stores, most of which are in Paris, are Au Bon Marché (the first department store in France, founded in 1852), Printemps (best for perfumes), Galeries Lafayette (famous for high fashion) and La Samaritaine, the largest department store in the capital.

Fashion is the forte of most Parisian department stores, many of which stage regular fashion shows. Most also specialise in cosmetics and provide money-changing services, export discounts (i.e. VAT refunds), a travel agency, and theatre and concert tickets. Many department stores also have a food (*alimentation*) department.

☑ **SURVIVAL TIP**

Some department stores, such as Printemps, give foreign visitors a 10 per cent discount on all purchases.

Department stores don't close for lunch and usually open from 09.30 until around 19.00, Mondays to Saturdays, with late-night shopping on one day until around 21.30. Most deliver goods within a certain radius and also ship goods overseas (for a fee). If you're making a number of purchases from different departments, you can often obtain a *carnet d'achats* and pay for everything at the same time.

Chain stores are rarer than in most other European countries. French chain stores include Bally and Eram (shoes), and FNAC (audio, books and video). Department stores such as Printemps, Au Bon Marché, Trois Quartiers, La Samaritaine and Nouvelles Galeries are also chain stores, with branches in several towns. Chain stores such as Monoprix and Prisunic (subsidiaries of Galeries Lafayette and Printemps respectively) and Uniprix, which are like budget department stores and known as *magasins populaires*, have outlets throughout France.

There are also a number of British and other foreign chain stores operating in France, including The Body Shop, Brentanos, Burton, C & A, Espirit, Gap, Habitat, Ikea, Jaeger, Toys 'R' Us, Virgin Megastore, WH Smith and Zara.

SUPERMARKETS & HYPERMARKETS

There are supermarkets (*supermarchés*) and hypermarkets (*hypermarchés*) – both often referred to as 'large areas' (*grandes surfaces*) – in or just outside most towns. Among the leading supermarket and hypermarket chains are Auchan/ATAC, Carrefour, Casino, Champion (most of which, since 2009, have become 'Carrefour Market' supermarkets), Intermarché, E. Leclerc, Prisunic and Super U/ Hyper U.

The last ten years has seen a steady increase in the number of low-price supermarkets known as *supermarchés hard discount*, e.g. Lidl and ED. They offer the usual range of foodstuffs and household goods you find in traditional supermarkets and hypermarkets, but without the frills of attractive presentation and shelving. Savings on a mixed-bag shopping basket can be as much as 10 per cent.

Hypermarkets are often located in a shopping or commercial centre (*centre commercial*) with many smaller shops, cafés and restaurants (often including a self-service restaurant), toilets, telephone booths, a huge free car park, and a petrol station (usually the cheapest local source).

Large supermarkets and hypermarkets are generally open all day from 08.00 until around 19.30 (some hypermarkets stay open later). However, some small supermarkets close for lunch, although not usually on Saturdays. Some supermarkets are open on Sunday mornings. Many supermarkets and hypermarkets have petrol stations which are open 24 hours a day if you have a credit or debit card.

One thing you won't find in supermarkets or hypermarkets is much in the way of medicines, which can only be purchased at a chemists (see **Medicines** on page 219), or any tobacco products, for which you must go to a *tabac* (see **Tobacconist** on page 334).

The French are keen on DIY (*bricolage*) and there are numerous DIY superstores, some of which (e.g. Castorama, Leroy Merlin) offer free telephone advice and DIY courses. There are also supermarkets for furniture (e.g. But, Monsieur Meuble) and electrical goods (e.g. Darty, Boulanger). France even has funeral supermarkets (Roc-Eclerc), where you can choose your coffin and headstone at your leisure.

The French are keen gardeners, and many hypermarkets have extensive garden departments, often selling plants as well as gardening equipment. There are also dedicated garden centres (*jardinerie*) and nurseries (*pépinerie*) in or on the outskirts of most towns.

⚠ Caution

When you enter a supermarket or hypermarket, there's often a counter, called a *consigne*, where you must leave goods purchased elsewhere, large bags and crash helmets; you're given a receipt. If there's no *consigne*, a security guard may heat seal you previous purchases in a plastic bag, which you can then take into the store with you.

At many supermarkets and hypermarkets, plastic bags aren't provided except for fruit and vegetables, and are now banned, although you can buy a biodegradable bag at checkout tills for a few cents. Checkout staff don't bag your purchases or take them to your car for you. It's essential to have a returnable €1 coin (or similar size token/*jeton*) to use a trolley (*caddie*).

Food

The range of food sold by French supermarkets and hypermarkets is similar to that in the UK (with the exception of vegetarian and vegan food – see below). Most supermarkets and hypermarkets have separate counters for meat, fish, bread and cheese. The French generally don't like to buy pre-packaged meat, fish, fruit or vegetables. Supermarkets sell few foreign foods, although some have sections (usually hidden) where imported products can be found (see **Foreign Food Shops** above). Some supermarkets also have a salad bar.

Fruit and vegetables may be sold individually (*la pièce*) or by the kilo (*le kg*). In the latter case, they may be weighed by an assistant or you weigh them yourself on scales with buttons depicting the various produce, although some supermarkets still weigh produce at the checkout. (If you're supposed to weigh produce and forget, you'll be sent by the checkout assistant to do so, while frustrated shoppers in the queue behind fume!).

As in other countries, perishable items have a sell-by date (*date limite de vente*) or use-by date (*date limite d'utilisation optimale/DLUO*), which may also be described as a 'consume-by-date' (*date limite de consommation/DLC*) or 'expiry date' (*date de péremption*). You should always check this, as it's common for out-of-date products to be left on the shelves.

Vegetarian & Vegan Food

France is a nation of carnivores, and vegetarian food (other than fruit and vegetables) is in short supply, although supermarkets are beginning to stock vegetarian prepared meals, and other products. Vegans have a difficult time living in France, where veganism isn't widely understood. Information about vegetarianism in France can be found on the website of the French vegetarian association, the Alliance Végétarienne de France (🖳 www.vegetarisme.fr). Vegetarians looking for French recipe ideas should consult 🖳 www.cuisine-vegetarienne.com.

Diet Food

There's less 'diet' (*diététique*, *minceur* or *lite*) food than in some other developed countries (e.g. the UK and US), although the French buy around four times more diet food than a decade ago. Low-fat yoghurts in particular have proliferated and other low-fat foods (e.g. cheeses, milk and cream) are widely available.

Organic, GM & 'Fair Trade' Food

There's an increasing amount of organic agriculture (*agriculture biologique*) in France, where there are now some 10,000 organic farms. Organic products, which are widely available in supermarkets and hypermarkets, are labelled '*bio*'. However, organic food tends to be 30 to 100 per cent more expensive than 'ordinary' food, and a new type of food called *agriculture raisonnée* is now available, offering a compromise (in both price and production methods).

France imposes strict regulations regarding the production and sale of genetically modified (GM) food (*organismes génétiquement modifies/OGM*). Certain French food manufacturers, including Danone, Knorr, Marie Surgelé and Nestlé claim not to use any GM products.

'Fair trade' food (*commerce équitable*) recently made an appearance in French supermarkets, although it hasn't yet caught on, as the French are concerned above all with quality.

DRINK

Drinking alcohol is an integral part of everyday life in France, where many people have a daily tipple. The days of cheap French booze, however, may be numbered, as the government is raising taxes on alcoholic drinks, ostensibly to reduce the incidence of alcoholism and its cost to the state, although even a 1 per cent tax increase will conveniently raise an extra €30m in revenue. There's also plenty of choice among non-alcoholic drinks.

Wine

France is, of course, world-famous for its wines, and one of the essential features of a civilised home is a large cellar (*cave*), where wines are left to mature for years (often far longer than is good for them). Despite its renown, the French wine industry is in crisis as more and more foreigners switch to 'new world' wines and the French themselves, although inseparably wedded to their own wines, drink less and less. Indeed, the popular view of the French as great drinkers could hardly be further from the truth: their alcohol consumption per head is relatively low (wine consumption has reduced by a third in the last 25 years) and there's a growing anti-alcohol lobby.

As even teetotallers are no doubt aware, there's more to wine than its colour, which may be red, white, pink or even yellow (e.g. *vin jaune* from the Jura and most dessert wines), and it's a well known fact that the more you know about wine, the more you'll enjoy it (it also make your more eloquent and a better driver!). There are numerous excellent books about French wine, and information about

wine-related tours and holidays can be found at 🖳 www.winetourisminfrance.com (available in English).

Merchants

France doesn't have the equivalent of a British 'off-licence', and there are few specialist wine merchants (*marchand de vins/caviste/négociant*), although there's usually at least one in most large towns. There are, however, a few chains of wine shops (such as Nicolas), where prices are fixed throughout the chain, and independent wine shops and local chains in Paris, such as Le Repaire de Bacchus. Most wine shops will deliver if you buy more than a few bottles. A good *épicerie* or *charcuterie* usually also sells wines, although they're generally considerably more expensive than supermarkets.

Most people buy their wine from supermarkets and hypermarkets, although the quality and range isn't usually outstanding. If you buy wine from your local supermarket, keep an eye open for their *Foire au Vin* special offers.

Nowhere are French stores more parochial and nationalistic than when it comes to selling wine. Most supermarkets and hypermarkets stock a wide selection of local wines, but may offer little from other regions of France apart from Bordeaux and, to a lesser extent, Burgundy. You're likely to find few (if any) non-French wines in your local supermarket, where they're normally segregated from French wines (e.g. hidden behind a pillar) and overpriced.

Buying Direct

Buying direct is the best way to buy wine in France, where many wine lovers buy the bulk of their wine direct from growers, either by making an annual visit to vineyards or by mail-order. Vineyards selling wine direct usually have signs inviting you to free tastings (*dégustation gratuite* or *dégustation et vente*), with the hope of selling you a few bottles or cases. Most vineyards and distillers are geared to receive visitors, particularly the great champagne and cognac houses, several of which make a small charge for a conducted tour and tasting. Appointments must be made to visit some smaller vineyards and most are closed during lunchtimes.

Beer

French beer (*bière*) is usually of the 'lager' variety and comes mainly from the northeast, e.g. Alsace, Lorraine, Picardie and Nord-Pas-de-Calais. As well as the well-known brands, there are many excellent, strong beers (e.g. top-fermented *bières de garde*) brewed by farmhouse breweries. The French also drink Belgian beer but rarely beer from any other country.

Beer is usually sold in packs of 6 to 24 x 25cl or 33cl bottles and is much cheaper than in most other European countries. Supermarkets have frequent offers on beer, although the practice of selling beer in returnable bottles (*bouteilles consignées/verres consignés*), which works out even cheaper than small bottles, has practically died out.

Spirits & Other Alcoholic Drinks

Spirits are cheaper in France than in many other European countries, although more expensive than in Italy and Spain. Among the many popular spirits in France are Cognac, Armagnac, Marc (a grape brandy made from the residue of wine production in wine-growing regions), Calvados (apple brandy from Normandy), Kirsch (cherry brandy from Alsace) and a wide variety of liqueurs, such as Bénédictine, Chartreuse, Cointreau and Grand Marnier. Imported gin and, especially, Scotch, Irish, American and Canadian whiskies are also popular.

> France is the world's largest whisky market after Spain, and the French buy 12 times as much whisky as brandy, whose sales are suffering as a result.

Brandy is classified by age, i.e. *vieux* or *réserve* (three years old), *vieille réserve* (four years old), *VSOP* (an abbreviation of the English 'very special old pale', indicating five years' ageing), and *hors d'âge* (literally 'ageless' but meaning over six years old).

Aniseed liqueurs (*pastis*) such as Pernod and Ricard are brewed in the south, and Alsace is home to Fleur de Bière – distilled malt beer. Absinthe, long banned (and for good reason), has recently been legalised. If your taste is for the really exotic, try Soho or Yachting Cocktail Litchi (made with lychees), Passoã (alcoholic passion fruit juice), Ortilette or Fleur de Pissenlit (the former made from nettle leaves, the latter from fermented dandelion flowers, whose reputed effect is indicated by the French name!).

Among the many other popular alcoholic drinks in France are apple and pear cider (brewed in Brittany and Normandy), and fortified wines, drunk as aperitifs. Alcohol flavoured with fruit and other things is common throughout France, every region having its own variations such as *crème de cassis* (which is added to white wine to make *kir*), *crème de menthe* and *crème de cacao*, Pineau des Charentes (grape juice and cognac), Floc de Gascogne (grape juice and Armagnac) and pommeau (apple juice and calvados).

Coffee & Tea

Coffee is cheaper and better in France than in many countries, and decaffeinated coffee (*café décaféiné* or simply *déca*) is widely available. Almost unbelievably, tea-drinking is on the increase in France, where almost a quarter of the population start the day with a cup of tea rather than coffee. Don't even think about buying 'French' (black) tea bags, which are expensive and taste of nothing, no matter how familiar-sounding the brand. Some British brands (e.g. Twinings and Lipton's) are becoming more common in supermarkets, although they often seem much weaker than the original.

Milk & Cream

Fresh milk is relatively expensive in France, and many supermarkets sell little or no fresh milk, as most French buy long-life (*UHT*) milk; this initially tastes awful in tea but most foreigners get used to it. It usually comes in skimmed (*écrémé*) and semi-skimmed (*demi-écrémé*) versions as well as full-cream (*entier*) and is sold in litre cartons or (plastic) bottles. 'Fresh' milk may be days old when purchased and consequently goes off quickly.

You may have difficulty finding the type of cream you're used to: *crème fraîche* isn't 'fresh cream' but slightly soured cream, and the nearest you'll get to British 'single' and 'double' cream are *crème entière* and *crème entière* épaisse, which, like milk, are usually sold in 'long-life' cartons (it may keep for only a few weeks even unopened). Sweetened 'whipped' cream (crème Chantilly) in an aerosol can (bombe) is also available.

Water

Although French tap water is safe to drink, most people prefer to buy bottled water (the average French person drinks 100 litres a year!), of which there's a bewildering variety in most supermarkets (France has over 100 spas). Most mineral water is still (plate or sans gaz), although sparkling water (eau gazeuse/pétillante) is also available, the most famous brand being Perrier.

> ### ☑ SURVIVAL TIP
>
> If you drink only bottled water, you're advised to change brands regularly, as each contains a preponderance of certain minerals rather than a healthy mixture.

TOBACCONIST

The tobacconist (bureau de tabac, commonly called simply tabac) is a unique French institution. They're identified by a vertical orange sign representing a carrot (which dates back to when slices of raw carrot were put in tobacco to keep it moist).

Not only are tabacs the sole authorised vendors of cigarettes and other tobacco products (see **Smoking** on page 231), they're also mini-stationers. A tabac sells postage stamps, postcards, single envelopes and writing paper, as well as gifts and souvenirs, cigarette lighters and other odds and ends. They also sell lottery tickets and may be agents for PMU off-track betting.

Oddly, a tabac is also the source of government forms and the official outlet for fiscal stamps (timbre fiscal) used to pay fines (e.g. parking tickets), government taxes and official fees such as those required for a residence permit (carte de séjour). Stamps are sold in denominations of €0.50, €1, €2, €5, €8, €10, €20, €30 and €90, although few tabacs stock the whole range of fiscal stamps and you may need to try a few to get the stamp

you need. A tabac is usually combined with a bar or newsagents, and there's often a post box (boîte aux lettres) outside. They're usually open late (some Parisian tabacs never seem to close).

CLOTHING

Clothing outlets range from street bazaars selling cut-price clothes to elegant boutiques offering the ultimate in chic. The flagship of the French fashion industry is haute couture: made-to-order clothes employing the best designers (many of them British!), craftsmanship and materials. Garments are outrageously expensive (costing from €3,000 to €8,000 or more). Not surprisingly, the worldwide clientele for haute couture clothing is estimated to be no more than a few thousand people, with just a few hundred regular customers.

Everyday clothes are expensive compared with those in other Western countries, mainly due to a lack of imports. As with other things in life, the French generally prefer quality to quantity, and 'classic' clothes are made to last and never go out of fashion. One of the best value ready-to-wear labels is Tati, who have their flagship store at boulevard Rochechouart in Paris and branches in a number of other cities.

Bargains can be found in cities if you're willing to hunt around or wait for the sales (see page 323). Last season's designer labels are usually sold at half-price, i.e. ridiculously instead of outrageously expensive. Most shops hold sales in January and at the end of June, and bargains can be found year round in Alésia, the major discount shopping district in Paris' 14th arrondissement. The Forum des Halles in Paris is a giant subterranean shopping centre where you can find every kind of clothing at bargain prices. There are also 'label villages' (ville de marques), where designer clothes and other luxury goods can be purchased at discounts of up to 30 per cent.

Popular women's ready-to-wear shops include Benetton, Cacharel, Caroll, Franck et Fils and Infinitif, while top men's shops include 100,000 Chemises, Alain Figaret, Cacherel, Cerrutti 1881, Charles Le Golf, Kenzo and New Man.

There are also many secondhand shops selling clothes, euphemistically referred to as 'twice twice' (*bis bis*), especially in Paris, e.g. the Magasin du Troc, which sells slightly used *haute couture* clothes and accessories, perhaps worn only by models. Here you can pick up a Chanel suit for as little as a third of the new price (merely excessively expensive). Second-hand clothing stores for men are also becoming increasingly popular among Parisians. Costume and formal wear hire is possible from many shops in Paris and other cities.

There are many excellent women's fashion magazines in France, including *Modes et Travaux* and *Vogue*.

For those unfamiliar with European sizing, a size-conversion table is included in **Appendix E**.

NEWSPAPERS, MAGAZINES & BOOKS

There are over 200 daily, weekly and monthly newspapers and magazines in France, not including trade magazines and reviews. However, there are few, if any, national newspapers, as the French generally prefer local news. Most daily newspapers are published for a region, such as *Le Progrès de Lyon*, *La Voix du Nord* (Lille), *Sud-Ouest* (Bordeaux) and *Ouest-France* (published in Rennes and France's largest-selling daily paper, with a circulation of over 1m). *Le Parisian* is the capital's daily newspaper (and the nearest France comes to a 'tabloid'), with regional editions named *Aujourd'hui*.

There are only three French newspapers that can claim to be national. The most famous is *Le Monde,* the most intellectual and respected, as well as the best-selling 'national' daily. It's centre-left and similar in prestige to the English *Times* (which is centre-right), and published in Paris in the afternoon and given the following day's date (which can be confusing!). Next in pecking order is *Le Figaro* (moderate right, conservative – similar to the UK's *Daily Telegraph*) and lastly *Libération* (known colloquially as *Libé*), an intellectual and one-time fashionable tabloid of the centre-left (it was co-founded by Jean-Paul Sartre).

Other popular newspapers include *l'Humanité* (known as *l'Huma* – the French will abbreviate anything), the recently revamped, official organ of the French Communist Party, *L'Equipe*, a daily newspaper devoted entirely to sport, and *La Croix*, a right-wing Catholic newspaper. There are also a number of financial newspapers, including *Les Echos* and *La Tribune* (France's answer to the *Financial Times* or *Wall Street Journal*); *Le Monde* has a number of offshoots, such as *Le Monde d'Education* and *Le Monde Diplomatique*, the latter a monthly international newspaper. Surprisingly, specialist Sunday newspapers are almost unknown apart from the undistinguished *Le Journal de Dimanche* and *L'Humanité Dimanche*, although many daily newspapers are also published on Sundays. As elsewhere, weekend papers often carry extra supplements, e.g. travel, fashion and TV programmes, and cost more than weekday issues.

Many newspapers provide excellent weekly magazines (see below) and reviews, and free local weekly newspapers full of advertisements are delivered to homes in many areas. A 'tabloid press' is also virtually nonexistent, as scandal-mongering is largely the preserve of magazines. France has strict laws regarding personal privacy, although this hasn't prevented the publication of a number of scandal sheets in recent years, including *Minute* and *Voici*, and there are two weekly satirical papers, *Le Canard Enchaîné* (similar to the UK's *Private Eye*) and *Charlie Hebdo* (more juvenile), both published on a Wednesday.

French newspapers are expensive in comparison with, for example, British papers, the 'nationals' costing €1.40 for *Le Figaro* and €1.50 for *Le Monde*. On the other hand, they contain 'real' news as opposed to magazine-style articles, and the standard of journalism is high.

Where the French excel is in the field of magazines and they produce a larger number than any other European country, with the possible exception of the UK, where the diversity of technical and trade magazines is unmatched, even in the USA. French publishers produce over a thousand monthly and even more weekly and quarterly titles. Popular weekly current affairs magazines include the best-selling *Paris Match* (largely 'celebrity' news), *Le Nouvel Observateur* (left), *Le Point* and *L'Express* (middle-of-the-road conservative), *Marianne* (left, tabloid-like) and *VSD* (semi-serious).

Business and financial titles include *Enjeux les Echos*, *L'Expansion* and *Le Nouvel Economiste*. Among the many women's magazines are *Biba*, *Elle*, *Femme Actuelle*, *Marie Claire* and *Marie France* and there are French versions of men's magazines such as *FHM* and *Men's Health*. Other popular magazines include *Figaro Magazine*, *Madame Figaro* and *Jours de France*.

Newspapers and magazines are sold at tobacconists (*tabac*), newsagents' (e.g. the Maison de la Presse chain) and railway station kiosks, and in supermarkets. Some are available online, e.g. ⌨ www.lecanardenchaine.fr, www.figaro.fr, www.liberation.fr, www.lemonde.fr, www.marianne2.fr and www.mondediplomatique.fr (or ⌨ http://mondediplo.com for the English version).

⚠ Caution

English-language books are expensive in France, where there are no discount bookshops, although you can buy books online from UK sellers such as Amazon.co.uk.

It used to be cheaper to buy bestselling books, such as Michelin guides, from hypermarkets. However, the French government introduced fixed prices to protect small bookshops from going out of business, thus restricting the availability of most books.

In small towns there are usually a few small shops selling a limited selection of books, rather than one large bookshop. There are secondhand bookshops in larger towns and cities. Second-hand and rare bookshops and markets are fairly common in Paris, notably the *bouquinistes* along the banks of the river Seine, although these tend to stock specialist books (at specialist prices).

English-language Publications

Major newspapers from other countries are available on the day of issue in Paris and a day or two later in the provinces. Some English-language daily newspapers are printed in France and widely available on the day of publication, including *USA Today*, *International Herald Tribune* (edited in Paris), *Wall Street Journal Europe*, the *Guardian*, the *Times* and the *European Financial Times* (printed in Frankfurt). Foreign newspapers are much more expensive than in their home countries (the price is stated in the newspaper, usually on the front or back page) and usually don't include many (if any) of the supplements normally carried in weekend issues (such as the *Sunday Times*). You can access most newspapers via the internet, which is usually free, although some such as the *Times/Sunday Times* require a subscription.

Many British and foreign newspapers produce weekly editions, including the *Guardian Weekly*, *International Express* and the *Weekly Telegraph*, which are available on subscription. *Le Monde* publishes a supplement in English on Saturdays. A number of other English-language publications are available in Maisons de la Presse, major supermarkets and on subscription (see **Appendix B**).

Note that the French for bookshop is *librairie*; a library is a *bibliothèque*.

Most French bookshops don't stock English-language books. There are, however, English-language bookshops in most large towns and cities, as well as in resort towns. English-language bookshops in Paris include the Abbey Bookshop (5th *arrondissement*), Librairie Albion (4th), Brentano's (2nd), Galignani (1st),

San Francisco Book Co. (6th), Shakespeare & Company (5th), WH Smith & Son (1st), Tea and Tattered Pages (6th), and the Village Voice (6th). English-language books are also sold at the Virgin Megastore on the Champs-Elysées. However, imported English-language books are expensive (except for this one, which is an absolute bargain!), usually costing around double their 'recommended' home country price. Americans in particular will be appalled. It's cheaper to buy them from Amazon via their UK website and to stock up when visiting the UK.

Many expatriate organisations and clubs run their own libraries or book exchange schemes, and some French public libraries keep a small selection of English-language books (see **Libraries** on page 308). Some bookshops also sell secondhand books, which may also be available from market stalls.

FURNITURE & FURNISHINGS

Furniture (*meubles*) is generally quite expensive in France compared with many other European countries and the choice is usually between basic functional furniture and high-quality designer furniture, with little in between. Exclusive (i.e. expensive) modern and traditional furniture is available everywhere, including bizarre pieces from designers such as Gaultier for those with money to burn and a need to impress. Many regions have a reputation for high-quality, hand-made furniture.

If you're looking for antique furniture at affordable prices, the best bargains are to be found at flea markets (*foire à tout*) in rural areas. However, you must arrive early and drive a hard bargain, as the asking prices are often a joke. You can often buy good secondhand and antique furniture at bargain prices from a *dépôt-vente*, where people sell their old furniture and courts sell repossessed household goods. Look under *Dépôts-vente*, *meubles*, *équipement pour la maison* in your local *Yellow Pages*. There are also companies selling furniture that has been repossessed from bankrupt businesses at bargain prices. A useful guide to antique buying is *Antiques en France: an English Buyer's Guide*.

Modern furniture is popular and is often sold in huge stores in commercial centres (inexpensive chain stores include But,

Conforama and Fly) and hypermarkets, some of which provide the free loan of a van. Pine furniture is inexpensive. Beware of buying complicated home-assembled furniture with indecipherable French instructions (translated from Korean) and too few screws. If you want reasonably priced, good quality, modern furniture, you need look no further than Ikea, a Swedish company manufacturing furniture for home assembly with a 14-day money-back guarantee. (The price of Ikea furniture varies with the country and most items are much cheaper in France than, for example, in the UK.) If you're buying a large quantity of furniture, don't be reluctant to ask for a discount, as many stores will give you one if you ask.

When buying furniture for a home in France, don't forget to take the climate into consideration. The kind of furniture you buy may also depend on whether it's a permanent or holiday home. Note also that, if you plan to furnish a holiday home with antiques or expensive furniture, you'll need adequate security and insurance.

HOUSEHOLD GOODS

Household goods are generally of good quality and the choice, although not as wide as in some other European countries, has improved considerably in the last decade. Not surprisingly for a nation that spends much of its time in the kitchen (the rest is spent in the dining room), French kitchenware in particular is among the best in the world. Prices are also competitive, with bargains to be found at supermarkets and hypermarkets. Apart from hypermarkets, one of the best stores for household appliances is Darty, which has outlets in most towns.

Interest-free credit or deferred payment is common and goods can usually be paid for in ten monthly instalments. If you choose to pay 'cash' for a product advertised with an interest-free credit period, you're entitled to a discount in proportion to the length of the credit period, e.g. around 2 per cent for a six-month period, 3.5 per cent for 12 months and 6.5 per cent for two years. You can also obtain an extended guarantee (for an extra charge), which enables you in effect to 'trade in' an almost new article for a state-of-the-art model.

Bear in mind when importing household appliances which aren't sold in France that it may be difficult or impossible to get them repaired or serviced locally. If you bring appliances with you, don't forget to bring a supply of spares and refills, such as bulbs for a refrigerator or sewing machine, and bags for a vacuum cleaner. Similarly, the standard size of kitchen appliances and cupboard units in France isn't the same as in other countries, and it may be difficult to fit an imported dishwasher or washing machine into a French kitchen. Check the size and the latest French safety regulations before shipping these items to France or buying them abroad, as they may need expensive modifications.

If you already own small household appliances, it's worthwhile bringing them to France, as all that's usually required is a change of plug. However, if you're coming from a country with a 110/115V electricity supply, such as the US, you'll need a lot of expensive converters or transformers, and it's better to buy new appliances in France. Small appliances such as vacuum cleaners, grills, toasters and electric irons aren't expensive and are of good quality (the label 'NF' indicates compatibility with French safety standards). Don't bring your TV without checking its compatibility first, as TVs from many countries don't work in France (see **Chapter 8**).

Subject to electricity supply compatibility, foreign computers will work. If you need to buy a computer while in France but don't want it to have a French operating system or an AZERTY keyboard, you can order one from an international supplier or buy one in the UK or Ireland. It's possible, however, to 'convert' a French computer to work with a QWERTY keyboard (although the on-screen instructions will still be in French).

If you need kitchen measuring equipment and cannot cope with decimal measures, you'll need to bring your own measuring scales, jugs, cups and thermometers (see also **Appendix E**). Pillows and pillowcases aren't the same size in France as, for example, in the UK or US, and the French use duvets and not blankets to keep warm in winter.

LAUNDRY & DRY CLEANING

Thanks to the French obsession with their appearance, all large towns have laundries (*blanchisserie*) and dry cleaners' (*nettoyage à sec/pressing*), most of which also do minor repairs, alterations and dyeing. (There are more dry cleaners' and laundries in Paris than in the whole of many other European countries!) Dry cleaning is expensive, however, and you must usually pay in advance. Cleaning by the kilo with no pressing is possible in some places, and you can also save money by having your clothes brushed and pressed, rather than cleaned. Note also that 'express' cleaning may mean a few days rather than hours, even at a dry cleaner's where cleaning is done on the premises. Some shops will collect and deliver items for a small fee.

Except in Paris, there are few self-service launderettes (*laveries automatiques*), as the French prefer not to wash their dirty linen in public. Launderette machines are usually operated by tokens (*jetons*) marked with the price and purchased from an attendant. Machines usually take around 7kg (15lb) of washing, although there are often machines of different sizes. Washing powder and softeners are available from vending machines, although it's much cheaper to provide your own. Launderettes have heavy-duty spin dryers (*super essorage*) that reduce the time required to dry clothes but may make them impossible to iron! Dryers can be very hot, so take care with delicate items requiring little drying.

In some villages, there are still communal *lavoirs*, usually located by a river or near a spring, although these aren't recommended for everyday use.

ONLINE & MAIL-ORDER SHOPPING

Shopping by mail-order (*vente par correspondance* or *vente à domicile*) and by telephone has long been popular in France, and shopping online has now taken off, accounting at the end of 2009 for around 5 per cent of retail sales. Online shopping in 2009 was almost €25bn and €37bn is projected for 2011. TV shopping (*téléachat*, 'abbreviated' to *TVHA*) is also popular.

When ordering goods outside France, ensure that you're dealing with a bona fide company and that the goods will work in France (if applicable). If possible, always pay by credit card when buying by mail-order or over the internet, as the credit card issuer may be jointly liable with the supplier if there's a problem. Also take into account shipping costs, duty and VAT. If you purchase a small item by post from outside the EU, you may need to pay French VAT (*TVA*) on delivery or at the post office on collection.

Mail-order shopping and online shopping is regulated in France by the Fédération du e-commerce et de la Vente à Distance, 60 rue de la Boétie, 75008 Paris (🖥 www.fevad.com).

Catalogues

The French mail-order catalogue business is the third-largest in Europe after Germany and the UK, and most French catalogue companies have an up-market, modern image, particularly when compared with the rather old-fashioned image of mail-order in some countries.

The leading companies include Camif (🖥 www.camif.fr); Amataï, formerly Neckermann (🖥 www.amatai.fr), cheap but reasonably quality; Quelle (🖥 www.quelle.fr), mid-price, medium quality and aimed mainly at women and children; La Redoute (🖥 www.laredoute. fr), with around 9m customers and specialising in fashion; 3Suisses (🖥 www.3suisses.fr), with an extensive clothing range; and Vert Baudet (🖥 www.vertbaudet.fr). Most of these also have stores in major cities and collection points throughout the country.

Many foreign companies will send goods anywhere in the world, e.g. Fortnum & Mason, Habitat and Harrods in the UK. Most provide account facilities, or payment can be made by international credit cards. Even if a foreign company won't send goods abroad, there's nothing to stop you obtaining a catalogue from a friend or relative and ordering through them.

DEPOSITS, RECEIPTS & CONSUMER RIGHTS

Under the French Civil Code, all products sold must be suitable for the use for which they're intended. If they aren't, you're entitled to exchange them or obtain a refund and it's illegal for traders to use 'small print' (*clauses abusives*) to try to avoid liability, although they'll often examine products to check that they haven't been misused. You have the same legal rights whether goods are puchased at the recommended retail price or at a discount during a sale.

Despite all this, obtaining an exchange, let alone a refund, can be a difficult, long-winded and frustrating experience, although most supermarkets and hypermarkets now have an automatic refund policy within a limited period (e.g. two weeks), provided you produce your receipt, and may even exchange goods or provide a voucher (*bon*) if you don't have a receipt.

You should always insist on a receipt (*quittance/ticket/reçu*) and retain it. This isn't just in case you need to return or exchange goods, but also to verify that you've paid if an automatic alarm sounds as you're leaving a shop or any questions arise. It's wise

to keep receipts and records of all major purchases made while you're resident in France, particularly if your stay is short. This may save you both time and money when you leave France and are required to declare your belongings in your new country of residence.

If you're asked to pay a deposit for an item, check whether this is an *acompte* or *arrhes*. With *arrhes* you have the right to cancel your order, although you'll lose your deposit (if the vendor cancels the agreement, he must return twice the amount of the deposit), whereas an *acompte* constitutes the first instalment payment for the item as part of a binding contract to pay the full amount. If you break something in a shop, you're legally liable to pay for it, although the shopkeeper may not wish to enforce the law.

CONSUMER PROTECTION

There are strict consumer protection laws (*code de la consommation*, which can be consulted at 🖳 www.legifrance.gouv.fr/waspad/uncode?code=cconsoml.rcv) in France, where the price of goods and services must be clearly displayed and indicate whether tax and service is included (as applicable). Refunds must be made for faulty or inadequate goods returned within seven days (or if a refund is requested within ten days in the case of goods installed in the home); after this period, a credit note, replacement or alternative product can be offered.

Each French department has a Direction Départementale de la Protection des Populations (DDPP) or Direction Départementale de la Cohésion Sociale et de la Protection des Populations (DDCSPP) – a departmental agency for competition, consumption and fraud repression – whose job is to prevent dishonest vendors from cheating consumers, although it deals only with 'minor' complaints. The addresses for each department can be found at 🖳 www.economie.gouv.fr/dgccrf:liste-des-directions-departementales-de-la-protect.

The national body, the Direction Générale de la Concurrence, de la Consommation et de la Répression des Fraudes (DGCCRF), can be contacted by telephone (☎ 01 40 27 16 00); if you write (in French) with details

of your complaint and supporting paperwork (e.g. receipts) to the DGCCRF, BP 5000, 75153 Paris Cedex 03, it will be forwarded to the relevant organisation. Information about your consumer rights can be obtained from the DGCCRF or its departmental offices (see 🖳 www.economie.gouv.fr/dgccrf – click on *Fiches pratiques* and then choose from the alphabetical list.) Some model letters (*lettre type*) are also provided on the DGCCRF website, although the mere threat of an official complaint often has the desired effect.

The Institut National de la Consommation (INC) is the umbrella organisation for all French national consumer associations. Its website (🖳 www.conso.net) provides links to regional consumer organisations, government agencies and other consumer sites, and around 100 model letters. It can provide you with the name of an appropriate consumer association if you require information or have a particular complaint or problem. Another consumer associations is the Union Fédérale des Consommateurs Que Choisir (🖳 www.quechoisir.org), which publishes a monthly magazine similar to *Which?* In the UK.

> The INC (see above) publishes a monthly magazine, *60 Millions de Consommateurs*, containing comparative product tests, practical and legal information, loan calculations and details of insurance surcharges. It's available on subscription, from newsagents or via a dedicated website (🖳 www.60millions-mag.com).

Rennes, Brittany

Lavendar fields, Provence

18.

ODDS & ENDS

This chapter covers miscellaneous information. Although not of vital importance, most of the topics covered are of general interest to anyone living or working in France, including everything you ever wanted to know about *toilettes* and *tutoiement* (but were afraid to ask).

CITIZENSHIP

There are three ways you can acquire French citizenship: by being born in France, through marriage and through naturalisation:

♦ **Birth:** France operates the *droit du sol*, whereby anyone born on French soil automatically becomes a French citizen at the age of 18 (unless he wishes not to), provided that he has lived in France for at least five years between the ages of 11 and 18. However, children born of foreign parents acquire their nationality until the age of 13, when they can choose to become dual nationality (French and their parents' nationality), provided they've lived in France for a total of at least five years since the age of eight, i.e. continuously from the age of 8 to 13. To register a child as a national of a foreign country, you must send certain documents to your embassy or consulate, which may include the following:

  – a *copie intégrale de l'acte de naissance* (see **Childbirth** on page 225);

  – the mother's and the father's birth certificates (originals);

  – their marriage certificate (original) if applicable;

  – two colour photographs (of the appropriate size) of the child's face on a white background;

  – the fee.

♦ **Marriage:** The marriage of a non-French citizen to a French citizen entitles him or her to French citizenship after four years of marriage, unless they have a child in France, in which case naturalisation is immediate. In the case of a non-French citizen who hasn't lived regularly in France for at least three years since their marriage, the post-marriage qualifying period for naturalisation is five years. Note that if you divorce soon after obtaining citizenship, you may be suspected of fraud!

♦ **Naturalisation:** To obtain French citizenship through naturalisation, as opposed to acquisition through marriage, you must have lived in France for at least five years, be at least 18 and satisfy the authorities that you're of good character and have an adequate knowledge of the French language. The period of residence may be reduced (e.g. to two years) if you've attended certain French institutions of higher education or have rendered special services to the country. An application for naturalisation takes between around 12 months and two years to be processed and must be made to the *préfet* of your local *département*. He will pass your file to your local mayor for investigation and, if you haven't committed mass murder and have paid your taxes, your application will be sent to the Ministry of Foreign Affairs with the *préfet*'s recommendation. The minister's decision is final and there's no appeal against a refusal to grant naturalisation.

Around 20 per cent of applications are rejected or postponed (usually because of inadequate language skills). Since 2006, citizenship has been conferred upon successful applicants at a solemn ceremony, along with information about citizens' rights and duties and, if appropriate, suggestions for the 'Frenchification' of your surname! Naturalisation confers French nationality upon the applicant, his spouse and his children aged under 18.

While awaiting naturalisation – and indeed to be entitled to remain in France – non-EU immigrants must meet certain 'citizenship' criteria, including the ability to speak French, and earn a minimum amount (which is higher than the normal minimum wage – see page 22) and must wait 18 months before being allowed to bring their family members to France.

Whether or not you must renounce your existing citizenship or can become a citizen of France as well as your home country depends on your nationality. For example, citizens of Norway and Spain must give up their original nationality. Both France and the UK allow dual (and even multi-nationality), but British subjects resident in France should note that they may retain a UK passport only for 15 years, although the period can be 'renewed' if they spend at least six months in the UK. A passport isn't obligatory for French citizens, although it's required for anyone travelling abroad. A valid passport, or identity card (*carte d'identité*), is also required for a French citizen travelling to EU countries that aren't in the Schengen Area, namely Bulgaria, Cyprus, Ireland, Rumania and the UK.

A passport can be obtained, within two to six weeks, from the local town hall and costs around €90. French passports are valid for ten years (with a possible extension for a further five years) at a time and can be renewed free of charge. *Cartes d'identité*, which are obligatory but free, are also valid for ten years and obtainable from your local town hall. You must obtain a new one if you change your marital status.

CLIMATE

France is the only country in Europe that experiences three distinct climates: continental, maritime and Mediterranean. It isn't easy to

generalise about the weather (*temps*), as many regions and areas are influenced by two of these as well as by micro-climates created by mountains, forests and other geographical features.

Generally the Loire river is considered to be the point where the cooler northern European climate gradually begins to change to the warmer southern climate. If you're planning to live in France and don't know whether the climate in a particular region will suit you, it's advisable to rent accommodation until you're absolutely sure, as some people find the extremes of hot and cold in some areas unbearable. Spring and autumn are usually fine throughout France, although the length of the seasons varies with the region and altitude.

The west and northwest (principally Brittany and Normandy but also parts of Poitou-Charentes) have a maritime climate tempered by the Atlantic and the Gulf Stream, with relatively mild winters and warm summers, and most rainfall in spring and autumn. The area around La Rochelle in the west enjoys a pleasant micro-climate and is the second sunniest region of France after the Côte d'Azur. Many people consider the western

Atlantic coast to have the best summer climate in France, with the heat tempered by cool sea breezes, although the wind can be less pleasant at other times of the year. The Atlantic coastal area, below Brittany, has had some exceptionally severe storms and unusually high tides (with inland flooding) in the last few years.

The Massif Central (which acts as a weather barrier between north and south) and eastern France have a moderate continental climate with cold winters and hot, stormy summers. However, the centre and eastern upland areas have an extreme continental climate with freezing winters and sweltering summers. The northern Massif is prone to huge variations in temperature and it was here that a record 41°C (106°F) minimum/maximum temperature difference occurred in one day (on 10th August 1885). In Paris, it's rare for the temperature to fall below minus 5°C (24°F) in winter or to rise above 30°C (86°F) in summer.

The Midi, stretching from the Pyrenees to the Alps, is hot and dry except for early spring, when there's usually heavy rainfall; the Cévennes region is the wettest in France with some 200cm (79in) of rain a year. Languedoc has hot, dry summers and much colder winters than the French Riviera, snow often remaining until May in the mountainous inland areas. The Riviera enjoys mild winters, daytime temperatures rarely dropping below 10°C (50°F), and humid and very hot summers, the temperature often rising above 30°C (86°F). The average daily sunshine on the French Riviera is five hours in January and 12 hours in July. Note, however, that it isn't always warm and sunny on the Riviera and it can get quite cold and wet in winter.

The higher you go, the colder it gets. The Alps and Pyrenees experience extremes of weather with heavy snow in winter and hot summers, although the western Pyrenees have surprisingly mild winters. The Alpine range disrupts normal weather patterns and there are often significant local climatic variations. Central and eastern France have the coldest winters.

Average annual sunshine hours and days' rainfall in selected towns and cities are shown in the table below.

France experiences many strong, cold and dry winds (vent violent) including the Mistral and the Tramontane. The Mistral is a bitterly cold wind that blows down the southern end of the Rhône valley into the Camargue and Marseille. The Tramontane affects the coastal region from Perpignan, near the Pyrenees, to Narbonne. Corsica is buffeted by many winds, including the two aforementioned plus the Mezzogiorno and Scirocco. There are over 800 other named winds in France – from the A de Pargues, a cold easterly wind felt in the northeast of France, to the Zéphyr, a warm westerly wind felt in the west – listed and

Climate Guide			
Town/City	**Region**	**Sunshine Hours**	**Days' Rainfall**
Bordeaux	Aquitaine	2,084	125
Carcassonne	Languedoc-Roussillon	2,506	94
Clermont-Ferrand	Auvergne	1,907	90
Limoges	Limousin	1,974	135
Nantes	Pays-de-la-Loire	1,956	118
Nice	Provence-Alpes-Côte-d'Azur	2,694	64
Paris	Ile-de-France	1,800	112
Poitiers	Poitou-Charentes	1,930	113
Quimper	Brittany	1,749	146
Rouen	Upper Normandy	1,687	131
Toulouse	Midi-Pyrénées	2,047	101
Vannes	Brittany	2,024	131

Temperature Guide

Location	Spring	Summer	Autumn	Winter
Bordeaux	17/6 (63/43)	25/14 (77/57)	18/8 (64/46)	9/2 (48/36)
Boulogne	12/6 (54/43)	20/14 (68/57)	14/10 (57/50)	6/2 (43/36)
Lyon	16/6 (61/43)	27/15 (81/59)	16/7 (61/45)	5/-1 (41/30)
Nantes	15/6 (59/43)	24/14 (75/57)	16/8 (61/46)	8/2 (46/36)
Nice	17/9 (63/48)	27/18 (81/64)	21/12 (70/54)	13/4 (55/39)
Paris	16/6 (61/43)	25/15 (77/59)	16/6 (57/43)	6/1 (43/34)
Strasbourg	16/5 (61/41)	25/13 (77/55)	14/6 (57/43)	1/-2 (34/28)

described in the *Petite Encyclopédie des Vents de France* (J C Lattès).

France occasionally experiences extreme and unpredictable weather, particularly in the south, where flash floods can be devastating. Wherever you live, if you're anywhere near a waterway you should ensure that you have insurance against floods.

Average daily maximum/minimum temperatures for selected cities in Centigrade and Fahrenheit (in brackets) are shown in the table above.

Weather forecasts (météo) are broadcast on TV and radio stations and published in daily newspapers. You can also obtain weather forecasts by telephone, e.g. ☎ 3201, 3250 or 08 92 68 08 08 (or 08 92 68 02 followed by a two-digit department code for a local forecast), 08 99 70 08 08, 08 99 70 11 00 or 08 99 70 12 34 (the French are as obsessed with the weather as the British!) or via the internet, e.g. 💻 www.meteo.fr or www.meteoconsult.fr. French weather forecasts now include an index for afternoon ultra-violet light levels: 1 is the lowest, 10 or 10+ the highest.

CRIME

France has a similar crime rate to most other European countries and in common with them, crime has increased considerably over the last 20 years; the number of reported crimes has almost doubled in a decade: an estimated 18m offences are reported to the police each year (over half of which are for noise nuisance!), 5m of which result in an official crime report (*procès verbal/PV*) and 1.3m in legal proceedings, 650,000 in court, although more than half of all cases are dropped. Such figures have been compiled only since 2003, when the government set up the Observatoire National de la Délinquance, and available to the public only since February 2006 (go to 💻 www.inhes. interieur.gouv.fr and click on '*Résultats et statistiques*' under '*ONDRP*'). Annual reports in English can be downloaded from the website.

Stiffer sentences have failed to stem the spiralling crime rate, and prisons are bursting at the seams with some 65,000 (2011) inmates (around 95 per cent men) – around 10,000 or 15 per cent more than their official capacity (some house almost twice as many prisoners as they were designed for). The 'occupancy rate' is, however, much lower than the UK's: around 90 prisoners per 100,000 population in France compared with 150 per 100,000 in the UK (and over 700 per 100,000 in the US!). Over 35 per cent of those sentenced to prison terms manage to avoid them, and over 2,000 convicted offenders are on parole wearing an electronic tag. There's no death penalty in France, where the maximum prison sentence is 30 years.

Although most crimes are against property, violent crime is increasing, particularly in the Ile-de-France. Mugging is on the increase throughout France, although it's still rare in most cities. In some towns in southern France pensioners have been the target of muggers and even truffle hunters have been robbed of their harvest at gunpoint. Sexual harassment (or worse) is fairly common in France, where women should take particular care late at night and never hitchhike alone.

The worst area for crime is the Mediterranean coast (one of the most corrupt and crime-ridden regions in Europe), particularly around Marseille and Nice, where most crime is attributable to a vicious underworld of racketeers and drug dealers. Marseille is still notorious as the centre of organised crime such as drug-trafficking, money-laundering, robbery and prostitution. There's a growing use of guns in urban crime, and gang killings are fairly frequent in Marseille and Corsica, where separatist groups such as the *Front Libéral National Corse* (*FLNC*), *Cuncolta Naziunalist* and the *Mouvement pour l'Autodétermination* (*MPA*) have become increasingly violent in recent decades.

Thefts are soaring (around half of crimes involve theft) and burglary has reached epidemic proportions in some areas (holiday or second homes are a popular target). Many people keep dogs as a protection or deterrent against burglars and fit triple-locked and steel-reinforced doors. However, crime in rural areas remains low and it's still common for those in villages and small towns not to lock their homes or cars.

Car theft and theft from cars is rife in Paris and other cities. Foreign-registered cars are a popular target, particularly expensive models, which are often stolen to order and spirited abroad. Car burning has become a popular 'sport' among urban youth gangs as well as

breaking shop windows and looting when there are otherwise peaceful demonstrations. Other 'games' include driving without lights at night and shooting at the first car to flash its headlights!

Pickpockets and bag-snatchers have long been a plague in Paris, where the 'charming' street urchins (often gypsies) are highly organised and trained. They surround and distract you, and when your attention is diverted pick you clean without your noticing. Keep them at arm's length, if necessary by force, and keep a firm grip on your valuables. Always remain vigilant in tourist haunts, queues and on the *métro*. Don't tempt fate with an exposed wallet or purse or by flashing your money around and hang on tight to your bags. One of the most effective methods of protecting your passport, money, travellers' cheques and credit cards, is with a money belt worn under your clothes. Tourists and travellers are the targets of some of France's most enterprising criminals, including highwaymen and train robbers.

Although the increase in crime isn't encouraging, the overall crime rate in France – especially in rural areas – is low, particularly that of violent crime.

You can usually safely walk almost anywhere at any time of day or night and there's no need for anxiety or paranoia about crime. However, you should be 'street-wise' and take certain elementary precautions. These include avoiding high-risk areas at night, such as tower block suburbs, which are inhabited or frequented by drug addicts, prostitutes and pickpockets.

Street people (*clochards*) in Paris and other cities may occasionally harass you, but they're generally harmless. You can safely travel on the Paris *métro* (and other *métros* in France) at any time, although some stations are best avoided late at night and you should be wary of pickpockets, who tend to snatch bags and jump off trains just as the doors are closing. When you're in an unfamiliar city, ask a policeman, taxi driver or other local person whether there are any unsafe neighbourhoods – and avoid them! Note that it's a criminal offence not to attempt to help someone who has been a victim of crime, at least by summoning assistance.

See also **Car Theft** on page 203, **Security** on page 94, **Household Insurance** on page

249, **Legal System** on page 352 and **Police** on page 361.

GEOGRAPHY

France, often referred to as *l'hexagone* on account of its hexagonal shape (the French are sometimes known as *les hexagonaux*), is the largest country in western Europe. Mainland France (*la métropole*) covers an area of almost 550,000km² (212,300mi²), stretching 1,050km (650mi) from north to south and almost the same distance from west to east (from the tip of Brittany to Strasbourg). Its land and sea border extends for 4,800km (around 3,000mi) and includes some 3,200km (2,000mi) of coast.

France is bordered by Andorra, Belgium, Germany, Italy, Luxembourg, Spain and Switzerland. Its borders are largely determined by geographical barriers, including the English Channel (*la Manche*) in the north, the Atlantic Ocean in the west, the Pyrenees and the Mediterranean in the south, and the Alps and the Rhine in the east.

Mainland France is divided into 22 regions and 94 departments, the Mediterranean island of Corsica (*Corse*) comprising a further two departments (see **Appendix F**). Corsica is 160km (99mi) from France and 80km (50mi) from Italy, covering 8,721km² (3,367mi²) and with a coastline of 1,000km (620mi). There are also five overseas departments (*département d'outre-mer/DOM*) – French Guyana (*Guyane*), Guadeloupe, Martinique, Mayotte and Réunion. – and four overseas territories (*territoires d'outre-mer/TOM*) – French Polynesia (*Polynésie-française*), New Caledonia (*Nouvelle Calédonie*), Saint-Pierre-et-Miquelon and the Wallis and Futuna islands. (Although situated within France, Monaco is an independent principality and isn't governed by France.)

The north and west of France is mostly low-lying. The basin in the middle of the country, with Paris at its centre, occupies a third of France's land area and is one of Europe's most fertile agricultural regions. The Massif Central to the south is noted for its extinct volcanoes, hot springs and rivers; it has many peaks rising above 1,500m (5,000ft). Mont Blanc – at 4,810m (15,781ft) western Europe's highest mountain – is in the French Alps. In general, the south and southeast of France are mountainous, although despite its many mountain ranges (Alps, Auvergne, Jura, Massif Central, Pyrenees and Vosges), France is largely a lowland country with most of its area less than 200m (650ft) above sea level.

Almost 90 per cent of France's land is productive, with around one-third cultivated, one-quarter pasture and almost a third forest.

> While other countries suffer deforestation, France has enjoyed a doubling of its forested area in the past two centuries and an increase of 35 per cent (to 16m hectares/40m acres) since 1945 – a growth of 30,000ha (75,000 acres) per year – so that forest now covers almost a third of the country.

France has a comprehensive network of rivers and canals comprising some 40 per cent of European waterways, including the Garonne, Loire, Rhine, Rhône and Seine. The Loire, 1,020km (634mi) in length, is France's longest river. In recent decades, however, France has lost half its wetlands (*zones humides*), which now account for a mere 2.5 per cent of the country's area.

GOVERNMENT

France has a republican form of government dating from 1792, three years after the Revolution, although it has been much modified and refined over the years and there have been five Republics (new constitutions) lasting from 3 to 70 years: the First from 1792 to 1795; the Second, after a revival of the monarchy, from 1848 to 1851; the Third from 1870 to 1940; the Fourth from 1946 to 1958; and the Fifth from 1958 to the present.

Since 1870, the government has been headed by a president with a prime minister and two houses of parliament. France's rulers are bound by a written constitution detailing the duties and powers of the president, government and parliament, and the conditions of election. Central government is divided into three branches: executive, legislature and judiciary. The executive is headed by the president, who's the head of state. The legislative branch is represented by parliament, comprising the national assembly and the senate. The constitution is protected by a nine-member constitutional council.

French government has traditionally been highly centralised, edicts regularly issuing from Paris and filtering down to local administrators. However, in accordance with a Decentralisation Law passed in August 2004, a number of responsibilities have been delegated to regional and departmental administrations. *Routes nationales* and minor airports, for example, are now under the control of departments, as are social housing, professional training, and certain other educational, cultural and healthcare functions.

The President

The French president – currently Nicolas Sarkozy, who was elected in May 2007 – wields more power than his US counterpart and can assume dictatorial powers in a national emergency. He 'leads and determines the policy of France' and appoints the prime minister and government. He can dissolve the house (once a year) should it pass a vote of no confidence against his prime minister and he has considerable powers in the fields of foreign affairs and defence. The French president lives, appropriately, like a king in the Elysée Palace in Paris.

Nicolas Sarkozy

The president is directly elected by the people and must have an absolute majority. Should a candidate not achieve an absolute majority on the first ballot, which is unusual, a second ballot is held two weeks later between the two candidates with the highest number of votes after the first ballot. Just two weeks' campaigning is allowed for the first ballot and one week for the second and there's also a strict limit on election expenses (Americans please note).

Although the president can dissolve parliament and call new elections, he cannot block legislation passed by parliament but can appeal directly to the people by calling a referendum. This is rarely done (there have been only nine referenda since 1789), the last two being in October 2000, when the presidential mandate was reduced from seven to five years, in line with that of the National Assembly (see below), and in May 2005, when the people rejected the EU constitution.

Parliament

Parliament plays a secondary role in France compared with many other democracies, and it meets in two sessions for a total of just 120 days a year. It has two houses, the National Assembly (*Assemblée Nationale*) and the Senate (*Sénat*). The National Assembly is the 'lower' house, to which its 577 deputies (*députés*) are directly elected by the people every five years. Although well paid, many deputies have other jobs as well. The Senate ('upper' house) is appointed indirectly by a college of some 130,000 local councillors. It consists of 318 senators (mostly local politicians), one third of whom are elected every three years. The Senate has limited powers to amend or reject legislation passed by the National Assembly; when an impasse is reached, the National Assembly has the final decision.

The French use a modified 'first-past-the-post' voting system for deputies. As with presidential elections, unless a candidate receives over 50 per cent of the votes on the first ballot, there's a second ballot a week later. Only candidates who received at least 12.5 per cent in the first round are eligible, although usually only the top two candidates contest the second round, while first round losers encourage their supporters to back their preferred candidate.

Politics is a popular subject for discussion, but when it comes to voting abstentionists are the largest electoral group.

Political Parties

The main political parties are as follows: the now dominant, right-wing *Union pour la Majorité Populaire* (*UMP*), which subsumed the *Rassemblement pour la République* (*RPR*), the conservative Gaullist party founded by de Gaulle, the *Démocratie Libérale* party and the *Parti Radical*; the centre-right-wing *Mouvement Démocratique (MODEM)* formerly the *Union pour la Démocratie Française* (*UDF*), incorporating the *Parti Républicain*, founded by former president Giscard d'Estaing; the left-wing *Parti Socialiste*, and *Parti Communiste Français*; the *Europe écologie – les Verts* (*EELV*) created in 2010, bringing together various political shades of Green; and the extreme right-wing party *Front National*, now led by Marine Le Pen, succeeding her father the notorious racist Jean-Marie Le Pen.

> The concept of 'left' and 'right' in politics originated in France where, after the 1789 Revolution, monarchists sat to the right and republicans to the left of the president of the Assemblée Constituante.

Recent years have seen growing support for the *Europe Ecologie-Les Verts*, which combines two environmentally-concerned parties. Its candidate for the 2012 presidency is Eva Joly, a popular former judge who specialised in anti-corruption investigations.

Local Government

For political and administrative purposes, France is divided into 22 regions (*région*), 96 departments (*département*), 3,509 cantons (*canton*) and 36,851 communes (*commune* or *municipalité*). The regions were created in 1972, each consisting of a number of *départements*. Many correspond (more or less) to the old provinces of France such as Burgundy, Normandy and Provence. Each region has an elected council (*conseil régional*) and executive (*conseillers*), its seat being the region's designated 'capital' town (*chef-lieu*). Each *commune* or *municipalité* (see below) contributes a number of *conseillers* according to its size (from a minimum of nine for a commune with under 100 inhabitants to a maximum of 69 for a town of over 300,000).

Regional elections take place in March and the term of office is six years. Regions are responsible for adult education and certain aspects of culture, tourism and industrial development. The state retains control of general education, justice and health services. Expatriates are entitled to vote in municipal elections and should register on the electoral roll at their *mairie*.

Departments

Each *département* has an elected council (*conseil général*), under the direction of the council's *président*, who vote on the development and budget for the department services for which they're responsible. The *conseil général* is distinct from the prefecture (*préfecture*) run by a prefect (*préfet*), which represents the state in the department. *Départements* are responsible for welfare and social services, while law enforcement through the national police force (*police nationale*), as opposed to the local (municipal) police, is the prefect's responsibility.

Departments are numbered roughly in alphabetical order with a two-digit number, from Ain (01) to Val d'Oise (95). There are also five overseas departments (*départements d'outre-mer/DOM*) – Guadaloupe (951), Martinique (972), Mayotte (976), French Guyana (973) and Réunion (974). The *département* number is used as the first two digits of post codes and the last two digits of vehicle registration numbers. Departmental elections are held every six years.

A major change will take place in 2014 when 3,500 councillors (*conseillers territoriaux*) will be elected for the first time in France. They'll replace the 6,000 previously elected *conseil général* and *conseil régional* executive councillors by sitting on both councils, thus streamlining local government at departmental and regional levels.

Communes

Communes vary in size from large cities to tiny villages with a handful of inhabitants and are governed by a municipal council headed by a mayor (*maire*), who's the most important person in the commune and definitely not someone you want to fall out with! Communes control their own town planning, including granting building permits, buildings and environment. The town hall (*hôtel de ville* in towns, *mairie* in villages) also functions as a registry of births, marriages and deaths, passport office, citizens' advice bureau, land registry, council headquarters and general information office.

Mayors

Mayors (*maires*) are both the elected head of the municipal council and representatives of the state and have wide powers, including acting as chief of the local police, issuing building permits and performing marriages as well as presiding over local social services, schools, and cultural and sports facilities.

Municipal elections are held to elect the local mayor, whose term of office is six years. Mayors are frequently re-elected and often serve a number of terms of office. The mayor works in conjunction with the municipal council (*conseil municipal*). Almost all prime ministers and presidents of France have been mayors of their home towns, as are most central government ministers: 80 per cent of deputies and 90 per cent of senators.

A controversial aspect of the French political system is the *cumul des mandats*, whereby individuals are allowed to hold more than one post, e.g. at local and national level. The law does, however, prevent you, for example, from being both an MP (*deputé*) and *sénateur* – you can't be in two places at the same time – and from holding two posts where one could favour the interests of the other.

France has three times as many mayors as any other EU country, and corruption is even more widespread in local municipal politics than at national level (which is saying something!); in recent decades there has been an increasing number of scandals involving mayors, a number of whom have absconded with public funds (Jacques Chirac allegedly among them). In addition, many towns and cities have been forced to increase taxes to pay for grandiose schemes embarked upon by megalomaniac mayors, costing local

taxpayers millions of euros. Unlike members of parliament, however, mayors don't enjoy *immunité parlementaire*, whereby they cannot be prosecuted!

Paris

Paris is unique in that it has 20 mayors, one for each *arrondissement*. Since 1977, Paris has also had an 'overall' mayor, chosen by the 163 councillors of the municipal council. Paris is both a *département* and a commune, and therefore its council sits as both a departmental council and a municipal authority. *Arrondissements* are shown on post codes (e.g. 75001 signifies the 1st *arrondissement*) and are also written as *1e*, *2e*, *3e* (1st, 2nd, 3rd) or *Xe*, *XVe* and *XXe* (10th, 15th, 20th).

Voting & Elections

Only French citizens aged 18 or older are permitted to vote in French elections, sensibly held on a Sunday. (In fact, they aren't eligible to vote until March of the year after they turn 18.) To register to vote you must have been resident for at least six months in a community.

Foreign EU citizens resident in France are eligible to vote in elections to the European Parliament and local municipal elections, provided they've registered at the town hall (first time registrations must be made between 1st September and 31st December), and they may also stand as candidates for councillors in municipal elections, but not as mayors or deputy mayors. To retain your right to vote in your native country, you may need to register as an 'overseas elector'.

British subjects should note that they may continue to vote in UK elections for only 15 years after moving abroad.

LEGAL SYSTEM

The French legal system is based entirely on written civil law. The system of administrative law was laid down by Napoleon and is appropriately called the *code Napoléon* (Napoleonic code). The code governs all branches of French law and includes the *code civil*, the *code fiscal* and the *code pénal*. It's regularly updated, for example in 1994 a new criminal code was introduced, including clauses on sexual harassment, ecological terrorism, crimes against humanity and maximum jail sentences, which are 30 years.

Judicial System

Franc has two judicial systems: administrative and judiciary. The administrative system deals with disputes between the government and individuals, while the judiciary handles civil and criminal cases. France doesn't have a jury system (abolished in 1941) but a mixed tribunal made up of six lay judges and three professional judges, with convictions decided by a two-thirds majority. However, in the *cour d'assises* (see below), nine ordinary citizens make up a *jury populaire*.

Under the French criminal law system, cases are heard by a variety of courts, depending on the severity of the alleged offence. Civil courts include a *tribunal d'instance* (for small claims up to around €5,000), a *tribunal de commerce* (for commercial disputes), a *tribunal de sécurité sociale* (for disputes over social security payments), a *tribunal de grande instance* (for cases relating to divorce and adoption, etc., as well as some criminal cases) and a *conseil de prud'hommes* (an arbitration service for labour disputes).

Criminal courts include a *tribunal de police* (for minor misdemeanours such as illegal parking), a *tribunal correctionnel* (for more serious offences), a *cour d'assises* (for major cases) and a *cours d'appel* (for appeals; the supreme appeal court is the *Cour de Cassation*). A new kind of judge called a *juge de proximité*, created in September 2002, can deal with claims of up to €4,000.

Under France's inquisitorial system of justice, suspects are questioned by an independent examining magistrate (*juge d'instruction*). Other types of judge include *juges du siège* (arbitration judges) and *juges d'instance* (presiding judges).

Legal Counsel

Never assume that the law in France is the same as in any other country, as this often isn't the case. Anyone charged with a crime is presumed innocent until proven guilty, and the accused has the right to silence. All suspects are entitled to see a lawyer immediately after their arrest, a person under judicial investigation must be notified in writing, and an examining magistrate may not

remand suspects in custody in a case he's investigating.

It's unnecessary to employ a lawyer or barrister (*avocat* – also the word for avocado pear) in a civil case heard in a *tribunal d'instance*, where you can conduct your own case (if your French is up to the task). If you use a lawyer, not surprisingly, you must pay his fee. In a *tribunal de grande instance* you must employ a lawyer. An *avocat* can act for you in almost any court of law. A legal and fiscal adviser (*conseil juridique et fiscal*) is similar to a British solicitor and can provide legal advice and assistance on commercial, civil and criminal matters, as well as on tax, social security, labour law and similar matters. He can also represent you before certain administrative agencies and in some courts.

A bailiff (*huissier*) deals with summonses, statements, writs and lawsuits, in addition to the lawful seizure of property ordered by a court. He's also employed to officially notarise documents and produce certified reports (*constats*) for possible subsequent use in legal proceedings, e.g. statements from motorists after a road accident.

If you need an English-speaking lawyer, you can usually obtain a list of names from your country's embassy or a local consulate in France (see **Appendix A**). Certain legal advice and services may also be provided by embassies and consulates in France, including an official witness of signatures (Commissioner for Oaths). French residents have the right to a free consultation with a lawyer; ask at your local Tribunal de Grande Instance for times. Legal aid (*aide juridictionnelle*) is available to EU citizens and regular visitors to France on low incomes.

Public Notary

A public notary (*notaire*, addressed as *Maître*) is a public official authorised by the Ministry of Justice and controlled by the Chambre des Notaires. Like a *conseil juridique*, he's also similar to a British solicitor, although he doesn't deal with criminal cases or offer advice concerning criminal law.

A *notaire* also informs and advises about questions relating to administrative, business, company, credit, family, fiscal and private law. In respect to private law, a *notaire* is responsible for administering and preparing documents relating to leases, property sales and purchases, divorce, inheritance, wills, loans, setting up companies, and buying and selling businesses. He guarantees the validity and safety of contracts and deeds, and is responsible for holding deposits on behalf of clients, collecting taxes and paying them to the relevant authorities. *Notaires'* fees are fixed by the government and therefore don't vary from one *notaire* to another, i.e. they're invariably astronomical!

Notaires have a monopoly in the areas of transferring property, testamentary and matrimonial acts, which by law must be in the form of an authentic document (*acte authentique*), verified and stamped by a *notaire*.

Documentation

Under French law, you're required to retain certain documents for a minimum period, which varies from six months to life. For example:

◆ **Six months:** hotel and restaurant bills;

◆ **One year:** receipts for chimney sweeping; telephone bills; *huissier*'s fees; removal bills; children's school attendance records (*certificats de scolarité*); proof of payment of fines;

◆ **Two years:** insurance receipts and cancellation letters; receipts for professional fees; standing order instructions and bank deposit slips; employment contracts; credit notes; water bills; bills for electric appliances and clothing; social security and complementary insurance refunds; property tax demands; receipts for family allowance payments;

◆ **Three years:** TV licence demands; currency exchange receipts;

◆ **Four years:** income and wealth tax bills and proofs of payment;

◆ **Five years:** life insurance receipts; pay slips other than salary statements; unemployment payment slips; divorce settlements; electricity and gas bills; rental charges and payment receipts; proof of payments to *notaires*; social security contribution records; receipts for non-salaried income;

♦ **Six years:** letters of dismissal; income tax demands and returns, plus supporting paperwork;

♦ **Ten years:** house and car insurance contracts; mortgage contracts; business account cheque stubs and bank statements; self-employment records; receipts for co-ownership charges; credit notes relating to property ownership or rental; receipts for repairs by a shop or for building work; invoices from private clinics; documents relating to a community property; estate agent's bills;

♦ **Eighteen years:** school reports; children's health records (for their first 18 years);

♦ **Thirty years:** building permits; architects' and builders' contracts; bills for building work; personal bank statements; loan and debt records; official papers relating to self-employment;

♦ **Life:** identity cards and residence permits; marriage and divorce certificates; education certificates; life insurance contracts; receipts for legal fees; salary statements; building and other work guarantees; unemployment registration; marriage contracts and divorce papers; co-ownership agreements; bills for valuables; records relating to gifts; education certificates; medical records and certificates; hospital bills; local tax bills; savings account books; *livret de famille*; pension payment receipts and related documents.

Personal pay slips from employment in France should be kept until retirement, as you must justify your earnings when applying for a French pension. Product guarantees and receipts should be kept for as long as you have the products, and rental agreements until the end of the rental period.

There are many books explaining the intricacies of French law, including *Un An de Chronique Juridique* and *Le Guide Juridique*, both published by VO Editions and *Principles of French Law* (OUP).

Disabled People

Since 11th February 2005, when the *Loi pour l'Egalité des Droits et des Chances des Personnes Handicapées* was passed, disabled people (unfortunately still known as *handicapés*) have – at least in the eyes of the law – had equal rights with the able-bodied regarding employment, education, leisure activities and access to public buildings and transport. Employers with 20 staff or more should have at least 6 per cent of posts filled by disabled people, although in practice the average percentage is between 4 and 5 per cent.

Specifically, the law provides for the creation of a *Maison des Personnes Handicapées* in each department, where information can be obtained, a nationwide assessment of facilities for the disabled. In particular these relate to public transport and improvements where necessary; the creation of financial allowances for disabled people to cover the cost of, for example, special equipment in the home or car; the enrolment of disabled children at their local school (rather than in 'special' schools); and a campaign against discrimination by employers when engaging staff.

Information relevant to disabled people is contained throughout this book.

MARRIAGE & DIVORCE

The legal age of consent in France is 18, but boys and girls aged between 15 and 18 can be married with the consent of parents. Non-French citizens are entitled to be married in France, but divorcees and widows must wait 300 days after their divorce or the death of their spouse before being allowed to remarry (in case of pregnancy).

Almost 7.5m French citizens live without a partner, around 1m of whom are divorcees, and the number is growing each year.

Only some 50 marriages are performed annually for each 10,000 citizens – the lowest per capita number in Europe. As in many other developed countries, the average age for marriage is increasing and is almost 30 for men and 28 for women, who on average give birth for the first time at just under 30.

The number of unmarried couples in France has quadrupled to around 2m in the last two

once did, and all children have the same rights; an unmarried mother (*mère célibataire*) is even paid a generous allowance by the state.

Procedure

To arrange a marriage in France, either partner must apply at least a month in advance to the town hall where they normally live (they must have lived there for at least 40 days). The bride and groom must each provide at least one witness and may provide two, whose names must be given to the town hall when the wedding is arranged.

Both partners must also provide passports, residence permits (if applicable), birth certificates (stamped by their country's local consulate not more than six months previously), proof of residence in France, and a medical certificate issued within the previous two months (see below). A divorced or widowed person must provide a divorce or death certificate. You may also be required to produce a *certificat de célibat* (proving that you aren't already married) no more than three months old, provided by your embassy and a notarised 'affidavit of law' (*certificat de coutume*), drawn up by a lawyer in your home country, to confirm that you're free to marry.

For a church ceremony, you may be asked to produce other documents, such as a baptism certificate. All documents must be 'legalised' in your home country and translated into French by an approved translator.

No more than two months before marrying, a couple must undergo a medical examination (*certificat d'examen médical prénuptial*), including a blood test and chest X-ray. The cost is reimbursed by social security. The medical was originally intended to check compatibility between the blood groups of a couple, although with the advent of AIDS it has taken on a new significance. The results are confidential and cannot prevent a wedding from taking place. If a divorced or widowed woman wishes to remarry within 300 days of the divorce or death, she must provide a medical certificate verifying that she isn't pregnant. For a church wedding, you may be required to attend a day's *préparation de*

decades (among Europeans only the Swedes are less keen on marriage). It's estimated that 40 to 50 per cent of couples who get married have already cohabited for up to two years. Many couples don't bother to get married and simply live together, but French law distinguishes between partners living together 'unofficially' (*en union libre*) and 'officially' (*en concubinage*). Those living together *en concubinage* have some of the same privileges in law as married couples, including social security. To qualify for these, you may need to obtain a (free) certificate from your town hall testifying that you're living together 'as man and wife' (take identification, proof of address and two witnesses), although town halls aren't obliged to issue them, in which case you can both sign a 'sworn declaration' (*attestation sur l'honneur*) that you live together.

The major disadvantage of *concubinage* is that it isn't recognised under French inheritance laws, so partners can inherit only the amount allowed to non-relatives (see **Wills** on page 280) and they receive no state pension when their partner dies. A *pacte civile de solidarité*, which is signed at a court, confers some but not all of the legal benefits of marriage (see **PACS** below). In certain parts of Paris, it's possible for couples to have an unofficial 'marriage' ceremony, although gay marriages aren't legal in France (a 2004 'union' in Bordeaux was declared unlawful).

It's reckoned that over 40 per cent of French children are born out of wedlock and a fifth are raised by a single parent (85 per cent women). Illegitimacy no longer carries the stigma it *mariage* course. You're then issued with a pre-marital certificate. Notification of an impending wedding (*bans*) must be published ten days before the ceremony at the town hall where the wedding is to take place.

A civil ceremony, presided over by the mayor or one of his deputies, must be performed in France to legalise a wedding. Although around 50 per cent of couples choose to undergo a church 'blessing' ceremony, it has no legal significance and must take place after the civil ceremony. There's no fee for a marriage in France, although most town halls make a collection in aid of local charities.

Married couples are given a 'family book' (*livret de famille*), in which all major family events such as the birth of children, divorce or death are recorded.

Matrimonial Regimes

Marriages are performed under a matrimonial regime (*régime matrimonial*) that defines how a couple's property is owned during marriage or after divorce or death. If you're married in France, the regime applies to all your land or land rights in France, irrespective of where you're domiciled, and your total assets if you're domiciled in France.

There are four regimes: two communal regimes (*régime communautaire*) and two 'separatist' regimes (*régime séparatiste*). Under a *communauté universelle*, all assets and all debts are jointly owned; under a *communauté réduite aux acquêts*, each spouse retains ownership of assets acquired before marriage (and assets acquired after marriage in the form of inheritances and gifts), while all assets acquired jointly after marriage are jointly owned. Under a *séparation de biens*, nothing is jointly owned; and under a *participation aux acquêts*, nothing is jointly owned but if the marriage is dissolved, assets acquired during the marriage are divided equally.

A marriage contract isn't obligatory but is strongly recommended. A *notaire* will charge at least €400 to draw one up. If you're married in France and you don't specify otherwise, you're usually subject to a communal regime. If you choose a separatist regime, it's usual to detail in a notarised contract how your assets are to be disposed of.

If you were married abroad and are buying a house in France, your *notaire* will ask you which matrimonial regime you were married under and whether there was a marriage contract. If there was no contract, you'll usually be deemed to be married under a communal regime. You can change your marital regime, but not within two years of drawing up a marriage contract. However, changing your marital regime is expensive (up to €4,000), and can take up to nine months, therefore it's advisable to set up the regime you want when you get married. If you're unsure about the implications of French marital regimes, you should seek advice from a *notaire*.

Divorce

As in most other developed countries, the divorce rate has risen alarmingly (by around 40 per cent) in France in the last decade, with over a third of marriages ending in divorce (there was even a best-selling *Divorce* magazine!). However, it's still lower than in some other European countries, e.g. the UK, and the US. You can be divorced under French law only when one spouse is a French citizen or when two non-French spouses are resident in France. To be divorced 'by mutual consent' (*divorce par consentement mutuel* or *divorce sur demande conjointe*), you must have been married for at least six months. Other types of divorce are 'consent to divorce but not to consequences' (*divorce sur demande acceptée*), divorce based on fault (*divorce pour faute*) such as adultery, and divorce based on termination of married life (*divorce pour rupture de la vie commune*).

The grounds for a divorce needn't be disclosed, provided both parties agree on the repercussions such as the division of property, custody of children, alimony and maintenance. A divorce is usually granted automatically by a judge, although he may order a delay of three months for reflection. A divorce becomes final one month after judgement or two months if it has gone to appeal. A contested divorce must be decided by a court of law.

PACS

Cohabiting partners (even those of the same sex) may sign a *pacte civile de solidarité* (*PACS*), which protects the individual rights of each party and entitles partners to share property rights and enjoy income tax benefits. To make a *PACS*, you must go to the local *tribunal d'instance* (listed in the phone book) and submit a written statement that you wish to draw up a *PACS* under law no. 99-944 of 15th November 1999, including details of the division of possessions between you. There's no standard form for this. You must also provide identification, birth certificates, a certificate from the relevant *tribunal d'instance* confirming your place of birth, and 'sworn statements' (*attestation sur l'honneur*) that you live in the area and that there are no legal impediments to your making a *PACS*, e.g. one of you being married. Inheritance rights are the same as for married couples (see **Inheritance & Gift Tax** on page 278), but a surviving partner cannot claim a 'widow's' or 'widower's' pension (*pension de réversion*).

MILITARY SERVICE

France is one of the leading military powers (*force de frappe*) in western Europe and a member of NATO. Defence spending accounted for approximately 13 per cent of the state budget and around 2.3 per cent of GDP in 2009.

Compulsory military service was suspended in 2001 and hasn't been reintroduced.

Instead of military service, males born after 1979 and females born after 1983 must attend a one-day training course, *Journée d' Appel de Préparation à la Défense* (*JAPD*). The course consists of lectures on the army and the country's defence systems, and literacy and numeracy tests. If proof of attending the course cannot be provided, you face a variety of sanctions ranging from being excluded from public examinations at school or university to being unable to obtain a driving licence or (far more seriously) a fishing or hunting licence.

If you're aged 18 to 26, you can become a part-time soldier (*volontaire militaire*) for a year, and 18 to 28-year-olds can become 'civil volunteers' (*volontaire civil*) and undertake various 'missions', e.g. protecting the environment, for between 6 and 24 months.

PETS

The French are generally unsentimental about pets (and animals in general) and keep them as much for practical purposes (e.g. to guard premises or catch vermin) or as fashion accessories as for companionship – although, of course, there are exceptions to this. Nevertheless, pets (*animal domestique* or *animal de compagnie*) are more widely tolerated than in many other countries. French hotels usually quote a rate for pets (e.g. €10 per night), and most restaurants allow dogs and many provide food and water (some even allow owners to seat their pets at the table!). There are even exclusive dog restaurants.

> Although food shops make an effort to bar pets, it isn't unusual to see a supermarket trolley containing a dog or two (the French don't take much notice of 'no dogs' signs).

There's usually no discrimination against dogs when renting accommodation, although they may be prohibited in furnished apartments. Paris has a pet cemetery (*cimetière des chiens*) at Asnières and there are others in Nice, Toulouse and Villepinte.

Exporting & Importing Pets

If you plan to take a pet to France, it's important to check the latest regulations. Make sure that you have the correct papers, not only for France but for all the countries you'll pass through to reach France. Particular consideration must be given before exporting a pet from a country with strict quarantine regulations in case you wish to re-import it later. For example, if you're exporting a cat or a dog or certain other animals from the UK, you should obtain a 'passport' for them confirming that they've been ISO micro-chipped and that their vaccinations are up to date. You must then continue to have them vaccinated regularly while in France. If you fail to do this and want to bring your pets back to the UK at any time, they'll need to be quarantined for six months.

The cost of a pet passport (i.e. the tests and vaccinations required to obtain one) is around GB£165, plus GB£60 per year for follow-up vaccinations and around GB£20 for a border check on re-entry to the UK.

Note that you may have to make arrangements well in advance; for example, a pet must be blood tested at least six months before it can be taken to the UK. Details of the scheme, known as PETS, can be obtained from the Department for Environment, Food and Rural Affairs (see **Information** below). An EU pet passport is now available from any vet.

You can take up to three animals into France at any time, one of which may be a puppy (three to six months old), although no dogs or cats under three months may be imported. Two psittacidae (parrot-like birds) can be imported into France and up to ten smaller species; all require health certificates issued within five days of departure. Other animals require import permits from the French Ministry of Agriculture.

If you're transporting a pet to France by ship or ferry, you should notify the ferry company. Some companies insist that pets are left in vehicles (if applicable), while others allow pets to be kept in cabins. If your pet is of a nervous disposition or unused to travelling, it's best to tranquillise it on a long sea crossing. Pets can also be transported by air and certain pets can be carried with you (in an approved container), for which there's a charge, e.g. around €120 one-way from the US.

There are companies which will accommodate your pets while you move, take care of all export requirements and ship them

to you when you've settled in, e.g. Pinehawk Kennels & Livestock Shippers (☎ 01223-290249) in the UK.

Vaccinations

France has almost eradicated rabies by vaccinating foxes, although there have recently been a number of reported cases in dogs. Although there's generally no quarantine period for animals imported into France, there are strict vaccination requirements for dogs in certain departments, where they must be vaccinated against rabies and have a *certificat contre la rage* or a health certificate (*certificat de bonne santé*), signed by an approved veterinary surgeon and issued no more than five days before their arrival.

Resident dogs need an annual rabies booster and it's recommended that they're also vaccinated (*vacciné*) against the following diseases:

◆ **Babesia canis**, also known as *Piroplasma canis* or Canine piroplasmosis (*piroplasmose*), a parasitic disease carried by ticks (*tiques**) that also affects horses and cattle. (Ticks are a problem in many parts of France and can be lethal. You should invest in a tick-remover (around €4 from vets) and treat your pets regularly with a preventive such as Frontline.)

◆ **Distemper** or Carré's disease (*la maladie de Carré*, also known as *la maladie des jeunes chiens* and *la maladie du jeune âge*, as it mainly affects young animals), a potentially fatal viral infection;

◆ **Hepatitis contagiosa canis** or Rubarth's disease (*hépatite de Rubarth*), an acute viral disease which attacks the liver;

◆ **Leptosporosis** (*leptospirose*), a bacterial disease which can be transmitted to humans and can be fatal;

◆ **Parvovirus** or Parvo (*parvovirose*), an intestinal virus;

◆ **Tracheobronchitis**, known as kennel cough (*toux de chenil*), which is one of the most common canine diseases and can lead to fatal complications.

Vaccinations (*vaccin*) are initially in two stages, a 'booster' (*rappel*) being administered three or four weeks after the initial injection (*piqure*); a single annual renewal is required. Each injection costs between around €35 and €60, depending on the vet. Serums must be administered separately.

Cats aren't required to have regular rabies vaccinations, although if you let your cat roam free outside your home it's advisable to have it vaccinated annually and a rabies vaccination is compulsory for cats entering Corsica or being taken to campsites or holiday parks. All cats must, however, be vaccinated against feline gastro-enteritis and typhus.

All vaccinations must be registered with your veterinary surgeon (*vétérinaire*) and be listed on your pet's vaccination card or (preferably) in a *livret international de santé* or the recently introduced EU pet passport, which, if you plan to take your pets abroad, must also certify that the animal has been confined to countries that have been rabies-free for at least three years.

Sterilisation

Sterilisation of pets isn't common practice in France, where stray dogs and cats are a problem in many areas and many people prefer to exterminate unwanted puppies and kittens. Nevertheless, vets are familiar with the procedures, which are usually straightforward.

Sterilisation of bitches and female cats not only prevents them from becoming pregnant but can also protect them against the canine equivalent of breast cancer (*cancer des mamelles*), provided the operation is carried out before the animal's first heat.

Sterilising a bitch costs between around €140 and €300 depending on the size of the animal, and the vet; sterilisation of female cats costs around €130. Castration of male dogs and cats costs approximately half as much and can be beneficial if an animal is aggressive or prone to running away.

Dogs

There are around 17 dogs to every 100 people in France, one of the highest ratios in the world. Around 40 per cent of French people list their dogs as the most important thing in their lives (even more important than their lovers!) and the French spend some €3bn on them annually; there's at least one 'poodle-parlour' (*salon de toilettage*) in every town and there's even a canine *pâtisserie* in Paris, called unimaginatively 'Mon Bon Chien', where pampered pooches can be kitted out with *haute couture* clothing as well as treated to *haute cuisine* 'cakes'. On the other hand, many dogs are kept outdoors and some are almost permanently penned. It's rare to see French people walking their dogs (except for 'show').

> Dogs don't wear identification discs and there's no system of licensing. However, all dogs born after 6th January 1999 must be given an official identifying number, either tattooed inside the ear or contained in a microchip inserted under the skin. This rule is designed to make it easier to find the owners of stray dogs and to reduce the incidence of 'dog trafficking'.

Around 100,000 dogs are abandoned by their owners each year, many at the start of the long summer holiday or after the hunting season is over, and stray dogs are regularly rounded up and taken to the local pound (*fourrière*) to be destroyed. A further 60,000 dogs are stolen each year and certain breeds are highly prized. It's therefore recommended to have your dog tattooed or chipped, even if it was born before this date. Some vets favour tattooing (*tatouage*) because the number is visible, whereas reading a microchip (*puce*) requires a machine. Others recommend micro-chipping because a tattoo can be removed or wear off. Identity numbers are kept in a central computer controlled by the French Society for the Protection of Animals (Société Protectrice des Animaux/SPA), which is organised on a departmental basis. Contact your nearest SPA office if you lose your pet.

Dogs must be kept on leads in most public parks and gardens and there are large fines for dog owners who don't comply. Dogs are forbidden in some parks, even when on leads, and on most beaches in summer. On public transport, pets weighing less than 6kg (13lb) must usually be carried in a basket or cage; larger dogs must wear a muzzle and be kept on a lead. Some 500,000 people are bitten by dogs each year in France, 60,000 of whom are hospitalised, and certain breeds of dog (e.g. pit-bull terriers) must be muzzled in public places.

The unpleasant aspect of France's vast dog population is abundantly evident on the pavements of towns and cities, where dogs routinely leave their 'calling cards' (officially known as *déjections canines*). You must watch where you walk: many pavements aren't *trottoirs* but '*crottoirs*'.

▲ Caution

Over 600 Parisians are hospitalised each year after slipping on dog dirt, and there's a national association of mothers called Inter-Mamans, who have in the past threatened to 'donate' their infants' soiled nappies to mayors throughout France unless they take action to clear the streets of dog mess!

In Paris and some other cities, there are dog toilet areas. However, most dog owners take their pets to a local park or car park or simply let them loose in the streets to do their business, although allowing your pooch to poop on the pavement is illegal and you can be fined if you don't 'scoop' up after it. (The fine for first-time offences is between €30 and €45, depending on the community.). At the very least, owners are required to take their pets to the kerb to relieve themselves; you're reminded by dog silhouettes on the footpath in Paris and other cities, where signs encourage owners to teach their dogs to use gutters ('*Apprenez-lui le caniveau*'), which are regularly cleaned and disinfected. The capital's patrols of motorised pooper-scoopers (*moto-crottes*), which once picked up four tonnes of doggy-do daily,

are being phased out in favour of 'hygiene inspectors' dishing out on-the-spot fines. (Although it's little consolation, it's supposedly good luck to tread in something unpleasant.)

Kennels & Catteries

There are many kennels and catteries, where fees are around €9 per day for cats and €13 for dogs; look in the *Yellow Pages* under *Pensions pour chiens, chats*. If you plan to leave your pet at a kennel or cattery, book well in advance, particularly for school holiday periods.

Health & Insurance

Veterinary surgeons (*vétérinaire*) are well trained in France, where it's a popular and well paid profession. Emergency veterinary care is available in major cities, where there are also animal hospitals (*hôpital pour animaux*) and vets on 24-hour call for emergencies. A visit to a vet usually costs €30 to €40. Some vets make house calls, for which there's a minimum charge of around €70 to €85. Taxi and ambulance services are also provided for pets.

Medical treatment for dogs can be just as expensive as human treatment, e.g. €300 for a scan and over €600 for a major operation – and it isn't reimbursed by social security. Health insurance for pets is available from a number of insurance companies, but usually provides only partial cover.

There are essentially two types of pet insurance: insurance against accidents and insurance against illness and accidents. The former costs around €80 or €90 per year and covers only medical and surgical costs resulting from accidental injury, e.g. a broken bone, poisoning or a bite by another dog. The latter, which costs at least twice as much, also covers the treatment of certain illnesses and diseases.

As with human health insurance, you should check exactly what is and isn't covered and what conditions apply. Certain treatment may be excluded, e.g. vaccinations, sterilisation or castration, dental treatment and cancer screening, as may certain hereditary diseases. Conditions may include an upper age limit (usually nine or ten years for dogs), a waiting period (of up to four months) before insurance becomes effective, an annual claim limit (generally between €800 and €1,600) and an excess or deductible (*franchise*), which often applies to every claim and can be as much as 30 per cent, i.e. not a horse!

Pet insurance doesn't cover you for third party liability, e.g. if your pet bites someone or causes an accident, which should be included in your household insurance (see page 249); check with your insurer.

If you wish to have your pet cremated, you must now pay around €165 (the service was previously free), although you may bury an animal weighing up to 35kg in your garden.

Information

For the latest regulations regarding the importation and keeping of pets in France, contact the Sous-Direction de la Santé et de la Protection Animales, Ministère de l'Agriculture et de la Pêche (☎ 01 49 55 49 55, 💻 www. agriculture.gouv.fr – click on '*Thèmatiques*' and then on '*Santé et Protection des Animaux*'). If you wish to import an exotic pet or more pets than the standard quota, contact the Direction Générale des Douanes (💻 www. douane.gouv.fr – the website has information in English about animal species threatened with extinction, which cannot be imported into France').

Further details of the British pet passport scheme can be obtained from the Department for Environment, Food and Rural Affairs (DEFRA, ☎ 020-7238 6951 or 0845-933 5577, 💻 www.defra.gov.uk).

A useful book is *Travel Tips for Cats and Dogs* by David Prydie (Ringpress Books).

From 1st January 2012, the UK's Pet Travel scheme harmonises with the regulations for animal movement operating throughout the EU, which means that quarantine will no longer be necessary for animals imported into the UK (provided they have satisfactory vaccination results) from the EU.

POLICE

There are three main police forces in France: the *police nationale*, the *gendarmerie nationale* and the *Compagnie Républicaine de la Sécurité* (*CRS*). All French police are addressed formally as *monsieur/madame l'agent* and colloquially called *flics* (cops), although there are many less polite names.

The *police nationale* are under the control of the Interior Ministry and are called *agents de police*. They deal with all crime within the jurisdiction of their police station (*commissariat de police*) and are most commonly seen in towns, distinguished by the silver buttons on their uniforms. At night and in rain and fog, they often wear white caps and capes.

The *gendarmerie nationale/gardes mobiles* is part of the army, trained by the Ministry of Defence, although it's at the service of and (since 2009) under the operational control of the Interior Ministry. *Gendarmes* wear blue uniforms and traditional *képis*, and are distinguished by the gold buttons on their uniforms. They deal with serious crime on a national scale and general law and order in rural areas and are responsible for motorway patrols, air safety, mountain rescue, and air and coastal patrols. *Gendarmes* include police motorcyclists (*motards*).

The *CRS* is often referred to as the riot police, as it's responsible for crowd control and dealing with public disturbances, although it also has other duties, including life-saving on beaches in summer. Over the years the *CRS* has acquired a notorious reputation for its violent response to demonstrations (*manifestations*) and public disturbances, although often under extreme provocation. The mere appearance of the *CRS* at a demonstration is enough to raise the temperature, although it has been trying to improve its public image.

In addition to the three kinds of national police mentioned above, most cities and medium size towns have municipal police (*police municipale/corps urbain*), who deal mainly with petty crime, traffic offences and road accidents. Municipal police traditionally wore a *képi* (like *gendarmes*), although this has been replaced by a flat, peaked cap. While officers of the *gendarmerie nationale*, the *police nationale* and the *CRS* are armed, *police municipale* aren't, unless the local *préfet* and *maire* decide that they should be.

There are also various special police forces, including the *Groupement d'Intervention de la Gendarmerie Nationale* (*GIGN*), a sort of SAS unit; the *Police de l'Air et des Frontières* (*PAF*), border guards; the *Direction Centrale des Renseignements Généraux* (*DCRG* or *RG*), the 'intelligence' squad; the *Police Judiciaire* (*PJ*), the criminal investigation department; *Surveillance du Territoire* (*SDT*), a counterespionage division; an anti-terrorist unit called *Recherche, Assistance, Intervention et Discussion* (*RAID*); and the *CSP*, antiterrorist police who guard embassies and government buildings in Paris, who wear blue windcheaters, carry machine guns and aren't the best people to ask directions to the Eiffel Tower!

In general, French police (of any type) aren't popular with the public and have an unenviable reputation, particularly among ethnic groups. Police 'brutality', usually directed towards racial minorities, has led to riots in some areas; in autumn 2005, the worst disturbances in Paris since 1968 were allegedly the outcome of police harassment.

In 2003, Nicolas Sarkozy, then Minister of the Interior, abolished neighbourhood policing (*le police locale*), but following outbreaks of serious violence, notably in some suburbs in Grenoble in 2010, reinforcement units were sent to help municipal police in hot spots. In April 2011, Claude Guéant, the current Minister of the Interior, announced the creation of patrolling units (*patrouilleurs*) from September

2011 to re-establish close police contact with the public.

 Caution

The police can stop you and demand identification at any time (*contrôle de papiers*), therefore it's advisable to carry your passport, residence permit (*carte de séjour*) or ID with proof of residence. If you don't have any identification you can be arrested.

If your identification documents are stolen or lost, you must report immediately to the nearest police station, where you must make a *déclaration de perte ou de vol*. You'll be given a receipt, which will be accepted by the authorities until new documents are issued. It's wise to keep copies of all important documents (e.g. passport, visa and *carte de séjour*) in a safe place so that replacements are easier to obtain.

If you're arrested, you're required to state your name, age and permanent address only. Never make or sign a statement without legal advice and the presence of a lawyer. Unless your French is fluent, you should make it clear that you don't understand French and, in any case, ask permission to call your lawyer or embassy. Someone from your embassy should be able to provide a list of English-speaking lawyers.

The police can hold you in custody for 24 hours, although you're entitled to see a lawyer immediately after arrest. After 24 hours they need the authority of a magistrate. A Council of Europe commission recently stated that suspects in France ran a 'not inconsiderable risk' of being mistreated while in police detention.

The police don't prosecute criminal cases in France, which is done by a public prosecutor. Police can fine offenders (and do so, particularly if they're non-residents) on the spot for motoring offences such as speeding and drunken driving, and fines must be paid in cash (see **Traffic Police** on page 195). You're entitled to ask the name and particulars of any policeman who stops you, although it may be better to do this after you've found out what you've been stopped for!

All French residents have a police record (even if it's blank!) and you may be asked to produce it, e.g. if you need to travel to or work in certain countries. To obtain a copy of your record (*extrait de casier judiciaire*), you should send details of your date and place of birth and a copy of your passport and *carte de séjour* to the Casier Judiciaire National, 44317 Nantes Cedex 3. (If you're in Nantes, you can go directly to 107 rue du Landreau).

If you lose anything or are the victim of a theft, you must report it in person at a police station and complete a report (*déclaration de vol/plainte*), of which you'll receive a copy. This must usually be done within 24 hours if you plan to make a claim on an insurance policy. Don't, however, expect the police to be the slightest bit interested in your loss.

If you need to contact the police in an emergency, dialling 17 will put you in touch with your local *gendarmerie* or *commissariat de police*, listed at the front of your local telephone directory.

POPULATION

It's estimated that the population of France on 1st January 2011 was 65,821,885; of these 63,136,180 lived in metropolitan France and the remainder in French overseas departments and territories. The census (*recensement*) system was changed in 2004 to an annual survey of approximately one-fifth of the population (communes of fewer than 10,000 inhabitants are surveyed every five years, while those over 10,000 are surveyed annually, but only around 8 per cent of the population each time). The effect has been to make estimated figures available more frequently. The present population figures suggests that government incentives to encourage families to have more children in order to reverse a declining birth rate are taking effect.

The average density of the population of mainland France is around 100 people per km² (260 per mi²), one of the lowest in Europe, although the density varies enormously from region to region. Paris is one of the most densely populated cities in the world, with over 20,000 inhabitants to the km² (over 52,000 per

mi²), while in many rural areas there are just a handful. When Paris is excluded, the average population density drops to around 50 people per km² (130 per mi²).

Over 70 per cent of the French population lives in the urban areas of the north, east and the Rhône valley, although the population of industrial cities such as Le Havre, Saint-Etienne and Toulon is in decline. France's urban population doubled between 1936 and 1999, since when the decline in rural population has been reversed: 72 of the 96 departments boast a 'positive migratory balance'. On the other hand, there's a worrying trend of population movement from the north to the south, with visible signs of de-industrialisation in the north and pressure on water and other resources. This is particularly apparent in the southeast, which, as a popular region for retirement, also faces a disproportionate imbalance in the age demographics. Steps have been taken in some areas to revive dying villages, e.g. by linking them to nearby large towns and industrial zones, to provide villagers with access to a wider range of facilities and services.

France has few large cities compared with other European countries with comparable populations, and Paris (2.2m) is the only city with over a million inhabitants, excluding its suburban areas. If these are included, Paris has a population of almost 11m, Lyon 1.6m, Marseille1.4m and Lille 1.1m. Only five other cities (Toulouse, Bordeaux, Nantes, Strasbourg and Nice) have more than half a million inhabitants, while there are over 32,500 villages with fewer than 2,000 inhabitants.

In the last 20 years there has been a shift away from the industrial regions of the north to the sunny south. There's also a drift away from the mountainous areas of central France and, for the first time in history, away from Paris, as young executives and technocrats head for Avignon, Grenoble, Lyon, Montpellier, Nice, Toulouse and, most recently, the area around Aix-en-Provence and Marseille.

The average age of the population is around 37 years, with some 15 per cent over 65. France is becoming increasingly popular with retirees, particularly those from the UK, Germany, the Netherlands and Scandinavian countries, which is putting additional strain on its state healthcare and pension systems (see **Chapters 13** and **14**).

France has around 6m immigrants (i.e. people not born in France), around 10 per cent of the population and a net increase of over half a million since 1999. Some 2m have become naturalised. Around 1.7m of the total are from EU countries, the vast majority Portuguese (the most numerous immigrants), Spanish and Italians. From the early 19th century until the late '50s/early '60s, Algeria was a French colony and Morocco and Tunisia protectorates, and there are around 1.5m North African immigrants in France, as well as around 400,000 people from sub-Saharan Africa and 700,000 from other parts of Africa and the Caribbean.

France also has a long tradition of welcoming political refugees, who number over 200,000 (most from Eastern Europe, Indo-China, the Middle East and Latin America). It's estimated that there are a further 400,000 illegal immigrants, mostly from Africa and all subject to the new policy of forcible repatriation. The majority of immigrants (around 60 per cent) settle in Ile-de-France, Provence-Alpes-Côte d'Azur and Rhône-Alpes.

The French preoccupation with equality means that official census figures don't include a breakdown of the population by race, ethnic origin or colour.

Immigration is a controversial and emotive subject in France, where there's a degree of 'racial tension' in some areas and overt racism is common – almost 20 per cent of the population regularly voted for racist former *Front National* party leader Jean-Marie Le Pen in presidential elections. (His daughter, Marine, succeeded him in January 2011 and will be the *Front National's* candidate in the 2012 French presidential elections.) EU immigrants are tolerated by most French people, although the same cannot be said of Africans and Arabs. The majority of North Africans, for example, exist in 'ghettos' in run-down suburbs, particularly north of Paris, with large families, on incomes well below the official poverty line and in a vicious circle of deprivation and lack of opportunity.

RELIGION

France has officially been a secular state since the Revolution and therefore has a long tradition of religious tolerance; residents have freedom of religion without hindrance from the state or community, and the majority of the world's religious and philosophical movements have religious centres or meeting places in Paris and other major cities.

Nevertheless, the majority of the population is Christian, by far the largest number belonging to the Catholic faith (around 62 per

cent of the population) and a mere 2 per cent Protestants. The second-largest religious group is Muslims (6 per cent), mostly immigrants from North Africa, and France is home to some 700,000 Jews.

> Details of mosques in France can be found on 🖥 http://mosquee.free.fr and a list of synagogues at 🖥 www.pagesjaunes.fr (enter *Synagogues* in the first box and then the name of the city or town where you're looking for a synagogue).

Religious observance continues to decline and attendance at mass has dropped to below 15 per cent (attendance is lowest in Paris, particularly among those aged 18 to 35). With well under 50 per cent of marriages consecrated in a church and only 45 per cent of babies baptised, parish priests have lost much of their traditional influence and there's a serious shortage of recruits for the priesthood. However, few French are atheists, although many are agnostics.

Church and state were officially divorced in 1905, since when all churches have been state owned and the church is responsible only for 'running' them. On the other hand, the Catholic church is prominent in education, where it maintains many private schools separate from the state education system, although largely funded by the state (see **Private Schools** on page 148). An attempt to abolish state funding for religious schools by the Socialists in the '80s generated fierce opposition and was quickly abandoned.

For information about local places of worship and service times, contact your local town hall or tourist information office. Churches and religious centres are listed in the *Yellow Pages* under *Églises* and *Cultes* (e.g. *Culte israélite* for synagogues), and include American and English churches in Paris and other major cities.

There are over 50 Anglican churches in France, and details of English-language services throughout France (and indeed the world) are contained in the *Directory of English-Speaking Churches Abroad*, published by the Intercontinental Church Society (☎ 01926-430347, 🖥 *www.ics-uk. org*).

SOCIAL CUSTOMS

All countries have strange social customs and France is no exception. As a foreigner you'll probably be excused if you accidentally insult your hosts, but it's better to be aware of accepted taboos and courtesies, especially as the French are much more formal than most foreigners (especially Americans and Britons) imagine.

Greeting

When you're introduced to a French person, you should say 'good day, Sir/Madam' (*bonjour madame/monsieur*) and shake hands (a single pump is enough – neither limp nor knuckle-crushing). *Salut* (hi or hello) is used only among close friends and the young. When saying goodbye, it's customary to shake hands again. In an office, everyone shakes hands with everyone else on arrival at work and when they depart (so that the amount of work done is in inverse proportion to the number of staff).

It's also customary to say good day or good evening (*bonsoir*) on entering a small shop and goodbye (*au revoir madame/monsieur*) on leaving. *Bonjour* becomes *bonsoir* around 18.00 or after dark, although if you choose *bonsoir* (or *bonjour*), don't be surprised if the response isn't the same. *Bonne nuit* (good night) is used when going to bed or leaving a house in the evening. On leaving a shop you may be wished *bonne journée* (have a nice day) or variations such as *bon après-midi*, *bonne fin d'après-midi*, *bon dimanche* or *bon week-end*, to which you should reply *merci*, adding *vous aussi*, *vous de même* or *et vous*. The standard and automatic reply to *merci* is *je vous en prie* (you're welcome).

Titles should generally be used when addressing or writing to people, particularly when the holder is elderly. The president of a company or institution should be addressed as *monsieur* (*madame*) *le président* (*la présidente*), a courtesy title usually retained in retirement. The mayor must be addressed as *Monsieur/Madame le Maire* (even female mayors are *le Maire*!).

Kissing

To kiss or not to kiss, that is the question. When negotiating this social minefield, it's best to take your cue from the French. You shouldn't kiss (*faire la bise*) when first introduced to an adult, although young children will expect to be kissed. If a woman expects you to kiss her, she'll offer her cheek. Note that men kiss women and women kiss women but men don't kiss men, unless they're relatives or very close friends. The 'kiss' isn't usually a proper kiss, more a delicate brushing of the cheeks accompanied by kissing noises, although some extraverts will plant a great wet smacker on each side of your face.

The next question is which cheek to kiss first. Again, take your cue from the natives, as the custom varies from region to region (and even the natives aren't always sure where to start). Finally, you must decide how many kisses to give. Two is the standard number, although many people kiss three or four or even six times. It depends partly on where you are in France.

The British travel agent Thomas Cook recently published a *French Kissing Guide*, according to which four kisses are the norm in northern France, three in the mid-west and southern central areas and two in the west, east and extreme south, a single kiss being acceptable only in the department of Charente-Maritime! Much also depends on how well you know the person concerned: acquaintances may kiss twice, friends four times and old friends six! Kissing usually takes place when you take your leave, as well as when you greet someone. It's also customary to kiss everyone in sight – including the men if you're a man – at midnight on New Year's Eve!

Vous & Tu

When talking to a stranger, use the formal form of address (*vous*). Don't use the familiar form (*tu/toi*) or call someone by his Christian name until you're invited to do so. Generally the older, senior (in a business context) or simply local person will invite the other to use the familiar *tu* form of address (called *tutoiement*) and first names; when it happens, the switch is often sudden and you should pick up on it immediately or you'll forever be stuck on formal terms.

The familiar form is used with children, animals and God, but almost never with your elders or work superiors. However, the French are becoming less formal and the under 50s often use *tu* and first names with work colleagues (unless they're of the opposite sex, when *tu* may imply a special intimacy!) and will quickly switch from *vous* to *tu* with new social acquaintances, although older people may be reluctant to make the change.

Some people always remain *vous*, however often you meet them, such as figures of authority (the local mayor) or those with whom you have a business relationship, e.g. your bank manager, tax officials and policemen.

Gifts

If you're invited to dinner by a French person (which is a sign that you've been accepted into the community), take along a small present of flowers, a plant or chocolates. Gifts of foreign food or drink aren't generally well received unless they're highly prized

in France such as Scotch whisky; foreign wine, however good the quality, isn't recommended!

Some people say you must never take wine, as this implies that your hosts don't know what wine to buy, but this isn't necessarily the case. If you do take wine, however, don't expect it to be served with the meal. It will almost certainly be put aside for a future occasion; your hosts will already have planned the wine for the meal and know that a wine needs to settle before it can be drunk. Flowers can be tricky, as to some people carnations signify bad luck, chrysanthemums are for cemeteries (they're placed on graves on All Saints' Day), red roses signify love and are associated with the Socialists and yellow roses have something to do with adultery – and marigolds (soucis) simply aren't de rigueur. If in doubt, ask a florist for advice.

Eating & Drinking

You shouldn't serve any drinks (or expect to be served one) before all the guests have arrived – even if some are an hour or more late! If you're offered a drink, wait until your host has toasted everyone's health (santé) before taking a drink. **Never** pour your own drinks (except water) when invited to dinner. If you aren't offered a(nother) drink, it's time to go home.

> ☑ **SURVIVAL TIP**
>
> **Always go easy on the wine and other alcohol; if you drink to excess you're unlikely to be invited back!**

The French say bon appétit before a meal and you shouldn't start eating until your hosts do. It's polite to eat everything that's put on your plate. Cheese is served before dessert.

Conversation

The French love detailed and often heated discussions, but there are certain topics of conversation that need handling with care or avoiding altogether. These include money, which is generally mentioned only when complaining about how expensive things are or boasting of how large a motoring fine has been incurred; it's a major faux pas to ask a new acquaintance what he does for a living, as his job title will often give an indication of his salary. Far safer to stick to discussions about food and drink (without, however, comparing French food and drink with that of your home country – unless your praising French gastronomy!). When conversing, even in the midst of a heated debate, avoid raising your voice, which is considered vulgar, although you may interrupt, which is considered normal. Note also that the French often stand close when engaging in conversation, which you may find uncomfortable or even threatening at first.

Greeting Cards

The sending of cards, other than birthday cards, isn't as common in France as in some other countries. It isn't, for example, usual to send someone a card following a bereavement or after passing a driving test. Instead of Christmas cards, the French send New Year cards, but only to people they don't usually see during the year.

The design of most French greetings cards is on a par with the worst in other countries. More acceptable cards may be found in some bookshops, although the range rarely goes much beyond reproductions of works of art.

Dress

Although the French are often formal in their relationships, their dress habits, even in the office, are often extremely casual. Note, however, that the French tend to judge people by their dress, the style and quality being as important as the correctness for the occasion (the French often wear 'designer' jeans to dinner). You aren't usually expected to dress for dinner, depending of course on the sort of circles you move in. On invitations, formal dress (black tie) is smoking exigé/tenue de soirée and informal dress is tenue de ville.

Phone Calls

Always introduce yourself before asking to speak to someone on the telephone. Surprisingly, it's common to telephone at meal times, e.g. 12.00 to 14.00 and around 20.00, when you can usually be assured of finding someone at home. If you must call at these times, you should apologise for disturbing the household.

Noise

It's common for there to be noise restrictions in French towns and villages, particularly with regard to the use of lawnmowers and other mechanical tools. Restrictions are imposed locally and therefore vary, but in general, noisy activities are prohibited before around 08.00 or 09.00 every day, after 19.00 on weekdays and Saturdays and after 12.00 on Sundays, and additionally at lunchtime on Saturdays.

Gesticulating

Like the Italians, the French talk with their hands – often more than with their tongues – but the art of gesticulation can be as difficult to master (and as full of pitfalls for the unwary) as the spoken language. A few tips that could help you avoid a *faux pas* include:

♦ never point with your index finger, which is considered rude, but use an open hand (which should also be used when 'thumbing' a lift);

♦ similarly, beckon with your four fingers, palm down;

♦ the thumb is used to mean 'one' when counting, not the index finger;

♦ to indicate boredom, rub your knuckles against your cheek, to show surprise, shake your hand up and down, and to convey scepticism pull down your lower eyelid;

♦ tapping your fingers on the opposite forearm while raising the forearm slightly indicates an impending or actual departure – usually as a result of boredom!

The classic French shrug is perhaps best left to the natives!

TIME DIFFERENCE

Like most of the continent of Europe, France is on Central European Time (CET), which is Greenwich Mean Time (GMT) plus one hour, from October to March and GMT+2 the rest of the year. The change to 'summer time' (*l'heure d'été*) takes place on the last Sunday in March and to winter time (*l'heure d'hiver*) on the last Sunday in October. Time changes are announced in local newspapers and on radio and TV, and officially take place at 02.00. (In 1997, the French tried to abolish the change of time but were overruled by Brussels!)

Times in France, for example in timetables, are usually written using the 24-hour clock (also in this book), when 10am is written as 10h or 10.00 and 10pm as 22h or 22.00. Midday (*midi*) is 12.00 and midnight (*minuit*) is 24.00 or 00.00; 7.30am is written as 7h30 or 07.30. However, the French use the 12-and 24-hour clocks interchangeably in conversation and it's wise to make sure you've understood. In some French towns, clocks strike twice, with a minute's pause in between, just in case you missed it the first time.

The time (in summer) in selected major foreign cities when it's midday in Paris is shown in the table below.

You can find the local time in any country or major city via the internet, e.g. 🖳 www.timeanddate.com/worldclock.

TIPPING

Tips (*pourboire*, literally 'in order to drink') aren't as freely offered as in the US or even the UK and have become less common since the introduction of the euro. In some places you may even come across signs forbidding tipping (*pourboire interdit*)! Whether or not you should tip depends largely on whether a service charge has already been included in the price. If service is included, this should be indicated by the words *service compris* (*SC*), *service et taxe compris* (*STC*) or *prix nets/ toutes taxes comprises* (*TTC*), which means that prices are inclusive of service and value added tax (*TVA*). If service is extra, *service*

Paris at Noon					
London	Jo'burg	Sydney	Auckland	Los Angeles	New York
1100	1300	2200	2400	0500	0800

stadiums, who traditionally relied on tips for a good part of their income, has virtually died out. While in old-fashioned venues, ushers may more or less demand a tip, elsewhere they may be prohibited from accepting tips. If in doubt, ask. In many modern cinemas, seats aren't numbered (you can sit anywhere) and there are no ushers. It's unnecessary to tip a petrol station attendant (*pompiste*) for cleaning your windscreen or checking your oil, although they're poorly paid and are pleased to receive a small gratuity.

Christmas is generally a time of giving tips to all and sundry, including the postman (*facteur*), garbage collectors (*éboueurs*) and firemen (*sapeurs-pompiers*), who will often call in early December or November (sometimes as early as October!) 'offering' you a calendar, for which you're nevertheless expected to pay – unless you don't want your post delivered, your rubbish collected or any house-fires extinguished for the following 12 months!

The size of such tips depends on how often someone has served you, the quality and friendliness of the service, your financial status and, of course, your generosity. Generally €5 to €15 is acceptable, although you may wish to give more to the *gardienne* of your apartment block (it pays to be nice to her). Large tips are, however, considered ostentatious and in bad taste (except by the recipient, who will be your friend for life).

If you're unsure who or how much to tip, ask your neighbours, friends or colleagues for advice (who will all tell you something different!).

non compris (*SNC*) or *service en sus* may be indicated.

Service is now automatically included in all restaurant bills, although you may still leave a tip if you've had exceptional service. In hotels a 15 per cent service charge is usually included in the bill. In bars and cafés, prices usually include service when you sit at a table but not when you stand at the bar (it should be shown on the menu or bill or the *tarif des consommations*). It's usual to leave your small change on the bar or in the dish provided.

Those who are usually tipped include porters (€1 to €2 per bag, which may be a fixed fee), group tour guides (€1 to €2 for a morning or afternoon), taxi drivers (10 to 15 per cent) and hairdressers (10 per cent). In top-class hotels it's normal to tip a bellboy, porter, chambermaid or other staff members if you ask them to perform extra services. In public toilets where there's an attendant, there's usually a fixed charge and you aren't required to tip, although when no charge is displayed, it's usual to leave €0.15 to €0.30.

The custom of tipping ushers (*ouvreuse*) in theatres, cinemas, concert halls and sports

TOILETS

French public toilets vary considerably in their modernity (or antiquity!), and in addition to some of the world's worst, France – always a country of stark contradictions – also has some of the best.

The French use a variety of names to refer to a toilet including *toilettes*, *WC* (bizarrely pronounced 'VC' – an abbreviation for *double-VC*), *waters*, *lavabos*, *cabinets* (all in the plural, even if there's only one – as there often is) and colloquially *petit coin* (the little corner) and other less polite terms. Public toilets are labelled *messieurs/hommes* and *dames/femmes*.

'Turkish' loos (*cabinets à la turque/siège turc*) – i.e. those consisting simply of a hole in the floor – are still found on basic campsites, at motorway rest areas, and in many cheap bars and restaurants. Care must be taken when flushing, as it's often difficult to keep your clothes and feet dry.

Urinals (properly termed *Vespasiens*, after the Emperor Vespasian, who introduced them to ancient Rome, but more commonly referred to as *pissoirs* or *pissotières*) are thankfully no more and have been replaced by unisex, 24-hour *sanisettes* or 'superloos': cylindrical metal booths topped with a *'Toilettes'* sign. In some towns and cities these cost up to around €1, although all 420 *sanisettes* in Paris have recently been made free. You're forbidden to allow small children (e.g. under ten) to use them on their own, as they may be unable to open the door (a small child was once swept into a sewer by the cleaning process and drowned!), and relieving yourself in public can earn you a fine. Plans are in hand to introduce a new type of automatic toilet, accessible by the disabled and incorporating a drinking water tap.

In cities and towns, public toilets are also found at railway and bus stations, in parking garages and in the street. In towns, there are often public toilets with attendants (commonly known as *'Dame Pipi'*), where there's a fixed charge of around €1. If no charge is displayed, it's normal to leave €0.50 to €1. Toilet paper may be dispensed (piece by piece) by the attendant. In some rural areas you're given a key or even a detachable door handle to an outside toilet.

In many restaurants and bars, men and women share a common WC and there may be a urinal next to the wash basin. In cheap bars and restaurants there may be no toilet paper. Some toilets have no light switch and the light is operated automatically when you lock the door (to prevent people leaving the light on when they leave). In private residences, Americans should ask for the toilet and not the bathroom (*salle de bains*), as the toilet is often separate from the bathroom.

Most French bathrooms have a *bidet* in addition to a toilet bowl; these are for 'intimate ablutions' and aren't footbaths, drinking fountains or toilets! They're also common in hotels, where rooms may have a wash basin and a *bidet* but no toilet bowl, although they're going out of fashion.

French toilets employ a variety of flushing devices including a knob on top of the cistern which is pulled upwards, a push button on the cistern behind the bowl (often with two 'settings': short and long flush), a chain, or even a foot-operated button on the floor (in public toilets).

If a building has a septic tank (*fosse septique*), certain items mustn't be flushed down the toilet, including sanitary towels, paper other than French toilet paper (which is designed to disintegrate), disposable nappies (diapers), condoms or anything made of plastic. You should also not use standard bleaches, disinfectants and chemical cleaners in systems with septic tanks (special products are available), as they can have a disastrous effect on their operation and create nasty smells!

In Paris, it's common to see young children (assisted by their parents) relieving themselves in the gutter (*caniveau*), which is where dogs are also supposed to do their business (the gutters are swept and washed daily). In rural areas, the lack of public toilets is no obstacle to many Frenchmen, who are happy to relieve themselves by the side of the road (and even in your garden!) whenever the urge strikes them (not advisable in a public place, such as on an aircraft!), and generally make little attempt to conceal themselves behind a tree or other object, often not even bothering to turn their backs to passing women or children. Those of a delicate disposition, beware!

Pont de Normandie

19.
THE FRENCH

Who are the French? What are they like? Let's take a candid and totally prejudiced look at them, tongue firmly in cheek, and hope they forgive my flippancy – or that they don't read this bit, which is why it's at the back of the book. (French readers and Francophiles, please note: this chapter isn't supposed to be taken too seriously!)

The typical French person is artificial, elitist, hedonistic, enigmatic, idle, civilised, insular, a hypochondriac, bloody-minded, spineless, a suicidal driver, misunderstood, inflexible, pseudo-intellectual, modern, lazy, disagreeable, seductive, complaining, a philosopher, authoritarian, cultured, gallant, provincial, educated, sophisticated, aggressive, flirtatious, unsporting, egocentric, unbearable, paternalistic, insecure, racist, an individual, ill-disciplined, formal, cynical, unfriendly, emotional, irritating, narrow-minded, charming, unhygienic, obstinate, vain, laid-back, a socialist and a rightwing conservative, serious, long-winded, indecisive, convivial, unloved, callous, bad-tempered, garrulous, inscrutable, ambivalent, infuriating, anti-American, incomprehensible, superior, ignorant, impetuous, a gastro-maniac, blinkered, decadent, truculent, romantic, extravagant, reckless, sensuous, pragmatic, aloof, chauvinistic, capitalistic, courteous, chic, patriotic, xenophobic, proud, passionate, fashionable, nationalistic, bureaucratic, conceited, arrogant, dishonest, surly, rude, impatient, articulate, chivalrous, brave, selfish, imaginative, amiable, debauched, boastful, argumentative, elegant, a lousy lover, egotistical, cold, a good cook, sexy, private, promiscuous, contradictory, political, intolerant, inhospitable, brusque, handsome, an Astérix fan, and above all – insufferably French!

You may have noticed that the above list contains 'a few' contradictions (as does life in France), which is hardly surprising as there's no such thing as a typical French person. Apart from the numerous differences in character between the inhabitants of different regions of France, the population encompasses a potpourri of foreigners from all corners of the globe. However, while it's true that not all French people are stereotypes (some are almost indistinguishable from 'normal' humans), I refuse to allow a few eccentrics spoil my argument...

Living among the French can be a traumatic experience, and foreigners are often shocked by French attitudes. One of the first things a newcomer needs to do is discover where he fits in, particularly regarding class and status. In many ways the French are even more class and status conscious than the British (it was the Normans who introduced class into the UK), with classes ranging from the aristocracy (*les grandes familles*, otherwise known as the guillotined or shortened classes) and upper bourgeoisie, through the middle and lower bourgeoisie to the workers and peasantry. The French class system is based on birthright rather than wealth, and money doesn't determine or buy status (so *ploucs nouveaux riches* needn't apply).

As in most developed countries, there's a huge and widening gap between the rich and the poor, e.g. business tycoons and the lowest-paid workers, particularly those living in rural areas.

The best way to become (and remain) rich in France is to be born with a platinum spoon in your mouth. However, the French don't generally flaunt their wealth, and many find the subject of money distasteful (especially the seriously rich).

The French are renowned for their insularity (worse than the Japanese!) and cannot stand foreigners. The butt of their jokes (when they aren't about bodily functions) are the Belgians and Swiss, whom they poke fun at out of jealousy for their linguistic versatility and superior cultural heritage. However, if it's any consolation, the French reserve their greatest enmity for their fellow countrymen (everybody hates Parisians – even other Parisians).

The French are Alsatians, Basques, Burgundians, Bretons, Corsicans, Normans, Parisians, Provençals, etc., first and French second. Parisians believe that anybody who doesn't live in Paris is a peasant (*plouc*) and beneath contempt. Paradoxically, most Parisians (half are interlopers) have a yearning to live in the country (*la France profonde*) and escape to it at every opportunity. Fortunately the French don't like to leave France (or at least the Francophone world), for which the rest of the world can be truly thankful.

There's a love-hate relationship between the French and the Germans (the former love to hate the latter), although the French reserve their greatest animosity for *les Anglo-Saxons*, i.e. the very same foreigners who rescued them (twice) from the dreaded Hun. France owes its liberty, independence and status as a great (small 'g') power to American and British intervention in two World Wars, a humiliating fact they would prefer to forget (although it doesn't hurt to remind them now and again!). Although it's understandable when you've had your butt kicked by the Krauts three times in two generations that you prefer not to dwell on it, they're still an ungrateful shower (next time the Germans can keep the damned place!).

Every setback is seen as part of an international conspiracy (naturally concocted by *les Anglo-Saxons*) to rob France of its farms, jobs, culture, language and very identity. The French bemoan the American influences seeping into their lives, such as *le fast food* (known as *le néfaste food* – 'unhealthy food'), American English, and worst of all, US 'culture', symbolised by Disneyland Paris (which patriotic French people are praying will go broke – again) and McDonald's 'restaurants' (known as *'macdos'*), which have become a target for self-styled cultural 'guardian angels', battling to prevent the Americanisation of France. However, French youth devours everything American including its clothes, films, music, food, drinks, toys, technology and culture, and French people of all ages pepper their speech with Anglicisms – often feigning ignorance that the words have been pinched from English.

Which brings us to a subject dear to every French person's heart – food. As everyone knows, food was a French invention (along with sex, the guillotine and VAT) and eating is the national pastime (more important than sex, religion and politics combined). The French are voracious carnivores and eat anything that walks, runs, crawls, swims or flies. They're particularly fond of all the nasty bits that civilised people reject including hoofs, ears, tails, brains, entrails and reproductive organs (the French are anything but squeamish). They also eat repulsive things such as snails and frogs' legs. The French are also partial to barbecued British lamb, which they prefer cooked alive over the embers of a burning truck. A nation of animal lovers, the French are particularly fond of the tastier species such as horses and songbirds, which are usually eaten raw with garlic (it's essential to develop a tolerance to garlic if you're to live in France). The French have an ambivalent attitude towards 'pets', and those they don't pamper are often treated abominably.

The French also know a thing or two about drinking and are among the world's most prolific consumers of alcohol (only the Luxembourgeois drink more), although you rarely see a legless French person. As every French person knows, intelligence, sexual prowess and driving skills are all greatly enhanced by a few stiff drinks.

Not surprisingly, they're obsessed with their livers (when not eating those of force-fed geese) and bowel movements, both of which have an intimate relationship with food and drink. The customary treatment for a liver crisis

their cows and sheep for a day out to Paris and other cities (they also regularly distribute free produce on the city streets for the poor town folk). The French, who are difficult to govern at the best of times, are impossible to rule in bad times. France always seems to be teetering on the edge of anarchy and revolution, and mass demonstrations have a special place in French political culture. The *CRS* (riot police) are the only people capable of communicating with rioting people, which they do by whacking them on the head with a large baton. Not surprisingly, the French are the world's leading consumers of tranquillisers, not to mention aspirins to counter the effects of being frequently bashed on the head.

The French complain loud and long about their leaders and the merest mention of politics is a cue for a vociferous argument. They're contemptuous of their politicians, which isn't surprising considering they're an incompetent, licentious and corrupt bunch of buffoons who couldn't organise a *soûlerie* in a vineyard. Politicians rate lower than prostitutes in the social order and the quality of the service they provide (prostitutes have morals and principles and do a sterling job – ask any politician!).

French politics are a bizarre mixture of extreme left and extreme right, although deep down most French are ultraconservative. The French (through Jean Monnet) invented the European Union (EU), a fact which should be patently obvious to anyone, considering it's one of the most bureaucratic and dictatorial organisations in the world. They believe that the EU was a splendid institution while it pursued French ambitions and was led by France, but are ambivalent about it since all the Eastern European rabble were admitted and are positively hostile to Turkey's proposed accession. General de Gaulle was adamant that the intractable British should never be allowed to join and the French have since been doing their utmost to keep them at arm's length (the French call the Channel 'the Sleeve').

(*crise de foie*) and most other ailments is the suppository, used to treat everything from the common cold to a heart attack (the French are a nation of hypochondriacs and, when not eating, they're popping pills). The French are never happier than when they're complaining about something, and protests (*manifestations*) are commonplace and an excuse for a good riot.

Civil disobedience is the national sport and the French take to the barricades at the drop of a beret. France has numerous self-help groups (called anarchists in other countries) and many French people, e.g. fishermen, hunters, farmers and truck drivers, are a law unto themselves. Obeying senseless edicts such as motoring laws, prohibitive signs (e.g. no parking, no smoking, no dogs, no riots) and other trivial rules is a matter of personal choice in France – and most French choose not to. Although France is ostensibly a country of written rules, regulations and laws, they exist solely to be waived, bent or adapted (*système débrouillard* or *système D*) to your own advantage.

Kind-hearted French farmers are famous for their love of animals and they often take

France is the most bureaucratic country in the world, with almost twice as many civil servants as Germany and three times as many as Japan. In order to accomplish anything remotely official in France, 98 forms must be completed in quintuplicate, each of which must be signed by 47 officials in 31 different government departments. Only then do you get your bus pass! When dealing with civil servants, however, you must never show your impatience, which is like a red rag to a bull. It's the fault of all those French cheeses; as de Gaulle so succinctly put it: "It's difficult to rule a nation with 265 cheeses" (or possibly 365, 400 or even 750). It's even harder to govern a country that has no idea how many cheeses it has!

The French aren't exactly noted for their humility and variously describe France (*la Grande Nation*) as the most cultured of countries, the light of the world, and a nation destined by God (who's naturally French) to dominate the continent. Naturally, Paris is the capital of civilisation and the city of light.

France lives on its past glories (*la gloire*) and clings tenaciously to its colonies (which it uses as a testing ground for its nuclear weapons) long after other colonists have seen the light. French history is littered with delusions of grandeur (*la grandeur française*), which spawned such infamous megalomaniacs as Charlemagne, Napoleon, de Gaulle, and the most famous Frenchman of all, Astérix.

France yearns for foreign adulation, the predominance of the French language and culture (Johnny Hallyday aside), and to be hailed as the undisputed leader of Europe. The French person's favourite word is appropriately *supérieur* (nobody **ever** accused the French of being modest).

⚠ Caution

The French language has divine status in France and is the language of love, food and the Gods. The French cling to it as their last vestige of individuality and its propagation by the foreign service is sacrosanct (mock it at your peril!).

The French love their language and habitually use it as a blunt instrument to intimidate uneducated foreigners, i.e. anyone who doesn't speak it (only in France are tourists treated with contempt for not speaking the language). To fully understand the French you need an intimate knowledge of their beautiful and romantic language, which is the key to their spirit and character. In practice this consists of learning just two words, *merde!* and *NON!*, which can be used effectively to deal with every situation, as was aptly demonstrated by General de Gaulle (see also *le bras d'honneur* below). The French say no to every request and only afterwards (may) consider possible alternatives.

Most French pretend not to speak English, usually because they speak it excruciatingly badly and have a gigantic inferiority complex about the English language, which they blame for the decline of the French language and empire (the ability to speak French is no longer the sign of a civilised person), while eagerly adopting English words, especially those ending in '-ing' (in fact, often inventing words ending in -ing that don't exist in English) in order to demonstrate their *sex-appeal*.

If you're unable to make yourself understood in English, you should resort to sign language, a scientific and highly developed art form in France. The supreme gesture is *le bras d'honneur*, meaning 'up yours' (or something less printable!): hold your right arm outstretched and smack your left hand against your right bicep, simultaneously bringing your right forearm smartly upwards. It isn't advisable, however, to make this gesture in the general direction of a *gendarme* or anyone with a gun.

When not eating, the French are allegedly making love. They're obsessed with sex and have a long tradition of debauchery. French men think they're God's gift to women and are in a permanent state of arousal. Every attractive woman is a potential conquest, especially foreign ones, some of whom have a reputation for being 'easy' (if you want to know how good your wife is in bed, the saying goes, ask your French friends!).

The French use sex to sell everything from cars to mineral water (what others find sexist, the French find sexy) and lack modesty in all things, discarding their clothes at every opportunity. French women enjoy being objects of desire and most care little for women's liberation and indulge their 'macho' (i.e. selfish) men, most of whom couldn't change a nappy if their lives depended on it. Flirting is an art form, where sexual overtones are part and parcel of everyday life.

The French are renowned for their sexual peccadilloes and are credited with inventing sadism (the Marquis de Sade), brothels (*bordellos*), French letters (Condom is a French town), masturbation and adultery. In France, *c'est normal* for a woman to seek lovers and for a man to have mistresses. If a married man is a philanderer it's a source of pride, a mark of respect and nothing to be ashamed of (a real vote-catcher for politicians!). A mistress is a status symbol, the absence of which casts grave doubts on a man's virility and sexual predilections.

As a by-product of this rampant free love, the French have record numbers of illegitimate children, whom they have been forced to legalise (along with their concubines). They even have the gall to call homosexuality 'the English vice' (*le vice anglais*), although

everyone knows why Paris, which is famous for its transvestites, is called gay Paris (France is the only country where the men wear more perfume than the women!).

Despite not washing, living on garlic and wearing their socks for weeks on end, Frenchmen have amazingly established a reputation for suave, seductive charm (surely women aren't still attracted to Alain Delon and Gérard Depardieu?). However, despite his formidable reputation, the Frenchman's performance in bed is similar to his performance in the battlefield: lots of pomp and ceremony, but when the pantaloons are down he empties his cannon out of range and rolls over.

Fittingly, the national symbol is the resplendent cockerel, which seduces and impregnates the submissive hens and then crows (*cocorico!*) triumphantly, even when it has nothing to boast about (after which it's cooked in wine and eaten). However, despite the fact that the rooster services many hens, the evidence is that he doesn't satisfy them (around half of French women declare their sex lives to be unsatisfactory).

The French are formidable sportsmen and have produced a long line of sporting heroes (although their names are difficult to recall and the most famous is better known for head-butting an opponent). Among the most popular French sports are sex; beating the system (e.g. fare evasion, cheating the tax man, claiming unlawful social security and defrauding the EU); stock-car racing on public roads; corruption, fraud and sleaze; falling off skis; running (away from the Germans); falling off bicycles while following Americans, Belgians, Spaniards and assorted other foreigners around France; losing at football (1998 was a temporary aberration); *boules* (a form of marbles played by southerners plastered on *pastis*); rioting; horse riding (to escape from rampaging Germans); shooting themselves in the feet; tennis and sex. It's widely acknowledged that the French are cheats, poor losers and have absolutely no notion of *le fair-play*. After all, how can a nation which doesn't play cricket or baseball possibly be trusted to play by the rules?

Enough frivolity – let's get down to serious business! Like most capitalist countries, France is a sorely divided nation. While the elite and privileged bourgeoisie luxuriate in the sun, the inhabitants of the poor suburbs and immigrant ghettos remain permanently in the gloom, plagued by poor transport, soaring crime levels, extremist politics, and an acute sense of dereliction and hopelessness. There's a festering racial problem, with suppressed and disadvantaged Africans and Arabs (enticed to France as cheap labour) locked in a vicious circle of poverty and deprivation.

The increasingly destitute farming communities and thousands of rural villages are also firmly anchored in second-class France. The human fallout from *la bonne vie* and high unemployment occupy the streets and *métro* tunnels of French cities. France also suffers from increasing drug abuse, alcoholism, racism and violence. However, by far the biggest challenge facing France's leaders is how to reform the economy (e.g. debt-ridden public companies, a yawning social security deficit and endless benefits, and workers addicted to time off and holidays) without provoking a(nother) revolution.

The French do, however, have a few good points. They've managed (largely) to preserve the splendour of their countryside and the charm and splendour of their villages, towns and cities. They enjoy the best (although least adventurous) cuisine in the world and many of the world's great wines (although their failure to admit that anyone else can make decent wine is costing them dear). They have good public services, fine schools, exceptional social security benefits (although the country cannot afford them), superb hospitals (with virtually no waiting lists), excellent working conditions and employee benefits, and a first class transport system with magnificent *autoroutes* and among the world's fastest trains. The country enjoys a generally high standard of living, low inflation and a relatively healthy economy (despite the gloom).

> The French (unlike many other nations) haven't turned their backs on their roots and strong family and community ties and loyalties are a prominent feature of French life.

France is one of the most cultured countries in the world and the French are renowned for their insatiable appetite for gastronomy, art, literature, philosophy and music – whether they understand it or not. Paris houses some of the world's greatest museums, monuments and architectural treasures, and is one of the world's most attractive and romantic cities, and its cleanest major capital (London and New York please note) – apart from the canine deposits on pavements.

France is highly competitive on the world stage, notably in foreign affairs, business, technology, sport and culture, and is one of the few developed countries with the vision and boldness to conceive and execute grandiose schemes (*les grands projets*). The French are justifiably proud of their achievements (critical foreigners are simply jealous) and France is no longer an island unto itself, its traditional insularity having been replaced by a highly developed sense of international responsibility. It remains one of the most influential nations in the world and a positive power for good, particularly in the field of medicine, where *Médecins sans Frontières* and *Médecins du Monde* do exemplary work.

While French bureaucracy is enough to discourage anybody, ordinary French people usually couldn't be more welcoming (apart from Parisians). If you're willing to meet them halfway and learn their language, you'll invariably be warmly received by the French, who will go out of their way to help you – and 'educate' you in the finer points of civilised living. Contrary to popular belief, they aren't baby-eating ogres and, provided you make an effort to be friendly, they're likely to overwhelm you with kindness. Although it's difficult to get to know the French, when you do you invariably make friends for life.

Anyone planning to make their permanent home in France should bear in mind that assimilation is all-important. If you don't want to live **with** the French and share their way of life, language, culture and traditions, you're probably better off going somewhere else (or staying at home).

The mark of a great nation is that it never breeds indifference in foreigners – admiration, envy, hostility or even blind hatred, but never indifference! Love it or hate it, France is a unique, vital, civilised, bold, sophisticated and challenging country.

In the final analysis, the French enjoy one of the world's best lifestyles and what many believe is the finest overall quality of life (French civilisation has been described as an exercise in enlightened self-indulgence). Few other countries offer such a wealth of intoxicating experiences for the mind, body and spirit – and not all out of a bottle! – or provide a more stimulating environment in which to live and work. (But don't tell the French – they insufferable enough as it is!)

Vive la différence! Vive la République! Vive la France! Vive les Français!

20.

MOVING HOUSE OR LEAVING FRANCE

When moving house or leaving France, there are numerous things to be considered and a 'million' people to inform. The checklists contained in this chapter will make the task easier and may even help prevent an ulcer or nervous breakdown – provided you don't leave everything to the last minute.

MOVING HOUSE

When moving house within France, bear in mind the following:

♦ If you're renting accommodation, you must usually give your landlord at least three months' notice (refer to your contract). Your resignation letter must be sent by registered post (*lettre recommandée avec accusé de réception*).

♦ Inform the following, as applicable:

– your employer;

– your present town hall and the town hall in your new community within a month of taking up residence. They'll change the address on your *carte de séjour,* if applicable.

– your local social security (Caisse Primaire d'Assurance Maladie/CPAM) and family allowance (Caisse d'Allocations Familiales) offices;

– your local income tax office (Centre des Impôts) and *trésorerie*;

– your local electricity/gas and water companies (at least two days in advance);

– France Télécom (and other phone companies) if you have a telephone. You can have your new number announced to callers for six months.

– your regional TV licence centre (Centre Régional de la Redevance Audiovisuelle) if you have a TV and other TV companies (cable, satellite);

– your insurance companies, e.g. health, car, house contents and public liability; hire purchase companies; lawyer; accountant; and local businesses where you have accounts. Obtain new insurance, if applicable.

– your banks and other financial institutions, such as stockbrokers and credit card companies. Make arrangements for the transfer of funds and the cancellation or alteration of standing orders. – your family doctor, dentist and other health practitioners. Health records should be transferred to your new practitioners. – your children's schools. If applicable, arrange for schooling in your new community (see **Chapter 9**). Try to give a term's notice and obtain copies of any relevant school reports and records from current schools as well as a *certificat de radiation.*

– all regular correspondents, publications to which you subscribe, including professional and trade journals, social and sports clubs, and friends and relatives. Arrange to have your post redirected by the post office by completing a permanent change of address card (*ordre de réexpédition définitif*), available from post offices, at least four days in advance.

– your local consulate or embassy if you're registered with them.

♦ If you have a French driving licence or a French-registered car and are remaining in the same department, you must return your licence and car registration document (*carte grise*) and have the address changed (see page 75). If you're moving to a new department, you must inform both your current and new *préfectures*. You must re-register your car and obtain a new licence from your new *préfecture* within three months of taking up residence.

♦ Return any library books or anything borrowed.

♦ Arrange removal of your furniture and belongings (or hire a vehicle if you're doing your own removal).

♦ If you live in rented accommodation, obtain a refund of your deposit from your landlord.

♦ Ask yourself (again): 'Is it really worth all this trouble?'

LEAVING FRANCE

Before leaving France for an indefinite period, you should do the following in addition to the things listed above under Moving House:

♦ Check that your own and your family's passports are valid.

♦ Give notice to your employer, if applicable.

♦ Check whether you qualify for a rebate on income tax and social security payments (see **Chapter 13**). Tax rebates are normally paid automatically. If you've contributed to a supplementary pension scheme, a percentage of your contributions will be repaid, although your pension company will require proof that you're leaving France permanently.

♦ Obtain a copy of your health and dental records and a statement from your health insurance company stating your present level of cover. You may wish to arrange health and dental check-ups before leaving France.

♦ Make arrangements to sell or let your house or apartment and other property in France.

♦ Arrange to sell anything you aren't taking with you (car, furniture, etc.) and to ship your belongings. Find out the procedure for shipping your belongings to your country of destination. Check with the local embassy or consulate in France of the country to which you're moving. Forms may need to be completed before arrival. If you've been living in France for less than a year, you're required to re-export all imported personal effects, including furniture and vehicles (if you sell them, you may have to pay tax or duty).

♦ If you have a French-registered car that you plan to take with you, you can drive on your French registration plates for a maximum of three months.

♦ Pets may require vaccinations or may need to go into quarantine for a period (see page 357), depending on your destination.

♦ Contact France Télécom (see **Chapter 7**) and anyone else well in advance if you need to recover a deposit.

♦ Arrange health, travel and other insurance (see **Chapter 13**). Terminate any French loans and lease or hire purchase contracts, and pay all outstanding bills (allow plenty of time, as some companies are slow to respond).

♦ Check whether you're entitled to a rebate on your car and other insurance. Obtain a letter from your French motor insurance company stating your no claims bonus.

♦ Check whether you need an international driving licence or a translation of your French or foreign driving licence for your country of destination.

♦ Give friends and business associates in France a temporary address, telephone number and email address where you can be contacted abroad.

♦ If you'll be travelling or living abroad for an extended period, you may wish to give someone 'power of attorney' over your financial affairs in France so that they can act on your behalf in your absence. This can be for a fixed period or open-ended and can be limited to a specific purpose only. You should, however, obtain expert legal advice before doing this.

♦ Buy a copy of the relevant book in our *Living and Working* series before leaving France. If we haven't published it yet, drop us a line and we'll get started on it right away!

Bon voyage !

Château de Chambord, Loire

APPENDICES

APPENDIX A: USEFUL ADDRESSES

Embassies & Consulates

Foreign embassies are located in the capital Paris (those for selected English-speaking countries are listed below), and many countries also have consulates in other cities (all British consulates are listed below). Embassies and consulates are listed in the *Yellow Pages* under *Ambassades, Consulats et Autres Représentations Diplomatiques*.

Australia: 4 rue Jean Rey, 15e (☎ 01 40 59 33 00).

Ireland: 4 rue Rude, 16e (☎ 01 44 17 67 00).

New Zealand: 7ter rue Léonard de Vinci, 16e (☎ 01 45 01 43 43).

South Africa: 59 quai Orsay, 7e (☎ 01 53 59 23 23).

United Kingdom: 35 rue Faubourg St Honoré, 8e (see below) and 18 bis rue Anjou, 8e (☎ 01 44 51 31 02).

United States of America: 2 rue St Florentin, 1e (☎ 08 10 26 46 26) and 2 avenue Gabriel, 1e (☎ 01 43 12 22 22).

British Consulates-General

Consulates-General are permanently staffed during normal office hours.

Bordeaux: 353 boulevard du Président Wilson, BP 91, 33073 Bordeaux (☎ 05 57 22 21 10). Covers the departments of Ariège, Aveyron, Charente, Charente-Maritime, Corrèze, Creuse, Dordogne, Haute-Garonne, Gers, Gironde, Landes, Lot, Lot-et-Garonne, Pyrénées-Atlantiques, Hautes-Pyrénées, Deux-Sèvres, Tarn, Tarn-et-Garonne, Vienne and Haute-Vienne.

Lille: 11 square Dutilleul, 59800 Lille (☎ 03 20 12 82 72). Covers the departments of Aisne, Ardennes, Nord, Pas-de-Calais and Somme.

Lyon: 24 rue Childebert, 69288 Lyon Cedex 1 (☎ 04 72 77 81 70). Covers the departments of Ain, Allier, Ardèche, Cantal, Côte d'Or, Doubs, Drôme, Isère, Jura, Loire, Haute-Loire, Puy-de-Dôme, Rhône, Haute-Saône, Saône-et-Loire, Savoie, Haute-Savoie and the Territoire de Belfort.

Marseille: 24 avenue du Prado, 13006 Marseille (☎ 04 91 15 72 10). Covers the departments of Alpes-de-Haute-Provence, Hautes-Alpes, Alpes-Maritimes, Aude, Bouches-du-Rhône, Gard, Hérault, Lozère, Pyrénées-Orientales, Var and Vaucluse, as well as Corsica.

Paris: 35 rue du Faubourg Saint Honoré, 75383 Paris (☎ 01 44 51 31 00). Covers the departments of Aube, Calvados, Cher, Côtes d'Armor, Eure, Eure-et-Loir, Finstère, Ille-et-Vilaine, Indre, Indre-et-Loire, Loir-et-Cher, Loire, Loire-Atlantique, Loiret, Maine-et-Loire, Manche, Marne, Haute-Marne, Mayenne, Meurthe-et-Moselle, Meuse, Morbihan, Moselle, Nièvre, Oise, Bas-Rhin, Sarthe and Vosges, as well as the whole of the Ile-de-France and the overseas departments and territories.

British Honorary Consulates

Honorary consulates aren't permanently staffed and should be contacted **in emergencies only,** e.g. for urgent passport renewals or replacements.

Boulogne-sur-Mer: c/o Cabinet Barron et Brun, 28 rue Saint Jean, 62200 Boulogne-sur-Mer (☎ 03 21 87 16 80).

Cherbourg-Octeville: BP 15, 50460 Querqueville (☎ 02 33 78 01 83).

Dunkerque: (☎ 03 28 66 11 98).

Le Havre: c/o LD Lines, Terminal de la Citadelle, BP 90746, 76060 Le Havre (☎ 02 35 19 78 88).

Montpellier: 271 Le Capitole, Bâtiment A, 64 rue Alcyone, 34000 Montpellier (☎ 04 67 15 52 07).

Nantes: 16 boulevard Gabriel Giust'hau, BP 22026, 44020 Nantes Cedex 1 (☎ 02 51 72 72 60).

Toulouse: c/o English Enterprises, 8 allée du Commingues, 317700 Colomiers, 31300 Toulouse (☎ 05 61 30 37 91).

Tours: 7, rue des Rosiers, 37510 Savonnières (☎ 02 47 43 50 58).

Miscellaneous

Alliance Française, 101 boulevard Raspail, 75270 Paris Cedex 06 (☎ 01 42 84 90 00, 🖳 www.alliancefr.org). Famous language-teaching school.

Brit Consulting, 11 rue Félix Faure, 75015 Paris (☎ 06 23 86 30 21, 🖳 www.britconsulting.com). A project management service for people building or renovating property in France.

British Association of Removers (BAR) Overseas, Tangent House, 62 Exchange Road, Watford, WD18 0TG, UK (☎ 01923-699480, 🖳 www.removers.org.uk).

Centre des Impôts de Non-Résidents, TSA 10010 -10 rue du Centre, 93160 Noisy-le-Grand Cedex (☎ 01 57 33 83 00).

Centre Renseignements Douaniers (🖳 www.douane.gouv.fr). Customs information.

Chambre des Notaires, 12 avenue Victoria, 75001 Paris (☎ 01 44 82 24 00, 🖳 www.paris.notaires.fr).

Compagnie Nationale des Experts Immobiliers, 18 rue Volney, 75002 Paris (☎ 01 42 96 18 46, 🖳 www.expert-cnei.com).

Conseil Supérieur du Notariat, 31 rue du Général Foy, 75383 Paris Cedex 08 (☎ 01 44 90 30 00, 🖳 www.notaires.fr).

Department for Environment, Food & Rural Affairs (DEFRA), Nobel House, 17 Smith Square, London SW1P 3JR, UK (☎ 020-7238 6951/0845-933 5577, 🖳 www.defra.gov.uk).

Fédération Nationale de l'Immobilier (FNAIM), 129 rue du Faubourg St Honoré, 75008 Paris (🖳 www.fnaim.fr).

Gîtes de France, 59 rue St Lazare, Paris 75439 Cedex 09 (☎ 01 49 70 75 75, 🖳 www.gites-de-france.fr).

Office du Tourisme, 25 rue des Pyramides, 75001 Paris (☎ 08 92 68 30 00, 🖳 www.parisinfo.com).

De Particulier à Particulier, 45 rue du Cardinal-Lemoine, 75239 Paris Cedex 05 (☎ 01 40 56 33 33, 🖳 www.pap.fr).

Société d'Aménagement Foncier et d'Etablissement Rural (SAFER), 91 rue du Faubourg St Honoré, 75008 Paris (☎ 01 44 69 86 00, 🖳 www.safer.fr).

Union Nationale des AVF (Accueils des Villes Françaises), 3 rue de Paradis, 75010 Paris (☎ 01 47 70 45 85, 🖳 www.avf.asso.fr).

APPENDIX B: FURTHER READING

This appendix contains a selected list of English-language publications about France and the French. Other books and magazines are mentioned in the relevant chapters.

English-language Newspapers & Magazines

The Connexion (☎ 04 93 32 16 59, 💻 www.connexionfrance.com). Monthly newspaper.

Brittany Pages (☎ 0800 91 77 56, 💻 www.brittanypages.com). Monthly newspaper.

Dordogne Advertiser (☎ 0800 91 77 56, 💻 www.dordogneadvertiser. fr). Free monthly newspaper.

France Magazine, Archant Life (UK ☎ 01242-216001, 💻 www. francemag.co.uk). Monthly lifestyle magazine.

French Property News, Archant Life (☎ 020-8543 3113, 💻 www. french-property-news.com). Monthly property magazine.

Languedoc Pages (☎ 0800 91 77 56, 💻 www.languedocpages.com). Monthly newspaper.

Living France, Archant Life (UK ☎ 01858-438832, 💻 www.livingfrance. com). Monthly lifestyle/property magazine.

Normandy Advertiser (☎ 0800 91 77 56, 💻 www.normandyadvertiser. fr). Free monthly newspaper.

The Riviera Reporter (☎ 04 93 45 77 19, 💻 www.riviera-reporter.com). Bi-monthly free magazine covering the Côte d'Azur.

The Riviera Times (☎ 04 93 27 60 00, 💻 www.rivieratimes.com). Monthly free newspaper covering the Côte d'Azur and Italian Riviera.

Books

The books listed below are just a selection of the hundreds written about France. The publication title is followed by the author's name and the publisher (in brackets).

Culture

Culture Wise France, Joe Laredo (Survival Books)

The Essence of Style, Joan Dejean (Free Press)

France, the Land (Lands, Peoples & Cultures), Greg Nickles (Crabtree Publishing).

French Cinema: From its Beginnings to the Present, Henri Fournier Lanzoni (Continuum International Publishing Group)

Paris Jazz: A Guide, Luke Miner (The Little Bookroom)

Savoir Flair, Polly Platt (Distri Books)

The Alps: A Cultural History, Andrew Beattie (Signal Books)

The Complete Merde, Genevieve (Harper Collins)

Food & Drink

Best Street Markets in France, M Anderson & R Fennell (Travellers Temptation Press)

Bistro, Laura Washburn, Ryland (Peters & Small)

The French Kitchen, Joanne Harris & Fran Warde (Doubleday)

The Great Wines of France, Clive Coates (Mitchell Beazley)

Love Food Love Paris, Kate Whiteman (AA Travel Publications)

Michelin Guide France (Michelin)

The Rubbish on our Plates, Fabien Perucca & Gérard Pouradier (Prion)

Truffles and Tarragon, Anne Gregg (Bantam)

Vegetarian France, Alex Bourke & Alan Todd (Vegetarian Guides)

Vintcents French Food Dictionary, Charles Vintcent (Harriman House Publishing)

Why French Women Don't Get Fat, Mireille Guiliano (Chatto & Windus)

History

Agincourt: A New History, Anne Curry (Tempus Publishing)

A Brief History, Cecil Jenkins (Robinson)

The French Revolution, Christopher Hibbert (Penguin)

The Measure of All Things: the Seven-year Odyssey that Transformed the World, Ken Alder (Little, Brown)

Napoleon, Vincent Cronin (HarperCollins)

That Sweet Enemy: The British and the French from the Sun King to the Present, Robert & Isabelle Tombs (Pimlico)

The Unfree French: Life under the Occupation, Richard Vinen (Penguin)

La Vie en Bleu: France and the French since 1900, Roderick Kedward (Penguin)

The White Cities, Joseph Roth (Granta Books)

Language

101 French Idioms, Jean-Marie Cassagne (Passport Books)

101 French Proverbs, Jean-Marie Cassagne (Passport Books)

Better French, Monique Jackman (Studymates)

Colloquial French, C. Kirk-Greene (Foulsham)

Conversational French Made Easy, Monique Jackman (Hadley Pager Info.)

French Idioms & Expressions, C. Kirk-Greene (Foulsham)

French Idioms and Expressions, C. Kirk-Greene (Foulsham)

French Language Survival Guide (Harper Collins)

Insider's French, Eleanor & Michel Levieux (The University of Chicago Press)

Rude French, Georges Pilard (Harrap)

Slang & Colloquialisms, Georgette Marks & Charles Johnson (Harrap)

Living & Working

Buying a Home in France, David Hampshire (Survival Books). All you'll ever need to know to successfully buy, rent or sell property in France.

Find Out About France, Duncan Crosbie (Barron's Educational)

Living in Provence, Dane McDowell & Christian Sarramon (Flammarion)

More France Please & **More More France Please**, Helena Frith-Powell (Gibson Square)

Renovating & Maintaining Your French Home, Joe Laredo (Survival Books). The best-selling book about maintaining French property.

Retiring in France, David Hampshire (Survival Books). All you need to know about enjoying your golden years in France.

Rural Living in France, Jeremy Hobson (Survival Books). Everything you need to know to create your very own French rural idyll.

People

50 Reasons to Hate the French, Jules Eden & Alex Clarke (Quetzal Publishing UK)

French or Foe, Polly Platt (Distri Books)

How to be French, Margaret Ambrose (New Holland Publishers)

Sixty Million Frenchmen Can't Be Wrong, Jean-Benoit Nadeau (Robson Books)

Tourist Guides

AA Explorer France (AA Publishing)

Cruising French Waterways, Hugh McKnight (Adlard Coles Nautical)

The Food Lover's Guide to France, Patricia Wells (Workman Publishing)

France and the Grand Tour, Jeremy Black (Palgrave Macmillan)

France: DK Eyewitness Travel Guides (Dorling Kindersley)

France: Lonely Planet Country Guide, Nicola Williams (Lonely Planet)

France: Rough Guide Travel Guides (Rough Guides)

Provence A-Z, Peter Mayle (Profile Books)

Via Ferrata: A Complete Guide to France, Philippe Poulet (Cordee)

Travel Literature

France in Mind: an Anthology, Powers Leccese (Vintage Books)

The House in France, Gully Wells (Bloomsbury)

Next Stop France, Claire Boast (Heinemann)

Paris: a Literary Companion, Ian Littlewood (Franklin Watts)

Paris & Elsewhere: Selected Writings, Richard Cobb (New York Review of Books)

This is Paris, Miroslav Sasek (Universe Publishing)

Something to Declare: Essays on France, Julian Barnes (Alfred A. Knopf)

A Summer in Gascony, Martin Calder (Nicholas Brealey)

Travels with a Donkey in the Cévennes, Robert Louis Stevenson (Oxford)

We'll Always Have Paris: American Tourists in France since 1930, H. Levenstein (University of Chicago Press)

A Year in Provence, Peter Mayle (Profile Books)

Miscellaneous

The Changing Face of France, Virginia Chandler (Raintree)

France, a Love Story: Women Write About the French Experience (Seal Press)

France: Country Insights, Teresa Fisher (Raintree)

France: Destination Detectives, Paul Mason (Raintree)

French Flea Bites (Mill of the Flea), George East (La Puce Publications)

The French Touch, Jan de Luz (Gibbs M. Smith)

How I Won the Yellow Jumper: Despatches from the Tour de France, Ned Boulting (Yellow Jersey)

My Life in France, Julia Child & Alex Prud'homme (Random House USA)

Paris, Shops & More, Vincent Knapp & Angelika Taschen (Taschen)

APPENDIX C: USEFUL WEBSITES

The following is a selection of websites about France and the French.

General Information

All About France (🖥 www.all-about-france.com).

Alliance Française (🖥 www.alliancefr.org). The famous French language school.

Alliance française in Paris (🖥 www.paris.alliancefr.fr).

Anglo Info (🖥 www.angloinfo.com). Information and forums specific to Aquitaine, Brittany, Normandy, Poitou-Charentes and Provence.

Bonjour (🖥 www.bonjour.com). French tuition.

British Association of Tour Operators to France (🖥 www.holidayfrance.org.uk).

Cityvox (🖥 www.cityvox.com). Information about eating out, accommodation, foreign food shops, etc. in selected towns in France.

Electricité de France (🖥 www.edf.fr).

L'Etudiant (🖥 www.letudiant.fr). Information for students in French.

Europa Pages (🖥 www.europa-pages.com). Directory of European language courses.

European Council for International Schools (🖥 www.ecis.org).

France Guide (🖥 www.franceguide.fr). Tourist information in English.

French-at-a-Touch (🖥 http://french-at-a-touch.com). General information on France and links to many other sites.

French Embassy in London (🖥 www.ambafrance-uk.org).

French Entrée (🖥 www.frenchentree.com). Information on every aspect of living in France and a useful forum.

French Tourist Board (🖥 www.franceguide.com).

INSEE (🖥 www.insee.fr). Office of national statistics: population, unemployment, salaries, etc. (in English and French).

Invest in France Agency (🖥 www.invest-in-france.org). Useful information on living and working in France.

Legifrance (⌨ www.legifrance.gouv.fr). Official legal information.

Living France (⌨ www.livingfrance.com). The site of the eponymous magazine, providing useful information about all aspects of living in France and a lively discussion forum with over 18,000 members.

Météo France (⌨ www.meteofrance.com). Weather and climate in France.

Ministry of Culture & Communications (⌨ www.culture.fr).

Moving to France Made Easy (⌨ www.moving-to-france-made-easy.com). Plenty of information about life in France.

Online Newspapers (⌨ www.onlinenewspapers.com/france.htm). Links to dozens of French newspaper publishers' sites.

Pages Jaunes (⌨ www.pagesjaunes.fr). The French *Yellow Pages*.

Paris Info (⌨ www.parisinfo.com). The site of the Paris Convention & Visitors' Bureau.

Paris Notes (⌨ www.parisnotes.com). A subscription newsletter about Paris, published ten times a year.

Pavillon Bleu (⌨ www.pavillonbleu.org). A list of 'blue flag' beaches in France (awarded by the Foundation for European Education and Environment).

Le Point (⌨ www.lepoint.fr). Articles and surveys on all aspects of French life from the consumer magazine *Le Point*.

Pratique (⌨ www.pratique.fr). Practical information about life in France (in French).

Le Progrès (⌨ www.leprogres.fr). General information in French.

Que Choisir (⌨ www.quechoisir.org). Reports and articles from the consumer magazine *Que Choisir*.

Radio France (⌨ www.radiofrance.fr).

Service Public (⌨ www.service-public.fr). Official French government portal, with links to all ministry and other sites.

This French Life (⌨ www.thisfrenchlife.com). Articles about setting up a variety of necessary services, from bank accounts to internet connection, as well as some of the more enjoyable things about life.

US Embassy in Paris (⌨ www.amb-usa.fr).

Webvivant (⌨ www.webvivant.com). Online community for English speakers in France and Francophiles everywhere.

Government Ministries

Ministries of the Economy and Finance and of Budgets and Accounting (🖳 www.finances.gouv.fr). Economic and tax information.

Ministry of Education (🖳 www.education.gouv.fr).

Ministry of Foreign & European Affairs (🖳 www.diplomatie.gouv.fr/en). Information (in English) about French foreign policy.

Prime Minister (🖳 www.premier-ministre.gouv.fr). Information (in English) about the French Prime Minister's role and function.

Employment

Agence pour la Création d'Entreprises (🖳 www.apce.com). Help for company founders in French.

Cadre Emploi/Cadres Online (🖳 www.cadremploi.fr and www.cadresonline. com). For executive or managerial positions

Pôle Emploi (🖳 www.pole-emploi.fr). French national employment agency.

Keljob (🖳 www.keljob.com). Job search portal

Property & Accommodation

Coast & Country (🖳 http://coast-country.com). English-speaking estate agents on the Côte d'Azur.

De Particulier à Particulier (🖳 www.pap.fr). Advertisements in the French property magazine *De Particulier à Particulier* (English-language version available).

Entre Particuliers (🖳 www.entreparticuliers.com). Property advertisements.

Faire Construire sa Maison (🖳 www.construiresamaison.com). Site of the magazine *Faire Construire sa Maison*.

FNAIM (🖳 www.fnaim.com). French federation of estate agents.

Foncia (🖳 www.foncia.fr). Rental accommodation specialists.

Gîtes de France (🖳 www.gites-de-france.com). Principal national organisation regulating self-catering accommodation.

Green-Acres Services (🖳 www.green-acres.com). Property agents.

Immonot (🖳 www.immonot.com). Property listed with *notaires* and information on buying.

Immoprix (🖳 www.immoprix.com). Average property and building land sale prices by type, size, town, area, department and region.

ImmoStreet (🖳 www.immostreet.com). Properties for sale and rent; also has automatic calculator showing repayment amounts for mortgage purchases.

Journal des Particuliers (🖳 www.journaldesparticuliers.com). Advertisements in the French property magazine *Le Journal des Particuliers*.

Logic-Immo (🖳 www.logic-immo.com). French estate agents' property advertisements.

Notaires de France (🖳 www.notaires.fr). Property listed with *notaires* and information on buying.

Salut France (🖳 http://salut-france.com). French property search agents.

Se Loger (🖳 www.seloger.com). Properties for sale and rent plus quotations for insurance, removals and building work.

Terrains (🖳 www.terrain.fr). Building land for sale and information on buying land.

Communications

Air

Aéroports Français (🖳 www.aeroport.fr). Details of and links to all French airports.

Air France (🖳 www.airfrance.com).

BMI (🖳 www.flybmi.com).

British Airways (🖳 www.britishairways.co.uk).

EasyJet (🖳 www.easyjet.com).

Flybe (🖳 www.flybe.com).

Ryanair (🖳 www.ryanair.com).

Sea

Brittany Ferries (🖳 www.brittanyferries.com).

Condor Ferries (🖳 www.condorferries.co.uk).

Norfolkline (🖥 www.norfolkline.com).

P&O Ferries (🖥 www.poferries.com).

Sea France (🖥 www.seafrance.com).

Transmanche (🖥 www.transmancheferries.com).

Other Public Transport

Eurolines (🖥 www.eurolines.com). International coach services.

Eurostar (🖥 www.eurostar.com). International rail services.

Eurotunnel/Le Shuttle (🖥 www.eurotunnel.com). Car transport through the Channel Tunnel.

Motorail (🖥 www.frenchmotorail.com). Travelling by rail with your car in France.

National Express (🖥 www.nationalexpress.com). International coach services.

Rail Europe (🖥 www.raileurope.com). Eurostar/*TGV* link.

RATP (🖥 www.ratp.fr). Parisian regional transport authority.

SNCF (🖥 www.sncf.fr). French national railways.

Trans'bus (🖥 www.transbus.org). Information about urban public transport in France.

Motoring

ASFA (🖥 www.autoroutes.fr). Information about French motorways and tolls.

Automobile Association/AA (🖥 www.theaa.co.uk).

Bison Futé (🖥 www.bison-fute.equipement.gouv.fr). French road traffic reports.

Mappy (🖥 www.iti.fr). Road route planning through France.

Royal Automobile Club/RAC (🖥 www.rac.co.uk).

APPENDIX D: WEIGHTS & MEASURES

France uses the metric system of measurement. Those who are more familiar with the imperial system will find the tables on the following pages useful. Some comparisons shown are only approximate, but are close enough for most everyday uses.

In addition to the variety of measurement systems used, clothes sizes often vary considerably with the manufacturer – as we all know only too well! Try all clothes on before buying and don't be afraid to return something if, when you try it on at home, you decide it doesn't fit (most shops will exchange goods or give a refund).

Women's Clothes

Continental	34	36	38	40	42	44	46	48	50	52
UK		8	10	12	14	16	18	20	22	24	26
US		6	8	10	12	14	16	18	20	22	24

Pullover's

	Women's							Men's					
Continental	40	42	44	46	48	50		44	46	48	50	52	54
UK	34	36	38	40	42	44		34	36	38	40	42	44
US	34	36	38	40	42	44		sm	med		lg	xl	

Men's Shirts

Continental	36	37	38	39	40	41	42	43	44	46
UK/US	14	14	15	15	16	16	17	17	18	-

Men's Underwear

Continental	5	6	7	8	9	10
UK		34	36	38	40	42	44
US		sm	med		lg	xl	

NB: sm = small, med = medium, lg = large, xl = extra large

Children's Clothes

Continental	92	104	116	128	140	152
UK	16/18	20/22	24/26	28/30	32/34	36/38
US	2	4	6	8	10	12

Children's Shoes

Continental	18	19	20	21	22	23	24	25	26	27	28	29	30	31	32
UK/US	2	3	4	4	5	6	7	7	8	9	10	11	11	12	13
Continental	33	34	35	36	37	38									
UK/US	1	2	2	3	4	5									

Shoes (Women's & Men's)

Continental	35	36	37	37	38	39	40	41	42	42	43	44	45	46	47
UK	2	3	3	4	4	5	6	7	7	8	9	9	10	11	12
US	4	5	5	6	6	7	8	9	9	10	10	11	11	12	12

Weight

Imperial	Metric	Metric	Imperial
1oz	28.35g	1g	0.035oz
1lb*	454g	100g	3.5oz
1cwt	50.8kg	250g	9oz
1 ton	1,016kg	500g	18oz
2,205lb	1 tonne	1kg	2.2lb

Area

British/US	Metric	Metric	British/US
1 sq. in	0.45 sq. cm	1 sq. cm	0.15 sq. in
1 sq. ft	0.09 sq. m	1 sq. m	10.76 sq. ft
1 sq. yd	0.84 sq. m	1 sq. m	1.2 sq. yds
1 acre	0.4 hectares	1 hectare	2.47 acres
1 sq. mile	2.56 sq. km	1 sq. km	0.39 sq. mile

Capacity			
Imperial	**Metric**	**Metric**	**Imperial**
1 UK pint	0.57 litre	1 litre	1.75 UK pints
1 US pint	0.47 litre	1 litre	2.13 US pints
1 UK gallon	4.54 litres	1 litre	0.22 UK gallon
1 US gallon	3.78 litres	1 litre	0.26 US gallon
NB: An American 'cup' = around 250ml or 0.25 litre.			

Length			
British/US	**Metric**	**Metric**	**British/US**
1in	2.54cm	1cm	0.39in
1ft	30.48cm	1m	3ft 3.25in
1yd	91.44cm	1km	0.62mi
1mi	1.6km	8km	5mi

Temperature	
°Celsius	**°Fahrenheit**
0	32 (freezing point of water)
5	41
10	50
15	59
20	68
25	77
30	86
35	95
40	104
50	122

Temperature Conversion

• **Celsius to Fahrenheit:** multiply by 9, divide by 5 and add 32. (For a quick and approximate conversion, double the Celsius temperature and add 30.)

• **Fahrenheit to Celsius:** subtract 32, multiply by 5 and divide by 9. (For a quick and approximate conversion, subtract 30 from the Fahrenheit temperature and divide by 2.)

NB: The boiling point of water is 100°C / 212°F. Normal body temperature (if you're alive and well) is 37°C / 98.6°F.

Power			
Kilowatts	Horsepower	Horsepower	Kilowatts
1	1.34	1	0.75

Oven Temperature		
Gas	Electric	
	°F	°C
-	225–250	110–120
1	275	140
2	300	150
3	325	160
4	350	180
5	375	190
6	400	200
7	425	220
8	450	230
9	475	240

Air Pressure	
PSI	Bar
10	0.5
20	1.4
30	2
40	2.8

APPENDIX E: MAPS

The map opposite shows the 22 regions and 96 departments of France (excluding overseas territories), which are listed below. The departments are (mostly) numbered alphabetically from 01 to 89. Departments 91 to 95 come under the Ile-de-France region, which also includes Ville de Paris (75), Seine-et-Marne (77) and Yvelines (78), shown in detail opposite. The island of Corsica consists of two departments, 2A and 2B.

01 Ain	32 Gers	64 Pyrénées-Atlantiques
02 Aisne	33 Gironde	65 Hautes-Pyrénées
2A Corse-du-Sud	34 Hérault	66 Pyrénées-Orientales
2B Haute Corse	35 Ille-et-Vilaine	67 Bas-Rhin
03 Allier	36 Indre	68 Haut-Rhin
04 Alpes-de-Hte-Provence	37 Indre-et-Loire	69 Rhône
05 Hautes-Alpes	38 Isère	70 Haute-Saône
06 Alpes-Maritimes	39 Jura	71 Saône-et-Loire
07 Ardèche	40 Landes	72 Sarthe
08 Ardennes	41 Loir-et-Cher	73 Savoie
09 Ariège	42 Loire	74 Haute-Savoie
10 Aube	43 Haute-Loire	75 Paris
11 Aude	44 Loire-Atlantique	76 Seine-Maritime
12 Aveyron	45 Loiret	77 Seine-et-Marne
13 Bouches-du-Rhône	46 Lot	78 Yvelines
14 Calvados	47 Lot-et-Garonne	79 Deux-Sèvres
15 Cantal	48 Lozère	80 Somme
16 Charente	49 Maine-et-Loire	81 Tarn
17 Charente-Maritime	50 Manche	82 Tarn-et-Garonne
18 Cher	51 Marne	83 Var
19 Corrèze	52 Haute-Marne	84 Vaucluse
21 Côte-d'Or	53 Mayenne	85 Vendée
22 Côte-d'Armor	54 Meurthe-et-Moselle	86 Vienne
23 Creuse	55 Meuse	87 Haute-Vienne
24 Dordogne	56 Morbihan	88 Vosges
25 Doubs	57 Moselle	89 Yonne
26 Drôme	58 Nièvre	90 Territoire de Belfort
27 Eure	59 Nord	91 Essonne
28 Eure-et-Loir	60 Oise	92 Hauts-de-Seine
29 Finistère	61 Orne	93 Seine-Saint-Denis
30 Gard	62 Pas-de-Calais	94 Val-de-Marne
31 Haute-Garonne	63 Puy-de-Dôme	95 Val-d'Oise

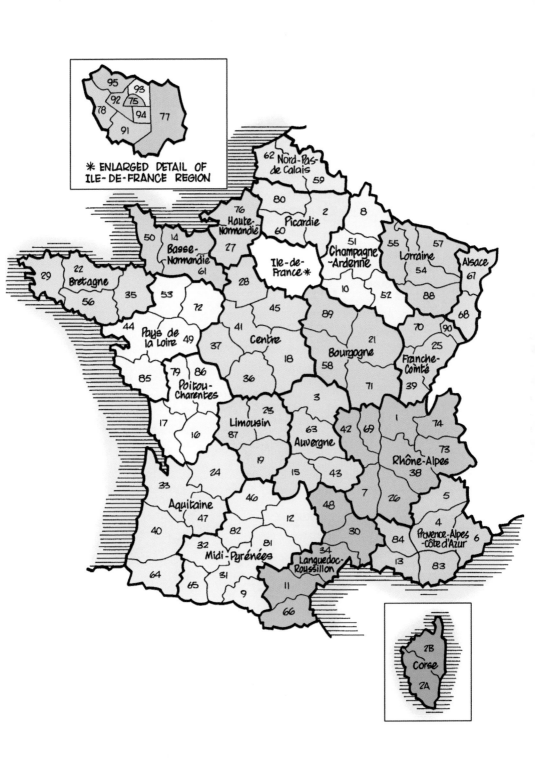

* ENLARGED DETAIL OF ILE-DE-FRANCE REGION

CITIES & AIRPORTS

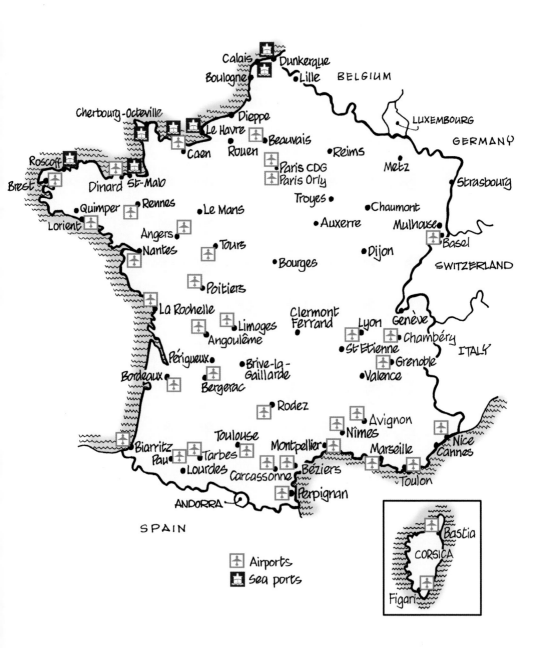

TGV RAIL LINES

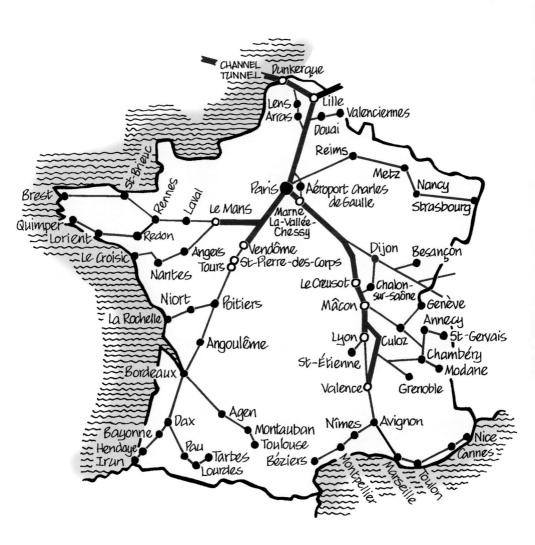

MOTORWAYS

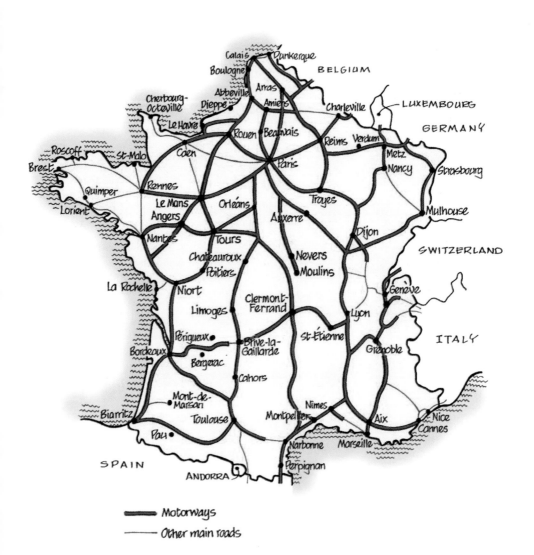

Motorways
Other main roads

INDEX

PHOTO CREDITS

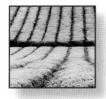

Culture Wise France

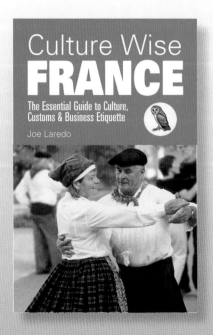

ISBN:978-1-905303-07-6

Joe Laredo

Travellers often underestimate the depth of cultural isolation they can face abroad, particularly in a country with a different language. To some people, France may seem an 'easy' option, with its millions of annual visitors and hundreds of thousands of foreign residents. However, sooner or later, most newcomers find many aspects of French life alien – bureaucracy, food and language, for example – and some come unstuck as a result. *Culture Wise France* will help you understand France and its people, and adapt to the French way of life. Most importantly, it will enable you to quickly feel at home.

£9.95

The Best Places to Buy a Home in France

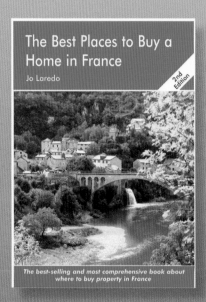

ISBN: 978-1-901130-14-0

Joe Laredo

The Best Places to Buy a Home in France is essential reading for anyone planning to buy property in France, and is designed to help you avoid costly mistakes and save endless hours researching local property prices and availability. It is the most comprehensive and up to date source of information available for anyone wishing to explore the property market in France before buying a home, and also includes important information about local amenities and services. Whether you are seeking a holiday or a permanent home, or buying for investment, business or pleasure, *The Best Places to Buy a Home in France* will guide you every step of the way.

£12.95

Retiring in France

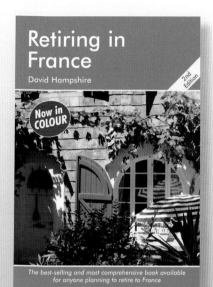

The best-selling and most comprehensive book available for anyone planning to retire to France

ISBN: 978-1-901130-61-8

David Hampshire

Retiring in France is mandatory reading for anyone planning to retire to France, whether permanently or for just part of the year, and is worth its weight in champagne. As with all life-changing decisions, the key to a successful retirement in France is extensive planning and research (research, research) before you go, which is where this book will prove invaluable. *Retiring in France* is the most comprehensive book available about all aspects of retiring to France – written by best-selling author David Hampshire – and is packed with vital information to help make the process as smooth and straightforward as possible.

£12.95

Running Gîtes & B&Bs in France

Everything you need to know to run a successful gîte and B&B business in France

ISBN: 978-1-905303-30-4

Jo Taylor

Running Gîtes & B&Bs in France is essential reading for prospective 'landlords' (landladies?) and provides readers with a step-by-step guide to establishing and running a successful gîte or bed and breakfast business. Whether you plan to do this from abroad, using a local agent or manager, or as a full- or part-time resident in France, this book will prove invaluable. *Running Gîtes & B&Bs in France* explains everything you need to know, including what property to buy and where; conversion and renovation; obtaining grants, loans and mortgages; legal considerations; record-keeping and taxation; equipment and provisions; advertising, marketing and publicity; dealing with enquiries and bookings; providing extra services; employing an agent; hiring staff; and much, much more.

£12.95

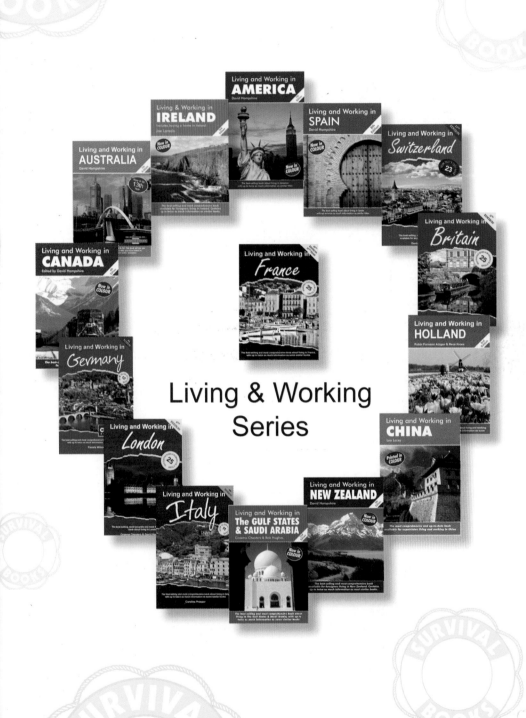

Living & Working
Series